Cryptography:

Breakthroughs in Research and Practice

Information Resources Management Association
USA

Published in the United States of America by
   IGI Global
   Information Science Reference (an imprint of IGI Global)
   701 E. Chocolate Avenue
   Hershey PA, USA 17033
   Tel: 717-533-8845
   Fax: 717-533-8661
   E-mail: cust@igi-global.com
   Web site: http://www.igi-global.com

                     Library of Congress Cataloging-in-Publication Data

Names: Information Resources Management Association, editor.
Title: Cryptography : breakthroughs in research and practice / Information
   Resources Management Association, editor.
Description: Hershey, PA : Information Science Reference, 2020. | Includes
   bibliographical references. | Summary: ""This book examines novel
   designs and recent developments in cryptographic security control
   procedures to improve the efficiency of existing security mechanisms
   that can help in securing sensors, devices, networks, communication, and
   data"-- Provided by publisher.
Identifiers: LCCN 2019034135 (print) | LCCN 2019034136 (ebook) | ISBN
   9781799817635 (h/c) | ISBN 9781799817642 (eISBN)
Subjects: LCSH: Cryptography. | Data transmission systems--Security
   measures. | Computers--Access control.
Classification: LCC TK5102.94 .C776 2020 (print) | LCC TK5102.94 (ebook)
   | DDC 005.8/24--dc23
LC record available at https://lccn.loc.gov/2019034135
LC ebook record available at https://lccn.loc.gov/2019034136

British Cataloguing in Publication Data
A Cataloguing in Publication record for this book is available from the British Library.

The views expressed in this book are those of the authors, but not necessarily of the publisher.

For electronic access to this publication, please contact: eresources@igi-global.com.

List of Contributors

Abdelkader, Gafour / *Djellali Liabes University, Algeria* 129

Agarwal, Sugandha / *Amity University, India* 39

Agrawal, Nitesh Kumar / *Indian School of Mines, India* 449

Akojwar, Sudhir Gangadharrao / *Government College of Engineering, India* 159

Alam, Naved / *Jamia Hamdard, India* 180

Ali, Syed Taqi / *National Institute of Technology Kurukshetra, India* 214

Amine, Filali Mohamed / *Djellali Liabes University, Algeria* 129

Anghelescu, Petre / *University of Pitesti, Romania* 99

Annamalai, Murugan / *Dr. Ambedkar Government Arts College, India* 48

Ayyappan, Sonal / *SCMS School of Engineering and Technology, India* 458

Babu, Anna / *M. G. University, India* 458

Babu, Erukala Suresh / *K.L. University, India* 72

Banerjee, Anurag / *M. S. Ramaiah Institute of Technology, India* 193

Barari, Adrita / *Defence Institute of Advanced Technology, India* 498

Bhasin, Harsh / *Jawahar Lal Nehru University, India* 180

Bhat, G.M. / *University of Kashmir, India* 1

Bhatia, Mahinder Pal Singh / *Netaji Subhas Institute of Technology, India* 373

Bhatia, Manjot Kaur / *University of Delhi, India* 373

Biswas, G. P. / *Indian Institute of Technology (Indian School of Mines), India* 120, 306

Dey, Nilanjan / *Techno India College of Technology, India* 1

Dhavale, Sunita V. / *Defence Institute of Advanced Technology, India* 498

Dhawale, Chitra A. / *P. R. Pote College of Engineering and Management, India* 332

Ding, Wanmeng / *Hefei Electronic Engineering Institute, China* 416

Driss, El Ouadghiri / *MoulaySmail University, Morocco* 316

Fathimal, P. Mohamed / *Manonmaniam Sundaranar University, India* 438

G. M., Siddesh / *M. S. Ramaiah Institute of Technology, India* 193

Gao, Lin / *Tianjin Chengjian University, China* 480

Gao, Tiegang / *Nankai University, China* 480

Guo, Teng / *University of International Relations, China* 537

Gupta, Daya Sagar / *Indian Institute of Technology (ISM) Dhanbad, India* 306

Haldar, Manas Kumar / *Swinburne University of Technology, Malaysia* 391

Hassan, Naanani / *Ben'msik University, Morocco* 316

Hiriyannaiah, Srinidhi / *M. S. Ramaiah Institute of Technology, India* 193

Ibtihal, Mouhib / *MoulaySmail University, Morocco* 316

Issac, Biju / *Teesside University, UK* 391

Jacob, Grasha / *Rani Anna Government College, India* 48

Jambhekar, Naveen D. / *S. S. S. K. R. Innani Mahavidyalaya, India* 332

Jiao, Jian / *University of International Relations, China* 537

K. G., Srinivasa / *M. S. Ramaiah Institute of Technology, India* 193

Khan, Zafar Jawed / *RCERT Chandrapur, India* 159

Khare, Ayush / *Indian School of Mines, India* 449

Kumari, R. Shantha Selva / *Mepco Schlenk Engineering College, India* 277

Liu, Feng / *Chinese Academy of Sciences, China* 428, 537

Liu, Hanlin / *Hefei Electronic Engineering Institute, China* 416

Liu, Lintao / *Hefei Electronic Engineering Institute, China* 416

Liu, Xin / *Harbin Institute of Technology, China & Harbin University of Science and Technology, China* 545

Lu, Yuliang / *Hefei Electronic Engineering Institute, China* 416

Manna, G. C. / *BSNL, India* 142

Moh, Melody / *San Jose State University, USA* 257

Mohit, Prerna / *Indian Institute of Technology (Indian School of Mines), India* 120

Mondal, Jayanta / *KIIT University, India* 556

Morappanavar, Anusha / *M. S. Ramaiah Institute of Technology, India* 193

Muñoz, Melesio Calderón / *Cupertino Electric, Inc., USA* 257

Muttoo, Sunil Kumar / *University of Delhi, India* 373

Nagaraju, C. / *Y.V. University, India* 72

Nagaria, Deepak / *Bundelkhand Institute of Engineering and Technology, India* 39

Nidhyananthan, S. Selva / *Mepco Schlenk Engineering College, India* 277

Pal, Arup Kumar / *Indian School of Mines, India* 449

Parah, Shabir A. / *University of Kashmir, India* 1

Prajapat, Shaligram / *Maulana Azad National Institute of Technology, India & Devi Ahilya University, India* 239

Prasad, M. / *Mepco Schlenk Engineering College, India* 277

Prasad, M.H.M. Krishna / *J.N.T. University, India* 72

Rani, P. Arockia Jansi / *Manonmaniam Sundaranar University, India* 438

Reddy, V. Lokeswara / *K.S.R.M College of Engineering, India* 355

Rura, Lauretha / *Swinburne University of Technology, Malaysia* 391

Sang, Jianzhi / *Harbin Institute of Technology, China* 545

Sawlikar, Alka Prasad / *RCERT Chandrapur, India* 159

Sharma, Dixit / *Guru Nanak Dev University, India* 22

Sharma, Rahul / *Indian School of Mines, India* 449

Sheikh, Javaid A. / *University of Kashmir, India* 1

Singh, Butta / *Guru Nanak Dev University, India* 22

Singh, Manjit / *Guru Nanak Dev University, India* 22

Singh, O.P. / *Amity University, India* 39

Suryavanshi, Vishnu / *GHRCE Nagpur, India* 142

Swain, Debabala / *KIIT University, India* 556

Thakur, Ramjeevan Singh / *Maulana Azad National Institute of Technology, India* 239

Wan, Song / *Hefei Electronic Engineering Institute, China* 416

Wang, Guangyu / *Chinese Academy of Sciences, China & Auckland University of Technology, New Zealand* 428

Wang, Shen / *Harbin Institute of Technology, China* 545

Wang, Wen / *Chinese Academy of Sciences, China* 537

Wei, Zhang / *Engineering University of Chinese Armed Police Force, China*............................... 295

Yan, Wei Qi / *Chinese Academy of Sciences, China & Auckland University of Technology, New Zealand*.. 428

Yan, Xuehu / *Hefei Electronic Engineering Institute, China*.. 416

Zhang, Weizhe / *Harbin Institute of Technology, China* 545

Zhao, Jie / *Tianjin Chengjian University, China* 480

Table of Contents

Preface...xi

Section 1
Chaotic and DNA-Based Cryptography

Chapter 1
Realization of a New Robust and Secure Watermarking Technique Using DC Coefficient
Modification in Pixel Domain and Chaotic Encryption...1
    Shabir A. Parah, University of Kashmir, India
    Javaid A. Sheikh, University of Kashmir, India
    Nilanjan Dey, Techno India College of Technology, India
    G.M. Bhat, University of Kashmir, India

Chapter 2
Chaotic Function Based ECG Encryption System...22
    Butta Singh, Guru Nanak Dev University, India
    Manjit Singh, Guru Nanak Dev University, India
    Dixit Sharma, Guru Nanak Dev University, India

Chapter 3
Biometric Image Security Using Chaos Algorithm...39
    Sugandha Agarwal, Amity University, India
    O.P. Singh, Amity University, India
    Deepak Nagaria, Bundelkhand Institute of Engineering and Technology, India

Chapter 4
DNA Sequence Based Cryptographic Solution for Secure Image Transmission 48
    Grasha Jacob, Rani Anna Government College, India
    Murugan Annamalai, Dr. Ambedkar Government Arts College, India

Chapter 5
IPHDBCM: Inspired Pseudo Hybrid DNA Based Cryptographic Mechanism to Prevent Against
Collabrative Black Hole Attack in Wireless Ad hoc Networks 72
    Erukala Suresh Babu, K.L. University, India
    C. Nagaraju, Y.V. University, India
    M.H.M. Krishna Prasad, J.N.T. University, India

Section 2
Cryptographic Algorithms

Chapter 6
Cryptographic Techniques Based on Bio-Inspired Systems 99
Petre Anghelescu, University of Pitesti, Romania

Chapter 7
Modification of Traditional RSA into Symmetric-RSA Cryptosystems 120
Prerna Mohit, Indian Institute of Technology (Indian School of Mines), India
G. P. Biswas, Indian Institute of Technology (Indian School of Mines), India

Chapter 8
Hybrid Approach of Modified AES 129
Filali Mohamed Amine, Djellali Liabes University, Algeria
Gafour Abdelkader, Djellali Liabes University, Algeria

Chapter 9
Cryptographic Algorithms for Next Generation Wireless Networks Security 142
Vishnu Suryavanshi, GHRCE Nagpur, India
G. C. Manna, BSNL, India

Chapter 10
Efficient Energy Saving Cryptographic Techniques with Software Solution in Wireless Network ... 159
Alka Prasad Sawlikar, RCERT Chandrapur, India
Zafar Jawed Khan, RCERT Chandrapur, India
Sudhir Gangadharrao Akojwar, Government College of Engineering, India

Chapter 11
Applicability of Cellular Automata in Cryptanalysis 180
Harsh Bhasin, Jawahar Lal Nehru University, India
Naved Alam, Jamia Hamdard, India

Section 3
Encryption Keys and Homomorphic Encryption

Chapter 12
A Novel Approach of Symmetric Key Cryptography using Genetic Algorithm Implemented on
GPGPU 193
Srinivasa K. G., M. S. Ramaiah Institute of Technology, India
Siddesh G. M., M. S. Ramaiah Institute of Technology, India
Srinidhi Hiriyannaiah, M. S. Ramaiah Institute of Technology, India
Anusha Morappanavar, M. S. Ramaiah Institute of Technology, India
Anurag Banerjee, M. S. Ramaiah Institute of Technology, India

Chapter 13
Provable Security for Public Key Cryptosystems: How to Prove that the Cryptosystem is Secure ... 214
    Syed Taqi Ali, National Institute of Technology Kurukshetra, India

Chapter 14
Towards Parameterized Shared Key for AVK Approach 239
    Shaligram Prajapat, Maulana Azad National Institute of Technology, India & Devi Ahilya
        University, India
    Ramjeevan Singh Thakur, Maulana Azad National Institute of Technology, India

Chapter 15
Authentication of Smart Grid: The Case for Using Merkle Trees 257
    Melesio Calderón Muñoz, Cupertino Electric, Inc., USA
    Melody Moh, San Jose State University, USA

Chapter 16
Secure Speaker Recognition using BGN Cryptosystem with Prime Order Bilinear Group 277
    S. Selva Nidhyananthan, Mepco Schlenk Engineering College, India
    M. Prasad, Mepco Schlenk Engineering College, India
    R. Shantha Selva Kumari, Mepco Schlenk Engineering College, India

Chapter 17
A Pairing-based Homomorphic Encryption Scheme for Multi-User Settings 295
    Zhang Wei, Engineering University of Chinese Armed Police Force, China

Chapter 18
A Secure Cloud Storage using ECC-Based Homomorphic Encryption 306
    Daya Sagar Gupta, Indian Institute of Technology (ISM) Dhanbad, India
    G. P. Biswas, Indian Institute of Technology (ISM) Dhanbad, India

Chapter 19
Homomorphic Encryption as a Service for Outsourced Images in Mobile Cloud Computing
Environment 316
    Mouhib Ibtihal, MoulaySmail University, Morocco
    El Ouadghiri Driss, MoulaySmail University, Morocco
    Naanani Hassan, Ben'msik University, Morocco

Section 4
Steganography

Chapter 20
Digital Image Steganography: Survey, Analysis, and Application 332
    Chitra A. Dhawale, P. R. Pote College of Engineering and Management, India
    Naveen D. Jambhekar, S. S. S. K. R. Innani Mahavidyalaya, India

Chapter 21

Improved Secure Data Transfer Using Video Steganographic Technique 355
  V. Lokeswara Reddy, K.S.R.M College of Engineering, India

Chapter 22

Secure Group Message Transfer Stegosystem 373
  Mahinder Pal Singh Bhatia, Netaji Subhas Institute of Technology, India
  Manjot Kaur Bhatia, University of Delhi, India
  Sunil Kumar Muttoo, University of Delhi, India

Chapter 23

Implementation and Evaluation of Steganography Based Online Voting System 391
  Lauretha Rura, Swinburne University of Technology, Malaysia
  Biju Issac, Teesside University, UK
  Manas Kumar Haldar, Swinburne University of Technology, Malaysia

Section 5
Visual Cryptography

Chapter 24

Exploiting the Homomorphic Property of Visual Cryptography 416
  Xuehu Yan, Hefei Electronic Engineering Institute, China
  Yuliang Lu, Hefei Electronic Engineering Institute, China
  Lintao Liu, Hefei Electronic Engineering Institute, China
  Song Wan, Hefei Electronic Engineering Institute, China
  Wanmeng Ding, Hefei Electronic Engineering Institute, China
  Hanlin Liu, Hefei Electronic Engineering Institute, China

Chapter 25

Basic Visual Cryptography Using Braille 428
  Guangyu Wang, Chinese Academy of Sciences, China & Auckland University of Technology,
    New Zealand
  Feng Liu, Chinese Academy of Sciences, China
  Wei Qi Yan, Chinese Academy of Sciences, China & Auckland University of Technology, New
    Zealand

Chapter 26

Threshold Secret Sharing Scheme for Compartmented Access Structures 438
  P. Mohamed Fathimal, Manonmaniam Sundaranar University, India
  P. Arockia Jansi Rani, Manonmaniam Sundaranar University, India

Chapter 27

An Improved Size Invariant (n, n) Extended Visual Cryptography Scheme 449
  Rahul Sharma, Indian School of Mines, India
  Nitesh Kumar Agrawal, Indian School of Mines, India
  Ayush Khare, Indian School of Mines, India
  Arup Kumar Pal, Indian School of Mines, India

Chapter 28
A Methodological Evaluation of Crypto-Watermarking System for Medical Images.......................458
    Anna Babu, M. G. University, India
    Sonal Ayyappan, SCMS School of Engineering and Technology, India

Chapter 29
Reversible Watermarking in Medical Image Using RDWT and Sub-Sample 480
    Lin Gao, Tianjin Chengjian University, China
    Tiegang Gao, Nankai University, China
    Jie Zhao, Tianjin Chengjian University, China

Chapter 30
Video Saliency Detection for Visual Cryptography-Based Watermarking 498
    Adrita Barari, Defence Institute of Advanced Technology, India
    Sunita V. Dhavale, Defence Institute of Advanced Technology, India

Chapter 31
On the Pixel Expansion of Visual Cryptography Scheme 537
    Teng Guo, University of International Relations, China
    Jian Jiao, University of International Relations, China
    Feng Liu, Chinese Academy of Sciences, China
    Wen Wang, Chinese Academy of Sciences, China

Chapter 32
A Novel Pixel Merging-Based Lossless Recovery Algorithm for Basic Matrix VSS 545
    Xin Liu, Harbin Institute of Technology, China & Harbin University of Science and
        Technology, China
    Shen Wang, Harbin Institute of Technology, China
    Jianzhi Sang, Harbin Institute of Technology, China
    Weizhe Zhang, Harbin Institute of Technology, China

Chapter 33
A Contemplator on Topical Image Encryption Measures 556
    Jayanta Mondal, KIIT University, India
    Debabala Swain, KIIT University, India

Index..574

Preface

Technology in today's world has developed rapidly with the emergence of smart computation and artificial intelligence. These devices continue to integrate themselves into various fields of research and practice, making operations and tasks easier to accomplish. Despite the vast benefits technology has to offer, the swift development has created an array of vulnerabilities and unlocked a significant amount of security and privacy risks. The protection of valuable data and information has become a key topic of research because of this.

Cryptography is the practice of writing codes and developing secure communication techniques. The art of cryptography has emerged as a prevalent area of study as many practitioners and professionals are relying on this technology to keep their information safe from cyber attacks and hackers. Within this up-and-coming subject lies a diverse amount of methods and approaches that can be specifically applied to countless professions.

Because of cryptography's popularity, there are new studies and research findings being published at a rapid pace. It remains a challenge for the general public to keep up with the constant discoveries being made in this field. Researchers, universities, and professionals need a compilation of information that stays up to date on the latest findings and studies regarding cryptography and provides them with current advancements and future trends in this industry.

The everchanging landscape surrounding the diverse applications of different scientific areas can make it very challenging to stay on the forefront of innovative research trends. That is why IGI Global is pleased to offer this one-volume comprehensive reference that will empower academicians, graduate students, engineers, IT specialists, software engineers, security analysts, industry professionals, and researchers with a stronger understanding of cryptography.

This compilation is designed to act as a single reference source on conceptual, methodological, and technical aspects and will provide insight into emerging topics including but not limited to cybersecurity, encryption, information security, intrusion detection systems, authentication, and threat detection. The chapters within this publication are sure to provide readers the tools necessary for further research and discovery in their respective industries and/or fields.

Cryptography: Breakthroughs in Research and Practice is organized into five sections that provide comprehensive coverage of important topics. The sections are:

1. Chaotic and DNA-Based Cryptography;
2. Cryptographic Algorithms;
3. Encryption Keys and Homomorphic Encryption;
4. Steganography; and
5. Visual Cryptography.

The following paragraphs provide a summary of what to expect from this invaluable reference source:

Section 1, "Chaotic and DNA-Based Cryptography," opens this extensive reference source by highlighting the latest trends in DNA-based cryptography techniques and explores the application of the mathematical chaos theory to the practice of cryptography. The first chapter in this section, "Realization of a New Robust and Secure Watermarking Technique Using DC Coefficient Modification in Pixel Domain and Chaotic Encryption," by Profs. Shabir Parah and Javaid Sheikh from the University of Kashmir, India; Prof. Nilanjan Dey from Techno India College of Technology, India; and Prof. G.M. Bhat from the University of Kashmir, India, explores the security of digital watermarking using new encryption methods and embedded systems. Another featured chapter, "Chaotic Function Based ECG Encryption System," by Profs. Butta Singh, Manjit Singh, and Dixit Sharma from Guru Nanak Dev University, India, studies specific encryption structures for remote healthcare monitoring systems and protecting the integrity of medical data. The following chapter, "Biometric Image Security Using Chaos Algorithm," by Profs. Sugandha Agarwal and O.P. Singh from Amity University, India and Prof. Deepak Nagaria from Bundelkhand Institute of Technology, India, discusses experimental analyses that provide an efficient and secure algorithm for real-time image encryption and transmission. One of the closing chapters, "DNA Sequence Based Cryptographic Solution for Secure Image Transmission," by Prof. Grasha Jacob from Rani Anna Government College, India and Prof. Murugan Annamalai from Dr. Ambedkar Government Arts College, India, features research on an encryption scheme based on DNA sequences that enable secure transmission of images across the internet. The final chapter in this section is "IPHDBCM: Inspired Pseudo Hybrid DNA Based Cryptographic Mechanisms to Prevent against Collaborative Black Hole Attack in Wireless Ad hoc Networks," authored by Prof. Erukala Suresh Babu from K.L. University, India; Prof. C. Nagaraju from Y.V. University, India; and Prof. M.H.M. Krishna Prasad from J.N.T. University, India. This chapter addresses the detection and defense of blackhole attacks using hybrid DNA-based cryptography (HDC) mechanisms.

Section 2, "Cryptographic Algorithms," includes chapters on emerging innovations and applications for optimized algorithms within cryptography. The initial chapter in this section, "Cryptographic Techniques Based on Bio-Inspired Systems," by Prof. Petre Anghelescu from the University of Pitesti, Romania, provides an alternative to conventional security methods using bio-inspired techniques based on the cellular automata (CAs) and programmable cellular automata (PCAs) theory. The following chapter is "Modification of Traditional RSA into Symmetric-RSA Cryptosystems," authored by Profs. Prerna Mohit and G.P. Biswas from the Indian Institute of Technology, India. This chapter addresses the modification of RSA cryptography using extensive applications including digital signature and encryption. Another chapter in this section, "Hybrid Approach of Modified AES," by Profs. Filali Mohamed Amine and Gafour Abdelkader from Djellali Liabes University, Algeria, discusses the modification and transformation of advanced encryption standard algorithms using images as input data. The chapter that follows this, "Cryptographic Algorithms for Next Generation Wireless Networks Security," is written by Prof. Vishnu Suryavanshi from GHRCE Nagpur, India and Prof. G.C. Manna from BSNL, India. This chapter explores the encoding of information and communication security in next generation networks by using quantum cryptographic algorithms. Another chapter found within this section, "Efficient Energy Saving Cryptographic Techniques with Software Solution in Wireless Network," by Profs. Alka Prasad Sawlikar and Zafar Jawed Khan from RCERT Chandrapur, India and Prof. Sudhir Gangadharrao Akojwar from the Government College of Engineering, India, examines the application of conversion and encryption techniques to secure and compress transmitted data. The closing chapter, "Applicability of

Cellular Automata in Cryptanalysis," authored by Prof. Harsh Bhasin from Jawar Lal Nehru University, India and Prof. Naved Alam from Jamia Hamdard, India, explores the applicability of soft computing techniques within cryptanalysis and discusses the future scope of similar methods.

Section 3, "Encryption Keys and Homomorphic Encryption," presents coverage on novel strategies within the field of encryption and key technology. The opening chapter of this section, "Provable Security for Public Key Cryptosystems: How to Prove that the Cryptosystem is Secure," by Prof. Syed Taqi Ali from National Institute of Technology Kurukshetra, India, reviews the security proofs of well known public key cryptosystems as well as the multiple approaches for structuring these proofs. This chapter is followed by "Towards Parameterized Shared Key for AVK Approach," which is written by Prof. Shaligram Prajapat and Prof. Ramjeevan Singh Thakur from the Maulana Azad National Institute of Technology, India. This chapter examines the implementation of the automatic variable key (AVK) approach within symmetric key cryptosystems from various users' perspectives. The following chapter, "Authentication of Smart Grid: The Case for Using Merkle Trees," by Prof. Melesio Calderón Muñoz from Cupertino Electric, Inc., USA and Prof. Melody Moh from San Jose State University, USA, argues for the use of Merkle trees as opposed to public key encryption for the authentication and security of devices within smart grids. Another noteworthy chapter found in this section is "Secure Speaker Recognition using BGN Cryptosystem with Prime Order Bilinear Group," by Profs. S. Selva Nidhyananthan, Prasad M., and Shantha Kumari R. from Mepco Schlenk Engineering College, India. This chapter examines the efficiency of secure speaker recognition frameworks by implementing BGN Cryptosystems. One of the following chapters, "A Pairing-based Homomorphic Encryption Scheme for Multi-User Settings," by Prof. Zhang Wei from the Engineering University of Chinese Armed Police Force, China, provides detailed security analysis of a pairing-based multi-user homomorphic encryption scheme by adopting the idea of proxy re-encryption and focusing on the compatibility of computation. Also included in this section is the chapter "A Secure Cloud Storage using ECC-Based Homomorphic Encryption," by Profs. Daya Sagar Gupta and G.P. Biswas from the Indian Institute of Technology Dhanbad, India. This chapter presents a new homomorphic public-key encryption scheme based on elliptic curve cryptography, which allows public computation on encrypted data stored on a cloud. The closing chapter of this section, "Homomorphic Encryption as a Service for Outsourced Images in Mobile Cloud Computing Environment," written by Profs. Mouhib Ibtihal and El Ouadghiri Driss from MoulaySmail University, Morocco and Prof. Naanani Hassan from Ben'msik University, Morocco, proposes a two cloud approach, a private cloud dedicated to encryption and a public cloud dedicated to storage, for the security and protection of outsourced images in mobile cloud computing atmospheres.

Section 4, "Steganography," discusses coverage and research perspectives on the latest developments and implementations of steganographic methods. In the foremost chapter of this section, "Digital Image Steganography: Survey, Analysis, and Application," by Prof. Chitra A. Dhawale from P. R. Pote College of Engineering and Management, India and Prof. Naveen D. Jambhekar from S. S. S. K. R. Innani Mahavidyalaya, India, the authors discuss the basics of digital image steganographic techniques as well as types of images used, performance analysis of various steganographic algorithms used for attacks, and current applications. Following this chapter is "Improved Secure Data Transfer Using Video Steganographic Technique," authored by Prof. V. Lokeswara Reddy from K.S.R.M College of Engineering, India. This chapter explores the modern development of video steganography by using a double layered security technique. Another chapter presented in this section, "Secure Group Message Transfer Stegosystem," by Prof. Mahinder Pal Singh Bhatia from the Netaji Subhas Institute of Technology, India and

Profs. Manjot Kaur Bhatia and Sunil Kumar Muttoo from the University of Delhi, India, proposes a new secure message broadcasting system to hide the messages so attackers cannot sense the existence of messages, using steganography and image encryption. The closing chapter within this section, "Implementation and Evaluation of Steganography Based Online Voting System," by Prof. Lauretha Rura from Swinburne University of Technology, Malaysia; Prof. Biju Issac from Teesside University, UK; and Prof. Manas Kumar Haldar from Swinburne University of Technology, Malaysia, studies novel approaches to online voting by combining visual cryptography with image steganography to improve system security without damaging usability and performance.

Section 5, "Visual Cryptography," highlights the latest research findings pertaining to cryptographic techniques that allow visual information to be encrypted. The opening chapter of this section, "Exploiting the Homomorphic Property of Visual Cryptography," by Profs. Xuehu Yan, Yuliang Lu, Lintao Liu, Song Wan, Wanmeng Ding, and Hanlin Liu from the Hefei Electronic Engineering Institute, China, demonstrates the effectiveness and security of homomorphic visual cryptographic scheme (HVCS) with theoretical analysis and simulation results. This chapter is followed by "Basic Visual Cryptography Using Braille," which is authored by Profs. Guangyu Wang, Feng Liu, and Wei Qi Yan from the Chinese Academy of Sciences, China. In this chapter, the authors conduct an experiment in which they embed Braille into visual cryptography (VC) methods due to the similarities in both approaches, with the intent to enhance the security of VC shares. Another chapter featured in this section, "Threshold Secret Sharing Scheme for Compartmented Access Structures," written by Profs. P. Mohamed Fathimal and P. Arockia Jansi Rani from Manonmaniam Sundaranar University, India, discusses a new method of secret image sharing that eliminates the danger of image regeneration and misuse, as well as offers better visual quality of recovered images using a compartmented scheme. Another early chapter presented within this section, "An Improved Size Invariant (n, n) Extended Visual Cryptography Scheme," by Profs. Rahul Sharma, Nitesh Kumar Agrawal, Ayush Khare, and Arup Kumar Pal from the Indian School of Mincs, India, examines a protracted cryptography method using a distinct number of image shares that is able to generate a visually secret message without extending its size while also enhancing the visual quality. Also contained within this section is the chapter "A Methodological Evaluation of Crypto-Watermarking System for Medical Images," written by Prof. Anna Babu from M.G. University, India and Prof. Sonal Ayyappan from SCMS School of Engineering and Technology, India. This chapter presents the basic aspects of crypto-watermarking techniques and their application within the secure transmission of medical images. Following this chapter is "Reversible Watermarking in Medical Image Using RDWT and Sub-Sample," by Profs. Lin Gao and Tiegang Gao from Nankai University, China and Prof. Jie Zhao from Tianjin Chengjian University, China, which explores a reversible medical image watermarking scheme that uses redundant discrete wavelet transform (RDWT) and sup-sample in order to meet the high demand of perceptual quality as well as providing enhancement on the embedding capacity. Another noteworthy chapter, "Video Saliency Detection for Visual Cryptography-Based Watermarking," by Profs. Adrita Barari and Sunita V. Dhavale from the Defence Institute of Advanced Technology, India, reviews the application of visual cryptography techniques in non-intrusive video watermarking with an emphasis on saliency feature extraction in videos. One of the closing chapters in the section, "On the Pixel Expansion of Visual Cryptography Scheme," is written by Profs. Teng Guo and Jian Jiao from the School of Information Science and Technology, China and Profs. Feng Liu and Wen Wang from the Chinese Academy of Sciences, China. This chapter discusses the pixel expansion of visual cryptography methods within various kinds of graph access structures as well as graph decomposition techniques derived from these schemes. Another chapter featured in the culmination of this section, "A

Novel Pixel Merging-Based Lossless Recovery Algorithm for Basic Matrix VSS," authored by Profs. Xin Liu, Shen Wang, Jianzhi Sang, and Weizhe Zhang from Harbin Institute of Technology, China, analyzes a lossless recovery algorithm for visual secret share (VSS) that implements exclusive XOR operation and merging pixel expansion. The final chapter, "A Contemplator on Topical Image Encryption Measures," by Profs. Jayanta Mondal and Debabala Swain from KIIT University, India, illustrates a survey on image encryption in various domains providing an introduction to cryptography as well as developing a review of sundry techniques.

Although the primary organization of the contents in this work is based on its five sections, offering a progression of coverage of the important concepts, methodologies, technologies, applications, social issues, and emerging trends, the reader can also identify specific contents by utilizing the extensive indexing system listed at the end.

Section 1
Chaotic and DNA–Based Cryptography

Chapter 1
Realization of a New Robust and Secure Watermarking Technique Using DC Coefficient Modification in Pixel Domain and Chaotic Encryption

Shabir A. Parah
University of Kashmir, India

Nilanjan Dey
Techno India College of Technology, India

Javaid A. Sheikh
University of Kashmir, India

G.M. Bhat
University of Kashmir, India

ABSTRACT

The proliferation of information and communication technology has made exchange of information easier than ever. Security, Duplication and manipulation of information in such a scenario has become a major challenge to the research community round the globe. Digital watermarking has been found to be a potent tool to deal with such issues. A secure and robust image watermarking scheme based on DC coefficient modification in pixel domain and chaotic encryption has been presented in this paper. The cover image has been divided into 8×8 sub-blocks and instead of computing DC coefficient using Discrete Cosine Transform (DCTI, the authors compute DC coefficient of each block in spatial domain. Watermark bits are embedded by modifying DC coefficients of various blocks in spatial domain. The quantum of change to be brought in various pixels of a block for embedding watermark bit depends upon DC coefficient of respective blocks, nature of watermark bit (0 or 1) to be embedded and the adjustment factor. The security of embedded watermark has been taken care of by using chaotic encryption. Experimental investigations show that besides being highly secure the proposed technique is robust to both signal processing and geometric attacks. Further, the proposed scheme is computationally efficient as DC coefficient which holds the watermark information has been computed in pixel domain instead of using DCT on an image block.

DOI: 10.4018/978-1-7998-1763-5.ch001

1. INTRODUCTION

The advancement in communication and networked and multimedia technologies and exponential rise in the users of internet world-wide has resulted in reproduction and distribution of multimedia content likeaudio, images and videos easier. In such a protection of multimedia content has become one of the prominent issues. Various encryption techniques are being used to encrypt the multimedia information before actual data transmission to avert various security and Intellectual Property Right (IPR) problems. However, the disguised look of the scrambled data makes the attacker more suspicious and hence the chances of a malicious attack from the adversary get increased. Given the significance of the problem some serious work needs to be done in order to ensure security and maintain the easy availability of multimedia content. In recent years digital watermarking has received most attention for security and protect multimedia data (Cox et al, 1998; Djurovic et al, 2001; Parah et al, 2014a). A digital watermark is a special data such as logo, imperceptibly embedded in multimedia content like an image etc. to prove its ownership. Since images are one of the prominent members of multimedia content, most of the developed watermark schemes reported till date use images as cover media (Ghouti, et al, 2006). Depending upon visibility of watermark, watermarking schemes are classified into two classes viz.; visible and invisible techniques. Most generally invisible (imperceptible) watermarking is used for copyright protection. Ina typical imperceptible watermarking technique,the watermark or special information datais embedded inside a cover image in such a way that it is imperceptible. Thus, it does not catch the attention of human visual system and protectsthe cover image from common signal processing and geometric attacks. The aim is to create a watermarked image that looks precisely same to a human eye but ensures ownership claim whenever necessary. Digital watermarking has been successfully validated to be very suitable in identifying thesource; creator, owner and distributor of a digital multimedia object (Shih, 2008).

Digital image watermarking techniques are classified into various classes depending on various laid criteria. One of the prominent classifications is based on the domain of embedding the watermark. Based on this criteria watermarking is classified into spatial and transform domain (Shabir et al, 2013c; Parah et al, 2015d). Spatial domain watermarking techniques are the earliest and simplest. In spatial domain watermarking the watermark is embedded in some of the selected pixels (or all) of a cover image (Shabir et al, 2012b; Shabir et al, 2013c; Shabir et al, 2012c; Parah et al, 2015c). On the other hand, transform domain watermarking techniques involve modification of the transformed coefficients of the cover image. These transform domain watermarking makes use of various image transforms like Fourier Transform (FT) (Cintra et al, 2009; Liu and Zaho, 2010), Discrete Wavelet Transform (DWT) (Ghuti et al, 2006; Lu et al, 2012; Tsai, 2011; Wang et al, 2007), Singular Value Decomposition (SVD) (Djurovic et al, 2001; Lai and Tsai, 2010; Liu and Tan, 2002; Chen et al, 2013), Fractional Fourier Transform (FFT) (Bhatnagar and Ramman, 2011) and Contorlet transform. Pixel domain (spatial domain) watermarking schemes have least computational overhead; however they are fragile to various image processing and geometric attacks (Shabir et al, 2014a; Shabir et al, 2013a; Shabir et al, 2012a; Shabir et al, 2015; Shabir et al, 2014c). Transform domain methods on the other hand, are robust as compared to spatialdomain techniques. It is due to the underlying fact that when the inverse transformation is applied to a watermarked image, the watermark is irregularly distributed over the whole image. Thus it is very difficult for an attacker to extract or even modify the watermark. This paper presents a very intresting approach to watermarking, wherein we have successfully shown that a robust watermarking system can be implemented in spatial domain by embedding the watermark in DC component of Discrete Cosine Transfer (DCT) coefficients. Rest of the paper has been organised as follows. An extensive survey of literature has been presented in section 2. Mathematical preliminaries have been discussed in section 3. Proposed system has been discussed in detail in section 4. Section 5 presents experimental results and discussions. The paper concludes in section 6.

2. RELATED WORK

A lot of research has been reported in the field of digital watermarking. Parah et al, 2016 have proposed a robust and blind watermarking technique in DCT domain using inter-block coefficient differencing. The scheme utilises the difference between two DCT coefficients of the adjacent blocks to embed the watermark information. The scheme has been shown to be robust to various image processing andgeometric attacks. The authors show that besides singular attacks the scheme is robust to hybrid attacks as well. An adaptive blind image watermarking using edge pixel concentration has been reported in (Fazlali et al, 2016). A two-level Contourlet transform on the cover image has been used. Thefirst level approximate image is partitioned into blocks and edge information is extracted. This is followed by application of DCT Transform at the block level. Improved robustness has been guaranteed by embedding the watermark redundantly and using majority vote during extraction.A novel watermarking system for copyright protection and verification has been proposed in (Bhatnagr and Wu, 2015). The cover image has been segmented into non-overlapping blocks utilizing the means of space filling curve amount of DCT energy in the blocks. Multiple watermarks have been embedded in the cover image. Singular Value Decomposition (SVD) has been used to embed watermarks into the image. The scheme besides yielding good perceptual quality watermark images has been shown to be robust to various image processing attacks. A frequency domain adaptive digital image watermarking scheme has been reported in (Karla et al, 2015). The scheme has been designed for color images. Prior to watermark embedding Hamming codes are added to the intensity component of color image. Dual encryption has been used on watermark to ensure its security. The scheme makes use of DWT, DCT and Arnold transform and has been reported to be robust to various signal processing attacks.

A blind watermarking technique for images based on chaotic mixtures has been reported in (Niansheng et al, 2015). Logistic maps have been firstly used to scramble the watermark. DWT is used on cover image and watermark is embedded approximation coefficients. The authors proposed a technique displayingvery good properties with regard to imperceptibility, robustness and security.A blind watermarking scheme where middle frequency bands of the Fractional Fourier Transform (FrFT) of an image are used to embed watermark has been reported in (Lang and Zang, 2014). The scheme is robust to manyimageprocessing operations. But the proposed system has less robustness to JPEG compression.A secure and robust watermarking technique for gray scale images is presented in (Guo et al, 2015). Both cover image and logo are encrypted before embedding. However, the schemeperformance to JPEG compression waspoor.A DCT based watermarking technique has been reported in (Ma et al, 2012). Arnold transform has been used to reduce the correlation between pixels and enhance security. A watermarking technique based on the concept of mathematical remainder is reported in (Lin et al, 2010).The scheme was robust against various image processing attacks has lesser imperceptibility. A DCT based robust watermarking technique has been reported in (Das et al, 2014). The cover image was divided into 8 ×8 pixel blocks followed by computation of DCT of each block. The scheme has been reported to be robust to various image processing and geometric attacks.

All the above discussions reveal that watermarking is usually carried out in spatial domain or frequency domain with both the domains. The main advantage of former is lesser computational complexity and the later robustness to various attacks. In this paper we try to explore a watermarking system which has lesser computational complexity like spatial domain but offer robustness to various attacks as in transform domain. We have successfully shown that a robust watermarking system can be implemented in spatial domain by embedding the watermark in DC component of DCT. It is however important to mention that DCT has not been used for computation of DC component of a block, but it has been generated in spatial domain. It is in place to mention that (Shih and Wu, 2003) have already put forth watermarking scheme which uses both spatial domain and frequency domain concepts However, unlike the proposed scheme the authors make use of actual DCT transform to compute various coefficients.

Consequently, a new blind watermarking schemegrey scale images has been proposed in this paper. The scheme makes use of arithmetic mean of a selected block to compute its corresponding DC coefficient (without involving use of DCT, DC coefficient is computed). The watermark is embedded by modifying pixel values in accordance with watermark informationand the quantization step. The proposed system not only evades the errors resulting from the spectral transformation but also keepsthe distribution feature of frequency coefficients. As such the proposed scheme is computationally simpler.

3. MATHEMATICAL PRELIMINARIES

3.1. Computation DC Coefficients in Spatial Domain

Discrete Cosine Transform (DCT) is used for domain transformation of a given set of real numbers. The transform kernel of DCT is cosine function. DCT has been used widely in various multimedia watermarking applications due to the fact that famous compression standard JPEG also makes use of it. For the transformation of images from spatial domain to spectral domain 2-D DCT transform is used. Conversely for restoration of an image from its frequency components the inverse 2-D DCT is used.

For a $P \times Q$ image g (x, y) (x = 0, 1, 2,. . ., P-1, y = 0, 1, 2,. . ., Q-1),its 2-D DCT is given as follows:

$$C\left(u,v\right) = \alpha_u \alpha_v \sum_{x=0}^{P-1} \sum_{y=0}^{Q-1} g\left(x,y\right) \cos \frac{\pi\left(2x+1\right)u}{2P} \cos \frac{\pi\left(2y+1\right)v}{2Q} \qquad (1)$$

where P and Qrepresent the rows and columnsof g(x, y), u and v are the horizontal and vertical frequency components (u = 0, 1, 2,. . ., P-1, v = 0, 1, 2,. . .,Q-1), C(u, v) is the DCT coefficient of image g(x, y).

$$\alpha_u = \begin{vmatrix} \dfrac{1}{\sqrt{P}} & for\, u = 0 \\ \\ \sqrt{\dfrac{2}{P}} & for\, 1 \leq u < P-1 \end{vmatrix} \qquad (2)$$

$$\alpha_v = \begin{vmatrix} \dfrac{1}{\sqrt{Q}} & for\, v = 0 \\[2em] \sqrt{\dfrac{2}{Q}} & for\, 1 \le v < Q - 1 \end{vmatrix} \tag{3}$$

The inverse DCT is given by:

$$g(x,y) = \sum_{u=0}^{P-1}\sum_{v=0}^{Q-1} \alpha_u \alpha_v\; C(u,v) \cos\frac{\pi(2x+1)u}{2P} \cos\frac{\pi(2y+1)v}{2Q} \tag{4}$$

Expanding the above equation we get:

$$g(x,y) = \alpha_0 \alpha_0 C(0,0) + \alpha_0 \alpha_1 C(0,1)\cos\frac{\pi(2y+1)}{2Q} + \alpha_0 \alpha_2 C(0,2)$$
$$+ \ldots\ldots + \alpha_P \alpha_Q C(P,Q)\cos\frac{P\pi(2x+1)}{2P}\cos\frac{Q\pi(2y+1)}{2Q} \tag{5}$$

It is evident from the above expanded expression that spatial domain image can be obtained from various constituent frequency domain coefficients.

The DC coefficient in the DCT domain can be easily found using equation (1) and is given as:

$$C(0,0) = \frac{1}{\sqrt{PQ}}\sum_{x=0}^{P-1}\sum_{y=0}^{Q-1} g(x,y) \tag{6}$$

It is evident from Equation (6) that DC coefficient C(0,0) is simply averaged sum of all pixel values of g(x, y) in the pixel domain

The basic procedure of adding a watermark in DCT domain involves addition of watermark information to various DCT coefficients, followed by usage of inverse DCT to obtain watermarked image. It is a proven fact that the energy of signal added to DC coefficient does not suffer any loss after the application of inverse DCT. In order to elaborate the results, the authors can refer to (Qingtang et al, 2013). The outline of the whole process is that embedding watermark into the DC coefficient in DCT domain can be easily replaced in the pixel domain.

3.2. DC Component Modification

We have already shown that the DC coefficient can be obtained by using arithmetic average of a given image block in spatial domain. Further, watermark embedding the DC component of DCT domain can be achieved by adjusting the value of pixel in the spatial domain appropriately. It is however pertinent to mention that the modified total of all the picture elements in pixel domain must equal the altered value of DC coefficient in transform domain. It is significant to find the updating value of every pixel in the pixel domain in accordance with changed value of DC component in the transform domain.

From Equation (4), the inverse DCT can be rewritten as:

$$g(x,y) = \frac{1}{\sqrt{PQ}} C(0,0) + g^{\sim}(x,y) \tag{7}$$

where $g^{\sim}(x,y)$ represents the reconstructed image from AC components.

Assume that cover image is represented by number of non-overlapping blocks represented as:

$$g(x,y) = \left\{ g_{i,j}(m,n), 0 \leq i < \frac{M}{b}, 0 \leq j < \frac{N}{b}, 0 \leq m,n < b \right\} \tag{8}$$

Here M and N represent row and column dimensions of the cover image and b × b is size of each block (cover image is divided into (i × j) non-overlapped blocks). Let us assume that while embedding watermark bit into DC component of the (i, j)th block, the altered value of the said component is given by $\Delta A_{i,j}$.

Using Equations (4) and (6) the modified DC component of (i, j)th block is represented by:

$$C'i,j(0,0) = Ci,j(0,0) + \Delta A_{i,j} \tag{9}$$

and $$g'(m,n) = \frac{1}{b} C'i,j(0,0) + g^{\sim}_{i,j}(m,n) \tag{10}$$

Here $C'i,j(0,0)$ represents the altered DC coefficient with alteration factor $\Delta A_{i,j}$. It is further to be noted that $g^{\sim}_{i,j}(m,n)$ represents reconstructed image block from AC components while as $g'(m,n)$ represents cover image block with watermark data.

From the above equations the following expressions can be involved:

$$g'_{i,j}(m,n) = \frac{1}{b} C'i,j(0,0) + g^{\sim}_{i,j}(m,n) \tag{11}$$

$$= \frac{1}{b}(C_{i,j}(0,0) + \Delta A_{i,j}) + g^{\sim}_{i,j}(m,n) \tag{12}$$

$$= \frac{\Delta A_{i,j}}{b} + \frac{\Delta A_{i,j}}{b}(C_{i,j}(0,0) + g^{\sim}_{i,j}(m,n) \tag{13}$$

$$g'_{i,j}(m,n) = \frac{\Delta A_{i,j}}{b} + g_{i,j}(m,n) \tag{14}$$

Above equations (10) to (14) specify that each pixel has to be modified using an alteration factor of $\dfrac{\Delta A_{i,j}}{b}$.

4. METHODOLOGY

The block diagram of proposed system is shown in Figure 1. The watermark to be embedded is firstly encrypted using chaotic encryption. An adaptive key length is used for setting up initial conditions for the generation of chaos to encrypt the watermark. To enhance the security of the watermark encrypted watermark has been embedded in the cover images. Watermark encryption has been discussed in detail in section 4.1. The grey scale host image has been divided into 8×8 non-overlapping blocks. Cover image and encrypted watermark are inputted to watermark embedder for generation of watermarked image. It is pertinent to mention that 512×512 sized images have been used for testing the algorithm. Since a 512×512 image is composed of 4096, 8×8 blocks, we embed a 64×64 binary watermark in every cover image with a single bit of information embedded in each 8×8 block. The DC coefficient of each block has been computed in spatial domain as already discussed. The watermark has been embedded by modifying the DC component of each block. Watermark embedding has been described in section 4.2, while as extraction has been discussed in detail in section 4.3.

The detailed description of the proposed scheme block diagram is as follows.

4.1. Chaotic Encryption

Chaotic encryption was used to increase the security of the proposed system. Conventional data scrambling and encryption systems like DES, RSA etc. are not appropriate for encrypting digital images. This is due to high redundancy and bulk data involved with digital images. In such a scenario chaotic encryption has been found as a wonderful alternative. This is because the chaotic signals have been found to have

Figure 1. Block diagram of the proposed scheme

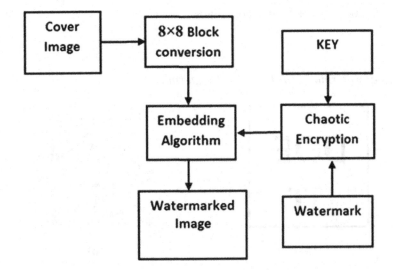

cryptographically enviable features like high sensitivity to initial conditions, high randomness and long periodicity etc. Due to presence of mentioned properties chaos-based image cryptosystems have been found to be highly robust to statistical attacks. Further the inherent properties of chaos like confusion and diffusion, balanced-ness and high randomness make it an ideal candidate to be used for encrypting image based data.

The pseudo- randomness and the non-linear dynamics of chaos were tapped for securing the watermark.An Analog non- linear chaotic system is represented by:

$$\frac{dX_i(t)}{dt} = f\left(X_j(t), \alpha\right) \tag{15}$$

Here $X_i(t) \in R^N$ represents the coordinate i of the system state at time instant t., f a parametric non-linear function, which controls evolution of the system and α is a vector that also the system evolution. For digital multimedia applications we make use of the discrete-time non-linear dynamic systems (NLDS). A discrete time NDLS is given by:

$$X_{i+1} = f\left(X_i, \alpha\right) \tag{16}$$

Typically, the time evolution of X can be calculated with given f, α initial state vector X(0). A 64×64 watermark for embeddingwas used. Figure 2(a) and 2(b) show the original watermark and its encrypted version using chaotic encryption.

The initial parameters for chaos generationwere definite by means of encryption key K. The pseudo-code for the generation of chaos is as follows:

Algorithm 1. Generation of chaos
Data = Original watermark (1: n); %% Read watermark
x = []; %% Memory allocation
x (1)=0.5; %% First element initialization
μ = 3.3; %% Variable initiation for chaos generation
p = []; %% Memory allocation for final chaotic data
for y=1:n

Figure 2. (a) Original watermark. (b) Encrypted Watermark

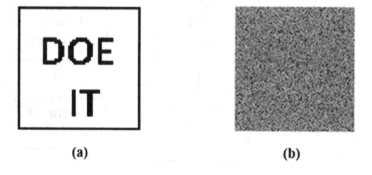

| (a) | (b) |

```
x(y+1)= µ *x(y)*(1-x(y));
if x(y)>0 && x(y)<0.5
ew(y)=~data(y);
elseif x(y)>=0.5
ew(y)=data(y); %% 'ew' stores the final encrypted watermark
end
end
```

4.2. Watermark Embedding

The applied embed the watermark in a cover image are as follows: 1) read the cover image and divide it into 8×8 non-overlapping pixel blocks, 2) encrypt the watermark (as per section 3.1), 3) directly compute DC coefficient $Cij(0,0)$ of each block according to Equation (6), and iv) asper encrypted watermark bit value ew(i, j) alteration factors magnitudes AF1and AF2 as shown below are chosen:

$$if \, ew(i,j) = 1, \begin{cases} AF1 = 0.5\beta \\ AF2 = -1.5\beta \end{cases} \tag{17}$$

$$if \, ew(i,j) = 0, \begin{cases} AF1 = -0.5\beta \\ AF2 = 1.5\beta \end{cases} \tag{18}$$

Afterward, use the alteration factors AF1 and AF2 to compute the quantized coefficient values as: $C1=2k\beta+AF1$, and $C2=2k\beta+AF2$, where $k = \text{floor(ceil}(Ci,j(0,0) / 2\beta)$.

Then, compute $C'i,j(0,0)$ for embedding the watermark in $Ci,j(0,0)$ using the following expression:

$$C'_{i,j}(0,0) = \begin{cases} C_2 & if \, abs\left(C_{i,j}(0,0) - C_2\right) < abs\left(C_{i,j}(0,0) - C_1\right) \\ C_1 & else \end{cases} \tag{19}$$

The modified value $\Delta Ci,j$ of the DC coefficient is then computedas follows:

$$\Delta Ci,j(0,0) = C'i, (0,0) - Ci,j(0,0) \tag{20}$$

Finally, in order to obtain the watermarked image, $\Delta Ci,j(0,0)/8$ is added to all the pixels of the block.

4.3. Watermark Extraction

The proposed scheme uses blind extraction. The following steps are followed to extract the watermark from thewatermarked image.

1.   Divide the watermarkedimage into non-overlapped 8×8 blocks.

2. Obtain the DC coefficient $Ci,j(0,0)$ of each block of watermarked image directly using equation (6).
3. Compute the encrypted watermark that was embedded in the watermarked imageusing the quantification step β as follows:

$$ew(i,j) = mod\left(ceil\left(\frac{Ci,j(0,0)}{\beta}\right),2\right) \tag{21}$$

4. Use same key K, at the receive for successful decryption of watermark

4.4. Proposed System Evaluation

The proposed system is analysed for these parameters using various subjective and objective image quality metrics. Some of the objective image quality metrics used to evaluate the scheme have been defined below. It is pertinent to mention that Cj,k and Wj,k respectively represent cover image and its watermarked version. P and Q are number of pixels in rows and columns while as wm and wme respectively denote embedded and extracted watermarks.

A. Peak Signal to Noise Ratio (PSNR)

$$PSNR = 10\log\frac{(2^n - 1)^2}{MSE} = 10\log\frac{(255)^2}{MSE} \tag{22}$$

B. Mean Square Error (MSE)

$$MSE = \frac{1}{PQ}\sum_{j=1}^{P}\sum_{k=1}^{Q}(C_{j,k} - W_{j,k})^2 \tag{23}$$

C. Normalized cross co-relation (NCC)

$$NCC = \frac{\sum_{j=1}^{P}\sum_{k=1}^{Q}(C_{j,k} * W_{j,k})}{\sum_{j=1}^{P}\sum_{k=1}^{Q}C^2_{j,k}} \tag{24}$$

$$\text{Bit Error Rate (BER)} = \frac{1}{PQ}\left[\sum_{i=1}^{P}\sum_{j=1}^{Q}w_m(i,j) \oplus w_{me}(i,j)\right]\times100 \tag{25}$$

5. EXPERIMENTAL RESULTS AND DISCUSSIONS

Digital image watermarking systems are supposed to satisfy some important requirements like imperceptibility, robustness and security.

5.1. Imperceptibility Analysis

Imperceptibility in a wartermarking system refers to the fact that addition of watermark shoud to add a perceptible artifacts to the original image. This section presents various subjective and objective experimental results obtained from the imperceptivity point of view of the proposed system. It is to be noted that the proposed scheme is tested on a number of standard grey scale test image of size (512 x512), while as size of the embedded watermark is 64× 64. The investigation has been carried out on Intel core i5-560M, 2.66 GHz processor with 4GB RAM using MATLAB 7 running on Windows platform. Figure 3 shows various original images and their respective watermarked imagesobtained using proposed scheme, while as objective metrics obtained are presented in Table 1.

It is evident from the subjective quality of the watermarked images that the proposed technique is capable of producing highly imperceptible watermarked images

From Table 1,it is seen that average PSNR obtained for the test images is 42.82 dB and NCC is 1.0000 showing that high quality imperceptible images are produced by the proposed scheme. A comparison of the PSNR of the proposed scheme with various state- of-art schemes for test image Lena is shown in Figure 4.

Figure 3. Original images and their corresponding watermarked versions

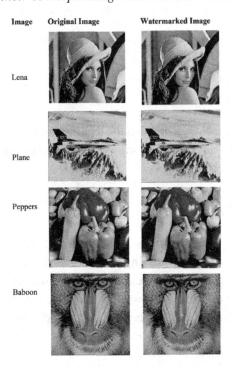

Table 1. Various Image quality metrics for watermarked images

Image	PSNR (dB)	NCC
Lena	42.83	1.0000
Baboon	42.89	1.0000
Peppers	42.84	1.0000
Plane	42.72	1.0000
Average	**42.82**	**1.0000**

Figure 4. Comparison of proposed scheme with state-of art- for "Lena"

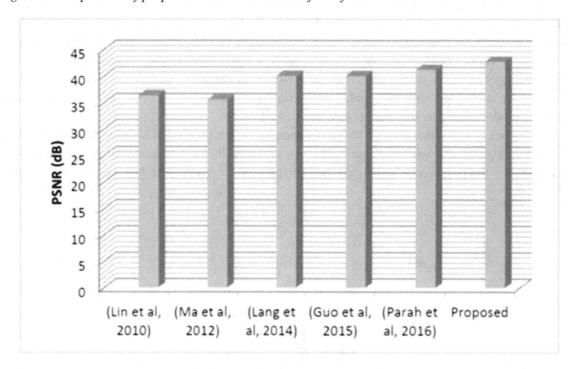

As shown the proposed scheme outperforms all the techniques under comparison. A further comparison of the proposed scheme with various a latest state-of-art schemesas depicted in Table 2, whichshows the superiority of the proposed scheme.

5.2 Robustness Analysis

Robustness refers to ability of a watermarking scheme to withstand various attacks. The watermarked images are subjected to various image processing and geometric attacks to investigate the robustness of the proposed scheme. Figure 5 shows subjective quality of watermarked images after different attacks, for test image Lena while as Table 3 shows various objective quality parameters obtained when watermarked Lena is subjected to various attacks alike, noise addition, filtering, histogram equalization and JPEG compression.

Table 2. Comparison of proposed scheme with (Parah et al, 2016)

Image	PSNR (dB)	
	(Parah et al, 2016)	**Proposed**
Lena	41.27	42.83
Baboon	41.21	42.89
Peppers	41.84	42.84
Plane	41.17	42.72
Average	**41.37**	**42.82**

Figure 5. Subjective quality of 'Lena' for various attacks

Table 3. Various Image quality parameters after different attacks on watermarked 'Lena'

Attack	PSNR (dB)	BER	NCC
No Attack	42.8312	0	1.0000
Median Filtering (3x3)	34.7958	0.0430	0.9886
Salt and Pepper Noise (d=0.01)	25.1388	0.1531	0.9718
Histogram Equalization	19.0975	0.4836	0.8859
Gaussian Noise (v=0.0002)	29.6893	0.0164	0.9963
JPEG (Quality Factor)			
10	29.5628	0.0188	0.9477
20	29.5628	0.0773	0.9505
30	30.5493	0.0674	0.9894
40	31.1212	0.0071	0.9994
50	31.5609	0.0012	0.9997
60	31.9095	0	1.0000
70	32.3640	0	1.0000
80	32.9650	0	1.0000
Low Pass Filtering (3x3)	30.7020	0.0583	0.9607
Sharpening (3x3)	25.8487	0.6943	0.7478
Rotation (Degrees)			
1	42.4311	0.0590	0.9882
10	42.8314	0.0640	0.9886
45	42.0314	0.1685	0.9880
Cropping			
Centre	42.8314	0.0918	0.9991
Top Left Corner	42.6780	0.1678	0.9993
Bottom left corner	42.2345	0.2322	0.9996
Top right Corner	42.7717	0.0918	0.9989
Bottom right corner	42.8022	0.1254	0.9979

Table 4. Various Image quality parameters after different attacks on watermarked 'Baboon'

Attack	PSNR (dB)	BER	NCC
No Attack	42.8945	0	1.0000
Median Filtering (3x3)	25.0021	0.0700	0.9501
Salt and Pepper Noise (d=0.01)	25.5055	0.3098	0.9321
Histogram Equalization	16.2279	0.5020	0.8632
Gaussian Noise (v=0.0002)	29.7877	0.1489	0.9736
JPEG (Quality Factor)			
10	24.2698	0.5479	0.8034
20	26.0754	0.3052	0.9014
30	27.1856	0.1152	0.9727
40	28.0265	0.0071	0.9924
50	28.7920	0	1.0000
60	29.6154	0	1.0000
70	31.5067	0	1.0000
80	32.8423	0	1.0000
Low Pass Filtering (3x3)	24.4918	0.1387	0.9665
Sharpening (3x3)	21.6806	0.4309	0.8856
Rotation (Degrees)			
1	42.8943	0.1007	0.9889
10	42.6945	0.1118	0.9848
45	42.8945	0.1703	0.9801
Cropping			
Centre	42.8933	0.0928	0.9968
Top Left Corner	42.8945	0.2039	1.0000
Bottom left corner	42.8712	0.2332	1.0000
Top right Corner	42.8815	0.2126	0.9996
Bottom right corner	42.8777	0.2364	0.9960

It is pertinent to mention that BER and NCC have been computed between original and extracted watermark, while as PSNR has been computed between Original and Watermarked images. The results in Figure 5 and Table 3 depict that the proposed scheme is robust to the image processing attacks. Tables 4, 5 and 6 respectively show the performance indices of the proposed scheme for test images 'Baboon', 'Peppers' and 'Plane'; respectively.

Table 5. Various Image quality parameters after different attacks on watermarked Pepper

Attack	PSNR (dB)	BER	NCC
No Attack	42.833	0	1.0000
Median Filtering(3x3)	34.5423	0.0291	0.9945
Salt and Pepper Noise (d=0.01)	25.1283	0.2874	0.9393
Histogram Equalization	20.5714	0.4827	0.8558
Gaussian Noise (v=0.0002)	29.8138	0.1423	0.9754
JPEG (Quality Factor)			
15	31.2246	0.5374	0.8504
25	32.6312	0.2197	0.9610
35	33.3813	0.0598	0.9898
45	33.8969	0.0095	1.0000
55	34.3289	0	1.0000
65	34.8219	0	1.0000
75	35.7234	0	1.0000
85	36.1135	0	1.0000
Low Pass Filtering (3x3)	31.2781	0.0754	0.9581
Sharpening (3x3)	26.8880	0.3079	0.9198
Rotation (Degrees)			
1	42.6716	0.0332	0.9919
10	42.8335	0.0632	0.9889
45	42.6331	0.1589	0.9938
Cropping			
Centre	42.8335	0.0938	0.9950
Top Left Corner	42.8515	0.02039	1.0000
Bottom left corner	42.8003	0.02017	0.9996
Top right Corner	42.6315	0.02014	0.9992
Bottom right corner	42.3641	0.0364	0.9660

Table 6. Various Image quality parameters after different attacks on watermarked 'Plane'

Attack	PSNR (dB)	BER	NCC
No Attack	42.7276	0	1.0000
Median Filtering (3x3)	34.0620	0.0735	0.9803
Salt and Pepper Noise (d=0.01)	25.0672	0.2769	0.9416
Histogram Equalization	13.4360	0.5393	0.8509
Gaussian Noise (v=0.0002)	29.7704	0.1436	0.9708
JPEG (Quality Factor)			
15	31.1593	0.4380	0.8020
25	33.0126	0.1912	0.9669
35	34.1132	0.0635	0.9945
45	34.8263	0.0059	0.9994
55	35.4286	0	1.0000
65	36.1732	0	1.0000
75	37.0012	0	+1.0000
85	37.6519	0	1.0000
Low Pass Filtering (3x3)	30.7850	0.1052	0.9442
Sharpening (3x3)	24.8422	0.3030	0.9191
Rotation (Degrees)			
1	42.8192	0.0542	0.9889
10	42.7276	0.0713	0.9841
45	41.1216	0.1848	0.9819
Cropping			
Centre	42.7276	0.0993	0.9956
Top Left Corner	42.1654	0.2039	1.0000
Bottom left corner	42.3213	0.2334	1.0000
Top right Corner	42.1843	0.2114	0.9992
Bottom right corner	42.0907	0.0371	0.9662

5.3. Brief Discussions on Robustness

A brief discussion on robustness of this system to various attacks has been carried out for the system and is presented below.

A. **Median Filtering:** We have subjected the watermarked images is subjected to Median Filtering attack with a kernel of (3×3).The BER to this attack varies from 2% to 7% for the various test images used for evaluating the scheme, showing that the proposed scheme shows a good degree of robustness to this attack.

B. **Salt and Pepper attack:** The watermarked images obtained using proposed scheme have been attacked with salt and pepper noise of (density=0.01). The observed values of BER for various test images vary from 27% to 30%.

C. **Histogram Equalization:** The performance of the proposed scheme is not as good for this attack compared to above mentioned attacks. This is substantiated by high values of BER obtained for various images.

D. **Additive White Gaussian Noise (AWGN):** The proposed scheme has been tested for Gaussian noise attack (variance=0.0002). It has been observed that BER for this attack varies for 14% to 16% for various used images. Thus the scheme is robust to this attack.

E. **Low Pass Filtering:** We have subjected our scheme to Low Pass Filtering attack with filter kernel size of (3×3). It has been seen that the scheme is robust to this attack as the observed BER varies from 5% to 13%.

F. **Sharpening:** The scheme has been subjected to sharpening (3×3) attack. It has been observed that the scheme is less robust to this attack as the observed BER ranges from 30% to 43%.

G. **Rotation:** It has been observed that the proposed scheme is also robust to rotation attack. The observed BER values show that, robustness is highest for lower rotational values while it decreases as rotation increases. As observed the BER varies from 3% to 18% as angle of rotation is increased from 1 degree to 45 degree.

H. **JPEG Compression:** JPEG is one of the mostly used compression standards,used to compress multimedia content like images and videos. It is generally used to save memory space for storing a multimedia object or to save bandwidth requirements. As such it forms on of the most important attacks (though unintentional at times) that a multimedia object like a digital image undergoes. We have exclusively tested our scheme for this attack for varying Quality Factor of JPEG compression. The Quality factor has been varied from 10 to 80. The experimental results show that the proposed scheme is highly robust to this attack. From Table 3 we observe that BER varies from 1% to 7% for quality factor values in the range of 10 to 30. It is pertinent to mention that smaller the quality factor higher the compression. However for any value of Quality factor above 50 the BER reduce to zero. From Table 4 it is observed that BER is 0 for quality factor of 50 or above. Similarly Tables 5 and 6 show that BER is zero for quality factor of 55 and above. It is as such concluded that the proposed scheme is absolutely robust to JPEG compression for a quality factor of 50 and above. This is one of the prominent advantages of the proposed scheme.

Various robustness parameters of the proposed technique are comparedwith that of (Parah et al, 2016) and (Das et al., 2014) . In addition, the results have been depicted in Tables 7 and 8 as shown below. From the tabulated results it is quite evident that proposed scheme is more robust compare various schemes under comparison.

Generally, security using several techniques such as watermarking is an interesting process that applied in several applications as reported in (Dey et al, 2013a; Parah et al, 2015a; Bose et al, 2014; Dey et al, 2013b; Dey et al, 2012a; Parah et al 2015a; Dey et al, 2012b; Parah et al, 2015b; Shabir et al, 2014b, Shabir et al, 2013b; Shabir et al, 2012b; Bhat et al, 2010; Bhat et al, 2009). The proposed approach establishes its efficiency, thus it can be applied with various applications.

Table 7. Robustness comparison of proposed scheme with (Parah et al, 2016) for 'Lena'

Attack	Normalized Cross-Correlation (NC)		PSNR (dB)	
	(Parah et al, 2016)	Proposed	(Parah et al, 2016)	Proposed
Median Filtering (3×3)	0.9445	0.9886	33.52	34.79
Salt and Pepper noise (0.01)	0.8598	0.9798	24.9	25.13
Histogram Equalization	0.9665	0.8893	11	19.09
AWGN (0.0001)	0.9375	0.9963	29.69	30.52
Sharpening	0.99731	0.9778	25.69	25.84

Table 8. Robustness comparison of proposed scheme with (Parah et al, 2016) and (Das et al., 2014) for cropping attack for test Image 'Lena'

CroppedArea	Normalized Cross-Correlation (NC)		
	(Das et al, 2014)	(Parah et al, 2016)	Proposed
25% Top-left corner	0.9954	0.9986	0.9993
25% Top-right corner	0.9973	0.9980	0.9996
25%Bottom-left corner	0.9924	0.9989	0.9989
25%Bottom-right corner	0.9981	0.9980	0.9979

6. CONCLUSION

This paper presented a robust and secure image watermarking scheme for grey scale images. The cover image was divided into 8×8 sub-blocks and instead of computing DC coefficient using DCT. TheDC coefficient of each block in spatial domain was computedand modified in to embed watermark. The quantum of change to be brought in various pixels of a block for embedding watermark bit depends upon DC coefficient of respective blocks, nature of watermark bit (0 or 1) to be embedded and the adjustment factor. Chaotic encryption was used for ensuring security of embedded watermark. Extensive experimental investigations were carried out for imperceptibility and robustness analysis of the scheme. Experimental investigations demonstrated that besides being highly secure,the proposed technique is robust to various signal processing and geometric attacks.

The most important advantage of the system is that it is absolutely robust to JPEG compression for quality factor of 50 and above. The proposed scheme was compared with some state-of- art schemes in the field and comparison results show that our scheme performs better. In addition to above facts it is imperative to understand that the proposed scheme is computationally efficient as DC coefficient which holds the watermark information has been computed in pixel domain instead of using DCT on an image block. The robustness of the proposed scheme to histogram equalization and sharpening, however, is low. The future work aims at modifying the algorithm so that it can withstand these attacks as well.

ACKNOWLEDGMENT

The authors acknowledge the support rendered by University Grants Commission (UGC) Government of India under its Minor Research Project grant number 41-1340/2012(SR) for conduct of this work.

REFERENCES

Bhat, G., Mustafa, M., Shabir, A., & Javaid, A. (2010). FPGA Implementation of Novel Complex PN Code Generator based data Scrambler and Descrambler. *International journal of Science and Technology, 4*(1), 125-135.

Bhat, G., Shabir, A., & Javaid, A. (2009). VHDL Modelling and Simulation of Data Scrambler and Descrambler for secure data communication. *Indian Journal of Science and Technology, 2*(10), 41–43.

Bhatnagar, G., & Raman, B. (2011). A new robust reference logo watermarking scheme. *Multimedia Tools and Applications, 52*(2), 621–640. doi:10.100711042-009-0433-2

Bhatnagar, G., & Wu, Q. (2015). A new robust and efficient multiple watermarking scheme. *Multimedia Tools and Applications, 74*(19), 8421–8444. doi:10.100711042-013-1681-8

Bose, S., Chowdhury, S. R., Sen, C., Chakraborty, S., Redha, T., & Dey, N. (2014). Multi-thread video watermarking: A biomedical application. *Proceedings of International Conference on Circuits, Communication, Control and Computing (I4C)* (pp. 242-246).

Chen, R., Luo, Y., Lan, Y., & Alsharif, R. (2013). A new robust digital image watermarking algorithm based on singular value decomposition and independent component analysis. *J. Com. Inf. Tech., 8*(5), 530–537.

Cintra, J., Dimitrov, S., Oliveira, M., & Campello, M. (2009). Fragile watermarking using finite field trigonometrical transforms. *Signal Processing Image Communication, 24*(7), 587–597. doi:10.1016/j.image.2009.04.003

Cox, I., Miller, L., Bloom, A., Fridrich, J., & Kalker, T. (2008). *Digital watermarking and steganography.* Elsevier.

Das, C., Panigrahi, S., Sharma, V., & Mahapatra, K. (2014). A novel blind robust image watermarking in DCT domain using inter-block coefficient correlation. *Int. J. Electron. Commun, 68*(3), 244–253. doi:10.1016/j.aeue.2013.08.018

Dey, N., Das, P., Chaudhuri, S. S., & Das, A. (2012c). Feature analysis for the blind-watermarked electroencephalogram signal in wireless telemonitoring using Alattar's method. *Proceedings of the Fifth International Conference on Security of Information and Networks* (pp. 87-94). 10.1145/2388576.2388588

Dey, N., Das, P., Roy, A. B., Das, A., & Chaudhuri, S. S. (2012a). DWT-DCT-SVD based intravascular ultrasound video watermarking. *Proceedings of Information and Communication Technologies* (pp. 224–229). WICT.

Dey, N., Mukhopadhyay, S., Das, A., & Chaudhuri, S. S. (2012b). Analysis of P-QRS-T components modified by blind watermarking technique within the electrocardiogram signal for authentication in wireless telecardiology using DWT. *International Journal of Image. Graphics and Signal Processing*, *4*(7), 33–36. doi:10.5815/ijigsp.2012.07.04

Dey, N., Nandi, B., Das, P., Das, A., & Chaudhuri, S. (2013a). Retention of electrocardiogram features insignificantly devalorized as an effect of watermarking. *Advances in Biometrics for Secure Human Authentication and Recognition*, *23*, 175–184. doi:10.1201/b16247-10

Dey, N., Samanta, S., Yang, X. S., Das, A., & Chaudhuri, S. S. (2013b). Optimisation of scaling factors in electrocardiogram signal watermarking using cuckoo search. *International Journal of Bio-inspired Computation*, *5*(5), 315–326. doi:10.1504/IJBIC.2013.057193

Djurovic, I., Stankovic, S., & Pitas, I. (2001). Digital watermarking in the fractional Fourier transformation domain. *Journal of Network and Computer Applications*, *24*(2), 167–173. doi:10.1006/jnca.2000.0128

Fazlali, H., Samavi, S., Karimi, N., & Shirani, S. (2016). *Adaptive blind image watermarking using edge pixel concentration*. Multimed Tools Appl. Doi:10.100711042-015-3200-6

Ghouti, L., Bouridane, A., Ibrahim, M., & Boussakta, S. (2006). Digital image watermarking using balanced multiwavelets. *IEEE Transactions on Signal Processing*, *54*(4), 1519–1536. doi:10.1109/TSP.2006.870624

Ghouti, L., Bouridane, A., Ibrahim, M., & Boussakta, S. (2006). Digital image watermarking using balanced multiwavelets. *IEEE Transactions on Signal Processing*, *54*(4), 1519–1536. doi:10.1109/TSP.2006.870624

Guo, J., Zheng, P., & Huang, J. (2015). Secure watermarking scheme against watermark attacks in the encrypted domain. *Journal of Visual Communication and Image Representation*, *30*, 125–135. doi:10.1016/j.jvcir.2015.03.009

Kalra, G., Talwar, R., & Sadawarti, H. (2015). Adaptive digital image watermarking for color images in frequency domain. *Multimedia Tools and Applications*, *74*(17), 6849–6869. doi:10.100711042-014-1932-3

Lai, C., & Tsai, C. (2010). Digital image watermarking using discrete wavelet transform and singular value decomposition. *IEEE Transactions on Instrumentation and Measurement*, *59*(11), 3060–3063. doi:10.1109/TIM.2010.2066770

Lang, J., & Zhang, Z. (2014). Blind digital watermarking method in the fractional Fourier transform domain. *Optics and Lasers in Engineering*, *53*, 112–121. doi:10.1016/j.optlaseng.2013.08.021

Lin, S., Shie, S., & Guo, J. (2010). Improving the robustness of DCT-based image watermarking gainst JPEG compression. *Computer Standards & Interfaces*, *32*(1-2), 54–60. doi:10.1016/j.csi.2009.06.004

Liu, R., & Tan, T. (2002). An SVD-based watermarking scheme for protecting rightful ownership. *IEEE Transactions on Multimedia*, *4*(1), 121–128. doi:10.1109/6046.985560

Liu, Y., & Zhao, J. (2010). A new video watermarking algorithm based on 1D DFT and Radon transform. *Signal Processing*, *90*(2), 626–639. doi:10.1016/j.sigpro.2009.08.001

Lu, W., Sun, W., & Lu, H. (2012). Novel robust image watermarking based on subsampling and DWT. *Multimedia Tools and Applications, 60*(1), 31–46. doi:10.100711042-011-0794-1

Ma, F., Zhang, J., & Zhang, W. (2012). A blind watermarking technology based on DCT do-main, *Proc. of the IEEE Int. Conf. on Computer Science and Service System* (pp. 398–401)

Niansheng, L., Huajian, L., Huaiyu, D., Donghui, G., & Deming, C. (2015). Robust blind image watermarking based on chaotic mixtures. *Nonlinear Dynamics, 80*(3), 1329–1355. doi:10.100711071-015-1946-z

Parah, S., Javaid, A., Farhana, A., & Bhat, G. (2015d). On the Realization of Robust Watermarking System for Medical Images. *Proc. of 12th IEEE India International Conference (INDICON) on Electronics, Energy, Environment, Communication, Computers, Control (E3-C3),* New Delhi, India (pp. 172-178).

Parah, S., Javaid, A., Jahangir, A., Nazir, L., Farhana, A., & Bhat, G. (2015c). A high Capacity Data Hiding Scheme Based on Edge Detection and Even-Odd Plane Separation. *Proceedings of 12th IEEE India International Conference (INDICON) on Electronics, Energy, Environment, Communication, Computers, Control (E3-C3),* New Delhi, India (pp. 1-6) 10.1109/INDICON.2015.7443595

Parah, S., Javaid, A., Nazir, L., Farhana, A., & Bhat, G. (2015b). Information Hiding in Medical Images: A Robust Medical Image Watermarking System for E-Healthcare. *Multimedia Tools and Applications.* doi:10.100711042-015-3127-y

Parah, S., Shazia, A., & Ayash, A. (2015a). Robustness analysis of a digital image watermarking technique for various frequency bands in DCT domain. *Proceedings of international 1st IEEE international symposium on nanoelectronic and information systems iNiS,* Indore India (pp. 71-76). 10.1109/iNIS.2015.41

Parah, S., Sheikh, J., Hafiz, M., & Bhat, G. (2014a). A secure and robust information hiding technique for covert communication. *International Journal of Electronics, 102*(8), 1253–1266. doi:10.1080/00207217.2014.954635

Parah, S., Sheikh, J., Loan, N., & Bhat, G. (2016). Robust and blind watermarking technique in DCT domain using inter-block coefficient differencing. *Digital Signal Processing, 53,* 11–24. doi:10.1016/j.dsp.2016.02.005

Qingtang, S., Yugang, N., Qingjun, W., & Guorui, S. (2013). A blind color image watermarking based on DC component in the spatial domain. *Optik (Stuttgart), 124,* 255–6260.

Shabir, A., Javaid, A., & Bhat, G. (2012a). Data hiding in ISB planes: A high capacity blind stenographic technique. *Proc. of IEEE sponsored Intl. Conference INCOSET '12, Tamilnadu, India* (pp. 192-197).

Shabir, A., Javaid, A., & Bhat, G. (2012b). On the realization of a secure, high capacity data embedding technique using joint top-down and down- top embedding approach. *Elixir Comp. Sci. & Engg., 49,* 10141–10146.

Shabir, A., Javaid, A., & Bhat, G. (2013a). On the Realization of a spatial Domain Data Hiding Technique based on Intermediate Significant Bit Plane Embedding (ISBPE) and Post Embedding Pixel Adjustment (PEPA). *Proceedings of IEEE International Conference on Multimedia Signal Processing and Communication Technologies IMPACT '13,* AMU, Aligargh, India (pp. 51-55)

Shabir, A., Javaid, A., & Bhat, G. (2013b). Data hiding in color images: A high capacity data hiding technique for covert communication. *Computer Engineering and Intelligent Systems*, *4*, 113–118.

Shabir, A., Javaid, A., & Bhat, G. (2013c). High capacity data embedding using joint intermediate significant bit and least significant technique. *International Journal of Information Engineering and Applications*, *2*, 1–11.

Shabir, A., Javaid, A., & Bhat, G. (2014a). A secure and efficient spatial domain data hiding technique based on pixel adjustment. *American Journal of Engineering and Technology Research*, *14*(2), 38–44.

Shabir, A., Javaid, A., & Bhat, G. (2014b). Data hiding in scrambled images: A new double layer security data hiding technique. *Computers & Electrical Engineering*, *40*(1), 70–82. doi:10.1016/j.compeleceng.2013.11.006

Shabir, A., Javaid, A., & Bhat, G. (2014c). Fragility Evaluation Of Intermediate Significant Bit Embedding (ISBE) Based Digital Image Watermarking Scheme For Content Authentication. *Proc. of International Conference on Electronics, Computers and Communication*, Banglore, India (pp. 198-203)

Shabir, A., Javaid, A., & Bhat, G. (2015). Hiding in encrypted images: A three tier security data hiding system. *Multidimensional Systems and Signal Processing*. doi:10.100711045-015-0358-z

Shabir, A., Javaid, A., & Bhat G. (2012c). On The Realization Of Secure And Efficient Data Hiding System using ISB & LSB Technique. *Engineering e-Transaction*, *7*(2), 48-53.

Shih, F., & Wu, S. (2003). Combinational image watermarking in the spatial and frequency domains. *Pattern Recognition*, *36*(4), 969–975. doi:10.1016/S0031-3203(02)00122-X

Shih, Y. (2008). *Digital watermarking and steganography: fundamentals and techniques*. FL: CRC Press. doi:10.1007/978-3-540-92238-4

Tsai, M. (2011). Wavelet tree based digital image watermarking by adopting the chaotic system for security enhancement. *Multimedia Tools and Applications*, *52*(2–3), 347–367. doi:10.100711042-010-0475-5

Wang, S., Zheng, D., Zhao, J., Tam, J., & Speranza, F. (2007). An image quality evaluation method based on digital watermarking. *IEEE Transactions on Circuits and Systems for Video Technology*, *17*(1), 98–105. doi:10.1109/TCSVT.2006.887086

This research was previously published in the Journal of Global Information Management (JGIM), 25(4); edited by Zuopeng (Justin) Zhang; pages 80-102, copyright year 2017 by IGI Publishing (an imprint of IGI Global).

Chapter 2
Chaotic Function Based ECG Encryption System

Butta Singh
Guru Nanak Dev University, India

Manjit Singh
Guru Nanak Dev University, India

Dixit Sharma
Guru Nanak Dev University, India

ABSTRACT

Remote health-care monitoring systems communicate biomedical information (e.g. Electrocardiogram (ECG)) over insecure networks. Protection of the integrity, authentication and confidentiality of the medical data is a challenging issue. This chapter proposed an encryption process having a 4-round five steps -encryption structure includes: the random pixel insertion, row separation, substitution of each separated row, row combination and rotation. Accuracy and security analysis of proposed method for 2D ECG encryption is evaluated on MIT-BIH arrhythmia database.

INTRODUCTION

The technology advancements in health care systems have dramatically increased the number of elderly patients. Remote health care monitoring of patients can decrease the traffic at specialized medical centers and provide reliable emergency services. The applications of remote healthcare technologies have also reduced the medical costs as well. In remote health care monitoring, body sensors acquire biological signals and other physiological parameters of the patient. The recorded signals and confidential side information or any urgent alerts are sent to the specialized hospital servers or medical cloud via the Internet. The security and privacy threats as well as crucial biomedical data integration issues are introduced with internet as a communication channel. Secure transmission of confidential biomedical data has become a common interest in both research and applications (Leeet al., 2008; Li et al., 2013; Hu et

DOI: 10.4018/978-1-7998-1763-5.ch002

al., 2007). Accordingly, it is essential to employ a security protocol which will have powerful information security. One method to protect information from unauthorized eavesdropping is to use an encryption technique. The encryption is the process by which the information is transformed into intelligible form to construct the encrypted data/cipher data. Decryption is the process to reconstruct the original information from encrypted data.

An electrocardiogram (ECG) is an important physiological signal required to transmit in remote health care system used not only to analyze cardiac diseases, but also to provide crucial biometric information for identification and authentication. The ECG signal which monitors the electrical activity of heart is usually characterized by its various set points (P, QRS, T) and intervals (PR interval, QT interval and RR interval) that reflects the rhythmic electrical depolarisation and repolarisation of atria and ventricles (Singh et al., 2014). With an ECG signal, various arrhythmias, degree of myocardial damage and the structure of the atrium and ventricle can also be analyze and identified. While transmitting biomedical information such as ECG through the internet, protection of patient's privacy and confidentiality is a challenging issue (Jero et al., 2015). The methods of computer software should guarantee the information security on the server and inside the communication channels. Several researchers have proposed various security protocols to secure patient confidential information (Enginet al., 2005; Ibaida et al., 2013). The Encryption algorithms based techniques are commonly used to secure data during the communication and storage. As a result, the final data will be stored in encrypted format (Wang et al., 2010; Maglogiannis et al., 2009).

In 1998, Fridrich proposed the chaos-based approach for image encryption (Fridrich 1998), since then there have been increasing researches on chaotic encryption techniques. Chaos based algorithms are developed and considered as the core of encryption processes due to ergodicity, mixing property, the high sensitivity of chaotic systems to parameters and initial conditions (Zhu et al., 2011; Fu et al., 2011; Zhu et al., 2012). Recently, conventional logistic map and tent map based1D chaotic maps, and coupled map lattice based 2D chaotic maps have been developed for substitution-only encryption methods (Soma et al., 2013; Radwan et al., 2016). Chaos-based algorithms have shown exceptionally superior properties in aspects such as security, speed and complexity and computational cost.

Many researchers have proposed ECG signal processing techniques by treating 1D ECG signal as a 2D image and exploiting the inter- and intra-beat correlations by encoder (Chou et al., 2006; Wang et al., 2008). The "cut and align beats approach and 2D DCT" and "period normalization and truncated SVD algorithm" are available preprocessing techniques to get good compression results in ECG (Wei et al., 2001; Lee et al., 1999). This kind of preprocessing are also often associated with the use of state-of-the-art image encoders, like JPEG2000. In (Chou et al., 2006), the authors proposed a lousy compression technique based on converting the 1D ECG signal into 2D ECG image. A period sorting preprocessing technique was introduced, which consists of a length-based ordering of all periods. The authors exploited inter and intra-beat dependencies to compress irregular ECG signals. The technique is based on the supposition that periods with similar lengths tend to be highly correlated, which is not a very strong assumption and may not be valid for pathological ECG signals. Another preprocessing technique consists of QRS detector, period length normalization, period preprocessing and image transform was proposed in (Filho et al., 2008).

This chapter introduces a simple and efficient chaotic system approach using a combination of two existing 1D chaotic maps to encrypt 2D ECG signal. Security analysis reveals the performance of proposed method for 2D ECG encryption. ECG is encrypted in a lossless manner so that after reconstruction there will be zero difference between the original and the reconstructed ECG signal.

MATERIAL AND METHODS

In the emerging field of medical engineering, research subjects like cardiac arrhythmia detection, heart rate variability, cardiovascular and pulmonary dynamics, artificial intelligence based medical decision support and ECG compression, etc. are of major interest (Singh et al., 2012a; Singh et al., 2012b). The Massachusetts Institute of Technology (MIT) supplies some valuable resources for such research projects. These resources include databases containing recorded physiological signals and software for analyzing, viewing and creating such recordings. In the present study, ECG samples from Arrhythmia Database (http://ecg.mit.edu) have been taken for investigation of the efficiency of the proposed method. The Database contains 48 half-hour excerpts of two-channel ambulatory ECG recordings, obtained from 47 subjects studied by the BIH Arrhythmia Laboratory. The 11-bit resolutions over 10 mV range with sampling frequency of 360 Hz per sample channel were recorded.

PROPOSED TECHNIQUE

1D ECG to 2D ECG Signal

Formation of 2D ECG signal broadly consist steps: QRS detection, ECG segmentation, pre-processing, and transformation (Chou et al., 2006; Filho et al., 2008). First stage of process is the acquisition of ECG data from standard MIT-BIH arrhythmia database, for comparative analysis and validation of proposed technique. Details of this database are already discussed in section 2. The second stage involved QRS detection and R peak based ECG segmentation. The peaks of QRS complex were detected to identify each RR interval and to map 1D ECG signal to 2D ECG image, Many QRS detection algorithms have been proposed in literature and in the present work the RR interval time series were estimated by the Tompkins method proposed in (Pan et al., 1985)for its simple implementation and high detection accuracy In ECG segmentation, ECG samples from one R peak to next R peak are retained in one segmented block and each block (Row wise) is vertically stacked to form 2D ECG image(Chou et al., 2006). The segmentation and reassembling of ECG signal as an image was accomplished by choosing R peak as its delineation boundary, leaving half peak at each end of the row. Further the row oriented assembly was performed by retaining the ECG samples from one R-peak to the next R-peak. Then this 2D ECG will be encrypted by 2D chaotic method. Figure 1 shows the ECG samples for the record of 100, 117 and 119 from MIT-BIH arrhythmia ECG database. Figure 2 shows the result of 2D array of row wise stacking with their histograms in Figure 3. The resulted image was encoded through standard bitmap encoder which provides progressive quality. The resulted encrypted 2D ECG can be transmitted over cloud or a base station from remote place and can be reconstructed at receiving end. The first stage of reconstruction process is to split the side information and encrypted ECG from the merged data coming from communication channel. The next stage of reconstruction process is R peak based incorporation and estimation of raw ECG data.

Chaos Based ECG Encryption

To investigate the proposed chaotic system in information security for ECG, using the Logistic Tent System as its example, we used 1D chaotic image encryption algorithm for ECG encryption.

Figure 1. First 2500 ECG samples of data 100, 117, and 119 of MIT-BIH arrhythmia database

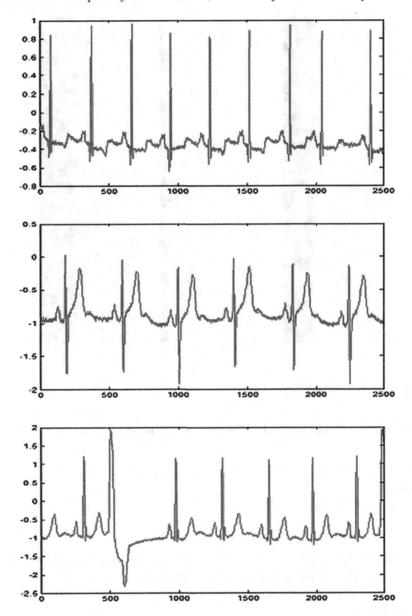

The proposed algorithm has a 4-round-encryption structure. Each encryption round includes five steps: the random pixel insertion, row separation, substitution of each separated row, row combination and rotation with 90° in anticlockwise direction (Figure 4). The algorithm first inserts a random pixel in the beginning of each row in the original 2D ECG, separates each row into a 1D data matrix, applies a substitution process to change data values in each 1D matrix, combines all 1D matrices back into a 2D data matrix according to their row positions in the original 2D ECG, and then rotates the 2D matrix 90° anti clockwise. Repeating these processes four times obtains the final encrypted ECG (Figure 5). The proposed algorithm is able to transform original 2D ECG randomly into different noise-like encrypted images with excellent confusion and diffusion properties.

Figure 2. 2D ECG formation of complete data records 100, 117, and 119 of MIT-BIH arrhythmia database

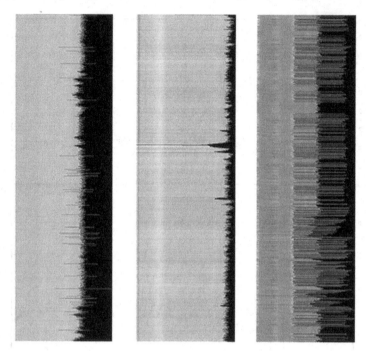

Random ECG Sample Insertion

One ECG sample with a random value is inserted in the beginning of each row in the original 2D ECG signal.

$$PE(x, y) = \begin{cases} Rand(x) & y = 1 \\ E(x, y-1) & otherwise \end{cases}$$

where *E* is the original 2D ECG with size of *M X N; PE(x,y)* is the processed ECG with size of *MX(N+1)*, *1≤x≤M, 1≤y≤N+1;* Random function *Rand(x)* produces random numbers.

Chaotic Substitution

The each row of PE is separated row by row into 1D array

row$_i$(j)=PE(x,y)

where *row$_i$* is the *ith* 1D row array with length of *(N+1)*

The chaotic substitution process replaces the samples in each 1D row array *row$_i$* by the following equation:

Figure 3. Histogram of 100, 117, and 119 data records of MIT-BIH arrhythmia database

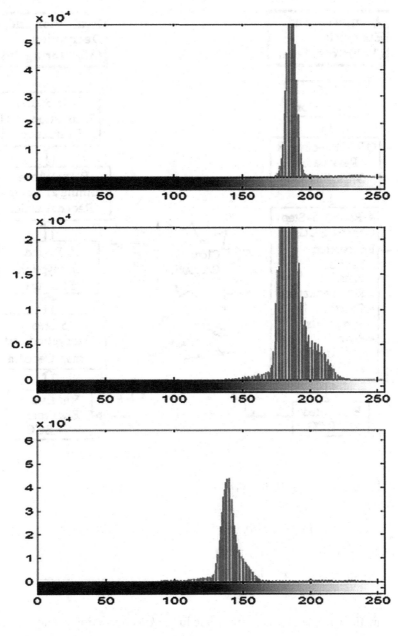

$$\phi_i(j) = \begin{cases} row_i(j) & j = 1 \\ \phi_i(j-1) \oplus row_i(j) \oplus \left(\left\lfloor S_k(i,j)X10^{10} \right\rfloor \bmod 256 \right) & otherwise \end{cases}$$

where $\oplus$ denotes the bit-level XOR operation, $\lfloor . \rfloor$ is the floor function, and $S_k(i,j)$ is the random sequence for the *kth* (k = 1, 2, 3, 4) encryption round, which is generated by the Logistic-Tent system(*LTS*) as defined by the following equation:

Figure 4. Description of proposed ECG encryption and decryption technique

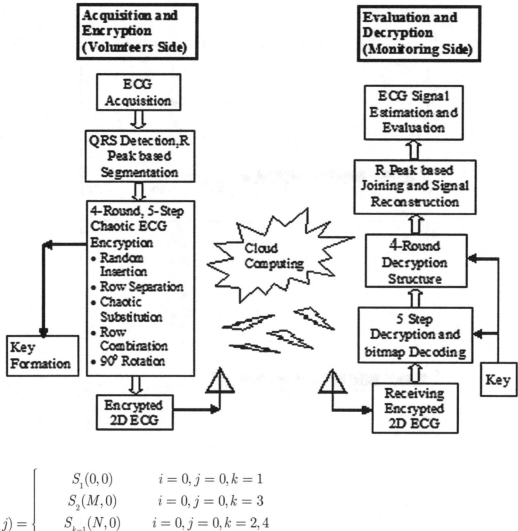

$$S_k(i,j) = \begin{cases} S_1(0,0) & i=0, j=0, k=1 \\ S_2(M,0) & i=0, j=0, k=3 \\ S_{k-1}(N,0) & i=0, j=0, k=2,4 \\ LTS(r_0, S_k(i-1,0)) & i>1, j=0 \\ LTS(r_k, S_k(i,j-1)) & i>1, j>0 \end{cases}$$

where r_k and $S_k(0,0)$ are the parameter and initial value in the *kth* encryption round, respectively; $S_1(0,0)$, r_o and r_k are defined by users.

We utilized the Logistic and Tent maps as seed maps to form the LTS system, as defined in the following equation:

$$X_{n+1} = \begin{cases} (rX_n(1-X_n) + (4-r)X_n/2) \bmod 1 & X_i < 0.5 \\ (rX_n(1-X_n) + (4-r)(1-X_n)/2) \bmod 1 & X_i \geq 0.5 \end{cases}$$

where parameter *r* is with range of (0,4).

Row Combination

After changing data values in each row matrix in the 1D substitution process, the row combination is an inverse process of the row separation and random insertion. It combines all 1D matrices back into a 2D matrix, and removes the first pixel in each row. The process is defined in the following equation:

$$C(i,j) = \phi_i(j+1)$$

where C is the 2D matrix with size of $M \times N$ and $j \leq N$.

Rotation

The process is to rotate the 2D ECG matrix 90 degrees counter clockwise as following equation:

$$E(i,j) = C(j, N - i + 1)$$

After the first encryption round, E is the feedback to the input of the random pixel insertion process. Final encrypted ECG obtained by four encryption rounds. In this algorithm, security keys are composed of six portions: the LTS parameter (r_0) and initial value $S_1(0.0)$, the LTS parameters in each encryption round (r_1, r_2, r_3, r_4).

In decryption stage, the authorized users should have correct security keys and follow the inverse procedures of encryption. The inverse 1D substitution is defined in the following equation:

$$R_i(j) = B_i(j-1) \oplus B_i(j) \oplus \left(\left\lfloor S_k(i, j) X 10^{10} \right\rfloor \bmod 256 \right)$$

Figure 5. Encrypted ECG of complete data records 100, 117, and 119 of MIT-BIH arrhythmia database

Figure 6. Histograms of encrypted 100, 117, and 119 data records of MIT-BIH arrhythmia database

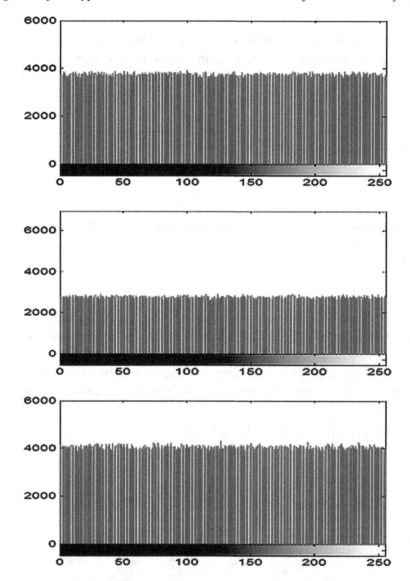

RESULT AND DISCUSSION

Having described the proposed encryption technique, we present in this section the performance evaluation and simulation parameters. The proposed method encrypt ECG signal with excellent confusion and diffusion properties and high security level. These can evade the confidential medical information from leakage.

Figure 7. Decrypted ECG of complete data records 100, 117, and 119 of MIT-BIH arrhythmia database with key $K_1(s_1=0.6; r_0=3.997; r_1=3.99; r_2=3.96; r_3=3.77; r_4=3.99)$

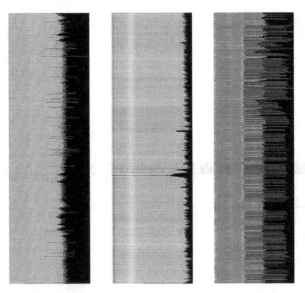

Accuracy Analysis

Percentage Root Mean Square Difference (PRD)

It is a measure of acceptable fidelity and degree of distortion introduced during encryption and decryption algorithm

$$PRD(\%) = 100 \times \sqrt{\frac{\sum_{n=1}^{N}(X_s(n) - X_r(n))^2}{\sum_{n=1}^{N}(X_s(n))^2}}$$

where $X_s(n)$ and $X_r(n)$ are the original and decrypted signal respectively of data length N.

Proposed method encrypt the ECG signal lossless way (PRD=0) for all the data records of MIT-BIH database (Table 1). From juridical and clinical point of view, the use of lossless encryption/decryption process is very much important.

Histogram Analysis

Histogram analysis shows the distribution of pixel values across the whole image where peaks for some specific gray scale value appear. For effectively encrypted images this distribution should be flat (Fuet al., 2011; Radwanet al., 2016). A visual investigation of the proposed method can be observed from the histograms of 2D ECG before and after the encryption (Figure 3 and Figure 6). After the encryption

Figure 8. Histograms of decrypted 100, 117, and 119 data records of MIT-BIH arrhythmia database with key $K_1(s_1=0.6; r_0=3.997; r_1=3.99; r_2=3.96; r_3=3.77; r_4=3.99)$

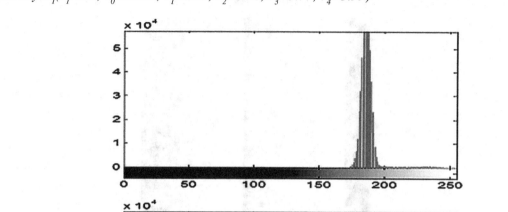
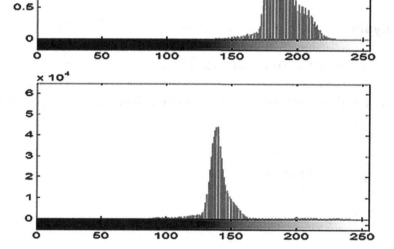

process all histograms became similar to a uniform distribution, independent of the nature of the original histogram, as expected for a strong encryption scheme.Figure 6 shows all encrypted ECG signals are noise- like ones.

Security Analysis

There are several statistical methods for evaluating the noise-like encrypted images, including the information entropy and correlation analysis. A good encryption should resist all kinds of known attacks, it should be sensitive to the secret keys, and the key space should be large enough to make brute-force attacks infeasible. Some security analysis has been performed on the proposed encryption scheme.

Table 1. Security analysis of proposed technique on MIT BIH arrhythmia database

Data	Correlation Coefficient (with -90^0 Rotation)	Correlation Coefficient (with +90^0 Rotation)	Original Information Entropy	Encrypted Information Entropy	Decrypted Information Entropy	PRD
100	0.006	-0.0014	3.9375	7.9914	3.9375	0
101	-0.0096	-0.0105	4.4612	7.993	4.4612	0
102	-0.0036	0.0071	4.6856	7.992	4.6856	0
103	-0.0022	-0.0144	4.6233	7.9922	4.6233	0
104	0.0005	-0.0034	4.8545	7.9928	4.8545	0
105	-0.0057	0.0082	4.2095	7.9947	4.2095	0
106	-0.0042	0.0068	4.7057	7.992	4.7057	0
107	0.0041	-0.0003	6.5215	7.9916	6.5215	0
108	-0.002	0.0017	3.3504	7.995	3.3504	0
109	-0.0033	-0.0038	5.4018	7.9927	5.4018	0
111	0.0029	0.0054	4.9472	7.9916	4.9472	0
112	-0.002	0.0002	5.1214	7.9903	5.1214	0
113	0.0139	0.0085	5.2189	7.992	5.2189	0
114	0.0034	0.0022	4.3191	7.9922	4.3191	0
115	0.0071	-0.0037	4.9676	7.9928	4.9676	0
116	0.0079	0.0023	5.3086	7.9912	5.3086	0
117	0.0099	-0.0006	5.021	7.9913	5.021	0
118	0.0063	0.0035	5.5502	7.9933	5.5502	0
119	0.0037	0.0106	4.6586	7.9944	4.6586	0
121	-0.002	0.0033	5.3168	7.9919	5.3168	0
122	0.0038	0.0018	4.8485	7.9917	4.8485	0
123	0.0017	-0.0056	4.4171	7.9937	4.4171	0
124	-0.0034	-0.0082	4.8685	7.991	4.8685	0
200	-0.0065	0	3.7793	7.9951	3.7793	0
201	-0.0015	0.0043	3.551	7.9935	3.551	0
202	-0.0006	0.0135	4.1958	7.9935	4.1958	0
203	0.0031	-0.0044	2.5367	7.9973	2.5367	0
205	0.0128	-0.0003	3.7393	7.9916	3.7393	0
207	-0.004	-0.0082	3.7522	7.995	3.7522	0
208	0.0009	-0.0131	4.6145	7.9945	4.6145	0
209	0.0107	-0.0027	4.708	7.9913	4.708	0
210	-0.0043	0.0013	3.1032	7.9963	3.1032	0
212	0.011	0.0092	5.3862	7.993	5.3862	0
213	0.0013	-0.0015	5.8204	7.9927	5.8204	0
214	-0.0078	-0.0113	4.2264	7.9944	4.2264	0
215	-0.0061	-0.0028	3.8604	7.9948	3.8604	0
217	-0.0041	-0.0102	6.1748	7.9921	6.1748	0

continues on following page

Table 1. Continued

Data	Correlation Coefficient (with -90° Rotation)	Correlation Coefficient (with +90° Rotation)	Original Information Entropy	Encrypted Information Entropy	Decrypted Information Entropy	PRD
219	0.0023	0.0033	4.3868	7.994	4.3868	0
220	0.0001	-0.0036	4.3864	7.9921	4.3864	0
221	-0.0024	-0.0029	3.632	7.9947	3.632	0
222	0.0028	0.0042	4.3512	7.9926	4.3512	0
223	0.0003	0.0033	3.4806	7.9954	3.4806	0
228	0.0024	-0.0073	3.6248	7.9957	3.6248	0
230	0.0027	-0.0031	4.9464	7.9912	4.9464	0
231	-0.0122	0.0034	3.7568	7.9942	3.7568	0
232	-0.0039	0.0021	2.618	7.9965	2.618	0
233	-0.0053	0.0016	4.9541	7.9945	4.9541	0
234	-0.0014	0.0032	4.8296	7.9911	4.8296	0

Information Entropy

Information entropy (IE) is a measure of uncertainty in a random variable and evaluates the randomness of an image (Fu et al., 2011; Zhu et al., 2012). Higher the IE of an image means the excellent random property.

$$IE = \sum_{l=0}^{F-1} P(L=l) \log_2 \frac{1}{P(L=l)}$$

where F is the gray level and $P(L=l)$ is the percentage of pixels with value equal to l. For a gray scale image maximum IE is 8. Table 1 shows the IE of original, encrypted and decrypted 2D ECG signals of MIT BIH arrhythmia database. IE values of original and decrypted signal are similar for all the data records. Whereas IE values of encrypted signal are very high (>7.9) for all the records which shows the level of randomness in encrypted signals.

Correlation

To verify the robustness of the proposed algorithm against statistic attacks, Pearson correlation coefficients of neighbouring (adjacent) pixels in the original and encrypted 2D ECG signals have been analyzed. The objective of encryption procedure is to transform highly correlated original images in to noise-like encrypted images with low correlations (Fu et al., 2011; Zhu et al., 2012).

The correlation can be computed by

$$corr_{xy} = E[(x-\mu_x)(y-\mu_y)]/(\sigma_x \sigma_y)$$

where μ and σ are the mean value and standard deviation, respectively.

Table 1 validate that the proposed method generated encrypted signal with sufficiently low correlation of adjacent pixels.

Security Key Analysis

Six parameters of encryption algorithm r_0, r_1, r_2, r_3 and $S_1(0,0)$ form the key space. In the key sensitivity test, ECG data from samples 100, 117 and 119 (Figure 1) are encrypted using proposed algorithm with an initial key set (K_1) as

$$s_1=0.6; r_0=3.997; r_1=3.99; r_2=3.96; r_3=3.77; r_4=3.99;$$

Figure 7 and 8 show the decrypted signals and corresponding histograms respectively for data samples 100, 117 and 119 with keys K_1, and then another key set K_2 is generated with a small change applied to r_0 while keeping all other parameters unchanged as

$$s_1=0.6; r_0=3.9970000001; r_1=3.99; r_2=3.96; r_3=3.77; r4=3.99;$$

Figure 9 and 10 show the decrypted signals and corresponding histograms respectively for data samples 100, 117 and 119 with keys K_2. It shows the high key sensitivity of the proposed method in both the encryption and decryption processes. Original signal can be reconstructed using correct key (K_1) only. Even a small change in the security key (e.g. K_2) will lead to the erroneous decryption process.

Figure 9. Decrypted ECG of complete data records 100, 117, and 119 of MIT-BIH arrhythmia database with wrong key K_2 ($s_1=0.6$; $r_0=3.9970000001$; $r_1=3.99$; $r_2=3.96$; $r_3=3.77$; $r_4=3.99$)

Figure 10. Histograms of decrypted 100, 117, and 119 data records of MIT-BIH arrhythmia database with wrong key K_2 (s_1=0.6; r_0=3.9970000001; r_1=3.99; r_2=3.96; r_3=3.77; r_4=3.99)

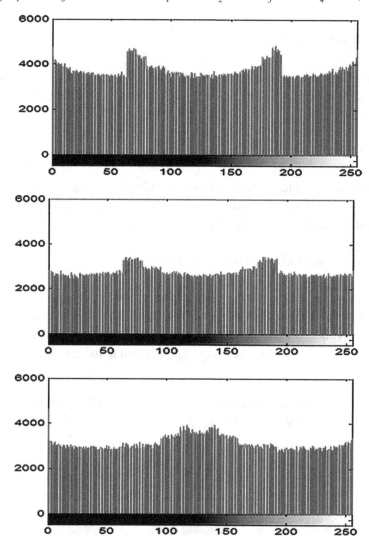

CONCLUSION

In view of E-health recognition and patient privacy, it is essential to encrypt biomedical signals. In particular, medical security is required to provide; confidentiality, integrity and authentication. In this chapter, we develop a chaos-based encryption system for applications to 2D ECG signals.

Excellent diffusion and confusion properties of proposed method can resist the chosen-plaintext attack. Particularly, encrypted signals of the proposed algorithm are random, non- repeated and unpredictable, even using the same set of security keys. The algorithm can also withstand the data loss and noise attacks. While arithmetic operations based encryption approaches have to deal round-off errors, our algorithm recover exact original information after an encryption/decryption procedure. The novelty of this method is that the reconstructed signal is an exact replica of the original one and has an excellent key sensitivity.

REFERENCES

Chou, H. H., Chen, Y. J., Shiau, Y. C., & Kuo, T. S. (2006). An effective and efficient compression algorithm for ECG signals with irregular periods. *IEEE Transactions on Bio-Medical Engineering, 53*(6), 1198–1205. doi:10.1109/TBME.2005.863961 PMID:16761849

Engin, M., Çıdam, O., & Engin, E. Z. (2005). Wavelet transformation based watermarking technique for human electrocardiogram (ECG). *Journal of Medical Systems, 29*(6), 589–594. doi:10.100710916-005-6126-0 PMID:16235811

Filho, E. B. L., Rodrigues, N. M. M., da Silva, E. A. B., de Faria, S. M. M., da Silva, V. M. M., & de Carvalho, M. B. (2008). ECG signal compression based on Dc equalization and complexity sorting. *IEEE Transactions on Bio-Medical Engineering, 55*(7), 1923–1926. doi:10.1109/TBME.2008.919880 PMID:18595813

Fridrich, J. (1998). Symmetric ciphers based on two-dimensional chaotic maps. *International Journal of Bifurcation and Chaos in Applied Sciences and Engineering, 8*(6), 1259–1284. doi:10.1142/S021812749800098X

Fu, C., Lin, B., Miao, Y., Liu, X., & Chen, J. (2011). A novel chaos-based bit-level permutation scheme for digital image encryption. *Optics Communications, 284*(23), 5415–5423. doi:10.1016/j.optcom.2011.08.013

Hu, F., Jiang, M., Wagner, M., & Dong, D. (2007). Privacy-preserving telecardiology sensor networks: Toward a low-cost portable wireless hardware/software codesign. *IEEE Transactions on Information Technology in Biomedicine, 11*(6), 619–627. doi:10.1109/TITB.2007.894818 PMID:18046937

Ibaida, A., & Khalil, I. (2013). Wavelet-based ECG steganography for protecting patient confidential information in point-of-care systems. *IEEE Transactions on Bio-Medical Engineering, 60*(12), 3322–3330. doi:10.1109/TBME.2013.2264539 PMID:23708767

Jero, S. E., Ramu, P., & Ramakrishnan, S. (2015). ECG steganography using curvelet transform. *Biomedical Signal Processing and Control, 22*, 161–169. doi:10.1016/j.bspc.2015.07.004

Lee, H., & Buckley, K. M. (1999). ECG data compression using cut and align beats approach and 2-D transforms. *IEEE Transactions on Bio-Medical Engineering, 46*(5), 556–564. doi:10.1109/10.759056 PMID:10230134

Lee, W., & Lee, C. (2008). A cryptographic key management solution for hipaa privacy/security regulations. *IEEE Transactions on Information Technology in Biomedicine, 12*(1), 34–41. doi:10.1109/TITB.2007.906101 PMID:18270035

Li, M., Yu, S., Zheng, Y., Ren, K., & Lou, W. (2013). Scalable and secure sharing of personal health records in cloud computing using attribute based encryption. *IEEE Transactions on Parallel and Distributed Systems, 24*(1), 131–143. doi:10.1109/TPDS.2012.97

Maglogiannis, I., Kazatzopoulos, L., Delakouridis, K., & Hadjiefthymiades, S. (2009). Enabling location privacy and medical data encryption in patient telemonitoring systems. *IEEE Transactions on Information Technology in Biomedicine, 13*(6), 946–954. doi:10.1109/TITB.2008.2011155 PMID:19171519

Pan, J., & Tompkins, W. J. (1985). A real-time QRS detection algorithm. *IEEE Transactions on Bio-Medical Engineering*, *32*(3), 230–236. doi:10.1109/TBME.1985.325532 PMID:3997178

Radwan, A. G., Abd-El-Haleem, S. H. & Abd-El-Hafiz, S. K. (2016). Symmetric encryption algorithms using chaotic and non-chaotic generators: A review. *Journal of Advanced Research*, *7*, 193–208. PMID:26966561

Singh, B., Sharma, D., Singh, M., & Singh, D. (2014). An improved ASCII character encoding method for lossless ECG compression. *Advances in Biomedical Science and Engineering*, *1*(2), 1–11.

Singh, B., & Singh, D. (2012a). Effect of threshold value r on multiscale entropy based heart rate variability. *Cardiovascular Engineering and Technology*, *3*(2), 211–216. doi:10.100713239-012-0082-x

Singh, B., Singh, D., Jaryal, A. K., & Deepak, K. K. (2012b). Ectopic beats in approximate entropy and sample entropy-based HRV assessment. *International Journal of Systems Science*, *43*(5), 884–893. doi:10.1080/00207721.2010.543478

Soma, S., & Sen, S. (2013). A non-adaptive partial encryption of grayscale images based on chaos. *Proc Technol*, *10*, 663–671. doi:10.1016/j.protcy.2013.12.408

Wang, H., Peng, D., Wang, W., Sharif, H., Chen, H., & Khoynezhad, A. (2010). Resource-aware secure ECG healthcare monitoring through body sensor networks. *IEEE Wireless Communications*, *17*(1), 12–19. doi:10.1109/MWC.2010.5416345

Wang, X., Meng, J., Tai, S. C., Sun, C. C., & Yan, W. C. (2008). A 2-D ECG compression algorithm based on wavelet transform and vector quantization. *Digital Signal Processing*, *18*(2), 179–188. doi:10.1016/j.dsp.2007.03.003

Wei, J., Member, S., Chang, C., Chou, N., & Jan, G. (2001). ECG data compression using truncated singular value decomposition. *IEEE Transactions on Information Technology in Biomedicine*, *5*(4), 290–299. doi:10.1109/4233.966104 PMID:11759835

Zhu, C. (2012). A novel image encryption scheme based on improved hyperchaotic sequences. *Optics Communications*, *285*(1), 29–37. doi:10.1016/j.optcom.2011.08.079

Zhu, Z., Zhang, W., Wong, K., & Yu, H. (2011). A chaos-based symmetric image encryption scheme using a bit-level permutation. *Information Sciences*, *181*(6), 1171–1186. doi:10.1016/j.ins.2010.11.009

This research was previously published in the Handbook of Research on Healthcare Administration and Management edited by Nilmini Wickramasinghe; pages 205-221, copyright year 2017 by Medical Information Science Reference (an imprint of IGI Global).

Chapter 3
Biometric Image Security Using Chaos Algorithm

Sugandha Agarwal
Amity University, India

O.P. Singh
Amity University, India

Deepak Nagaria
Bundelkhand Institute of Engineering and Technology, India

ABSTRACT

In this world of Advanced Technology, the Biometrics are proved to be a significant method for user identification. However, the use of biometric is not new, but these days, with the increase in multimedia applications, it has gained its popularity in analysing human characteristics for security purposes. Biometric Encryption using Chaos Algorithm is a technique used to make it more convenient to the user and to provide high level security. The most prominent physical biometric patterns investigated for security purposes are the fingerprint, hand, eye, face, and voice. In the proposed image encryption scheme, an external secret key of 160-bit is used. The initial conditions for the logistic map are derived using the external secret key. The results obtained through experimental analysis provide an efficient and secure way for real-time image encryption and transmission.

INTRODUCTION

In recent years, the communication has become easier, but hackers are smarter than anyone can think of. It is more important to get aware of and use the best techniques for secure image transfer. With the escalation of information exchange across the Internet, and the storage of sensitive data on an open network, cryptography has become an increasingly important feature of computer security. In this paper, we have focused on biometric encryption using chaos algorithm. A biometric is defined as a unique, measurable, physical or biological trait for automatically recognizing or authenticating the identity of a human being.

DOI: 10.4018/978-1-7998-1763-5.ch003

It includes data such as retina, iris, fingerprint, face, DNA, vein patterns, hand geometry, typing rhythm, mouse dynamics and voice. The main applications of biometrics are access controls, national ID card, passport control, border control, criminal investigation, and terrorist identification. Biometric is a very powerful tool for security purposes because of its property of uniqueness. Thus, biometric authentication can replace the use of passwords to secure a key. It provides a strong link between an individual and a claimed identity. This offers convenience and secure identity confirmation. If biometrics are used in most of the security systems for example bank locker systems, online transactions etc. then one can get a relief from remembering various passwords. It provides direct connection between the password and the user. A password is not tied to a user, the system running the cryptographic algorithm is unable to differentiate between the authorised user and an attacker who fraudulently acquires the password of an authorised user. As an alternative to password protection, biometric authentication provides a new mechanism for key security by using a biometric to secure the cryptographic key. Instead of entering a password to access the cryptographic key, the use of this key is guarded by biometric authentication. When a user wishes to access a secured key, he or she will be prompted to allow for the capture of a biometric sample. Biometric authentication is becoming the most popular and most reliable user authentication mechanism, even it is vulnerable to attacks.

LITERATURE REVIEW

Several encryption algorithms (Maniccam & Bourbakis, 2001; Jiun-In & Cheng, n.d.; Gu & Han, 2006; Seyedzade et al., 2010; Zhou et al., 2014; Younes & Jantan, 2008; Sinha & Singh, 2003; Zeghid et al., 2007; Xiao & Zhang, 2006; Alsafasfeh & Arfoa, 2011) have been proposed including Lossless image compression and encryption using SCAN by S.S.Maniccam, N.G. Bourbakis (Maniccam & Bourbakis, 2001), Mirror-like image encryption algorithm by Jiun-In Guo, Jui-Cheng Yen (Jiun-In & Cheng, n.d), Image encryption based on hash function by Seyed Mohammad Seyedzade, Reza Ebrahimi Atani and Sattar Mirzakuchak (Seyedzade et al., 2010) and Image encryption using Block-Based Transformation Algorithm by Mohammad Ali, Bani Younes and Aman Jantan (Younes & Jantan, 2008), but Chaos-based encryption techniques (Gu & Han, 2006; Zhou et al., 2014; Alsafasfeh & Arfoa, 2011) are considered good for practical use as these techniques provide a good combination of speed, high security, complexity and computational power etc. Consequently, the traditional ciphers like AES, DES, and RSA etc. are not suitable for real time image encryption as these ciphers require a large computational time and high computing power. For real time image encryption, only those ciphers are preferable which take lesser amount of time and at the same time without compromising security.

To ensure the privacy and security of the biometric system, many scholars have conducted researches to explore the possible risk of biometric network and feasible measurement to guarantee the security. Uludag et al. analysed the challenges involved in biometric application in authentication system and limitations of the biometric cryptosystems (Uludag et al., 2004). Many techniques have been introduced since to reduce the vulnerability of biometric data. Alok a Sinha and Kehar Singh introduced a technique for Image Encryption using Digital Signatures, Soutar et al. (1996), proposed an algorithm on biometric encryption. Alghamdi et al. (2010) states that image encryption cannot be used for large amount of data and high resolution images. Hao et al. (2005) presented a secure way to integrate iris biometric with cryptography. Chaos-based cryptography is the latest and efficient way to develop fast and secure cryptography for image encryption. The chaotic behaviour is the random behaviour of a nonlinear system and the important characteristics of chaos is its extreme sensitivity to initial conditions of the system. In Baptista (1988), Baptista explained cryptography with chaos.

A number of new techniques, extensions or improved versions of the earlier techniques, have been proposed in recent years. The main idea behind this paper is to develop a secure and reliable encryption technique using chaotic functions. In the proposed algorithm, we have used the Logistic-map for chaotic sequence generation. Then, a user intrinsic key is generated from the biometrics and used as the initial value of the chaotic sequence. The random sequence produced by the chaotic phenomenon is used to encrypt and secure the biometric image.

In Section III, we discuss the step by step procedure of image encryption and in Section IV, the experimental analysis of the proposed image encryption scheme such as histogram, PSNR, MSE, Correlation Coefficient and key space analysis etc. to prove its security against the most common attacks. Finally, in Section V, we conclude the paper.

PROPOSED METHOD

In this section, we discuss the step by step procedure used for encrypting as well as decrypting the biometric image. See the diagrams in Figure 1 and Figure 2.

Figure 1. Block diagram of encryption

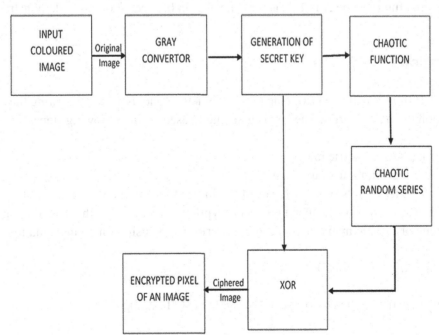

Figure 2. Block diagram of decryption

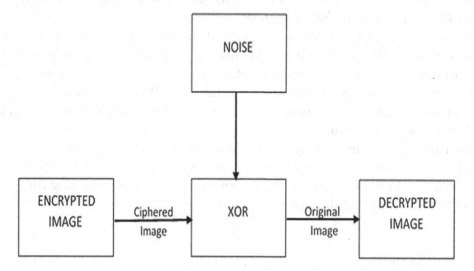

Chaotic Function

Chaotic functions are similar to the noise signal. Chaotic signal plays very important role in case of encryption because of their advantages as sensitivity to primary condition, high key space, control parameters, ergodicity, and randomness. The chaotic function logistic map equation (Zhou et al., 2014) is as follows:

$$Xn+1= rXn (1-Xn) \tag{1}$$

where r can be a value between 0 and 4. The parameter r and initial value Xn may represent the key, and determines the future value Xn+1. When r is a value in between 3.6 to 4, it demonstrates a chaotic behaviour.

Key Generation

A secret key of 160-bit is extracted from the user's biometrics and used for generating the initial values for the formation of chaotic series. The key is generated based on the following steps:

- Obtain processed biometric image;
- Divide the image into four equal parts;
- Select the first five pixels from each part of the image to form initial value;
- These selected five pixels are then used as encryption key to encrypt the part of image;
- Initial value of logistic map function can be determined by using following equation:

P = [P1, P2, P3, P4, P5] (Decimal)

- Following equation is then used to convert P into ASCII number as follows:

B = [P1,1, P1,2, P1,3, . . ., P2,1, P2,2, . . ., P5,7, P5,8] (ASCII) (Pareek et al., 2006)

- Equation is used to determine initial value of chaotic map function as follows:

$$U_{ok} = \frac{P_{1,1} \times 2^{39} + P_{1,2} \times 2^{38} + ... + P_{2,1} \times 2^{31} + ... + P_{5,7} \times 2^{1} + P_{5,8} \times 2^{0}}{2^{40}} \qquad (2)$$

For each part of plain image step b is repeated. For encrypting pixels in each part of plain image following equation is used:

New Value=round ($U_{ik} \times 255$) $\otimes$ Old Value $\qquad (3)$

Encryption and Decryption Algorithm

The steps of proposed encryption and decryption algorithms are presented below:

1. From each channel of image, extract the key as explained in the Key Generation algorithm;
2. The initial values for the chaotic map are obtained from the extracted key as explained above;
3. Encrypt each shuffled pixel by XORing with respective chaotic sequence generated.

An encrypted image is obtained after performing the above steps. To decrypt the encrypted image, repeat the same steps as in encryption by reversing the process.

EXPERIMENT ANALYSIS

- **Histogram:** The histogram of the original image (Figure 3) and encrypted image (Figure 4) is shown in this section;
- **Correlation Coefficient:** Correlation between two adjacent pixels is able to break the high correlation among the pixels. Therefore, the proposed technique is robust against statistical attacks. The lesser the correlation coefficient, the best is the ciphered image. We have calculated the correlation coefficient by using the following formula:

$$Correlation = \rho = \frac{\text{cov}(X,Y)}{\sigma_x \sigma_y} \qquad (4)$$

where Covariance is obtained by this formula:

$$Cov_{xy} = \frac{\Sigma(x - \bar{x})(y - \bar{y})}{(n-1)} = \frac{\Sigma xy - n\overline{xy}}{(n-1)} \qquad (5)$$

- Peak signal-to-noise ratio (PSNR) is the ratio between the maximum possible power of a signal and the power of corrupting noise. The higher PSNR means good quality of image. In this case, the PSNR value is 7.2393 and it is high enough which shows the image possess good quality;
- **MSE:** The Mean Square Error is the average squared difference between a reference image and a reconstructed (encrypted) image. The MSE is less i.e., 1.2279e+04, so we can conclude that the obtained ciphered image is the best image;
- **Key Space:** The key space size is the total number of different keys that can be associated with the encryption framework. For a secure encryption framework, the key space should be large enough to make the system vulnerable to brute-force attacks. From the cryptographic point of view, the size of the key space should not be smaller than 2100. In the proposed technique, we use 160-bit space key, therefore the key space is 2160. So, the-e key space is large enough to resist the brute-force attacks.

Simulation

The schematic flow chart in Figure 5 represents how the biometric image is acquired from the source, encrypted and decrypted using the chaotic function, for the use in various applications. See also Table 1.

Figure 3. Histogram of original image

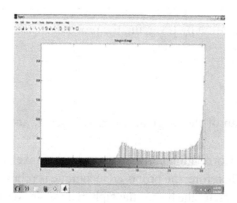

Figure 4. Histogram of encrypted image

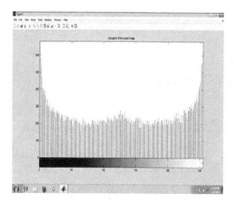

Figure 5. Simulation result

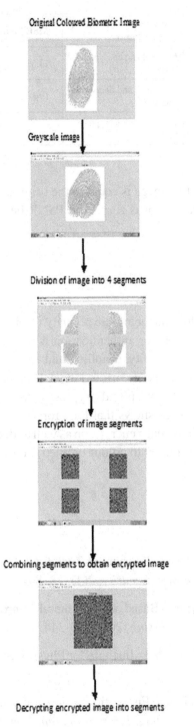

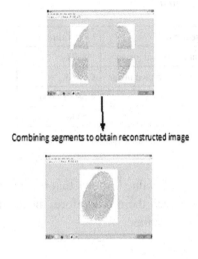

Combining segments to obtain reconstructed image

Table 1. Corresponding values obtained between original and encrypted image

Parameters	Values
Correlation coefficient of original image	0.8971
Correlation coefficient of encrypted image	0.6490
Mean Square Error	1.6892e+004
Peak Signal-To-Noise Ratio	5.8540

Table 2. MSE and PSNR values

MSE and PSNR Found Between	MSE Values	PSNR Values
Original and encrypted image	1.6892e+004	5.8540
Encrypted and decrypted image	1.6892e+004	5.8540
Original and decrypted image	0	infinite

From Table 2, MSE value 0 shows that reconstructed image is equal to the original image and there is no difference between them. Therefore, mean square error is zero. And PSNR being inversely proportional to MSE it is finite.

CONCLUSION

In this paper, we have proposed a chaotic algorithm for enhancing the security of biometric data using the chaotic map. The importance of biometric approaches for authentication is increasing day by day because of the advantages such as security, accuracy, reliability, usability, and friendliness, etc. Some significant parameters in analysing the biometric data are lesser correlation coefficient, low MSE, high PSNR and large key space increase the robustness of the proposed cryptosystem. The experimental analysis including histogram, PSNR, MSE and Key Space shows that the proposed image encryption scheme provides an efficient and secure way for real-time image encryption as well as decryption process using chaos logistic map. The proposed system is not limited to colour biometric data and is extended to secure grey scale biometric data also.

REFERENCES

Alghamdi, A. S., & Ullah, H. (2010). A Secure Iris Image Encryption Technique Using Bio-Chaotic Algorithm. *International Journal of Computer and Network Security, 2*(4), 78–84.

Alsafasfeh, Q. H., & Arfoa, A. A. (2011). Image Encryption Based on the General Approach for Multiple Chaotic Systems. *Journal of Signal and Information Processing, 2*(3), 238-244.

Baptista, M. S. (1988). *Cryptography with chaos.* College Park: Institute for Physical Science and Technology: University of Maryland.

Gu, G., & Han, G. (2006). An Enhanced Chaos Based Image Encryption Algorithm. *Proceedings of the IEEE First International Conference on Innovative Computing, Information and Control.*

Hao, F., Anderson, R., & Daugman, J. (2005). *Combining cryptography with biometrics effectively* (Tech. Rep. No. 640). Cambridge, United Kingdom: University of Cambridge, Computer Laboratory.

Jiun-In, G., & Cheng, Y.J., A new mirror-like image encryption algorithm and its VLSI architecture. *Department of Electronics Engineering National Lien-Ho College of Technology and Commerce.*

Maniccam, S. S., & Bourbakis, N. G. (2001). Lossless image compression and encryption using SCAN. *Pattern Recognition, 34*(6), 1229–1245. doi:10.1016/S0031-3203(00)00062-5

Pareek, N.K., Patidar, V., & Sud, K.K. (2006) Image encryption using chaotic logistic map. 926–934.

Seyedzade, S. M., Atani, R. E., & Mirzakuchaki, S. (2010). A Novel Image Encryption Algorithm Based on Hash Function. *Proceedings of the 6th Iranian Conference on Machine Vision and Image Processing.* 10.1109/IranianMVIP.2010.5941167

Sinha, A., & Singh, K. A. (2003). Technique for Image Encryption using Digital Signatures. *Optics Communications, 218*(4-6), 229–234. doi:10.1016/S0030-4018(03)01261-6

Soutar, C., & Tomko, G. J. (1996). Secure private key generation using a fingerprint. *Proceedings of CardTech/SecurTech Conference* (Vol. 1, pp. 245–252).

Uludag, U., Pankanti, S., & Jain, A. K. (2004). Biometric cryptosystems: issues and challenges. *Proceedings of the IEEE, 92*(6).

Xiao, H. P., & Zhang, G. J. (2006). An Image Encryption Scheme Based On Chaotic Systems. *IEEE Proceedings of the Fifth International Conference on Machine Learning and Cybernetics*, Dalian (pp. 2707-2711).

Younes, A. M. B., & Jantan, A. (2008). *Image Encryption Using Block-Based Transformation Algorithm.* IAENG International Journal of Computer Science.

Zeghid, M., Machhout, M., Khriji, L., Baganne, A., & Tourki, R. (2007) A Modified AES Based Algorithm for Image Encryption. World Academy of Science, Engineering and Technology.

Zhou, Y., Bao, L., & Chen, C. L. P. (2014). A new 1D chaotic system for image encryption. *Signal Processing, 97*, 172–182. doi:10.1016/j.sigpro.2013.10.034

ADDITIONAL READING

John, J., & Raj, A. S. (2015). Reliable Biometric Data Encryption Using Chaotic Map. *International Journal of Advanced Research in Computer and Communication Engineering, 4*(11).

Khan, M. K., & Zhang, J. (2007). An intelligent fingerprint-biometric image scrambling scheme. *Proceedings of International Conference on Intelligent Computing* (Vol. 2, pp. 1141–1151).

Kocarev, L. Chaos-based cryptography: a brief overview. Circuits and Systems Magazine, 1(3), 6–21.

Ratha, N. K., Connell, J., & Bolle, R. (2001). Enhancing security and privacy in biometrics based authentication systems. *IBM Systems Journal, 40*(3), 614–634. doi:10.1147/sj.403.0614

Chapter 4
DNA Sequence Based Cryptographic Solution for Secure Image Transmission

Grasha Jacob
Rani Anna Government College, India

Murugan Annamalai
Dr. Ambedkar Government Arts College, India

ABSTRACT

With the advent of electronic transactions, images transmitted across the internet must be protected and prevented from unauthorized access. Various encryption schemes have been developed to make information intelligible only to the intended user. This chapter proposes an encryption scheme based on DNA sequences enabling secure transmission of images.

INTRODUCTION

Internet has become ubiquitous, faster, and easily manageable by anyone on the earth. Social Networking enables people of all ages and strata to interact with each other in any part of the world through sites like Facebook, Twitter, Linked-In, YouTube, Blogs, Wikis and so on. In today's information epoch, individuals, businesses, corporations, and countries are interconnected and Information on demand is practically inevitable anytime, anywhere. The essence of global economy is influenced by the internet being available, and it is tough to imagine a day without email or social networking. The idea of being connected anytime, anywhere and having instant information and data sharing certainly comes out with a substantial risk. Security has become more and more of an issue in recent years. Data in transit can be regarded as secure if and only if both the sender and the receiver are capable of protecting the data and the communication between the two hosts is identified, authenticated, authorized and private, meaning that no third party can eavesdrop on the communication between them. Hackers constantly find ways of stealing sensitive data using various techniques. It is estimated that the number of devices connected

DOI: 10.4018/978-1-7998-1763-5.ch004

to Internet will reach to more than 50 billion around the year 2020. Corporate Espionage has become a reality in this age of the Internet and the global economy. E-commerce transactions are currently plagued with cyber-attacks and are a serious deterrent to the growth of e-commerce globally. In 2008, 4.8 million credit cards were compromised in USA. Revenue losses to the tune of $ 3.3 billion were reported in 2009 from US alone due to cyber-attacks. Successful penetration of Web sites has become the trend of the day. Unfortunately, security issues are more complex no matter how much technology is used.

Data Security and Cryptography go hand in hand as cryptography is an accepted and effective way of protecting data. Though cryptography is used commonly in transit, it is now increasingly being used for protecting data at rest as well. Encryption consists of changing the data located in files into unreadable bits of characters unless a key to decode the file is provided. The security of the sensitive information transmitted through an insecure public communication channel poses a great threat by an unintended recipient. Cryptographic techniques help in ensuring the security of such sensitive information. Cryptography enables the sender to securely store or transmit sensitive information across insecure networks so that it can be understood only by the intended recipient. A cryptographic system applies encryption on the information and produces an encrypted output which will be meaningless to an unintended user who has no knowledge of the key. Knowledge of the key is essential for decryption.

Defense organizations often use encryption systems to ensure that secret messages will be unreadable if they are intercepted by unintended recipients. Encryption methods can include simple substitution codes, like switching each letter for a corresponding number, or more complex systems that require complicated algorithms for decryption. As long as the coding is kept secret, encryption can be a good method for securing information. On computers systems, there are a number of ways to encrypt images in order to make them more secure.

An encryption scheme is unconditionally secure if the ciphertext generated does not contain enough information to determine uniquely the corresponding plaintext no matter how much ciphertext is available or how much computational power the attacker has. With the exception of the one-time pad, no cipher is unconditionally secure.

The security of a conditionally secure algorithm depends on the difficulty in reversing the underlying cryptographic problem such as how easy it is to factor large primes. All ciphers other than the one-time pad fall into this category.

An encryption scheme is said to be computationally secure if the cost of breaking the cipher exceeds the value of the encrypted information the time required to break the cipher exceeds the useful lifetime of the information Shannon introduced two fundamental properties for any cipher to be perfectly secure - diffusion and confusion. The idea of diffusion is to hide the relationship between the cipher text and plain text. Diffusion implies that each bit in the cipher text is dependent on all bits in the plain text i.e., if a single bit in the plain text is changed several or all bits in the cipher text will be changed. The idea of confusion is to hide the relation between the cipher text and the key. This will infuriate the adversary who tries to use the cipher text to find the key. The diffusion effect can be introduced on cipher text by permutation. The confusion effect can be introduced on cipher text by substitution box or S-box.

In secure cryptographic schemes, the legitimate user should be able to decipher the messages and the task of decrypting the cipher text should be infeasible for an adversary. But today, the breaking task can be easily performed by a non-deterministic polynomial-time machine.

The Data Encryption Standard (DES) is an algorithm with approximately 72 quadrillion possible keys. The security of the DES is based on the difficulty of picking out the right key after the 16-round nonlinear function operations. Boneh et al. describe in detail a library of operations which were useful when working with a DNA computer. They estimated that given one arbitrary (plain-text, cipher-text) pair, one could recover the DES key in about 4 months of work. Furthermore, they showed that under chosen plain-text attack it was possible to recover the DES key in one day using some preprocessing. Their method could be generalized to break any cryptosystem which uses keys of length less than 64 bits. This clearly indicates that molecular computing has the ability to break DES. Though cryptography enables in ensuring security to sensitive information, code breakers have come up with various methods to crack the cryptographic systems being developed. Though computational power offered by the revolution in Information Technology paved the way to build new and strong algorithms in cryptography, it is also a strong tool used by cryptanalysts to break the cryptosystems. Hence the subject of finding new and powerful ciphers is always of interest and new directions in cryptography are explored. As traditional cryptographic methods built upon mathematical and theoretical models are vulnerable to attacks, the concept of using DNA computing in the field of cryptography has been identified as a possible technology that brings forward a new hope for unbreakable algorithms.

In cryptography, a one-time pad (OTP) is an encryption technique that cannot be cracked when used correctly. In this technique, a plaintext is paired with a random secret key (or *pad*) using an XOR operation. Then, each bit or character of the plaintext is encrypted by combining it with the corresponding bit or character from the pad using modular addition. If the key is truly random - at least as long as the plaintext, is never reused in whole or in part, and is kept completely secret, then the resulting ciphertext will be impossible to decrypt or break. It has also been proven that any cipher with the perfect secrecy property must use keys with effectively the same requirements as OTP keys. The OTP properties correspond to the characteristics of the unbreakable encryption system defined by Shannon.

The XOR operation is reversible. Consider two images – a plaintext image, P and a Key image, K of the same size (dimension) as that of the plain text image. Let E be the resultant image obtained when an XOR operation is performed on P and K. The original image P is obtained (regained or restored) when an XOR operation is once again performed on E and K.

$$E \leftarrow P \oplus K$$

$$P \leftarrow E \oplus K \tag{1}$$

The key image used as one time pad must be of the same size as that of the plaintext image to prevent information from being leaked. The primary merit of XOR operation is that it is simple to implement, and that it is computationally inexpensive.

DNA COMPUTING

DNA stands for Deoxyribo Nucleic Acid. DNA represents the genetic blueprint of living creatures. DNA contains instructions for assembling cells. Every cell in the human body has a complete set of DNA. DNA is unique for each individual. DNA is a polymer made of monomers called deoxy-ribo nucleotides. Each nucleotide consists of three basic items: deoxyribose sugar, a phosphate group and a nitrogenous base. The nitrogenous bases are of two types: purines (Adenine and Guanine) and pyrimidines (Cytosine and Thymine). The key thing to note about the structure of DNA is its inherent complementarity proposed by Watson and Crick. A binds with T and G binds to C. All DNA computing applications are based on

Watson-Crick complementarity. DNA computing is an inter disciplinary area concerned with the use of DNA molecules for the implementation of computational processes. The main features of DNA are massive parallelism, intense storage capacity and energy efficiency. Adleman's pioneering work gave an idea of solving the directed Hamiltonian Path Problem (Travelling Salesman Problem) of size n in O(n) using DNA molecules. The principle used by Adleman lies in coding of information (nodes, edges) in DNA clusters and in the use of enzymes for the simulation of simple calculations. The various operations performed on DNA are synthesized, cutting, ligation, translation, substitution, polymerase chain reaction, detection using gel electrophoresis and affinity purification. Adleman's work urged other researchers to develop DNA-based logic circuits using a variety of approaches. The resulting circuits performed simple mathematical and logical operations, recognized patterns based on incomplete data and played simple games. Molecular circuits can even detect and respond to a disease signature inside a living cell, opening up the possibility of medical treatments based on man-made molecular software. Lipton extended the work of Adleman and investigated the solution of Satisfiability of Propositional Formula pointing to new opportunities of DNA computing. Research work is being done on DNA Computing either using test tubes (biologically) or simulating the operations of DNA using computers (Pseudo or Virtual DNA computing). In 1997, L. Kari gave an insight of the various biological operations concerning DNA.

DNA Cryptography

Taylor (1999) et al. proposed a substitution cipher for plaintext encoding where base triplet was assigned to each letter of the alphabet, numeral and special characters and demonstrated a steganographic approach by hiding secret messages encoded as DNA strands among multitude of random DNA. Decryption was difficult with the use of sub-cloning, sequencing and there was a need of an additional triplet coding table.

In 2000, Gehani et al. introduced a trial of DNA based Cryptography and proposed two methods: i) a substitution method using libraries of distinct one time pads, each of which defines a specific, randomly generated, pair-wise mapping and ii) an XOR scheme utilizing molecular computation and indexed random key strings were used for encryption. They used the natural DNA sequences to encode the information and encrypted an image by using the XOR logic operation. Such experiments could be done only in a well-equipped lab using modern technology, and it would involve high cost.

Leier et al. (2000) also presented two different cryptographic approaches based on DNA binary strands with the idea that a potential interceptor cannot distinguish between dummies and message strand. The first approach hid information in DNA binary strands and the second designed a molecular checksum. Decryption was done easily using PCR and subsequent gel electrophoresis without the use of sub-cloning, sequencing and additional triplet coding table. Although the approach of generating bit strands shown here had advantages such as rapid readout, it also had practical limitations. One of the limitations was the resolution of the used agarose-gels.

Chen (2003) presented a novel DNA-based cryptography technique that took advantage of the massive parallel processing capabilities of biomolecular computation. A library of one time pads in the form of DNA strands was assembled. Then, a modulo-2 addition method was employed for encryption whereby a large number of short message sequences could be encrypted using one time pads.

A novel public-key system using DNA was developed by Kazuo et al. (2005) based on the one-way function. The message-encoded DNA hidden in dummies could be restored by PCR amplification, followed by sequencing.

The YAEADNA algorithm proposed by Sherif et al. (2006) used a search technique in order to locate and return the position of quadruple DNA nucleotide sequence representing the binary octets of plain text characters. Plain text character and a random binary file were given as input and the output PTR was a pointer to the location of the found quadruple DNA nucleotide sequence representing the binary octet. The encryption process was tested on images to show how random the selection of DNA octet's locations is on the encrypting sequence.

Cui et al. (2008) designed an encryption scheme by using the technologies of DNA synthesis, PCR amplification, DNA digital coding and the theory of traditional cryptography. The data was first pre-processed to get completely different ciphertext to prevent attack from a possible word as PCR primers. Then, the DNA digital encoding technique was applied to the ciphertext. After coding sender synthesizes the secret-message DNA sequence which was flanked by forward and reverse PCR primers, each 20-mer oligo nucleotides long. Thus, the secret-message DNA sequence was prepared and at last sender generated a certain number of dummies and put the sequence among them. Once the data in encrypted form reached the receiver's side the reverse procedure was followed to decrypt it. Biological difficult issues and cryptography computing difficulties provided a double security safeguard for the scheme. The intended PCR two primer pairs used as the key of this scheme was designed by the complete cooperation of sender and receiver to increase the security of this encryption scheme.

Ning (2009) explained the pseudo encryption methodology based upon the work of Gehani. The plain text was converted to DNA sequences and these sequences were converted to the spliced form of data and protein form of data by cutting the introns according to the specified pattern and it was translated to mRNA form of data and mRNA was converted into protein form of data. The protein form of data was sent through the secure channel. The method did not really use DNA sequences, but only the mechanisms of the DNA function; therefore, the method was a kind of pseudo DNA cryptography methods. The method only simulates the transcription, splicing, and translation process of the central dogma; thus, it was a pseudo DNA cryptography method.

Sadeg et al. (2010) proposed a symmetric key block cipher algorithm which included a step that simulated ideas from the processes of transcription (transfer from DNA to mRNA) and translation (from mRNA into amino acids). Though the encryption algorithm (OTP) proposed was theoretically unbreakable, it experienced some disadvantages in its algorithm. These drawbacks had prevented the common use of its scheme in modern cryptosystems.

Qinghai (2010) had also proposed a method to protect information, including representing information using biological alphabets to enhance the security of traditional encryption, using DNA primer for secure communication and key distribution, and using the chemical information of DNA bases for steganography. Alice and Bob share a secret DNA sequence codebook. Alice can design a sequence that can maximally match one of the sequences in the codebook and then send the designed sequence to Bob through a public channel. When Bob receives the sequence he would use the non-matching letters in the private sequence as the encryption key. Knowing the public string only, an attacker cannot decrypt the transmitted information.

Xuejia et al. (2010) also proposed an asymmetric encryption and signature cryptosystem by combining the technologies of genetic engineering and cryptology. It was an exploratory research of biological cryptology. DNA-PKC uses two pairs of keys for encryption and signature, respectively. Using the public encryption key, everyone can send encrypted message to a specified user, only the owner of the private decryption key can decrypt the ciphertext and recover the message; in the signature scheme, the owner of the private signing key can generate a signature that can be verified by other users with the public verification key, but no else can forge the signature. DNA-PKC differs from the conventional cryptology in that the keys and the ciphertext are all biological molecules. The security of DNA-PKC relies on difficult biological problems instead of computational problems; thus DNA-PKC is immune from known attacks, especially the quantum computing based attacks.

In 2010, in the image encryption algorithm based on DNA sequence addition operation combined with logistic chaotic map to scramble the location and value of pixel of an image presented by Qiang et al., a DNA sequence matrix was obtained by encoding the original image and it was divided into some equal blocks and two logistic maps. DNA complementarity and DNA sequence addition operations were utilized to add these blocks. DNA sequence matrix was decoded to get the encrypted image. The experimental results and security analysis showed that the proposed algorithm had larger key space and resisted exhaustive, statistical and differential attacks.

Qiang et al. (2012) presented a novel image encryption algorithm based on DNA subsequence operations that uses the idea of DNA subsequence operations (such as elongation operation, truncation operation, deletion operation, etc.) combining with the logistic chaotic map to scramble the location and the value of pixel points from the image. The experimental results and security analysis showed that the proposed algorithm was easy to be implemented, had good encryption effect and a wide secret key's space, strong sensitivity to secret key, and had the abilities of resisting exhaustive attack and statistic attack but the defect was its weak ability of resisting differential attack.

DNA Coding

An electronic computer needs only two digits, 0 and 1 for coding information. As a single strand of DNA is similar to a string consisting of a combination of four different symbols, A, C, G and T, DNA coding should reflect the biological characteristics of the four nucleotide bases- A, C, G and T along with the Watson-Crick complementary rule (A is complementary to T and C is complementary to G) [46]. Out of the twenty four combinations of the four nucleotides, only eight combinations given within parenthesis satisfy the complementary rule of the nucleotides. (00011011 - C T A G, 00011011 - C A T G, 00011011 - G T A C, 00011011 - G A T C, 00011011- T C G A, 00011011- T G C A, 00011011 - A C G T, 00011011 - A G C T). Figure 1 represents the molecular structure of the four nucleotides. In accordance with the increasing molecular weight of the four nucleotides, (C -111.1 g/mol, T - 126.1133 g/mol, A - 135.13 g/mol and G - 151.13 g/mol)C T A G, is the best coding pattern and is used as DNA Coding. According to DNA Coding Technology, C denotes the binary value 00, T denotes 01, A denotes 10 and G denotes 11 so that Watson-Crick complementary also holds good. Table 1 gives the DNA Coding. This pattern could perfectly reflect the biological characteristics of the four nucleotide bases and has biological significance.

Figure 1. a) Cytosine b) Thyminec) Adenine d) Guanine

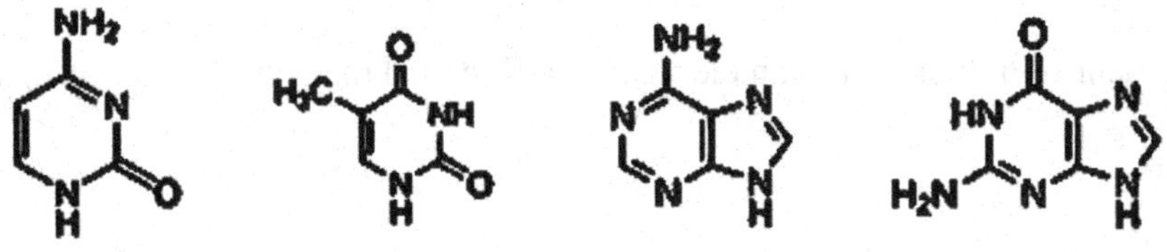

Table 1. DNA coding

Digital Value	DNA Base	Molecular Weight g/mol
00	C	111.1
01	T	126.11
10	A	135.13
11	G	151.13

Axiomatic Definition of DNA Algebra

DNA algebra is an algebraic structure defined on a set of elements B{C, T, A, G} together with two binary operators 'V' and '^' provided the following Huntington postulates are satisfied.

1a. Closure with respect to the operator V.
1b. Closure with respect to the operator ^.
2a. An identity element with respect to V, designated by C: '

$$x \text{ V } C = x, \forall x \in B \tag{2}$$

2b. An identity element with respect to ^, designated by G:

$$x \wedge G = x, \forall x \in B \tag{3}$$

3a. Commutative with respect to V.

$$x \text{ V } C = C \text{ V } x, \forall x \in B \tag{4}$$

3b. Commutative with respect to ^ .

$$x \wedge G = G \wedge x, \forall x \in B \tag{5}$$

4a. V is Distributive over ^.

$$x \text{ V } (y \wedge z) = (x \text{ V } y) \wedge (x \text{ V } z), \forall x,y,z \in B \tag{6}$$

4b. V is Distributive over ^.

$$x \wedge (y \text{ V } z) = (x \wedge y) \text{ V } (x \wedge z), \forall x,y,z \in B \tag{7}$$

For every element $x \in B$, there exists an element x' $\in B$ (called the complement of x) such that

$x \text{ V } x' = G$ and

$$x \wedge x' = C \tag{8}$$

There exists atleast two elements x, y ∈*B*, such that x ≠ y.
The following De' Morgan's laws also hold good.

$$(x \vee y)' = x' \wedge y', \forall x,y \in B \tag{9}$$

$$(x \wedge y)' = x' \vee y', \forall x,y \in B \tag{10}$$

The primitive logic operations OR, AND, NOT and XOR can be carried out and the results will be obtained as given in the characteristic tables Table 2, Table 3, Table 4 and Table 5.

DNA Sequence Based Image Representation

The term image refers to a two-dimensional light intensity function, denoted by f(x,y), where the value of f at spatial coordinates(x,y) gives the intensity(brightness) of the image at that point. As light is a form of energy f(x,y) must be nonzero and finite, that is f(x) must lie between zero and infinity (0 < f(x,y) < ∞). A digital image is an image f(x,y) that has been discretized both in spatial coordinates and brightness. A digital image can be considered a matrix (two dimensional array) whose row and column indices identify a point in the image and the corresponding matrix element value identifies the gray level at that point. The elements of such a picture array are called pixels. Each pixel of the image consists of 8 bits. Using DNA coding principle, substituting C for 00, A for 01, T for 10 and G for 11, each pixel of the DNA image is represented as a quadruple nucleotide sequence.

Table 2. AND characteristic table

>	C	T	A	G
C	C	C	C	C
T	C	T	C	T
A	C	C	A	A
G	C	T	A	G

Table 4. XOR characteristic table

⊕	C	T	A	G
C	C	T	A	G
T	T	C	G	A
A	A	G	C	T
G	G	A	T	C

Table 3. OR characteristic table

V	C	T	A	G
C	C	T	A	G
T	T	T	G	G
A	A	G	A	G
G	G	G	G	G

Table 5. NOT characteristic table

X	C	T	A	G
~X	G	A	T	C

Arithmetic and Logic Operations on Images

Arithmetic and logic operations between pixels are used extensively in most of the branches of image processing and are generally carried out on images pixel by pixel. The principle use of image addition is for image averaging - to reduce noise. Image addition is mainly done using XOR operation for brightening the image and for image security applications. Image subtraction is a basic tool in medical imaging where it is used to remove static background information. Image multiplication or division is used to correct gray level shading resulting from non-uniformities in illumination or in the sensor used to acquire the image. Arithmetic operations can be done "in place" such that the result of performing an operation can be stored in that location in one of the existing images. With DNA computing, two DNA images can be added using parallel addition of the rows of the two images.

Biological Operations on DNA Sequences

The following biological operations can be performed on DNA sequences in a test tube to program the DNA computer.

Synthesis

In standard solid phase DNA synthesis, a desired DNA molecule is built up nucleotide by nucleotide on a support particle in sequential coupling steps. For example, the first nucleotide (monomer), say A, is bound to a glass support. A solution containing C is poured in, and the A reacts with the C to form a two-nucleotide (2-mer) chain AC. After washing the excess C solution away, one could have the C from the chain AC coupled with T to form a 3-mer chain (still attached to the surface) and so on.

Separation

Separation is the process of separating the strands by length using gel electrophoresis.

Merging

Merging or mixing is the process of pouring the contents of two test tubes into a third one to achieve union. Mixing can be performed by rehydrating the tube contents (if not already in solution) and then combining the fluids together into a new tube, by pouring and pumping.

Extraction

Extraction is the process of extracting those strands that contain a given pattern as a substring by using affinity purification.

Annealing

Annealing is the process of bonding together two single-stranded complementary DNA sequences by cooling the solution. Annealing in vitro is also known as hybridization.

Melting

Melting is the process of breaking apart a double-stranded DNA into its single-stranded complementary components by heating the solution. Melting in vitro is also known as denaturation.

Amplification

Amplifying is making copies of DNA strands by using the Polymerase Chain Reaction. PCR is an in vitro method that relies on DNA polymerase to quickly amplify specific DNA sequences in a solution. PCR involves a repetitive series of temperature cycles, with each cycle comprising three stages: denaturation of the guiding template DNA to separate its strands, then cooling to allow annealing to the template of the primer oligonucleotides, which are specifically designed to flank the region of DNA of interest and finally, extension of the primers by DNA polymerase. Each cycle of the reaction doubles the number of target DNA molecules, the reaction giving thus an exponential growth of their number.

Cutting

Cutting is the process of cutting DNA double-strands at specific sites by using restriction enzymes.

Ligation

Ligation is the process of pasting DNA strands with complementary (compatible) sticky ends using ligase.

Substitute

Substitute is the process of substituting - inserting or deleting (cutting and ligation) DNA sequences by using PCR site-specific oligonucleotide mutagenesis.

Marking/ Unmarking

Single strands are marked by hybridization, that is, complementary sequences are attached to the strands, making them double-stranded. The reverse operation is unmarking of the double-strands by denaturing, that is, by detaching the complementary strands. The marked sequences will be double-stranded while the unmarked ones will be single-stranded.

Destroying

The marked strands are destroyed by using exonucleasesor by cutting all the marked strands with a restriction enzyme and removing all the intact strands by gel electrophoresis.

Detecting and Reading

Given the contents of a tube, say "yes" if it contains at least one DNA strand, and "no" otherwise. PCR may be used to amplify the result and then a process called sequencing is used to actually read the solution.

Operations and Functions Used

The operations of molecular biology and functions that are used for this work can be equivalently formalized as follows:

Synthesis

Creation of DNA sequences for the image data is referred to as Synthesis. DNA sequences are made up of four bases – A, C, G and T. According to the DNA Coding Technology, C denotes 00, A – 01, T - 10 and G – 11.Each pixel of eight bits is converted into a quadruple nucleotide sequence.

$$10010011 \rightarrow TACG \tag{11}$$

Translation

When the positions of sequences are translated, the sequences are interchanged. Translation is represented as

$$P_1P_2P_3P_4 \leftrightarrow P_5P_6P_7P_8 \tag{12}$$

Substitution

Each quadruple nucleotide sequence is substituted by the value returned by the DNA Sequence Crypt function. Substitution is represented by the following expression.

$$V \leftarrow DNASequenceCryptfn(P_1P_2P_3P_4) \tag{13}$$

Detect

Detect searches for a quadruple nucleotide sequence of the image starting from a random position in the DNA sequence file and returns true if a match is found and false otherwise.

Re-Substitution

Each value, V in the encrypted image is replaced by the corresponding quadruple nucleotide sequence from that position in the DNA Sequence File.

$$P_1P_2P_3P_4 \leftarrow V \tag{14}$$

Re-Synthesis

Re-synthesis is the process of converting each sequence into its digital form.

$$TACG \rightarrow 10010011 \tag{15}$$

DNA Sequence Crypt Function

DNA Sequence Crypt function is a function that returns one of the many positions of the quadruple DNA sequence in the key DNA sequence file.

A one to many DNA Sequence Crypt function is a one-to-many function d(x), which has the following three properties:

1. A pointer, h maps an input quadruple nucleotide sequence, x to one of the many positions obtained in random in the key DNA sequence file.
2. Ease of computation: Given d and an input x, d(x) is easy to compute.
3. Resistance to guess: In order to meet the requirements of a cryptographic scheme, the property of resistance to guess is required of a crypt function with input x, x_1 and outputs y, y_1.

As similar quadruple nucleotide sequence that occur in a plain text are mapped to different positions in the DNA nucleotide sequence file(one to many mapping), it is difficult for a recipient to guess the plain-text.

DNA Sequence Database

DNA sequences can be obtained from GenBank®, the NIH genetic sequence database, an annotated collection of all publicly available DNA sequences. GenBank is part of the International Nucleotide Sequence Database Collaboration, which comprises the DNA DataBank of Japan (DDBJ), the European Molecular Biology Laboratory (EMBL), and GenBank at NCBI. These three organizations exchange data on a daily basis.

Query sequence(s) to be used for a BLAST search should be pasted in the 'Search' text area. It accepts a number of different types of input and automatically determines the format or the input.

A sequence in FASTA format begins with a single-line description, followed by lines of sequence data. The description line (defline) is distinguished from the sequence data by a greater-than (">") symbol at the beginning. It is recommended that all lines of text be shorter than 80 characters in length.

In cryptographic applications, long DNA sequences are generally used.

HYBRID ENCRYPTION SCHEME

Hybrid encryption scheme proposed is a symmetric encryption scheme. Symmetric encryption algorithms use an identical secret key for encryption and decryption process and the key is sent to the receiver through a secure communication channel.

$$K_e = K_d = K \tag{16}$$

The requirement of a symmetric algorithm is that both the sender and the receiver know the secret key, so that they can encrypt and decrypt the information easily.

The proposed hybrid encryption scheme is a combination of a cryptosystem using XOR-OTP and substitution proposed by Gehani et al. and the DNA-based Implementation of YAEA Encryption Algorithm proposed by Sherif et al given in Figure 2.

Figure 2. The DNA YAEA Encryption Algorithm proposed by Sherif et al.

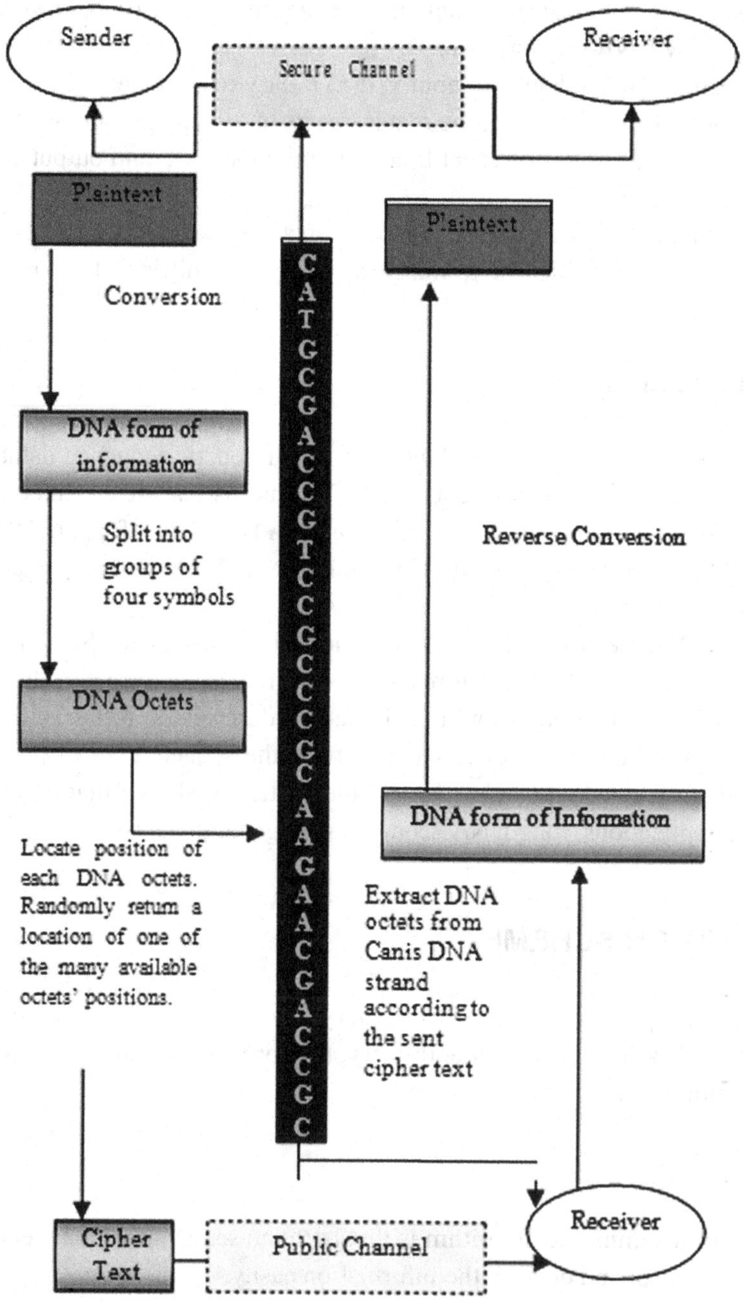

Principle

In the hybrid encryption scheme, the image to be encrypted and the key image are synthesized - transformed into DNA images and XOR One-Time Padding is performed using the substitution operation (a complex operation which is a combination of cutting and ligating operations) and an intermediate image is obtained. Both cutting and ligation use the same enzymes that organisms use for the maintenance of their own DNA. Cutting uses a restriction endonuclease. Table 4 represents the truth table for the XOR operation on DNA nucleotides. The intermediate image is scanned for four nucleotides at a time and one of the many positions (index) of the same quadruple DNA nucleotides sequences as that of the scanned nucleotides of the image in the gene sequence file is detected. The index is stored as a double dimensional array and the resultant encrypted image (2D array) is sent to the receiver. The key image used for OTP is sent to the receiver through a secure communication channel. The sender and receiver should also agree upon the same DNA sequence file that is used for encryption and hence decryption.

Since this is a symmetric key encryption scheme, the same DNA sequence file is used during the decryption process. In the decryption process, the received image (2D array) is actually pointers (index) to the DNA sequence file. The indices are substituted by quadruple nucleotide sequences starting from that index and the DNA image thus obtained is XOR-ed with the key DNA image (synthesized- converted into DNA image) and the resultant decrypted image is the original image that was transmitted in the encrypted form. The encryption and decryption algorithms of the hybrid encryption scheme are pictorially represented in Figure 3 and Figure 4.

ALGORITHM 1. HYBRID_CRYPT

```
Input: X [image file] to be encrypted, Y [image file] -key image,
R[Binary file that contains DNA nucleotides sequence],
Output: Encrypted image E
```

1. SYNTHESIS

a. Convert image file X into its DNA sequence

X ← DNA [X]

b. Convert key image file Y into its DNA sequence

Y ← DNA [Y]

2. SUBSTITUTION // OTP

X ← X ⊕ Y

3. DETECTION and SUBSTITUTION

For each quadruple DNA nucleotide sequence in X search from a random location RND (Z) in a binary file are represented in the form of a single strand DNA sequence.

If the correct pattern is found, its location **I** is then recorded

If the search is successful

Then store I in E;

Else

Repeat step 3

End Algorithm

ALGORITHM 2. HYBRID_DECRYPT

```
Input: Encrypted image E, Y [image file] - key image,
R [Binary file that contains DNA nucleotides sequence]
Output: Decrypted image X
1. SYNTHESIS
      Convert E into DNA sequence
2. DETECTION and RE-SUBSTITUTION
      F ← DNA sequence represented by E [I] in the binary file R
3. SUBSTITUTION and RE-SYNTHESIS
      F ← F ⊕ Y // O TP
      Convert F into its binary equivalent and display the image X.
End Algorithm.
```

Experimental Results

Matlab R2008a was used to simulate the DNA operations on a MiTAC Notebook PC with Intel® Core™ 2Duo CPU T6400 @ 2.00 GHz, 2 GB RAM, 32 bit operating system. Experiments were performed using different images of different sizes to prove the validity of the proposed algorithm. Figure 5 shows an example of an original image (plaintext), key image, encrypted image (Ciphertext) and the decrypted image (Figures 3-5).

Figure 3. Encryption process

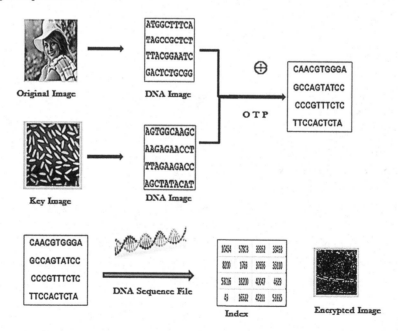

Figure 4. Decryption process

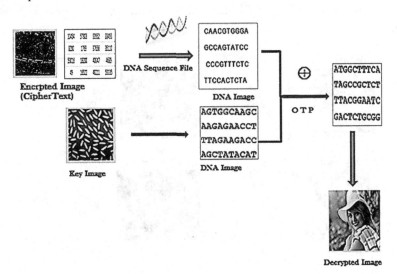

Figure 5. a) Original image of size 128 x 128b) Key image of size 128 x 128 c) encrypted image d) decrypted image

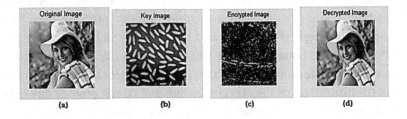

Cryptanalysis

A good information security system should be able to protect confidential images and should be robust against statistical, cryptanalytic and brute-force attacks. The level of security that the hybrid encryption algorithm offers is its strength. The proposed method is examined through statistical analysis, sensitivity to key changes and key space analysis.

Statistical Analysis

The encrypted image should not have any statistical similarity with the original image to prevent the leakage of information. The stability of the proposed method is examined via statistical attacks - the histogram and correlation between adjacent pixels.

Histogram Analysis

An image histogram is a graphical representation of the number of pixels in an image as a function of their intensity and describes how the image-pixels are distributed by plotting the number of pixels at each intensity level.

Figure 6. a) Original image (Elaine) b) histogram of original image c) encrypted image d)histogram of encrypted image e)original image (Elaine) f)histogram of original image g)encrypted image h) histogram of encrypted image

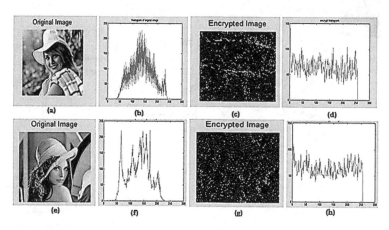

An attacker will find it difficult to extract the pixels statistical nature of the original image from the encrypted image if the histograms of the original image and encrypted image are different. Figure 6 a) - h) show the original Elaine.bmp of size 128 x 128, its histogram, the encrypted image, its histogram and the original Lena.bmp of size 128 x 128, its histogram, the encrypted image and its histogram. The histograms of the encrypted images (Figure 6 d) and h)) are fairly uniform and significantly different from the histograms of the original images (Figure 6 a) and e)). It is clearly observed that the histograms of the encrypted images look quite similar (though the original images are different) and are completely different from that of the histograms of the original images and do not provide any information regarding the distribution of gray values to the attacker; Hence the proposed algorithm can resist any type of histogram based attacks and this strengthens the security of encrypted images significantly.

Correlation Coefficient Analysis

In most of the plaintext-images, there exists high correlation among adjacent pixels, while there is a little correlation between neighboring pixels in the encrypted image. It is the main task of an efficient image encryption algorithm to eliminate the correlation of pixels. Two highly uncorrelated sequences have approximately zero correlation coefficient. The Pearson's Correlation Coefficient is determined using the formula:

$$\gamma = \frac{n\sum xy - (\sum x)(\sum y)}{\sqrt{n(\sum x^2)(\sum x)^2}\sqrt{n(\sum y^2)(\sum y)^2}} \tag{17}$$

where x and y are the gray-scale values of two adjacent pixels in the image and n is the total number of pixels selected from the image for the calculation. Table 6 tabulates the correlation coefficient calculated for the original and encrypted images. If there is no linear correlation or a weak linear correlation, γ is close to 0. A value near zero means that there is a random, nonlinear relationship between the two adjacent pixels and a value near one indicates that there is a linear relationship between adjacent pixels. It is

Table 6. Correlation coefficient

Image	Correlation Coefficient					
	Horizontal		Vertical		Diagonal	
	Original	Encrypted	Original	Encrypted	Original	Encrypted
Elaine.bmp	0.93076	-0.00801	0.94215	0.00918	0.88403	-0.02338
Lena.bmp	0.88875	0.00024	0.95104	0.00724	0.86972	0.01820
Camera.bmp	0.90886	-0.03015	0.94411	-0.01280	0.88152	-0.01162

Figure 7. Correlation coefficient relationships

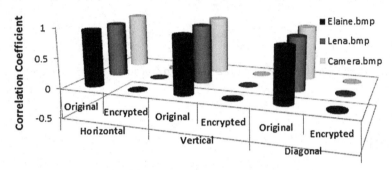

clear from Figure 7 that there is negligible correlation between the two adjacent pixels in the encrypted image. However, the two adjacent pixels in the original image are highly correlated as the correlation coefficient value is close to 1.

Differential Attacks

Attackers often make a slight change for the original image, use the proposed algorithm to encrypt the original image before and after changing, and compare two encrypted images to find out the relationship between the original image and encrypted image. This is known as differential attack.

Known-Plaintext and Chosen Plaintext Attacks

For encryption with a higher level of security, the security against both known-plaintext and chosen-plaintext attacks are necessary. Chosen/Known-plain text attacks are such attacks in which one can access/choose a set of plain texts and observe the corresponding encrypted texts. Figure 8a) is the mask image obtained by the XOR operation of a Plain image and its encrypted image. Figure 8b) shows an unsuccessful chosen/known-plain text attack using the proposed algorithm.

Algorithm Test

```
Input:  C,Z - Plain Images, C1, Z1 - Cipher image
Output T - Boolean
Step 1:M← C ⊕ C₁// Mask Image
```

Figure 8. a) XOR Mask b) Failed attack to crack the encrypted image

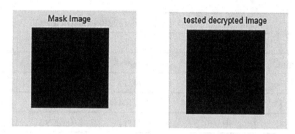

```
Step 2: If Z = M  ⊕Z₁ //Z₁ - encrypted image of the plain image Z
then
T ← True//Unknown encrypted image is decrypted
        else
                    T ← False  //resists Chosen/ Known Plain Text attack
end if
End Algorithm
```

Brute Force Attack

A Brute Force Attack or exhaustive key search is a strategy that can be used against any encrypted data by an attacker who is unable to take advantage of any weakness in an encryption system that would otherwise make his task easier. It involves systematically checking all possible keys until the correct key is found. The key to this encryption algorithm is an image which is of the same size as that of the image to be encrypted. Moreover, the aspect of bio-molecular environment is more difficult to access as it is extremely difficult to recover the DNA digital code without knowing the correct coding technology used. When an intruder gets the encrypted image and tries to decrypt the encrypted image without knowing the correct DNA digital coding technology, it would not be decrypted at all. An incorrect coding will cause biological pollution, which would lead to a corrupted image.

Key Sensitivity Analysis

The key sensitivity is an essential feature for any good cryptographic algorithm to guarantee the security of the proposed system against the brute-force attack. The key sensitivity of a proposed method can be observed in two different ways: i) the cipher image cannot be decrypted correctly if there is a small difference between the encryption and decryption keys and ii) if a different sequence file is used for encryption and decryption.

Figure 9 and Figure 10 clearly show that the decryption depends on the key image and DNA sequence file used for encryption. A different key image or a different DNA sequence file will not decrypt the encrypted image.

Figure 9. Decryption when a different sequence is used

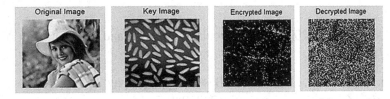

Figure 10. Decryption when a different key image is used

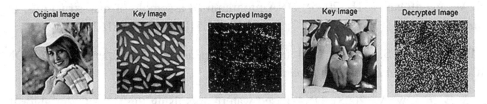

CONCLUSION

DNA based encryption is the beneficial supplement to the existing mathematical encryption. DNA binary strands support feasibility and applicability of DNA-based Cryptography. The security and the performance of the DNA based cryptographic algorithms are satisfactory for multi-level security applications of today's network. The proposed hybrid encryption scheme using DNA technology can resist brute-force, statistical and differential attack.

REFERENCES

Adleman, L. (1994). Molecular Computation of Solutions to Combinatorial Problems. *Science, 266*(5187), 1021–1024. doi:10.1126cience.7973651 PMID:7973651

Amos, M., Paun, G., Rozenberg, G., & Salomaa, A. (2002). Topics in the theory of DNA computing. *Theoretical Computer Science, 287*(1), 3–38. doi:10.1016/S0304-3975(02)00134-2

Chen, J. (2003). A DNA-based biomolecular cryptography design. *IEEE International Symposium on Circuits and Systems*, (pp. 822–825).

Cui, G. Z., Qin, L. M., Wang, Y. F., & Zhang, X. (2007). Information Security Technology Based on DNA Computing. *IEEE International Workshop on Anti-counterfeiting, Security, Identification*. 10.1109/IWASID.2007.373746

Cui, G. Z., Qin, L. M., Wang, Y. F., & Zhang, X. (2008). An Encryption Scheme using DNA Technology. *International Conference on Bio-Inspired Computing: Theories and Applications*.

Forouzan, B. A., & Mukhopadhyay, D. (2007). *Cryptography and Network Security*. Tata: McGraw Hill.

Gao, Q. (2010). *Biological Alphabets and DNA-based Cryptography*. American Society for Engineering Education.

Garzon, M. H., & Deaton, R. J. (2000). Biomolecular computing and programming: A definition. *Kunstliche Intelligenz*, *1*, 63–72.

Gehani, A., LaBean, T., & Reif, J. (2000). DNA Based Cryptography. *DIMACS Series in Discrete Mathematics and Theoretical Computer Science.*, *54*, 233–249.

Gifford, D. K., & Winfree, E. (2000). *DNA Based Computers V*. American Mathematical Society.

Gothelf, K. V., & LaBean, T. H. (2005). DNA-programmed assembly of nanostructures. *Organic & Biomolecular Chemistry*, *3*(22), 4023–4037. doi:10.1039/b510551j PMID:16267576

Gupta, V., Parthasarathy, S., & Zaki, M. J. (1997). Arithmetic and logic operations with DNA. *Proc. 3rd DIMACS Workshop on DNA-based Computers.*

Heider, D., & Barnekow, A. (2008). DNA-based watermarks using the DNA Crypt algorithm. *BMC Bioinformatics*, *8*(1), 176. doi:10.1186/1471-2105-8-176 PMID:17535434

Kahn, D. (1967). *The Code breakers*. New York: McMillan.

Kari, Daley, Gloor, Siromoney, & Landweber. (1999). How to Compute with DNA. *Foundations of Software Technology and Theoretical Computer Science*, 269-282.

Kari, L. (1997). From Micro-soft to Bio-soft. *Biocomputing and Emergent Computation Publications, World Scientific*, *26*, 146–164.

Leier, A., Richter, C., Banzhaf, W., & Rauhe, H. (2000). Cryptography with DNA binary strands. *Bio Systems*, *57*(1), 13–22. doi:10.1016/S0303-2647(00)00083-6 PMID:10963862

Li, J., Zhang, Q., Li, R., & Shihua, Z. (2008). Optimization of DNA Encoding Based on Combinatorial Constraints. *ICIC Express Letters ICIC International*, *2*, 81–88.

Ning, K. (2009). A pseudo DNA cryptography Method. *CoRR*. Retrieved from http://arxiv.org/abs/0903.2693

Norcen, R., Podesser, M., Pommer, A., Schmidt, H. P., & Uhl, A. (2003). Confidential storage and transmission of medical image data. *Computers in Biology and Medicine*, *33*(3), 273–292. doi:10.1016/S0010-4825(02)00094-X PMID:12726806

Qiang, Z., Xue, X., & Wei, X. (2012). A Novel Image Encryption Algorithm based on DNA Subsequence Operation. *The Scientific World Journal*.

Reif, J. (1997). Local Parallel Biomolecular Computation. *3rd DIMACS workshop on DNA based computers*.

Richa, H. R., & Phulpagar, B. D. (2013). Review on Multi-Cloud DNA Encryption Model for Cloud Security. *Int. Journal of Engineering Research and Applications*, *3*(6), 1625–1628.

Richter, C., Leier, A., Banzhaf, W., & Rauhe, H. (2000). Private and Public Key DNA steganography. *6th DIMACS Workshop on DNA Based Computers*.

Risca, V. I. (2001). DNA-based Steganography. *Cryptologia, Taylor and Francis, 25*(1), 37–49. doi:10.1080/0161-110191889761

Rothemund. (1996). A DNA and restriction enzyme implementation of Turing machines. *DNA Based Computers, 6,* 75-120.

Rothemund, P. W. K., Papadakis, N., & Winfree, E. (2004). Algorithmic self-assembly of DNA Sierpinski triangles. *PLoS Biology, 2*(12), e424. doi:10.1371/journal.pbio.0020424 PMID:15583715

Rozenberg, G., Bäck, T., & Kok, J. (2012). *Handbook of Natural Computing.* Springer. doi:10.1007/978-3-540-92910-9

Rozenberg, G., & Salomaa, A. (2006). DNA computing: New ideas and paradigms. Lecture Notes in Computer Science, 7, 188-200.

Sadeg, S. (2010). An Encryption algorithm inspired from DNA. *IEEE International Conference on Machine and Web Intelligence.*

Sakakibara, Y. (2005). Development of a bacteria computer: From in silico finite automata to *in vitro* and *invivo. Bulletin of EATCS, 87,* 165–178.

Sánchez, R., Grau, R., & Morgado, E. (2006). A Novel Lie Algebra of the Genetic Code over the Galois Field of Four DNA Bases. *Mathematical Biosciences, 202*(1), 156–174. doi:10.1016/j.mbs.2006.03.017 PMID:16780898

Shannon, C. E. (1949). Communication theory of secrecy system. *Journal of Bell System Technology, 28*(4), 656–715. doi:10.1002/j.1538-7305.1949.tb00928.x

Sherif, T. A., Magdy, S., & El-Gindi, S. (2006). A DNA based Implementation of YAEA Encryption Algorithm. *IASTED International Conference on Computational Intelligence.*

Siromoney, R., & Bireswar, D. (2003). DNA algorithm for breaking a propositional logic based crypto-system. *Bulletin of the European Association for Theoretical Computer Science, 79,* 170–177.

Stallings. (n.d.). *Cryptography and Network Security – Principles and Practice* (5th ed.). Prentice Hall.

Susan, K. L., & Hellman, M. E. (1994). Differential-Linear Cryptanalysis. *LNCS, 839,* 17–25.

Tausif, A., Sanchita, P., & Kumar, S. (2014). Message Transmission Based on DNA Cryptography [Review]. *International Journal of Bio-Science and Bio-Technology, 6*(5), 215–222. doi:10.14257/ijbsbt.2014.6.5.22

Taylor, C., Risca, V., & Bancroft, C. (1999). Hiding messages in DNA Microdots. *Nature, 399*(6736), 533–534. doi:10.1038/21092 PMID:10376592

Terec. (2011). DNA Security using Symmetric and Asymmetric Cryptography. *International Journal of New Computer Architectures and their Applications,* 34-51.

Udo, Saghafi, Wolfgang, & Rauhe. (2002). DNA Sequence Generator: A program for the construction of DNA sequences. *DNA Computing,* 23-32.

Vazirani, V. (2004). *Approximation Algorithms.* Berlin: Springer.

Volos, C. K., Kyprianidis, I., & Stouboulos, I. (2013). Image encryption process based on chaotic synchronization phenomena. *Signal Processing, 93*(5), 1328–1340. doi:10.1016/j.sigpro.2012.11.008

Wang, X., & Wang, Q. (2014). A novel Image Encryption Algorithm based on Dynamic S-Boxes constructed by chaos. *Nonlinear Dynamics, 75*(3), 567–576. doi:10.100711071-013-1086-2

Wang, Z., & Yu, Z. (2011). Index-based symmetric DNA encryption algorithm. *Fourth International Congress on Image and Signal Processing.*

Watson, J. D., & Crick, F. H. C. (1953). Molecular structure of nucleic acids: A structure for De-oxy ribose nucleic acid. *Nature, 25*(4356), 737–738. doi:10.1038/171737a0 PMID:13054692

Weichang, C., & Zhihua, C. (2000). Digital Coding of the Genetic Codons and DNA Sequences in High Dimension Space. *ACTA Biophysica Sinica, 16*(4), 760–768.

Westlund, B. H. (2002). NIST reports measurable success of Advanced Encryption Standard. *Journal of Research of the National Institute of Standards and Technology.*

Winfree. (1980). *The Geometry of Biological Time.* Academic Press.

Winfree, E. (1996). On the Computational Power of DNA Annealing and Ligation. *1st DIMACS workshop on DNA based computers.*

Wu, Y., Noonan, J. P., & Agaian, S. (2011). NPCR and UACI Randomness Tests for Image Encryption. *Journal of Selected Areas in Telecommunications, 4,* 31–38.

Wu, Y., Zhou, Y., Noonan, J. P., & Agaian, S. (2013). Design of Image Cipher Using Latin Squares. *Information Sciences, 00,* 1–30.

Xiao, G., Lu, M., Qin, L., & Lai, X. (2006). New field of cryptography: DNA cryptography. *Chinese Science Bulletin, 51,* 1139–1144.

Xiao, J. H., Zhang, X. Y., & Xu, J. (2012). A membrane evolutionary algorithm for DNA sequence design in DNA computing. *Chinese Science Bulletin, 57*(2), 698–706. doi:10.100711434-011-4928-7

XueJia. (2010). Asymmetric Encryption and signature method with DNA technology. *Information Sciences, 53,* 506–514.

Youssef, Emam, & Saafan, & AbdElghany. (2013). Secured Image Encryption Scheme Using both Residue Number System and DNA Sequence. *The Online Journal on Electronics and Electrical Engineering, 6*(3), 656-664.

Yunpeng, Z., Fu, B., & Zhang, X. (2012). DNA cryptography based on DNA Fragment assembly. *IEEE International Conference Information Science and Digital Content Technology.*

Zhang, M., Sabharwal, L., Tao, W., Tarn, T.-J., Xi, N., & Li, G. (2004). Interactive DNA sequence and structure design for DNA Nano applications. *IEEE Transactions on Nanobioscience*, *3*(4), 286–292. doi:10.1109/TNB.2004.837918 PMID:15631140

Zhang, X. C. (2008). Breaking the NTRU public key cryptosystem using self-assembly of DNA tilings. *Chinese Journal of Computers*, *12*, 2129–2137.

Chapter 5
IPHDBCM:
Inspired Pseudo Hybrid DNA Based Cryptographic Mechanism to Prevent Against Collabrative Black Hole Attack in Wireless Ad hoc Networks

Erukala Suresh Babu
K.L. University, India

C. Nagaraju
Y.V. University, India

M.H.M. Krishna Prasad
J.N.T. University, India

ABSTRACT

Secure communication is one of the basic requirements for any network standard. Particularly, crypto-graphic algorithms have gained more popularity to protect the communication in a hostile environment. As the critical information that is being transferred over the wireless adhoc networks can be easily acquired and is vulnerable to many security attacks. However, several security communication threats had been detected and defended using conventional symmetric and asymmetric cryptographic mechanism, which are too difficult and resource consuming for such mobile adhoc networks. Recently, one of the severe security threats that have to be detected and defend in any type of network topology is blackhole attack and cooperative blackhole. Because of its severity, the black hole attack has attracted a great deal of attention in the research community. Comprehensively the results of the existing system conclude that the black hole attack on various mobile adhoc networks is hard to detect and easy to implement. This paper addresses to detect and defend the blackhole attack and cooperative blackhole attack using hybrid DNA-based cryptography (HDC) mechanism. Moreover, the proposed method upsurge the security issue with the underlying AODV routing protocol. Eventually, This Hybrid DNA-based Cryptography (HDC) is one of the high potential candidates for advanced wireless ad hoc networks, which require less communication bandwidth and memory in comparison with other cryptographic systems. The simulation results of this proposed method provide better security and network performances as compared to existing schemes.

DOI: 10.4018/978-1-7998-1763-5.ch005

1. INTRODUCTION

There is a necessity to design and develop a secure wireless mobile ad hoc network (SWMANETs), particularly useful for battlefield applications in order to perform security-sensitive operations. Unlike wireless network with fixed infrastructure that makes use of access points to communicate, a MANET is an infrastructure less network does not require any centralized administration. however, network elements of these networks are needed to be deployed rapidly with reasonably low cost. One of the primary concerns of these networks requires resilient security service, which are more vulnerable to limited physical insecurity of mobile nodes, as these nodes are disposed to attacks. These attacks are performed in both reactive and proactive routing protocols, which can roughly be relegated into two major categories such as active and passive attacks (Konate, K., 2011; Gopi, A. P et al., 2015 ; Kumar, S. A et.al 2015). The malicious nodes pretend to be as a trusted router by advertising the spurious service requests to disrupt the normal routing operation and to deny the services to authorized nodes, which leads to a DOS attack. In active attack, the malicious router originates the attack by modifying the information in the network. The black hole attack is one such type of active assaults that can be performed against both reactive and proactive routing protocols. To be more specific, each black hole node impersonates the source and destination node by sending an imitated path request to the destination node and imitated path reply to the source node that was taking place in route discovery phase to claim that, it has the optimal route information. Finally, the black hole node consumes the packet, and simply drops the packets, that reduce the network performance *as shown in figure-1*. On the other hand, under the context of information and network security domain, it is necessary to provide an unbreakable cryptosystem to protect the data that we transmit over the network; Open Systems Interconnection (OSI) security architecture provided a systematic security solution for different layers of networks. In the routing layer of the OSI model, it is essential to design a secure protocol that can defend the black hole attack and cooperative black hole attack against on-demand routing protocol (Osathanunkul, 2011; Dasgupta, 2012). More importantly, the security services such as authentication, data confidentiality, nonrepudiation and data integrity services must be incorporated into these on-demand routing protocols.

The following are some of the challenging issues to secure against black hole attack and cooperative black hole attack. The first challenging issue is to secure the routing protocols against the black hole attack. This problem has not properly addressed in most of the existing secure routing protocols or if addressed, there are very expensive in terms of bandwidth and limited computational capabilities. The second challenging issue is to defend the black hole attack against adhoc routing protocols that dynamically changes the topology, (i.e., what kind of key management and authentication schemes are needed? Unlike of Wireless networks, MANET cannot use any certificate authority (CA) server).The third challenging issue is the existing secure routing protocols may not efficient or feasible to scale, as these protocols produce heavy traffic load and requires intensive computations.

This paper mainly addresses all the above issues using hybrid DNA based cryptographic mechanism to defend and detect a black hole attack and cooperative black hole attack against AODV routing protocol. We call this protocol, as Secure Routing Protocol using Hybrid DNA-based Cryptography (SRP-HDC) that establishes cryptographically secure communication links among the communicating mobile nodes.

The rest of the paper is as follows. Section-II specifies the related work that had proposed a large class of ad-hoc routing protocols and attacks against MANET in the literature. Section-III enumerates the hybrid cryptosystem that prevents the collaborative black hole attack against on-demand routing protocols by authentication and encryption mechanism. Section-IV presents the detection mechanism

Figure 1. Illustrates the black hole scenario

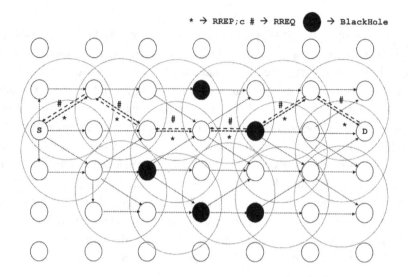

against collabrative black hole attack which will be incorporated into the secure routing route discovery procedures. Section-V specifies the security analysis and the simulation results for better evaluation of our theoretical work using network simulator NS-2. Finally, conclusion with future work are presented in Section-VI

2. RELATED WORK

The proposed SRPHDC protocol for mobile adhoc network may fall broadly into two categories, first, integrating the Inspired Pseudo Biotic DNA predicated Cryptographic approach into the existing AODV routing protocol and second, detecting the black hole attack against AODV in MANETs.

This section will discuss the revolution of the Black hole problem, which is a genuine security issue in mobile adhoc network that affect its performance. In this problem, a malevolent node makes use of the weakness of the AODV routing protocol to advertise itself having the optimal path to the destination with the aim of intercepting the packets. This malevolent node will drop all the packets or drops selectively to accomplish a denial-of-service (DOS) attack. Recently, many proposals had been proposed in defending, avoiding and detecting black hole nodes in mobile adhoc networks(Woungang, 2012 ; Lu, 2009; Bindra, 2012). In this paper, we collect and introduce the mechanisms that are proposed in recent years. In (Tsou et al., 2011). introduced a reverse tracing technique to detect and prevent the black hole nodes against DSR routing protocol. In (Baadache, A & Belmehdi A, 2010), Baadache et al. proposed a novel method based on the principle of Merkle tree to detect the black hole nodes against adhoc networks. However, their method experiences more computational overhead on routing. In (Jain et al., 2010). proposed a mechanism for detecting the cooperative malicious nodes based neighborhood monitoring of data blocks between source and destination. In (Anita et al., 2010) proposed a certificate based authentication method for recognizing the black hole attacks in mobile ad hoc networks. In (Lu, S et al., 2009) proposed a Secure AODV routing protocol against black hole attack for MANETS by showing the security limitations of AODV. In (Raj et al.,2009) proposed a strategy to identify and separate the blackhole attacks in mobile ad hoc networks. In their methodology, the algorithm experiences extreme overhead due to the handling of ALARM control messages and the threshold value should be updated at every time interval. In (Weerasinghe et al., 2007) introduces a system to prevent the cooperative black-hole attacks in mobile ad hoc networks. However, in their solution, black hole attack can be prevented; the extra control packets will cause more overhead in the network and high latency in the network. In (Deng et al., 2002) projected a mechanism to keep away the black hole nodes in mobile adhoc networks. However, this technique suffers from a cooperative black hole attack. (Shurman et al.,2004) proposed two different techniques to detect the black hole attack against MANETS. However, their solution cannot handle to detect multiple black hole attack. (Marti et al., 2000) proposed the misbehavior detection using the watchdog and the path rater. However, their solution cannot handle partial dropping of packets. (Tissieres et al., 2003) proposed the confidant protocol, which, monitor the neighbor nodes that makes use of reputation system. (Kozma et al.,2009) proposed a detection mechanism using the REACT system. However, in their solutions only gives the information of transmitting packets, but no information about forwarding path. (Woungang et al.,2012) introduced a mechanism to identify a black hole attack against the DSR routing protocol. However, in their solutions cannot handle cooperative black hole attacks and computation overhead is present.

Most of the solutions discussed above are used to detect or avoid black hole attacks on reactive routing protocols in the mobile ad hoc networks. However, most of the methods are used to either detect or preventing the black hole attacks. In this paper, a novel method is presented based on the AODV protocol in which the adversaries are detected based upon the close neighborhood of the range and avoiding the black hole using multiple path between source and destination and finally defending by integrating inspired pseudo biotic DNA based cryptographic mechanisms to the existing AODV routing protocol.

3. SECURE ROUTING AGAINST AODV PROTOCOL

In the layer-5 of the OSI network model, most of the possible attacks will be either on routing information or data tampering. The prevention of these attacks against on-demand routing protocols can be performed using authentication and encryption mechanism.

3.1. Overview of AODV Routing Protocol:

In brief, to summarize the AODV(Perkins et al., 2001; Babu, E. S et al., 2013) routing protocol. AODV is the predominant on-demand routing protocol that offers low processing, low network utilization, ability to adapt the dynamic conditions and low memory overhead.

We used this AODV as an underlying protocol to protect from the black hole attack. The functionality of AODV is usually initiated with the route discovery process, whenever a valid route is not present, and another mechanism is route maintenance, as AODV fails to maintain lifelong route between the sending node and receiving node, due to the high mobility by nature. During the route discovery process, if the originator needs of a route, broadcasts route request (RREQ) packet (with regular information and security related information) to its neighboring nodes, which is described in the next section-III(C). Once the neighbor node obtains a RREQ message from the originator, it broadcast the same RREQ message to its next hop with its current route. This process will be continual until it acquires the actual destination.

Figure 2. Illustrates route discovery process of modified AODV

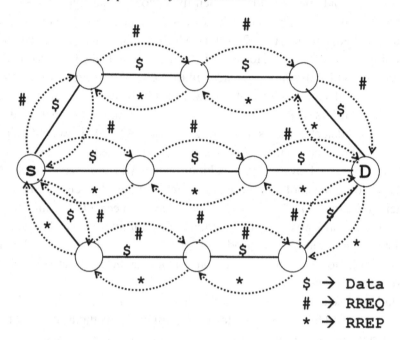

This proposed work modifies the original AODV protocol. The slight modification is done at the destination side. To be more specific, the destination node broadcast the Route Reply (RREP) packet back to all its neighbor nodes with the current route until reaches to the source node to create multiple route, instead of unicasting as in the original AODV routing protocol, as shown figure-2. To adapt the dynamic topology environment in the route discovery process of AODV in adhoc networks, we used multiple, possibly disjoint, routes/path (Kim et al., 2006; E. S et al., 2013) between source and destination. This modified AODV routing protocol has an ability to discover responds by unicasting the RREP packet to the source node. Instead of unicasting with single RREP packet, it broadcasts RREPs Reply (RREP) packet back to all its neighbor nodes with the current route until reaches to the source node. Once the first RREP message received by the source node, then it can begin sending the data to the destination, late arrived RREPs will be reserved or saved for future purpose. The alternative multiple paths between source and destination can be used for two purpose, first if the primary path fails to send the packets to the destination. Second, after detection of black hole node (both single and cooperative black hole node), source node will diverted the traffic with alternate route to the destination. Finally, once the path is entrenched, the nearest neighbor nodes will monitor the link status for the active routes. The nodes that do not conformed the neighbor rating based on neighbor profile will be eliminated from the route as described from Section-D(i,ii).

3.2. Background of DNA Cryptography:

In order to understand the rudimentary principles of DNA Cryptography (Gehani at al., 2003 ; Leier et al., 2000; Ning et al 2009) in a emerge area of DNA Computing, it is necessary to address the background details of central dogma of molecular biology, that is, how a DNA sequence is actually transcript and translated into a protein sequence as shown in figure-3. DNA (Deoxyribo Nucleic Acid) is the fundamental hereditary material that stores genetic information found in almost every living organisms ranging from very small viruses to complex human beings. It is constituted by nucleotides which forms polymer chains. These chains are also known as DNA strands. Each DNA nucleotides contains a single base and usually consists of four bases, specifically, Adenine (A), Guanine (G), Cytosine(C), and Thymine (T) represent genetic code. These bases reads from the start promoter which forms the structure of DNA strand by forming two strands of hydrogen bonds, one is A with T and another is C with G; These DNA sequences are eventually transcript and interpreted into chains of amino acids, which constitutes proteins.

3.3. Node Authentication using Hybrid DNA based Cryptosystem:

This section describes the hybrid DNA based cryptosystem (Babu et al., 2015), which is used to verify the data integrity and authenticate the mobile nodes. Moreover, this hybrid approach makes use of both the public and private key-based schemes.

- First, In order to authenticate the mobile nodes, public-key cryptography is used with a key pair of DNA based public keys, DNA based private keys, and it is used to establish the session keys.
- Second, pseudo DNA based symmetric cryptography is used to verify the data integrity. This can be achieved with the private key, which is shared by the two nodes.

In other words, symmetric encryption will be used to achieve integrity and confidentiality, while asymmetric encryption will provide to authenticate the members of mobile nodes. Subsequently, the above method can be succeed with the following assumption.

- First, clearly, according the characteristics of MANETS, initial trustees must exist among the mobile nodes.
- Second, pairwise DNA based mutual secret keys must exist between the nodes.
- Third, during the initialization phase of the network, we embed the unique ID, an initial key pair of DNA based private key, and DNA based public key for every node.
- Finally, the shared secret keys are used to reboot from PKI, which can distribute and generate a key pair of DNA based private key and DNA based public key for every node.

Next, In order to authenticate the mobile nodes and to establish the session keys, the following framework is used.

- Initially, a node 'S' generates a pair of DNA secret key K(PR,S) and public key K(PU,S) and distributed the public key K(PU,S) to the node 'D' by using Public Key Infrastructure or Trusted Authority.
- Similarly, a node 'D' also generates a pair of DNA private key K(PR,D) and public key K(PU,D) and distributed the DNA public key K(PU,D) to the node 'S' by using PKI or CA.
- If the node 'S' and node 'D' are 1-hop neighbors then Node 'S' can authenticate the node 'D' by issuing a signed certificate with its DNA private key. Here certificate is a proof of node 'D' ID and DNA public key with 'S' signature.

Figure 3. Central dogma of molecular biology

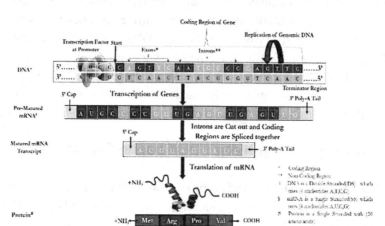

- If any of the intermediate nodes 'w' want the read the signed certificate, he/she should hold 'S' DNA public key and then node 'w' can read and trust that node by bind it along its DNA public key.

- Finally, N-hop one to one intermediate nodes can quickly create a DNA private key by using three-way handshake based on the key information and availability of certificates in the PKI (Capkun, S et al., 2003)

i.   Secure Route Discovery Process on AODV routing protocol:

Whenever, source node wants to send the data to the destination. It initiates the path discovery process only, when no valid route is present to the destination. Consequently, it broadcasts Route Request (RREQ) packet by creating pairwise DNA private key/shared key (the procedure of symmetric DNA based cryptography is discussed in section III-C(iii) with neighbor nodes, until RREQ reaches to the destination node. To achieve this, first, source node generates pseudo random number and signs that number to create the certificate with its DNA secret key using asymmetric cryptosystem, subsequently the RREQ packet is secured by a Message Digest (MD5) algorithm (Babu, E. S., 2015, September ; Babu, E. S., (2015).), finally, the signature and generated hash value is attached to the RREQ control packet, and forwards to its intermediate nodes. Second, the intermediate node having source node DNA public key will verify the signed certificate and then decrypt the message that contains the shared secret key that can be summarized as.

$$cm_{q,i} + h\left(cm_{q,i} + K_{(sk,j)}\right) + \mathrm{E}\left(\mathrm{E}\left(K_{(sk,j)}, \quad K_{(i,pub)}\right)K_{(i,pri)}\right) \tag{1}$$

Where cm_q is RREQ control message that contains original message (M), identity Number (IN) of a node that forwards the original message and sequence number (SeqNo) of the message, which can be written in (2). $h(cm_{q,i}+K_{(sk,j)})$ represents the keyed hash Message algorithm with a shared key $K_{(sk,s)}$ on message $cm_{q,i}$ which can be written in (3). Finally '+' denotes the concatenation of strings; the suffix 'i' is the number of intermediate nodes form source to destination $i=1,2,3,4,...,n$ and suffix 'j' is the number of keys created the source node 's' which is usually represented as $j=k_1,k_2,k_3,...,k_n$.

$$h\left(cm_{q,i} + K_{(sk,j)}\right) \tag{2}$$

$$h(cm_{q,i}+K_{(sk,j)}) \tag{3}$$

Once RREQ control packet reaches with the valid route to the destination, then it verifies the signature and decrypts the shared key with its private key and reply with a RREP control packet that transmits back to the source which can be summarized as

$$K_{(sk,s)} \tag{4}$$

ii.   To Authenticate the Communications between nodes using Pseudo DNA Asymmetric Cryptography:

Definition of Public Key Cryptography: An Asymmetric Cryptosystem is mathematical function with three-tuple $i = 1,2,3,4,....n$ where: ε is the encryption algorithm and $j = k_1, k_2, k_3, ..., k_n$ is the Decryption algorithm and $cm_{q,i} = \mathcal{M} + \left(IN_f\right) + SeqNo$ is a randomized key generation algorithm. It returns two keys in which one is a DNA public key denoted by K(Dpub,s) and another DNA private key denoted by K(Dpri,s); we write $a_1 \leftarrow K_{(Dpub,s)}$ and $a_2 \leftarrow K_{(Dpri,s)}$; $h\left(cm_{q,i} + K_{(sk,j)}\right)$ is a stateful public key algorithm. The deterministic encryption algorithm takes a plaintext 'p' along with the random key 'a_1' and returns a cipher text 'q'; we denote as q←E_a(p); $cm_{p,i} + h\left(cm_{p,i} + K_{(sk,j)}\right) + E\left(E\left(K_{(sk,j)}, K_{(i,pub)}\right)K_{(i,pri)}\right)$ is a decryption algorithm which takes the cipher text 'q' along with DNA private key 'a_2' and returns the equivalent plaintext 'p' ; we denote as p←D_a(q) where $p \in \{0,1,A,G,T,C\}^*$: finally we represent the stateful public key algorithm with $D_{a2}(E_{a1}(p))$=p for all p∈{0,1,A,G,T,C}*.

Suppose, a source node 's' want to send the data to the destination. It initiates with path discovery process with one of the 1-hop intermediate node 'r', then it generates the random key (Here, the Key will number of the splices, the starting code of the frame and removed length of the pattern codes) which will provided as shared DNA private key between source 's' and destination 'r'. and then source node encrypts the DNA shared secret key 's_k' by utilizing its neighbor DNA public key K(pub,r) and then once again source node encrypts the encrypted DNA based shared secret key 's_k' by utilizing its own private key K(pub,s). The output of encrypted shared key 's_k' provides signature for the RREQ control packet and secured by a Message Digest (MD5) algorithm. Once the RREQ control packet reaches with the valid route to the destination, then it verifies the integrity of message (signature) and decrypts the shared key with its private key and reply with a RREP control packet that transmits back to the source node. Hence, source node 's' can authenticate all intermediate node up to the destination node by creating the shared key 's_k' and distribute to all the nodes.

Figure 4. shows the architectural diagram of asymmetric cryptography used as a part of SRP-HDC work

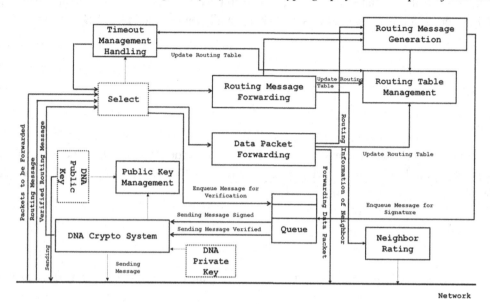

iii. Communications model for exchanging the shared key using Pseudo DNA based symmetric cryptography:

In (Babu, E. S et al., 2016; Nagaraju, C et al., 2016) We proposed a novel method called pseudo symmetric DNA based cryptographic mechanisms. Particularly, whenever a node needs to transmit the packet, first, the node should share the unique DNA based secret key with the source. i.e. private key are shared by the two participating nodes. Moreover, to protect the control or data traffic, the source node 's' can simple use the DNA based shared key and sent to the destination 'd'. The complete format is shown below:

$$M + h(M + SK_{sd}) \tag{5}$$

where SK_{sd} is the shared key which is the part of the message M that is shared between source 's' and destination 'd' .Here pseudo DNA based symmetric cryptography is mainly used to achieve data integrity and confidentiality. To perform the above communications model, the following steps can be described briefly as shown in figure-5.

1. Alice takes the plaintext (Secret Key) and it converts into binary form which in turn converts into DNA form
2. Alice will scan DNA form of information to generate the variable length random key by generating the No of the splices from the specified DNA pattern, the starting code of the DNA frame to find out the introns, introns places and removed length of the pattern codes i,e. introns are removed from the specified DNA sequence as the first round of Key Generation.
3. With the help of random key (splicing system), Alice will transcript the DNA sequence into the mRNA strand

4. After Generating mRNA Strand, Alice also generate the variable length random sub key by generating the No of the splices from the specified mRNA pattern, the starting code of the mRNA frame, introns places and removed length of the pattern codes as the second round of processing

5. Again, the spliced mRNA strand are translated into the amino acids, which forms protein sequence, as shown in Algorithm-5 (Hint: The mapping of codons to amino acids is done with the help of genetic code table. Usually table consists of 61 codons, which are mapped 20 amino acids)

6. Next, the protein sequence (Cipher Text) will be sent to the Bob through public channel.

7. The random variable length key is comprised of number of splices, the starting index, pattern codes length of the introns, the positions and places of the introns, the cut out the introns, random mapping of codon-amino acids will form the symmetric key to decrypt the cipher text (protein sequence), which is also sent to the Bob through a secure channel

8. On Bob's (Receiver) side, when he receives random keys and protein form (Cipher text) of data from Alice through the secure channel, then he can perform the decryption process.

9. Bob decrypts the cipher text message using the random key reversible translation to recover mRNA sequence from protein sequence, and then recover DNA form of information, in the reverse order as Alice encrypt the information.

10. Bob can then recover then binary form of information, and finally gets what Alice sent him.

Figure 5. Pseudo DNA symmetric cryptosystem

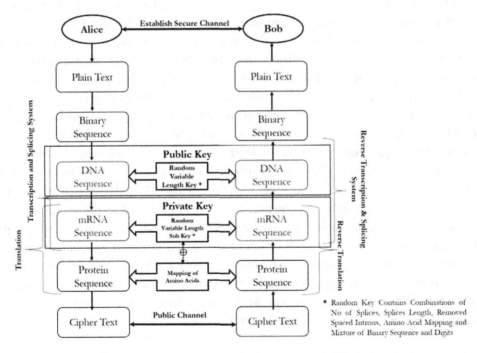

4. DETECTION OF BLACK HOLE ATTACK AGAINST AODV PROTOCOL:

This sub-section performs the next task, after developing the secure route discovery process on AODV routing protocol, the detection scheme against black hole attack should be incorporated into secure route discovery procedures. To detect the black hole attack, we assume and summarize the following.

1. Every node has an exclusive unique identifier and a pair of DNA based public/secret keys.
2. Initially a compromised participating node will be in routing until it is detected.
3. The source node will establish the DNA shared key with the destination via with all its intermediate nodes by utilizing the hybrid DNA key management scheme as discussed in Section-III(C).
4. There are sufficient uncompromised intermediate nodes in the arbitrary network. so that packets can reach with different routes to the destination.
   a. Detection of Single Black hole attack:

Initially, the nodes are allowed to build up with the trust, based on neighbor profile and behaviors of the nodes. Specifically, neighborhood profile includes all the features such as number of data packets or RREQ control packets sent as well as received, number of ACK or RREP packets are sent or forwarded and received from/to the neighbors, number of RREQ/RREP/data packets dropped. To detect the misbehaving nodes, first, the neighbor profile approach is used. In this approach, the nearest node can identify the misbehaving nodes by monitoring the network traffic of its neighboring nodes. Here, a profile is used to detect abnormal behavior in the network. Second, the nearest node makes use of the responses, such as (No response, Shutdown and Blacklisting) to detect the misbehavior of nodes. In our work, first two cases (No response, shut down response) of responses were chosen, as these two cases are more suitable for ad-hoc networking. The nearest node waits for the response from the neighbor nodes, the neighbor node communicates back to the nearest node in the form of response (i.e. nearest neighbor will response back (shut down or no responses) to the source node or intermediate nodes). To achieve this k-Nearest Neighbor algorithm (describe below) is used to compute the k nearest neighbor by calculating the distance between the nodes. To be more specific, let us assume that source node 's' sends the protected message to the destination node 'd' via intermediate node 'M'. We also assume that even though the intermediate node 'M' is initially authenticated, it can be compromised, during the route discovery phase. According to the authentication, malicious node 'M' could not tamper the packets that was received from source, but simply drop the packets instead of forwarding the packets to the destination. Meanwhile one of the nearest node 'NN' of the intermediate node 'M' response with shut down or no responses packet back to the source node or intermediate nodes. Based upon the response received and neighbor profile, the source node assume that intermediate node 'M' is misbehaving, however, the source node sends the packet through different path or route to the destination. Moreover, a Destination node also able to detect intermediate node 'M' is misbehaving. Finally, the source node gives the neighbor rating (described below) based on neighbor profile.

Nearest Neighbor (NN) Problem:

It is an optimization problem (Andoni A, 2009) that achieves the distance to the requested neighbor. To shorten this problem, we convey that a node 'x' is a K-nearest neighbor of a node 'y' i.e. the radius between node 'x' and node 'y' is at most K. This NN algorithm, either gives back K-nearest neighbor

Figure 6. An illustration of a K-near neighbor query

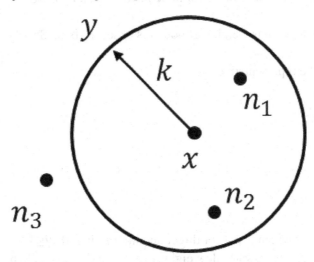

node or no such nodes exists. The requested nearest neighbor of the node 'y' is the node 'x'. However, both the nodes n₁ and n₂ are K-nearest neighbors of 'y' as illustrated in figure-6.

Neighbors Rating

Neighbor rating is usually calculate with the Beta distribution function.The probability distributions function of any two events is more often represented with Beta function, which is defined as

$$\Pi = \left(\mathcal{E}, \mathcal{D}, \mathcal{K} \right) \tag{6}$$

where $0 \le e \le 1$, $\alpha > 0$, $\beta > 0$

Let us assume the formation of nodes with two possibilities $\mathcal{E}$, the probability of 'e' is estimated by Beta distribution function based on past observations of $\mathcal{D}$, and it is resresented with α and β

$\alpha = 1 +$ observed value of e

$\beta = 1 +$ observed value of $\mathcal{K}$

Here, the binary process is normally corresponds like a node's behavior, the number of positive events 'e' and number of negative events $a_1 \leftarrow K_{(Dpub,s)}$ are measured over a period of time accordingly. To calculate the neighbor rating, it is necessary to assign flexible weights to different events; for instance, more importance will be given for data packet dropping rathen than control packet dropping.

"Case-1: if the direct neighbor rating from the node 'j' to node 'i' is of 1-hop neighbor, then direct neighbor rating (DR) is calculated based on its observations which is defined as:

$$a_2 \leftarrow K_{(Dpri,s)} \tag{7}$$

$P_{i,j}$ = latest positive variable actions weights of node j is observed by node i

$n_{i,j}$ = latest negative variable actions weights of node j is observed by node i

The direct rating can be represented as,

$$\mathcal{E}(\mathcal{M}, \mathcal{K}) \tag{8}$$

where

$$\mathcal{D}(C, \mathrm{K})$$

where γ is the past behavior which is part of direct neighbor rating; $0 \leq \gamma \leq 1$

In this work, we had added more variable weights to monitor the current behavior rather than the past behavior, which is denoted as small 'γ', because the malicious node (blackhole attack) can misuse the positive rating by limiting the weights. However, the past history will be deleted, as the time progresses to make effective rating. Finally, the entire computation is based upon the neighbor profile history. Moreover, this technique gives the efficient results in high mobility network."

The total rating is usually denoted as $TR_{i,j}$ that gathers all the direct neighbor rating $DR_{i,j}$ for the set of one-hop neighbors N, which is represented as $DR_{n,j}$ for every $n \in N$. Here, either N is the neighbors set that can trusted, or their information on rating will be sent for the abnormality test. The abnormality test of a node i checks the behavior based on given rating value $DR_{n,j}$, if the difference of $DR_{n,j}$ is large than the expected rating value $TR_{i,j}$ then it is reject otherwise it will accept. This condition makes more robust detection method against black hole attack. The abnormality test is defined as:

$$p \leftarrow D_a(q) \tag{9}$$

After detecting the malicious node based on neighbor direct rating, the source node will diverted the traffic with different route to the destination. Hence, intrusion of malicious node effect to network becomes weaker. Therefore, we can conclude that more paths reduce malicious node intrusion to network.

ii.   Detection of Cooperative Blackhole attack:

The below figure-7 depicts the cooperative black hole attack (Babu, E. S et al., 2016 ; Ramaswamy, S et al., 2003 ; Su, M. et al., 2010 ; Swarna, M. et al, 2016). which is more challenging attack to detect. In our design, source node has transfer its shared secret key with all its k-hop-neighbors using key management schemes. Suppose, source node 's' sends the protected message to the destination node 'd' via intermediate node 'M_1 and M_2'. We also assume that even though the intermediate node 'M_1 and M_2' is initially authenticated, it can be compromised, during the route discovery phase. According to the authentication, malicious node 'M_1' could not tamper or drop the message that was received from source, nevertheless, it may forward the message to M_2 node. In this case, M_2 is also comprised and may drop the message instead of forwarding the message to the destination or intermediate node. To detect

Figure 7. Illustration of an indirect foreign neighbor pair (n_j, n_k)

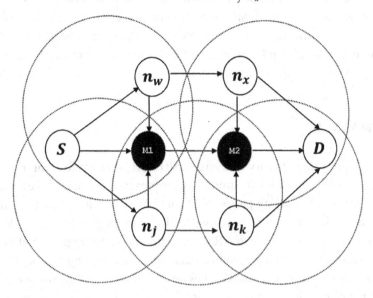

the cooperative misbehaving nodes, first, the nearest foreign neighbor profile approach is used. In this approach, each node finds its closest nearest foreign neighbor (2-hop-neighbor) by establishing DNA shared keys between the sender and neighbor nodes. To be more specific, Let n_j be the nearest node to M_1 and n_k be nearest neighbor node to M_2 and it is nearest foreign neighbor to s that estimate the history by neighbor rating of M_2 with the help of n_k. This setup is depicted below:

The node n_j is the neighbor to M_2 but cannot reach to M_2, and node n_k completely know the profile of M_2 since n_k is already neighbor to n_j, who gives opinion (misbehaving) about M_2. Subsequently, In a future behavior between M_1 and M_2 will be monitored by both n_j and n_k, the probability of this nodes behavior will be rated by both the nodes n_j and n_k is:

m_1 and m_2 is monitored by n_k

$X_{m1,m2}(y)$ = indicator variable for node n_j for the confirmation of malicious node m_2 at encounter y

$$p \in \{0,1, A, G, T, C\}^{*} ;$$
(10)

Let $D_{s,m1}(n)$ all the encounters (neighbor rating) between S and m_1 is monitored by n_j

$X_{s,m1}(n)$ = indicator variable for node s for the confirmation of malicious node m_1 at encounter y

$$D_{a2}\left(E_{a1}\left(p\right)\right) = p \text{ for all}$$
(11)

The interpretation of the equations 10th and 11th which gives the probability of n_j and n_k, that agree and approves the nodes M_1 and M_2 is misbehaving. Hence, the nearest foreign neighbor can identify the misbehaving nodes by monitoring the network traffic of its neighboring nodes. After detecting the malicious node based on foreign neighbor indirect rating, the source node will diverted the traffic with different route to the destination. Eventually, intrusion of malicious node effect to network becomes weaker. Once again, we can conclude that more paths reduce malicious node intrusion to the network. In summary, the single black hole and cooperative black hole intrusion can be identified without the need of expensive signatures, as these signatures, which can be used to defend the route from end to end.

5. SECURITY ANALYSIS

In this section, we investigate the security analysis of SRPHDC (Secure Routing Protocol using Hybrid DNA based Cryptography) by evaluating its strength in the presence of a black hole attack and cooperative black hole attack against AODV routing protocol which is described in Section-D(i,ii)5.3.3. Moreover, we also compared a SRPHDC routing protocol with ARAN (Sanzgiri, K et al., 2005.) protocols. It is observed that SRPHDC is more secure than ARAN. Additionally, this approach effectively reduces the processing power requirements in comparison of existing secure routing protocols, which might take excessive processing power for different kinds of mobile ad hoc networks. As discussed earlier, SRPHDC assumes public key management sub-system, which is capable of securely verifying the identity and public key for a given node. Furthermore, SRPHDC provides the basis of security services such as authentication, confidentiality, and nonrepudiation and data integrity.

Finally, we deliberate, how this proposed method satisfies the basic requirements in comparison of several existing (including ARAN) secure routing protocol. We also considered general routing attacks such as Blackhole attacks, participation of unauthorized nodes, Securing Shortest Paths, fabricated routing messages, Spoofed Route Signaling Attack parameters etc.

Figure 8. Throughput of AODV Vs SRPHDC

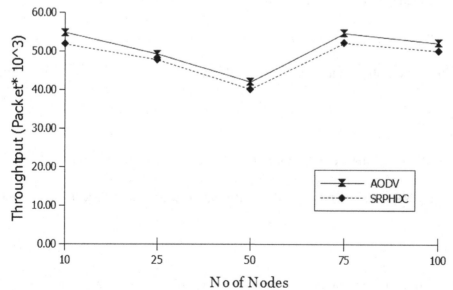

Figure 9. Throughput of modified AODV Vs SRPHDC

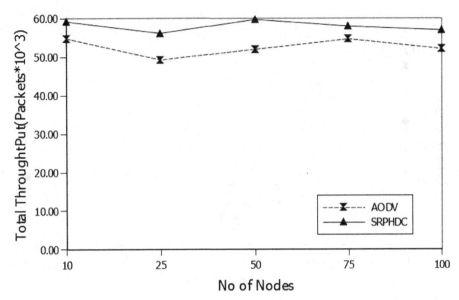

Figure 10. Throughput of AODV Vs SRPHDC in the presence of black hole nodes

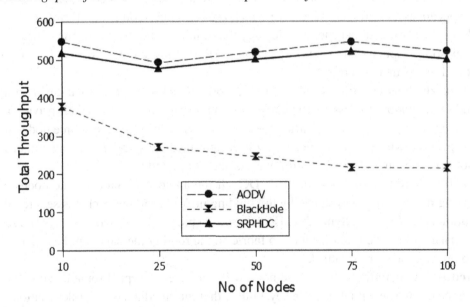

- **Black Hole Attacks:** In SRPHDC, a node is monitored by its nearest neighbor nodes, which calculates the neighbor rating, based on neighbor profile. If the node is misbehaving, the nearest neighbor nodes will identify and notify to the source node, then the source node will send the packets with alternate routes with different DNA public keys. In particular, to formally characterize the security offered by SRPHDC, we proposed secure route discovery process which is successful with hybrid biotic cryptosystem based on DNA based cryptography which makes use of both the symmetric key (to achieve the data integrity) and asymmetric key-based schemes (to

Figure 11. Throughput of modified AODV Vs SRPHDC in the presence of black hole nodes

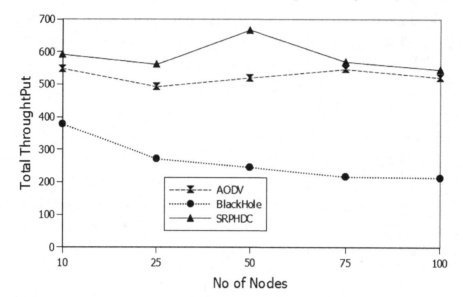

authenticate the mobile nodes and to establish the session keys). Moreover, DNA based cryptography appears as a rapidly growing field which provides ultra-compact information storage, vast parallelism, and exceptional energy efficiency that minimize the major overhead produced by the major existing cryptosystem. On the other hand, ARAN fails to defend the cooperative blackhole attack and incurs more overhead.

- **Unauthorized Participation:** In SRPHDC, authorized nodes are performed during route discovery and computation process. Particularly, only authorized nodes have both private and public key (asymmetric or shared key). During the route discovery process, the source node encrypts the control packets, which is authenticated by each intermediate node. Hence, unauthorized nodes will not generate any fallacious control packets and prohibited to join a route.

- **Fabricated Routing Messages:** In SRPHDC, all the authorized intermediate nodes will verify the routing message that was signed by the sending node, as routing packet is secured through an encryption key. Moreover, Symmetric DNA based cryptography is used to secure the session key, which make more difficult for intruder to fabricate the routing message, on the other side ARAN fails to prevent such type of attack.

- **Spoofed Route Signaling:** The source node will issue the encrypted route discovery packets by signing the certificate with its private key. Only either intermediate node or destination node, who have the right key can respond to the route discovery process and decrypt them. Hence, the spoofing node cannot launch any type of attack. This prevents completely the impersonation attacks.

- **Securing Shortest Paths:** In SRPHDC, during the route discovery process, the source and destination node can built multiple paths. The destination node can choose a secure minimum path among different route from the source as described in Section-III(A). Moreover, This SRPHDC scheme is designed in such a way, only the authenticated immediate neighbors can access the routing packets, which ensures that an intruder cannot inject false routing packets into secure route discovery process. While ARAN does not guarantee a shortest path, but offers a quickest path to the destination.

Figure 12. Routing load of AODV Vs SRPHDC in the presence of black hole nodes

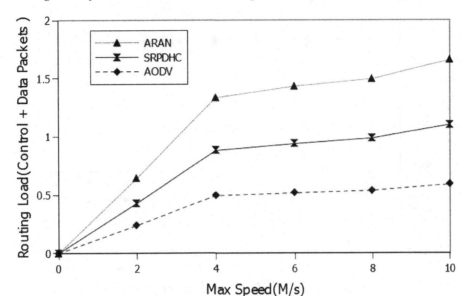

Figure 13. Routing load of modified AODV Vs SRPHDC in the presence of black hole nodes

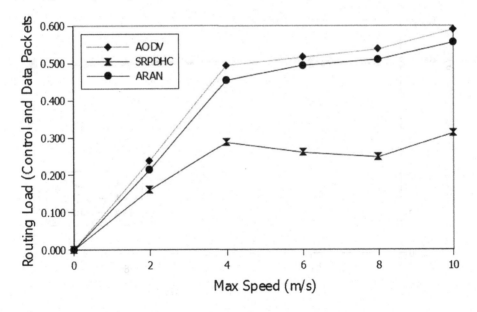

6. SIMULATION RESULTS AND PERFORMANCE ANALYSIS

To study the feasibility of our theoretical work, we have implemented and evaluated the Secure Routing Protocol Using Hybrid Biotic DNA based Cryptography method using network simulator [NS2],which is a software program running in Ubuntu-13.04 and conducted a series of experiments to evaluate its effectiveness. The experiment results show that this method is more efficient and increase the power against black hole attacks.

Figure 14. Packet delivery ratio of AODV Vs SRPHDC in the presence of black hole nodes

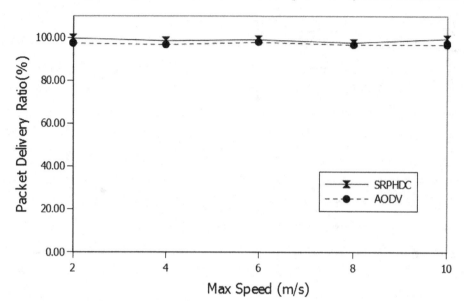

Figure 15. Packet delivery ratio of AODV, SRPHDC, ARAN

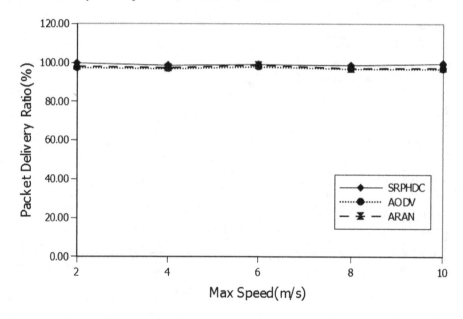

The experimental values were obtained by evaluating the SRPHDC with the current version of the AODV routing protocol, by including the behavior of malicious (black hole) nodes into the simulations. Moreover, to improve the performance of SRPHDC, we had modified AODV routing protocol with the following assumptions are made on the misbehaving node.

1.   The source node will establish the session keys on demand, during the route-discovery process of AODV routing protocol.

Table 1. NS-2 simulation parameters of SRPDHC

NS-2 Parameters	
Propagation model	Two Ray Ground
No of Nodes	10, 25, 50,75,100
Transmission Range	250m
Simulation Time	500 Seconds
Simulation Area	750m X 750m
Node Mobility	Model Random Waypoint
Traffic Type	FTP/TCP
Data Payload Size	512 Bytes/Packet
Node Pause Time	0-20s
Maximum node speed	1-20m/s
Key Size	1024 bits Key

2. Once the route is established between the source and destination, then one of the intermediate nodes acts as a black hole node that drops both the data and routing packets.

Our simulations are mainly used to compare between SRPHDC with AODV routing protocol with and without the presence of malicious nodes. Moreover, we also compare SRPHDC with modified AODV with and without the presence of malicious nodes and ARAN respectively. To evaluate the SRPHDC, we considered various performance metrics.

-   **Packet Delivery Ratio (PDR):** It is the ratio between the number of application layer data packets that are received correctly by all the destination node, and the number of application layer data packets originated by the source node.
-   **Average End-to-End-Delay:** The Average delay is usually measured in all the correctly received packets. The average time taken to deliver a data packet from the source node and the time taken to be received a data packet at the destination.
-   **Routing Overhead:** The total number of application layer data packets that have been received by the destination node at a given simulation time t.
-   **Total Overhead:** The total number of control (non-data) packets that have been delivered by the nodes in the network at the simulation t.

In our first scenario, the experimental values were obtained by evaluating the SRPHDC with the current version of the AODV routing protocol, by including the behavior of malicious (black hole) nodes into the simulations. Here, SRPHDC is compared to original AODV routing protocol because the implementation of SRPHDC is based on AODV.

The following Table-1 gives the simulation parameters, which are used to compare SRPHDC with AODV, SRPHDC with modified AODV and ARAN respectively. Particularly, In order to calculate the performance of this proposed work, we had collect the simulated data by running the simulation up to 500 second with an input of 10, 25, 50, 75, 100 nodes.

Specifically Figure-8 depicts the total throughput of SRPHDC in comparative to AODV without presence of black hole nodes with various simulating nodes by 10,25,50,75,100 respectively. It is observed that, if the number of misbehaving nodes is very less, then AODV continues delivering the packets correctly to the destination without the need of SRPHDC, because, in this case packet dropping is not serious between source and destination.

The figure-9 shows total throughput of SRPHDC and modified AODV without presence of black hole nodes with various simulating nodes by 10,25,50,75,100 respectively. In this case, it gives more throughput with modified AODV and SRPHDC compared to normal AODV routing protocol.

Figure-10 depicts the throughput of SRPHDC and AODV routing protocol in the presence of 2, 4, 6, 8, 10 black hole nodes out of 10, 25, 50, 75, and 100 nodes respectively. It is observed that AODV drastically decreases the throughput in the presence of 10% to 40% black hole nodes, the black hole will be part of the route in AODV that result in a low packet delivery ratio (PDR) or high packet drop. While, SRPHDC still delivers the data packets with almost the same amount of data as depicted in the figure-8 and figure-9.

Figure-11 depicts the throughput of SRPHDC and modified AODV routing protocol in the presence of 2, 4, 6, 8, 10 black hole nodes out of 10, 25, 50, 75, 100 nodes respectively. Indeed, it is observed that modified AODV will drop the packets less than normal AODV in the presence of 10% to 40% black hole nodes. Whereas SRPHDC still delivers the data packets with almost the same amount of data as normal AODV and modified AODV routing protocol. Moreover, SRPHDC tries to detect the black hole nodes and forwards the packets in alternate path that assures successful packet delivery.

The figure-12 and figure-13 depicts the total overhead of SRPHDC in comparison with AODV and SRPHDC in comparison with modified AODV respectively. Here, it is observed that SRPHDC gives slight overhead than AODV due to the security mechanism and less overhead than modified AODV in the presence of different numbers of blackhole nodes. The reason is that SRPHDC can detect the blackhole nodes based on neighbor rating and remove them from routing. Moreover, SRPHDC gives less overhead than ARAN, because SRPHDC make use of DNA computing which provides parallel computation and efficient storage capacity .

As shown in figure-14, the packet delivery fraction of SRPHDC is higher in all scenarios (10, 25, 50, and 75,100) and almost identical in AODV routing protocol at different speeds. However, AODV drastically decreases in the presence of malicious node, which delivers fewer data packets and routing packets to the destination.

Figure 16. End-to-end delay of AODV Vs SRPHDC in the presence of black hold nodes

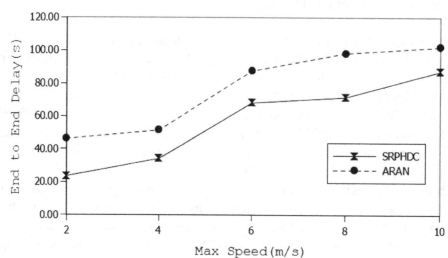

Figure 17. End-to-end delay of SRPHDC and ARAN

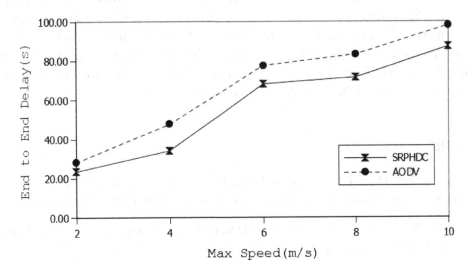

While, SRPHDC detects the black hole nodes and removed from the routing based on neighbor rating. Hence, SRPHDC using modified AODV is extremely efficient in the route discovering, monitoring the routing process and maintaining multiple path for delivery of data packets in the presence of malicious node. Furthermore, it is also seen that SRPHDC always outperforms normal AODV.

The figure-15 depicts the packet delivery ratio of ARAN and SRPHDC with different pause times. While, SRPHDC has a higher PDR than ARAN. Since, it delivers more data packets than ARAN to the destination

As shown in figure-16. End to End Delay of SRPHDC and AODV at different speeds. AODV reduces the PDR in high mobility (maximum speed increases from 1.5 and 10 milliseconds) conditions, because more link breakage between source and destination, Therefore, as maximum speed increases the PDR decreases. As compared to AODV,

SRPHDC always has a lower End-to-End packet latency in high mobility conditions. Moreover, SRPHDC make use of multipath routing, if one path fails, an alternate path will immediately be available.

The figure-17 shows the End-to-End packet latency of SRPHDC and ARAN. In this case, it is observed that SRPHDC has lower latency than ARAN, Since, SRPDHC make use of DNA computing which provides parallel computation that causes less overhead of cryptographic operations than ARAN. In ARAN, while processing the control packets, each and every node has to verify the signature and replace with its own digital signature that cause more overhead using conventional cryptography and additional delays at each node. Therefore, the End-to-End packet latency increases.

7. CONCLUSION

In this paper, we have proposed a scheme for defending and detecting the blackhole attack against modified AODV routing protocol in mobile ad-hoc wireless networks. This SRPHDC protocol which establishes cryptographically secure communication among the nodes. Hybrid DNA-based Cryptography (HDC) is one of the high potential candidates for advanced wireless ad hoc networks which require less computational power, communication bandwidth and memory in comparison with other cryptographic systems. The simulation results of this work provide better security, less computation overhead and network performances as compared to existing AODV and ARAN schemes. As a conclusion, DNA cryptography is an emerge new idea and very promising field where research can be done in great innovation and development. but these DNA cryptography lacks the related theory which is nevertheless still an open problem to model the good DNA cryptographic schemes.

REFERENCES

Al-Shurman, M., Yoo, S. M., & Park, S. (2004, April). Black hole attack in mobile ad hoc networks. *Proceedings of the 42nd annual Southeast regional conference* (pp. 96-97). ACM. 10.1145/986537.986560

Andoni, A. (2009). Nearest neighbor search: the old, the new, and the impossible [Doctoral dissertation]. Massachusetts Institute of Technology.

Baadache, A., & Belmehdi, A. (2010). Avoiding black hole and cooperative black hole attacks in wireless ad hoc networks. arXiv preprint arXiv:1002.1681.

Babu, E. S., Nagaraju, C., & Prasad, M. H. M. (2015, September). A Secure Routing Protocol against Heterogeneous Attacks in Wireless Adhoc Networks. *Proceedings of the Sixth International Conference on Computer and Communication Technology 2015* (pp. 339-344). ACM.

Babu, E. S., Nagaraju, C., & Prasad, M. K. (2013). An Implementation and Performance Evaluation Study of AODV, MAODV, RAODV. *Mobile Ad hoc Networks, 4*, 691–695.

Babu, E. S., Nagaraju, C., & Prasad, M. K. (2013). An Implementation and Performance Evaluation of Passive DoS Attack on AODV Routing Protocol in Mobile Ad hoc Networks. *International Journal of Emerging Trends & Technology in Computer Science, 2*(4), 124–129.

Babu, E. S., Nagaraju, C., & Prasad, M. K. (2015). Analysis of Secure Routing Protocol for Wireless Adhoc Networks Using Efficient DNA Based Cryptographic Mechanism. *Procedia Computer Science, 70*, 341–347. doi:10.1016/j.procs.2015.10.029

Babu, E. S., Nagaraju, C., & Prasad, M. K. (2016). Efficient DNA-Based Cryptographic Mechanism to Defend and Detect Blackhole Attack in MANETs. *Proceedings of International Conference on ICT for Sustainable Development* (pp. 695-706). Springer Singapore. 10.1007/978-981-10-0129-1_72

Babu, E. S., Nagaraju, C., & Prasad, M. K. (2016). Inspired Pseudo Biotic DNA based Cryptographic Mechanism against Adaptive Cryptographic Attacks. *International Journal of Network Security, 18*(2), 291–303.

Babu, E. S., Nagaraju, C., & Prasad, M. K. (2016). *Light-Weighted DNA-Based Cryptographic Mechanism Against Chosen Cipher Text Attacks. InAdvanced Computing and Systems for Security* (pp. 123–144). Springer India.

Babu, E. S., Nagaraju, C., & Prasad, M. K. (n. d.). Light-Weighted DNA Based Hybrid Cryptographic Mechanism Against Chosen Cipher Text Attacks. *International Journal of Information Processing.*

Bindra, G. S., Kapoor, A., Narang, A., & Agrawal, A. (2012, September). Detection and removal of cooperative blackhole and grayhole attacks in MANETs. *Proceedings of the 2012 International Conference on System Engineering and Technology (ICSET)* (pp. 1-5). IEEE.

Capkun, S., Buttya, L., & Hubaux, J. P. (2003). Self-organized public-key management for mobile ad hoc networks. *IEEE Transactions on* Mobile Computing, 2(1), 52–64.

Dasgupta, M., Santra, D., & Choudhury, S. (2012, November). Network Modelling of a Blackhole prevention mechanism in Mobile Ad-hoc Network. *Proceedings of the 2012 Fourth International Conference on Computational Intelligence and Communication Networks (CICN)* (pp. 734-738). IEEE. 10.1109/CICN.2012.153

Deng, H., Li, W., & Agrawal, D. P. (2002). Routing security in wireless ad hoc networks. *Communications Magazine, 40*(10), 70–75. doi:10.1109/MCOM.2002.1039859

Gehani, A., LaBean, T., & Reif, J. (2003). DNA-based cryptography. In *Aspects of Molecular Computing* (pp. 167–188). Springer Berlin Heidelberg. doi:10.1007/978-3-540-24635-0_12

Gopi, A. P., Babu, E. S., Raju, C. N., & Kumar, S. A. (2015). Designing an Adversarial Model Against Reactive and Proactive Routing Protocols in MANETS: A Comparative Performance Study. *Iranian Journal of Electrical and Computer Engineering, 5*(5).

Jain, S., Jain, M., & Kandwal, H. (2010). Advanced algorithm for detection and prevention of cooperative Black and Gray hole attacks in mobile ad hoc networks. *International Journal of Computers and Applications, 1*(7), 37–42. doi:10.5120/165-290

Kim, C., Talipov, E., & Ahn, B. (2006). A reverse AODV routing protocol in ad hoc mobile networks. In *Emerging Directions in Embedded and Ubiquitous Computing* (pp. 522–531). Springer Berlin Heidelberg. doi:10.1007/11807964_53

Konate, K., & Abdourahime, G. (2011, January). Attacks Analysis in mobile ad hoc networks: Modeling and Simulation. *Proceedings of the 2011 Second International Conference on Intelligent Systems, Modelling and Simulation (ISMS)* (pp. 367-372). IEEE.

Kozma, W., & Lazos, L. (2009, March). REAct: resource-efficient accountability for nodemisbehavior in ad hoc networks based on random audits. *Proceedings of the second ACM conference on Wireless network security* (pp. 103-110). ACM. 10.1145/1514274.1514290

Kumar, S. A., Babu, E. S., Nagaraju, C., & Gopi, A. P. (2015). An Empirical Critique of On-Demand Routing Protocols against Rushing Attack in MANET. *Iranian Journal of Electrical and Computer Engineering, 5*(5).

Leier, A., Richter, C., Banzhaf, W., & Rauhe, H. (2000). Cryptography with DNA binary strands. *Bio Systems, 57*(1), 13–22. doi:10.1016/S0303-2647(00)00083-6 PMID:10963862

Lu, S., Li, L., Lam, K. Y., & Jia, L. (2009, December). SAODV: a MANET routing protocol that can withstand black hole attack. *Proceedings of the 2009 International Conference on Computational Intelligence and Security* (pp. 421-425). IEEE. 10.1109/CIS.2009.244

Marti, S., Giuli, T. J., Lai, K., & Baker, M. (2000, August). Mitigating routing misbehavior in mobile ad hoc networks. *Proceedings of the 6th annual international conference on Mobile computing and networking* (pp. 255-265). ACM. 10.1145/345910.345955

Ning, K. (2009). *A pseudo DNA cryptography method*. arXiv preprint arXiv:0903.2693.

Osathanunkul, K., & Zhang, N. (2011, April). A countermeasure to black hole attacks in mobile ad hoc networks. *Proceedings of the 2011 IEEE International Conference on Networking, Sensing and Control (ICNSC)* (pp. 508-513). IEEE. 10.1109/ICNSC.2011.5874910

Perkins, C. E., & Royer, E. M. (2001, March). The ad hoc on-demand distance-vector protocol. In *Ad hoc networking* (pp. 173–219). Addison-Wesley Longman Publishing Co., Inc.

Raj, P. N., & Swadas, P. B. (2009). Dpraodv: A dyanamic learning system against blackhole attack in aodv based manet. arXiv preprint arXiv:0909.2371.

Ramaswamy, S., Fu, H., Sreekantaradhya, M., Dixon, J., & Nygard, K. E. (2003, June). Prevention of Cooperative Black Hole Attack in Wireless Ad Hoc Networks. *Proceedings of the International conference on wireless networks* (Vol. 2003).

Sanzgiri, K., LaFlamme, D., Dahill, B., Levine, B. N., Shields, C., & Belding-Royer, E. M. (2005). Authenticated routing for ad hoc networks. *IEEE Journal on* Selected Areas in Communications, *23*(3), 598–610.

Su, M. Y., Chiang, K. L., & Liao, W. C. (2010, September). Mitigation of black-hole nodes in mobile ad hoc networks. *Proceedings of the 2010 International Symposium on Parallel and Distributed Processing with Applications (ISPA)* (pp. 162-167). IEEE. 10.1109/ISPA.2010.74

Swarna, M., Umar, S., & Babu, E. S. (2016). A Proposal for Packet Drop Attacks in MANETS. In Microelectronics, Electromagnetics and Telecommunications (pp. 377-386). Springer India. doi:10.1007/978-81-322-2728-1_33

Tissieres, C., Buchegger, S., & Le Boudec, J. Y. (2003). A Test-Bed for Misbehavior Detection in Mobile Ad-hoc Networks---How Much Can Watchdogs Really Do? (No. LCA-REPORT-2003-011).

Tsou, P. C., Chang, J. M., Lin, Y. H., Chao, H. C., & Chen, J. L. (2011, February). Developing a BDSR scheme to avoid black hole attack based on proactive and reactive architecture in MANETs. *Proceedings of the 2011 13th International Conference on Advanced Communication Technology (ICACT)* (pp. 755-760). IEEE.

Weerasinghe, H., & Fu, H. (2007, December). Preventing cooperative black hole attacks in mobile ad hoc networks: Simulation implementation and evaluation. In *Future generation communication and networking (fgcn 2007)* (Vol. 2, pp. 362–367). IEEE. doi:10.1109/FGCN.2007.184

Woungang, I., Dhurandher, S. K., Peddi, R. D., & Obaidat, M. S. (2012, May). Detecting blackhole attacks on DSR-based mobile ad hoc networks. *Proceedings of the 2012 International Conference on Computer, Information and Telecommunication Systems (CITS)* (pp. 1-5). IEEE.

This research was previously published in the International Journal of Information Security and Privacy (IJISP), 10(3); edited by Michele Tomaiuolo and Monica Mordonini; pages 42-66, copyright year 2016 by IGI Publishing (an imprint of IGI Global).

Section 2
Cryptographic Algorithms

Chapter 6
Cryptographic Techniques
Based on Bio-Inspired Systems

Petre Anghelescu

University of Pitesti, Romania

ABSTRACT

In this chapter, bio-inspired techniques based on the cellular automata (CAs) and programmable cellular automata (PCAs) theory are used to develop information security systems. The proposed cryptosystem is composed from a combination of a CA as a pseudorandom number generator (PRNG) and a PCA that construct the ciphering functions of the designed enciphering scheme. It is presented how simple elements named „cells" interact between each other using certain rules and topologies to form a larger system that can be used to encrypt/decrypt data sent over network communication systems. The proposed security system was implemented in hardware in FPGA devices of type Spartan 3E – XC3S500E and was analyzed and verified, including NIST statistical tests, to assure that the system has good security and high speed. The experimental results proves that the cryptographic techniques based on bio-inspired algorithms provides an alternative to the conventional techniques (computational methods).

INTRODUCTION

Because the communications and computer systems become each time more pervasive, cryptographic techniques plays an essential role, requiring new solutions, in order to provide *data authentication, integrity* and *confidentiality* in insecure environments. The interconnection of these pervasive devices leads to Mark Weiser's famous vision of ubiquitous computing (Weiser, 1999) and in this way within any minute, a huge amount of information is exchanged through the Internet or over other insecure communication channels. Many kinds of information exchanges, for example text, audio/video content, in multimedia communications, should be protected from *unauthorized copying, intercepting* and *tampering* as they are traversing on public digital networks. Accordingly, cryptography has become more important in data security. Also, in the recent years, researchers have remarked the similarities between bio-inspired systems (particularly cellular automata), chaos and cryptography (Dachselt, & Schwarz,

DOI: 10.4018/978-1-7998-1763-5.ch006

2001; Fuster-Sabater, & Cabalerro-Gil, 2010; Kocarev, & Lian, 2011). Some of the cellular automata features as *ergodicity* and *sensibility to the initial conditions* and *control parameters* can be correlated with the cryptographic properties as *confusion* and *diffusion*.

The essence of the theoretical and practical efforts which are done in this new field is represented by the idea that bio-inspired based encryption techniques are capable to have similar performances regarding the classic methods based on computational techniques. In this paper is presented an encryption system that uses a combination of two cellular automata: *a first class of cellular automaton* that generates the evolution rules for the second class of *five programmable cellular automata* arranged in pipeline. The entire security system was implemented both in software using C# programming language and in hardware on a FPGA of type Spartan 3E – XC3S500E in which the plaintext/ciphertext is received/transmitted using User Datagram Protocol (UDP).

This chapter is organized in eight sections. In the *background section*, are described some basic theoretical foundations of the proposed work that includes CAs and PCAs. The *third section*, provides a brief overview of the classical cryptography and bio-inspired systems in cryptography. The *next section*, on *reconfigurable hardware devices*, introduces the existing reconfigurable hardware devices approaches for supporting bio-inspired algorithms and presented also the reasons for using them in the application presented in this chapter. Then, the section *bio-inspired based algorithm for cryptography*, describes the proposed bio-inspired encryption algorithm used to encrypt and decrypt data sent over the communication networks. Additionally, in section *testing and experimental results*, are made the investigations of statistical properties of the encrypted sequences (performed using NIST statistical tests), distribution of text (plaintext and ciphertext) and encryption/decryption speed. In the next section, are presented the future research direction of the research presented in this chapter. Finally, section eight, conclude the chapter.

BACKGROUND

The intersection of biology and computer science has been a productive field for some time. On one hand, CAs is a bio-inspired paradigm highly addressing the soft computing and hardware for a large class of applications including information security. On the other hand, PCAs is a modified CAs structure including switches in order to allow the self-organizing of the cellular structure.

Cellular Automata (CA)

CAs, first introduced by von Neumann and Stanislav Ulam (Neumann, 1966) in the '50s, exhibit useful and interesting characteristics and has attracted researchers from different field of interests, who applied it in different ways. The most notable characteristics of CAs are: *massive parallelism, locality of cellular interactions* and *simplicity of basics components*. CAs perform computations in a distributed way on a spatial grid and differ from a standard approach to parallel computations whereby a problem is split into independent sub-problems later to be combined in order to yield a final solution. CAs suggest a new approach in which a complex global behavior can be modelled by non-linear spatially extended local interactions.

Thus far, CAs have been used primarily to model the systems consisting of a number of elements obeying identical laws of local interactions (e.g. problems of fluid dynamics, plasma physics, chemical systems, crystals growth, economics, two-directional traffic flow, image processing and pattern recognition, parallel processing, random number, evolution of spiral galaxies, modeling of very complicated physical or chemical processes, molecular computing) (Adamatzky, 1994; Ilachinski, 2001; Wolfram, 2002).

The wide applicability of CA is somehow limited because the methodologies for designing CA, intended to solve specific predefined tasks, are still underdeveloped. Such designing techniques would be extremely useful since there exist many problems for which local interactions, that would drive CA to solve these problems, are not known in advance. To the best of my knowledge, some works has already been done in this area, mainly using genetic algorithms to find evolution rules for the specific CAs.

CAs are mathematical idealizations of physical systems in terms of discrete time and space, where interactions are only local and where each cell can assume the value either 0 or 1 (Sung-Jin, 2004). In fact, CA represents a particular class of dynamical systems that enable to describe the evolution of complex systems with simple rules, without using partial differential equations. Each cell of the CA is restricted to local neighborhood interactions only, and as a result it is incapable of immediate global communication. The neighborhood of the cell is taken to be the cell itself and some or all of the immediately adjacent cells. The CA evolves in discrete steps, with the next value of one site determined by its previous value and that of a set of sites called the neighbor sites. The extent of the neighborhood can vary, depending among other factors upon the dimensionality of the CA under consideration. Classical examples for cell neighborhoods are presented in *Figure 1* (left side, von Neumann Neighborhood - with 3 cells for one-dimensional CA respective 5 cells for bi-dimensional CA and right side, Moore neighborhood with 3 cells for one-dimensional cellular automata respective 9 cells for bi-dimensional cellular automata considers both kinds the direct and the diagonal neighbors).

The state of each cell is updated simultaneously at discrete time steps, based on the states in its neighborhood at the preceding time step. The algorithm used to compute the next cell state is referred to as the CA local rule.

Typically, a CA consists of a graph where each node is a finite state cell. This graph is usually in the form of a two-dimensional lattice whose cells evolve according to a global update function applied uniformly over all the cells. As arguments, this update function takes the cell's present state and the states of the cells in its interaction neighborhood as shown in Figure 2.

Figure 1. CA classical neighborhoods (a) von Neumann neighborhood, (b) Moore neighborhood

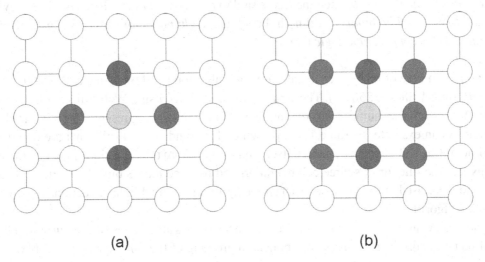

(a)   (b)

Figure 2. CAs state transitions depending on the neighborhood states

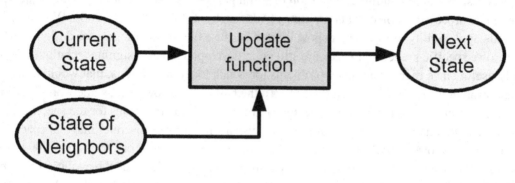

The next-state function describing a rule for a three neighborhood CA cell where assuming that

i is *position of an individual cell in an one dimensional array*,
t is *time step*, and
$a_i(t)$: *output state* of the *i-th cell* at *the t-th time step*

can be expressed as follows:

$$a_i(t+1) = f\left[a_i(t), a_{i+1}(t), a_{i-1}(t)\right] \tag{1}$$

where *f* denotes the *local transition function* realized with a combination logic and is known as a rule of the CA.

If the *rule of a CA* involves *only XOR logic*, then it is called a *linear rule*.
Rules involving *XNOR logic* are referred to as *complement rules*.
A CA with all its cells having *linear rules* is called a *linear CA*, whereas a CA having a *combination of XOR and XNOR rules* is called *additive CA*.
If *all the cells obey the same rule*, then the CA is said to be a *uniform CA*, *otherwise*, it is a *hybrid CA*.
A CA is said to be a *null boundary CA* if both the *left* and *right neighbor* of the *leftmost* and *rightmost terminal cell* is connected to logic *0-state*.

For example, in case of one-dimensional, three neighborhood and two-state cell, the number of all possible *uniform CA* rules is 256 (2^8). These rules are enumerated using Wolfram's naming convention (Wolfram, 1986) from rule number 0 to rule number 255 and can be represented by a 3-variable Boolean function. As an example, in Table 1, are presented five fundamental rules that are obtained using 3-neighborhood (the cell on the left, the cell itself and the cell from the right side of the cell in question). This means that the rule for this three cell neighborhood must contain 8 bits. These rules, arranged in a certain mode, are used in the proposed encryption system presented in later sections to construct the cryptographic algorithm.

The space of evolution rules depends on the number of possible states of the current cell and the number of its neighbors. This leads to an exponential growing of the rules space (see Table 2).

Table 1. An example of CA evolution rules construction

Rules (Decimal Number)	7 111	6 110	5 101	4 100	3 011	2 010	1 001	0 000
90	0	1	0	1	1	0	1	0
150	1	0	0	1	0	1	1	0
51	0	0	1	1	0	0	1	1
60	0	0	1	1	1	1	0	0
102	0	1	1	0	0	1	1	0
	2^7	2^6	2^5	2^4	2^3	2^2	2^1	2^0

Table 2. The size of the rules in function of neighborhood dimension

Size of the Cell Neighborhood	Decimal Rule Size (Maximum Value)	Rule Bit Size
2	16	4
3	256	8
4	65536	16
5	4294967296	32
6	18446744073709551616	64
7	3.40E+38	128
8	1.16E+77	256
9	1.34E+154	512

The systematic study of CA was initialized by S. Wolfram in (Wolfram, 2002) in which he studied the relationships between CA and different dynamical systems. According to (Wolfram, 2002) there are four classes of CA whose comportment can be compared with the similar behavior of the dynamic systems (given in parenthesis):

Class I: The CA evolution from all initial configurations reaches the same final state and stays there (limit points).

Class II: The CA encounters simple or cyclic structures, but which one depends on the initial configuration (limit cycles).

Class III: The CA from majority of initial states lead to arbitrary patterns (chaotic behavior of the kind associated with strange attractors).

Class IV: The CA from some of initial configurations generates global complex structures (very long transients with no apparent analog in continuous dynamic systems). This behavior basically means that CA can be shown to be capable of universal computation.

This classification mainly refers to 1-D CAs, but similar ones can be made for 2-D or 3-D cases. Classifications of CA are done by means of empirical observations of CA evolutions (space-time patterns). The very large phenomenology of the CA model, its apparently big complexity and massive parallelism (however, this parallelism, when emulated in software or in sequential hardware, disappears) offer a good basis for applications in cryptography and not only.

Programmable Cellular Automata (PCA)

The programmable cellular automata (PCA) was firstly introduced in (Nandi et al., 1994) as a modified CA structure. These PCA allows spatial and temporal variations in the state transition rules within a CA according to some external control scheme and signals. Practically, PCA dynamically change the CA rules. As an example, using such a cell structure as in Figure 3, all possible non-complemented additive rules can be achieved through the combinations of the control signals of C_1, C_2 and C_3 switches.

Thus the PCA architecture is very much flexible and enable to emulate via control signals different hybrid CA configurations (Anghelescu et al., 2010). In practice, a control program, stored in memory, can be employed to activate the switches. For example, the state 1 or 0 of the bit i-th of a memory word either opens or closes the switch that controls that cell. Basically, such a structure is referred as a PCA. In this paper, PCA is used to implement the proposed encryption algorithm.

All in all, the CAs and PCAs offer a good basis for applications in cryptography and represent a "converse pole" as computing architecture in comparison with sequential model: are parallel systems without central processing unit in which the computation powerful of his elements are much reduced.

LITERATURE REVIEW

In present, promising applications for cryptographic algorithms may be classified into two categories:

Category I: Processing of large amount of data at real time potentially in a high speed network. Examples include telephone conversations, telemetry data, video conferencing, streaming audio or encoded video transmissions and so forth.

Figure 3. PCA with 3-neighbors and all non-completed additive evolution rules

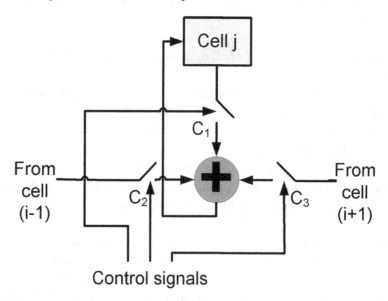

Category II: Processing of very small amount of data at real time in a moderately high-speed network transmitted unpredictably. Examples include e-commerce or m-commerce transactions, bank account information extraction, e-payments and micro-browser-based (WAP-style), HTML page browsing and so forth.

Cryptographic realizations could be done in software or in hardware (Henriquez et al., 2006). In *software platforms* can be used for those security applications where the data traffic is not too large and thus low encryption rate is acceptable. On the other hand, *hardware methods* offer high speed and bandwidth, providing real time encryption if needed.

A good overview on the all major cryptographic techniques can be found in reference (Menezes et al., 1996; Stallings, 2003; Cusick & Stanica, 2009; Koc, 2009). Accordingly, the cryptographic methods are divided into two categories: symmetric-key (or secret-key) and asymmetric-key (or public-key). In symmetric cryptography the same key is used for both encryption and decryption, whereas in asymmetric cryptography there are two keys: one for encryption (which is public known), and other for decryption (which must remain secret). Based on these algorithms there are mainly two classes of symmetric-key encryption schemes: block ciphers and stream ciphers. Block ciphers breaks up the message into blocks of the fixed length and encrypt one block at a time. On the contrary, the stream ciphers encrypt a single bit of plain text at a time. Encryption is accomplished by combining the cipher sequence with the plaintext, usually with the bitwise XOR logic operation. There are several methods in order to generate the cipher sequence beginning from the secret key: LFSR (Linear Feedback Shift Register) generator, BBS (Blum Blum Shub) generator, and so forth (Menezes et al., 1996).

As we said above, there are several mathematical techniques that can be used for cryptographic purpose, and one of them is the use of bio-inspired systems or discrete dynamical systems (Schmitz, 2001). In the domain of researches having as subject the association between the cellular automata and cryptography was reported more encryption systems based on the cellular automata theory. CA were proposed for both secret-key and public-key cryptography. Remarkable is the fact that the relationship between the CA and cryptography was revealed by Shannon in his fundamental early work (Shannon, 1949):

Good mixing transformations are often formed by repeated products of two simple non-commuting operations. Hopf has shown, for example, that pastry dough can be mixed by such a sequence of operations. The dough is first rolled out into a thin slab, then folded over, then rolled, and the folded again, etc.

It seems that Shannon discusses about a system composed from simple components that interaction between them – with a transparent local comportment – but the global comportment of the entire system unsuspected, things that are well known in the CA theory.

So that, a very simple variant used for encryption using cellular automata is reported by Stephen Wolfram in (Wolfram, 1986) and (Wolfram, 2002) and is based on the fact that the CA from class III (conform the Wolfram classification) are dynamical chaotic systems. In this case, the evolution of the cellular automaton depends considerable of the initial state, but we can say that after some time the state is forgotten in sense in which cannot be found from current configuration analyses. Anyway, if we repeat the initial state, the evolution will be the same. Wolfram use a uniform 1D CA with three neighborhoods, and rule 30 to generate pseudorandom number sequences (CA-PRNG). The encryption system proposed by Wolfram can be included in category "Chaotic stream ciphers based on the pseudorandom number generator" (PRNG). The based principle of these ciphers is to obtain the encryption text by mixing the output of these pseudorandom number generators with the message (Lee et al., 2003; Koc, 2009).

Another solution used for encryption with cellular automata is presented in (Hortensius et al., 1989) and (Nandi et al., 1994). These used non-uniform CA with two rules 90 and 150, and it was found that the quality of pseudorandom number generated was better that the quality of the Wolfram system. (Tomassini & Perrenoud, 2000) proposed to use non-uniform, 1D CAs with four rules 90, 105, 150 and 165, which provide high quality pseudorandom number sequences and a huge space of possible secret keys which is difficult for cryptanalysis.

Another variant of encryption system based on the cellular automata, which consider also the inverse iteration, is presented in (Adamatzky, 1994) and (Martin, 2004). Here is used a bi-dimensional cellular automaton and the dates are the initial state of the cellular automaton. Using a reversible evolution rule the initial message is modified progressive. The message is decrypted rolling the inverse rule the same number of iterations as to encryption. This encryption system can be included in category of "Stream ciphers based on inverse iteration-with reaction". These systems can be also based on a series of evolution rules that served as chaotic system, rules used for encryption and decryption (Lu et al., 2004).

Other cryptosystem realized with the help of cellular automata combine the direct and inverse iteration (Gutowitz, 1994), "Block ciphers based on the direct and inverse iteration" (Masuda & Aihara, 2002) – these ciphers was as a general rule proposed for image encryption. Here is used a bi-dimensional cellular automaton, the message being the initial state of this. The codification implied the inverse iteration of a rule, the key is a rule. This rule is not necessary to be reversible: for inverse iteration is chosen randomly one of the possible states of the cellular automaton. For decryption we must know the rule that is direct iterated and use the same number of steps (Anghelescu et al., 2010; Anghelescu et al., 2013).

(Tripathy & Nandi, 2009) have designed a lightweight CA-based symmetric-key encryption that supports 128-bit block size with 128-, 192- and 256-bit keys. The motivation for embarking on CA for their cipher design is due to the fact that CA provides a high level of parallelism and therefore, able to achieve high speeds. The cipher has also been proved to be resistant against timing analysis attacks.

A hybrid CA with 2 rules 30 and 134 is proposed as cryptographic hash functions in (Jamil et al., 2012), in which elementary CA rules are used for mixing bits of the message. The cipher has also been analyzed using NIST tests and passes all the statistical tests.

The deterministic chaotically dynamic of CA is similar with pseudorandom systems used in classical methods and the complexity of a dynamical system that determine the efficiency of the entire information protection process is equivalent with the algorithm complexity from classical encryption methods.

Wolfram (Wolfram, 2002) pointed out that the future researches in this domain must be oriented to find solutions to complete the classical encryption systems with the other based on the bio-inspired systems (for example cellular automata theory), and less to design work of new methods developed "ad-hoc".

From the above discussion, seeing the promised potential of using of the CA in the field of cryptography, we believe that research on bio-inspired cryptography will be helpful to benefit the conventional cryptology and open a broader road to the design of ciphers with very good properties.

RECONFIGURABLE HARDWARE AND CA

The reconfigurable devices as piece of hardware able to dynamically adapt to algorithms and become through electrically program, almost any kind of digital circuit or system, was firstly introduced by G. Estrin in 1960. His invention consists on a hybrid machine composed by a general purpose microprocessor interconnected with programmable logic devices (Bobda, 2007). In general, reconfigurable devices tend to be a good choice when dealing with algorithms that implies high parallelism as CA based algorithms are. VLSI (also known as ASIC - Application Specific Integrated Circuit) and FPGAs (Field Programmable Gate Arrays) are two distinct alternatives for implementing cryptographic algorithms in hardware. An electronic device is said to be configurable (or programmable) when its functionality is not pre-defined at fabrication-time, but can be further specified by a configuration bit-stream (or a program). Reconfigurable devices permit configuration several times, supporting system upgrades and refinements in a relatively small time scale. Given this architectural flexibility and upgradeability, they constitute the best candidate for supporting bio-inspired architectures: they offer a set of features that permit the implementation of flexible architectures, while still guaranteeing high performance execution (Upegui, 2010).

A FPGA consists of an array of logic elements together with an interconnect network which can be configured by the user at the point of application. The basic structure of a FPGA circuit that contain an array/matrix of configurable logic blocks of potentially different types, including general logic, memory and multiplier blocks, surrounded and connected via programmable interconnects is presented in Figure 4.

User programming specifies both the logic functions of each block and the connections between the blocks. In one sense, FPGAs represent an evolutionary improvement in gate array technology which offers potential reductions in prototype system costs and product time-to-market. However, recent applications of FPGA technology suggest their impact on electronic systems may be much more profound. Consider the fact that reprogrammable FPGAs are capable of dynamically changing their logic and interconnect structure to adapt to changing system requirements. This offers a new computing paradigm which blurs the traditional lines between hardware and software. The main advantage of FPGAs is their re-configurability, i.e., they can be used for different purposes at different stages of a computation and they can be, at least partially, reprogrammed on run-time. The two most popular FPGA manufacturers are Xilinx and Altera. Today, due to cost decreases and the flexibility of a programmable solution, high-density FPGAs are often employed for system-level prototyping.

All in all, the using of FPGA devices for bio-inspired based cryptosystems is motivated by *four reasons*: *encryption speed* (encryption algorithms based on multiple cells interconnected contain many operations on that uses communications between adjacent cells and these can be executed in parallel or pipelined mode in hardware, while not suitable in software); *security assured* (there is no physical protection for an encryption algorithm written by software and an intruder can go in with various debugging tools to modify the algorithm without anyone ever realizing it; hardware encryption devices can be securely encapsulated to prevent this.); *flexibility* (all the implemented functions could be upgraded at any time); *analogy between the re-configurability and CA (*all the CA cells could be updated in parallel, in a single time clock*)*.

Figure 4. Basic FPGA structure

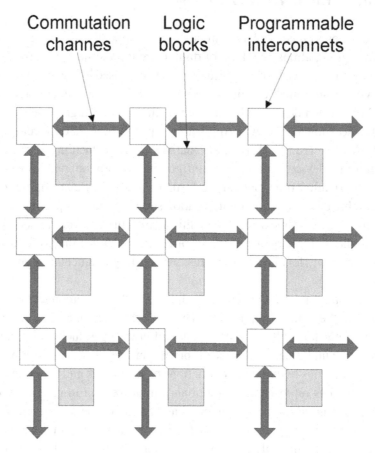

BIO-INSPIRED BASED ALGORITHM FOR CRYPTOGRAPHY

In this section is presented the proposed cryptosystem used to encrypt/decrypt data sent over the communication networks. This cryptosystem uses a *one-dimensional CA* and a *combination of five one-dimensional PCAs* arranged in pipeline and a *control logic* that manage all the operations of the CA and PCAs. The basic structure of the cryptosystem is presented in Figure 5.

Because a lot of simulations and research has been carried out using 8-bit PCAs, an 8-bit PCAs was chosen for this project. In the block cipher scheme, one 8-bit message block is enciphered by one enciphering function. The enciphering function has five fundamental transformations (FTs) in order to operate on 8-bit data. This FTs are constructed using five PCAs arranged in pipeline. The block cipher scheme can be mathematically expressed as follows:

If

M is a *block of text* (*8 bits plaintext*),
C is a *block of text* (*8 bits ciphertext*),
E is an *enciphering function*

Figure 5. Basic structure of the cryptosystem

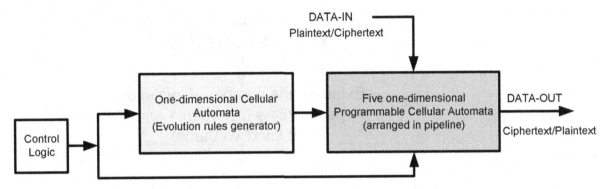

Then encryption:

$$C = E \bullet M \tag{2}$$

Decryption:

$$M = E^{-1} \bullet C \tag{3}$$

where: ● denotes a function symbol.

The algorithm discussed here to encrypt/decrypt data sent over communication networks can be divided into two-phases: an *encryption phase* and a *decryption phase*.

In the *encryption phase* the initial PCA configurations that practically contain inside the plaintext are evolved a number of predefined steps (between 1 and 7). The PCAs control signals are generated using the interconnections with the first CA that acts like a pseudo-random number generator (PRNG). The encryption phase for the pipelined PCAs block cipher is presented in Figure 6.

In the *decryption phase* the initial PCA configurations that contain inside the ciphertext are evolved a number of steps that must be accordingly with the differences between 8 and number of steps used for encryption phase. The diagram of the decryption phase for the pipelined PCAs block cipher is presented in Figure 7.

In the decryption phase *decrEvolSteps is 8 - encrEvolSteps* because the PCAs discovered and used in this cryptosystem generates for any initial state (that could be plaintext or ciphertext) cycles of even length that will repeat themselves after 8 steps. The PCAs used in this cryptographic algorithm is a *hybrid PCA* and is configured with the combination of the rules 51, 60 and 102 presented in the Table 1. In Figure 8 is presented an example of cycles generated by the PCA configured with rules cell 1 – rule 60, cell 2 – rule 51, cell 3 – rule 60, cell 4 – rule 60, cell 5 – rule 60, cell 6 – rule 51, cell 7 – rule 51, cell 8 – rule 51 and initial states 128 in the left side and 242 in the right side.

As it is shown in Figure 8, the PCA has two equal cycles of length 8. This property is a basic requirement of the cryptographic scheme. For example, in the enciphering phase, if it is used this PCA as enciphering function and define a plaintext as its initial state, it goes to its intermediate state after four cycles. In the deciphering phase, after running another four cycles, the intermediate state returns back to its initial state, so the cipher text is deciphered into plaintext. Because the PCA does not generate se-

Figure 6. The diagram of the encryption phase

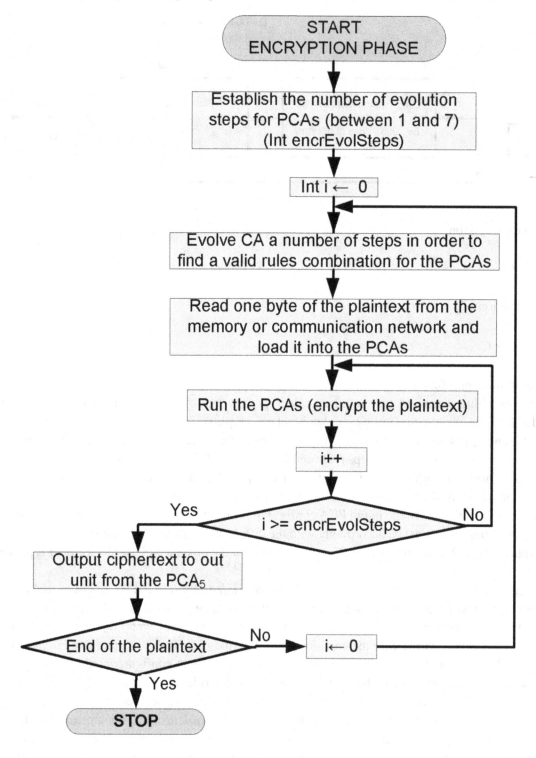

Figure 7. The diagram of the decryption phase

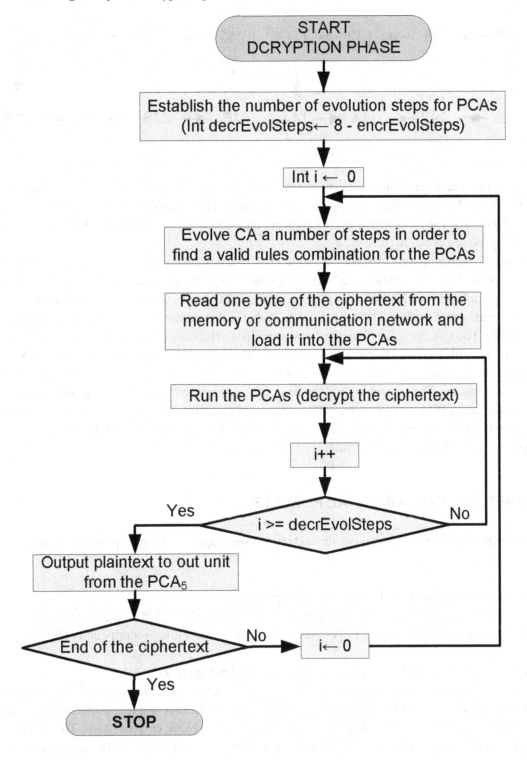

Figure 8. The transitions diagram of the PCA with initial states 128 (left side) and 242 (right side)

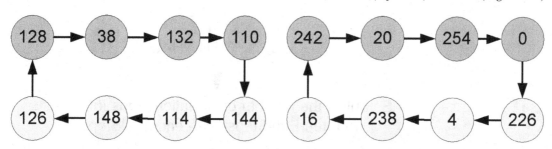

quences of maximum-length for all the possible combinations (512) of the rules it is necessary to apply from the first CA used as PRNG only the combinations of the three rules 51, 60 and 102 that generate cycles of length 8. The rules with 8-cycle length are only 156 and are presented in detail in my previous paper (Anghelescu et al., 2010).

In concordance with the CA theory, a single PCA cell was designed and then was multiplied in the FPGA circuits. The cell consists of a D flip-flop and a logic combinational circuit (LCC). The LCC includes multiplexers and XNOR logic gates to implement the rules of CA and to control the loading of data and operation of the CA. The entire scheme of that cell is presented in detail in paper (Anghelescu et al., 2013). The CA that select which rules are applied to the cells of the PCAs is realized by using a combination of rules 90 and 150 presented in Table 1. It has established in paper (Hortensius & Podaima, 1990) that the maximum-length CAs with rules 90 and 150 generates patterns having a high quality of pseudo-randomness. The control logic is the heart of the design and includes the communication interface between the FPGA and PC using UDP protocol and controls all operations of the cryptosystem. UDP is a simple to implement protocol because it does not require keeping track of every packet sent or received and it does not need to initiate or end a transmission.

TESTING AND EXPERIMENTAL RESULTS

A lot of experiments were carried out throughout the development of the cryptosystem, motivated by three reasons:

First: For investigation of the CA and PCA comportment,
Second: For assuring that the generated sequences respect the CA and PCA theory and
Third: To assure that the pipeline PCA based cryptosystem has a good security and high speed.

The general structure of the cryptosystem is presented in Figure 9.

In order to put in practice the principle of working of the cryptosystem was proposed an architecture which is able to satisfy both of the requirements for communication and for specifications related on PCA. FPGA circuits are used to implement the pipeline PCA block cryptosystem. The cryptosystem is implemented using VHDL code and is written in Xilinx ISE and Active HDL using structural and behavioral specifications. The hardware implementation of the PCA cryptosystem was realized using a Spartan 3E XC3S500E FPGA board from Xilinx (Xilinx, 2011) (see Figure 10).

Figure 9. Bio-inspired cryptosystem: general architecture

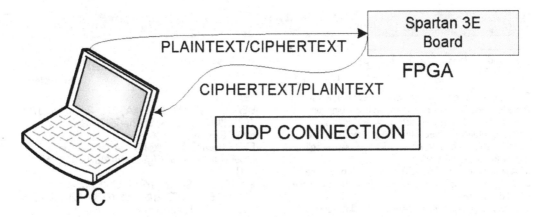

Figure 10. FPGA board used for test the bio-inspired based cryptosystem

The FPGA board is interfaced with a host computer using RJ-45 connector and UDP protocol. The UDP allows high speed data transfer from the PC to the cryptosystem and inverse. In Figure 11 is presented an illustrative example for the cryptographic phases (encryption and decryption process) applied to a text file.

The message (plaintext or ciphertext) is divided into 1Kb packages and is sent to the FPGA board using the UDP client – server connection. As the bytes reaches destination they are immediately encrypted using the correspondent bytes of the PCA's state and then saved into the 1Kb RAM memory of the board. In the FPGA, the message received is treated character by character as we explained above and the encryption/decryption results are sent back by the FPGA to the PC to be displayed, stored and analyzed. In hardware, the encryption rules are applied using the CA as PRNG or are downloaded to the RAM memory before encryption. When the encryption process begins, rules are generated or read out in sequence and sent to the PCAs. The process of generated or read rules does not introduce delays in the cryptographic algorithm because are generated/read in parallel with the encryption/decryption of a block of message.

Figure 11. Results for encryption and decryption phases

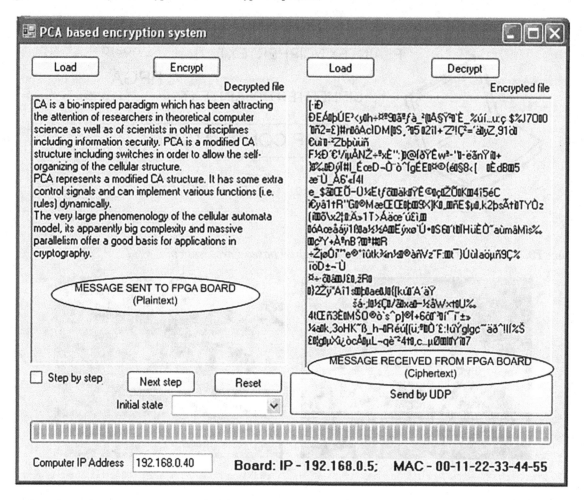

To show that the bio-inspired based cryptosystem has the property of *confusion* specific for classical cryptography it is possible to identify the distribution of the plaintext and ciphertext in ASCII intervals. This cryptosystem will map the given plaintext into a random ciphertext, which means that no pattern appears in the ciphertext. In the Figure 12 and Figure 13, the distribution of the ASCII values for a plaintext and ciphertext is presented. In Figure 12, plaintext distribution, most of the characters are lowercase, so the distribution is dense in the interval 97 and 122. In Figure 13, ciphertext distribution, the ciphertext is distributed almost uniform in the complete interval of ASCII values, and not only in the *zone of alphanumeric intervals,* and hence the developed cryptosystem also maps plaintext to a random ciphertext.

In the PCA encryption algorithm, the same ciphertext may be generated from different plaintext, and any ciphertext may give rise as well to different plaintext depending on the different PCA's rule configuration.

The PCA based encrypted sequences was tested using a set of 16 statistical tests conceived by the National Institute of Standards and technology (NIST) (Rukhin et al., 2010). The NIST test generates probabilistic results with respect to some characteristics that describe the pseudo-random number generators. The encrypted sequences pass the NIST tests and the system is accepted as possible random (Table 3).

Figure 12. Distribution of the plaintext in ASCII interval

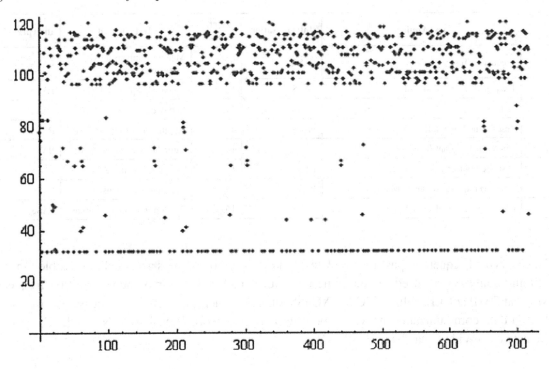

Figure 13. Distribution of the ciphertext in ASCII interval

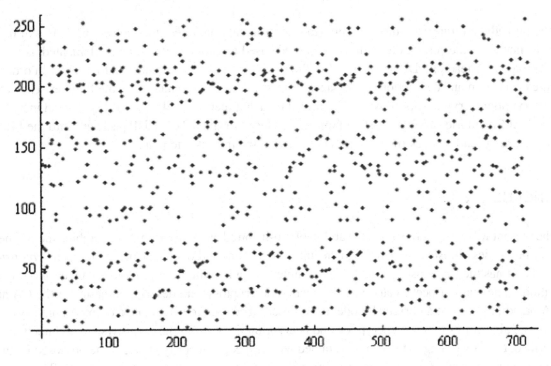

Table 3. Results for NIST statistical tests

Crt. No.	Test Applied	Interpretation	Crt. No.	Test Applied	Interpretation
1.	Frequency Test	PASS	9.	Maurer's Universal Statistical	PASS
2.	Frequency Test within a Block	PASS	10.	Linear Complexity Test	PASS
3.	Runs Test	PASS	11.	Serial Test	PASS
4.	Test for the Longest Run of Ones in a Block	PASS	12.	Approximate Entropy Test	PASS
5.	Binary matrix Rank Test	PASS	13.	Cumulative Sums Forward	PASS
6.	Discrete Fourier Transform	PASS	14.	Cumulative Sums Reverse	PASS
7.	Non-Overlapping Template Matching Test	PASS	15.	Random Excursions Test	PASS
8.	Overlapping Template Matching Test	PASS	16.	Random Excursions Variant	PASS

The encrypted sequences pass the NIST tests and the cryptosystem is accepted as possible random. The timing analyzer was used to determine the critical path and the maximum operating frequency (33Mbps at 50MHz CLK Xilinx FPGA – XC3S500E). The encryption system discussed above can be applied in data communication networks, both in private network (Local Area Network – LAN) and public network (Wide Area Network – WAN).

FUTURE RESEARCH DIRECTIONS

In the immediate future, in order to assure flow control and guarantees that all sent packets will reach the destination in the correct order, the bio-inspired based cryptosystem will be implemented using the TCP protocol instead of UDP protocol. Also, the FPGA board will be connected to a router in order to assure encryption and decryption of messages from any computer connected to the Internet. The value for encryption/decryption speed will be improved by using increased FPGA clock speed and increased space RAM memories in order to store more encrypted/decrypted TCP/UDP packages into the FPGA before starting sending back the messages to the PC in the transmission phase.

CONCLUSION

In the present work, is demonstrated the ability of bio-inspired based algorithms to combine the two necessary properties *diffusion* (sensitivity to the initial conditions and/or control parameters) and *confusion* (the output has the same distribution for any plaintext used like input) in order to obtain cryptographic solutions. The major aspect treated in this paper is the cryptosystem description based on the CA and PCA paradigms, where an original model is proposed to cooperate and create a cryptographic system. The basic algorithms for each encryption and decryption involved in the cryptosystem architecture are described, too. According to the results obtained with respect to security analysis, the proposed method is expected to be useful for real-time encryption/decryption and transmission applications. The general conclusion of this work is that it is possible to build evolutionary cryptosystems based on a simple mathematical models specific of CA and PCA by introducing the local interaction between cells, local evolution rules, and massive parallelism.

REFERENCES

Adamatzky, A. (1994). *Identification of Cellular Automata*. London: Taylor & Francis Ltd.

Anghelescu, P., Ionita, S., & Iana, V. (2013). High-speed PCA Encryption Algorithm using Reconfigurable Computing. *Journal of Cybernetics and Systems*, 44(4), 285–304.

Anghelescu, P., Ionita, S., & Sofron, E. (2010). Encryption Technique with Programmable Cellular Automata. *Journal of Cellular Automata*, 5(1-2), 79–106.

Bobda, C. (2007). *Introduction to Reconfigurable Computing – Architectures, algorithms and applications*. Springer.

Cho, S.-J., Choi, U.-S., Hwang, Y.-H., Kim, H.-D., Pyo, Y.-S., Kim, K.-S., & Heo, S.-H. (2004). Computing Phase Shifts of Maximum-Length 90/150 Cellular Automata Sequences. Proceeding of the *6th International Conference on Cellular Automata for Research and Industry, ACRI 2004*, Amsterdam (pp. 31-39). 10.1007/978-3-540-30479-1_4

Cusick, T., & Stanica, P. (2009). *Cryptographic Boolean functions and applications*. Elsevier.

Dachselt, F., & Schwarz, W. (2001). Chaos and Cryptography. *IEEE Transactions on Circuits and Systems*, 48(12), 1498–1509. doi:10.1109/TCSI.2001.972857

del Rey, Á.M. (2004). A Novel Cryptosystem for Binary Images. *Grant SA052/03, Studies in Informatics and Control*, 13(1).

Fuster-Sabater, A., & Cabalerro-Gil, P. (2010). Chaotic Cellular Automata with Cryptographic Application. Proceedings of the 9th *International Conference on Cellular Automata for Research and Industry* (pp. 251–260). Springer-Verlag Berlin Heidelberg

Gutowitz, H. (1994). *Methods and Apparatus for Encryption, Decryption and Authentication using Dynamical Systems*.

Rodriguez-Henriquez, F., Saqib, N.A., Días Pérez, A.D., & Koc, C.K. (Eds.), (2006). Cryptographic algorithms on reconfigurable hardware. Springer Science + Business Media, LLC.

Hortensius, P.D., McLeod, R.D., & Card, H. (1989). Parallel Random Number Generation for VLSI Systems using Cellular Automata. *IEEE Transactions on Computers*, 38(10), 1466–1473. doi:10.1109/12.35843

Hortensius, P. D., & Podaima, R. D. (1990). Cellular Automata Circuits for Built-in Self-test. *IBM Journal of Research and Development*, 34(2/3), 389–405. doi:10.1147/rd.342.0389

Ilachinski, A. (2001). Cellular Automata – A Discrete Universe. Singapore: World Scientific Publishing Co. Pte. Ltd.

Jamil, N., Mahmood, R., & Muhammad, R. (2012). A New Cryptographic Hash Function Based on Cellular Automata Rules 30, 134 and Omega-Flip Network. Proceedings of the *2012 International Conference on Information and Computer networks (ICICN 2012)*, Singapore (Vol. 27, pp. 163-169). IACSIT Press.

Koc, C.K. (Ed.), (2009). Cryptographic engineering. Springer Science + Business Media, LLC. doi:10.1007/978-0-387-71817-0

Kocarev, L., & Lian, S. (2011). *Chaos-Based Cryptography – Theory, Algorithms and Applications*. Springer-Verlag Berlin Heidelberg. doi:10.1007/978-3-642-20542-2

Lee, P. H., Pei, S. C., & Chen, Y. Y. (2003). Generating chaotic stream ciphers using chaotic systems. *The Chinese Journal of Physiology*, *41*, 559–581.

Lu, H., Wang, S., Li, X., Tang, G., Kuang, J., Ye, W., & Hu, G. (2004). A new spatiotemporally chaotic cryptosystem and its security and performance analyses. *Chaos (Woodbury, N.Y.)*, *14*(3), 617–629. doi:10.1063/1.1772731 PMID:15446972

Masuda, N., & Aihara, K. (2002). Cryptosystems with discretized chaotic maps. *IEEE Trans. Circuits Syst. I*, *49*(1), 28–40. doi:10.1109/81.974872

Menezes, A., Oorschot, P., & Vanstone, S. (1996). *Handbook of applied cryptography*. CRC Press. doi:10.1201/9781439821916

Nandi, S., Kar, B. K., & Chaudhuri, P. P. (1994). Theory and applications of cellular automata in cryptography. *IEEE Transactions on Computers*, *43*(12), 1346–1356. doi:10.1109/12.338094

Rukhin, A., Soto, J., Nechvatal1, J., Smid, M., Barker, E., Leigh, S., Levenson, M., Vangel, M., Banks, D., Heckert, A., Dray, J., Vo, S. (2010). *A Statistical Test Suite for Random and Pseudorandom Number Generators for Cryptographic Applications* (NIST Special Publication 800-22).

Schmitz, R. (2001). Use of Chaotic Dynamical Systems in Cryptography. *Journal of the Franklin Institute, 338*(4), 429-441.

Shannon, C. (1949). Communication Theory of Secrecy Systems. *Bell Sys. Tech. J., 28*, 656–715. Retrieved from netlab.cs.ucla.edu/wiki/files/shannon1949.pdf

Stallings, W. (2003). *Cryptography and Network Security* (3rd ed.). Prentice Hall.

Tomassini, M., & Perrenoud, M. (2000). Stream Ciphers with One- and Two-Dimensional Cellular Automata. In M. Schoenauer at al. (Eds.), Parallel Problem Solving from Nature - PPSN VI, LNCS (Vol. 1917, pp. 722-731).

Tripathy, S., & Nandi, S. (2009). LCASE: Lightweight cellular automata-based symmetric key encryption. *International Journal of Network Security*, *8*(2), 243–252.

Upegui, A. (2010). Dynamically Reconfigurable Hardware for Evolving Bio-Inspired Architectures. In R. Chiong (Ed.), *Intelligent Systems for Automated Learning and Adaptation: Emerging Trends and Applications* (pp. 1–22). doi:10.4018/978-1-60566-798-0.ch001

von Neumann, J. (1966). *Theory of Self -Reproducing Automata* (Ed., Burks, A.W.). London: Univ. of Illinois Press.

Weiser, M. (1999). The computer for the 21st century. *Mobile Computing and Communications Review*, *3*(3), 3–11. doi:10.1145/329124.329126

Wolfram, S. (1986). Cryptography with Cellular Automata. *Springer, Advances in Cryptology: Crypto '85 Proceedings. LNCS, 218*, 429–432.

Wolfram, S. (2002). *A new kind of science*. Champaign, IL: Wolfram Media Inc.

Xilinx. (2011). Spartan 3E Starter kit board data sheet. Retrieved from http://www.xilinx.com/support/documentation/boards_and_kits/ug230.pdf

This research was previously published in the Handbook of Research on Advanced Hybrid Intelligent Techniques and Applications edited by Paramartha Dutta, Pinaki Banerjee, Dipankar Majumdar, and Siddhartha Bhattacharyya; pages 59-77, copyright year 2016 by Information Science Reference (an imprint of IGI Global).

Chapter 7
Modification of Traditional RSA into Symmetric– RSA Cryptosystems

Prerna Mohit

Indian Institute of Technology (Indian School of Mines), India

G. P. Biswas

Indian Institute of Technology (Indian School of Mines), India

ABSTRACT

This paper addresses the modification of RSA cryptography namely Symmetric-RSA, which seem to be equally useful for different cryptographic applications such as encryption, digital signature, etc. In order to design Symmetric-RSA, two prime numbers are negotiated using Diffie-Hellman key exchange protocol followed by RSA algorithm. As the new scheme uses Diffie-Hellman and RSA algorithm, the security of the overall system depends on discrete logarithm as well as factorization problem and thus, its security is more than public-key RSA. Finally, some new cryptographic applications of the proposed modifications are described that certainly extend the applications of the existing RSA.

1. INTRODUCTION

As the popularity of internet technology is increasing, more and more numbers of users are using it. In addition, its security protection is also very important. Hence, to provide security protection, data need to be encrypted before transmitting over a public channel. Two basic technologies are used for the encryption of data, i.e. symmetric key encryption and asymmetric key encryption (Mohit et al., 2015; Mohit et al., 2016; Sun et al., 2007). One of the very well-known cryptography scheme is RSA algorithm (Sun et al., 2007; Peng et al., 2016; Ambedkar et al., 2011; Minni et al., 2013). In broad terms the security of traditional public-key cryptosystem either depend on the factorization problem or the discrete logarithm problem. The RSA-type algorithm comes under the factorization problem and the Diffie-Hellman (DH) comes under discrete logarithm problem. We modify the RSA encryption technology using a combination

DOI: 10.4018/978-1-7998-1763-5.ch007

of DH, RSA and presented a more efficient encryption/decryption technology. In 1998, Takagi (Takagi et al., 1998) showed the extension of RSA to multi-prime algorithm with modulus p^kq and reduced the decryption time by using Quisquater-Couvreur method. After a few years in 2002, Elkamchouchi et al. (Elkamchouchi et al., 2002) proposed extended RSA, where RSA algorithm is implemented using Gaussian integers over real and imaginary numbers.

Later on, several versions of the extended RSA are developed that shows the validity of executing RSA algorithm over the complex numbers (El-Kassar et al. 2005) (Verkhovsky et al., 2011), however its competence is lesser than the existing RSA. In 2015 M. Thangavel (Thangavel, 2015) proposed an enhanced version of RSA, which uses several parameters such as four prime numbers, three Euler functions, multiple public and private exponents that increase the overall computational complexity and overhead of the scheme.

In this paper, a modification of the RSA algorithm is proposed. The public-key RSA is converted into a Symmetric-key RSA (SYM-RSA) cryptosystem, where two prime numbers are securely exchanged using a hybrid of Diffe-Hellman key exchange, RSA and used them for the generation of a secret key between two participants.

The rest of the paper is presented as follows. Section 2 gives preliminaries of some existing schemes considered in order to understand the proposed protocol. Section 3 explains the proposed symmetric-RSA (SYM-RSA) followed by its security analysis in Section 4. Section 5 contains the conclusion of the paper.

2. PRELIMINARIES

Since the modifications of RSA are proposed using Diffie-Hellman (DH) key exchange protocol, thus DH and RSA techniques are introduced below.

2.1. Diffie-Hellman (DH) Protocol

In (Diffie et al., 1976), Whitfield Diffie and Martin Hellman published an elementary article for secure exchange of a contributory common key between two remote participants over public channels. It does not require any prior information and is known to be the first public-key cryptosystem. In DH protocol, a finite multiplicative group $<Z_p, \times>$ with a generator g are publicly assumed, and two public messages are exchanged for negotiation of a secret key. Let A and B are two participants, who exchange the following two public messages, where $A \rightarrow B: C$ means A sends message C to B:

$A \rightarrow B: X = g^x \pmod P$, where $1 < x < P$ and x is a random secret chosen by A

$B \rightarrow A: Y = g^y \pmod P$, where $1 < y < P$ and y is a random secret chosen by B

The common contributory secret key K (say) is calculated by the participants independently as

$K = Y^x \pmod P = (g^y)^x \pmod P = X^y \pmod p = (g^x)^y \pmod P$

This key K is secure, because the DHP (DH problem) and the underlying DLP (discrete logarithm problem) as given below are intractable in polynomial time for a large prime modulus P.

DHP: Given public values $(X = g^x, Y = g^y)$, the computation of $K = g^{xy}$ (mod P)
DLP: Given either of the public values $(X = g^x$ or $Y = g^y)$, the computation of random secrets x or y

This protocol has huge applications in designing other useful cryptosystems and some of them are Secure Socket Layer (SSL), Transport Layer Security (TLS), Internet Protocol Security (IPSec), Public Key Infrastructure (PKI), Digital Signature Standard (DSS), PGP (Pretty Good Privacy), SET (Secure Electronic Transaction) etc. Although the DH protocol has numerous applications, it is vulnerable to several attacks like man-in-the-middle, Denial-of-Service (DoS) etc.

2.2. RSA Algorithm

The RSA was developed by Ron Rivest, Adi Shamir and Len Adleman in the year 1976 (Rivest et al., 1976), and is the most widely used public key algorithm in cryptography. It comprises following four steps:

(1)   Choose two large distinct prime numbers p and q
(2)   Compute $n = p \times q$, Euler function $\Phi(n) = (p-1) \times (q-1)$ and delete p and q
(3)   Select a number e such that $1 < e < \Phi(n)$ and relative prime to $\Phi(n)$
(4)   Compute multiplicative inverse d such that $e \times d \equiv 1 \bmod \Phi(n)$

   Encryption:

(1)   Choose any k-bit plaintext m such that $k \leq \log_2(n)$, where n is the public modulus.
(2)   Compute cipher-text $c = m^e (mod\ n)$

   Decryption: Compute plaintext $m = c^d (mod\ n)$

3. MODIFIED ELGAMAL OVER INTEGERS PROPOSED MODIFICATION OF PUBLIC RSA TO SYMMETRIC RSA (SYM-RSA)

As we know, Diffie- Hellman (DH) protocol supports negotiation of a secret key between two remote participants through the exchange of two public values, where pre-negotiation of a finite multiplicative large prime order group and a generator are necessary. Using these public values, both the parties calculate a common key independently. On the other hand, a user through RSA algorithm can generate public-private key pair for message encryption and other purposes. Now, we propose a technique to negotiate two prime numbers between two remote users using DH protocol and establish same public-private key pair by using RSA algorithm. Since two users have same RSA private key, the proposed scheme becomes a symmetric (SYM-RSA). In brief, SYM-RSA uses DH for secure negotiation of two prime numbers and then each user uses RSA for the generation of a common secret private key between them. Now, the details of the proposed scheme are described.

3.1. Design of Proposed SYM-RSA

It consist of two steps- (1) Use of DH key exchange protocol for secure negotiation of two prime numbers and (2) Use of RSA algorithm for generation of a common secret key. The step-1 is given below in Box 1. where two remote users A and B assume a finite multiplicative group with a generator and exchange four messages publicly.

Note that two users A and B securely negotiate two prime numbers P_1 and P_2 using DH protocol, because two integers y, $t < P$, which are selected arbitrarily, cannot be expected to be considered by opponents although the public values R_{A1}, R_{B1} are known. Each user then uses RSA with these two prime numbers and generates two common secret keys. In fact, the proposed scheme is framed in such a way that both the private- and public-key of the RSA including the common modulo become secret and only known to the users A and B, and hence, termed as SYM-RSA. The proposed scheme is explained through a flow-diagram as provided below in Box 2.

As shown, the private- and public-key pair of RSA becomes secret, i.e., *(e, n)* and *(d, n)* are both secret and only known to the users A and B. As an application of the proposed SYM-RSA, user A may encrypt a message m using RSA algorithm using either of the two secret keys and send to user B. User B, on receiving the cipher-text, can decrypt easily using RSA and the remaining secret key as provided below:

User A: Let the plaintext is m, so the cipher-text $C = m^e \bmod n$, here the secret key *(e, n)* is used for encryption (similarly, the secret *(d, n)* is also applicable). The cipher-text C is sent to B.

User B: On receiving, user B decrypts C using the secret key *(d, n)* and gets plaintext as $m = C^d \bmod n$.

Similarly, other applications of the traditional RSA can be implemented using our SYM-RSA cryptosystem. However, it may be noted that some new applications, which are not supported by existing RSA, could also be developed. For instance, simultaneous message security and integrity are easily possible in SYM-RSA, where the same is not supported in existing RSA. The diagrammatic view of the proposed signature process is given in Figure 1. and explained below.

Let the plaintext be m, its simultaneous encryption and signature for integrity/authentication in one way can be done using SYM-RSA as follows:

Encryption: $C = m^e \bmod n$

Signature generation: $Sig = h^d \bmod n$, where *Sig* stands for signature and $h = H(m)$ for a hash function H.

Final message: *(C, Sig)*

Verification: $m' = C'^d \bmod n$, $h' = (Sig')^e \bmod n$, where C' and Sig' are the received messages. Now, if $h' = H(m')$, message security and integrity are verified, otherwise not.

Note that if either of two secret keys is compromised, the SYM-RSA becomes a public-key RSA, which is exactly similar to the existing RSA.

Box 1. Negotiation of two prime numbers using DH

[Negotiate finite multiplicative group $G(P)$ and a generator g]	
User A	User B
1) Randomly select x	1) Randomly select s
2) Compute and send to B:	
$\xrightarrow{\quad R_{A1}=g^x \bmod P \quad}$	
	2) Compute and send to A:
$\xleftarrow{\quad R_{B1}=g^s \bmod P \quad}$	
3) Compute $P_1 = R_{B1}^{y}\ mod\ P$	3) Compute $P_2 = R_{A1}^{t}\ mod\ P$
$= g^{sy} \bmod P$	$= g^{xt} \bmod P$
(y and t are randomly selected such that both P_1 and P_2 become primes)	
4) Compute and send to B:	
$\xrightarrow{\quad R_{A2}=g^y \bmod P \quad}$	
	4) Compute and send to A:
$\xleftarrow{\quad R_{B2}=g^t \bmod P \quad}$	
5) Compute $P_2 = R_{B2}^{x}\ mod\ P$	5) Compute $P_1 = R_{A2}^{s}\ mod\ P$
$= g^{xt}\ mod\ P$	$= g^{sy}\ mod\ P$

Box 2. Negotiation of two common secret keys using RSA

(Prime numbers P_1 and P_2 are known)	
User A	User B
1) Calculate $n = P_1 \times P_2$	1) Calculate $n = P_1 \times P_2$
2) $\Phi(n) = (P_1-1)(P_2-1)$	2) $\Phi(n) = (P_1-1)(P_2-1)$
3) Select e, where $gcd(e, \Phi(n)) = 1$	
	[Steps 3 and 4 may be executed by B as well and similarly, the value of r be sent by B to A]
4) Compute $r \equiv P_1 \times e \bmod P_2$ and send to B	
$\xrightarrow{\qquad\qquad r \qquad\qquad}$	
	3) Compute e from r as $e \equiv r \times P_1^{-1} \bmod P_2$
5) Calculate d as $e \times d \equiv 1 \bmod \Phi(n)$	4) Calculate d as $e \times d \equiv 1 \bmod \Phi(n)$

Figure 1. Simultaneous message security and signature using SYM-RSA

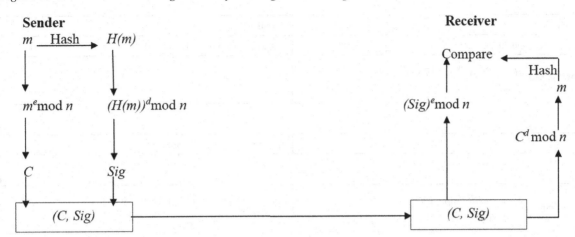

4. IMPLEMENTATION

This section shows the practical implementation of SYM-RSA using the mathematical example. However, for understanding purpose small numbers are taken, but practically it is considered as secure for < 512-bits.

Example: Let us suppose two users A and B pre-negotiated a multiplicative group of prime order $p=7853$ with a generator $g=3607$. The required computations and message exchange are given below in Box 3.

As shown, both e and d for the users A and B are unique and never be disclosed to others in our scheme.

5. SECURITY ANALYSIS

As stated in the previous section, the proposed SYM-RSA uses DH and RSA public-key cryptosystems. The DH key exchange protocol is secured, because the underlying DHP (DH Problem) is computationally intractable. The DHP in the context of proposed SYM-RSA is restated below:

As shown, two pair of messages $(R_{A1} = g^x \bmod P, R_{B2} = g^t \bmod P)$ and $(R_{A2} = g^y \bmod P, R_{B1} = g^s \bmod P)$ are publicly exchanged between two users A and B. Thus, a DHP, which exists corresponding to each pair, can be defined as the computation of $P_1 = g^{xt} \bmod P$ (or $P_2 = g^{ys} \bmod P$) by knowing the corresponding message pairs. This problem is not solvable in real time as no polynomial time algorithm is available. Also, as we know the hardness of DHP depends on the computation of either x or t (similarly either y or s), the solution of DHP is actually the solution of DLP (discrete logarithm problem) which is not tractable in polynomial time.

Alternatively, the computation of P_1 and/or P_2 by an opponent on iteration over R_{A1} and R_{B1} for large prime modulo P is not feasible for having exact matching with secrets y and t, because these secrets are random and several such values exist for generating prime numbers from R_{A1} and R_{B1}. Thus, the proposed prime numbers negotiation procedure is secure. On the other hand, the generation of two secret keys using RSA is also secured as explained below.

Box 3. Negotiation of Two Prime Numbers Using DH

User-A:	User-B:
1) Select a random number $x=1239$,	1) select a random number $s=976$
2) Compute $R_{A1} = 3607^{1239} \bmod 7853$ $= 546$	
$\xrightarrow{\quad R_{A1}=546 \text{ to } B \quad}$	
	2) Compute $R_{B1} = 3607^{976} \bmod 7853$
$\xleftarrow{\quad R_{B1}=7807 \text{ to } A=7807 \quad}$	
3) Compute $P_1 = 7807^{779} \bmod 7853$ $= 3697$	3) Compute $P_2 = 546^{129} \bmod 7853$ $= 2749$
4) Compute $R_{A2} = 3607^{779} \bmod 7853$ $= 3155$	
$\xrightarrow{\quad \text{Send } R_{A2}=3155 \text{ to } B \quad}$	
	4) Compute $R_{B2} = 3607^{129} \bmod 7853$ $= 543$
$\xleftarrow{\quad \text{Send } R_{B2}=543 \text{ to } A \quad}$	
5) Compute $P_2 = 543^{1239} \bmod 7853$ $= 2749$	5) Compute $P_1 = 3155^{976} \bmod 7853$ $= 3697$

Box 4. Negotiation of two common secret keys using RSA

1) Compute $n = 2749 \times 3697$ $= 10163053$	1) Compute $n = 2749 \times 3697$ $= 10163053$
2) Compute $\Phi(n) = (2749-1)(3697-1)$ $= 10156608$	2) Compute $\Phi(n) = (2749-1)(3697-1)$ $= 10156608$
3) Compute $e= 991$ such that $gcd\,(991, 10156608)=1$	
4) Compute $r \equiv 2749 \times 991 \bmod 3697= 3267$	
$\xrightarrow{\quad \text{Send } r=3267 \text{ to } B \quad}$	
	3) Compute $e \equiv 3267 \times 2749^{-1} \bmod 3697$ $= 991$
5) Compute $d = 991^{-1} \bmod 10156608$ $= 9080479$	4) Compute $d = 991^{-1} \bmod 10156608$ $= 9080479$

As we know, the existing RSA with a modulus greater than or equal to 512-bit number is secured, because no polynomial time algorithm in factorization of publicly known RSA modulus is available. Since the modulus n of the proposed SYS-RSA is not publicly known, our RSA modification in this respect is more secure than the existing one. Also, the computations of e, $\Phi(n)$ and d are hard as

1. Computation of e involves the solution of the congruence $r = P_1 \times e \bmod P_2$, where P_1 and P_2 are unknown (r is known).
2. Computation of $\Phi(n)$ involves on the availability of P_1 and P_2, however they are kept secret in our scheme.
3. Computation of d involves on the availability of e and $\Phi(n)$, which as shown in 1) and 2) are not computable.

Thus, the proposed SYM-RSA as a whole is secured.

6. CONCLUSION

This article presented a modification of existing RSA public-key cryptography and presented in the form of Symmetric-RSA (SYM-RSA) i.e. symmetric-key RSA is designed using the combination of DH and RSA algorithm. One of the application of proposed SYM-RSA is described i.e. message integrity. In addition, security analysis proves the security of proposed SYM-RSA in this paper as well. In future, the work will be extended and implement in real life scenario such as entity authentication.

REFERENCES

Ambedkar, B. R., Gupta, A., Gautam, P., & Bedi, S. S. (2011, June). An Efficient Method to Factorize the RSA Public Key Encryption. *Proceedings of the 2011 International Conference on Communication Systems and Network Technologies (CSNT)* (pp. 108-111). IEEE. 10.1109/CSNT.2011.29

Diffie, W., & Hellman, M. (1976). New directions in cryptography. *IEEE Transactions on Information Theory, 22*(6), 644–654. doi:10.1109/TIT.1976.1055638

El-Kassar, A. N., Haraty, R. A., Awad, Y. A., & Debnath, N. C. (2005, November). *Modified RSA in the Domains of Gaussian Integers and Polynomials Over Finite Fields* (pp. 298–303). CAINE.

Elkamchouchi, H., Elshenawy, K., & Shaban, H. (2002, November). Extended RSA cryptosystem and digital signature schemes in the domain of Gaussian integers. *Proceedings of the 8th International Conference on Communication Systems* (Vol. 1, pp. 91-95). 10.1109/ICCS.2002.1182444

Minni, R., Sultania, K., Mishra, S., & Vincent, D. R. (2013, July). An algorithm to enhance security in RSA. *Proceedings of the 2013 Fourth International Conference on Computing, Communications and Networking Technologies (ICCCNT)* (pp. 1-4). IEEE. 10.1109/ICCCNT.2013.6726517

Mohit, P., & Biswas, G. P. (2015, March). Design of ElGamal PKC for encryption of large messages. *Proceedings of the 2015 2nd International Conference on Computing for Sustainable Global Development (INDIACom)* (pp. 699-703). IEEE.

Mohit, P., & Biswas, G. P. (2016, March). Modification of Symmetric-Key DES into Efficient Asymmetric-Key DES using RSA. *Proceedings of the Second International Conference on Information and Communication Technology for Competitive Strategies* (p. 136). ACM. 10.1145/2905055.2905352

Peng, L., Hu, L., Lu, Y., Xu, J., & Huang, Z. (2016). Cryptanalysis of Dual RSA. *Designs, Codes and Cryptography*.

Rivest, R. L., Shamir, A., & Adleman, L. (1983). A method for obtaining digital signatures and public-key cryptosystems. *Communications of the ACM, 26*(1), 96–99. doi:10.1145/357980.358017

Sun, H. M., Wu, M. E., Ting, W. C., & Hinek, M. J. (2007). Dual RSA and its security analysis. *IEEE Transactions on Information Theory, 53*(8), 2922–2933. doi:10.1109/TIT.2007.901248

Sun, H. M., Wu, M. E., Ting, W. C., & Hinek, M. J. (2007). Dual RSA and its security analysis. *IEEE Transactions on Information Theory, 53*(8), 2922–2933. doi:10.1109/TIT.2007.901248

Takagi, T. (1998, August). Fast RSA-type cryptosystem modulo p k q. *Proceedings of the Annual International Cryptology Conference* (pp. 318-326). Springer Berlin Heidelberg. 10.1007/BFb0055738

Thangavel, M., Varalakshmi, P., Murrali, M., & Nithya, K. (2015). An Enhanced and Secured RSA Key Generation Scheme (ESRKGS). *Journal of Information Security and Applications, 20*, 3–10. doi:10.1016/j.jisa.2014.10.004

Verkhovsky, B. (2011). Cubic Root extractors of Gaussian integers and their application in fast encryption for time-constrained secure communication. *Int'l J. of Communications, Network and System. The Sciences, 4*(4), 197.

This research was previously published in the International Journal of Business Data Communications and Networking (IJB-DCN), 13(1); edited by Zoubir Mammeri; pages 66-73, copyright year 2017 by IGI Publishing (an imprint of IGI Global).

Chapter 8
Hybrid Approach of Modified AES

Filali Mohamed Amine
Djellali Liabes University, Algeria

Gafour Abdelkader
Djellali Liabes University, Algeria

ABSTRACT

Advanced Encryption Standard is one of the most popular symmetric key encryption algorithms to many works, which have employed to implement modified AES. In this paper, the modification that has been proposed on AES algorithm that has been developed to decrease its time complexity on bulky data and increased security will be included using the image as input data. The modification proposed itself including alteration in the mix column and shift rows transformation of AES encryption algorithm, embedding confusion-diffusion. This work has been implemented on the most recent Xilinx Spartan FPGA.

INTRODUCTION

It is important aspect to protect the confidential multimedia data from unauthorized access. Multimedia content can be text, audio, still images, animation and video. Such contents are protected by multimedia security method. Commonly, this is attained by techniques that are profoundly based on cryptography. These schemes facilitate communication security, piracy and shelter (Chang, 2014).

Large size of images causes certain challenges for encryption. Normally a typical image has a very large size. Using traditional encryption algorithm will make encryption difficult for large volume of multimedia data (Chang et al, 2016). For the encryption of any multimedia data, we need such algorithms that require less computation because of large size of data. Symmetric-key algorithms are fewer computationally serious than any Asymmetric key algorithms. Typically, symmetric key algorithms are thousands of times sooner than those of the asymmetric algorithms. So, the better suitable method to encrypt the multimedia data is, to encrypt it with symmetric key encryption algorithms.

DOI: 10.4018/978-1-7998-1763-5.ch008

Our research is concerned with optimizing the existing standards of cryptography (AES) for the images and data encryption. It is also slanting towards exploiting the huge amount of data, in order to attain preferred speed.in this work proposes a modified version of AES algorithm and demonstrates that executions can accomplish superior and high throughput (Chang, et al., 2016).

STATE OF ART

There are several modified in AES to improve speed the performance, increase the security and addition same complexity on algorithm steps. (Mohammad, et al., 2015) The reason development is appeared many different the implementation on software and hardware. Each implementation has need to modified AES according to the specific proposes.

In (Xu, et al., 2013) a modified AES by used longer key length and data matrix. That extended the data matrix to eight row and variable number of column (6, 8, 12 and 16) the input data block (48, 64, 96 and 128), and extended the key length to (384,512, 768 and 1024). This paper not change the first and fourth stages (substitution byte, Add Round Key), third stage shift row change from shift third row to seventh row shifted left and four stages (mix column) change the static matrix 3x3 to new matrix 8x8, should be calculate inverse static matrix used in Mix column on GF (28). This modification is increase robustness and use a few times for encryption and decryption processing.

In (Kaur, et al., 2014) modified the AES algorithm by reduce the calculation, computation overhead, and reduce the time encryption process. It replaces the mix column stage in AES algorithm into permutation stage (like the permutation table (IP) that used in DES algorithm) because the mix column is take large calculation time and that makes the encryption process are slow. The other stages in AES algorithm don't change.

Finally, modification used simple S-box for encryption and decryption to reduce the computation amount, the new S-box has some properties, simple generation and same S-box used for encryption and decryption (Rashidi, 2014).

The Advanced Encryption Standard (AES)

The AES is a block cipher that is the standard version of Rijndael. It has a fixed block length of 128bits and variable key lengths. The number of internal rounds of the AES depends on the key size, which is 10, 12 and 14 for the key length 128,192 and 256 respectively. In our design, we consider the case of 128 bits for the key length and 10 rounds. Before the first round, the main key is added to the plaintext. Then, inrounds1–9, all four operations are performed to the state array. In the last round (10th round), the Mix-columns transformation is not used, which makes encryption and decryption symmetric (Daemen et Rijmen, 2001) (see Figure 1).

Sub Bytes

Function performs a non-linear transformation independently on each byte of the input state. This transformation is performed by substituting each byte of the state with a value from substitution box (also termed as S-box). There are 16 parallel S-boxes each with eight inputs and eight outputs. The S-box operation is the only nonlinear transformation of the AES algorithm. It is an invertible operation and can be used for decryption processes too.

Figure 1. The AES-128 encryption algorithm

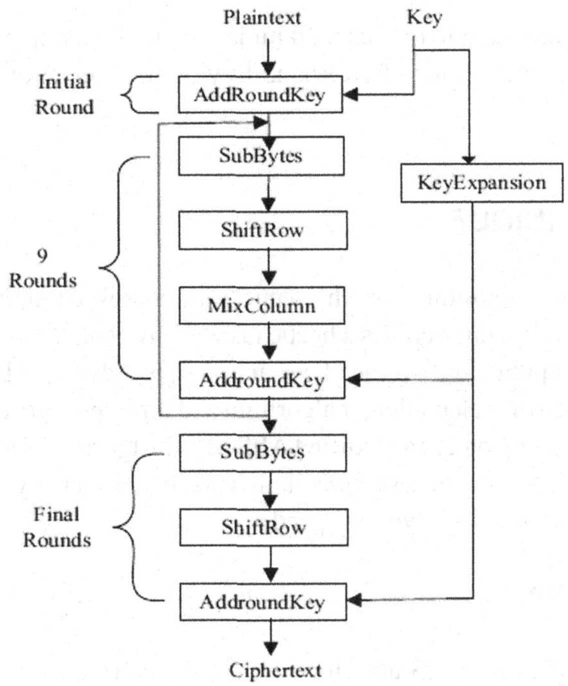

Shift Row

Shift Row operation is the cyclic shifting of each row of the state to the left. The shifting numbers are depended on the number of the row. The top row is not shifted and the last three rows are cyclically shifted over 1, 2, and 3 bytes, respectively

Mix Column

This process is for mixing up of the bytes in each column separately during the forward process. The corresponding transformation during decryption is de noted InvMix-Columns and stands for the inverse mix column transformation (Ichikawa et al, 2000). The goal here is to further scramble up the 128-bit input block.

Key Addition

In this operation, the round key is applied to the State by simple bit-by-bit XOR. Key-Addition is the same for the decryption process. Before the first round, a key addition layer is applied to the cipher data. This transformation is stated as the algorithm initial round key addition. The final round of the cipher is equal to the basic round with the Mix-Column step removed. A key expansion unit is defined in order to generate the appropriate key, for every round, from the initial key value. When all rounds of transformation are completed, a cipher data block with the same length as the plain data has been generated.

Key Expansion

The task of the key expansion module is to expand initial key for generating a series of Round Keys. In AES-128, this module generates a total of 10 Round Key of 16 bytes in order to be employed respectively in rounds of AES.

AES MODIFIED TECHNIQUE

When we use the encryption algorithms for the security of complex multimedia data, computational overhead is so large that encryption becomes a hectic task (Wang et al, 2016). To overcome the problem of high calculation and computational overhead, we analyze the Advanced Encryption Standard (AES) and modify it, so as to reduce the calculation of algorithm and for improving the encryption performance security. So, we develop and implement a modified AES based Algorithm for all kinds of data. The basic aim of modifying the AES is to provide less computation and better security for data. The modified AES algorithm adjusts to provide better encryption speed.

Modified Aes Algorithm

The present research modifies the AES algorithm (makes modification in Shift Row trans-formation and Mix-Columns) in order to make the AES algorithm more secure and faster. The four phases of the conventional AES constituting the round function are Sub Bytes, Shift-Rows, Mix-Columns and AddRoundkey. But the modified AES proposed is using Permutation in place of the Mix Column step.

There are 10 rounds for full encryption. The four different stages that we use for Modified-AES Algorithm (see Figure 2) are:

- Substitution bytes
- M-ShiftRows
- Permutation
- AddRoundKey

Modified Shift Row Transformation

1. When the round number is odd, the Shift Rows transformation operates on the rows of the state array (as normal Shift-Row transformation) (Abdulkarim, 2013) (see Figure 3);
2. When the round number is even, the Shift-Row transformation operates on the column of the state array; it shifts the bytes in each column by a certain offset in circle. The first column unchanged, the second column is shift cyclically shifted to the bottom by one byte, the third column is shifted cyclically to the bottom by two bytes and the last column is cyclically shifted to the bottom by three bytes.

Figure 2. AES modified algorithm flow

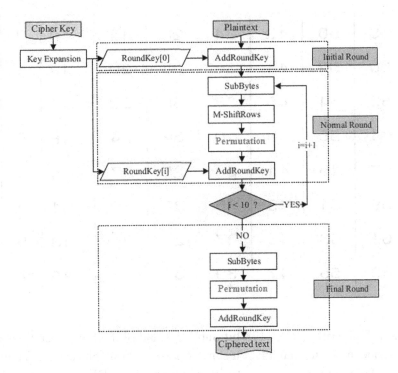

Figure 3. Modified shift row transformation Case 2

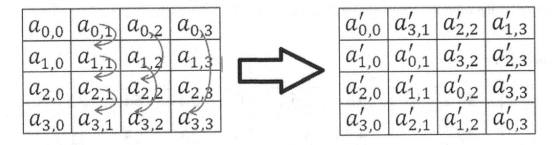

Modified MixComls

Permutation is widely used in cryptographic algorithms. Permutation operations are interesting and important from both the cryptographic and the architectural points of view.

The inputs to the IP table consist of 64 bits. Modified-AES algorithm takes 128 bits as input. The functions Substitution Bytes and Shift Rows are also interpreted as 128 bits whereas the Permutation function takes 64 bits (Vandana, 2013). We divide the consequential bits of Shift Rows function into two parts of 64 bits, then take each part of 64 bits as input of permutation tables, and shift bits one by one according to that table. We fetch one bit from the source, and put it into the correct position in the destination. Each bit of a block is subject to initial permutation, which can be represented by the initial permutation (IP) table shown in Figure 4.

Figure 4. IP table

58	50	42	34	26	18	10	2
60	52	44	36	28	20	12	4
62	54	46	38	30	22	14	6
64	56	48	40	32	24	16	8
57	49	41	33	25	17	9	1
59	51	43	35	27	19	11	3
61	53	45	37	29	21	13	5
63	55	47	39	31	23	15	7

This Modified AES algorithm takes 128-bit Sub bytes and Shift Rows operations also work data, there is a need to divide the sequential bits stage into 2 portions of 64 bits each and then part of 64 bits as an input of permutation tables according to IP table taken from DES algorithm. One bit from the source is fetched and then placed into position in target destination. Each bit is interpreted to IP table. After having completed the permutation of the 128 bits, we again repeat it for another 128-bit remaining operation of algorithm are executed (see Figure 5).

Figure 5. IP¹ table

40	8	48	16	56	24	64	32
39	7	47	15	55	23	63	31
38	6	46	14	54	22	62	30
37	5	45	13	53	21	61	29
36	4	44	12	52	20	60	28
35	3	43	11	51	19	59	27
34	2	42	10	50	18	58	26
33	1	41	9	49	17	57	25

For the full decryption of the Modified-AES algorithm, the transformation processes are, Inv-Bytesub, Inv-Shiftrows, Inv-Permutation, and the Addroundkey, which are performed in 10 rounds as it is in the encryption process.

RESULTS AND COMPARISONS

The proposed modified AES encryption algorithm used to test and evaluate some bases image, which uses in encryption process based on software simulation (Chang et al., 2017).

To test the algorithm, we take the different size of image and compare the calculated time of both the Modified-AES with Advanced Encryption Standard (AES). The result is shown in Table 1.

Digital Image Formats

There are many types of digital image formats like .bmp, .gif, .jpg, .pict, .eps, and .png. This project can use any kind of format. The results obtain in this paper are mainly using .gif format only (Chang, et al, 2017) (see Figure 6).

Table 1. Comparison of performance of AES with MAES

Image Size (Pixel)	Image Size(kb)	AES-Time/ms	MAES-Time/ms
256*256	192	6.510	6.338
512*512	250	8.710	8.221
512*512	742	25.225	25.101
1024*1024	2.35 Mb	76.800	75.001

Figure 6. Encryption results time for different size of image

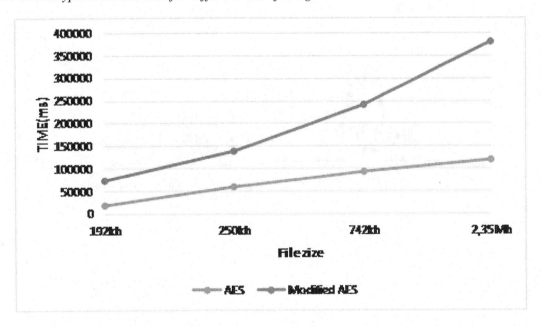

Histograms of Encrypted Images

We select grey-scale images (256×256) having different contents, and we calculate their histogram. One typical example among them is shown in Figure. 7. We can see that the histogram of the ciphered image is uniform and is significantly different from that of the original image. Therefore, it does not provide any indication to employ any statistical attack on the image under consideration. Moreover, there is no loss of image quality after performing the encryption/decryption steps.

Correlation of Two Adjacent Pixels

Testing the correlation between two horizontally adjacent pixels, and two vertically adjacent pixels respectively, in a ciphered image. First, select n pairs of two adjacent pixels from an image randomly. Then the correlation coefficient of each pair uses the formula calculated in Figure 8.

The results of the correlation coefficients for horizontal, vertical and diagonal adjacent pixels for the plain-image and its cipher-image are show in Table 2. The visual testing of the correlation distribution of two vertically adjacent pixels and the cipher image produced by the proposed scheme is shown in Figure 9.

Figure 7. Histogram of original image and cipher image

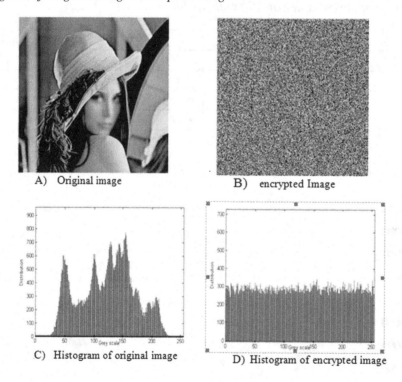

A)   Original image   B)   encrypted Image

C)   Histogram of original image   D) Histogram of encrypted image

Figure 8. Equation for calculating image correlation

$$r_{xy} = \frac{\frac{1}{N}\sum_{i=1}^{N}(x_i - \overline{x})(y_i - \overline{y})}{\sqrt{\left(\frac{1}{N}\sum_{i=1}^{N}(x_i - \overline{x})^2\right)\left(\frac{1}{N}\sum_{i=1}^{N}(y_i - \overline{y})^2\right)}},$$

$$\overline{x} = \frac{1}{N}\sum_{i=1}^{N}x_i, \qquad \overline{y} = \frac{1}{N}\sum_{i=1}^{N}y_i,$$

Table 2. Correlation coefficient of two adjacent pixels in original and encrypted image

Direction	Plain Image	Ciphered Image
horizontal	0.9401	0.0093
vertical	0.9470	-0.0613
Diagonal	0.9122	-0.0081

Figure 9. Correlation of original image and cipher image

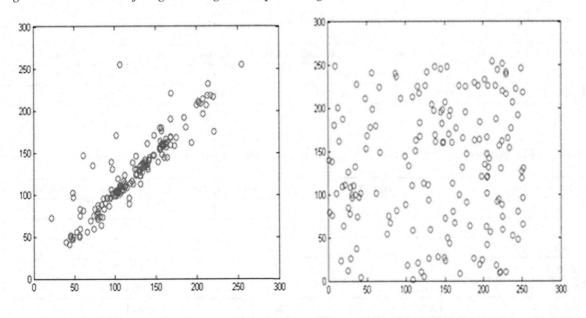

A) Correlation of Original image   B) Correlation of image cipher

FPGA IMPLEMENTATION

The implementation of AES algorithm is performed on the Spartan 6 device, which is a member of Xilinx family. The VHDL code of the design is synthesized placed and routed using Xilinx ISE 14.1.

Table 3 shows the results of the implementations of MAES in FPGA kit Spartan 6. It is clear from the table that increases the throughput. Because we optimized and modified the algorithm AES for speed, we can achieve 98.3 *Gbps* on a Xilinx device Spartan-6. Although our implementation needs more area, it has better area-speed utilization.

For the sake of completeness, we have also compared results of our technique with the recent state-of-the-art results. For that purpose, we implemented our design on Xilinx Virtex-5 FPGA, since most of the recent work uses this FPGA as target device. We have compared the results of our technique and recent work against a number of area and performance parameter.

Table 4 compares FPGA implementation results of our design to other selected designs. It is clear form Table 4 that our architecture Similarly, when we compare the best frequency results of existing technique, our technique gives comparable (in case of Virtex-5 implementation) or better results (in case of Virtex 5) while consuming much less device resources.

CONCLUSION

The various modified AES algorithms proposed are more robust than the original AES as they have been tested on various parameters of security and the modified algorithm has proved to give better encryption results with reduced time complexity. A good encryption algorithm should resist various kinds of attacks say, known plain-text attack, and several other brute–force attacks.

Table 3. Implementation results of our AES modified and AES classic

Encryption Algorithm	Latency	Frequency (MHZ)	Throughput (Gbps)	Area %
M-AES	3.354	886.64	98.3	49.4
AES	1.538	650.364	68.1	64.2

Table 4. Comparison between our implementations and other previous implementations

Design	Type FPGA	Frequency Mhz	Throughput(Gb/s)
Wang et Ha	Virtex5	312.80	70.9
Soliman et al.	Virtex5	50.20	73.37
Van et al.	Virtex5	619	64.7
Qu et al.	Virtex5	258.5	18.5
Rahimunnisa et al.	Virtex5	/	20.3
Our design	**Virtex5**	**886.64**	**88.1**

Future Work

We will perform the security analysis of MAES, to see how; much more or less secure it is, as compare to the different AES implementation. Moreover, we will compare it with other Modified versions of AES, work done by other researchers.

REFERENCES

Anwar, H., Daneshtalab, M., Ebrahimi, M., Plosila, J., & Tenhunen, H. (2013, December). FPGA implementation of AES-based crypto processor. In *Proceedings of the 2013 IEEE 20th International Conference on Electronics, Circuits, and Systems (ICECS)* (pp. 369-372). IEEE.

Chang, V., Amin, R., Islam, S. H., Vijayakumar, P., & Khan, M. K. (2017). A robust and efficient bilinear pairing based mutual authentication and session key verification over insecure communication. *Multimedia Tools and Applications*.

Chang, V., Amin, R., Kumar, N., Biswas, G. P., & Iqbal, R. (2016). A light weight authentication protocol for IoT-enabled devices in distributed Cloud Computing environment. *Future Generation Computer Systems*.

Chang, V., Campbell, J., & Et Hosseinian-Far, A. (2016). Philosophising data: a critical reflection on the 'hidden' issues. In *Big Data: Concepts, Methodologies, Tools, And Applications* (pp. 302–313). Hershey, PA: IGI GLOBAL.

Chang, V., Kuo, Y. H., & Ramachandran, M. (2016). Cloud computing adoption framework: A security framework for business clouds. *Future Generation Computer Systems, 57*, 24–41. doi:10.1016/j.future.2015.09.031

Chang, V., & Ramachandran, M. (2014, January). A proposed case for the cloud software engineering in security. In *Proceedings of the International Workshop on Emerging Software as a Service and Analytics, ESaaSA 2014-In Conjunction with CLOSER 2014* (pp. 71-79).

Daemen, J., & Rijmen, V. (2001, November). Advanced Encryption Standard. National Institute for Standards and Technology (NIST). Retrieved from http://csrc.nist.gov/publictions/fips/fips-197

Hoang, T. (2012, February). An efficient FPGA implementation of the Advanced Encryption Standard algorithm. In Proceedings of the 2012 IEEE RIVF International Conference on Computing and Communication Technologies, Research, Innovation, and Vision for the Future (RIVF), (pp. 1-4). IEEE. 10.1109/rivf.2012.6169845

Hodjat, A., & Verbauwhede, I. (2004, April). A 21.54 Gbits/s fully pipelined AES processor on FPGA. In *Proceedings of the 12th Annual IEEE Symposium on Field-Programmable Custom Computing Machines FCCM '04* (pp. 308-309). IEEE.

Huang, C. W., Chang, C. J., Lin, M. Y., & Tai, H. Y. (2007, October). Compact FPGA implementation of 32-bits AES algorithm using Block RAM. In Proceedings of the TENCON 2007 IEEE Region 10 Conference (pp. 1-4). IEEE.

Ichikawa, T., Kasuya, T., & Matsui, M. (2000, April). Hardware Evaluation of the AES Finalists. In Proceedings of the AES candidate conference (pp. 279-285).

Järvinen, K. U., Tommiska, M. T., & Skyttä, J. O. (2003, February). A fully pipelined memoryless 17.8 Gbps AES-128 encryptor. In *Proceedings of the 2003 ACM/SIGDA eleventh international symposium on Field programmable gate arrays* (pp. 207-215). ACM.

Kaur, A., Bhardwaj, P., & Kumar, N. (2013). Fpga implementation of efficient hardware for the Advanced Encryption Standard. *International Journal of Innovative Technology and Exploring Engineering*, 2(3), 186–189.

Koradia, V. (n. d.). Modification in Advanced Encryption Standard. *Journal of Information, Knowledge and Research in Computer Engineering*, 2(2), 358.

Mohammad, O. K. J., Abbas, S., El-Horbaty, E. S. M., & Salem, A. B. M. (2015). Innovative method for enhancing key generation and management in the aes-algorithm. arXiv:1504.03406

National Institute of Standards and Technology (U.S.). (n. d.). Advanced Encryption Standard. Retrieved from http://csrc.nist.gov/publication/drafts/dfips-AES.pdf

Qin, H., Sasao, T., & Iguchi, Y. (2006). A design of AES encryption circuit with 128-bit keys using look-up table ring on FPGA. *IEICE Transactions on Information and Systems*, 89(3), 1139–1147. doi:10.1093/ietisy/e89-d.3.1139

Qu, S., Shou, G., Hu, Y., Guo, Z., & Qian, Z. (2009, May). High throughput, pipelined implementation of AES on FPGA. In *Proceedings of the International Symposium on Information Engineering and Electronic Commerce IEEC '09* (pp. 542-545). IEEE. 10.1109/IEEC.2009.120

Rahimunnisa, K., Karthigaikumar, P., Rasheed, S., Jayakumar, J., & SureshKumar, S. (2014). FPGA implementation of AES algorithm for high throughput using folded parallel architecture. *Security and Communication Networks*, 7(11), 2225–2236. doi:10.1002ec.651

Rahimunnisa, K., Karthigaikumar, P., Rasheed, S., Jayakumar, J., & SureshKumar, S. (2014). FPGA implementation of AES algorithm for high throughput using folded parallel architecture. *Security and Communication Networks*, 7(11), 2225–2236. doi:10.1002ec.651

Rashidi, B., & Rashidi, B. (2013). Implementation of an optimized and pipelined combinational logic rijndael S-Box on FPGA. *International Journal of Computer Network and Information Security*, 5(1), 41–48. doi:10.5815/ijcnis.2013.01.05

Saggese, G. P., Mazzeo, A., Mazzocca, N., & Strollo, A. G. (2003, September). An FPGA-based performance analysis of the unrolling, tiling, and pipelining of the AES algorithm. In FPL (pp. 292-302).

Saggese, G. P., Mazzeo, A., Mazzocca, N., & Strollo, A. G. (2003, September). An FPGA-based performance analysis of the unrolling, tiling, and pipelining of the AES algorithm. In FPL (pp. 292-302).

Saqib, N. A., Rodríguez-Henríquez, F., & Díaz-Pérez, A. (2003, September). AES algorithm implementation-an efficient approach for sequential and pipeline architectures. In *Proceedings of the Fourth Mexican International Conference on Computer Science ENC '03* (pp. 126-130). IEEE. 10.1109/ENC.2003.1232885

Shtewi, A. A., Hasan, B. E. M., & Hegazy, A. E. F. A. (2010, February). An Efficient MAES Adapted for Image Cryptosystems. *International Journal of Computer science and Network Security, 10*(2).

Soliman, M. I., & Abozaid, G. Y. (2011). FPGA implementation and performance evaluation of a high throughput crypto coprocessor. *Journal of Parallel and Distributed Computing, 71*(8), 1075–1084. doi:10.1016/j.jpdc.2011.04.006

Soliman, M. I., & Abozaid, G. Y. (2011). FPGA implementation and performance evaluation of a high throughput crypto coprocessor. *Journal of Parallel and Distributed Computing, 71*(8), 1075–1084. doi:10.1016/j.jpdc.2011.04.006

Van Dyken, J., & Delgado-Frias, J. G. (2010). FPGA schemes for minimizing the power-throughput trade-off in executing the Advanced Encryption Standard algorithm. *Journal of Systems Architecture, 56*(2), 116–123. doi:10.1016/j.sysarc.2009.12.001

Verbauwhede, I., Schaumont, P., & Kuo, H. (2003). Design and performance testing of a 2.29-GB/s Rijndael processor. *IEEE Journal of Solid-State Circuits, 38*(3), 569–572. doi:10.1109/JSSC.2002.808300

Wang, Y., & Ha, Y. (2013). FPGA-based 40.9-Gbits/s masked AES with area optimization for storage area network. *IEEE Transactions on Circuits and Systems, 60*(1), 36–40. doi:10.1109/TCSII.2012.2234891

Wang, Z., Cao, C., Yang, N., & Chang, V. (2016). ABE with improved auxiliary input for big data security. *Journal of Computer and System Sciences.*

Xu, P., Jin, H., Wu, Q., & Wang, W. (2013). Public-key encryption with fuzzy keyword search: A provably secure scheme under keyword guessing attack. *IEEE Transactions on Computers, 62*(11), 2266–2277. doi:10.1109/TC.2012.215

This research was previously published in the International Journal of Organizational and Collective Intelligence (IJOCI), 7(4); edited by Victor Chang; pages 83-93, copyright year 2017 by IGI Publishing (an imprint of IGI Global).

Chapter 9
Cryptographic Algorithms for Next Generation Wireless Networks Security

Vishnu Suryavanshi
GHRCE Nagpur, India

G. C. Manna
BSNL, India

ABSTRACT

At present a majority of computer and telecommunication systems requires data security when data is transmitted the over next generation network. Data that is transient over an unsecured Next Generation wireless network is always susceptible to being intercepted by anyone within the range of the wireless signal. Hence providing secure communication to keep the user's information and devices safe when connected wirelessly has become one of the major concerns. Quantum cryptography algorithm provides a solution towards absolute communication security over the next generation network by encoding information as polarized photons, which can be sent through the air security issues and services using cryptographic algorithm explained in this chapter.

INTRODUCTION

Does increased security provide comfort to paranoid people? Or does security provide some very basic protections that we are naive to believe that we don't need? During this time when the Internet provides essential communication between tens of millions of people and is being increasingly used as a tool for commerce, security becomes a tremendously important issue to deal with. There are many aspects to security and many applications, ranging from secure commerce and payments to private communications and protecting passwords. One essential aspect for secure communications in next generation wireless network is that of cryptography, which the focus of this chapter is.

DOI: 10.4018/978-1-7998-1763-5.ch009

Security in computer world determines the ability of the system to manage, protect and distribute sensitive information (Abdel-Karim R. Al Tamimi 2006). The most attractive and fast growing network is 802.11 in wireless networks. In 1997IEEE 802.11 introduced standards for wireless local network (WLAN) communication, some of these standards are:

- Using the 2.4 GHz radio spectrum and 11 Mbps max data rate is 802.11b.
- Using the 5 GHz radio spectrum and 54 Mbps max data rate is 802.11a.
- Using the 2.4 GHz radio spectrum and 54 Mbps max data rate is 802.11g.

Wireless Robust Security Network is 802.11i (Quality of service). It is used in quality of service for traffic prioritization to give delay sensitive application such as multimedia and voice communication priority(SANS, 2005).Next generation wireless technology 3G, 4G and more has been gaining rapid popularity in recent years.

They have ubiquitous wireless communications and services as Integration of multi-networks is using IP technology; similar technology to the wired Internet where users are freed from their local networks, not just IP end-to-end but over-the-air packet switching, high bandwidth / high-speed wireless and highly compatible with wired network infrastructures like ATM, IP.

These technologies are facing security problems in the software products used to access the vast Internet, operating systems, www browsers and e-mail programs(Chandra, et al., 2008).For secure data transformation cryptographic algorithms plays a key role.

A cryptographic technique provides three forms of security namely confidentiality, data integrity and authentication. Confidentiality refers to protection of information from unauthorized access (Daemean & Rijmen, 1999). Information has not been manipulated in any unauthorized way is ensured by data integrity. Authentication can be explained in two groups as entity authentication and message authentication. Detecting any modifications to the message provides message authentication. Entity authentication assures the receiver of a message, about both the identity of the sender and his active participation (Kumar & Purohit, 2010)

Need of a standard depends on the ease of use and level of security which it provides. Here, the distinction between wireless usage and security standards show that the security is not maintained well up to with the growth past of end user's usage. The hackers monitor and even change the integrity of transmitted data in current wireless technology. Lack of rigid security standards has caused companies to invest millions on securing their wireless networks.

Securing Next Generation Wireless Networks is an extremely challenging and interesting area of research. Unprotected wireless networks are vulnerable to several security attacks including eavesdropping and jamming that have no counterpart in wired networks. Moreover, many wireless devices are resource limited, which makes it challenging to implement security protocols and mechanisms.

The main objective of this chapter to study and analyze use of Cryptographic Algorithms for Next Generation wireless networks Security in terms confidentiality, Confidentiality, Integrity, Availability, Anti-virus, anti-spyware software, firewall, Authentication, Access control, and Cryptanalysis.

BACKGROUND

Information is an important asset and resource for business and needs to be protected like any other asset. The protection of information is usually known as information security. A basic and classical model of security objectives include the so called CIA triad which stands for confidentiality, integrity and availability. In this chapter we tried to notify security issues and services and use of cryptographic algorithms.

1. SECURITY ISSUES AND SERVICES

Signal fading, mobility, data rate enhancements, minimizing size and cost, user security and (Quality of service) QoS are the key challenges in wireless networks (Kumar & Jain, 2012).Handheld devices which are used in embedded application have not generally been viewed as posing security threats, their increased computing power and the ease with which they can access networks and exchange data with other handheld devices introduce new security risks to an agency's computing environment. This section describes how the security requirements for confidentiality, integrity, authenticity, and availability for handheld device computing environments can be threatened. In a sizable geographic area, Wireless Mesh Networks (WMNs) presents a good solution to provide wireless Internet connectivity (Siddiqui & Seon, 2007).

2. SECURITY ISSUES

2.1 Loss of Confidentiality

Confidentiality assures only the knowing recipients is accessible to the information transmitted across the network. On the handheld device, the storage module, or the PC or while being sent over one of the Bluetooth, 802.11, IR, USB, or serial communication ports; confidentiality of information can be compromised. Moreover, most handheld devices are shipped with connectivity that is enabled by default. These default configurations are typically not in the most secure setting and should be changed to match the agency's security policy before being used.

Confidentiality is the privacy of a useful thing. Specifically, confidentiality can be defined as which people, under what conditions are authorized to access a useful thing. The confidentiality of this information is extremely important because the subjection of this information could bring embarrassment and heavy penalties. Confidentiality can be achieved through strong asymmetric cryptographic solutions in wired networks (Anjum & Salil, 2009)

2.2 Loss of Integrity

Information secrecy, data integrity and resource availability of users are to be provided by security services. To prevent improper modification of data and resource availability preventing denial of services is data integrity (Liang & Wang, 2004).

The integrity of the information on the handheld device and of the handheld device hardware, applications, and underlying operating system are also security concerns. Information stored on, and software and hardware used by, the handheld device must be protected from unauthorized, unanticipated, or unintentional modification. Information integrity requires that a third party be able to verify that the content of a message has not been changed in transit and that the origin or the receipt of a specific message be verifiable by a third party

Integrity is evaluated by two primary properties. First, there is the notion that a useful thing should be trusted; that is, there is an expectation that a useful thing will only be modified in appropriate ways by appropriate people. For example, a hospital patient's allergy information is stored in a database. The doctor should be able to trust that the allergy information is correct and up-to-date.

If data is damaged or incorrectly altered by authorized or unauthorized personnel then you must consider how important it is that the data be restored to a trustworthy state with minimum loss; which is the second part of integrity. For example, suppose a nurse who is authorized to view and update a patient's allergy information is upset with his/her employer and wants to disrupt a patient's data to make the hospital look bad. How important is it that the hospital be able to catch this error and trace it back to the person(s) who caused it?

Data integrity is guaranteed because required keys may be generated during the authentication process for data encryption and message authentication.

2.3 Loss of Availability

In the modeling and design of fault tolerant wireless systems, availability for wireless mobile systems has presented great challenges. There are high expectations from customer for level of availability and performance from wireless communication system as with the rapid growth of wireless communication services (Kishor, Trivedi, Ma & Dharmaraja, 2003).

Authorized person, entity, or device can access a useful thing represented by availability. For example, an organization has a system which provides authentication services for critical systems, applications, and devices on campus. An interruption in this service could mean the inability for customers to access computing resources and staff to access the resources they need to perform critical tasks. Therefore a loss of the service could quickly translate into a large financial loss in lost employee time and potential customer loss due to inaccessibility of resources. Because of this, the availability of this authentication system would be considered 'High'.

The outage-and-recovery of its supporting functional units can affect the performance and availability of a wireless system.

2.4 Anti-Virus and Anti-Spyware Software, and a Firewall

Now a day's antivirus solution became a normal component of computer system. Just like other components or services of computer system antivirus software can be targeted. Anti-virus software is the most cumbersome implementation. It has to pass with hundreds of file types and formats like executables, documents, compressed archives, executable packers and media files. Such formats are quite complex. Hence to implement such software on these formats is extremely difficult (Feng, 2008). Install anti-virus and anti-spyware software, and keep them up-to-date.

For any program that tracks user's online activities and secretly transmits information to a third party is a spyware. Annoying interruptions like pop-ups ads to security breaches and loss of intellectual property are the effects of spyware (Webroot Software Inc., 2004)

Unauthorized access to or from a network is prevented by firewall which is hardware or software system. It can be implemented in both hardware and software, or a combination of both. Firewalls are used to prevent unauthorized Internet users from accessing private networks connected to the Internet. All data entering or leaving the Intranet pass through the firewall, which examines each packet and blocks those that do not meet the specified security criteria (Okumoku-Evroro & Oniovosa, 2005) If your firewall was shipped in the "off" mode, turn it on.

3. SECURITY SERVICES

3.1 Authentication

Entity authentication (or "peer entity authentication" as it is referred to in ISO 7498-2) provides corroboration to one entity that another entity is as claimed. This service provides confidence, at the time of use only, that an entity is not attempting to impersonate another entity or that the current communications session is an unauthorized replay of a previous connection.

To protect credit card transactions on the Internet the Secure Electronic Transaction is used. IBM, Microsoft, Netscape, RSA, Terisa and Verisign these companies are collaborated in the development of SET. This system is designed for

Wired networks and does not meet all the challenges of wireless network. Multifactor Authentication techniques can be used to provide secure web transactions using cell phones. This multifactor technique is based on TIC's and SMS confirmation (Tiwari & Sudip, 2007)

Authentication is a process which a user gains the right to identify him or her. Passwords, biometric techniques, smart cards, certificates, etc. are the key techniques to authenticate a user. These techniques namely come under Multifactor Authentication techniques. Usually within one institute, a user may have a single identity; however, if a user has rights to identify himself in several different organizations or systems, more than one identity from a person may cause problems.

There are four major scenarios based on different degrees of trust:

1. The right of an individual to self-determination as to the degree to which personal information will be shared among other individuals or organizations to control the collection, storage, and distribution of personal or organizational information.
2. The right of an individual to self-determination as to the degree to which the individual is willing to share with others information about himself that may be compromised by unauthorized exchange of such information among other individuals or organizations
3. The right of individuals and organizations to control the collection, storage, and distribution of their information or information about themselves.
4. The right of individuals to control or influence what information related to them may be collected and stored and by whom and to whom that information may be disclosed.

Authentication mechanisms differ in the assurances they provide:

1.   Data was generated by the Principal at some point in the past.
2.   The Principal was present when the data was sent.
3.   The data received was freshly generated by the Principal.

Mechanisms also differ in the number of verifiers:

1.   Support for single verifier per message.
2.   Support for multiple verifiers.

Whether the mechanism supports the ability of the verifier to prove to a third party that the message originated with the Principal. We divide the authentication policy into three major categories:

1.   Personal/system;
2.   Internet;
3.   Network authentication.

3.2 Access Control

To control the flow of information between subject and object where subject is always an active entity while object is a passive entity this mechanism is called access control. Access control is a three-step process which includes identification, authentication and authorization. There are three access control modes which have their own merits and demerits. These are

- Discretionary Access Control (DAC).
- Mandatory Access Control (MAC).
- Role Based Access Control (RBAC).

The first step in any access control solution is identification or authentication.

Authentication are often discussed in terms of "factors" of proof, such as a PIN, a smart card and a fingerprint. Access Control Techniques and Technologies are Rule Based Access Control, Menu Based Access Control (Vinay, 2007).

Over the years security practitioners have developed a number of abstractions in dealing with access control. Protection of objects is the crucial requirement, which in turn facilitates protection of other resources controlled via the computer system. Access control provides a secure solution for web services (WS). To find syntactic and semantic errors administrators of WS can specify access control policies and validate them (Yague & Javier, 2005).

- For the transmission of data the users belonging to the same multicast session form a Data Group (DG). One DG contains the users that can access to a particular resource. According to access privilege the users are also divided into non-overlapping Service Groups (SG).

- Access control on manipulation of resources via "Hyper Text Transfer Protocol" Adam's user agent attempts the reading, writing, or deletion of an information resource identified by a Universal Research Locator (URL);
- Adam's user agent attempts the use of a processing resource to execute programs.

3.3 Data Confidentiality

Robust Security Network Association (RSNA) provides two data confidentiality protocols, called the Temporal Key Integrity Protocol (TKIP) and the Counter-mode/CBC-MAC Protocol (CCMP). Confidentiality protection schemes are:

- **Data Privacy:** The data produced by each sensor node should be only known to itself.
- **Data Confidentiality:** In addition to data privacy, partially or fully aggregated data should only be known by the sink.
- **Efficiency:** After the confidentiality protection schemes are introduced, the system overhead should be kept as small as possible (Taiming, 2001).

Guidelines have been issued in a number of specific areas to help to protect the confidentiality of personal data held in the department.

1. The first stage in establishing policies and procedures to ensure the protection of personal data is to know:
   a. What data is held?
   b. Where it is held, and
   c. What are the consequences would be when data is lost or stolen.

With that in mind, as a first step identifying the types of personal data held within the department, identifying and listing all information repositories holding personal data and their location should conduct an audit.

The storage, handling and protection of this data should be included in the Department's risk register these are associated with risks. The security measures in place are appropriate and proportionate to the data being held can be established by department.

2. All data centers and server rooms used to host hardware and software on which personal data is stored should be restricted to access. This can be done using entail swipe card and/or PIN technology to the room(s) in question – such a system should record when, where and by whom the room was accessed. Such access records and procedures should be reviewed by management frequently.
3. Those computer systems which are no longer in active use and which contain personal data should be removed.
4. Passwords used to access PCs, applications, databases, etc. should be of sufficient strength. A password should include numbers, symbols, upper and lowercase letters. If possible, password length should be around 12 to 14 characters but at the very minimum 6 to 8 characters. Repetition, dictionary words, letter or number sequences, usernames, or biographical information like names or dates must be avoided as Passwords. They should be changed on a regular basis (CMOD, 2008).

It defines four types of data confidentiality service:

3.4 Connection Confidentiality

This service provides for the confidentiality of all user data transferred using a connection.

- **Connectionless Confidentiality:** This service provides for the confidentiality of all user data transferred in a single connectionless data unit (i.e. a packet).
- **Selective Field Confidentiality:** This service provides for the confidentiality of selected fields within user data transferred in either a connection or a single connectionless data unit.
- **Traffic Flow Confidentiality:** This service provides for the confidentiality of information which might be derived from observation of traffic flows.

4. CRYPTOLOGY AND ITS CLASSIFICATION

Cryptology has two main branches cryptography and cryptanalysis.

4.1 Cryptanalysis

The mathematical science that deals with analysis of a cryptographic system to gain knowledge needed to break or circumvent the protection that the system is designed to provide. Attacks, in the context of network security, can be classified in two main classes, active and passive. The many known attacks against WEP can be categorized into different groups according to their goals:

Cryptosystems come in 3 kinds:

1. Those that have been broken (most).
2. Those that have not yet been analyzed (because they are new and not yet widely used).
3. Those that have been analyzed but not broken. (RSA, Discretelog cryptosystem, AES).

Most common ways to turn cipher text into plaintext:

1. Steal/purchase/bribe to get key
2. Exploit sloppy implementation/protocol problems (hacking/cracking) examples someone used spouse's name as key, someone sent key along with message. The main goal of a cryptanalyst is to obtain maximum information about the plaintext (original data).
    a. **Message Decryption:** Allows the attacker to obtain the plaintext corresponding to the cipher-texts of messages intercepted in the network.
    b. **Message Injection:** Allows the attacker to actively generate new valid messages and send them to stations associated with the network.
    c. **Key Recovery:** Is the process of obtaining the pre-shared WEP key. This is the most interesting attack type, because successfully executed it allows the attacker full access to the network

5. LINEAR CRYPTANALYSIS

High probability occurrences of linear expressions involving plaintext bits, "ciphertext" bits, and sub-key bits will be the advantage of linear cryptanalysis. It is a known plaintext attack: that is, it is premised on the attacker having information on a set of plaintexts and the corresponding ciphertexts. However, the attacker has no way to select which plaintexts (and corresponding ciphertexts) are available. The attacker has knowledge of a random set of plaintexts and the corresponding ciphertexts in many applications and scenarios.

The basic idea is to approximate the operation of a portion of the cipher with an expression that is linear where the linearity refers to a mod-2 bit-wise operation (i.e., exclusive-OR denoted by "$\oplus$"). Such an expression is of the form:

$$Xi_1 \oplus Xi_2 \oplus \ldots \oplus Xi_n \oplus Yj \oplus Yj_1 \oplus Yj_2 \oplus \ldots Yj_n = u \ v \qquad (1)$$

where Xi represents the i-th bit of the input $X = [X1, X2, \ldots]$ and Yj represents the j-th bit of the output $Y = [Y1, Y2, \ldots]$. This equation is representing the exclusive-OR "sum" of u input bits and v output bits.

6. DIFFERENTIAL CRYPTANALYSIS

High probability of certain occurrences of plaintext differences and differences into the last round of the cipher exploits the Differential cryptanalysis. For example, consider a system with input $X = [X1 \ X2 \ldots Xn]$ and output $Y = [Y1 \ Y2 \ldots Yn]$. Let two inputs to the system be X' and X'' with the corresponding outputs Y' and Y'', respectively. The input difference is given by $\Delta X = X' \oplus X''$ where "$\oplus$" represents a bit-wise exclusive-OR of then-bit vectors and, hence,

$$[\Delta X] = [\Delta X_1 \ \Delta X_2 \ldots \Delta X_n]$$

where $\Delta X_i = X'_i \oplus X''_i$ with Xi' and Xi'' representing the i-th bit of X' and X'', respectively.

Similarly, $\Delta Y = Y' \oplus Y''$ is the output difference and

$$[\Delta Y] = [\Delta Y_1 \ \Delta Y_2 \ldots \Delta Y_n]$$

where $\Delta Yi = Y' \oplus Y''$.

In an ideally randomizing cipher, the probability that a particular output difference ΔY occurs given a particular input difference ΔX is $\frac{1}{2}^n$ where n is the number of bits of X.

A particular ΔY occurs given a particular input difference ΔX with a very high probability pD (i.e., much greater than $(1/2^n)$ seeks to exploit a scenario in Differential cryptanalysis

The pair $(\Delta X, \Delta Y)$ is referred to as a differential.

The Differential cryptanalysis which is a chosen plaintext attack, the attacker is able to select inputs and examine outputs in an attempt to derive the key. For differential cryptanalysis, the attacker will select pairs of inputs, X' and X'', to satisfy a particular ΔX, knowing that for that ΔX value, a particular ΔY value occurs with high probability (Heys, 2001)

7. CRYPTOGRAPHY

Cryptography is the study of how to design algorithms that provide confidentiality, authenticity, integrity and other security related services for data transmitted in insecure communication environments. Confidentiality protects data from leaking to unauthorized users. Authenticity provides assurance regarding the identity of a communicating party, which protects against impersonation. Integrity protects data against being modified (or at least enables modifications to be detected).

For the encryption and decryption of algorithm if we are using same key (i.e. for encryption and decryption) then it is called symmetric key cryptography or it is also called one key algorithm, where as in asymmetric or public key cryptography requires two keys one is used to encrypt the plaintext and other to decrypt the cipher text. One of these keys is published or public and the other is kept private.

Cryptography is classified into four categories.

7.1 Symmetric Key Cryptography

Symmetric-key encryption is that both the sender and the receiver of an encrypted message have a common secret key k (see Figure 2.). In order to encrypt the message m, also referred to as plaintext, the sender uses the function E together with the key

$$c = E_k(m)$$

D and secret key k (m = message, c = encrypted message).

One should assume that E and D are known to the public in that way an encryption scheme is designed, and obtaining the message m from ciphertext c merely depends on the secret key k (principle of Kerckhoff). In practice, the principle of Kerckhoff is not always used. That means that the encryption scheme is kept secret. There are two reasons for this: one can adopt an even higher security through this additional secrecy, to protect a system not only against cryptographic attacks but also against attacks on

Figure 1. Evolution of cryptography

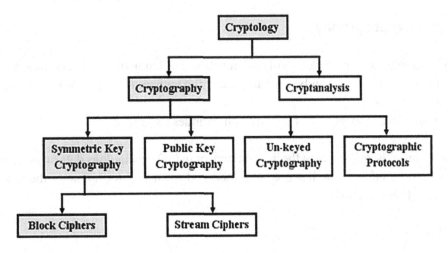

Figure 2. Symmetric-key encryption system with encryption function E, decryption function

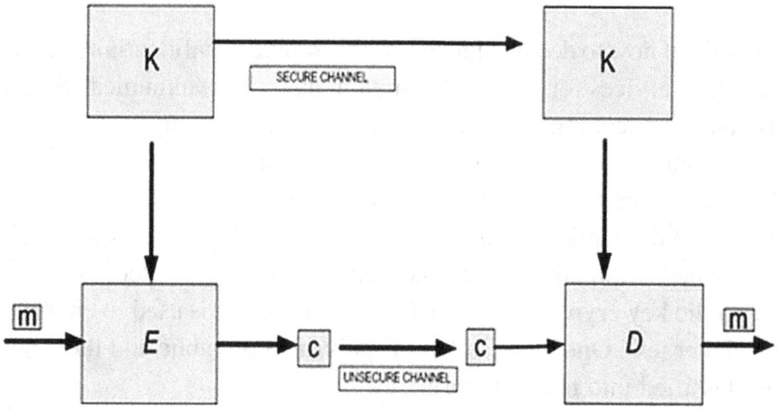

the hardware. Secondly, the use of a weak and inadequately examined algorithm is concealed through secrecy. Based on symmetric keys a new robust cryptography algorithm to increase security and prevent from unauthorized access to the contents of encrypted files is developed. It depends on structure of files; creation method of keys and resultantly the secret file cryptography using each of them are the key factors (Mohammad, 2013).

7.2 Public Key Cryptography

From the last 300-400 years Public-key cryptography (PKC) is the most significant new development in cryptography. Modern PKC was first described publicly by Stanford University professor Martin Hellman and graduate student Whitfield Diffie in 1976. Public-key introduces another concept involving key pairs: one for encrypting, the other for decrypting. This concept is very clever and attractive, and provides a great deal of advantages over symmetric-key:

- Simplified key distribution;
- Digital Signature;
- Long-term encryption.

7.3 Un-Keyed Cryptography

Un-keyed cryptography study gives details of hash function. Hash functions are very important primitives in cryptography. Hash functions can be used to protect the authenticity of information and to improve digital signature schemes.

The protection of the authenticity of information includes two aspects:

- The protection of the originator of the information, or in ISO terminology data origin authentication,
- The fact that the information has not been modified or in ISO terminology the integrity of the information (Preneel, 2003).

Hash function in cryptography is classified in two types:

- Un-keyed hash functions, and
- Keyed hash functions.

Cryptography un-keyed hash functions should satisfy preimage resistance and second preimage resistance and collision resistance. Preimage resistance means that, given an output it is infeasible to obtain an input which produces the output. Second preimage resistance is that, given an input it is infeasible to obtain an input which produces the same output as the given input. Lastly it is infeasible to obtain two different inputs which produce the same output as given input is called collision resistance.

8. CRYPTOGRAPHIC PROTOCOLS

A security protocol (cryptographic protocol or encryption protocol) is that performs a security-related function and applies cryptographic methods, often as sequences of cryptographic primitives. Security protocols are small programs that aim at securing communications over a public network, like Internet. A variety of such protocols has emerged and is seeing increasing use. SSL/TLS, SSH, and IPsec are used in internet traffic (Como, Cortier, & Zalinescu, 2009). How the algorithms should be used describes a protocol. A sufficiently detailed protocol includes details about data structures and representations, at which point it can be used to implement multiple, interoperable versions of a program.

Cryptographic protocols are widely used for secure application-level data transport, some of these aspects:

- Key agreement or establishment;
- Entity authentication;
- Symmetric encryption and message authentication material construction;
- Secured application-level data transport;
- Non-repudiation methods;
- Secret sharing methods;
- Secure multi-party computation.

9. STREAM CIPHERS AND BLOCK CIPHERS

Secret key cryptography schemes are generally categorized as stream and block cipher.

9.1 Stream Cipher

Stream ciphers, which belong to the symmetric encryption techniques. Design and analysis of stream cipher systems as well as the most well-known encryption systems are introduced. When a block cipher is used, a long message m is divided into blocks $m = m_0, m_1, \ldots, m_{N-1}$ of the same length. Here the blocks have usually a length of $n = 64$, 128 or 256 bits, depending on the processing length n of the block cipher.

When stream ciphers are used, the message to be encrypted m is also divided into blocks. Here, however, only short blocks of length n occur. In this case we do not speak of a division into blocks, but into symbols. Usually, n = 1 or n = 8 bit. The encryption of the single symbols mt is carried out through a state dependent unit. Stream ciphers are slower than block and the Transmission error in one cipher text block have effect on other block such that if a bit lost or a altered during transmission the error affect the nth character and cipher re-synchronous itself after n correct cipher text characters as well as not suitable in the software. In synchronous stream cipher if a cipher text character is lost during transmission the sender and receiver must re-synchronous their key generators before they can proceed further.

9.1.1 Classification of Stream Ciphers

The symmetric stream encryption systems are classified in

1. Synchronous stream ciphers, and
2. Self-synchronizing stream ciphers.

The sender can be found on the left and the receiver on the right side. When a synchronous stream cipher is used, the sender and the receiver of an encrypted message have to compute the keystream z_t synchronously at any time $t \geq 0$ for encryption and decryption

9.1.1.1 Synchronous stream ciphers

Figure 3 depicts a symmetric, synchronous stream encryption system. The sender can be found on the left and the receiver on the right side. When a synchronous stream cipher is used; the sender and the receiver of an encrypted message have to compute the keystream z ciphers for time t, synchronously at any time $t \geq 0$ for encryption and decryption.

The keystream zt is generated independently from the plaintext message and the ciphertext. The encryption of the message symbols m_t, $t \geq 0$, can be described by the following equations:

$\sigma_t + 1 = f(\sigma_t, k),$

$z_t = g(\sigma_t, k),$

$c_t = h(z_t, m_t),$ Where $t \geq 0$ is valid.

The system has a state variable σ_t whose initial state σ_0 can either be known publicly or be determined from the secret key k. In order to be able to carry out the encryption, the encryption function h must clearly be invertible. The function f is called the next state function and g is called the output function. The functions f, g and h are known publicly.

9.1.1.2 Self-synchronizing stream ciphers

Besides synchronous stream ciphers, there are also self-synchronizing stream ciphers, but they are hardly used in information and communication systems. In this case the keystream z_t depends on the key k and a fixed number l of previously generated ciphertext symbols.

Figure 3. Synchronous, symmetric stream cipher

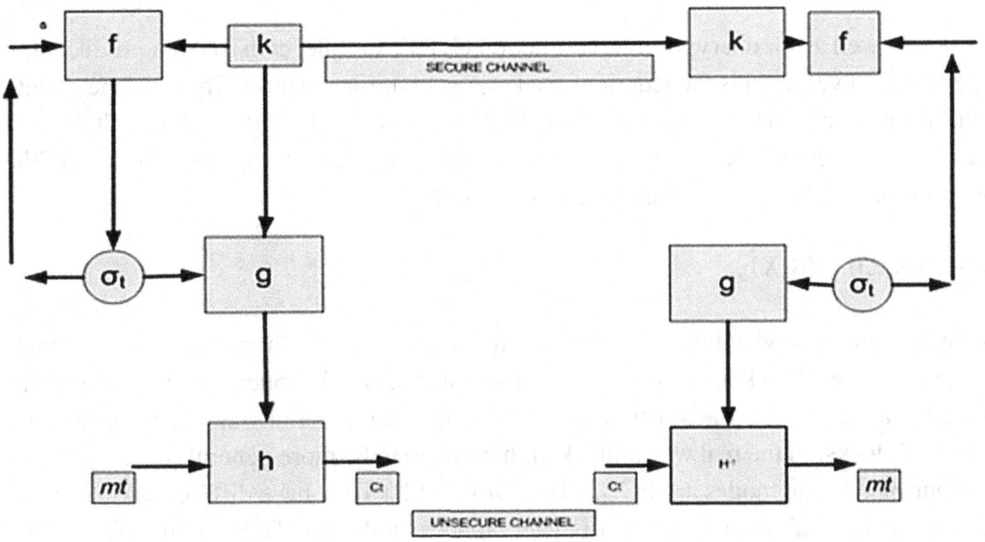

The encryption of a sequence of plaintext symbols m_t, $t \geq 0$, can be described by the following equations:

$$\sigma t = (ct-l, ct-l+1,..., ct-1),$$

$$zt = g(\sigma t, k),$$

$$ct = h(zt, mt).$$

Stream ciphers have several advantages which make them suitable for some applications. Most notably, they are usually faster and have a lower hardware complexity than block ciphers. They are also appropriate when buffering is limited, since the digits are individually encrypted and decrypted. Moreover, synchronous stream ciphers are not affected by error-propagation.

9.2 Block Cipher

Encryption systems can be subdivided in symmetric and asymmetric systems as well as in block and stream ciphers. When block ciphers are used, a long message m is divided into blocks $m = m_0, m_1, \ldots, m_{N-1}$ of the same length. Here the blocks have usually a length of $n = 64$, 128 or 256 bits, depending on the processing length n of the block cipher. Padding mechanisms are used to fill the last block when the message m is not long enough so that the last block m_{N-1} is also an n-bit block. Then the single blocks mt, $0 \leq t \leq N-1$ are assigned to a time-invariant encryption function f in order to obtain ciphertext $c_t = E_k(m_t)$, where k is the secret, symmetric key.

The parameters block length n and key length l should be chosen at least so large that a data complexity of 2^n as well as a processing complexity of 2^l is large enough not to allow an attacker to carry out an exhaustive key search in 10 or 20 years. Today, a block length of $n = 64$, 128 and 256 bits and an equally sized key length are used. The Feistel cipher is based on the idea of using the same function

$G: GF(2)^l \times GF(2)^{n/2} \rightarrow GF(2)^{n/2}$

for encryption as well as for decryption. The function G, for example, consists of a product cipher. Here we assume that n is even and l is the length of the key k or a sub-key derived from it. The plaintext block m of length n bit is split into two equally sized blocks L and R, each having a length of n/2 bit: m = (L,R). Thenthe ciphertext block c is, as shown in Fig. 4.2, put together from the block R andthe bitwise XOR operation of block L with the function value G(k,R):

$c = (R, L + G(k,R)) = (R,X)$.

Block ciphers are somewhat faster than stream cipher each time 'n' characters executed, transmission errors in one cipher text block have no effect on other blocks. Block ciphers can be easier to implement in software, because the often avoid time-consuming bit manipulations and they operate on data in computer-sized blocks. In the real world block ciphers seem to be more general (i.e. they can be used in any of the four modes, the modes are ECB, CBC, OFB, CFB). They have different structure like Feistel Network, for e.g. Kasumi and Clefia. In a Feistel cipher (see Figure 4), the plaintext is split into two halves. The round function is applied to one half, and the output of the round function is bitwise ex-or-ed with the other half finally, the two halves are swapped, and become the two halves of the next round. Another is Substitution-permutation network e.g. AES. In Substitution-Permutation (SPN) cipher, the round function is applied to the whole block, and its output becomes the input of the next round.

Although both stream ciphers and block ciphers belong to the family of symmetric encryption ciphers, there are some key differences. Block ciphers encrypt fixed length blocks of bits, while stream ciphers combine plain-text bits with a pseudorandom cipher bits stream using XOR operation. Even though block ciphers use the same transformation, stream ciphers use varying transformations based on the state of the engine. Stream ciphers usually execute faster than block ciphers. In terms of hardware complexity, stream ciphers are relatively less complex. Stream ciphers are the typical preference over block ciphers when the plain-text is available in varying quantities (for e.g. a secure wifi connection),

Figure 4. Encryption principle of a Feistel cipher with one round

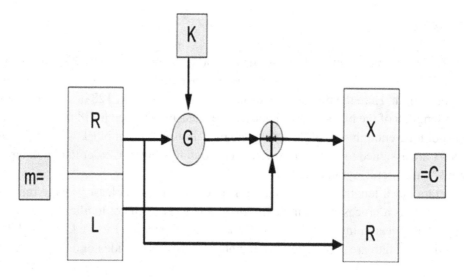

because block ciphers cannot operate directly on blocks shorter than the block size. But sometimes, the difference between stream ciphers and block ciphers is not very clear. The reason is that, when using certain modes of operation, a block cipher can be used to act as a stream cipher by allowing it to encrypt the smallest unit of data available.

10. CONCLUSION AND FUTURE WORK

A cryptographic algorithm is an essential part in network security. Most of the sensitive information in the wireless communication has latent security problems. An End-to-end security has been an issue in next generation wireless networks and hence a solution has to be proposed for the same using Secure Socket Layer/ Transport Layer Security (SSL/TLS), Virtual Private Network (VPN), or a similar mechanism should be provided for security of data. Cryptographic algorithms are utilized for security services in various environments in which low cost and low power consumption are key requirements. Wireless Local Area Networks (WLAN), Wireless Personal Area Networks (WPAN), Wireless Sensor Networks (WSN), and smart cards are examples of such technologies. Security is the most important part in Next Generation Wireless communication system, where more randomization in secret keys increases the security as well as complexity of the cryptography algorithms.

REFERENCES

Al Tamimi. (2006). *Security in Wireless Data Networks: A Survey Paper*. Academic Press.

Anjum, N., & Salil, K. (2009). Article. *Authentication and Confidentiality in Wireless Ad Hoc Networks, 21*, 28.

Ayu, T., & Sudip. (2007). A multi-factor security protocol for wireless payment- secure web authentication using mobile devices. *IADIS International Conference Applied Computing*.

Chandra, D.V., Shekar, V.V., Jayarama, & Babu. (2008). Wireless security: A comparative analysis for the next generation networks. *Journal of Theoretical and Applied Information Technology*.

Como, L. H., Cortier, V., & Zalinescu, E. (2009). Deciding security properties for cryptographic protocols. Application to key cycles. *ACM Transactions on Computational Logic, 5*, 1–38.

Daemean, J., & Rijmen, R. (1999). *AES Proposal: Rijndeal version 2*. Available at http://www.esat.kuleuveb.ac.be/rijmen/rijndeal

Feng. (2008). *Attacking Antivirus*. Nevis Networks,Inc.

Heys, H. M. (2001). *A Tutorial on Linear and Differential Cryptanalysis*. Academic Press.

Kishor, S., Trivedi, Y. Z., Ma, & Dharmaraja, S. (2003). Performability modeling of wireless communication systems. *International Journal of Communication Systems, 16*, 561–577.

Kumar, Y., & Prashant. (2010). Hardware Implementation of Advanced Encryption Standard. In *Proceedings of International Conference on Computational Intelligence and Communication Networks*. IEEE. 10.1109/CICN.2010.89

Liang & Wang. (2004). *On performance analysis of challenge/responsebased authentication in wireless networks*. Elsevier.

Mohammad, S. (2013). A New Secure Cryptography Algorithm Based on Symmetric Key Encryption. *Journal of Basic and Applied Scientific Research*. Retrieved from www.textroad.com

Muhammad & Seon. (2007). Security Issues in Wireless Mesh Networks. In *Proceedings of International Conference on Multimedia and Ubiquitous Engineering* (MUE'07). IEEE.

Okumoku-Evroro &Oniovosa. (2005). *Internet Security: The Role Of Firewall System*. Department Of Computer Science Delta State Polytechnic Otefe-Oghara.

Preneel, B. (2003). *Analysis and Design of Cryptographic Hash Functions*. Academic Press.

Protecting the confidentiality of Personal Data. (2008). CMOD Department of Finance.

SANS Institute (2005) "SANS Institute Info Sec Reading Room"

Singh & Jain. (2012). Research Issues in Wireless Networks. *International Journal of Advanced Research in Computer Science and Software Engineering, 2*(4).

Sun & Liu. (2004). *Scalable Hierarchical Access Control in Secure Group Communications*. IEEE.

Taiming, F., Chuang, W., Wensheng, Z., & Lu, R. (2001). *Confidentiality Protection for Distributed Sensor Data Aggregation*. Retrieved from http://www.cs.iastate.edu/

Vinay. (2007). *Authentication and Access Control The Cornerstone of Information Security*. Trianz White Paper.

Webroot Software Inc. (2004). *Anti-spyware software: Securing the corporate network*. Academic Press.

Yagüe, Mana, & Lopez. (2005). *A metadata-based access control model for web services*. Retrieved from www.emeraldinsight.com/researchregister

This research was previously published in Next Generation Wireless Network Security and Privacy edited by Kamaljit I. Lakhtaria; pages 265-285, copyright year 2015 by Information Science Reference (an imprint of IGI Global).

Chapter 10
Efficient Energy Saving Cryptographic Techniques with Software Solution in Wireless Network

Alka Prasad Sawlikar
RCERT Chandrapur, India

Zafar Jawed Khan
RCERT Chandrapur, India

Sudhir Gangadharrao Akojwar
Government College of Engineering, India

ABSTRACT

To reduce communication costs, to protect our data from eavesdropping and from unauthorized users, cryptographic algorithms are used. Cryptographic module has to be developed for combining the operation of compression and encryption synchronously on the file. The information file is preliminary processed and then converts into one intermediary form so that it can be compressed with better efficiency and security. In this paper an optimized approaching coding technique which deals with both the issues of size and security is introduced and characterized experimentally using the performance measurement approach java in which file of any data length can be practically compressed and encrypted using new encryption technique and a novel energy saving technique in wireless communication network with efficient hardware solution is presented. To improve the strength and capability of algorithms and to compress the transmitted data an intelligent and reversible conversion technique is applied.

DOI: 10.4018/978-1-7998-1763-5.ch010

INTRODUCTION

From last consecutive years we have seen an unrivalled explosion in the amount of information or text data which is transmitted via many digital devices and for reducing the traffic, there is a need of strong cryptographic techniques so that large amount of information can be transmitted. For this a number of novel compression algorithms have been proposed earlier such as LZW, RLE, DWT, DCT and HUFF-MAN. However, few of the above algorithms have been able to achieve best compression ratio.

Advantage of security is to ensure that our information remains confidential and only access by authorized user and ensure that no one has been able to change that one, so it provide full accuracy. Compression is used to compress and secure the data, because it uses less space and saves money. It increases speed of data transfer from disk to memory. Requirements for data security are confidentiality, authentication, integrity and freshness. It involves transforming data of a given frame, called source message to data of a reduced sized frame called code word.

There are different security techniques which are existing like AES, DES, ECC, RSA. Cryptography is valuable for protecting sensitive data online, especially in a world in which an increasing more systems are connected and unsafe to outside attack. It is also a valuable tool for authentication, allowing a user to verify his identity and statements using a public key encryption system. The main advantage of cryptography is as a security tool. Because any system connected wirelessly is bound to eventually be attacked by adversary, and it can be extremely tough to create a system that is invulnerable to outsiders. However, the mathematical analysis involved in encryption is complex enough that even if enemies manage to steal an encrypted file; he may never be able to break the code and access the contents. Strong encryption can be a last line of defense against outsiders, and can protect data even when it is being transferred through a connection that is not secure.

The public and private keys associated with public key cryptography which offers unique advantages to their users like if a user encrypts data with his private key, anyone can get original intelligent data with his public key, verifying that he and only he could have sent the transmission. A public key can also encode data that only that specific user can decode, creating secure one-way communications on the Internet.

Currently compression and encryption methods are doing simultaneously. Combination of two processes into one provides more security by this hybridization.

While combining both compression and encryption data will be first compressed using compression techniques and then encryption techniques will applied and then comparative analysis will be done. If encryption and compression are done at the same time then it takes less processing time and more speed.

Security of information is always been in demand since past few years and plenty of occurrences highlight the importance of the security of text data. As it is known, cryptography is a skill of hiding data and has been known from a long time, e.g. credit cards, debit cards, saving accounts, important documents and what not, everything needs protection. The most principal issue in world today is the large amount of valuable information that is flowing among various networks and present network development demands swap of information with more compression and security in both the time and space for data transmission for data storage (Jain, Lakhtaria, & Srivastav, 2013). This can be done by compression and encryption, such type of scheme is known as encryption compression crypto scheme. This ciphering or encryption is indeed a secure coding technique, whose purpose is to reduce the space for data storage and time for data transmission and thus compression ratio becomes an most important parameter which we have to always keep in mind. So the data, which needs to be protected, is increasing on a fast and rapid rate and can be handled a bit if we can reduce its size or can remove the redundancy and for this both encryption algorithm and compression technique have to be merged, combined and made them work on precious information so that our message or file will be of compressed and encrypted form and secure and is easy to handle because of its reduced size and encrypted form which extends many advantages like saves space, manageable, easily transferrable, practical, and feasible.

Take a look around we observed that the rapid adoption of network technologies and computing systems has brought newer risks and threats such as stealing, unauthorized access service, interruptions and reversing of information, and so on. This becomes more intense to suggest the importance of security and presents every organization with the legal and ethical responsibility to properly secure its information by using appropriate processes and measures. Imposing security at all states promises that information is processed, stored, or transmitted with integrity, reliability, and authenticity and available to all authorized entities.

For a protected and reduced transfer of text information, the algorithms of compression must be combined with the encryption of text data. The techniques of compression removes the redundancies contained in the text file in order to reduce the amount of information and on the other hand, the techniques of encryption

Due to its precious facts like object oriented, platform independent, simple, secure, portable, robust, architectural neural, multi-threaded, interpreted, dynamic, high performance, distributed etc JAVA is highly used for developing software. Here we are using Eclipse editor developed by eclipse open source community.

(Dey, 2017) Some applications required to transmit same message or information which contains signal over channels. When there is a high percentage of unreliability of transmission of any information then at that time some special types of modes of transmission should be selected. So, to overcome the effects of collision or interference multichannel signaling is introduced in wireless communication systems. By doing so one can transmit same message or information which contains signal over channels so that the information can be recovered. To reduce storage cost by eliminating redundancies which occurs in number of files, data compression techniques are used. For storage of data and for transmission we have to pay money and this cost increases with the quantity of data available. But this cost can be reduced by processing the data so that it takes less transmission time and less memory.

Well-known data compression algorithms are available and this paper deals with various data compression and encryption algorithms. The analysis of these algorithms can be used for finding various parameters which is applied in this proposed system. The new data compression technique has been proposed in this paper which is based on bit quantization level.

MATLAB simulation for the best crypto system is shown and the results were observed. This crypto system is then applied to wireless communication network using NS2 software. Observation shows that the new proposed compression technique when combined with cryptographic technique gives the best results in terms of various parameters like delay, throughput and energy.

New wireless sensor network (WSN) applications are growing up with recent technological advances in wireless communication and micro-electronics. The emergence of low cost multimedia devices and low-power such as microphones and micro-cameras has stimulated the development of the next generation of WSNs, known as wireless multimedia sensor network (WMSN).

The use of WMSN suggests a big interest for a wide variety of applications such as object detection, localization, tracking and counting. In fact, these systems can be applied to assist the elderly people, to intensify and complement existing surveillance systems against crime and to extend the ability of law enforcement agencies to monitor areas, public events, private properties and borders (Kaddachi & Soudani, (2010))

The data transmission, as a potential application on WMSN, is still limited to some problems related to energy consumption and storage capacity in nodes, as well as to the available bandwidth of the wireless links. Nodes in WMSN should ensure ad-hoc routing packets for other communication processes, so when sensing image or data, the CPU's of [INSERT FIGURE 001]these nodes can be heavily loaded with data processing tasks, and may be out of their capacities (Culurciello & Andreou, 2006; Akyildiz, Tommaso, & Chowdhury, 2007)

The data compression at the source node is being considered to be the efficient solution to protect the physical capacities of the node and to enhance its life-time. However, a big attention should be paid when building up an efficient and strong compression scheme that avoid weighty processing tasks falling down the available energy and making the node out of its capacities to relay with its neighbors.

A big mismatch comes into sight between the complexities of these compression algorithms and the available physical resources of WSN node for TinyOS-based implementation. However, most recent sensor platforms are software-based, as is the Cyclops platform. Some works have shown that popular algorithms such as JPEG, JPEG2000 or SPIHT are generally not efficient in software simulations because they lead to greater energy consumption and storage than the transmission of the uncompressed image. That is due to the stock limitation of the software-based platforms in terms of processor speed.

A hardware solution for data compression at source node can achieve dynamic compression rate according to the end user requirements. This solution represents a hardware circuit, which is intended to be embedded in the source and destination node. It will be considered as a co-processor for tasks related with compression to unload the node microcontroller giving it more computational bandwidth for wireless network interactions. Further, it will enhance time processing and achieve low power consumption. (Akyildiz, Tommaso, & Chowdhury, 2007; Duran-Faundez & Lecuire, 2008)

LITERATURE SURVEY

Several researchers have been carried cryptography. In literature survey found various compression and encryption algorithms for finding different energy efficient parameters. But still not found satisfactory solution for said problem so developed an algorithm for efficient energy saving. Following are some cryptographic techniques which have been studied.

In the paper "A Comparative Study of Lossless Compression Algorithm on Text Data," Jain, Lakhtaria, & Srivastav (2013) shows the comparison of different lossless compression algorithm over text data which contain different text patterns and had drawn compression ratio of all the algorithm by considering the compression time, decompression time and from comparison they concluded that the Huffman Encoding is considered as the most efficient algorithm. Authors have taken different file sizes using RLE, Adaptive Huffman and Shannon Fano algorithms done comparison based on compression ratio and found how compression ratio getting varied and observed that the size of compressed file created by Adaptive Huffman algorithm is very less in comparison to other algorithms (Jain, Lakhtaria, & Srivastav, 2013).

Med Lassaad Kaddachi, Adel Soudani (2010), in the paper "Efficient hardware solution for low power and adaptive image-compression in WSN", have presented a hardware solution for low power image compression which is based on Loeffler DCT transform. This solution is intended to be machine embedded as a coprocessor to the main WSN CPU. This solution provides powerful compression settings at run time according to the node state and the user requirements. It saves energy and grants short processing time compared to a software implementation of the image compression scheme. Authors have concluded that this solution can be enhanced with the integration of a CMOS image sensor that will reduce the energy and the acquisition time of the image. With this the image is compressed and then avoids energy loss and lengthy processing time. They proposed architecture for compression circuit at the source node and outline the image quality analysis and provide the characteristics of the proposed solution using FPGA and CMOS Standard-Cell and finally done comparison with the TinyOS by implementing. (Kaddachi & Soudani, 2010)

E. Culurciello, and A.G. Andreou, in "CMOS image sensors for sensor networks," discusses about two generations of CMOS image sensors with digital output fabricated. Collision on the output is displayed using contention detector circuits. The image sensors present very high dynamic range and ultra-low power operation. These characteristics allow the sensor to operate in different illuminating conditions and for years on the sensor network node power budget. Authors have concentrated on power saving technique of sensor nodes. (Culurciello & Andreou, 2006.)

In "A survey on wireless multimedia sensor networks," Ian F. Akyildiz, Tommaso Melodia, Kaushik R. Chowdhury, outlined the main research challenges. Algorithms, protocols, and hardware for the development of WMSNs were surveyed, and open research issues discussed in detail. Authors classified currently off-the-shelf hardware as well as available research prototypes for WMSNs. Furthermore, they discussed current solutions and open research issues at the application, transport, network, link, and physical layers of the communication stack, along with possible cross-layer synergies and optimizations. Further pointed out how recent work undertaken in Wyner–Ziv coding at the application layer, specialized spatio-temporal transport layer solutions, delay bounded routing, multi-channel MAC protocols, and UWB technology and amongst others, seems most promising research directions in developing practical WMSNs. (Akyildiz, Tommaso, & Chowdhury, 2007)

N. Dey, A.S. Ashour, in book "Intelligent Techniques in Signal Processing for Multimedia Security", proposes new algorithms to ensure secured communications and prevent unauthorized data exchange in secured multimedia systems. Focusing on numerous applications algorithms and scenarios, it offers an in-depth analysis of data hiding technologies including watermarking, cryptography, encryption, copy control, and authentication. The authors present a framework for visual data hiding technologies that resolves emerging problems of modern multimedia applications in several contexts including the medical, healthcare, education, and wireless. (Dey, 2017)

Duran-Faundez, and V. Lecuire, in "Error Resilient Image Communication with Chaotic Pixel Interleaving for Wireless Camera Sensors," discusses about new applications of wireless sensor networks which requires vision capabilities. They had considered the high loss rates found in sensor networks and the limited hardware resources of current sensor nodes, low-complexity robust image transmission must be implemented, avoiding as much as possible the need for retransmission or redundancy. They proposed a pixel interleaving scheme based in Torus Automorphisms, thus, neighboring pixels are transmitted in different packets. Hence, if packets are lost, authors found a high probability of retrieving enough information to obtain an approximation of the original value. Their results showed an increase of the image quality in comparison with a sequential raw image transmission approach, while preserving similar energy consumptions, time and low-complexity. (Duran-Faundez & Lecuire, 2008.)

In "Data compression algorithms for energy-constrained devices in delay tolerant networks," Sadler, Christopher M. and Margaret Martonosi, focused on collecting additional significant energy improvements by planning computationally-efficient lossless compression algorithms on the source node which reduces the amount of information that must be passed through the network to the sink, and thus have energy advantages that are multiplicative with the number of hops the data travels through the network. Upon observation, they comment if sensor system designers want to compress obtained data, they must either develop application-specific compression algorithms or use off-the-shelf algorithms not designed for resource-constrained sensor nodes. In this paper, they discusses the design issues involved with implementing, adapting, and customizing compression algorithms specifically made ready for sensor nodes. While enlarging sensor LZW (S-LZW) and some simple, but effective, variations to this algorithm, they showed how different amounts of compression can lead to energy savings on both the compressing node and throughout the network and that the savings depends heavily on the radio hardware .So to validate and evaluate their work, they had applied it to datasets from several different real-world deployments and showed that their approaches can reduce energy consumption by up to a factor of 4.5X across the network.(Sadler & Martonosi, 2006.)

Made Agus Dwi Suarjaya (2012) in "A New Algorithm for Data Compression Optimization", presented that when the storage nears it limit, they then try to reduce those files size to minimum by using data compression software so they proposed a new algorithm for data compression, called jbit encoding (JBE) which manipulates each bit of data inside file to minimize the size without losing any data after coding which is classified to lossless compression. This basic algorithm is intended to be combining with other data compression algorithms to optimize the compression ratio. The performance of their algorithm is measured by comparing combination of different data compression algorithms. (Suarjaya, 2012)

After detail study of above literature, design different algorithms for finding better solutions.

PROPOSED DATA COMPRESSION AND ENCRYPTION ALGORITHM

This section presents a new compression and encryption technique which was not proposed earlier. Following is the proposed algorithm which compresses and encrypts the message:

Step 1: Create a table for encoding the input symbols.
The upper bound limit and lower bound limit of each new symbol can be calculated or values can assigned as
a.   Initially load lower bound limit = 0, upper bound limit = 1
b.   Code all the symbols like a, b, c, d…...
c.   Find new values for current range, upper limit and lower limit

Current range = upper bound limit – lower bound limit
higher_ limit = lesser limit + (current range * higher limit of new symbol)
lesser_ limit = lesser limit + (current range * lesser limit of new symbol)

Step 2: The string can be encoded by fetching any value within the range of probability and after that convert the output decimal number into its binary format.
Step 3: Limit the number of bits by using the formula and anyways cancel it or floor it or put it in bracket

Table 1. Representation of characters along with its probability occurrence

Symbol	Probability	Range (lower limit, upper limit)
a	40%	(0.00, 0.40)
l	15%	(0.40, 0.55)
k	25%	(0.55, 0.80)
p	20%	(0.80, 1.00)

Also, No of bits = log [2/upper bound limit of last encoded symbol - lower bound limit of last encoded symbol]

Step 4: In this way compression can be finished and the number of bits are used to reduce the number of bits obtained in step2.

Step 5: Now for encryption choose any one binary key pad and EX-OR it with above.

Step 6: Then rotate right 4 bits means we will get rotating resulted bits.

Step 7: Convert above result into decimal format again.

The result which we will get output is floating point number and that is corresponding to the input symbol. Now here is the algorithm which decompresses and decrypts the text

Step 1: *Convert the received data and information into binary form.*

Step 2: Rotate bits to left.

Step 3: Selected binary key pad and EX-OR it with above result.

Step 4: Convert the result back into decimal form and result should be noted as encoded value.

Step 5: Encoded_value or Coded value = Encoded input

Still string is not fully decoded so match the symbol containing encoded value within its range

Current range = higher limit of new symbol - lesser limit of new symbol
Encoded value = (encoded value - lower bound limit of new symbol) ÷ current range at the output we will found the original string.

DETAIL MATHEMATICAL ANALYSIS OF AN ALGORITHM

Take following example to explain the above algorithm in a better way and following Table 1 represents number of characters with its probability.

Compression and Encryption have been done in a following manner.

Data to be encoded and encrypted is "alkp"

Step 1: Code 'a' as
current_ range = 1 - 0 = 1
upper limit bound = 0 + (1 × 0.4) = 0.4

lower limit bound = 0 + (1 × 0.0) = 0.0
Code 'l'
current_ range = 0.4 - 0.0 = 0.4
upper limit bound = 0.0 + (0.4 × 0.55) = 0.22
lower limit bound = 0.0 + (0.4 × 0.4) = 0.16
Encode 'k'
Current_ range = 0.22-0.16 = 0.06
upper limit bound = 0.16 + (0.06 × 0.8) = 0.208
lower limit bound = 0.16+ (0.06 × 0.55) = 0.193
Encode 'p'
current _range = 0.208-0.193 = 0.015
upper limit bound = 0.193 + (0.015 × 0.90) = 0.2065
lower limit bound = 0.193+ (0.015 × 0.80) = 0.205

Step 2: The string "alkp" may be encoded by any value within the range [0.2065, 0.205]. Now our output is 0.20425 whose binary equivalent = 0.0011010010010011011101

Step 3: No_ of_ bits = [log_2/0.0015] = [log1333.33] = 8bits

Step 4: So, after minimizing number of bits binary value is 0.00110100.

Step 5: Let Our One time key pad is – 0.10101010
Data- 0.00110100 from step 4. After EX-ORing we get the output as 10011110

Step 6: Rotate 4 bits right the result is 11101001

Step 7: 0 .11101001 in decimal is 0.91015625

Decompression and Decryption have been done in a following manner:

Step 1: Received main data is 0.91015625 and binary format of received data is 0.11101001

Step 2: Apply 4 times left shifts to result of step1 the result is 10011110

Step 3: Apply selected one time key pad i.e. 10101010 and logical EX-OR it with the result of step2 the result is 0.00110100

Step 4: Convert 0.00110100into decimal i.e. 0.203125

Step 5: See the probability ranges from table and decodes the four-character string encoded as 0.203125
Decode first symbol 'a'
0.20312 5 is within [0.00, 0.40) 0.203125
encodes 'a'
Remove effects /changes of 'a' from encode value
Current _range = 0.40 - 0.00 = 0.40
Coded or Encoded _value = (0.203125- 0.0) ÷ 0.40 = 0.50775
Decode next symbol 'l'
0.50775is within [0.40, 0.55) 0.50775
encodes 'l'
Remove effects/changes of 'l' from encode value
current range = 0.55 - 0.40 = 0.15
encoded value = (0.50775 - 0.40) ÷ 0.15 = 0.71833
Decode next that is third symbol 'k'
0.71833is within [0.55, 0.80) 0.71833encodes'k'

Remove effects/changes of 'k' from encode value
current range = 0.80 - 0.55 = 0.25
encoded value = (0.71833-0.55) ÷ 0.25=0.67332
Decode next third symbol 'p'
0.67332 is within [0.80, 0.90]
0.67332 encodes 'p'

IMPLEMENTATION OF NEW SYMMETRIC CRYPTOGRAPHIC TECHNIQUE USING JAVA

Computer security is concerned with the preservation of information in environments where there is a possibility of intrusion or malicious action. A vital technology that underpins the security of information in computer networks is known as Cryptography. The new trend in cryptography emphasizes the design of efficient cryptographic primitives that are provably secure in the standard model. For improving security systems government agencies are investing a considerable amount of resources because of recent terrorist activities that dangerously exposed flaws and weaknesses in today's system safety mechanisms.

Java is an object-oriented programming language with its own runtime environment. This is originally developed by Sun Microsystems and now merges into ORACLE Corporation. They can be run on any operating system that's why said as platform independent. Java code is famous as WORA that is writing once run anywhere. Now a day's three billion devices are running java as it is adopted as platform independent programming language. It is used to develop dynamic web pages, in standalone application, enterprise application as well as in mobile. (Bisht & Singh, 2015)

Due to its precious facts like object oriented, platform independent, simple, secure, portable, robust, architectural neural, multi-threaded, interpreted, dynamic, high performance, distributed etc it is highly used for developing software. Here we are using Eclipse editor developed by eclipse open source community. (Idrizi, Florim, Dalipi et al., 2013)

STEPS OF SYMMETRIC CRYPTOGRAPHIC ALGORITHM

Encryption Algorithm

1. Take input in the form of text. This message can be any text file with random data size including characters, symbols and numbers.
2. Operations are performed on every symbol of input: Stream cipher.
3. Generate any key of any length. This key should be same for both encryption and decryption.
4. Perform XOR operation of message with key but not directly. First calculate length of that key used which is constant throughout and take modulus of key length and each key character. Note the remainder.
5. Then XOR remainder with each character of message. Thus, the message will get encrypted.

Decryption Algorithm

Only single secret key has been exercised in the encryption. It is a symmetric algorithm, so same key is used for encryption and decryption. Decryption method of the algorithm is the reverse of their encryption method.

1. Take input as encrypted message.
2. Key is same
3. Perform XOR operation of message with key but not directly. First calculate length of that key used which is constant throughout and take modulus of key length and each key character. Note the remainder.
4. Then XOR remainder with each character of message. Thus, message will get decrypted.

Stages for Program

The following are the essential steps for reading file, compressing and encrypting

```
Public void start compression (String file Path){
//Read File
Array List<Integer> data Into ASCII = read File(file Path);
//Compress File
String compressed Data = compression Algorithm(data Into ASCII, file Path
//Encrypt File
String encryptedData = EncryptDecrypt.getInstance().
encryptData(compressedData);
//Write final encrypted file
WriteDataIntoFile(encryptedData,filePath,"FinalEncryptedData.txt");}
```

IMPLEMENTATION OF PROPOSED ENCRYPTION ALGORITHM

The above are the essential steps for reading file, compressing and encrypting.

In encryption and decryption process we had taken single key and XOR operation. The reason behind it is if we used multiple keys and more operations then time as well as size of encryption will increase.

Read file is a method to go to declaration where the logic is written which will convert each character into corresponding ASCII number. When it enters into declaration for read file it will check every character in the line and also checks whether that file is present in that path and if not then it will give error. Thus, the file reading process is going on and once it will finish we can observe size as above and then return the ASCII values.

This ASCII data have to send to compression algorithm along with file path and finally this method will return compressed data. Compression algorithm will fetch ASCII along with file, logically compressed and add into compressed file and send for encryption.

Since encryption, decryption and decompression is created in another file, we have to call the algorithm only. Then in encryption process first set key, give null, means void means nothing no compressed message neither key is present so no performance will occur so it has to be confirmed that both key and message should be available. Once it is confirm then split it into character, observe length in integer and then XOR.

Save as base 64 encode which is a file where actual encoding takes place and then performs encryption on it. For decryption reverse process occurs, decrypted data send for decompression we will get decompressed ASCII data then finally convert ASCII integer to original data. Decryption is done on direct encrypted file only with same key which is used in encryption then send to base 64 decoder then XOR so that we will get exactly decoded data which we had used for encrypted.

For implementation any file of infinite length can be chosen. Using compression and encryption technique we get following results. Figure 1 shows text file fetched from notepad, Figure 2, Figure 3, Figure 4, Figure 5 shows fetched file with size, ASCII, compressed and encrypted values.

With the help of programming we can see its size, ASCII values, compressed file, encrypted data and decrypted data as follows:

Similarly, we can observe size of every decrypted file, decompressed data and ASCII to original file in reverse manner as follows. Figure 6, Figure 7, Figure 8 and Figure 9 shows the values of decrypted file, decompressed data and ASCII to original.

INNOVATIVE ENERGY SAVING TECHNIQUE IN WIRELESS NETWORK

To reduce storage cost by eliminating redundancies which occurs in number of files, data compression techniques are used. As we know two types of data compression techniques are there: one is lossy and another is lossless and for reducing file size after decoding, lossy compression technique is used for video, audio and text compression. For storage of data and for transmission we have to pay money and this cost increases with the quantity of data available. But this cost can be reduced by processing the data so that it takes less transmission time and less memory space. Different data types consist of many lumps of repeated data. Such fresh data can be altered into a compressed data which saves a lot of storage and transmission costs.

Figure 1. Text File fetched from Notepad

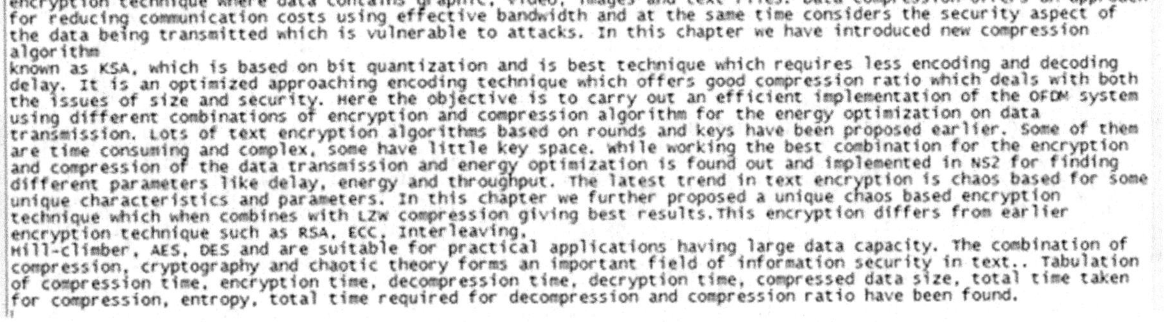
Untitled - Notepad

File Edit Format View Help

with the increasing demand of secure multimedia, there is a need to develop a new secured compression and encryption technique where data contains graphic, video, images and text files. Data compression offers an approach for reducing communication costs using effective bandwidth and at the same time considers the security aspect of the data being transmitted which is vulnerable to attacks. In this chapter we have introduced new compression algorithm
known as KSA, which is based on bit quantization and is best technique which requires less encoding and decoding delay. It is an optimized approaching encoding technique which offers good compression ratio which deals with both the issues of size and security. Here the objective is to carry out an efficient implementation of the OFDM system using different combinations of encryption and compression algorithm for the energy optimization on data transmission. Lots of text encryption algorithms based on rounds and keys have been proposed earlier. Some of them are time consuming and complex, some have little key space. While working the best combination for the encryption and compression of the data transmission and energy optimization is found out and implemented in NS2 for finding different parameters like delay, energy and throughput. The latest trend in text encryption is chaos based for some unique characteristics and parameters. In this chapter we further proposed a unique chaos based encryption technique which when combines with LZW compression giving best results.This encryption differs from earlier encryption technique such as RSA, ECC, Interleaving,
Hill-climber, AES, DES and are suitable for practical applications having large data capacity. The combination of compression, cryptography and chaotic theory forms an important field of information security in text.. Tabulation of compression time, encryption time, decompression time, decryption time, compressed data size, total time taken for compression, entropy, total time required for decompression and compression ratio have been found.

Figure 2. Fetched file with size, ASCII, Compressed and Encrypted values

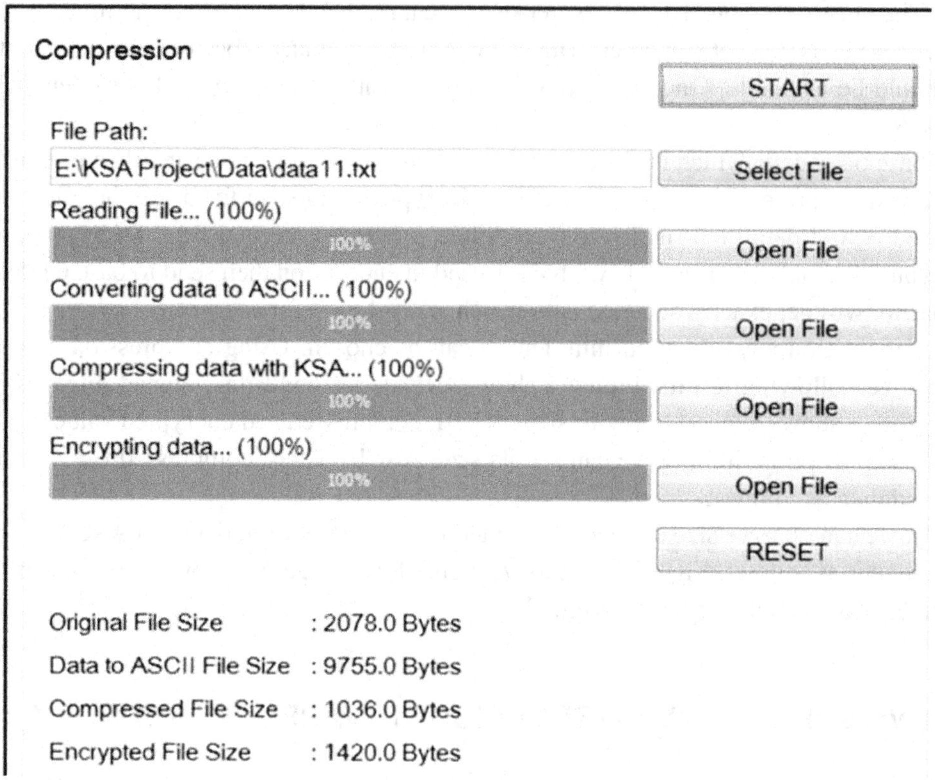

Figure 3. ASCII values of original file

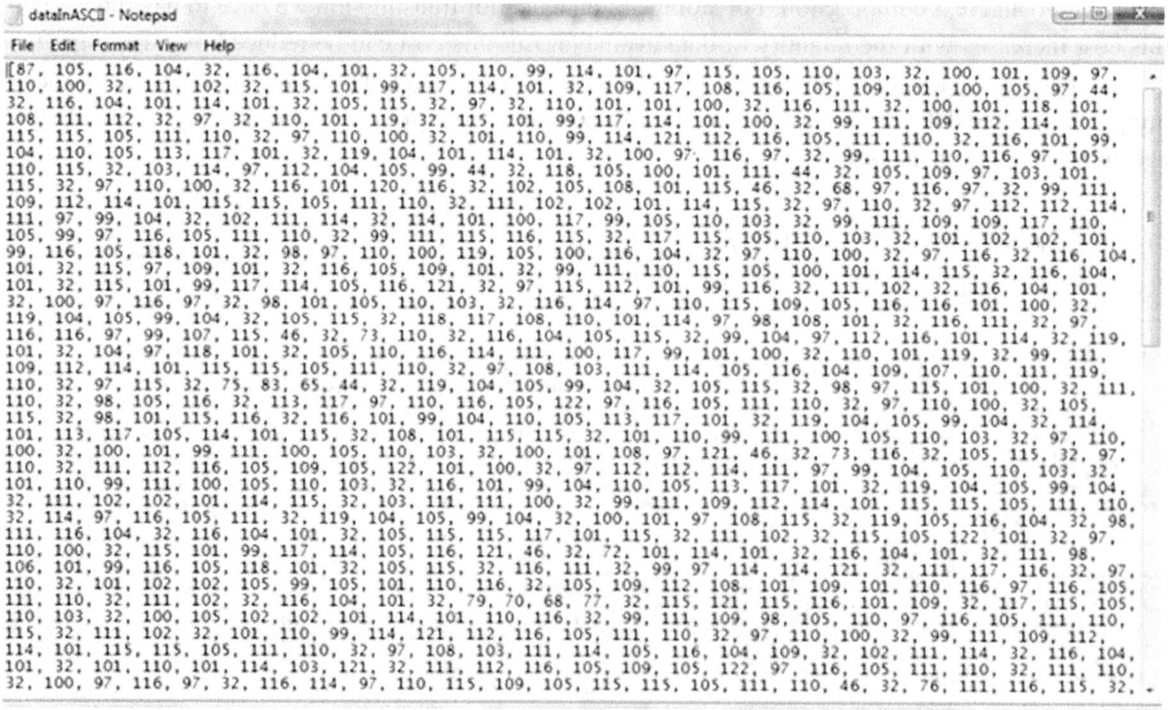

Figure 4. Compressed data of original file

Figure 5. Encrypted file after compression using proposed encryption technique

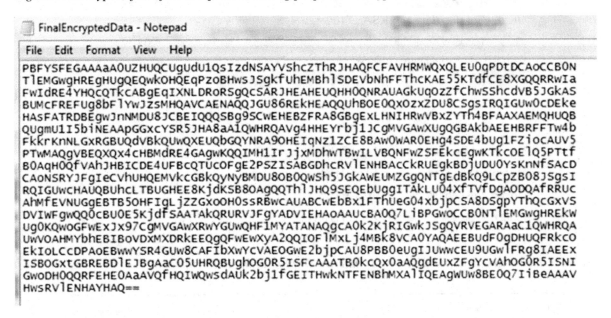

Sensor network establishes sensor network between neighboring nodes with radio range transmission and during communication one node exchanges their information to the neighboring node and thus easily discovers new nodes.

In addition, a power source often consists of a battery with a limited energy budget. In a well-designed network, the sensors in a certain area exhibit homogeneous behaviors to achieve energy balance. In other words, when one sensor dies, it can be expected that the neighbor of this node will give out energy very soon, since they will have to take the responsibilities of that died sensor and expects the lifetime of several months to be converted into several years. Thus, energy saving is crucial in designing life time wireless sensor networks.

Figure 6. Values of decrypted file, decompressed data and ASCII to original

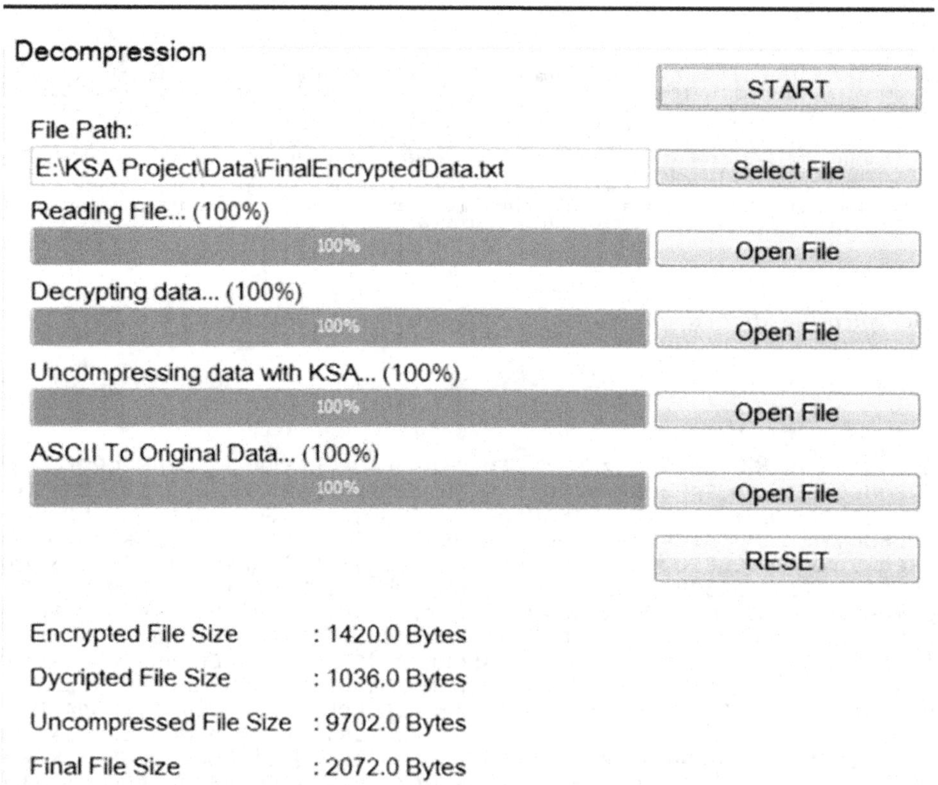

Figure 7. Decrypted data file with new symmetric cryptographic algorithm

Figure 8. ASCII values of decompressed data

uncompressedToASCII - Notepad

File Edit Format View Help

[86, 87, 116, 115, 33, 33, 104, 103, 33, 33, 110, 109, 114, 113, 97, 97, 105, 105, 102, 101, 101, 101, 108, 107,
110, 109, 33, 33, 102, 101, 114, 113, 99, 99, 114, 113, 33, 33, 116, 115, 116, 115, 108, 107, 101, 101, 96, 95, 33,
33, 104, 103, 114, 113, 33, 33, 114, 113, 96, 95, 110, 109, 100, 99, 33, 33, 110, 109, 101, 101, 118, 117, 109,
109, 112, 111, 96, 95, 110, 109, 118, 117, 114, 113, 99, 99, 114, 113, 100, 99, 99, 99, 109, 109, 114, 113, 115,
115, 105, 105, 110, 109, 97, 97, 100, 99, 101, 101, 99, 99, 120, 119, 116, 115, 110, 109, 33, 33, 100, 99, 105,
105, 105, 105, 116, 115, 33, 33, 104, 103, 114, 113, 33, 33, 97, 97, 96, 95, 99, 99, 111, 111, 97, 97, 111, 111,
33, 33, 114, 113, 112, 111, 104, 103, 44, 43, 118, 117, 101, 101, 110, 109, 33, 33, 108, 107, 102, 101, 114, 113,
97, 97, 100, 99, 116, 115, 120, 119, 33, 33, 105, 105, 101, 101, 46, 45, 69, 69, 116, 115, 33, 33, 110, 109, 113,
113, 101, 101, 114, 113, 110, 109, 33, 33, 102, 101, 101, 101, 114, 113, 97, 97, 33, 33, 112, 111, 114, 113, 97,
97, 104, 103, 103, 103, 114, 113, 114, 113, 101, 101, 99, 99, 110, 109, 33, 33, 110, 109, 109, 109, 110, 109, 98,
97, 116, 115, 110, 109, 33, 33, 111, 111, 116, 115, 33, 33, 114, 113, 110, 109, 33, 33, 102, 101, 100, 99, 116,
115, 118, 117, 33, 33, 97, 97, 101, 101, 104, 103, 116, 115, 33, 33, 110, 109, 33, 33, 116, 115, 116, 115, 100, 99,
114, 113, 108, 107, 33, 33, 105, 105, 100, 99, 99, 99, 111, 111, 104, 103, 101, 101, 114, 113, 116, 115, 100, 99,
114, 113, 99, 99, 114, 113, 117, 117, 33, 33, 114, 113, 100, 99, 116, 115, 110, 109, 33, 33, 104, 103, 33, 33, 97,
97, 96, 95, 99, 99, 105, 105, 102, 101, 116, 115, 97, 97, 114, 113, 105, 105, 116, 115, 100, 99, 118, 117, 104,
103, 104, 103, 105, 105, 33, 33, 116, 115, 110, 109, 114, 113, 99, 99, 100, 99, 116, 115, 33, 33, 116, 115, 97, 97,
107, 107, 46, 45, 73, 73, 33, 33, 105, 105, 114, 113, 99, 99, 97, 97, 116, 115, 114, 113, 118, 117, 33, 33, 97, 97,
100, 99, 105, 105, 116, 115, 110, 109, 116, 115, 100, 99, 33, 33, 101, 101, 33, 33, 110, 109, 113, 113, 101, 101,
114, 113, 110, 109, 33, 33, 108, 107, 111, 111, 105, 105, 105, 105, 107, 107, 111, 111, 110, 109, 97, 97, 33, 33,
82, 81, 44, 43, 118, 117, 104, 103, 104, 103, 105, 105, 33, 33, 97, 97, 100, 99, 33, 33, 110, 109, 99, 99, 116,
115, 113, 113, 97, 97, 116, 115, 122, 121, 116, 115, 110, 109, 33, 33, 110, 109, 33, 33, 114, 113, 99, 99, 115,
115, 33, 33, 100, 99, 105, 105, 105, 105, 116, 115, 33, 33, 105, 105, 99, 99, 33, 33, 101, 101, 116, 115, 114, 113,
114, 113, 108, 107, 115, 115, 33, 33, 110, 109, 110, 109, 105, 105, 102, 101, 97, 97, 100, 99, 101, 101, 99, 99,
101, 101, 110, 109, 33, 33, 101, 101, 97, 97, 46, 45, 73, 73, 33, 33, 114, 113, 97, 97, 33, 33, 113, 113, 105, 105,
105, 105, 100, 99, 33, 33, 112, 111, 114, 113, 97, 97, 105, 105, 110, 109, 33, 33, 110, 109, 110, 109, 105, 105,
102, 101, 116, 115, 99, 99, 110, 109, 113, 113, 100, 99, 118, 117, 104, 103, 104, 103, 110, 109, 102, 101, 115,
115, 33, 33, 111, 111, 100, 99, 99, 99, 109, 109, 114, 113, 115, 115, 105, 105, 110, 109, 114, 113, 116, 115, 110,
109, 118, 117, 104, 103, 104, 103, 101, 101, 97, 97, 114, 113, 118, 117, 116, 115, 33, 33, 111, 111, 104, 103, 116,
115, 100, 99, 105, 105, 115, 115, 101, 101, 33, 33, 102, 101, 114, 113, 122, 121, 33, 33, 110, 109, 33, 33, 100,
99, 116, 115, 105, 105, 120, 119, 33, 33, 101, 101, 100, 99, 116, 115, 100, 99, 110, 109, 106, 105, 99, 99, 105,
105, 100, 99, 105, 105, 33, 33, 110, 109, 98, 97, 114, 113, 120, 119, 111, 111, 116, 115, 97, 97, 33, 33, 102, 101,
104, 103, 104, 103, 111, 111, 33, 33, 109, 109, 108, 107, 108, 107, 111, 111, 97, 97, 105, 105, 110, 109, 110, 109,
33, 33, 104, 103, 33, 33, 70, 69, 76, 75, 115, 115, 115, 115, 101, 101, 33, 33, 114, 113, 110, 109, 33, 33, 104,
103, 102, 101, 114, 113, 111, 111, 33, 33, 110, 109, 99, 99, 110, 109, 116, 115, 110, 109, 114, 113, 110, 109, 33,
33, 110, 109, 115, 115, 113, 113, 105, 105, 110, 109, 97, 97, 100, 99, 99, 99, 109, 109, 114, 113, 115, 115, 105,
105, 110, 109, 97, 97, 103, 103, 114, 113, 116, 115, 108, 107, 103, 103, 114, 113, 116, 115, 100, 99, 101, 101,
101, 101, 103, 103, 33, 33, 113, 113, 105, 105, 105, 105, 97, 97, 105, 105, 110, 109, 110, 109, 33, 33, 97, 97, 96,
95, 116, 115, 97, 97, 114, 113, 105, 105, 114, 113, 110, 109, 46, 45, 77, 77, 116, 115, 33, 33, 102, 101, 116, 115,

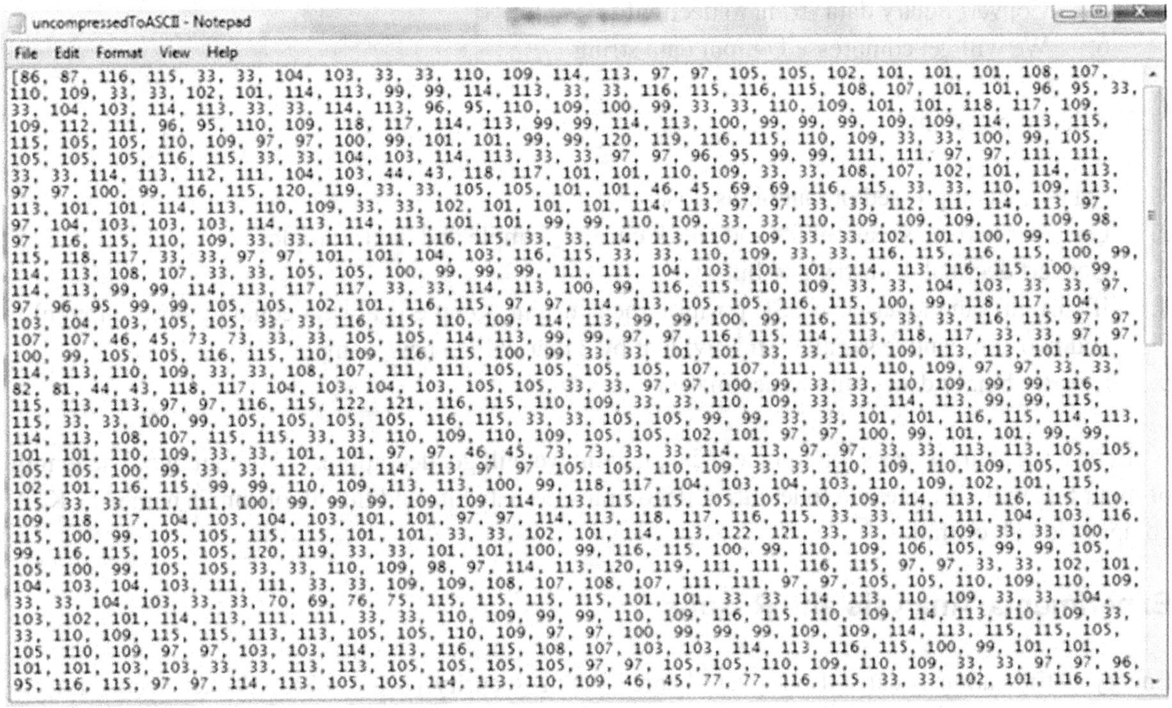

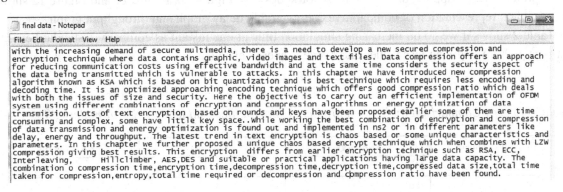

Figure 9. ASCII to Original converted file

final data - Notepad

File Edit Format View Help

With the increasing demand of secure multimedia, there is a need to develop a new secured compression and encryption technique where data contains graphic, video images and text files. Data compression offers an approach for reducing communication costs using effective bandwidth and at the same time considers the security aspect of the data being transmitted which is vulnerable to attacks. In this chapter we have introduced new compression algorithm known as KSA which is based on bit quantization and is best technique which requires less encoding and decoding time. It is an optimized approaching encoding technique which offers good compression ratio which deals with both the issues of size and security. Here the objective is to carry out an efficient implementation of OFDM system using different combinations of encryption and compression algorithms or energy optimization of data transmission. Lots of text encryption based on rounds and keys have been proposed earlier some of them are time consuming and complex, some have little key space..While working the best combination of encryption and compression of data transmission and energy optimization is found out and implemented in ns2 or in different parameters like delay, energy and throughput. The latest trend in text encryption is chaos based or some unique characteristics and parameters. In this chapter we further proposed a unique chaos based encrypt technique which when combines with LZW compression giving best results. This encryption differs from earlier encryption technique such as RSA, ECC, Interleaving, Hillclimber, AES,DES and suitable or practical applications having large data capacity. The combination o compression time,encryption time,decompression time,decryption time,compressed data size,total time taken for compression,entropy,total time required or decompression and cpmpression ratio have been found.

Advanced Compression and Decompression Algorithm

The different steps of the proposed algorithm are:

1. Take input data string of random length or specified length.
2. Decimate the data length by 2
3. Convert decimal data string to binary
4. Find the polarity of consecutive input sample as
   If next_sample > current_sample
   Make LSB bit of current output as '1'

Else make LSB bit of current output as '0'
5. Convert binary data string to decimal
6. We will get compressed output data string

For decompression:

1. Take first compressed output bit as it is.
2. Consider two consecutive bits and check current_sample and next_sample
3. Convert decimal data string to binary
4. If current_sample has 1 in LSB position then current_sample is always equal to new_output else add two consecutive samples and divide it by 2 that will be new_sample
5. Convert binary data string to decimal.

Repeat the same process for complete data length; we will get decompressed output bits. The length of input bits will always equal to length of decompressed data bits and this algorithm is named as KSA compression algorithm.

Experimental Analysis and Results

Energy optimization is carried out over channels using security protocol SSL(Socket Secure Layer) and NS2 software. The number of nodes can be varied, start and stop time can also be varied and can observe various parameters like energy, delay and throughput. Table 2 shows energy comparison table when protocol is not applied and using KSA for nodes=30. Figure 10, Figure 11 and Figure 12 shows the graphical representation of comparative energy graph, delay graph and throughput graph.

Table 2 shows if we go on increasing simulation time at one instant as compare to standard energy parameters KSA is giving less values and hence is energy efficient.

Table 2. Energy Comparison table when protocol is not applied and using KSA for nodes=30

Simulation Time	O-Energy	Energy	KSA_Energy
0	110	82	50
5	200	142	92
10	210	170	99
15	220	178	99
20	230	180	100
25	220	182	100
30	210	180	100

Figure 10. Comparative energy graph with number of nodes = 50 and stop time = 0.1sec

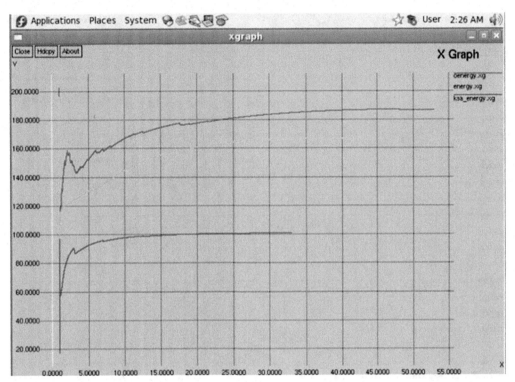

Figure 11. Comparative delay graph with number of nodes = 50 and stop time = 0.1sec

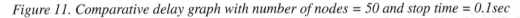

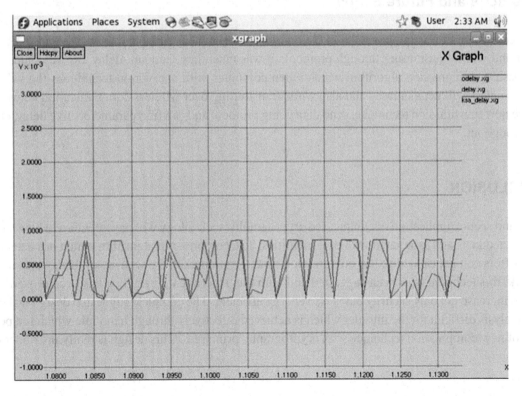

Figure 12. Comparative throughput graph with number of nodes = 50 and stop time = 0.1sec

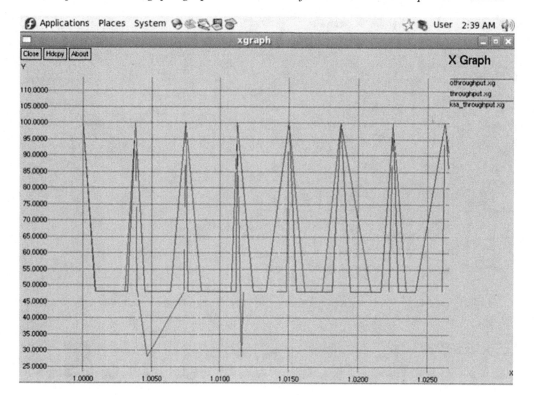

Limitations and Future Scope

Lossy compression was implemented in the complete work where editable data was dumped, difficult to edit and while transmitting through protocols it was taken large amount delay. So we could design new lossless compression algorithm which when combines with encryption techniques the values of the parameters will get increased and also while transmitting over wireless communication network we can use new transmission technique, send data using protocol and can find parameters like delay, energy and throughput.

CONCLUSION

A safe and secure application of compressed cryptographic technology will pay attention to how hackers are detected keys and associated with user identities. The compression algorithm which has been introduced offers compression with less compression time. To strengthen the security of the communication network, this technique has been suggested and with the experimental results it has been proved that it leads to increase not only security but is also energy efficient. The complete suggested design makes the cryptanalysis difficult for the intruder which is achieved effectively through a module which is a perfect blend of new compression technique with cryptography principles. This design is really instrumental in providing very big challenge to the intruders who attempt to break the algorithms by any means. The encryption technique introduced in this paper is implemented using Java by giving example and is showing practical results of how data gets read, compressed, converted in to ASCII, encrypted, what is exact size of original file, compressed, encrypted, decrypted and decompressed file. The complete suggested encryption algorithm makes the cryptanalysis difficult for the intruder which is achieved effectively through a module and is a perfect blend of new symmetric encryption technique with modular cryptographic principles. This design is really instrumental in providing very big challenge to the intruders who attempt to break the algorithms by any means. Thus, it can be concluded that the secret data can be transmitted securely in an insecure media using this module. Proposed algorithm is viewed best in terms of speed, cost, throughput, security and power consumption.

REFERENCES

Akyildiz, I. F., Melodia, T., & Chowdhury, K. R. (2007). A survey on wireless multimedia sensor networks. *Elsevier. Computer Networks*, *51*(4), 921–960. doi:10.1016/j.comnet.2006.10.002

Idrizi, F., Dalipi, F., & Rustemi, E. (2013). Analyzing the speed of combined cryptographic algorithms with secret and public key. *International Journal of Engineering Research and Development*, *8*(2), 4.

Bisht, N., & Singh, S. (2015). A Comparative Study of Some Symmetric and Asymmetric Key Cryptography Algorithm. *International Journal of Innovative Research in Science. Engineering and Technology*, *4*(3), 102.

Bisht, N., & Singh, S. (2015). A Comparative Study of Some Symmetric and Asymmetric Key Cryptography Algorithms. *International Journal of Innovative Research in Science*, *4*(3), 10281.

Brumley, B.B., & Hakala, R.M. (2009). Cache-timing template attacks. In *ASIACRYPT* (Vol. 5912, pp. 667-684).

Celikel, E., & Dalkilic, M. E. (2004). Experiments on a secure compression. *Proceedings of the International Conference on Information Technology: Coding and Computing ITCC '04* (Vol. 2, pp. 150-152). IEEE.

Charfi, Y., Wakamiya, N., & Murata, M. (2009). Challenging issues in visual sensor networks. *IEEE Wireless Communications*, *16*(2), 44–49. doi:10.1109/MWC.2009.4907559

Culurciello, E., & Andreou, A. G. (2006). CMOS image sensors for sensor networks. *Analog Integrated Circuits and Signal Processing*, *49*(1), 39–51. doi:10.100710470-006-8737-x

Dey, N. S. (2017). *Intelligent Techniques in Signal Processing for Multimedia Security*. Switzerland: Springer International. doi:10.1007/978-3-319-44790-2

Duran-Faundez., & Lecuire, V. (2008.). Error Resilient Image Communication with Chaotic Pixel Interleaving for Wireless Camera Sensors. *Proceedings of the Workshop on Real-World Wireless Sensor Networks (REALWMSN'08)*, Glasgow, Scotland.

Jain, A., Lakhtaria, K. I., & Srivastav, P. (2013). A Comparative Study of Lossless Compression Algorithm on Text Data. *Proceedings of the International Conference on Advances in Computer Science* (p. 536). AETACS Elsevier Digital Library.

Jain, Y. K., & Gosavi, P. B. (2008). Email Security using Encryption and Compression. *Proceedings of the IEEE Int. Conf. of Comput. Intel. Model. Control Autom.* (p. 136).

Kaddachi, M. L., & Soudani, A. (2010). *Efficient hardware solution for low power and adaptive image-compression in WSN. Proceedings of ICECS* (pp. 583–586). IEEE.

Lenstra, A. K., Hughes, J. P., Augier, M., Bos, J. W., Kleinjung, C.T., & Wachter. (2012). Public keys. In *Crypto, LNCS* (Vol. 7417, pp. 626-642).

Marcelloni, F. (2008). A Simple Algorithm for Data Compression in Wireless Sensor Networks. IEEE communications letters, 12(6), 411-413.

Motgi, N., & Mukherjee, A. (2001). Network Conscious Text Compression Systems (NCTCSys). *Proceedings of International Conference on Information and Theory: Coding and Computing*, Las Vegas, USA. IEEE Computer Society.

Nadeem, A. (2006). A performance comparison of data encryption algorithms. Proceedings of the First international conference on Information and communication technologies ICICT '05 (pp. 84-89).

Patil, M. V. (2014). SMS text Compression and Encryption on Android O.S. *Proceedings of the International Conference on Computer Communication and Informatics (ICCCI)*. 10.1109/ICCCI.2014.6921767

Sadler, C. M., & Martonosi, M. (2006.). Data compression algorithms for energy-constrained devices in delay tolerant networks. *Proceedings of the ACM Conference on Embedded Networked Sensor Systems (SenSys)*. 10.1145/1182807.1182834

Sagheer, A.M., Al-Ani, M.S., & Mahdi, O.A. (2013). Ensure Security of Compressed Data Transmission. *Proceedings of the Sixth International Conference on Developments in eSystems Engineering* (pp. 270-275). IEEE Computer Society of India. 10.1109/DeSE.2013.55

Sangwan, N. (2013). Combining Huffman text compression with new double encryption algorithm. *Proceedings of the IEEE International Conference on Emerging Trends in Communication, Control, Signal Processing & Computing Applications (C2SPCA)*.

Savari, M., Montazerolzohour, M., & Thiam, Y. E. (2012). Combining Encryption Methods in Multi-purpose Smart Card. *Proceedings of the IEEE Int. Conf. CyberSec.*

Shahi, G., & Singh, C. (2013). Securing and Compressing Transmission over LAN by using Public Key Cryptography. *International Journal of Innovative Research in Computer and Communication Engineering, 1*(7), 2320–9798.

Stallings & William. (2005). *Cryptography and Network Security: Principles and Practices (4ᵗʰ ed., Vol. 8)*. Prentice Hall International .

Suarjaya, M. A. (2012). A New Algorithm for Data Compression Optimization. *International Journal of Advanced Computer Science and Applications*, *3*(8), 14–17.

Ukhopadhyay, B. A. (2010). Cryptography and network security (2nd ed.). New Delhi: Mc Graw Hill Education.

This research was previously published in the International Journal of Synthetic Emotions (IJSE), 7(2); edited by Amira S. Ashour and Nilanjan Dey; pages 78-96, copyright year 2016 by IGI Publishing (an imprint of IGI Global).

Chapter 11
Applicability of Cellular Automata in Cryptanalysis

Harsh Bhasin
Jawahar Lal Nehru University, India

Naved Alam
Jamia Hamdard, India

ABSTRACT

Cryptanalysis refers to finding the plaintext from the given cipher text. The problem reduces to finding the correct key from a set of possible keys, which is basically a search problem. Many researchers have put in a lot of effort to accomplish this task. Most of the efforts used conventional techniques. However, soft computing techniques like Genetic Algorithms are generally good in optimized search, though the applicability of such techniques to cryptanalysis is still a contentious point. This work carries out an extensive literature review of the cryptanalysis techniques, finds the gaps there in, in order to put the proposed technique in the perspective. The work also finds the applicability of Cellular Automata in cryptanalysis. A new technique has been proposed and verified for texts of around 1000 words. Each text is encrypted 10 times and then decrypted using the proposed technique. The work has also been compared with that employing Genetic Algorithm. The experiments carried out prove the veracity of the technique and paves way of Cellular automata in cryptanalysis. The paper also discusses the future scope of the work.

1. INTRODUCTION

One of the most important factors responsible for the development of human race is the ability to communicate. The development and the design of communication system has become one of the most contentious issues. The security of communication is, therefore, one of the most essential attributes in any communication system. The development in the field of cryptography has helped achieve the dream of a secured communication. However, the system becomes vulnerable in one of the following cases. The intruder might want to 'listen' to the communication, which is referred to as eavesdropping. The

DOI: 10.4018/978-1-7998-1763-5.ch011

intruder might want to change data or worse might use it for some other purpose. A sound cryptography technique prohibits any of these. One of the easiest methods of cryptography is to apply XOR function on the data (plaintext) and key. The resultant is referred to as cipher-text. The key when XOR-ed with the plaintext again produces plaintext (Bruce, 1995; & Rothe, 2002). The soundness of a system, though, is not easy to ascertain. The breakability of the key can be one of the major factors in determining the goodness of a system.

One of the ways of doing so is to find how good a system is to diversified attacks. Given the cipher-text, the process of finding the plaintext is referred to as Cryptanalysis. Cryptanalysis has been one of the most researched topics in the field of Network Security. Various researchers have devised different methodologies to accomplish the task. Owing to the importance of the topic, it is therefore necessary to carry out an extensive literature review of the techniques and find the gaps therein. The review is also important to justify the applicability of soft computing techniques, especially Cellular Automata (CA), to handle the problem. The work intends to achieve the above goals.

The goals of this paper are as follows.

- To carry out a literature review of cryptanalysis using soft computing
- To find the gaps in the existing techniques
- To propose a technique using CA
- To verify and validate the technique

The paper has been organized as follows. The second section explains the literature review, the third section explains the concepts of CA, the fourth section explains the proposed work, the fifth section gives the results and the last section concludes. The work paves way of CA in cryptanalysis.

2. LITERATURE REVIEW

Cryptography is one of the most researched topics in Computer Science. The topic is not only important in securing essential data from eavesdropping and theft but has also been used to win wars. The power of cryptography was demonstrated in World War II. Cryptanalysis is the crafting of key, given a set of data and corresponding encrypted code. The researchers developed many models for cryptanalysis during the Second World War. These models proved instrumental in proving a strategic edge to Britain. The development in the field continued there-after, when the world was divided into two groups, both wanting to gain as much information as possible from the other. The turn of events would remind the fraternity of the importance of the cryptography. The breaking of PURPLE by William Friedman, breaking of ENIGMA by Alan Turing, problems faced in accessing the contents of Bin Laden's drive was the constant reminders of the importance of this topic.

The conventional techniques of Cryptanalysis include frequency counts, in order to ascertain the most frequently used syllabi. The use of letters and words in English gives a cue of what to expect from a given text. Another technique of cryptanalysis uses the study and analysis of patterns. Some of the researchers have used side chain attacks for accomplishing the above task but the method works only in constrained environment.

The present work deals with the problem using the power of CA and Neural Networks. In order to put the things in proper perspective, a review of the techniques has been carried out. The review was done to find the gaps in the existing techniques. The summary of the review has been provided in Table 1.

The review points to the fact that techniques like CA have seldom being used by researchers. Moreover, even those who used it have not performed requisite experimentation to verify and validate the work.

Table 1. The summary of the review

S. NO.	Name of Author	Techniques
1.	Bhateja, A	The method uses Genetic Algorithms to break Vigenere cipher. The technique uses Roulette wheel selection; two points cross over and cross mutation.
2.	Luthra J	The work uses the statistical data of the language as the premise. The work combines Genetic Algorithms with the Firefly Algorithm for cryptanalysis of the mono alphabetic substitution cipher.
3.	Shujun Li et al	The work breaks the permutation multimedia cipher. The work has been verified and validated using Quantitative cryptanalysis
4.	Omran, S.S.; Al-Khalid, A.S.; Al-Saady, D.M.	The work breaks then poly alphabetic substitution cipher (Vigenère cipher) by applying genetic algorithms. The work uses frequency analysis as its base
5.	Jun song et al.	The work assigns fitness values to the keys and produces higher fitness value keys. The work proves that a 4 round DES can be broken by the model.
6.	Uddin M. F. and Youness A. M.	The work uses Particle Swarm Optimization (PSO) in the cryptanalysis of classical simple substitution ciphers.
7.	Feng-Tse Lin and Cheng-yan kao	The work presents a cipher text only attack. Genetic Algorithm has been used to break the Vernam cipher. The proposed approach is a cipher-text only attack in which we don't know any plaintext. The only thing we have to know is that the plaintext is an English document.
8.	Girish Mishra, Saravjeet Kaur	The work breaks transposition cipher using Hill Climbing, Simulated annealing and combination of these.
9.	Xingyuan Wang, Qian Wang, Yingqian Zhang	This technique uses a logistic map to generate the keys. The results of the paper points to the fact that this method is better as compared to differential attacks.
10.	Chengqing Li, Shujun-Li, Gonzalo alvarez, Guanrong chen, Kwok Tund Lo	The work uses circular bit shift and XOR operations to generate the data. The work uses Chaotic System for control of pseudorandom bit sequences
11.	Mohammed M. Alani	The work uses a Neural Network based model. The work has been verified for DES and triple DES.
12.	R. Manjula, R. Anitha	the work tests various algorithms and designed a new one. According to the author, the success rate of the is 70 to 75 percent.
13.	Maiya Din, Ashok K Bhateja, Ram Ratan	The work uses Geffe generator, which is a non-linear binary key sequence generator. In this technique, the initial states are the secret key bits that maintain the security of Geffe generator.
14.	S. Franciszek, et., al.	The paper proposes a symmetric key cryptographic design based on 1-D cellular automata with radius 1 and 2. The quality of the system has been tested using standard attacks.
15.	Jaecchul Sung, et., al.	This paper implements self-invertible cellular automata based structure for cryptanalysis and uses the conjugate property as the base.
16.	M. Tomassini, & Mathieu Perrenoud.	The paper proposes 1-D and 2-d non-uniform cellular automata base system for cryptanalysis and discuss its hardware implementation.
17.	Feng Bao	The paper combines affine transformation with cellular automata to produce cryptanalysis system whose security has been tested using standard attacks.
18.	H. Nhasin & N. Arora	The paper proposes genetic algorithm based key generation algorithm and explains the implementation of the system and discusses the results of various attacks on the system.

3. CELLULAR AUTOMATA

The story of CA starts from "A New Kind of Science", a book by Wolfram (1984). The book initiated an intestate in the field, which was reflected in the works of Ulam and Von Neumann (Ulam, 1970) and numerous research papers published thereafter. Since then, CA has been successfully applied to various fields ranging from Artificial Life to Sociology. This paper explores the applicability of this fascinating field in cryptanalysis.

On the face of it, the concept appears naive to some and 'non-scientific' to many. However, rigorous mathematical analysis has proved these skeptics wrong. The simplicity of the concept has made it very popular. The idea that local interactions can generate results which are globally good is fascinating.

"The concept of CA was initiated in the early 1950's by J. Von Neumann and S. Ulam (1970). Von Neumann showed that a cellular automaton can be universal. He devised a CA, each cell of which has a state space of 29 states, and showed that the devised CA can execute any computable operation".

"A cellular automaton is a collection of "colored" cells on a grid of specified shape that evolves through a number of discrete time steps according to a set of rules based on the states of neighboring cells. The rules are then applied iteratively for as many time steps as desired. von Neumann was one of the first people to consider such a model, and incorporated a cellular model into his "universal constructor." Cellular automata were studied in the early 1950s as a possible model for biological systems" (Wolfram 2002).

Cellular Automata is a system which generates patterns that replicate themselves. The astonishing evolution of the development of these patterns forced the scientists to look at it with a whole a new perspective and not just as a game as proposed by John Horton Conway. CA generates complex pattern by simple rules and has been successfully used to reproduce any machine described in the program including a copy of itself (Wolfram, 1984). This amazing ability led a new lease of life to the theory of self-replication and the scientific fraternity has been inching closer to creating machines that can generate machines like themselves.

The mechanism of working of CA is as follows. In a CA, the state of an individual cell changes with time. The state at an instance depends on the present state of that cell and that of the neighbors. These local interactions result in fascinating patterns. These states are governed by rules.

Elementary CA is one dimensional automaton with two possible states per cell. These states are 1 or 0. 1 represents a live cell and 0 represents a dead cell. A cell's neighbors defined as the cell on either side of it. A cell and its two neighbors form a neighborhood of 3 cells, so there are 2^3 i.e. 8 possible patterns for a neighborhood. So, there are 2^8 i.e. 256 possible rules. However, there are versions of CA which consider more than two neighbors also. The rules generate fascinating pattern which are not just stunning but can also form the basis of generating initial population for GAs after minor modification. The above concept has been used as the starting point of the work proposed.

The number of rules depends on the number of neighbors. For instance, a three neighborhood CA would have 2^3 possible combinations and hence 2^8, that is 256 rules. The Universal nature of CA has been proved by Von Neumann. As a matter of fact, the rules given by Von Neumann were never implemented.

The present popularity of CA's can be attributed to "The Game of Life", given by Convoy (Gardner, 1970). The formulation of the present set of rules is attributed to Stephen Wolfram (Wolfram, 1984). The detailed and involved work of Wolfram formed the basis of the practical implementations on which many complex simulations were based.

As per Biswas (Sikdar, 2000) researchers should be able to predict the global behavior from the local CA rules. Once this goal is achieved, one should be able to design the local rules/initial conditions from a given prescribed global behavior.

4. PROPOSED WORK

The work proposes a model to find the key, given a sample having plaintext and cipher text, by making use of a model based on CA. Primarily, the task reduces to finding the requisite patterns. Here it may be stated that, regression using a machine learning technique can also accomplish the above task. However, the task here is to develop a mechanism for regression using CA. The work is based on the ability of Cellular automata to generate and identify patterns. The task has been accomplished as follows.

First of all, the bit string for the plaintext and the cipher text are converted into patterns (note that the strings are only 0^s and 1^s). The crafting of these patterns would form the basis of the rest of the work.

These patterns are then mapped to the most similar ones using a neural network based pattern recognizer. The step relies on the ability of a Neural Network to locate similar patterns. The appropriate rule number and the row number of the most similar pattern are then extracted. In the results section it has been stated that rule number 110 (Figure 1) proved to be one of the most useful rule for accomplishing this task (Figure 1).

Figure 1. Rule 110

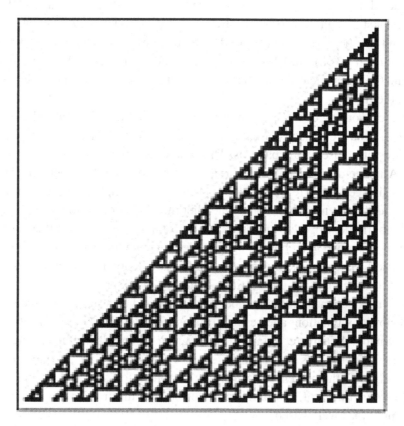

This is followed by preparation of a table consisting of the above data. This data forms the basis of the further analysis.

To summarize the formation of patterns using the given text and the corresponding cipher text is followed by the identification of the row number and the rule number of CA. This precarious task can be carried out using Neural Networks.

The model is trained using 70% of the data collected. The trained model is then verified and validated using 30% of the above data.

4.1. Analysis of the Data

The collected data was a set of a 3,000 plaintext (16 bit) and corresponding cipher text (16 bits), the key (16 bit) was also used in order to train the model.

The data was divided into two parts. 70% data was used for training the model and 30% for verification. The data used for training had three fields: plaintext, cipher text and the key. A connectionist, back propagation model using the CA rule and the cipher text was then developed, the key obtained and the actual key were XORed to find the Hamming distance between them. Less the Hamming distance, better the model. The coefficients of the model were assigned and modulated using the above Hamming distance. The process has been depicted in Figure 2. The model was then used to find the keys for the rest of 30% data (Figure 3). The procedure has been elucidated in Algorithm 1.

The above process has been summarized in the following Algorithm (Algorithm 1) which takes a set of Plaintexts and Cipher texts as input. The process has been explained in the above discussion and depicted in Figure 2 and 3.

Algorithm 1. *Cellular Automata Based Cryptanalysis System*
        Input: Plaintext (P_i), Key (K_i), Ciphertext (C_i)
1. Apply Neural Network Based Pattern similarity module to find the appropriate rule number (r_i) and row number (row_i) from the repository of the CA based patterns.
2. Populate the data table from rule number (r_i) and row number (row_i) and the K_i.
3. Apply NN Based Regression analyser
4. Find the Hamming distance between the unknown keys obtained and the K_is.
5. Reconfigure the NN Feedback model as per the above results.

The above model has been implemented and results are encouraging. The results obtained have been discussed in the next section.

5. RESULTS

The proposed model has been implemented and the results have been reported in this section. The discussion, conclusions and future scope have been presented in the next section.

Figure 2. CA based cryptanalysis system (CABCS): Training Phase

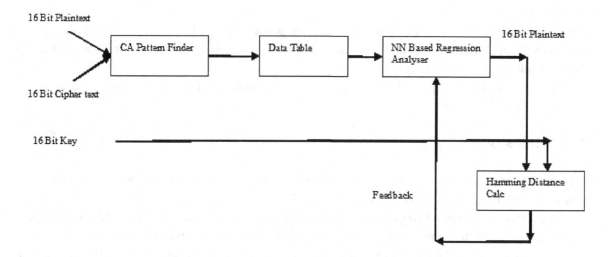

Figure 3. CA based cryptanalysis system (CABCS): Verification Phase

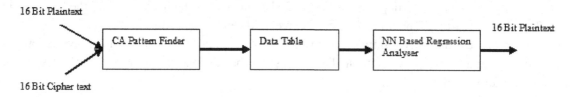

5.1. Data Collection

As stated in the previous section, the data collection was done with utmost care and through analysis. The data was collected as follows. 100 English text documents of about 500 words were collected. This was followed by randomly selecting around 3000 syllables. These were then converted into ASCII values and the sum was converted into a 16-bit binary number.

5.2. Encryption

The data was encrypted using a modified DES simulator developed in C#. The text obtained was of 16 bits. The binary data was then XORed with the keys to obtain the cipher text.

5.3. Model Application

The Cellular Automata Based Cryptanalysis System (as explained in the previous section) was then applied to the data. The results obtained were as follows.

5.4. Results

The system used pre-crafted tools for NN based pattern recognizer, and modified regression analyzer. The results were as follows (Table 2). As stated earlier 3000 sets were taken. The model, after training, produced 1372 correct keys. The number of keys that were differing in just one bit were 654. The number of keys having Hamming distance 2 were 214, and those having a Hamming distance 3 to 5 were 721. The results have been summarized in Figure 4 and Figure 5.

As against this, in the model employing genetic algorithms 1201 correct keys were obtained. The number of keys differing in a single bit were 543. The comparison has been shown in Figure 6. In the figure the dark columns depict the data of the proposed work and the light colored columns depict the data of the model that uses GA.

The results obtained were encouraging and pave way of the application of Neural Networks and Cellular Automata in cryptanalysis. Moreover, as compared to the model employing genetic algorithms, the results are better.

Table 2. Results

Result	Number	Percentage
Number of Plaintext, keys and Ciphertexts	3000	
Correct results Obtained	1372	45.73333333
Results obtained with 1 incorrect bit	654	21.8
Results obtained with 2 incorrect bit	214	7.133333333
Results obtained with 3-5 incorrect bits	721	24.03333333
Rest	39	1.3

Figure 4. The results (Pi Chart)

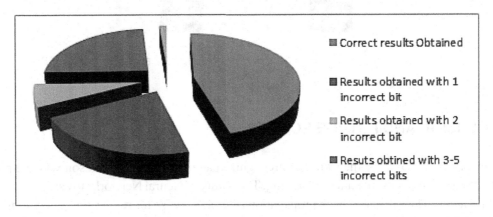

Figure 5. Number of results obtained in various categories

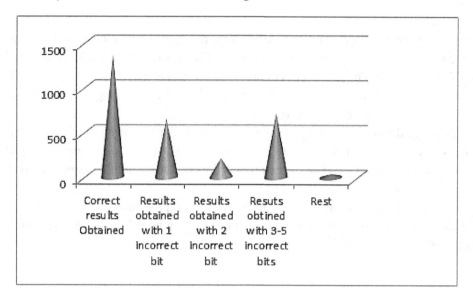

Figure 6. Comparison of the proposed technique and the technique that uses GA

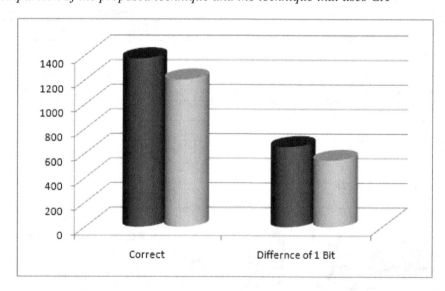

6. CONCLUSION AND FUTURE SCOPE

Neural networks are known for their knack to recognize patterns. This is the reason why the proposed model uses Neural Networks for pattern matching. The ability of Neural Networks to carry out regression is also well known. The work uses back propagation Neural Network for regression. The premise of the work is the ability of the CA to map patterns, which has ability to map and reproduce data. This ability has been used in various disciplines including social sciences. This makes a good case for using CA in cryptanalysis. The proposed model was developed, implemented, trained and verified. The results have been presented in the previous section and are encouraging. Though the exact keys were not obtained in all the cases, the work at establishes the ability of CA based model to predict the keys, given sufficient data. The work is now been extended and the various types of Neural Network based models are being used both for pattern matching and regression. The extension of this work would test the model with AES keys. Moreover, the number of bits in the new setup would be increased to 128. It is also being analyzed so as to why some patterns are more helpful in cryptanalysis as compared to others. A novel model involving Diploid Genetic Algorithm (DGA) is being developed. In order to extend the work, a comprehensive literature review has already been carried out (Bhasin, 2015). The technique has also been applied on a NP Hard problem and the results are encouraging (Bhasin, 2015). The future work would work on a model which uses DGA and CA to carry out cryptanalysis. The data for verification and validation has also been collected.

REFERENCES

Alani, M. M. (2012). Neuro Cryptanalysis of DES and Triple DES. *Neural Information Processing, 7667*, 637–646. doi:10.1007/978-3-642-34500-5_75

Bao, F. (2004). Cryptanalysis of a partially known cellular automata cryptosystem. *IEEE transaction on computers, 53*(11), 1493-1497.

Bhasin, H., & Mehta, S. (2015). On the applicability of diploid genetic algorithms. AI & society, 31(2), 265-274.

Bhasin, H., & Arora, N. (2010). Cryptography using genetic algorithms.

Bhateja, A. (2014). Genetic Algorithm with elitism for cryptanalysis of vigenere cipher, Issues and challenges. Paper presented at ICICT (pp. 373-377).

Gardner, M. (1970). Mathematical Games – The fantastic combinations of John Conway's new solitaire game "life". Scientific American. 223, 120–123.

Girish, M., & Kaur, S. (2015). Cryptanalysis of transposition cipher using hill climbing and simulated annealing. *Proceedings of International conference on soft computing for problem solving, Advances in intelligent systems and computing* (Vol. 336, pp. 293-302). DOI:10.1007/978-81-322-2220-0_23

H. Bhasin et., al. (2015). On the applicability of diploid genetic algorithms in dynamic environments. Proceedings of the 2014 international conference on Soft computing and machine intelligence (pp. 94-97).

Li, S., Li, C., Chen, G., Bourbakis, N.G., & Lo, K.-T. (2008). A general quantitative cryptanalysis of permutation-only multimedia ciphers against plaintext attacks. *Signal Processing Image Communication, 23*(3), 212-223. DOI:1016/j.image.2008.01.003

Lin, F.-T., & Kao, C.-Y. (1995). A genetic algorithm for cipher text only attack in cryptanalysis, Systems, man and cybernetics. In *Intelligent systems for the 21st century* (Vol. 1, pp 650-654). DOI:. doi:10.1109/ICSMC.1995.537837

Luthra J. (2011, December). A Hybrid firefly algorithm using genetic operators for the cryptanalysis of a mono alphabetic substitution cipher. *Proceedings of the Information and communication technologies* (pp. 202-206). Doi:10.1109/WICT.2011.6141244

M. din et., al. (2014). Cryptanalysis of Geffe Generator Using Genetic Algorithm. *Proceedings of the third international conference on soft computing for problem solving, advances in intelligent systems and computing* (pp. 509-514). Doi:10.1007/978-81-322-1768-8_45

Manjula, R., & Anitha, R. (2011). Identification of Encryption Algorithm using Decision tree. *Advanced computing communications in computer and information science*, 133, 237-246. Doi:10.1007/978-3-642-17881-8_23

Omran, S., Al-Khalid, A.S., & Alsaady, D. (2010, December). Using Genetic Algorithm to Break a Mono-Alphabetic Substitution Cipher. *Proceedings of ICOS IEEE Conference* (pp. 63-67). DOI:10.1109/ICOS.2010.5720065

Li, C., Li, S., Alvarez, G., Chen, G., & Lo, K.-T. (2007). Cryptanalysis of two chaotic encryption schemes based on circular bit shift and XOR operations. *Physics Letters. [Part A]*, 369(1-2), 23–30. doi:10.1016/j.physleta.2007.04.023

Rothe, J. (2002). Some facets of complexity theory and cryptography: A five-lecture tutorial. *ACM Comput. Surv.* 34(4), 504-549. Doi:10.1145/592642.592646

Schneier, B. (1995). Applied cryptography (2nd ed.). New York: John Wiley & Sons, Inc.

Seredynski, F., Bouvry, P., & Zomaya, A. Y. (2004). Cellular automata computation and secret key cryptography. *Parallel Computing*, 30(5-6), 753–766. doi:10.1016/j.parco.2003.12.014

Sikdar, B. K., Paul, K., Biswas, G. P., Yang, C., Boppana, V., Mukherjee, S., & Pal Chaudhuri, P. (2000, January). Theory and 28 Application of GF(2p) Cellular Automata as On-Chip Test Pattern Generator. *Proceedings Intl. Conf. on VLSI Design*, India (pp. 556–561).

Song, J., Zhang, H., Meng, Q., & Wang, Z. (2007). Cryptanalysis of four-round DES Based on Genetic algorithm. *Wireless communications. Networking and Mobile Computing.* Doi:10.1109/WICOM.2007.580

Sung, J., Hong, D., & Hong, S. (2007). Cryptanalysis of an involutional block cipher using cellular automata. *Information processing letters, 104*(5), 183-185.

Tumassini, M., & Perrenoud, M. (2001). Cryptography with cellular automata. *Applied soft computing, 1*(2), 151-160.

Uddin, M.F., & Youseef, A.M. (2006). Cryptanalysis of simple substitution ciphers using particle swarm optimization. *Evolutionary computation* (pp. 677-680). Doi:10.1109/CEC.2006.1688376

Ulam, S. (1970). Some mathematical problems connected with patterns of growth figures. In A. W. Burks (Ed.), *Essays on Cellular Automata*. Illinois: Univ. Illinois Press.

Wang, X., Wang, Q., & Zhang, Y. (2015). A fast image algorithm based on rows and columns switch. *Nonlinear Dynamics*, 79(2), 1141-1149. Doi:10.100711071-014-1729-y

Wolfram, S. (1984). Computation theory of cellular automata. *Communications in Mathematical Physics*, *96*(1), 15–57. doi:10.1007/BF01217347

Wolfram, S. (2002). *A new kind of science*. Champaign, IL, USA: Wolfram Media.

This research was previously published in the International Journal of Applied Metaheuristic Computing (IJAMC), 8(2); edited by Peng-Yeng Yin; pages 38-48, copyright year 2017 by IGI Publishing (an imprint of IGI Global).

Section 3
Encryption Keys and Homomorphic Encryption

Chapter 12
A Novel Approach of Symmetric Key Cryptography using Genetic Algorithm Implemented on GPGPU

Srinivasa K. G.
M. S. Ramaiah Institute of Technology, India

Siddesh G. M.
M. S. Ramaiah Institute of Technology, India

Srinidhi Hiriyannaiah
M. S. Ramaiah Institute of Technology, India

Anusha Morappanavar
M. S. Ramaiah Institute of Technology, India

Anurag Banerjee
M. S. Ramaiah Institute of Technology, India

ABSTRACT

The world of digital communication consists of various applications which uses internet as the backbone for communication. These applications consist of data related to the users of the application, which is confidential and integrity needs to be maintained to protect against unauthorized access and use. In the information hiding field of research, Cryptography is one of the wide techniques used to provide security to the internet applications that overcome the challenges like confidentiality, integrity, authentication services etc. In this paper, we present a novel approach on symmetric key cryptography technique using genetic algorithm that is implemented on CUDA architecture.

DOI: 10.4018/978-1-7998-1763-5.ch012

INTRODUCTION

In the internet era of applications, confidentiality, security, integrity and authentication services are increasingly becoming more important (Viega & McGraw, 2001). One of the key techniques used for providing secure communication is cryptography. Cryptography generally deals with exchange of messages between the sender and the receiver using some secure keys with encryption (encoding) and decryption (decoding). A brief introduction of cryptography, key components of it and its different types are discussed in section 1.

In the evolution of nature, a biological entity that adapts to the changes in the environment has better chances of survival according to the Darwin's theory of evolution. This analogy is applied to genetic programming, which uses theory of evolution steps to draw a better solution to a problem being solved by an algorithm (Kahn, 1996). The steps involved in genetic algorithm or programming is discussed in section 2.

With the advent of increasing multi-core processors, applications being developed need to utilize the threads functionality of these processors. Compute Unified Device Architecture (CUDA), a unified programming model was introduced by Nvidia, which facilitates programming both sequential and parallel portions of a program within a single unit (Nickolls et al., 2008). The different components of CUDA and its architecture are discussed in section 3.

Random numbers are generally used in cryptography for encryption and decryption. Many methods can be used in generating random numbers. The method of creating pseudo- random numbers using genetic algorithms involves more computation power, which can be processed using GPU using CUDA architecture. These pseudo random numbers are generated with linear congruential method. With the help of genetic algorithms implemented using CUDA architecture, the pseudo random numbers are used for encryption and decryption. The algorithm is compared with computation time spent on the CPU and the results are encouraging with CUDA. The paper is organized as follows. In section 1 we discuss briefly concepts related to cryptography, section 2 on genetic algorithms, section 3 on CUDA, section 4 on pseudo random generation and in the later sections, proposed approach and experimental results are discussed.

1. CRYPTOGRAPHY

In our daily life of internet applications and email systems, keeping data and messages confidentially is more important, for example in the launch of nuclear codes and other mission critical systems, in spy's profession the data confidentiality is not compromised. The science of protection of data and communications is called Cryptography (Viega & McGraw, 2001) and (Stinson, 2005). There are many applications where cryptography is applied currently in the fields of e-commerce transactions where examples include purchase using credit cards, wire money transfer etc. In this section, we discuss basic terminologies that are used in cryptography.

The transmission of a message involves two key elements namely the sender and the receiver. In Cryptography the messages are sent between sender and the receiver using encryption and decryption techniques, ensuring the information is received by the intended receivers without any intruders in the middle of the communication (Kessler, 2015). The basic model and different terminologies used in the cryptography are as shown in the Figure 1.

- **Plain Text:** The message that needs to be transmitted from the sender to the receiver in the original form.
- **Encryption:** A phase where the original message is encoded using a key.
- **Cipher Text:** The text that is the result of the encryption phase.
- **Decryption:** A phase of extracting the original message from the encoded message using a key.

The two basic methods of cryptography are *symmetric* and *asymmetric* cryptography (Stanoyevitch, 2010) and (Hellman, 2002). In symmetric cryptography, both sender and the receiver share the same key for encryption and decryption respectively as shown in the Figure 2 (Hellman, 2002). Thus, the key shared in this method needs to be more secure and powerful. In asymmetric cryptography, both sender and the receiver share different public and private keys for encryption and decryption respectively.

Cipher text plays an important role in cryptography, which must be kept secret and secure from the intruders. The analysis and study of breaking cipher text is called cryptanalyis (Barak et al., 2001). In order to generate keys required for the encryption and decryption, random numbers can be generated and same can be used as keys. These random numbers should be large in number and feasible enough to keep away from the intruders (Koblitz, 1994). Genetic programming can be used in evolving the population of random numbers using different techniques of it (Barker & Kelsey, 2012). In our approach, the random numbers are generated using linear congruential method and population is evolved using genetic algorithms. We discuss some of the basic steps followed in developing a genetic algorithm in the next section.

Figure 1. Basic model of cryptography

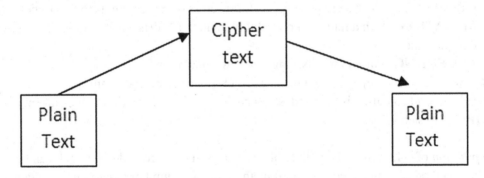

Figure 2. Symmetric key cryptography

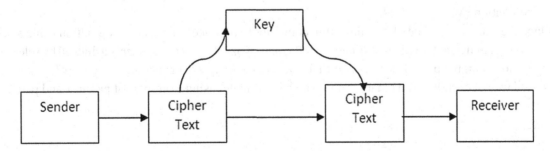

2. GENETIC ALGORITHMS

In nature, in the evolution of life, adaptation is always a key survival entity related to any biological life. Darwin's theory of evolution is applied for the survival of the fittest in the environment where biological entities exist. This theory of evolution can be applied to solving computer problems called as Genetic programming (Mitchell, 1999). The degree of adaptation of a solution to a given problem determines the fitness of the solution for a given population of inputs to the problem. A new population of solution might emerge that depends on the degree of adaptation determined (Thede, 2004). In this section, we describe in brief about genetic programming and its steps.

A genetic algorithm is a type of searching algorithm that uses the concept of survival of the fittest in the theory of evolution [10]. It searches a solution for a given problem using a list of the populations of solutions. It starts initially with a population of solutions, then evolves this population of solution using techniques of genetic evolution (cross over & mutation) in (Thede, 2004) and (Koza, 1992). The algorithm is terminated with a suitable condition when the best solution of population is achieved. The generic steps involved in the genetic algorithm are as follows and is as shown in the Figure 3.

1. **START:** Generate random population of n individuals (using some suitable method).
2. **FITNESS:** Evaluate the fitness $f(x)$ of each individual x in the population.
3. **NEW POPULATION:** Create a new population by repeating following steps until the new population is complete.
   a. **SELECTION:** Select two parent individuals from a population according to their fitness (the better fitness, the bigger chance to be selected).
   b. **CROSSOVER:** With a crossover probability, cross over the parents to form a new offspring.
   c. **MUTATION:** With a mutation probability, mutate the offspring at some locus (position in chromosome).
   d. **ACCEPTING:** Place new offspring in a new population.
4. **REPLACE:** Use new generated population for a further run of algorithm
5. **TEST:** If the end condition is satisfied, stop and return the best solution in the current population.
6. **LOOP:** Go to step 2.

The *population* of solutions is the initial collection of solutions considered which can be generated using random methods like linear congruential method, random number streams etc. An *individual* solution is a single solution in the population. The fitness of an individual solution produces the absolute value of the solution, which evaluates the fitness priority of the individual over other individual solutions in the population (Mitchell, 1999).

Once the fitness is evaluated, the algorithm continues to produce a new set of population using selection, crossover and mutation methods (Thede, 2004) and (Koza, 1992). *Crossover* is achieved by selecting a random locus on the pair of parents and their bits are exchanged to generate two new offspring. The most used way of encoding is a binary string which is as shown using examples of parent 1 and parent 2.

```
Parent 1 = 1101100100110110
Parent 2 = 1101111000011110
```

Figure 3. Steps in genetic algorithm

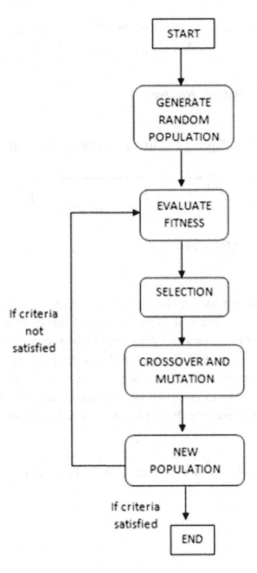

One of the ways to do crossover is to choose some crossover point randomly. Everything before this point is copied from first parent and everything after this point is copied from second parent [10] [11]. An example is as shown below.

Example: If the crossover point is chosen as the position after 5ᵗʰ bit, then crossover looks like:

```
Parent 1        11011 | 00100110110
Parent 2        11011 | 11000011110
Offspring 1     11011 | 11000011110
Offspring 2     11011 | 00100110110
```

Box 1.

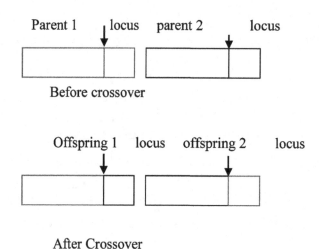

This is known as Single point crossover (Koza, 1992)– one crossover point is selected, binary string from the beginning of the chromosome to the crossover point is copied from one parent and the binary string from the crossover point to the end is copied from another parent (Box 1).

Mutation is achieved by selecting a random bit in the offspring and inverting it. The new offspring generated are placed in the next generation (Mitchell, 1999), (Thede, 2004) and (Koza, 1992). After a crossover is performed, mutation takes place. Mutation changes the new offspring randomly. For binary encoding, we can switch a few randomly chosen bits from 1 to 0 or from 0 to 1 which as shown in the example below.

Example: If bit 5 is chosen randomly then, mutation would be as follows:

```
Offspring      1100011100000111
```

After mutation,

```
Offspring      1100111100000111
```

Genetic algorithms require faster computation time, as it involves generating initial population, apply cross over and mutation techniques on it. In this regard, we can use CUDA a GPU programming model that facilitates in carrying out large computations with more number of threads. We discuss the CUDA programming model in the next section.

3. CUDA

With the advent of the multi core processors and many core GPUs and their increasing speed, applications needs to be developed that are scalable enough on these processors. In 2007, nvidia released CUDA, a scalable programming model that allows computation to be carried out both on CPU and many core GPUs (NVIDIA, 2007). Many applications related to computation, searching, bio-medical imaging sparse matrices etc are being rapidly developed using the CUDA programming model (Luebke, 2008). In this section, we briefly discuss some of the related key concepts to CUDA.

The three basic features that are offered by CUDA are hierarchy of thread groups, shared memories and barrier synchronization (Nickolls et al., 2008). In developing a parallel algorithm for a problem using CUDA, first the portion of the problem that can be done independently needs to be identified, and further execute these parts across independent parallel threads (Kirk & Hwu, 2012). CUDA is a minimal extension to C and C++ where the functions or full program are kernels. The kernels are executed across parallel threads that are organized using thread blocks and grids. A thread block is a set of threads that executes with barrier synchronization and a shared private memory space among themselves (Nickolls et al., 2008) and (Kirk & Hwu, 2012). A grid is a set of thread blocks that executes independently and parallel. A basic organization of the CUDA with threads, blocks and grids is as shown in the Figure 4. The programmer has to specify the number of threads per block and the number of blocks in the grid. CUDA supports 512 threads in one thread block. Each thread is given a unique id *threadIdx* numbered from *0,1…..blockdim-1* within a thread block. Each block is given a unique id *blockIdx* in the grid.

In order to execute the kernels on CUDA, the data that resides on the host needs to be transferred to the device or GPU first, invoke the kernel with appropriate number of threads and then finally execute it on the device (Kirk & Hwu, 2012). To perform these operations certain keywords are used that suggest the kernels are executed on the device and not on the host. Some of the keywords used are cudaMemcopy(), _global_, <<<>>> .We discuss some of them below that have been used in carrying out in our approach.

A CUDA kernel is recognized by the keyword *__global*. The specifications regarding the number of blocks in the grids and the number of threads in the blocks are provided in the kernel call. To compute in parallel, a number of threads need to be generated while invoking the kernel. CUDA uses dimGrid and dimBlock as the keywords for the parameters in the kernel function to specify the number of threads (NVIDIA, 2015). The kernel call is of the form

```
Kernel<<<dimGrid, dimBlock>>>(parameters..)
```

dimGrid indicates the number of blocks to be invoked in a grid while dimBlock indicates the number of threads to be invoked in a block. More the number of threads, more computation are done in parallel. Once dimGrid and dimBlock are fixed, the threads have to be assigned with their index value to ensure that each thread handles its own data. CUDA provides some keywords like *threadIdx, blockIdx* and *blockDim (*NVIDIA, 2015).

For a one-dimensional array, the index can be assigned as,

```
int tid = threadIdx.x + blockIdx.x * blockDim.x
```

These indices can be incremented as,

```
tid += blockDim.x * gridDim.x;
```

Figure 4. CUDA thread blocks and grids

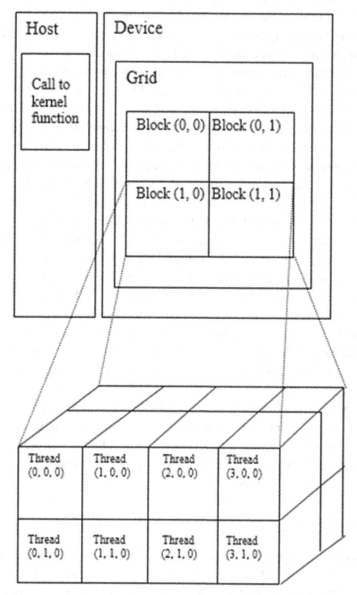

This makes sure that all the threads compute on their respective data without interfering with other data. As these threads work simultaneously, the entire computation can be done much faster than its sequential counterpart.

The kernel gets its input data from the host and the result must be sent back to the host. To accomplish this, data needs to be transferred between the host and the device. *cudaMemcpy()* allows the data transfer between host and the device (NVIDIA, 2015).

```
cudaMemcpy(dest,src,size,type_of_transfer)
```

It copies "*size*" bytes from the memory area pointed to by "*src*" to the memory area pointed to by "*dest*", where "*type_of_transfer*" specifies the direction of transfer.

The CPU and GPU do not have shared memory. They compute on variables that are allocated in their own memory. In CPU, memory can be allotted to variables by simple declaration or by using C function malloc(). The variables to be used in the kernel function must be allocated memory in the host code before invoking the kernel function. This is done by using the function cudaMalloc(). We may want to transfer data from host variables to device variables so that they can be sent as parameters to the kernel function. To do this, cudaMemcpy() is used. Once memory is allotted and data transfer is complete, the kernel is invoked by calling the kernel function. In this function call, number of blocks and number of threads should be specified. Parameters can also be sent. The variables allocated using cudaMalloc() must be sent as pointers. After the execution of kernel function, the data from device variables must be transferred to host variables for further processing. This is again done using cudaMemcpy() function.

The maximum overhead incurred in a GPU code is during the data transfer between host and device. To overcome this overhead, CUDA provides streams to hide the latency(Kirk & Hwu, 2012). The data to be transferred is allocated in the host pinned memory. Copies between pinned memory and device memory can be performed concurrently with kernel execution. Pinned memory can be mapped into the address space of the device, eliminating the need to copy. Allocation in pinned memory is done using *cudaHostAlloc*() function. Simultaneous data transfer can be done by creating CUDA streams. Instructions in the same stream cannot be executed simultaneously. Instructions in different streams can overlap to hide the data transfer latency. *cudaMemcpyAsync*() function is used to carry out simultaneous data transfer (NVIDIA, 2015).

In our approach on the parallel implementation of the encryption and decryption using genetic algorithms CUDA model is used for faster computation which is discussed in section 5 and 6.

4. LINEAR CONGRUENTIAL METHOD OF GENERATING PSEUDO RANDOM NUMBERS

A cryptographic algorithm requires a series of numbers to be produced for encryption and decryption phases. Random number generators are used to produce a stream of numbers for cryptographic algorithms [20]. The random numbers generated usually have two properties namely, uniformity and independence i.e. the random numbers generated are independent from the given continuous sample range. The random numbers generated for computer algorithms are called as pseudo-random numbers that deceive the user; the random numbers does not appear random. One of methods used to generate pseudo-random numbers is linear congruential method (Barker & Kelsey, 2012).

The Linear Congruential Method requires four parameters namely Xn, a, c and m. The random numbers are generated by using the following equation iteratively:

$$Xn+1 = (aXn+c) \bmod m$$

Therefore, generation 1 will be

$$Xo = Xn$$

Xn+1 = (aXo+c) mod m etc.

where Xo is the initial seed, 'a' is constant multiplier, c is the increment and m is modulus.

5. PROPOSED APPROACH

The project consists of two parts: encryption and decryption on the sender and receiver side respectively. Both encryption and decryption require the generation of the array of pseudorandom numbers. We make use of a structure to store the binary representation of the chromosomes and their respective fitness values.

```
typedef struct Chrom
{
        int bit[64];
            int fit;
        int value;
}chrom;
```

The sender and receiver exchange 8 parameters through a secure link. These are:

- **Xn, a, c, and m:** These are used in Linear Congruential Method.
- **Start_number and end_number:** These are used to obtain a subset of the pseudorandom numbers
- **Remainder and Modulus:** These are used to enforce another level of security.

Pseudo random numbers are generated using linear congruential method- sequential. The sequence of random numbers are dependent on one another, hence it is sequentially programmed. These random numbers are selected by evaluating their fitness using GA with steps on cross over and mutation, and done on CUDA architecture. Algorithms 1 to 5 discusses different operations that are followed in genetic algorithms, are presented below which are represented as kernels in CUDA program.

- **Fitness:** Once the array of pseudorandom numbers is created, they are stored in the structure in their binary representation. Their fitness value is calculated by checking if the number is a prime, if it is a prime, a fitness value of 1 is assigned to its structure. If not, a fitness value of 0 is assigned to it. The algorithm for fitness is shown in Algorithm 1.

Algorithm 1. Fitness function

```
Input: array of N numbers
1. for i=0 to N
2. flag=0
3. for j=2 to array[i]
4. if (array[i] % j = 0)
5. flag  = 1
6. if (flag = 0)
```

```
7. chromosome[i].fit = 1
8. else
9. chromosome[i].fit = 0
```

Once the first generation is created, it undergoes genetic algorithm operations to create the next generation of new pseudorandom numbers. The first generation numbers are used in three operations namely survival of the fittest, crossover and mutation.

- **Survival of the Fittest:** The first generation is passed as an argument to the kernel function and the pseudorandom numbers are selected based on their fitness value. The algorithm for the survival is shown in Algorithm 2 (Delman, 2004).

Algorithm 2. Survival of the fittest

```
Input: Array of N numbers with fitness value
1. size=0
2. for i=0 to N
3. if (chromosome[i].fit = 1)
4. array[size] = chromosome[i]
5. size = size + 1
```

Thus, the chromosomes of current population are selected according to their fitness value.

- **Crossover:** The selected generation undergoes crossover (Algorithm 3). The simplest way to do this is to choose some crossover point randomly. Everything before this point is copied from the first parent and everything after the crossover point is copied from the second parent (Bergmann et al., 2008).

Algorithm 3. Crossover

```
Input: Array of selected numbers
1. k = 0
2. Choose a random point in the chromosome
3. for j=0 to size
4. for i =0 to random
5. next[k].bit[i]=current[k].bit[i]
6. next[k+1].bit[i]=current[k+1].bit[i];
7. for i = random to 63
8. next[k].bit[i]=current[k+1].bit[i];
9. next[k+1].bit[i]=current[k].bit[i];
10. calculate fitness
```

Thus, the result of crossover is stored in next population.

- **Mutation:** This generation of numbers undergoes mutation with at low probability of 2%. Single point mutation occurs i.e. a random point is chosen and that bit is inverted (Algorithm 4).

Algorithm 4. Mutation

```
Input: New population
1. Choose a random point
2. row = random%size
3. col = random%66
4. if (next[row].bit[col] = 1)
5. next[row].bit[col] = 0
6. else
7. next[row].bit[col] = 1
8. calculate fitness
```

Thus, the result of mutation is stored in the new population.

Finally, the current population and next population are put together to form an array of pseudorandom numbers.

To form the key, a subset of this array is selected depending on the *start_number* and *end_number* given by the sender and receiver (Algorithm 5). To enforce another level of security, only those numbers which leave remainder *remainder* when divided by *modulus* are selected (Dorrendorf et al., 2007).

Algorithm 5. Creating sub-array

```
Input: Array of pseudorandom numbers
1. for i=0 to array_size
2. if array[i]>=start_number
3. if array[i] <= end_number
4. if array[i]%modulus = remainder
5. store array[i] in the subset array
```

This subset array is used as the key for encryption and decryption. These algorithms are used on sender as well as receiver's side to ensure that the sender and receiver share the key for encryption and decryption. The algorithms for encryption and decryption are presented as below.

Encryption

The encryption algorithm takes an input file which contains the plaintext to be secured. The plaintext is read from a text file in the host code itself. The ascii value of each character is stored in an array called *ascii*. The array of pseudorandom numbers created by using the above mentioned technique is stored in another array called *key*.

To encrypt within a kernel, the required data inputs must be transferred from the host to the device. The *ascii* array and the key array have to be transferred from the host to the device. As these are independent transfers, we create two CUDA streams. Each stream contains one of the transfers. Thus, data transfer is done in parallel and most of the overhead is hidden successfully. To get this done, the *ascii* array and *key* array must be allocated in host pinned memory. The algorithm for encryption is as shown in the Figure 5 and Algorithm 6.

Algorithm 6. Encryption

```
1. int tid= threadIdx.x + blockIdx.x * blockDim.x;
2. For every ascii value
3. r = (key[tid])%ascii[tid];
4. q = (key[tid])/ascii[tid];
5. tid+= blockDim.x * gridDim.x;
```

This computation is of the type SIMD. The same computation is done on a large set of data and can be easily parallelized by invoking many threads. Thus, the kernel function is

```
Encrypt<<<dimGrid,dimBlock>>>(....)
```

Example: If dimGrid = 512, that means 512 blocks are invoked and if dimBlock = 512, each block generates 512 threads. This is where high performance is achieved.

Once the control returns back to the host, the array of quotients and remainders have to be transferred back to the host by using *cudaMemcpy*() function.

Thus, *Cipher text = quotients followed by remainders.*

This array of quotient and remainders is written back to an output file. This output file contains the cipher text and is sent to the receiver. Any intruder who accesses this file sees only the sequence of quotients and remainders. Without guessing all 8 parameters of the key, it is very difficult to decrypt this ciphertext.

Decryption

The receiver receives the cipher text and considers the first half of the array to be quotients and the second half as remainders. Pair of quotients and remainders is taken together, and the key is applied to it to obtain the plaintext.

To decrypt within the kernel, the cipher text and the key have to be transferred to the device. As these are independent transfers, two CUDA streams are created. Each stream contains one of the transfers. Thus, these transfers are done simultaneously and most of the data transfer latency is hidden. The algorithm for decryption is as shown in the Figure 6 and Algorithm 7.

Algorithm 7. Decryption

```
1. int len = cipher_length/2
2. int tid=threadIdx.x + blockIdx.x * blockDim.x;
3. while(tid<len)
4. ascii[tid]=(key[tid]-cipher[tid+len])/cipher[tid]
```

Figure 5. Algorithm for encryption

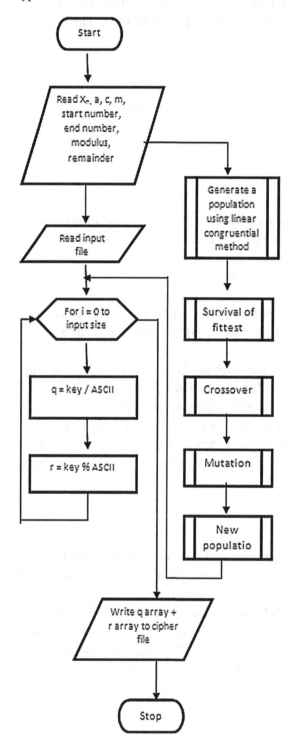

```
5. tid+= blockDim.x * gridDim.x;
```
Like encryption, decryption is parallelized by
```
Decrypt<<<dimGrid,dimBlock>>>(…)
```
The ascii numbers are converted into corresponding characters and stored in an output file.

6. RESULTS AND DISCUSSIONS

It is found that the implementation of this algorithm on GPU is better than its implementation on CPU in two ways: i.e. the generation of pseudorandom numbers and encryption and decryption.

Generation of Pseudorandom Numbers

The algorithm starts by creating 10000 pseudorandom numbers by Linear Congruential numbers. Each of these 10000 is assigned a fitness value of 1 or 0 depending on if it is a prime or not. Only primes are selected for further processing. These primes undergo crossover and mutation to create the next generation. Both generations are processed to check if they fall within a given range. Another level of security is added by checking if these numbers produce the same remainder when divided by a given number.

An experiment was conducted to compare the performance of CPU and GPU codes to generate the array of pseudorandom numbers. Table 1 shows key generation execution times on CPU and GPU. The parameters chosen were:

$X_n = 3562$
a= 23
c = 51
m = 6600
start_number = 4
end_number = 6600
modulus = 3
remainder = 2

A final array of 40908 pseudorandom numbers was generated with the following execution times.

Encryption

The algorithm starts with an array of input ascii values and an array of pseudorandom numbers that acts as the key. A pair of quotient and remainder is obtained by dividing a pair of key and ascii values. The algorithm runs sequentially in CPU version whereas many threads compute concurrently in GPU version. The Table 2 shows the result obtained when the code was run on a 100 Mb input file.

Figure 6. Flowchart for decryption

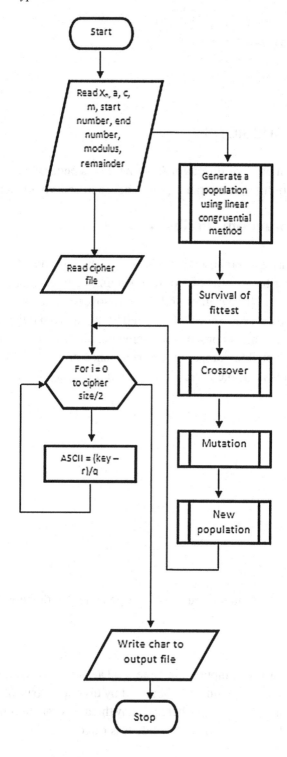

Table 1. Key generation execution times

	CPU (Seconds)	GPU (Seconds)	Speedup
Sender	1.47	0.06	24.5x
Receiver	1.47	0.06	24.5x

Table 2. Encryption execution times

CPU (Seconds)	GPU (Seconds)	Speedup
1.58	0.66	2.4x

Decryption

The algorithm starts with an array of input cipher values and an array of pseudorandom numbers that acts as the key. The ascii value is generated by subtracting the key with the remainder and then dividing it by the quotient. The algorithm runs sequentially in CPU version whereas many threads compute concurrently in the GPU versions. The Table 3 shows the results obtained when the code was run on a 100 Mb input file.

Performance

Initially, 10000 pseudorandom numbers are generated by Linear Congruential method. After selecting primes and carrying out crossover and mutation, a final array of 40908 pseudorandom numbers form the key. The input file size is 10MB and the output file at the receiver end is 10MB. Table 4 shows overall execution times achieved on CPU and GPU with speedup gained.

Fermi vs. Kepler

This section shows a comparison of two GPU architectures namely Fermi and Kepler that have discussed by NVIDIA Corporation, USA in (NVIDIA, 2015) . Table 5 and Figure 7 shows the results obtained when a 40 Mb file was given as input and run on both the architectures.

Input File Size

The algorithm was run on a Tesla machine. An experiment was carried out to analyse the performance as the input file size increases. Table 6 shows execution times of the CPU and GPU versions for different file size.

Table 3. Decryption execution times

CPU (Seconds)	GPU (Seconds)	Speedup
1.15	0.74	1.55x

Table 4. Overall execution times

	CPU (Seconds)	GPU (Seconds)	Speedup
Sender	3.58	2.1	1.7x
Receiver	3.35	1.9	1.76x

Figure 7. Fermi vs. Kepler

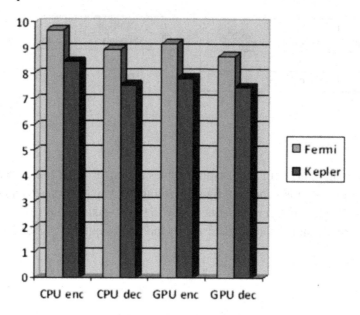

Table 5. Execution times for Fermi and Kepler

		Fermi	Kepler	Speedup
CPU	Encryption	9.7	8.47	1.14x
	Decryption	8.94	7.56	1.18x
GPU	Encryption	9.16	7.82	1.17x
	Decryption	8.68	7.46	1.16x

Table 6. Execution times for different file sizes in sec

MB	CPU		GPU	
	Encryption	Decryption	Encryption	Decryption
10	0.15	0.11	0.07	0.07
20	0.3	0.22	0.14	0.14
30	0.45	0.45	0.2	0.2
40	0.6	0.46	0.26	0.26
50	0.75	0.58	0.34	0.36
100	1.58	1.15	0.66	0.74

Constraints

To achieve successful encryption and decryption, the array of pseudorandom numbers is very important. The pseudorandom numbers generated must be large and should not repeat often.

- *Xn*: Since it is the first number, it must be large (>1000)
- *a*: This number is multiplied by *Xn*, it must not be too large so that the product *a* * *Xn* does not exceed memory limits (<100)
- *c*: This number is added to the product *a*Xn* (<500)
- *m*: This number is used to extract the modulus, if this is too small then all pseudorandom numbers fall under a small range and this may lead to repetition of numbers(>60 and <150)
- *start_number and end_number:* This range must be as wide as possible(start_number<9 and end_number>150)
- *modulus and remainder:* These two numbers should be small so that more number of pseudorandom numbers are selected in the final array (modulus<10 and remainder<10).

Example: Let the parameters exchanged by sender and receiver be:
$Xn = 3562$
$a = 23$
$c = 51$
$m = 6600$
$start\_number = 4$
$end\_number = 6600$
$remainder = 3$
$modulus = 2$

An array of 40908 pseudorandom numbers was generated by using the above parameters. Let us consider that the message sent by the sender is "hello!" This input string is read from the input file and the ascii value of each character is stored. This forms the input of the encryption algorithm. Tables 7 and 8 represents the corresponding encoding and decoding of the cipher text.

Table 7. Encryption

Char	Ascii	Key	Quotient	Remainder
H	104	5000	48	8
E	101	11000	108	92
L	108	17000	157	44
L	108	23000	212	104
O	111	5000	45	5
!	33	11000	333	11

Cipher text = 48 108 157 212 45 333 8 92 44 104 5 11.

Table 8. Decryption

Quotient	Remainder	Character
48	8	h
108	92	e
157	44	l
212	104	l
45	5	o
333	11	!

7. CONCLUSION

This paper proposes a secure method of cryptography by making use of genetic algorithms implemented on GPU using CUDA. The use of genetic algorithms helps us to create an array of pseudorandom numbers efficiently. Genetic algorithms are deterministic and also fast.

We see a dramatic improvement in performance in GPU implementation compared to CPU implementation. The GPU implementation is much faster than the CPU implementation. The drawback of this method is that it needs twice the amount of storage space for a message (quotient + remainder). Thus, the use of CUDA looks promising and is capable of efficiently handling large computations. We aim to implement this algorithm on a cluster of GPU. We aim to build a cluster of many Tesla Graphic cards so that the computation can be distributed among these cards in order to obtain better results. The overhead incurred in GPU version is the data transfer between host and device; we aim to reduce this overhead by distributing data over the cluster.

REFERENCES

Barak, B., Goldrecih, O., Impagliazzo, R., Rudich, S., Sahai, A., Vadhan, S., & Yang, K. (2001). *On the (im)possibility of obfuscating programs*. Paper presented at Springer 21st Annual International Cryptology Conference, Santa Barbara, California, USA (pp.1-18). 10.1007/3-540-44647-8_1

Barker, E., & Kelsey, J. (2012). *Recommendation for random number generation using deterministic random bit generators* [NIST Special Publication 800-90]. US Department of Commerce. doi:10.6028/NIST.SP.800-90a

Bergmann, K. P., Scheidler, R., & Jacob, C. (2008). Cryptanalysis using Genetic Algorithms. Paper presented at 10th annual conference on Genetic and evolutionary computation (GECCO), Geogia, USA (pp. 1099-1100).

Delman, B. (2004). *Genetic algorithms in cryptography* [Master's Dissertation]. Rochester Institute of Technology, New York, NY, USA.

Dorrendorf, L., Gutterman, Z., & Pinkas, B. (2007). *Cryptanalysis of the windows random number generator*. Paper presented at 14th ACM conference on Computer and communications security (pp. 476-485). 10.1145/1315245.1315304

Hellman, M. E. (2002). An overview of public key cryptography. *IEEE Communications Magazine, 40*(5), 42–49. doi:10.1109/MCOM.2002.1006971

Kahn, D. (1996). The Code-breakers: The comprehensive history of secret communication from ancient times to the internet. New York, NY, USA: SCRIBNER (Simon & Schuster).

Kessler, G. C. (2015). *An overview of cryptography*. Retrieved from http://www.garykessler.net/library/crypto.html

Kirk, D. B., & Hwu, W. W. (2012). *Programming massively parallel processors: a hands-on approach.* Burlington, MA, USA: Morgan Kauffman.

Koblitz, N. (1994). *A Course in Number Theory and Cryptography.* New York, NY, USA: Springer-Verlag. doi:10.1007/978-1-4419-8592-7

Koza, J. R. (1992). *Genetic Programming: On the Programming of Computers by Means of Natural Selection.* Cambridge, MA: MIT Press.

Luebke, D. (2008). *CUDA: Scalable parallel programming for high-performance scientific computing.* Paper presented at 5th IEEE International Symposium on Biomedical Imaging (ISBI) (pp. 836-838). 10.1109/ISBI.2008.4541126

Mitchell, M. (1999). *An Introduction to Genetic Algorithms.* Cambridge, MA: MIT Press.

Nickolls, J., Buck, I., Garland, M., & Skadron, K. (2008). Scalable parallel programming with CUDA. *ACM Queue; Tomorrow's Computing Today, 6*(2), 40–53. doi:10.1145/1365490.1365500

NVIDIA Corporation. (2007). CUDA Parallel Computing Platform. Retrieved from: http://www.nvidia.com/object/cuda_home_new.html

NVIDIA Corporation. (2015). *CUDA Toolkit Documentation.* Retrieved from: http://docs.nvidia.com/cuda/index.html#axzz3lsTcA8ft

Stanoycvitch, A. (2010). Introduction to cryptography with Mathematical Foundations and Computer Implementations. Boca Raton, FL, USA: CRC Press (Taylor & Francis Group).

Stinson, D. R. (2005). Cryptography- Theory and Practice. Boca Raton, FL, USA: CRC Press (Taylor & Francis Group).

Thede, S. M. (2004). An Introduction of Genetic Algorithms. *Journal of Computing Sciences in Colleges, 20*(1), 115–123.

Viega, J., & McGraw, G. (2001). *Building secure software: how to avoid security problems the right way.* USA: Addison & Wesley.

This research was previously published in Emerging Research Surrounding Power Consumption and Performance Issues in Utility Computing edited by K. G. Srinivasa, Ganesh Chandra Deka, G.M. Siddesh, and L.M. Patnaik; pages 283-303, copyright year 2016 by Information Science Reference (an imprint of IGI Global).

Chapter 13
Provable Security for Public Key Cryptosystems:
How to Prove that the Cryptosystem is Secure

Syed Taqi Ali
National Institute of Technology Kurukshetra, India

ABSTRACT

In the early years after the invention of public key cryptography by Diffie and Hellman in 1976, the design and evaluation of public key cryptosystems has been done merely in ad-hoc manner based on trial and error. The public key cryptosystem said to be secure as long as there is no successful cryptanalytic attack on it. But due to various successful attacks on the cryptosystems after development, the cryptographic community understood that this ad-hoc approach might not be good enough. The paradigm of provable security is an attempt to get rid of ad hoc design. The goals of provable security are to define appropriate models of security on the one hand, and to develop cryptographic designs that can be proven to be secure within the defined models on the other. There are two general approaches for structuring the security proof. One is reductionist approach and other is game-based approach. In these approaches, the security proofs reduce a well known problem (such as discrete logarithm, RSA) to an attack against a proposed cryptosystem. With this approach, the security of public key cryptosystem can be proved formally under the various models viz. random oracle model, generic group model and standard model. In this chapter, we will briefly explain these approaches along with the security proofs of well known public key cryptosystems under the appropriate model.

DOI: 10.4018/978-1-7998-1763-5.ch013

INTRODUCTION

In the early years after the invention of public key cryptography by Diffie and Hellman in 1976 (Diffie & Hellman, 1976), design and evaluation of public key cryptosystems has been done merely in an ad-hoc manner. That is the fact that the cryptosystem which withstood cryptanalytic attacks for several years is considered to be a secure cryptosystem. But there are many cryptosystems which have been broken after long time of their design. For example, Chor-Rivest cryptosystem (Chor & Rivest, 1985), (Lenstra, 1991), based on the knapsack problem, took more than 10 years to break totally (Vaudenay, 1998), whereas, before this attack it was believed that it is strongly secure. Due to various similar successful attacks on the cryptosystems, the cryptographic community understood that the lack of attacks at some time should never be considered as a security validation and demands the mathematical proof which guarantees the security of cryptosystems.

Provable Security

The paradigm of "provable" security is an attempt to solve this issue. The first public key encryption scheme which provides the mathematical proof of security was proposed by Rabin (Rabin, 1979) in 1979. Later, idea of provable security was introduced in the work of Goldwasser and Micali (Goldwasser, & Micali, 1984) in 1984. Rabin (Rabin, 1979) formally relates the difficulty of breaking the scheme (in some security model) to the difficulty of factoring an integer (a product of two large primes). The basic goals of provable security are, to define appropriate models of security on the one hand and to develop a cryptographic designs that can be proven to be secure within defined model on the other.

The formal security model consists of two definitions; firstly, it must specify how a polynomial-time adversary can interact with legitimate users of a cryptosystem and secondly, it must state what adversary should achieve in order to "break" the cryptosystem. For example, in encryption schemes as an adversary achievement - we define either to recover the message from ciphertext or to distinguish two ciphertexts whether they belong to same plaintext or to correctly map a ciphertext with the appropriate plaintext among the two given, etc.. And, as an adversarial interaction - we define that either adversary can get the decryption of any ciphertext of her choice or can only get the decryption of predefined ciphertexts or cannot get any decryption facility, etc.. Similarly, for digital signature schemes, we have such security models. The strength of the cryptosystem depends on how strong the security model is, under which it is proven secure. Detailed security models of public key encryption and digital signature schemes are discussed in subsequent sections.

Often, building a cryptographic scheme requires some particular atomic primitive(s). In order to prove the security of the scheme, one needs to provide the polynomial-time reduction procedure, which shows that the only way to break the scheme is to break the underlying atomic primitive(s). In other words, they must mathematically relate the security of the cryptosystem to the security of the atomic primitive(s) (such as one-way function or permutation or any hard problem on which scheme is built). Now a days cryptographic schemes are developed based on some well-studied problem(s) (such as integer factorization, discrete logarithm problem or any NP problem) and they provide *reductionist procedure* as a security proof to link the security of the scheme with the underlying well-studied problem. Eventually, if there exists some adversary who can break the proposed scheme then one can use that adversary with the help of devised reductionist procedure to solve the claimed well-studied problem, which is believed to be hard. As a consequence, since the well-studied problem is very hard to solve in polynomial-time, thus the proposed scheme is very hard to break by any polynomial-time adversary.

Another way of looking at these *reductions* is, when I give you a reduction from the integer factorization problem (or any appropriate NP problem) to the security of my cryptosystem, I am giving you a transformation with the following property. Suppose, any adversary claims that she is able to break my cryptosystem. Let $\mathcal{A}$ be the algorithm that does this. Then, my transformation uses $\mathcal{A}$ and puts some appropriate steps around it, results in a new algorithm $\mathcal{B}$ and this $\mathcal{B}$ provably solve integer factorization problem. Thus, as long as we believe that there exists no such algorithm which solves integer factorization, then there could be no such $\mathcal{A}$ possible. In other words, my cryptosystem is secure.

This is similar to the basic idea of reduction in NP-completeness. Where we provide a reduction from SAT (satifiability) to some problem; that is we are saying that some problem is hard unless SAT is easy.

Exact Security

The significant part is to provide the reductionist proof with fewer gaps (or with fewer assumptions) between the proposed scheme and the underlying chosen well-studied problem. Otherwise, in some cases it may take reasonably less time to break the proposed scheme and with the help of provided reduction steps takes many years to solve the underlying problem. This is possible when the security proof is designed by assuming that the scheme uses the longer length parameters such as large length secret keys. Obliviously, if in practice the proposed scheme is used with the shorter length keys then attacker can break it in less time without even solving the underlying problem.

Random-Oracle Model

Also the possibility occurs if one assumes for example, the underlying hash function is collision free (i.e. no two inputs have same output), which is difficult to believe since the output domain is lesser than the input domain. Truly, there will be more than one input which maps to one particular output but it is difficult to find such maps. Here the developer of the scheme assumes that the underlying hash function is a pure random function which on every input gives random output which is not so always. The security proof with such assumption comes under the different category called *Random-Oracle Model* (Ran, Oded & Shai, 2004), we will see it later in detail.

Generic Group Model

Sometimes, while proving security of the cryptosystem we assume that the attacker has no information about the specific representation of the group being used. That is, we assume that attacker tries to focus on the algorithm of the cryptosystem to exploit and does not exploit the special properties of the group, which is used to implement the scheme. This model is known as *Generic Group Model* and it is proposed by Shoup (Shoup, 1997) to give exact bounds on the difficulty of the discrete logarithm problem. In this security model, the attacker is not given direct access to group elements, but to the images of group elements with the consistent random one-to-one mapping. And the attacker is given access to certain oracles (a black box whose internal details are unknown) to perform group operations with images of group elements as inputs to it. In this way, we hide the exact details of the group being used in security proof.

In the subsequent sections, we explain the various security models in detail with the well-known cryptosystems as in example. Firstly, we define the public key cryptosystems then we give formal security models detail. Next, we prove the security of the ElGamal encryption scheme with reductionist proof as well as with game-based approach. Subsequently, we show the exact security of the RSA signature scheme and also show how to get the tight security with minor modification in the scheme. Then, we show the hardness of q-Strong Diffie Hellman assumption in the generic group model. Lastly, we conclude the chapter.

PUBLIC KEY CRYPTOGRAPHY

Public key cryptography or asymmetric cryptography is a group of algorithms or protocols where two, related and distinct keys are involved, one is called secret (or private) key and other is called public key. Public-key encryption schemes and signature schemes are examples of public key cryptography. In public-key encryption scheme, anybody who knows the public key of Alice can send a message securely to her, i.e. by encrypting it with the public key of Alice and only who possess the corresponding secret key, (ofcourse) Alice, can decrypt (recover) to obtain message. Whereas, in signature scheme, Alice can prove the authenticity and integrity of the message by producing the digital signature of the message using her secret key and anybody who knows the related public key of Alice can verify it with the help of verification process of the signature scheme.

Public Key Encryption Scheme

It is formally defined as a triple of possibly probabilistic polynomial-time algorithms ($\mathcal{G}$, $\mathcal{E}$, $\mathcal{D}$). The key generation algorithm $\mathcal{G}$ takes security parameter k as input and outputs a public-secret key pair (pk, sk). The encryption algorithm $\mathcal{E}$ takes input as the public key pk and a message $m \in \mathcal{M}$, a message space, and outputs a ciphertext C. The decryption algorithm $\mathcal{D}$ takes input as the secret key sk and the ciphertext C, and outputs either the message $m \in \mathcal{M}$ or the error symbol $\perp$. Decryption algorithm is necessarily deterministic.

$$\mathcal{G}\left(1^k\right) \xrightarrow{\$} \left(pk, sk\right)$$

$$\mathcal{E}\left(pk, m\right) \xrightarrow{\$} C$$

$$\mathcal{D}\left(sk, C\right) \rightarrow m \text{ or } \perp$$

where, $A \xrightarrow{\$} B$ implies A is generating a non deterministic output B.

Correctness: We say that the scheme is correct if the following condition holds;

For all $m \in \mathcal{M}$ and for all $(pk, sk) \xleftarrow{\$} \mathcal{G}(1^k)$, $\mathcal{D}(sk, \mathcal{E}(pk, m)) \rightarrow m$. That is, for all properly generated key pairs the decryption procedure correctly decipher the properly generated ciphertexts.

Signature Scheme

It is formally defined as a triple of possibly probabilistic polynomial-time algorithms $(\mathcal{G}, \mathcal{S}, \mathcal{V})$. The key generation algorithm $\mathcal{G}$ takes security parameter k as input and outputs a public-secret key pair (*pk,sk*). The signing algorithm $\mathcal{S}$ takes input as secret key *sk* and a message $m \in \mathcal{M}$, from message space, and outputs a signature σ. The verification algorithm $\mathcal{V}$ takes public key *pk*, message *m* and the signature σ as input and outputs either 1, denoting σ as a valid signature, or 0, denoting as invalid signature. Verification algorithm is necessarily deterministic.

$$\mathcal{G}(1^k) \xrightarrow{\$} (pk, sk)$$

$$\mathcal{S}(sk, m) \xrightarrow{\$} \sigma$$

$$\mathcal{V}(pk, m, \sigma) \rightarrow 1/0$$

Correctness: We say that the signature scheme is correct if the following condition holds;

For all $m \in \mathcal{M}$ and for all $(pk, sk) \xleftarrow{\$} \mathcal{G}(1^k)$, $\mathcal{V}(pk, m, \mathcal{S}(sk, m)) \rightarrow 1$. That is, for all properly generated key pairs the verification procedure correctly validate the properly generated signature.

FORMAL SECURITY MODELS

In order to prove the security of a cryptosystem, a formal security model should be described. A formal security model of any cryptosystem consists of two definitions. Firstly, it must specify how a polynomial-time adversary can interact with the legitimate users of the cryptosystem. Secondly, it must state that what attacker/adversary should achieve in order to break the cryptosystem. For example, in most of the encryption schemes, the adversary can get the ciphertext of his own messages by interacting with the system (an encryption oracle) – a kind of interaction, and at last she should correctly identify that the challenge ciphertext (not produced previously) is the encryption of which plaintext among the two given plaintexts – a kind of achievement. Similarly, in signature scheme, adversary can accumulate message-signature pairs by interacting with the system (a signing oracle) and at last she has to produce a new such pair of her choice, in order to break the signature scheme.

Security Model of Public Key Encryption Scheme

The well-known adversarial goals of any public key encryption scheme are: *indistinguishability of encryptions* (Goldwasser, & Micali, 1984) and *non-malleability* (Dolev, Dwork & Naor, 1991). Indistinguishability (IND), a.k.a. *semantic security,* requires that an adversary given a challenge ciphertext be unable to learn any information about the underlying plaintext. Non-malleability requires that an adversary given a challenge ciphertext be unable to modify it into another different ciphertext such that the plaintexts underlying these two ciphertexts are "meaningfully related" to each other.

On the other side, there are three different types of attacks defined on public key encryption schemes, depending on the level of facilitation given to the adversary, viz. Chosen-Plaintext Attack (CPA), non-adaptive Chosen-Ciphertext Attack (CCA1) and adaptive Chosen-Ciphertext Attack (CCA2) (Bellare, Desai, Pointcheval & Rogaway, 1998). In CPA, adversary knows only the public key, through which she can only encrypt messages of her choice, and later allowed to choose two challenge messages, after which she is given a challenge ciphertext (which is the encryption of one of the challenge messages). We say a public key encryption scheme is secure under CPA if it is hard for an adversary to relate the challenge ciphertext to its plaintext. In CCA1, in addition to the above facilities an adversary is given access to decryption oracle (through which she can get the decryption of ciphertext of her choice) before the challenge ciphertext is produced. Similar to the case of CPA, we say public key encryption scheme is secure under CCA1. In CCA2, adversary has access to decryption oracle even after the challenge ciphertext is given to her, but with the restriction that she cannot query challenge ciphertext to the decryption oracle. Similar to the case of CPA and CCA1, we say that the public key encryption scheme is CCA2 secure if it is hard for an adversary to relate the challenge ciphertext to its original plaintext.

To prove the security of encryption scheme we need to use some formal notion of confidentiality which is widely acceptable. One such definition is *indistinguishability under adaptive chosen ciphertext attack* (IND-CCA2), proposed by Rackoff and Simon (Rackoff & Simon, 1991).

Definition [IND-CCA2] We say that the encryption scheme ($\mathcal{G}$, $\mathcal{E}$, $\mathcal{D}$) is secure against IND-CCA2 adversary $\mathcal{A}$, if the probability that $\mathcal{A}$ wins the following game is negligible:

Note: Here $\mathcal{C}$ is the challenger who challenge that the underlying encryption scheme is secure and $\mathcal{A}$ is the adversary who claim that the encryption scheme in not secure against IND-CCA2 attack. The function $\upsilon: N \rightarrow R$ is *negligible* if it vanishes faster than the inverse of any polynomial. Formally, υ is negligible if for every constant $c \geq 0$ there exists an integer k_c such that $\upsilon(k) < k^c$ for all $k \geq k_c$.

Setup: The challenger $\mathcal{C}$ runs $(pk, sk) \overset{\$}{\leftarrow} \mathcal{G}(1^k)$ and gives public key *pk* to $\mathcal{A}$.

Phase-1: $\mathcal{A}$ can request the decryption of any ciphertext C_i of her choice. $\mathcal{C}$ runs

$m_i \leftarrow \mathcal{D}(sk, C_i)$ and returns m_i.

Challenge: $\mathcal{A}$ outputs two messages m_0 and m_1. $\mathcal{C}$ randomly choose $b \overset{\$}{\leftarrow} \{0,1\}$ and returns encryption of m_b, $C^* \overset{\$}{\leftarrow} \mathcal{E}(pk, m_b)$.

Phase-2: $\mathcal{A}$ can make similar queries as in Phase-1 with the restriction that the $\mathcal{A}$ cannot make query on C^*.

Output: Finally, $\mathcal{A}$ outputs a bit b' and wins if $b' = b$.

An adversary's advantage is defined to be $Adv_{\mathcal{A}}^{IND-CCA2}(k) = \left| Pr[b = b'] - 1/2 \right|$.

The alternate way of formally defining the security model in mathematical way is as follows.

Definition [IND-CCA2] An adversary $\mathcal{A}$, against the IND-CCA2 security of an encryption scheme $(\mathcal{G}, \mathcal{E}, \mathcal{D})$, is a pair of probabilistic polynomial-time algorithms ($\mathcal{A}_1, \mathcal{A}_2$). The success of the adversary is defined through the following IND-CCA2 game:

$$\left(pk, sk\right) \xleftarrow{\$} \mathcal{G}\left(1^k\right)$$

$$(m_0, m_1, state) \xleftarrow{\$} \mathcal{A}_1^{\mathcal{D}}\left(pk\right)$$

$$b \xleftarrow{\$} \{0,1\}$$

$$C^* \xleftarrow{\$} \mathcal{E}\left(pk, m_b\right)$$

$$b' \xleftarrow{\$} \mathcal{A}_2^{\mathcal{D}}(C^*, m_0, m_1, state)$$

where $\mathcal{A}_i^{\mathcal{D}}$ denotes that the algorithm $\mathcal{A}_i$ has access to decryption oracle, through which adversary can get the decryption of any ciphertext of her choice. The decryption oracle returns $m \leftarrow \mathcal{D}\left(sk, C\right)$. C^* is the challenge ciphertext on which adversary will not make query to decryption oracle. The adversary **wins** the game if $b = b'$. An adversary's advantage is defined to be

$$Adv_{\mathcal{A}}^{IND-CCA2}(k) = \left| Pr[b = b'] - 1/2 \right|.$$

Equivalently,

$$Adv_{\mathcal{A}}^{(IND-CCA2)}(k) = | Pr[\mathcal{A}(C^*, m_0, m_1, pk) \rightarrow b : \left(pk, sk\right) \xleftarrow{\$} \mathcal{G}\left(1^k\right); \; (m_0, m_1) \xleftarrow{\$} \mathcal{A}^{\mathcal{D}}(pk);$$

$$b \xleftarrow{\$} \{0,1\}; C^* \xleftarrow{\$} \mathcal{E}\left(pk, m_b\right) [-1/2|$$

We require that the adversary's advantage to be *negligible* in order to guarantee the security of the encryption scheme. Events which occur with negligible probability remain negligible even if the experiment is repeated for polynomially many times. Thus we require,

$$Adv_{A}^{IND-CCA2}\left(k\right) \leq \frac{1}{Q\left(k\right)}$$

where Q is some polynomial.

Note: The scheme is said to be IND-CCA1 secure if the adversary can make decryption oracle queries only before receiving the challenge ciphertext C^*, i.e. A cannot make decryption queries in phase-2 or algorithm A_2 does not have access to decryption oracle. Similarly, the scheme is said to be IND-CPA secure if the adversary do not make any decryption oracle queries at all, i.e. in both phase-1 and phase-2 or both the algorithm (A_1, A_2) do not have access to decryption oracle.

Security Model of Signature Scheme

The well-known adversarial goals of any signature scheme are: *existential forgery, selective forgery, universal forgery* and *total break*. Existential forgery says that adversary succeeds if she is able to forge the signature of at least one message of her choice. Selective forgery says that the adversary succeeds if she is able to forge the signature of some message selected prior to the attack. Universal forgery says that the adversary succeeds in breaking the underlying signature scheme only if she is able to forge the signature of any given message. In total break the adversary is able to compute the signer's secret key.

On the other side, there are three different types of attacks on signature schemes, similar to public key encryption schemes, depending on the level of facilitation given to the adversary, viz. key-only attack, known signature attack (KSA) and chosen message attack (CMA). In key-only attack, the adversary knows only the public key of the signer and therefore she can only check the validity of signatures of messages given to her. In KSA, the adversary knows the public key of the signer and has list of message/signature pairs, not of her choice. In CMA, the adversary is allowed to get the signature of number of messages, of her choice, from the signer. For more finer divisions of attacks refer (Goldwasser, Micali & Rivest, 1988).

Clearly, the best digital signature scheme is the one which is secure against *existential forgery under chosen message attack* (EF-CMA).

Definition [EF-CMA] An adversary A against the EF-CMA security of a signature scheme (G, S, V) is a probabilistic polynomial-time algorithm. The success of the adversary is defined through the following EF-CMA game:

$$\left(pk, sk\right) \xleftarrow{\$} G\left(1^k\right)$$

$$\left(m^*, \sigma^*\right) \xleftarrow{\$} A^S\left(pk\right)$$

where $\mathcal{A}^S$ denotes that the algorithm $\mathcal{A}$ has access to signature oracle, through which adversary can get the signature of any message of her choice. The signature oracle returns $\sigma \xleftarrow{\$} \mathcal{S}(sk, m)$. Finally adversary outputs the pair (m^*, σ^*) claiming that σ^* is the signature of the message m^*. The adversary *wins* the game if $\mathcal{V}(pk, m^*, \sigma^*) \rightarrow 1$. An adversary's advantage is defined to be

$$Adv_{\mathcal{A}}^{EF-CMA}(k) = Pr\left[\mathcal{V}(pk, m^*, \sigma^*) \rightarrow 1 : (pk, sk) \xleftarrow{\$} \mathcal{G}(1^k); (m^*, \sigma^*) \xleftarrow{\$} \mathcal{A}^S(pk)\right]$$

We require that the adversary's advantage to be negligible in order to guarantee the security of the signature scheme against EF-CMA adversary, i.e.

$$Adv_{\mathcal{A}}^{EF-CMA}(k) \leq \frac{1}{Q(k)}$$

where Q is some polynomial.

EXAMPLE OF PUBLIC KEY ENCRYPTION SCHEME

ElGamal Encryption Scheme ($\mathcal{G}, \mathcal{E}, \mathcal{D}$):

1. KeyGen; $\mathcal{G}(1^k)$:

        Select a random prime q of size k, i.e. $|q|=k$.
        Select an algebraic group G of order q.
        Choose randomly a generator $g \in_R G$.
        Choose a random $x \in_R \mathbb{Z}_q$
        Compute $g_1 = g^x$
Outputs, public key $pk = (g_1, g)$ and secret key $sk = x$.

2. Encryption; $\mathcal{E}(pk, m)$:

        Here message $m \in G$
        Choose $y \in_R \mathbb{Z}_q$
        Compute $C_2 = g^y, g_3 = g_1^y, C_1 = g_3.m$
Outputs, ciphertext $C = (C_1, C_2)$

3. Decryption; $\mathcal{D}(sk, C)$:

$$m = C_1 / C_2^x$$

Correctness: We can observe that, for all $pk = (g_1, g)$ and $sk = x$ generated from $\mathcal{G}(1^k)$, the following condition holds,

$$\mathcal{D}\left(sk,C\right)=\mathcal{D}\left(x,\left(C_{1},C_{2}\right)\right)=\frac{C_{1}}{C_{2}^{x}}=\frac{g_{3}m}{g_{2}^{x}}=\frac{g_{1}^{y}m}{g_{2}^{x}}=\frac{g^{xy}m}{g^{yx}}=m$$

Decisional Diffie-Hellman (DDH) Assumption: It says that it is hard to distinguish triples of the form (g^{x},g^{y},g^{xy}) from triples of the form (g^{x},g^{y},g^{z}), where x,y and z are random elements of $\mathbb{Z}_{q}$ and $g \in G$. More precisely it can be formulated as, let H be an algorithm that takes as input triples of group elements, and outputs a bit. The *DDH-advantage* of H is,

$$\left| Pr\left[x,y \xleftarrow{\$} \mathbb{Z}_{q}:H\left(g^{x},g^{y},g^{xy}\right)=1\right] - Pr\left[x,y,z \xleftarrow{\$} \mathbb{Z}_{q}:H\left(g^{x},g^{y},g^{z}\right)=1\right]\right|$$

The DDH assumption in G says that any efficient algorithm's *DDH-advantage* is negligible.

Security Analysis of above Public Key Encryption Scheme

Theorem 1: ElGamal encryption scheme is IND-CPA secure under the Decisional Diffie-Hellman (DDH) assumption.

Informally, it says that as long as there exists no PPT (probabilistic polynomial time) algorithm to solve DDH problem there cannot exists PPT adversary to break the ElGamal encryption scheme. Suppose if PPT adversary exists then we can utilize it to solve the DDH problem in polynomial time.

DDH_Challenger $\rightleftarrows$ ElGamal_Challenger $\mathcal{B}$ $\rightleftarrows$ CPA_Adversary $\mathcal{A}$

First we give proof using reductionist approach then we give proof using game-based approach.
Proof A (using Reductionist approach): The following lemma implies the Theorem 1.
Lemma 1. Suppose an adversary $\mathcal{A}$ breaks the ElGamal encryption scheme with the advantage ϵ. Then, we can construct an algorithm $\mathcal{B}$ that breaks the DDH assumption.
Proof. The input of $\mathcal{B}$ is a DDH challenge tuple $(h,h^{x},h^{y},h^{z}) \in G^{4}$, where G is an algebraic group of prime order q, $(x,y,z) \in \mathbb{Z}_{q}^{*}$ and either $z=xy$ or a random element. Now $\mathcal{B}$ tries to answer the given DDH challenge with the help of an adversary $\mathcal{A}$'s output in breaking the ElGamal encryption scheme. Let the challenge ciphertex be $C^{*}=\left(C_{1}^{*},C_{2}^{*}\right)$.

Setup: Algorithm $\mathcal{B}$ simulates the ElGamal encryption scheme as follows,

1. Sets the public key, $pk=(g_{1}=h^{x}, g=h)$ and secret key, $sk=x$ (unknown).
2. $\mathcal{B}$ gives pk to $\mathcal{A}$.

Phase-1: $\mathcal{A}$ can encrypt messages of her choice using the public key, pk. This is according to CPA definition.

Challenge: $\mathcal{A}$ outputs two messages m_0 and m_1 of her choice. i.e. $(m_0, m_1) \leftarrow \mathcal{A}(pk)$. $\mathcal{B}$ selects $b \in_R \{0,1\}$ and computes $C_1^* = h^z.m_b$, $C_2^* = g^y$. $\mathcal{B}$ gives $C^* = \left(C_1^*, C_2^*\right)$ as a challenge ciphertext to $\mathcal{A}$

Output: Finally $\mathcal{A}$ outputs $b' \in \{0,1\}$ with advantage ϵ, claiming that m_b, is the corresponding message of C^*. Then $\mathcal{B}$ outputs 1 if $b = b'$ otherwise outputs 0. $\mathcal{B}$'s output 1 implies that $z=xy$ and 0 implies z is a random, an answer for the DDH challenge input.

If an adversary $\mathcal{A}$ answers correctly with ϵ probability then with same ϵ probability $\mathcal{B}$ solves the DDH challenge. As DDH problem is known to be hard thus the ϵ is negligible and the ElGamal encryption scheme is secure under CPA.

Proof B (using Game based approach): Now we give the same proof using sequence of games (Shoup, 2004).

Let q be a prime of size k, i.e. $|q|=k$, where k is the security parameter. Let G be a group of order q and g be the generator of G.

Game 0: This is the real game as defined in the security model. The challenger $\mathcal{C}$ sets up the scheme and defines the parameters, $pk=(g_1,g)$, $sk=x$ similar to $\mathcal{G}\left(1^k\right)$ procedure. $\mathcal{C}$ gives public key $pk=(g_1,g)$ to an adversary $\mathcal{A}$.

At Challenge phase, $\mathcal{A}$ outputs two messages m_0 and m_1 of her choice i.e. $(m_0, m_1) \leftarrow \mathcal{A}(pk)$. $\mathcal{C}$ selects $b \in_R \{0,1\}$, $y \in_R \mathbb{Z}_q$ and computes $C_2^* = g^y, g_3 = g_1^y, C_1^* = g_3.m_b$. $\mathcal{C}$ gives $C^* = \left(C_1^*, C_2^*\right)$ as a challenge ciphertext to $\mathcal{A}$.

Finally in the Output phase, $\mathcal{A}$ ouputs $b' \in \{0,1\}$. Let S_0 be the event that $b' = b$, then the advantage of $\mathcal{A}$ in this game is,

$$Adv_{\mathcal{A}}^{IND-CPA}(k) = \left|Pr[b = b'] - 1/2\right| = \left|Pr[S_0] - 1/2\right|.$$

Game 1: We now make one small change to the Game 0. Namely, instead of computing g_3 as g_1^y we compute it as $g_3=g^z$, for some random $z \in_R \mathbb{Z}_q$. In this game, all the steps are same as Game 0 except as mentioned above $\mathcal{C}$ gives $pk=(g_1,g)$ to $\mathcal{A}$.

In Challenge phase, $\mathcal{C}$ computes $C_1^* = g_3.m_b$, where $g_3=g^z$ as above. $\mathcal{C}$ gives $C^* = \left(C_1^*, C_2^*\right)$ as a challenge ciphertext to $\mathcal{A}$.

Finally, $\mathcal{A}$ outputs $b' \in \{0,1\}$.

Let S_1 be the event that $b' = b$, then $Pr[S_1]=1/2$. This is because g_3 is effectively a one-time pad and adversary's output b' is independent of the hidden bit b. Since the distribution of g_3 is uniform distribution on G. And from this, one can see that the conditional distribution of C_1^* is the uniform distribution on G.

Claim 1. $|Pr[S_0] - Pr[S_1]|=\epsilon_{ddh}$ where ϵ_{ddh} is the DDH-advantage of some efficient algorithm which solves DDH problem. (and it is negligible due to DDH assumption)

The proof is the observation that in Game 0, the triple $\left(g_1, C_2^*, g_3\right)$ is of the form (g^x, g^y, g^{xy}), and in Game 1, it is (g^x, g^y, g^z). Thus, by the DDH assumption the adversary should not able to notice this difference. To make it more precise, we can observe that in challenge phase, $\mathcal{C}$ is using g^{xy} in Game 0 and

g^z in Game 1 for computing the challenge ciphertext field C_1^*. Thus, if there exists an adversary who can identify the correct message, m_0 or m_1, corresponding to the ciphertext C^* in Game 0 then when $\mathcal{C}$ uses g^z in place of g^{xy} in Game 1 the same adversary is able to notice the difference. That is, the behavior (or response) of the adversary in both the game can use to answer the DDH problem.

From the above $Pr[S_1]=1/2$, thus $|Pr[S_0] - Pr[S_1]| = |Pr[S_0] - 1/2| = \in_{ddh}$ and this is negligible. That completes the proof of security of ElGamal encryption scheme.

EXAMPLE OF SIGNATURE SCHEME

Full Domain Hash (FDH) Signature Scheme $(\mathcal{G}, \mathcal{S}, \mathcal{V})$ (Bellare & Rogaway, 1993):

It is a basic RSA signature scheme with full domain hash function, i.e. $H : \{0,1\}^* \rightarrow \mathbb{Z}_N^*$, where N is a RSA modulus.

```
KeyGen;  𝒢(1ᵏ):
Select two distinct odd primes of k/2 bits, say p and q.
Compute N=pq and φ(N)=(p - 1)(q - 1).
```
Choose $e \in_R \mathbb{Z}_{\varphi(N)}^*$ and compute $d \in \mathbb{Z}_{\varphi(N)}^*$: $ed \equiv 1 \bmod \varphi(N)$.

Define the full domain hash function, $H : \{0,1\}^* \rightarrow \mathbb{Z}_N^*$.
```
Outputs, public key pk=(N,e) and secret key sk=d.
```
Sign; $\mathcal{S}(sk, m)$:
```
Get y←H(m)
Computes signature, σ=yᵈmodN
Outputs σ
```
Verify; $\mathcal{V}(pk, m, \sigma)$:
```
Compute y=σᵉmodN
```
Get $y' \leftarrow H(m)$
```
Outputs 1 if y=y' else outputs 0.
```

Correctness: To prove that the FDH signature scheme is correct, we need to show that for all $pk=(N,e)$ and $sk=d$ generated from $\mathcal{G}(1^k)$, $\sigma^e=H(m)$, that's all.

Consider, LHS $= \sigma^e = (y^d \bmod N)^e = y^{ed} \bmod N = y$, ($\because ed \equiv 1 \bmod \varphi(N)$) and RHS $= H(m) = y$.

Thus, the FDH scheme is correct.

RSA Assumption: It says that it is hard to compute $x=y^{1/e}$ when RSA challenge (N,e,y) is given, $N=p.q$, where p and q are distinct primes, $e \in \mathbb{Z}_{\varphi(N)}^*$ and $y \in \mathbb{Z}_N^*$. More precisely it can be formulated as, let R be an algorithm that takes as input RSA challenge, and ouputs x. The *RSA-advantage* of R is,

$$Pr\left[N = p.q, e \xleftarrow{\$} \mathbb{Z}_{\varphi(N)}^*, y \xleftarrow{\$} \mathbb{Z}_N^* : R(N,e,y) = y^{1/e}\right]$$

The RSA assumption says that any efficient algorithm's *RSA-advantage* is negligible.

SECURITY ANALYSIS OF ABOVE SIGNATURE SCHEME

Theorem 2: The FDH signature scheme is secure in the random oracle model from the chosen-message attack by an existential forger under the RSA assumption.

Proof A (using Reductionist approach): The following lemma implies the Theorem 2.

RSA_Challenger $\rightleftarrows$ FDH Scheme_Challenger $\mathcal{B} \rightleftarrows$ CMA_Adversary $\mathcal{A}$

Lemma 2. Suppose an existential forger $\mathcal{A}$ forges the signature of FDH scheme under chosen-message attack with the advantage ϵ_{fdh} in time t_{fdh} then we can construct an algorithm $\mathcal{B}$ that breaks the RSA assumption with advantage ϵ_{rsa} in time t_{RSA}, where

$$\epsilon_{rsa} = \frac{1}{\left(q_{sig} + q_{hash} + 1\right)}.\epsilon_{fdh}$$

and $t_{rsa} = t_{fdh} + (q_{sig} + q_{hash} + 1)\theta(k^3)$. Where q_{sig} and q_{hash} are total number of signature queries and hash queries that $\mathcal{A}$ can make, respectively.

Proof. The input of $\mathcal{B}$ is a RSA challenge tuple (N^*, e^*, y^*), where $N^* = pq, e^* \in \mathbb{Z}^*_{\varphi(N^*)}$ and $y^* \in \mathbb{Z}^*_{N^*}$, p and q are distinct primes (unknown to $\mathcal{B}$). $\mathcal{B}$ tries to find $x^* \in \mathbb{Z}^*_{N^*} : x^{*e} mod N^* = y^*$, with the help of a forger $\mathcal{A}$'s output on forging FDH scheme.

Setup: Algorithm $\mathcal{B}$ simulates the FDH scheme as follows,

1. Sets the public key, $pk = (N = N^*, e = e^*)$ and secret key, sk is unknown.
2. $\mathcal{B}$ gives pk to $\mathcal{A}$.

Phase-1. $\mathcal{A}$ makes at most q_{hash} hash queries and q_{sig} signature queries on messages of her choice. This is according to CMA definition. Let $q = q_{sig} + q_{hash}$, $\mathcal{B}$ selects $j \in_R \{1, ..., q\}$, assuming that $\mathcal{A}$ may forge the signature on some message m^* for which she make the j-th hash query to $\mathcal{B}$. $\mathcal{B}$ answers to various queries as follows,

Hash query: $\mathcal{A}$ makes hash query m. $\mathcal{B}$ increments i and sets $m_i = m$. If $i = j$ then it sets $y_i = y^*$ and respond with y_j. Else chooses $x_i \in_R \mathbb{Z}^*_N$, sets $y_i = x_i^e mod N$ and respond with y_i. Note that for this computation $\theta(k^3)$ operations are needed, i.e. one RSA computation for each y_i.

Signature query: $\mathcal{A}$ makes signature query m. If there is already a hash query on m, i.e. $m = m_l$ for some $l \in \{1, ..., q\}$ then $\mathcal{B}$ respond with x_l as the signature ($\because (x_l)^e = y_l mod N$, $y_l = H(m)$ and is a valid signature). Further, if $l = j$ then $\mathcal{B}$ aborts. Else if no hash query were made on m then $\mathcal{B}$ implicitly makes the hash query on m and respond with the corresponding x_i.

Output: $\mathcal{A}$ outputs a valid signature $\hat{\sigma}$ for message $\hat{m}$. If $\hat{m} = m_j$ then we have a solution $\hat{\sigma} = y_j^{\ d} = y^{*d} = x^*$. And this will happen if $\mathcal{B}$'s guess is correct, i.e. with probability $\dfrac{1}{q} = \dfrac{1}{q_{sig} + q_{hash} + 1}$.

If a forger $\mathcal{A}$ forges the signature of FDH scheme with ϵ_{fdh} advantage then $\mathcal{B}$ solves the RSA challenge with $\epsilon_{rsa} = \dfrac{\epsilon_{fdh}}{q_{sig} + q_{hash} + 1}$ advantage. The running time of $\mathcal{B}$ is that of $\mathcal{A}$ plus the time to choose y_i values in hash queries. Thus, $t_{rsa} = t_{fdh} + (q_{sig} + q_{hash} + 1)\theta(k^3)$, where t_{fdh} is the running time of $\mathcal{A}$.

As RSA assumption holds, ϵ_{rsa} should be negligible and thus ϵ_{fdh} will be negligible for appropriate bounds on q_{sig} and q_{hash}, therefore FDH scheme is secure under CMA with existential forger in the random oracle model.

Proof B (using Game based approach): We now give a proof using sequence of games (Shoup, 2004). We start with the real game according to the security model then will switch to the other games with slight modifications and at last will relate it with the RSA problem.

Let the RSA challenge tuple be (N^*, e^*, y^*), $N^* = pq, e^* \in \mathbb{Z}^*_{\varphi(N)}$ and $y^* \in \mathbb{Z}^*_N$, where p and q are distinct primes (unknown to challenger). Let denote the signature in output phase in each game with $\hat{\sigma}$ and its message with $\hat{m}$. Let q_{hash} and q_{sig} be the maximum number of hash queries and signature queries, respectively, that an adversary $\mathcal{A}$ can made in any game. Note that each signature query implicitly needs a hash query, thus the total number of hash queries including for forge signature is $q = q_{sig} + q_{hash} + 1$. Let the adversary wins in the game G_i with advantage Adv_i.

G_0: This is the real game according to the security model of existential forger under the chosen-message attack. The challenger $\mathcal{B}$ sets up the FDH scheme and defines the scheme parameters, $pk(N,e)$ and $sk=d$ as in the real scheme. $\mathcal{B}$ gives public key pk to a forger $\mathcal{A}$.

Queries: $\mathcal{A}$ makes hash queries and signature queries. For hash query, $\mathcal{B}$ replies with a random value consistently, i.e. for same hash query reply with the same random value. For signature query, $\mathcal{B}$ respond according to the real scheme.

Output: In the output phase, $\mathcal{A}$ produces a valid signature $\hat{\sigma}$ for some message $\hat{m}$.

Thus, the advantage of adversary winning in this game is $Adv_0 = \epsilon_{fdh}$ and the adversary takes time t_{fdh} to win the game.

G_1: We modify the game G_0. Here $\mathcal{B}$ selects $j \in_R \{1,\ldots,q\}$, assuming that $\mathcal{A}$ may forge the signature on some message m^* for which she make the j-th hash query to $\mathcal{B}$.

Queries: For hash query on m. $\mathcal{B}$ increments i (initially 0) and sets $m_i = m$ and respond with a random value, say $y_i \in_R \mathbb{Z}^*_N$. Further, if $m = m_i$ for some existing i then $\mathcal{B}$ respond with the respective y_i, to maintain the consistency. This takes almost same time compared to previous game.

For signature query on m. If there is already a hash query on m, i.e. $m = m_l$ for some $l \in \{1,\ldots,q\}$ then $\mathcal{B}$ respond with $x_l = (y_l)^d \bmod N$ as the signature. Further, if $l = j$ then $\mathcal{B}$ aborts. Else if no hash query were made on m then $\mathcal{B}$ implicitly makes the hash query on m and respond with the corresponding x_i. This takes almost same time when compare to previous game.

Output: In the output phase, $\mathcal{A}$ produces a valid signature $\hat{\sigma}$ for some message $\hat{m}$ and if $\hat{m} \neq m_j, \mathcal{B}$ aborts the game. $\mathcal{A}$ successfully forge the signature with advantage Adv_1.

In this game, $\mathcal{B}$ aborts with the probability $\frac{1}{q}$. Thus, the $Adv_1 = \frac{\epsilon_{fdh}}{q}$ and time taken is same as previous game, i.e. t_{fdh}.

G_2: We modify the game G_1. Here $\mathcal{B}$ inserts RSA challenge tuple in one of the hash query in order to get the solution of it from $\mathcal{A}$'s output. Let (N^*, e^*, y^*) be the RSA challenge tuple for which $\mathcal{B}$ has to find the solution, where $N^* = pq, e^* \in \mathbb{Z}^*_{\varphi(N)}$ and $y^* \in \mathbb{Z}^*_N$, p and q are distinct primes (unknown to $\mathcal{B}$). The challenger $\mathcal{B}$ sets up the FDH scheme and defines the sets, $pk=(N=N^*, e=e^*)$ and $sk=(d=d^*)$, where d^* is unknown, thus sk is unknown to $\mathcal{B}$. $\mathcal{B}$ gives public key pk to a forger $\mathcal{A}$.

Queries: For hash query m. $\mathcal{B}$ increments i and sets $m_i=m$. If $i=j$ then it sets $y_i=y^*$ and respond with y_j. Else chooses $x_i \in_R \mathbb{Z}^*_N$, sets $y_i = x_i^e modN$ and respond with y_i. Note that for this computation $\theta(k^3)$ operations are needed, i.e. one RSA computation for each y_i. This is the extra operations as compare to previous game.

For signature query m. If there is already a hash query on m, i.e. $m=m_l$ for some $l\in\{1,...,q\}$ then $\mathcal{B}$ respond with x_l as the signature ($\because (x_l)^e = y_l modN$, $y_l=H(m)$ and is a valid signature). Further, if $l=j$ then $\mathcal{B}$ aborts. Else if no hash query were made on m then $\mathcal{B}$ implicitly makes the hash query on m and respond with the corresponding x_i. This takes almost same time when compared to previous game.

Output: $\mathcal{A}$ outputs a valid signature $.\hat{\sigma}.$ for message $\hat{m}$ and if $\hat{m} \neq m_j$, $\mathcal{B}$ aborts the game. $\mathcal{A}$ successfully forge the signature with advantage Adv_2.

Note that the games G_1 and G_2 are indistinguishable to $\mathcal{A}$. Thus, $Adv_2 = Adv_1 = \frac{\epsilon_{fdh}}{q}$ and time taken in this game is $t_{fdh}+(q_{sig}+q_{hash}+1)\theta(k^3)$.

If $\hat{m} = m_j$ then $\mathcal{B}$ have a solution to RSA challenge, i.e. $\hat{\sigma} = y_j^{\,d} = y^{*d} = x^*$. Let ϵ_{rsa} be the advantage of any algorithm in solving RSA problem, then $Adv_2 = \epsilon_{rsa}$ and let t_{rsa} be the time needed for the algorithm. Thus, we have

$$\epsilon_{rsa} = \frac{\epsilon_{fdh}}{q} = \frac{\epsilon_{fdh}}{q_{sig} + q_{hash} +1}$$

and $t_{rsa}=t_{fdh}+(q_{sig}+q_{hash}+1)\theta(k^3)$.

The above scheme is secure under random oracle model because we are generating hash queries response randomly in the security model but it is not the case when we replace it with some practical hash function in FDH construction. As we assume the hash function to be a pure random function, which is not always true, so we say that the scheme is secure in the random oracle model. Moreover, we gave the exact security of the FDH scheme but it is not *tight security* with respect to RSA assumption, since it is possible that $\epsilon_{RSA} \ll \epsilon_{FDH}$ and $t_{RSA} \gg t_{FDH}$. With the small modification in the FDH scheme we can achieve tight security bounds i.e. $\epsilon_{rsa} \approx \epsilon_{fdh}$ and $t_{rsa} \approx t_{fdh}$. The modified scheme is as detailed below.

EXAMPLE OF EXACT SECURITY OF A CRYPTOSYSTEM

Katz-Wang Signature Scheme $(\mathcal{G}, \mathcal{S}, \mathcal{V})$:

It is the improvement of FDH signature scheme with tight security.

KeyGen; $\mathcal{G}(1^k)$:

Select two distinct odd primes of $k/2$ bits, say p and q.

Compute $N=pq$ and $\varphi(N)=(p - 1)(q - 1)$.

Choose $e \in_R \mathbb{Z}^*_{\varphi(N)}$ and compute $d \in \mathbb{Z}^*_{\varphi(N)}$: $ed \equiv 1 \bmod \varphi(N)$.

Define the full domain hash function, $H:\{0,1\}^* \to \mathbb{Z}^*_N$.

Outputs, public key $pk=(N,e)$ and secret key $sk=d$.

Sign; $\mathcal{S}(sk,m)$:

Choose a random bit, $b \in_R \{0,1\}$

Get $y \leftarrow H(m \| b)$, concatenating message with a random bit

Computes signature, $\sigma = y^d \bmod N$

Outputs, (σ, b)

Verify; $\mathcal{V}(pk, m, (\sigma, b))$:

Compute $y = \sigma^e \bmod N$

Get $y' \leftarrow H(m \| b)$

Outputs, 1 if $y = y'$ else outputs 0.

Correctness: To prove that the above signature scheme is correct, we need to show that for all $pk=(N,e)$ and $sk=d$ generated from $\mathcal{G}(1^k)$, $\sigma^e = H(m \| b)$.

Consider, LHS $= \sigma^e = (y^d \bmod N)^e = y^{ed} \bmod N = y$, ($\because ed \equiv 1 \bmod \varphi(N)$) and RHS $= H(m \| b) = y$.

Thus, the Katz-Wang signature scheme is correct.

SECURITY ANALYSIS OF ABOVE SIGNATURE SCHEME

Theorem 3: The Katz-Wang signature scheme is secure in the random oracle model from the chosen-message attack by an existential forger under the RSA assumption.

Proof (using Game based approach): The following lemma implies the Theorem 3.

Lemma 3. Suppose an existential forger $\mathcal{A}$ forges the signature of Katz-Wang scheme under chosen-message attack with the advantage ϵ_{kw} in time t_{kw} then we can construct an algorithm $\mathcal{B}$ that breaks the RSA assumption with advantage ϵ_{rsa} in time t_{rsa}, where $\epsilon_{rsa} = \epsilon_{kw}$ and $t_{sa} = t_{kw} + (q_{sig} + q_{hash} + 1)\theta(k^3)$. q_{sig} and q_{hash} are total number of signature queries and hash queries that $\mathcal{A}$ can make, respectively.

Proof: We now give a proof using sequence of games. We start with the real game according to the security model then will switch to the other games with slight modifications and at last will relate it with the RSA problem.

Let the RSA challenge tuple be (N^*, e^*, y^*), where $N^* = pq, e^* \in \mathbb{Z}^*_{\varphi(N^*)}$ and $y^* \in \mathbb{Z}^*_{N^*}$, p and q are distinct primes (unknown). Let we denote the signature in output phase in each game with $\hat{\sigma}$ and its message with $\hat{m}$. Note that the q_{hash} and q_{sig} is the maximum number of hash queries and signature queries, respectively, that an adversary $\mathcal{A}$ can make in any game. Note that each signature query implicitly needs a hash query, thus the total number of hash queries including for forge signature is $q_{sig} + q_{hash} + 1$. Let the adversary wins game G_i with advantage Adv_i.

G_0: This is the real game according to the security model of existential forger under the chosen-message attack. The challenger $\mathcal{B}$ sets up the Katz-Wang scheme and defines the scheme parameters, $pk=(N,e)$ and $sk=d$ as in the real scheme. $\mathcal{B}$ gives public key pk to a forger $\mathcal{A}$.

Queries: $\mathcal{A}$ makes hash queries and signature queries. For hash query, $\mathcal{B}$ replies with a random value with consistent, i.e. for same hash query reply with the same random value. Without loss of generality we may assume that $\mathcal{A}$ also gets $H(m\|b')$ along with the $H(m\|b)$, where b' is the complement of b. For signature query, $\mathcal{B}$ respond according to the real scheme.

Output: In the output phase, $\mathcal{A}$ produces a valid signature $\hat{\sigma}$ for some message $\hat{m}$.

Thus, the advantage of adversary winning in this game is $Adv_0 = \epsilon_{kw}$ and the adversary takes time t_{kw} to win the game.

G_1: We modify the game G_0. Here $\mathcal{B}$ inserts RSA challenge tuple in the hash query in order to get the solution of it from $\mathcal{A}$'s forgery. Let (N^*, e^*, y^*) be the RSA challenge tuple for which $\mathcal{B}$ has to find the solution, where $N^* = pq, e^* \in \mathbb{Z}^*_{\varphi(N^*)}$ and $y^* \in \mathbb{Z}^*_{N^*}$, p and q are distinct primes (unknown to $\mathcal{B}$). The challenger $\mathcal{B}$ setups the Katz-Wang scheme and defines the scheme parameters as, $pk=(N=N^*, e=e^*)$ and $sk=(d=d^*)$, where d^* is unknown, thus sk is unknown to $\mathcal{B}$. $\mathcal{B}$ gives public key pk to a forger $\mathcal{A}$.

Queries: For hash query on (m,b). $\mathcal{B}$ selects a random bit c and two random integers t_1 and t_2 from $\mathbb{Z}^*_N$. If $c=b$, then $\mathcal{B}$ responds with $H(m\|b) = t_1^e y^*$ and $H(m\|b') = t_2^e$ and if $c = b'$, then $\mathcal{B}$ responds with $H(m\|b) = t_2^e$ and $H(m\|b') = t_1^e y^*$. Here we assume that adversary wont query same hash query twice. Note that for this computation $\theta(k^3)$ operations are needed, i.e. two RSA computation for each query. This is the extra operations as compare to previous game.

For signature query on m. If there is already a hash query on m, then $\mathcal{B}$ responds with the corresponding value of t_2. Else if no hash query were made on m then $\mathcal{B}$ implicitly makes the hash query on m and respond with the corresponding t_2.

Output: In the output phase, $\mathcal{A}$ produces a valid signature $\hat{\sigma}$ for some message $\hat{m}$. $\mathcal{A}$ successfully forge the signature with advantage Adv_1.

Note that the games G_0 and G_1 are indistinguishable to $\mathcal{A}$. Thus, $Adv_1 = Adv_0 = \epsilon_{kw}$ and time taken in this game is $t_{kw} + 2*(q_{sig} + q_{hash} + 1)\theta(k^3)$.

In this game, $\mathcal{B}$ have a solution to RSA challenge with the probability $\frac{1}{2}$. That is, the forge signature $\hat{\sigma}$ is either an e-th root of t_2^e or and e-th root of $t_1^e y^*$ for some values t_1 and t_2, known to $\mathcal{B}$. Thus, we have $\epsilon_{rsa} = \frac{Adv_1}{2} = \frac{\epsilon_{kw}}{2}$ and $t_{rsa} = t_{kw} + 2*(q_{sig} + q_{hash} + 1)\theta(k^3)$. This gives the tight reduction from RSA problem to the signature forgery problem.

EXAMPLE OF GENERIC GROUP MODEL

Now we look how to prove the security of a scheme or hardness of any assumption in generic group model. First, we look at certain definitions then we see the proof of q-SDH assumption.

Bilinear Groups and Map

- $(\mathbb{G}_1, *), (\mathbb{G}_2, *)$ and $(\mathbb{G}_T, *)$ are the three cyclic groups of prime order p;
- g_1 and g_2 are the generators of $\mathbb{G}_1$ and $\mathbb{G}_2$, respectively.
- e is a bilinear pairing $e : \mathbb{G}_1 \times \mathbb{G}_2 \to \mathbb{G}_T$, i.e., a map satisfying following properties:
  - Bilinearity: $\forall u \in \mathbb{G}_1, \forall v \in \mathbb{G}_2, \forall a, b \in \mathbb{Z}_p, e(u^a, v^b) = e(u, v)^{ab}$;
  - Non-degeneracy: $e(g_1, g_2) \neq 1$ and is thus a generator of $\mathbb{G}_T$.
- There are three types of bilinear maps depending on whether the group isomorphims $\psi : \mathbb{G}_1 \to \mathbb{G}_2$ and its inverse $\psi^{-1} : \mathbb{G}_2 \to \mathbb{G}_1$ are efficiently computable. We say that $(\mathbb{G}_1, \mathbb{G}_2)$ is of:
  - "Type 1" – if both Ψ and Ψ^{-1} are efficiently computable.
  - "Type 2" – if only Ψ is efficiently computable.
  - "Type 3" – if neither is efficiently computable.

Strong Diffie-Hellman Assumption (Boneh & Boyen, 2007):

Let $\mathbb{G}_1$ and $\mathbb{G}_2$ be two cyclic groups of prime order p and their respective generators are g_1 and g_2. In the bilinear group pair $(\mathbb{G}_1, \mathbb{G}_2)$, the q-SDH problem is stated as follows:

Given as input a $(q+3)$- tuple of elements $\left(g_1, g_1^{x}, g_1^{(x^2)}, \ldots, g_1^{(x^q)}, g_2, g_2^{x} \right) \in \mathbb{G}_1^{q+1} \times \mathbb{G}_2^2$, output a pair $\left(c, g_1^{1/(x+c)} \right) \in \mathbb{Z}_p \times \mathbb{G}_1$ for a freely chosen value $c \in \mathbb{Z}_p \setminus \{-x\}$.

An algorithm $\mathcal{A}$ solves the q-SDH problem in the bilinear group pair $(\mathbb{G}_1, \mathbb{G}_2)$ with advantage ϵ if

$$Adv_{\mathcal{A}}^{q-SDH} = Pr\left[\mathcal{A}\left(g_1, g_1^{x}, g_1^{(x^2)}, \ldots, g_1^{(x^q)}, g_2, g_2^{x} \right) = \left(c, g_1^{\frac{1}{(x+c)}} \right) \right] \geq \epsilon$$

where the probability is over random choices of generators $g_1 \in \mathbb{G}_1$ and $g_2 \in \mathbb{G}_2$, the random choice of $x \in \mathbb{Z}_p^*$ and the random bits consumed by $\mathcal{A}$.

PROVING THE q-SDH ASSUMPTION IN GENERIC GROUP MODEL

To gain more confidence in the SDH assumption, Boneh et al. (Boneh & Boyen, 2007) prove that it holds in generic group model by giving a lower bound on the computational complexity of the q-SDH problem for generic groups.

In the generic group model, elements of groups $\mathbb{G}_1, \mathbb{G}_2$ and $\mathbb{G}_T$ appear to be encoded as random unique strings, so that no property other than equality the adversary can exploit. In this adversary performs operations on group elements by interacting with respective oracles. There are three oracles for the group operations in each of the three groups $\mathbb{G}_1, \mathbb{G}_2$ and $\mathbb{G}_T$, two oracles for the homomorphism Ψ and its inverse Ψ^{-1}, and one oracle for the bilinear pairing $e : \mathbb{G}_1 \times \mathbb{G}_2 \to \mathbb{G}_T$. Thus there are total 12 oracles.

The working of the oracles in $\mathbb{G}_1$ is simulated by encoding the elements of $\mathbb{G}_1$ using an injective function $\xi_1 : \mathbb{Z}_p \to \{0,1\}^{\log_2 p}$, where p is the group order. Internally, the simulator $\mathcal{B}$ represents the elements of $\mathbb{G}_1$ not as actual but as their discrete logarithms relative to some arbitrary generator g_1. That is the function ξ_1 maps an integer $a \in \mathbb{Z}_p$ to the external string representation $\xi_1(a) \in \{0,1\}^{\log_2 p}$ of the elements $g_1^a \in \mathbb{G}_1$. Similarly, define an other functions $\xi_2 : \mathbb{Z}_p \to \{0,1\}^{\log_2 p}$ and $\xi_T : \mathbb{Z}_p \to \{0,1\}^{\log_2 p}$ to represent $\mathbb{G}_2$ and $\mathbb{G}_T$, respectively. Then, the adversary interacts with the oracles using the string representation of the group elements exclusively. Note that adversary knows $p = |\mathbb{G}_1| = |\mathbb{G}_2| = |\mathbb{G}_T|$.

The following theorem proves the unconditional hardness of the q-SDH problem in the generic bilinear group model.

Theorem 4: Suppose $\mathcal{A}$ is an algorithm that solves the q-SDH problem in generic bilinear groups of order p, making at most q_G oracle queries for the group operations in $\mathbb{G}_1, \mathbb{G}_2$ and $\mathbb{G}_T$, the homomorphisms Ψ and Ψ^{-1}, and the bilinear pairing e, all counted together. Suppose also that the integer $x \in \mathbb{Z}_p^*$ and the encoding functions ξ_1, ξ_2, ξ_T are chosen at random. Then, the probability, ϵ, that $\mathcal{A}$ on input $(p, \xi_1(1), \xi_1(x),\dots,\xi_1(x^q), \xi_2(1), \xi_2(x))$ outputs $\left(c, \xi_1\left(\dfrac{1}{x+c}\right)\right)$ with $c \in \mathbb{Z}_p \setminus \{-x\}$,

$$\epsilon = Pr\left[\mathcal{A}^G\left(\begin{array}{c} p, \xi_1(1), \xi_1(x),\dots,\xi_1(x^q), \\ \xi_2(1), \xi_2(x) \end{array} \right) = \left(c, \xi_1\left(\dfrac{1}{x+c}\right)\right) \right]$$

is bounded as

$$\epsilon \leq \frac{(q_G + q + 3)^2 (q+1)}{p-1}$$

Asymptotically we have, $\epsilon \leq O\left(\dfrac{q_G^2 q + q^3}{p}\right)$.

Proof: The proof is from (Boneh & Boyen, 2007). Let the algorithm $\mathcal{B}$ plays the following game with $\mathcal{A}$.

Setup Phase

$\mathcal{B}$ maintains three sets of pairs $L_1 = \{(P_{1,i}, \xi_{1,i}): i=1,\ldots,\omega_1\}$, $L_2 = \{(P_{2,i}, \xi_{2,i}): i=1,\ldots,\omega_2\}$ and $L_T = \{(P_{T,i}, \xi_{T,i}): i=1,\ldots,\omega_T\}$, such that, at step ω in the game, $\omega_1 + \omega_2 + \omega_3 = \omega + q + 3$. $P_{j,i}$ are the univariate polynomials in $\mathbb{Z}_p[X]$ and $\xi_{j,i}$ are the strings given to the adversary. The degree of the polynomial $P_{1,i}$ and $P_{2,i}$ is $\leq q$ and for $P_{T,i}$ is $\leq 2q$.

The sets are initialized at step $\omega=0$ by setting $\omega_1 = q+1$, $\omega_2 = 2$, and $\omega_T = 0$, and assigning $P_{1,i} = X^{i-1}$ for $i=1,\ldots,q+1$ and $P_{2,i} = X^{i-1}$ for $i=1,2$. And the corresponding $\xi_{1,i}$ and $\xi_{2,i}$ are set to random distinct strings.

At the start of the game $\mathcal{B}$ gives $\mathcal{A}$ the $q+3$ strings $\xi_{1,1},\ldots,\xi_{1,q+1},\xi_{2,1},\xi_{2,2}$ that correspond to the challenge SDH instance. Then $\mathcal{B}$ answers $\mathcal{A}$'s queries as follows.

Query Phase

$\mathcal{A}$ makes oracle queries on strings $\xi_{j,i}$ obtained from $\mathcal{B}$. Given any query string $\xi_{j,i}$, it is easy for $\mathcal{B}$ to determine its index i into the list L_j, and from there the corresponding polynomial $P_{j,i}$.

Group Operations: $\mathcal{A}$ may query a multiplication or division operation in $\mathbb{G}_1$. $\mathcal{B}$ increments the counter ω_1 by one. $\mathcal{A}$ gives $\mathcal{B}$ two operands $\xi_{1,i}, \xi_{1,k}$ with $1 \leq i,k < \omega_1$, and a multiply/divide selection bit. Then, $\mathcal{B}$ creates a polynomial $P_{1,\omega_1} \in \mathbb{Z}_p[X]$ which it sets to $P_{1,\omega_1} \leftarrow P_{1,i} + P_{1,k}$ for a multiplication or to $P_{1,\omega_1} \leftarrow P_{1,i} - P_{1,k}$ for a division. If the result is identical to an earlier polynomial $P_{1,l}$ for some $l<\omega_1$, the simulator $\mathcal{B}$ duplicates its string representation, $\xi_{1,\omega_1} \leftarrow \xi_{1,l}$ (in order to maintain consistency); otherwise, it selects a fresh random string $\xi_{1,\omega_1} \in \{0,1\}^{log_2 p}$. The simulator appends the pair $\left(P_{1,\omega_1}, \xi_{1,\omega_1}\right)$ to the set L_1 and gives string ξ_{1,ω_1} to $\mathcal{A}$.

Group operation queries in $\mathbb{G}_2$ and $\mathbb{G}_T$ are answered in a similar manner, based on their corresponding list L_2 and L_T.

Homomorphisms: $\mathcal{A}$ may query a homomorphism query from $\mathbb{G}_2$ to $\mathbb{G}_1$. $\mathcal{B}$ first increments the counter ω_1 by one. $\mathcal{A}$ gives a string operand $\xi_{2,i}$ with $1 \leq i \leq \omega_2$. Then, $\mathcal{B}$ makes a copy of the associated L_2 polynomial into L_1: it sets $P_{1,\omega_1} = P_{2,i}$. If L_1 already contained a copy of the polynomial, i.e., $P_{1,\omega_1} = P_{1,l}$ for some $l<\omega_1$, then $\mathcal{B}$ duplicates its existing string representation, $\xi_{1,\omega_1} \leftarrow \xi_{1,l}$; otherwise, it sets ξ_{1,ω_1} to a random string in $\{0,1\}^{log_2 p} \setminus \{\xi_{1,1},\ldots,\xi_{1,\omega_1 - 1}\}$. The pair $\left(P_{1,\omega_1}, \xi_{1,\omega_1}\right)$ to the list L_1 and the string ξ_{1,ω_1} is given to $\mathcal{A}$ as answer to the query.

Inverse homomorphism queries from $\mathbb{G}_1$ to $\mathbb{G}_2$ are answered similarly.

Pairing: $\mathcal{A}$ may query a pairing operation which consists two operands $\xi_{1,i}$ and $\xi_{1,k}$ with $1 \leq i \leq \omega_1$ and $1 \leq k \leq \omega_2$ for the current values of ω_1 and ω_2. $\mathcal{B}$ increments the counter ω_T by one and computes the product of polynomials $P_{T,\omega_T} \leftarrow P_{1,i} \cdot P_{2,k}$. The result is a polynomial of degree at most $2q$ in $\mathbb{Z}_p[X]$. If the same polynomial was already present in L_T, i.e., if $P_{T,\omega_T} = P_{T,l}$ for some $l<\omega_T$, then $\mathcal{B}$ simply clones the associated string, $\xi_{T,\omega_T} = \xi_{T,l}$; otherwise, it sets ξ_{T,ω_T} to a new random string in $\{0,1\}^{\log_2 p} \setminus \{\xi_{T,1}, \dots, \xi_{T,\omega_T-1}\}$. $\mathcal{B}$ adds the pair $(P_{T,\omega_T}, \xi_{T,\omega_T})$ to the list L_T, and gives the string ξ_{T,ω_T} to $\mathcal{A}$.

Note that $\mathcal{A}$ can get the exponentiation generically using $O(\log p)$ calls to the group operation oracles. Similarly, $\mathcal{A}$ can obtain the identity element in each group by requesting the division of any element into itself. Also note that the following invariant preserved throughout the game, where ω is the total number of oracle queries that have answered at any given time:

$$\omega_1 + \omega_2 + \omega_T = \omega + q + 3 \tag{1}$$

Output Phase

$\mathcal{A}$ returns a pair $(c, \xi_{1,l})$ where $c \in \mathbb{Z}_p$ and $1 \leq l \leq \omega_1$. Let $P_{T,l}$ be the corresponding polynomial in the set L_1.

$\mathcal{A}'s$ output is correct according to simulation framework if

$$P_{T,*}(x) = 1 \tag{2}$$

where

$$P_{T,*} = P_{1,l} \cdot \left(P_{2,2} + c.P_{2,1} \right) = P_{1,l} \cdot \left(X + c \right)$$

and $x \in \mathbb{Z}_p$ is a SDH exponent. This equality corresponds to DDH relation $e\left(A, g_2^x g_2^c \right) = e\left(g_1, g_2 \right)$ where A denotes the element of $\mathbb{G}_1$ represented by $\xi_{1,l}$.

Observe that since the constant monomial "1" has degree 0 and $P_{T,*} = P_{1,l} \cdot (X + c)$ where $(X+c)$ has degree 1, the above relation (2) cannot be satisfied in $\mathbb{Z}_p[X]$ unless $P_{1,l}$ has degree $\geq p-2$. We know that the degree of polynomial $P_{1,l}$ is at most q, therefore it is deduced that there exists an assignment in $\mathbb{Z}_p$ to the variable X for which equation (2) does not hold. Since equation (2) is thus a non-trivial polynomial equation of degree $\leq q+1$, it admits at most $q+1$ roots in $\mathbb{Z}_p$.

At this point, $\mathcal{B}$ chooses a random $x \in \mathbb{Z}_p^*$ as the secret SDH exponent, and evaluates all the polynomials under the assignment $X \leftarrow x$. If the assignment causes two non-identical polynomials within either of the sets L_1, L_2 and L_T to assume the same value, then the simulation provided by $\mathcal{B}$ to $\mathcal{A}$ was flawed since it is presented as distinct two group elements that were in fact equal. If it causes the non-trivial equation (2) to be satisfied, then the adversary has won the game. However, if no non-trivial equality emerges from the assignment, then $\mathcal{B}'s$ simulation was perfect and nonetheless resulted in $\mathcal{A}'s$ failure to solve the instance it was given.

From the above argument, the success probability of $\mathcal{A}$ in the generic model is bounded by the probability that at least one equality among the following is satisfied, for random $x \in \mathbb{Z}_p^*$:

1. $P_{1,i}(x){=}P_{1,j}(x)$ in $\mathbb{Z}_p$ - for some i,j such that $P_{1,i}{\neq}P_{1,j}$ in $\mathbb{Z}_p[X]$,
2. $P_{2,i}(x){=}P_{2,j}(x)$ in $\mathbb{Z}_p$ - for some i,j such that $P_{2,i}{\neq}P_{2,j}$ in $\mathbb{Z}_p[X]$,
3. $P_{T,i}(x){=}P_{T,j}(x)$ in $\mathbb{Z}_p$ - for some i,j such that $P_{T,i}{\neq}P_{T,j}$ in $\mathbb{Z}_p[X]$,
4. $P_{1,i}(x).(x{+}c){=}1$ in $\mathbb{Z}_p$.

Since each non-trivial polynomial $P_{1,i}$-$P_{1,j}$ has degree at most q, it vanishes at a random $x \in \mathbb{Z}_p^*$ with probability at most $q/(p-1)$. In a similar way, each non-trivial polynomial $P_{2,i}$-$P_{2,j}$ vanishes with probability $\leq q/(p-1)$, and $P_{T,i}$-$P_{T,j}$ with probability $\leq 2\,q/(p-1)$ since polynomials in L_T can have degree up to $2q$. The last equality holds with probability$\leq(q{+}1)/(p-1)$, as already shown. Summing over all valid pairs (i,j) in all four cases, it is deduced that $\mathcal{A}$ wins the game with probability,

$$\epsilon \leq \binom{\omega_1}{2}\frac{q}{p-1} + \binom{\omega_2}{2}\frac{q}{p-1} + \binom{\omega_T}{2}\frac{2q}{p-1} + \frac{q+1}{p-1}$$

It follows from equation (1) that the game ended with $\omega_1{+}\omega_2{+}\omega_T = q_G{+}q{+}3$, and we obtain:

$$\epsilon \leq (q_G+q+3)^2 q/(p-1) = O\left(q_G^2 q/p+q^3/p\right).$$

CONCLUSION

In this chapter, we understood that along with the design of cryptosystem its security proof is also necessary. We have seen two types of methods in proving the security of a cryptosystem viz. reductionist proof and game based proof. Game based proof is preferred when a cryptosystem is complex and when its security is based on multiple number theoretic assumptions, because it makes the probability analysis simple. We have seen security models for public key encryption schemes and signature schemes. The security of any cryptosystem can be proven secure in the standard model, random oracle model or in the generic group model. Among these, cryptosystems in the standard model are preferred, since it does not assume any randomness for any function in the construction of cryptosystem (as it is done in random oracle model) nor it assumes that the adversary wont exploit the special properties of underlying group (as it is assumed in generic group model secure schemes). We gave precise explanation for each of the said models with an example viz. Elgamal encryption scheme in standard model, FDH signature scheme in random oracle model and q-SDH assumption in generic group model. Similar to q-SDH assumption proof any cryptosystem security proof can be written in the generic group model.

REFERENCES

Bellare, M., Desai, A., Pointcheval, D., & Rogaway, P. (1998). Relations among notions of security for public-key encryption schemes. *Lecture Notes in Computer Science, 1462*, 26–45. doi:10.1007/BFb0055718

Bellare, M., & Rogaway, P. (1993). Random oracles are practical. *Proceedings of the 1st ACM Conference on Computer and Communications Security - CCS '93*. 10.1145/168588.168596

Boneh, D., & Boyen, X. (2007). Short Signatures Without Random Oracles and the SDH Assumption in Bilinear Groups. *Journal of Cryptology, 21*(2), 149–177. doi:10.100700145-007-9005-7

Chor, B., & Rivest, R. (1985). A Knapsack Type Public Key Cryptosystem Based On Arithmetic in Finite Fields (preliminary draft). Lecture Notes in Computer Science, 196, 54-65. doi:10.1007/3-540-39568-7_6

Diffie, W., & Hellman, M. (1976). New directions in cryptography. *IEEE Trans. Inform. Theory IEEE Transactions on Information Theory, 22*(6), 644–654. doi:10.1109/TIT.1976.1055638

Dolev, D., Dwork, C., & Naor, M. (1991). Non-malleable cryptography. *Proceedings of the Twenty-third Annual ACM Symposium on Theory of Computing - STOC '91*. 10.1145/103418.103474

Goldwasser, S., & Micali, S. (1984). Probabilistic encryption. *Journal of Computer and System Sciences, 28*(2), 270–299. doi:10.1016/0022-0000(84)90070-9

Goldwasser, S., Micali, S., & Rivest, R. (1988). A Digital Signature Scheme Secure Against Adaptive Chosen-Message Attacks. *SIAM J. Comput. SIAM Journal on Computing, 17*(2), 281–308. doi:10.1137/0217017

Lenstra, H. Jr. (1991). On the Chor-Rivest knapsack cryptosystem. *Journal of Cryptology, 3*(3), 149–155. doi:10.1007/BF00196908

Rabin, M. (1979). *Digitalized Signatures And Public-Key Functions As Intractable As Factorization*. MIT-Technical Report.

Rackoff, C., & Simon, D. (1991). Non-Interactive Zero-Knowledge Proof of Knowledge and Chosen Ciphertext Attack. *Lecture Notes in Computer Science, 576*, 433–444. doi:10.1007/3-540-46766-1_35

Ran, C., Oded, G., & Shai, H. (2004). The random oracle methodology, revisited. *Journal of the ACM, 51*(4), 557–594. doi:10.1145/1008731.1008734

Shoup, V. (1997). Lower Bounds for Discrete Logarithms and Related Problems. *Lecture Notes in Computer Science, 1233*, 256–266. doi:10.1007/3-540-69053-0_18

Shoup, V. (2004). *Sequences of Games: A Tool for Taming Complexity in Security Proofs*. Retrieved October 28, 2015, from IACR Eprint archive.

Vaudenay, S. (1998). Cryptanalysis of the Chor-Rivest cryptosystem. *Lecture Notes in Computer Science, 1462*, 243–256. doi:10.1007/BFb0055732

KEY TERMS AND DEFINITIONS

Adaptive Chosen-Ciphertext Attack (CCA2): In CCA2, adversary knows the public key (through which she can only encrypt messages of her choice) and has access to decryption oracle even after the challenge ciphertext is given to her, but with the restriction that she cannot query challenge ciphertext to the decryption oracle. Later adversary chooses two challenge messages, after which she is given a challenge ciphertext (which is the encryption of one of the challenge messages). We say a public key encryption scheme is secure under CCA2 if it is hard for an adversary to relate the challenge ciphertext to its plaintext.

Chosen Message Attack (CMA): In the signature scheme, adversary is allowed to get the signature of number of messages, of her choice, from the signer (i.e. has access to signature oracle).

Chosen-Ciphertext Attack (CCA1): In CCA1, adversary knows the public key (through which she can only encrypt messages of her choice) and also given an access to decryption oracle (through which she can get the decryption of ciphertext of her choice) before the challenge ciphertext is produced. Later adversary chooses two challenge messages, after which she is given a challenge ciphertext (which is the encryption of one of the challenge messages). We say a public key encryption scheme is secure under CCA1 if it is hard for an adversary to relate the challenge ciphertext to its plaintext.

Chosen-Plaintext Attack (CPA): In CPA, adversary knows only the public key, through which she can only encrypt messages of her choice, and later allowed to choose two challenge messages, after which she is given a challenge ciphertext (which is the encryption of one of the challenge messages). We say a public key encryption scheme is secure under CPA if it is hard for an adversary to relate the challenge ciphertext to its plaintext.

Exact Security: Proving the security of the cryptosystem with exact bounds and relations with respect to its input key length.

Existential Forgery: Adversary succeeds in breaking the underlying signature scheme if she is able to forge the signature of at least one message of her choice.

Generic Group Model: Proving the security of the cryptosystem with the assumption that the attacker did not utilize the special properties of the underlining implementation details or she is unaware of the underlining implementation details at the time of breaking the cryptosystem.

Indistinguishability or Semantic Security: Unable to learn any information about the underlying plaintext when given a challenge ciphertext in the public key encryption scheme.

Key-Only Attack: In the signature scheme, adversary knows only the public key of the signer and therefore she can only check the validity of signatures of the messages given to her.

Known Signature Attack (KSA): In the signature scheme, adversary knows the public key of the signer and has list of message/signature pairs, not of her choice.

Negligible Function: The function $\upsilon: N \rightarrow R$ is *negligible* if it vanishes faster than the inverse of any polynomial. Formally, v is negligible if for every constant $c \geq 0$ there exists an integer k_c such that $v(k) < k^c$ for all $k \geq k_c$.

Provable Security: Provable security in cryptosystem is formally proving the security of the underline cryptosystem.

Public Key Cryptography: Public key cryptography or Asymmetric cryptography is a group of algorithms or protocols where two, related and distinct, keys are involved, one is called secret (or private) key and other is called public key. Public-key encryption schemes and signature schemes are examples of public key cryptography.

Random-Oracle Model: Proving the security of the cryptosystem with the assumption that the underlining primitives, such as hash functions, works in an ideal form, i.e. assuming it to be a pure random function.

Selective Forgery: Adversary succeeds in breaking the underlying signature scheme if she is able to forge the signature of some message selected prior to the attack.

Total Break: The signature scheme is said to be total bread is adversary is able to compute the signer's secret key.

Universal Forgery: Adversary succeeds in breaking the underlying signature scheme only if she is able to forge the signature of any given message.

This research was previously published in the Handbook of Research on Modern Cryptographic Solutions for Computer and Cyber Security edited by Brij Gupta, Dharma P. Agrawal, and Shingo Yamaguchi; pages 317-341, copyright year 2016 by Information Science Reference (an imprint of IGI Global).

Chapter 14
Towards Parameterized Shared Key for AVK Approach

Shaligram Prajapat
Maulana Azad National Institute of Technology, India & Devi Ahilya University, India

Ramjeevan Singh Thakur
Maulana Azad National Institute of Technology, India

ABSTRACT

"Key" plays a vital role in every symmetric key cryptosystem. The obvious way of enhancing security of any cryptosystem is to keep the key as large as possible. But it may not be suitable for low power devices since higher computation will be done for longer keys and that will increase the power requirement which decreases the device's performance. In order to resolve the former specified problem an alternative approach can be used in which the length of key is fixed and its value varies in every session. This is Time Variant Key approach or Automatic Variable Key (AVK) approach. The Security of AVK based cryptosystem is enhanced by exchanging some parameters instead of keys between the communicating parties, then these parameters will be used to generate required keys at the receiver end. This chapter presents implementation of the above specified Mechanism. A model has been demonstrated with parameterized scheme and issues in AVK approach. Further, it has been analyzed from different users' perspectives. This chapter also highlights the benefits of AVK model to ensure two levels of security with characterization of methods for AVK and Estimation of key computation based on parameters only. The characteristic components of recent styles of key design with consideration of key size, life time of key and breaking threshold has also been pointed out. These characteristics are essential in the design of efficient symmetric key cryptosystem. The novel approach of AVK based cryptosystem is suitable for low power devices and useful for exchanging very large objects or files. This scheme has been demonstrated with Fibonacci-Q matrix and sparse matrix based diffused key information exchange procedures. These models have been further tested from perspective of hackers and cryptanalyst, to exploit any weakness with fixed size dynamic keys.

DOI: 10.4018/978-1-7998-1763-5.ch014

INTRODUCTION

"Sending and receiving information securely" is the sole objective of every communication system. The medium on which information is propagated has been transformed drastically due to growth in communication technology. As the transmission over public network takes places between unknown entities, ensuring security of information is a challenging task due to vulnerability of the public systems (Diffe & Hellman, 1977). Hence, ensuring security of information between participating entities is essential. Similarly, protection of data of interconnected machines within networked system from malicious damage is also desirable aspect of a successful cryptosystem. Since, the cryptosystem is exposed publicly in networked system. All of its components like plaintext, cipher text, key, enciphering algorithm and deciphering algorithms are available on the network either in hidden formats or exposed in some other way(depending upon mechanism) (Chakrabarti, et. al., 2008). Except the original text i.e. the plain text before leaving sender's machine, all other information is available in encrypted or hidden format. Among these components of symmetric key based cryptosystem, secrecy of key is important because if key is compromised, then rest other components are of no use. Using brute force attacks mechanism, weakness of these cryptosystems can be exploited, where cryptanalyst or attacker tries each possible key until the right key is found to decrypt the message (Prajapat & Thakur, *2015*). According to Moore's law, the power of personal computers has historically doubled approximately every 18 months. In addition, well equipped attackers often develop new techniques and algorithms to improve the efficacy of key search attacks. Therefore, estimate of the time required for successful key search attacks must be revised downward as the computing power and resources which are available to attacker's increases. Most of the time they are successful due to: availability and accessibility of fast computing resources, capability to use power of AI enabled algorithms, availability of sender/receiver's personal information to prune the search space making task of cryptanalyst and hacker's job easier (A. Nadeem et. al., 2005). With the growth of multi course processing, availability of CPU-GPU pairs parallel and grid based computing algorithms, the search time can be reduced to polynomial time from exponential (infeasible) in near future. Presently, to enhance the success rate of brute force attack best alternatives are:

- Reduce the life time of key.
- Increase the key length. In former approach by choosing the shorter key lifetime, one can reduce the possible potential damage even if one of the keys is known.

In later approach, choosing longer key length one can decrease the probability of successful attacks by increasing the number of combinations that are possible (Prajapat & Thakur, *2015*). The state of art symmetric key based cryptosystem trends towards increasing length of key for enhancing security, but it has certain side effects. It increases processing, resource utilization, and time consumption. In the next section of this chapter, we will learn the model of AVK, as a solution to the above problem. And subsequently we will learn to add extra security provision for this model of key exchange using exchange parameters only mechanism. The chapter also highlights novel methods for generating keys using parameterized key based cryptosystem.

BACKGROUND OF KEY SIZE SELECTION PROBLEM

The traditional approach of choosing key is actually deciding the string of characters consisting of digits, numbers, special symbols etc. (depending upon the type of implementation and system need) which is checked by source or destination. If the supplied key matches with the one which is associated with the actual user's resource (files, databases, etc), access is granted to all the resources of the authorized user (Shaligram Prajapat, R.S. Thakur, 2015).

- **Worst Case:** It is obvious, simple, straightforward and inexpensive style of choosing key length. In this scheme, user will be frequently choosing a relatively short string of characters. The user may be allowed to choose these keys, but, in such situations, the chosen key would be easy to remember. It implies that key can be easily cracked with a predictable set of permutations and combinations. Thus, it becomes easier for an intruder to guess the key and breach into system.
- **Best Case:** In this scheme, when difficult key or less obvious key is chosen, it breaks the comfort zone of user. The key is difficult to remember. So, the users save the key in the form of writing or recording the key somewhere noted on paper or may be in the system also, thus making it equally vulnerable.

One alternative to above mentioned problems is that, we can increase the length of key making the system relatively more secure against exhaustive search performed by cryptanalyst. But, before dealing with increment aspects of key length, it would be worth mentioning the notion of Safe Period and Breaking Period. The concept of probable expected *Safe period* and *Breaking period* or *Threshold* to prevent a key from systematic attacks can be computed from equation(1) and(2), This can be used as an indicator of the effectiveness of a selected length of key used in a given cryptosystem.

- **Safe Period:** It is the maximum time required to guess actual key using brute force method. It can be computed from following expression.

$$\text{Safe Time} = \frac{\text{Total number of keys} \ \times \ \text{Time to enter one key}}{2} \tag{1}$$

- **Breaking Period:** For any given key, it is the *optimistic time* to break the key, selected from characters set domain of size N, *Breaking period* for a given key can be computed from following expression:

$$\text{Breaking Threshold} = \frac{N^x \ * \ L}{R} \tag{2}$$

where:

x = length of key (in number of characters)
R = Character transmission rate. *R* characters per minute. (Computed from time required to enter data)

N = Size of character-set (domain-set) (i.e. number of letters and numeric from which the key is selected in number of characters involved for entry and replying in a log- in attempt is N characters)

Situation: 1

Consider a hypothetical cryptic communication system where sender or receiver uses keys of length 6 characters with the key entry rate 60 characters per minute. The key is constructed from a character set, a domain of size 20 characters (this means that only a limited set of infrequent characters are being used), the key-length x is 6 characters(Bytes), and the number of characters L in the session log-in is 15 characters(Bytes). For an operator working on a keyboard for the exhaustive key search, the expected Safe period would be:

$$\text{Safe Time} = \frac{\text{All number of keys} \quad * \quad \text{Time to enter a key}}{2}$$

$$\text{Safe Time} = \frac{20^6 \quad * \quad 15}{2 * 60} \text{ Minutes}$$

Safe Time = $8 * 10^6$ Minutes

Safe Time $\approx$ 15 Years

Situation: 2 (Usage of Parallel Node)

Further, extending the idea of previous case, with the assumption of using more systems (for simplicity, n=2). If two systems are used in parallel to solve the problem of situation-1, what would be effect over the performance of Safe period? Obviously, this may result in reduction in computation of expected Safe period because exhaustive search is empowered by the use of additional computing node connected to the first computing node.

We further assume that the two computers are connected by a high-speed line on which the data transmission rate (R) *is* 1200 characters per second (CPS) the expected Safe period would be:

$$\text{Safe Time} = \frac{20^6 \quad * \quad 15}{2 * 36000} \text{ Minutes}$$

Safe time= 13334.34 minutes

Safe time $\approx$ 9.523 days.

This reduces the effort from infeasible (result of situation 1) to feasible region (result of situation 2).

Situation: 3 (Using Delay to Prevent Guessing)

Allowing 'delay' between successive failure attempts also has an impact on breaking threshold. In other words, by adding automatic delay after each unsuccessful attempt can enhance the security, this can be elucidated as follows:

If a delay of 5 seconds is added between 2 unsuccessful attempts, then the time for each entry increases from 0.0125 second to 5.0125 second and the expected Safe period becomes greater than 5 years. In this way, the delay between each unsuccessful guessing makes it harder or infeasible to guess.

Formulation of Basis for Deciding the Length of a Key

The discussion of situation-1, situation-2 and situation-3 can be extended to form the baseline for deciding optimum key size. To compute the key length of suitable performance, let us assume that p is the probability that a correct key will be found by a cryptanalyst, *a*nd the time period in months over which systematic attempts are to be made over each 24 hours per day of operation is *M,* so *p* will have an upper bounded of $p_0$where:

$$P_0 = \frac{\text{Number of possible attempts to break the key in M months}}{\text{Number of Possible Keys}} \tag{3}$$

The number of possible attempts in M months $= \dfrac{T * M * 30 * 24 * 60}{L}$

The number of possible key is N^x, Therefore

$$p = \frac{4.32 * 10^4 * T * M}{L * N^x}$$

The probability that a proper key will be found is *p,* where $p \geq p_0$, which gives

$$N^x \geq \frac{4.32 * 10^4 * T * M}{L * p_0} \tag{4}$$

This is Anderson's formula and can be used to decide the length of key i.e. x, so that an intruder has a limited possibility of guessing the valid key, that is not greater than p. This can be explained with following illustrations:

Example 1

Consider a set of alphabets with 26 characters to create a key, it is desirable that it will have the probability of not greater than 0.001 of being discovered or interpolated after systematic attack of one month. If data entry rate is 300 characters per minute (CPS) and maximum key entry requires 15 characters, then estimate the length of a key. Using the equation (4),

$$20^x \geq \frac{4.32 * 10^4 * 300 * 1}{15 * 0.001}$$

$$20^x \geq 8.64 * 10^8$$

For

$x=2$, $26^2 \leq 8.64 * 10^8$
$x=3$, $26^3 \leq 8.64 * 10^8$
$x=4$, $26^4 \leq 8.64 * 10^8$
$x=5$, $26^5 \leq 8.64 * 10^8$
$x=6$, $26^6 \leq 8.64 * 10^8$
$x=7$, $26^7 \geq 8.64 * 10^8$

Thus optimum key size is 7 and above situations infer following facts can be inferred.

1. The critical factor for preventing an intruder from discovering a key by an exhaustive search is the length of the key.
2. For optimum key size, only five or six characters in length are relatively safe from systematic attack,
3. Key will generally not fail because of systematic attack, but, as a result of the carelessness of person who is using it.

MAIN FOCUS OF THE CHAPTER

Enhancement of Symmetric Key Based Cryptosystem by Increasing Key Size

Consider the following table, showing some symmetric key based cryptosystems and key size for encryption and decryption of plaintext information. DES was used widely in the financial industries. DES is a block cipher with 64-bit block size and 56-bit keys (Nadeem et. al., 2005; Prajapat & Thakur, 2014). This algorithm is still strong but, new versions with increased key length; 3DES have been developed to make it more secure. International Data Encryption Algorithm –IDEA uses 128 bit key and is considered very secure. RC2, RC4 are also fast cipher but, requires large keys. It accepts keys of variable length (Elminaam at. al., 2008).

Table 1. Some Symmetric algorithms and their key lengths

S.no.	Algorithm	Key Length
1	DES	64-bit block size and 56-bit keys
2	3DES	64 bit block size with 192 bits key size
3	RC2	64-bits block size with a variable key size, ranges from 8 to128 bits
4	Blowfish	64-bit block –size with variable length key, ranging from 32 bits to 448 bits; default 128
5	AES	128-bit block size with variable key length of 128, 192, or 256 bits; default 256.
6	RC6	128 bit block size of with key sizes of 128, 192 and 256 bits.

(Shaligram Prajapat at. al.,2013)

AVK Based Model for Symmetric Key Based Cryptosystem

In literature, various studies have been conducted to analyze the performance of algorithms for fixing the key and varying its length like 128 bit, 192 bit and 256 bit key. The significant observation was that increasing key size requires more battery and time consumption (D. S. A. Elminaam at. al., 2008). Simulation based results also shows that effect of changing the key size of AES on power consumption reduces performance .The performance comparison for AES and RC6 algorithm (with128 bit, 192 bits and 256 bit keys) over processing time and energy also highlights similar impact on increasing key sizes. It can be seen that going from 128 bits key to 192 bits causes increase in power and time consumption about 8% and going from 192 bits to 256 bits, key causes an increase of 16% .Results were similar in case of RC6. Alternative approach for improving security instead of using long keys of variable length to minimize time complexity and high power consumption AVK concept can be introduced, where the secret key will vary from session to session. Subsequent section will discuss this alternative AVK based strategy, where efficient transmission of data from source to destination will be achieved by using dynamic key.

Table 2. AVK approach for Symmetric key based cryptosystem (P.Chakrabarti. 2007)

Session ID	Alice Sends	Bob Receives	Bob Sends	Alice Receives	Remarks
1	Secret key (say 2)	2	Secret key (say 6)	6	For next slot, Alice will use 6 as key and Bob 2 as key for transmitting data.
2	Alice sends Bob first data as: 3 xor 6	Bob gets back original data as: (3 xor 6)xor 6 = 3	Bob sends first data as: 7 xor 2	Alice gets back original data as: (7 xor 2) xor 2 = 7	Alice will create new key 6 xor 7 for next slot. Bob will create new key (2xor 3).
3	Alice sends next data as: 4 xor (6 xor7)	Bob gets back original data as: ((4 xor(6xor 7)) (6 xor 7)) = 4	Bob sends next data as: 8xor (2xor 3)	Alice recovers data as: ((8 xor(2xor 3)) (2 xor 3)) = 8	Thus, Alice and Bob respectively exchange data 34 and 78.

Fibonacci-Q Matrix Based Information Exchange

The working of encryption based on Fibonacci-Q matrix based cryptosystem (Shaligram at. al. 2012) is described below.

Encryption Process

Step 1: $M = \begin{bmatrix} m_1 & m_2 \\ m_3 & m_4 \end{bmatrix}$ where $m_i > 0$ and i=1,2,3,4,...

Step 2: With parameters n=4 we construct keys as

$$Q^4 = \begin{bmatrix} 00005 & 00003 \\ 00003 & 00002 \end{bmatrix} \text{ or key} = \begin{bmatrix} 00000101 & 00000011 \\ 00000011 & 00000010 \end{bmatrix}$$

Step 3: Generate Cipher text matrix $C = M*K = \begin{bmatrix} m_1 & m_2 \\ m_3 & m_4 \end{bmatrix} * \begin{bmatrix} 00000101 & 00000011 \\ 00000011 & 00000010 \end{bmatrix}$

$e_1 = 00000101*m_1 + 00000011*m_2$
$e_2 = 00000011*m_1 + 00000010*m_2$
$e_3 = 00000101*m_3 + 00000011*m_4$
$e_4 = 00000011*m_3 + 00000010*m_4$

Decryption Process

Stakhov (2006), have explained the decryption process as follows:

Step 1: $E = \begin{bmatrix} e_1 & e_2 \\ e_3 & e_4 \end{bmatrix}$ where $m_i > 0$ and i=1,2,3,4...

Step 2: Compute the reversible deciphering function with shared parameters n=4 we construct keys as

$$Q^{-4} = \begin{bmatrix} 00002 & -00003 \\ -00003 & 00005 \end{bmatrix} \text{ or key} = \begin{bmatrix} 00000010 & -00000011 \\ -00000011 & 00000101 \end{bmatrix}$$

Step 3: Recover plain text matrix $M = C*K = \begin{bmatrix} e_1 & e_2 \\ e_3 & e_4 \end{bmatrix} * \begin{bmatrix} 00000010 & -00000011 \\ -00000011 & 00000101 \end{bmatrix}$

$m_1 = 00000101*e_1 + 00000011*e_2$
$m_2 = 00000011*e_1 + 00000010*e_2$
$m_3 = 00000101*e_3 + 00000011*e_4$
$m_4 = 00000011*e_3 + 00000010*e_4$

Above process has been analyzed, implemented and tested. (See details Shaligram et.al. 2012, 2013, 2014 and 2015).The algorithm has been analyzed, implemented and tested in the form of a symmetric key from both user and hackers or cryptanalyst's perspective. To support AVK model, it is recommended that parameter n and p must be changed from session to session to compute key of a particular session. In the next section, another approach for AVK based symmetric cryptosystem is discussed.

Sparse Matrix Based Information Exchange

Consider secure transmission of information of moving objects over noisy channel. Assume that desirable data of our interest are the non-zero entries of sparse matrix, using row major form (assuming standard representation scheme) at transmission end. The location coordinate (i, j) of nonzero element would serve as a key for encryption/ decryption using a linear curve, where a and b are row and column indexes of non-zero data respectively (Shaligram Prajapat, at. al., 2014). The assumption of proposed algorithms is that row and column indexes starts from 1.so reconsidering the original compact sparse matrix representation:

Linear AVK (LAVK) Based Encryption Scheme

Algorithm LSAVK-Encrypt (Matrix CSM[ ])

{ // Receive plain text from sender with location information, generate cipher and transmit

    for each i from 1 to CSM[0][3] in steps of 1 do

      { a ← CSM[i][0], b ← CSM[i][1], plaintext ← CSM[i][2];

      Generate Cipher Text CSM'[i][2] ← a+b*plaintext;

      Transmit Cipher Text(CSM'[ ])

      }

}

Algorithm LSAVK-Decrypt (Matrix CSM'[ ])

{ // Receive compact sparse matrix(cipher text) and recover plaintext information

    for each i from 1 to CSM[0][2] in steps of 1 do

      { a ← CSM'[i][0], b ← CSM'[i][1], plaintext ← CSM'[i][2];

      Generate Plain Text CSM'[i][3] ← $(CSM'[i][3] - CSM'[i][0]) / CSM'[i][1]$;

      return Plain-Text(CSM'[ ])

      }

}

The LAVK-Encrypt() is a linear method that accepts compact form of sparse matrix entries (containing information to be transmitted)and uses location (index position) as parameter for Cipher generation i.e. it exploits information of nonzero element(information content) and converts the information into cipher text in linear time. Similarly, LAVK-Decrypt () receives cipher text of data item and based on its key (using position co-ordinate of element as parameter).It recovers plaintext information. Since, key is diffused into the block of data (Compact Sparse Matrix) which is being transferred and no key exchange takes place separately, so it becomes highly difficult to interpolate any information regarding plaintext or key.

Each element or datum (data) is having a different location, such as the key. The location index or coordinate will act as parameter to construct key for encryption or decryption of data. Following table demonstrates the working of proposed scheme:

The sparse matrix recovered by intruder or hacker would by as follows:

[1,3,19; 2,1,15; 2,4,11; 2,6,18; 3,2,12; 3,5,14; 4,2,11; 4,3,29; 5,1,11; 5,2,15; 5,5,16; 6,3,9]

The advantage of LAVK based algorithms can be studied from the above table. It is noticed that for similar data, (Row-id. 3, 7 and 9) encrypted information would be different-bit strings, so patterns of original plain text cannot be generated; this adds an addition level of security. The data is encrypted by position of the device; hence, the key would be different for different locations. So, same information would have different ciphers making position based variability in data items. The algorithm is memory efficient $O(p+1)=O(p)$ and takes $O(n)$ time for processing, where p is number of nonzero items.

Table 3. LAVK approach for secure information transmission

Index	I	Generated Cipher by (Man in middle)	M(i,j)	Data from Node-1 (Binary Plaintext)	Message bits on Noisy Channel	Decimal Equivalent	Data Received by Node-2 (Received Plaintext)
00	06	06	12	00001100	01001110	078	00001100
01	01	03	19	00010011	00111010	058	00010011
02	02	01	15	00001111	00010001	017	00001111
03	02	04	11	00001011	00101110	046	00001011
04	02	06	18	00010010	01101110	110	00010010
05	03	02	12	00001100	00011011	027	00001100
06	03	05	14	00001110	01001010	073	00001110
07	04	02	11	00001011	00011010	026	00001011
08	04	03	29	00011101	01011011	091	00011101
09	05	01	11	00001011	00010000	016	00001011
10	05	02	15	00001111	00100011	035	00001111
11	05	05	16	00010000	01010101	085	00010000
12	06	03	09	00001001	00100001	033	00001001

PARAMETERS ONLY SCHEME FOR AUTOMATIC VARIABLE KEY

So far during the discussions, in the previous sections, we have pointed out about state-of-art crypto-graphic algorithms that rely on increasing the key size. Thus, it would require more time, computation and battery power. Automatic Variable Key (AVK) has been devised to explore alternative approach. Two methods have been discussed to demonstrate how AVK based cryptosystem can be developed. Both methods use some parameters to construct key. Fibonacci method (for a particular session, with given n and p values computations can be done for f_{n-1}, f_n and f_{n+1}) (Shaligram Prajapat, R.S.Thakur., 2015) and Sparse Matrix (Location co-ordinate (i, j) will act as parameter for encryption /Decryption) based approach can be modeled for automatic variability of key for secure information exchange. For these AVK based cryptosystem, parameters (n, p) or location (i, j) can vary from session to session. So, even if the intruder gets unwanted access to the key of session at time slot t, it would not be valid for original message extraction in session slot at time (t+1) onwards. In this model, since key is not transmitted in the data transfer. So, it becomes highly difficult to interpolate any information regarding plaintext or key. This entire process can be modeled in the form of parameterized-AVK model as Figure 1:

In this model, (shown below) node-1 and node-2 (Can be extended to node-n) are communicating with each other by sharing parameters instead of key exchange. The model also demonstrates that for same parameters different approaches may generate same key. Thus, additional level of security may be achieved by parameterized model. The two approaches for computation of key from parameters have been demonstrated by approach-1 and approach-2.

Computing Keys from Geometric Mean

Following algorithm demonstrates working of information exchange based on 'parameters only' scheme:

$Algorithm\ parameters4Key - node - 1\left(parameters\ p_1,\ p_2\right)$

{

1. Sense parameters p_1, p_2;

2. Compute the key for information exchange by: $key_i = \left(p_1 * p_2\right)^{1/2}$;

3. Sense the information to exchange $= D_i$;

Figure 1. Parameterized-AVK model

Node A

AVK Keys K $_1$, K$_2$,.....

AVK Keys K $_1$, K$_2$,.....

Node B

Parameters P$_1$, P$_2$,.....

Key Computation using Parameter Only

4.   If $\left(mode == transmit\right)$ Generate Cipher text $C_i = Encrypt\left(D_i, \ key_i\right)$;
Transmit Ci;

　　　Receive Plain text $P_i = Decrypt\left(D_i, \ key_i\right)$;

5. *else Use* P_i;

　　　}

Computing Keys from Arithmetic and Harmonic Mean

Algorithm Parameters4Key – node – 2 $\left(parameters \ p_1, \ p_2\right)$
{

1.   *Sense parameters* p_1, p_2;

2.   *Compute the Arithmetic Mean A.M. =* $\left(p_{1+}p_2\right)/2$;

3.   *Compute the Harmonic Mean H.M. =* $2 * \ p_1 \ * p_2 \ /\left(p_1 + p_2\right)$

4.   *Compute the* $Key_i = \left(A.M.*H.M\right)^{1/2}$

5.   *If* $\left(mode == transmit\right)$ *Generate Cipher text* $C_i = Encrypt\left(D_i, \ key_i\right); Transmit \ C_i;$

　　　Receive Plain text $P_i = Decrypt\left(D_i, \ key_i\right)$;

6.   *else Use* $P_{i;}$

　　　}

The major advantage of approach-1 and approach-2 can be noted here, without exchanging entire key, node-1 and node-2 will securely communicate with each other. Both the nodes are computing the same key using different function, which in turn enhances the level of security.

Hence, even if the parameters or method at any one node for key computation is known, it will not work for next node or parameter set (Shaligram Prajapat, R.S.Thakur, 2014).

EVALUATION OF CRYPTOSYSTEM: HACKERS / CRYPTANALYST PERSPECTIVE

The strength and weakness of cryptosystem can be evaluated by exploiting them and identifying degree of damage or loss of information. Harder the exploitation of system, weakness will make the cryptosystem more secure. By collecting or recording parameter information in log, noticing availability of captured cipher text, some guessed plaintext may be used by cryptanalyst or hacker for pattern discovery, and guessing the vulnerability of system, will measure the degree of success.

Table 4. Types of patterns needed by cryptanalysis

Input for Cryptic Mining	Information assumed to be available for pattern mining		
	Encryption Algorithm	Cipher text (for decoding)	Addition Requirements
Cipher text only	Yes	Yes	Only patterns from cipher text have to be explored or scanned, due to randomization of ciphers, it is relatively harder, but some information like key size can be interpolated.
Known plaintext	Yes	Yes	Identification of patterns from log of (P, C) pairs, where: P = plain text, C= Cipher text
Chosen plaintext	Yes	Yes	Patterns for CP can be explored i.e. Cipher text chosen by cryptanalyst and corresponding decrypted plain text i.e. (C, p = (C)) and learning from these patterns for future prediction can be attempted.
Chosen text	Yes	Yes	Patterns for training and cross validation are decided by cryptanalyst. Plain text chosen by cryptanalyst corresponding cipher text(PC), Cipher text chosen by cryptanalyst & corresponding decrypted plain text(CP)

Analyzing Parameter Passing through Queries

Consider log of session information in the form of a database consisting of information about key with corresponding set of parameters, $P=\{p_1, p_2, p_3, p_4\}$ and it is possible to submit queries about the composition of key for any key, then a series of request and replies in the following format can be achieved:

$\text{Request}_1(p_1 + p_2 + p_3)$ Reply key k_1
$\text{Request}_2(p_1 + p_2 + p_4)$ Reply key k_2
$\text{Request}_3(p_1 + p_3 + p_4)$ Reply key k_3
$\text{Request}_4(p_2 + p_3 + p_4)$ Reply key k_4

The augmented matrix of request response set would be:

$$\begin{bmatrix} 1 & 1 & 1 & 0 & key_1 \\ 1 & 1 & 0 & 1 & key_2 \\ 1 & 0 & 1 & 1 & key_3 \\ 0 & 1 & 1 & 1 & key_3 \end{bmatrix}$$

Simplification of these four equations values of all the unknowns can be solved, for example:

$p_1 = (key_1 + key_2 + key_3 - 3*key_4)/3$
$p_2 = (key_1 + key_2 - 2*key_3 + 2*key_4)/3$
$p_3 = (key_1 + key_3 + key_4 - 2*key_2)/3$
$p_4 = (key_2 + key_3 + key_4 - 2*key_1)/3$

Thus, it is clear that parameters p_1, p_2, p_3, p_4 are known, that are being propagated over the network. Known parameters, known cipher text pairs log can be used to predict future parameters. Hence, several attempts will be made to predict the probable key or plain text.

- **Improvement:** For protecting the system, request must be set small and with zero or minimum overlapping. If requests have no overlapping the database cannot be compromised through the use of simultaneous equations. Following algorithm may be used for solving n equations or n parameters,

$$Algorithm\, GEMSAE\left(A[\ ],\ n,\ X \right)$$
$$Begin$$
$$for\ i = 1\ to\ n\ in\ steps\ of\ 1\ do$$
$$\quad for\ j = 1\ to\ \left(n+1\right)\ in\, steps\ of\ 1\ do$$
$$\quad\quad Read\ A_{ij}$$
$$\quad end\ for$$
$$end\ for$$

//Forward elimination with partial pivoting

$$for\ k = 1\ to\ n-1\ in\ steps\ of\ 1\ do$$
$$max \leftarrow \left| A_{kk} \right|$$
$$p \leftarrow k$$
$$for\ m = \left(k+1\right)\ to\ n\ in\ steps\ of\ 1\ do$$
$$\quad if\ \left(\left| A_{mk} \right| > max \right)\ then$$
$$\quad \{ max \leftarrow \left| A_{mk} \right|;\ p \leftarrow m;\ \}$$

$$end\ for$$
$$if\ \left(max\ \leq\ e \right)$$
$$\quad \{ Print\ "Ill-Conditioned\ matrix";exit\}$$
$$else\ if\ \left(p = k\right) then\ go\ to\ ****$$
$$for\ q = k\ to\ \left(n+1\right)\ in\ steps\, of\ 1\ do$$
$$\quad \{ tmp \leftarrow A_{kq};\ A_{kq} \leftarrow A_{pq};\ A_{pq} \leftarrow tmp\ ;\}$$

$end\ for$

$for\ m\ =\ \left(k+1\right)\ to\ n$

$***\quad for\ i=\left(k+1\right)\ to\ n\ in\ steps of\ 1\ do$

$\qquad u \leftarrow A_{ik}\ /\ A_{kk}$

$\qquad for\ j=\ k\ to\ \left(n+1\right)\ in\ steps of\ 1\ do$

$\qquad\qquad A_{ij} \leftarrow A_{ij}\ -u*A_{kj}$

$\qquad end\ for$

$\quad endfor$

$endfor$

// Back Substitution

$X_{n} \leftarrow A_{n(n+1)}\ /\ A_{ii};$

$for\ i=\left(n-1\right)\ to\ 1\ in\ steps\ of\ -1\ do$

$sum \leftarrow 0;$

$\qquad for\ j=\left(\ i+1\right)\ to\ n\ in\ steps\ of\ 1\ do$

$\qquad\qquad sum \leftarrow sum\ +\ A_{ij}*X_{j}$

$\qquad end\ for$

$X_{i} \leftarrow \left(\ A_{i(n+1)}-sum\ \right)/A_{ii}$

$end\ for$

End

GEMSAE receives linear equations $Ax=b$ and converts it into upper triangular system $Ux = b'$. The matrix 'U' occupies upper triangular element positions of A. The algorithm ensures that $A_{kk}=0$.

- **Complexity Analysis:** For k from 0 to n-1, GEMSAE systematically eliminates variable $X[k]$ from equations (k+1) to n-1, so that coefficient matrix becomes upper triangular. In k^{th} iteration, an appropriate multiple is subtracted from each of equation k+1 to n-1. The multiple of kth equation is selected in such a manner that the kth coefficient becomes zero from k+1 to n, eliminating X_k from these equations.
- **Computations:** Assume that each scalar arithmetic takes a unit time. The kth iteration of the outer loop does not involve any computation on rows 1 to k-1; or columns 1 to k-1. So, only lower right F_{n-1}, F_n and F_{n+1} $(n-k)*(n-k)$ sub matrix of A will be computationally active. GEMSAE involves approx. $n^2/2$ divisions and approx. $[(n^3/3) - (n^2/2)]$ subtractions and multiplications. For large n, sequential run time of the GEMSAE is approx. $2n^3/3$. So, sequential complexity $T(n)=O(n^3)$.

CONCLUSION

This chapter highlights the significance of key, key size, life time of key and breaking threshold with suitable examples. These characteristics are essential in the design of every symmetric key cryptosystem. Both key length, key life time play a crucial role in security of cryptosystems. The obvious way of enhancing security of any cryptosystem is to keep the key as large as possible which may be suitable for low power devices. AVK scheme is in development phase, and various models are being evolved and suggested with fixed size dynamic keys empowered by 'parameters only' approach. Various parameterized security models without key exchange among communicating entities has been discussed with their merits and demerits. These schemes have been discussed in the light of exploiting patterns of ciphers, parameters and log of session wise captured information. This chapter also paves way for application of mining algorithms in cryptographic domain.

FUTURE RESEARCH DIRECTIONS

The choice of key length must be from 4 to 6 characters for optimum size with respect to time and power issue. Larger size of AVK would not be significant, and shorter key length would compromise the strength of cryptosystem. Performance analysis of AVK approach with state of art methods needs to be analyzed carefully. Choosing key as Fibonacci Q matrix may have several issues, such as, over what range of n and p cryptosystem will give optimum performance, beyond which it may have slow performance and easy guessing issues. From security point of view, it would be better to have matrix elements of 4 to 6 digits that is minimum 32 bit to maximum key size of 48 bits. The Sparse approach for AVK can be extended for three and higher dimensions. For cipher generation of any input size, encryption of plaintext or decryption of cipher text can be explored with various nonlinear curves and can be compared for efficiency with LAVKencrypt() and LAVKdecrypt(). Any cryptosystem which is working properly for encryption and decryption task always needs to be passed through proper screen-test from hackers or intruder's perspective to rectify against weaknesses. So, for how long it fights against brute force attack and AI based tests? It needs to be investigated. It is assumed that output of encryption process is always random, free from patterns. But, in reality this is not the case. Patterns may be discovered, attempts can be made based on: cipher classification and similarity. Ciphers may be arranged into clusters based upon key size, plaintext-cipher text correlations, association rule base can be formulated for predictions based on frequent patterns. So, metric to describe efficiency of cryptosystem w.r.t. systematic attack has to be tested also from these AI based tests.

REFERENCES

Nadeem, A., & Javed, M. Y. (2005, Aug). A Performance comparison of data encryption algorithms. *IEEE-International Conference of Information and Communication Technologies*. 10.1109/ICICT.2005.1598556

Schneier. (1996). *Applied cryptography: Protocols, Algorithms, and Source Code in C*. Wiley.

Elminaam, Kader, & Hadhoud. (2008). Performance Evaluation of Symmetric Encryption Algorithms. *International Journal of Computer Science and Network Security, 8*(12), 280–286.

Sutherland et al. (2010). *Cracking Codes and Cryptograms for Dummies*. Wiley.

Hellman. (2002). An Overview of Public Key Cryptography. IEEE Communication Magazine, 16(6), 24-32.

Chakrabarti, P., Bhuyan, B., Chowdhuri, A., & Bhunia, C. (2008). A novel approach towards realizing optimum data transfer and Automatic Variable Key (AVK) in cryptography. IJCSNS, 8(5), 241-250.

Prajapat, S., & Thakur. (2015a). Optimal Key Size of the AVK for Symmetric Key Encryption. *Covenant Journal of Information & Communication Technology, 71.*

Prajapat, S., & Thakur. (2015b). Various Approaches towards Crypt-analysis. *International Journal of Computer Applications, 127*(14), 15-24.

Prajapat, S., & Thakur, R. S. (2016a). Cryptic Mining for Automatic Variable Key Based Cryptosystem. *Elsevier Procedia Computer Science, 78*(78C), 199–209. doi:10.1016/j.procs.2016.02.034

Prajapat, S., & Thakur. (2016b). Realization of information exchange with Fibo-Q based Symmetric Cryptosystem. *International Journal of Computer Science and Information Security.*

Prajapat, S., & Thakur. (2016c). Cryptic Mining: Apriori Analysis of Parameterized Automatic Variable Key based Symmetric Cryptosystem. *International Journal of Computer Science and Information Security.*

Chakrabarti. (2007). Application of Automatic Variable Key (AVK) in RSA. *International Journal HIT Transactions on ECCN, 2*(5), 301-305.

Chakraborty, Mondal, Chaudhuri, & Bhunia. (2006). Various new and modified approaches for selective encryption (DES, RSA and AES) with AVK and their comparative study. International Journal HIT Transaction on ECCN, 1(4), 236-244.

Prajapat, Parmar, & Thakur. (2015). Investigation of Efficient Cryptosystem Using SGcrypter. *IJAER,* 853-858.

Prajapat et al. (2012). A Novel Approach For Information Security With Automatic Variable Key Using Fibonacci Q-Matrix. *International Journal of Computer & Communication Technology, 3*(3).

Prajapat, Rajput, & Thakur. (2013, Oct). Time variant approach towards Symmetric Key. *IEEE- Science and Information Conference 2013.*

Prajapat, & Thakur. (2014a, Mar). Time variant key using exact differential equation model. *National Conference in Emerging Trends in cloud Computing and Digital Communication* (ETCDC-2014).

Prajapat, & Thakur. (2014b, Jun). *Sparse approach for realizing AVK for Symmetric Key Encryption.* Presented on second days, International Research Conference on Engineering, Science and Management (IRCESM 2014), Dubai, UAE.

Prajapat, & Thakur. (2014c, Oct). *Time variant key using Fuzzy differential equation model.* Oriental Bhopal, India.

Prajapat, & Thakur. (2015a). Towards Optimum size of key for AVK based cryptosystem. Covenant Journal of Informatics and Communication Technology, 3(2).

Prajapat, & Thakur. (2013, Sep). *Recurrence relation approach for key prediction.* 18th International Conference of Gwalior Academy of Mathematical Science (GAMS), MANIT, Bhopal, India.

Prajapat, Swami, Singroli, Thakur, Sharma, & Rajput. (2014). Sparse approach for realizing AVK for Symmetric Key Encryption. *International Journal of Recent Development in Engineering and Technology, 2*(4), 13-18.

Prajapat, & Thakur. (2015b, Jun). Markov Analysis of AVK Approach of Symmetric Key Based Cryptosystem. *LNCS, 9159,* 164-176.

Prajapat, & Thakur. (2014d, Oct). Association Rule Extraction in AVK based cryptosystem. *International Conferences on Intelligent Computing and Information System* (ICICIS-2014).

Ross. (2010). Introduction to Probability models (10th ed.). Academic Press.

Stakhov, A. P. (2006). Fibonacci matrices, a generalization of the 'Cassini formula', and a new coding theory. Chaos, Solutions & Fractals, 30(1), 56–66.

Chapter 15
Authentication of Smart Grid:
The Case for Using Merkle Trees

Melesio Calderón Muñoz
Cupertino Electric, Inc., USA

Melody Moh
San Jose State University, USA

ABSTRACT

The electrical power grid forms the functional foundation of our modern societies, but in the near future our aging electrical infrastructure will not be able to keep pace with our demands. As a result, nations worldwide have started to convert their power grids into smart grids that will have improved communication and control systems. A smart grid will be better able to incorporate new forms of energy generation as well as be self-healing and more reliable. This paper investigates a threat to wireless communication networks from a fully realized quantum computer, and provides a means to avoid this problem in smart grid domains. We discuss and compare the security aspects, the complexities and the performance of authentication using public-key cryptography and using Merkel trees. As a result, we argue for the use of Merkle trees as opposed to public key encryption for authentication of devices in wireless mesh networks (WMN) used in smart grid applications.

ORGANIZATION BACKGROUND

Cupertino Electric Inc. is a private company founded in 1954 and headquartered in San José, CA. It provides electrical engineering and construction services.

San José State University (SJSU) was founded in 1857 as a normal school and has matured into a metropolitan university in the Silicon Valley. It is one of 23 campuses in the California State University system, offering more than 145 areas of study with an additional 108 concentrations.

DOI: 10.4018/978-1-7998-1763-5.ch015

INTRODUCTION

The electrical power grid has served humanity well up to now, but as we seek new ways to generate energy and improve efficiency, we find that the existing grid will not be able to meet our needs. It is expected that by 2050 worldwide consumption of electricity will triple (Kowalenko, 2010). Furthermore, power grids are still susceptible to large-scale outages that can affect millions of people (U.S.-Canada Power System Outage Task Force, 2004). These are the motivations for the creation of an "advanced decentralized, digital, infrastructure with two-way capabilities for communicating information, controlling equipment and distributing energy" (National Institute of Standards and Technology (NIST, 2010). This infrastructure will be better able to incorporate new forms of energy generation, as well as be self-healing and more robust. Each device in a smart grid will likely have its own IP address and will use protocols like TCP/IP for communication. Thus they will be vulnerable to similar security threats that face present day communication networks (Yan, Qian, Sharif, Tipper, 2012); however, the stakes will be much higher. That is to say, in the information technology industry the highest priority is the confidentiality, integrity and availability of information. In the electrical power industry the highest priority is human safety. For the smart grid cyber security measures must not get in the way of safe and reliable power system operations (NIST, 2010).

Problem Statement

"The smart grid is a long-term and expensive resource that must be built future proof" (NIST, 2014). That is to say it must be designed and implemented to be able to meet future scalability and functionality requirements. At the same time it also needs to be able to survive future malicious attacks. With this in mind, and with our knowledge of the threat posed to some types of public key encryption from the quantum computer, it must be concluded that if the quantum computer is realize and public key encryption is extensively used in the smart grid we will have a very serious situation on our hands.

While many may still think that the era of quantum computing is in the far horizon, according to the Wall Street Journal, China launched the world's first quantum communication satellite in August 16 2016 (Wall Street Journal, August 2016). While this has "set to launch Beijing far ahead of its global rivals in the drive to acquire a highly coveted asset in the age of cyber espionage: hack-proof communications," it has also shown that cyber attacks that are based on quantum computing may be more eminent that what many initially thought. Finding alternatives to public key encryption that is vulnerable to quantum-computing based attacks for smart grid at this stage is therefore timely, and is in line with NIST goals of making the smart grid "future proof."

This chapter looks at the threat to public key encryption systems from the quantum computer in the context of smart grid security. The authors argue for the use of Merkle (Hash) trees as opposed to public key on the smart grid, specifically when used to authenticate devices in WMN. Results of this chapter have been presented as a poster (Muñoz, Moh, & Moh, October 2014) and a conference paper (Muñoz, Moh, Moh, December 2014). This is a continuation of our research effort in smart grid (Kapoor & Moh, 2015) and in mobile network and cloud security (Wong, Moh, & Moh, 2012; Yang, & Moh, 2012; Gaur, Moh, & Balakrishnan, 2013).

For this chapter a Merkle tree authentication scheme is implemented, and incorporated into the ns-3 Network Simulator. It is then compared to the performances of a publicly available version of RSA, a public key encryption system. The goal is to show that Merkle trees are a reasonable alternative to public key cryptography system for smart grid networks.

Current State of Affairs

The evolution of the power grid is already under way. We see the development and discussions today around the Internet of Things (IoT) and smart buildings are already starting to show up on the landscape. Smart buildings are defined as buildings that use technology and processes to effectively control their environments. This is accomplished through the use of IT-aided sensors and controls that allow for better building management and maintenance. These sensors and controls are developed using open systems and protocols and it is understood that "all cybersecurity defense are potentially breakable." Therefore, it is necessary to develop back-up plans that identify the minimum level of functionality, particularly when it comes to the safety of human life. Hardwired equipment with hands-on controls should also be a part of this functionality. Industry is taking note of these issues. "Investigating the issue of cyber threats in smart buildings is timely and pertinent" (Khaund, 2015).

A recent work (Fernandes, Jung, & Prakash, 2016) gives a good evaluation of the Samsung-owned SmartThings. This is currently the largest smart home platform. It supports motion sensors, fire alarms and door locks. SmartThings is comprised of three main components namely, hubs, the cloud backend and a smart phone app. This work focuses on design flaw vulnerabilities, not bugs and oversights. The findings showed a number of problems related to controls, privilege and access to devices. As a result of these flaws the authors were able to steal lock pin-codes, disable vacation mode, and cause fake fire alarms. SmartApps was not *allowed* to carry out these operations, nor was physical access to the home required. This study has demonstrated how insecure smart homes can be.

The study described above looked at over-the-shelf smart home appliances. On top of the flaws demonstrated, one cannot ignore the cyber threats brought by quantum computing technologies. An evident is the recent launch of quantum satellite by China, which has shown that the era of quantum computing (and therefore its enabling of cybersecurity attacks) is no longer in a far-distant future (Wall Street Journal, August 2016).

BACKGROUND

The Threat of Quantum Information Processing

Today's computer architecture is based on the transistor and the binary number system. Invented in 1948 at Bell Labs, within 10 years the solid-state transistor completely replaced its predecessor the vacuum tube (Tanenbaum, 1990). The transistor opened the door to the modern computer age by allowing computers to do more with smaller and smaller components. In recent years the trend has been to increase computing power by increasing the number of cores on a processor, i.e., increasing computing power by adding more transistors. Multicore processors do indeed seem to be the future for computers in the near term, and the potential for greater computational power seems close at hand as a result of the progress of miniaturization, "but this trend cannot continue indefinitely" (Stajic, 2013). Yet for the security of public key there is a greater threat; namely, a fully realized quantum computer that can break the factorization and discrete log problems with a brute force attack.

The quantum computer is not bound to the limits of transistors or the binary system architecture. Quantum Information Processing (QIP) uses atoms held in a magnetic field instead of transistors. These units are called qubits. The underlying principle behind the quantum computer involves Einstein's wave-particle duality. QIP exploits the laws of quantum mechanics and as a consequence a single qubit can take infinitely many quantum states. This "allows for a much more powerful information platform than is possible with conventional components" (Stajic, 2013). It is more than just that a quantum computer would be faster, it is that in the realm of quantum physics a computer can solve the factorization or discrete log problem in polynomial time rather than exponential time (Shor, 1997).

The modern computer's design closely resembles the classic conceptual model called the Turing machine. Developed by the British computer scientist Alan Turing in the 1930s, the Turing machine can effectively compute any function that is computable (Kozen, 1997). It can only have a finite amount of states and it can only read and write one symbol at a time on a one-dimensional tape (Rosen, 1995). This is how modern computers work, executing instruction after instruction, linearly on a CPU; even multicore processors work like this. The classic Turing machine can be thought of as having a single fixed state at any given time; the quantum machine on the other hand "has an internal wave function, which is a superposition of a combination of the possible basis states." Transforms of the wave function can then alter the entire set of states in a single operation (Schneier, 1996).

The quantum computer is currently in its infancy, and it will be a great challenge to get hundreds and thousands of atoms to act in unison and function correctly (Kaku, 2008). Large-scale quantum computer hardware requires that each qubit be extremely well isolated from the environment, yet precisely controlled using external fields. These problems are far from trivial (Monroe, Kim, 2013) and currently beyond our technological capabilities to overcome. That being said, "no fundamental physical principles are known that prohibit the building of large-scale and reliable quantum computers" (Rieffel, Polak, 2011).

Public key encryption systems are secure today, but in 1994 Peter Shor of Bell Labs showed that factorization and discrete logarithm based public key systems could be broken with a brute force attack by a quantum computer (Kaku, 2008). Shor's algorithm attacks the problem of finding the period of a function. It uses quantum parallelism to produce a superposition of all the values of this function in a single step. It then uses a quantum Fourier transform and, measuring the yields, gives the period. This is then used to factor (Rieffel, Polak, 2011).

Electrical Power Grid

Electrical equipment is installed with the intention that it will be in service for many years, even decades. To do otherwise would not be efficient or acceptable. Computer and communication technologies advance at a much more rapid pace. As a result, technology on the grid tends to lag. Many functions in the grid today continue to use communications technologies similar to those that were used in the 1980s and 90s, such as dial-up connections used for personal computers (IEEE-USA Board of Directors, 2010). Considering the expense, potential for disruption, and difficult to reach locations of some of this equipment, it seems clear why it is not updated with the latest trends in the computer world; the electrical power grid does not abide by Moore's Law.

In the U.S., *The Energy Independence and Security Act of 2007* established that the NIST has "primary responsibility to coordinate development of a framework that includes protocols and model standards for information management to achieve interoperability of smart grid devices and systems" (NIST, 2010). NIST is a part of the U.S. Department of Commerce, and issues standards and guidelines in the hope that they are adopted by industry. This promotes interoperability that will in turn promote economic development (Schneier, 1996).

In recent years NIST has generated many important documents related to the smart grid, particularly the *NIST Framework and Roadmap for Smart Grid Interoperability Standards* and the *NIST Guidelines for Smart Grid Cyber Security*. Updated revisions for documents are ongoing.

Wireless Mesh Networks

WMN have become popular network topologies in recent years due to their cost effectiveness and robustness. WMN are already being used in the Advanced Metering Infrastructure (AMI) component of the smart grid. Some smart meters currently being used in the AMI are using the ZigBee protocol to form WMN.

The ZigBee standard defines a set of communications protocols for low-data-rate short-range wireless networking (ZigBee Alliance, 2008). ZigBee beholds to the IEEE 802.15.4 standard, which defines the two bottom layers of the protocol, but then goes beyond that to implement two additional layers. ZigBee is well suited for controls applications because it is a low power, low data communications protocol, which can support a mesh topology. ZigBee is simple and inexpensive when compared to WiFi and Bluetooth (http://www.youtube.com/watch?v=BkVcElfOVyw).

In a WMN nodes are peers that forward messages for the network. Each node is connected to several other nodes, thus improving reliability since multiple routes exist from source to sink. WMN do have drawbacks, particularly they are vulnerable to attacks to their dynamically changing topology, their lack of conventional security infrastructure and wireless nature (Siddiqui & Huong, 2007).

When a node joins the network establishing trust among the devices is done through the process of authentication. Authentication allows a node to ensure the identity of the peer it wants to communicate with. Public key encryption, as well as Merkle trees, offers means by which nodes in networks can authenticate. However, the Merkle tree based scheme's security rests on the use of cryptographically secure hash functions, which we understand to be resistant to a quantum computer attack (Stallings, 1999).

Authentication Using Public Key Encryption

Public key encryption uses a public-private key pair; one used to encrypt, the other to decrypt. This has many advantages. The strength of public key encryption rests on difficult to solve math problems. For this chapter the authors are concerned with those based on the factorization problem and the discrete logarithms problem. The experiment will deal specifically with the factorization problem.

Public key can be used to authenticate two devices in the following manner. For clarity call one device *Alice* and the other *Bob*. *Alice* sends a message to *Bob* claiming to be *Alice*. *Bob* needs more proof than this, so *Bob* encrypts a message *R* using *Alice*'s public key. Since the public key is public, anybody can encrypt a message, but only the holder of the private key can decrypt the message. Alice receives the message *R*, decrypts it then sends it back to Bob. Since she is the only holder of her private key, she has authenticated herself (Stamp, 2011).

It is not known for certain at this point if factoring is "difficult" (Stamp, 2011). That is to say, the best factoring algorithm asymptotically is the *number field sieve*, which is an exponential-time algorithm (Shor, 1997). Solving the factorization problem in a timely manner today is beyond the reach of the most powerful computers and most efficient algorithms (Cormen, Leiserson & Rivest, 2009).

The concern with information security is not just is it safe today, but will it be safe in the future? At one time the German Enigma machine was the state of the art in data encryption; today, breaking it is a challenging graduate level homework problem.

The probability that modern cryptographic algorithms will become completely insecure is low. However, technological and theoretical breakthroughs are always possibilities (NIST, 2014). In 2018 the European Commission is set to start a 10-year, €1 billion effort called the Quantum Technology Flagship to support and coordinate the research and development of the quantum computer. Elsewhere governments, academia, and industry are also investing and seeking to develop this revolutionary technology (Hellemans, 2016)

RSA

This chapter focuses on factorization problem based public key encryption systems, but several well-known and widely used discrete log problem systems are worth mentioning, namely Diffie-Hellman, El Gamal, and elliptic curve cryptography (ECC) (Rieffel & Polak, 2011). NIST approves of their use in smart grid and some are already finding use (https://www.certicom.com/index.php/device-authentication-service/smart-energy-device-certificate-service). All of these systems are vulnerable to a quantum attack.

RSA is a public key encryption system that is based on the factoring problem. The system works with the use of public-private key pairs. To create a key pair two large prime numbers *p* and *q* are multiplied together to generate *N*.

That is,

$$N = pq$$

Then a value *e* is chosen at random that is the relative prime (i.e., their greatest common divisor is 1) of the product *(p -1)(q - 1)*.

Then we compute the private key, such that

$$ed \equiv 1 \bmod (p-1)(q-1)$$

That is,

$$d = e^{-1} \bmod ((p-1)(q-1))$$

Note that *d* and *n* are also relative prime. At this point *p* and *q* can be discarded.

The RSA key pairs then are:

Public Key: (N, e)
Private Key: d

Now let *M* represent our plaintext message and let *C* be our cipher text. To encrypt we calculate the following:

$$C = M^e \bmod N$$

To Decipher we calculate:

$$M = C^d \bmod N$$

Here is a simple example (Schneier, 1996):

$$p = 47, q = 71$$

Then

$$N = p\,q = 3337$$
$$(p - 1)(q - 1) = 46 * 70 = 3220$$

Choose a random number e (must be relative prime to 3220) say 79. Then

$$d = 79^{-1} \bmod 3220 = 1019$$

e and N are published and d is kept secret.
Then to encrypt a message say:

$$M = 688232$$

Break into blocks:

$$M^1 = 688$$
$$M^2 = 232$$

Then:

$$688^{79} \bmod 3337 = 1570 = C^1$$
$$232^{79} \bmod 3337 = 2756 = C^2$$

Then your cipher text is *1570 2756*.
To decipher:

$$1570^{1019} \bmod 3337 = 688 = M^1$$
$$2756^{1019} \bmod 3337 = 232 = M^2$$

RELATED STUDIES

This section presents first related works on the justification of using WMN for smart grid, followed by a security framework of smart grid, and finally some relevant studies on using Merkel trees for smart grid authentication.

Modeling Smart Grid Using WMN

Smart grid technologies have gradually been developed through the combined efforts of electronic control, metering, and monitoring. Early experiments used the term broadband over power lines (BPL) to represent networks that connect millions of homes via smart meters, yet researchers used the WMN technology, notably for more reliable connections to home devices as well as supporting metering of other utilities (gas, water, etc.) (Burger & Iniewski, 2012). This was partly prompted by the successful initial deployments of smart grids using WMNs, such as the 2003 implementation in Austin, Texas (Sectoral e-Business Watch, 2009).

An important work of justifying the use of WMN model for smart grid network is by Xu and Wang (Xu & Wang, 2013). Recognizing the importance of providing time-critical communications in the power system, they modeled the smart grid network as a WMN, and provided the delay analysis in typical deployment scenarios. They specified the delay bounds, which would be useful for guiding smart grid network design to meet its communication demands.

One early theoretical study of using WMN as the communication environment of smart grid is by Zhang et al (Zhang, 2011). Recognizing that such environment needs to be robust, reliable, and efficient, the authors proposed a smart grid communication network, deploying WMN technologies including 802.15.4 Zigbee (Zigbee Alliance, 2008), 802.11s WLAN WMN standard (IEEE 802.11s, 2011) in different levels of smart grid networks, and verified its reliability through robust, efficient primal-dual routing.

Another theoretical study using WMN to model smart grid network is by Kim et al (Kim, Kim, Lim, Ko, Lee, 2012). The authors suggested using IEEE 802.11s standard (IEEE 802.11s, 2011) as the backbone for smart grid infrastructure, and analyzed the default routing protocol for the 802.11s standard, Hybrid Wireless Mesh Protocol (HWMP). They then proposed an enhancement, HWMP-RE (HWMP-Reliability Enhancement) for improving the routing reliability.

Smart Grid Security Framework

An important work on smart grid, or smart distribution grid (SDG), security was by Wang and Yi (Wang, Yi, 2011). They investigated two issues. First, they proposed a security framework for SDG based on a WMN topology and analyzed the potential security attacks and possible counter-attack measures. Next, they developed a new intrusion detection and response scheme (smart tracking firewall). They evaluated its performance and found that the smart tracking firewall can detect and respond to security attacks in real-time, and thus is a good fit for use in SDG.

The authors note that NIST guidelines document the usefulness and importance of WMN for smart grid. By their nature WMN are robust and economic so they are well suited for SDG applications. For an SDG to function properly they must meet the following requirements:

1. Collect power usage information
2. Monitor the status of electrical equipment
3. Send control messages from the control centers to electrical devices
4. Send pricing information to customers

WMN are vulnerable to signal jamming, eavesdropping and attacks from inside the network. It is argued that WMN need to cooperate with wired networks to deliver critical messages via secure and reliable paths within the shortest time. It is currently unknown if existing security of WMN can meet SDG requirements. Further research on this point is required.

Smart Grid Authentication using Merkel Trees

A recent work (Hu & Gharavi, 2014) evaluates authentication schemes for multi-gate mesh network in smart grid applications. This work provides additional support for the use of Merkle trees in smart grid. The most recently adopted IEEE 802.11s standard supports simultaneous authentication of equals (SAE) for its security protocol. This protocol uses one password shared by all devices. The standard also offers efficient mesh security association (EMSA) as an alternative approach. Both protocols use 4-way handshaking during which a network is vulnerable to denial of service (DoS) attacks.

The first step of the four-way handshake is to use a pre-shared key (PSK) or an authentication server to establish the authentication of the server. From this a secret key is generated that is called the pairwise master key (PMK). The client and server then exchange encrypted messages and decrypt them to authenticate themselves. 4-way hand shaking is a means for the client and server to independently prove to each other that they know the PSK/PMK, without disclosing it. The PMK usually lasts the entire session, but the traffic between needs to be encrypted as well. The handshake establishes a new key called the Pairwise Transient Key (PTK). It is prior to the establishment of the PTK that a denial of service could be launched. The goal of the attack would be to prevent the establishment of the PTK key. It is assumed that the attacker can eavesdrop and is able to forge messages. The Merkle tree is used during the exchange of the first message and without the PTK information the attacker is unable to derive the Merkle tree root. By using new Merkle trees during subsequent four-way hand shakings, this scheme is also able to prevent replay attacks.

The authors used ProVerif to analyze the vulnerabilities of the network and the resilience added by use of Merkle trees to defend against DoS attacks. This work does not look at quantum computer attacks on WMN.

Additional research has been done (Li, Lu, Zhou, Yang, & Shen, 2013) that uses Merkle trees for authentication to defend against message injection, message modification, message analysis and replay attacks. The work stresses the importance of authentication to the proper function of the smart grid. This work continues the discussion related to performance and security of Merkle trees in a smart grid application.

PROPOSED SOLUTION

This section describes the proposed solution. First, the Merkle tree and its construction are explained. As Merkle tree authentication scheme rests on a secure hash function, the second subsection expounded on secure hash functions and their desired properties. An important strength of hash functions is its resistance on birthday attack, which is illustrated in the last subsection.

Merkle Trees

A Merkle tree is a complete binary tree constructed from a set of secret leaf tokens where each internal node of the tree is a concatenation, then a hash of its left and right child. The leaves consist of a set of m randomly generated secret tokens. Since it is a complete binary tree, $m = 2^h$ where h is the height of the tree and m is the number of leaves. The root is public, and is the result of recursive applications of the one-way hash function on the tree, starting at the leaves (Santhanam et al., 2008).

Merkle trees offer low cost authentication for mesh clients. Compared to public key, they are lightweight, quick to generate and are resistant to quantum attacks (http://en.wikipedia.org/wiki/Merkle_tree). The strength of the Merkle tree authentication scheme rests on having a secure hash function and practical cryptographic hash functions do exist. The purpose of a hash function is to produce a "fingerprint" of a message, that is, a hash function $s()$ is applied to a file M and produces $s(M)$, which identifies M, but is much smaller (Stamp, 2011).

Figure 1 shows a Merkle tree with 8 leaves ($m = 8$). This tree therefore has 8 one-time authentication tokens to offer. In a mesh application the client generates the tree, and the root of the tree is made public. The client can prove its identity to any mesh router, by comparing the published root against the root that is generated when the hash function and authentication path are provided. Note that it is computationally infeasible to determine the secret token from the published root of the tree (Santhanam et al., 2008).

Here is an example of a client authenticating itself with leaf Y_5 (referring to Figure 1):

Let F be a mapping function that we define by:

$$F(i,i) = s(Y_i)$$

$$F(i, j) = s(F(i,k), F((k+1), j))$$

$$\text{where } k = \frac{i+j}{2}$$

Figure 1. A Merkel tree with authentication path

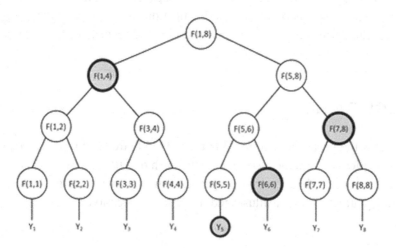

1. *F(1,8)* is the root and is public, made known by the router
2. The client sends F(1, 4) and F(5, 8) and the router computes: s(F(1, 4), F(5, 8)) = F(1, 8)
3. The client sends F(5, 6) and F(7, 8) and the router computes: s(F(5, 6), F(7, 8)) = F(5, 8)
4. The client sends F(5, 5) and F(6, 6) and the router computes: s(F(5, 5), F(6, 6)) = F(5, 6)
5. The client sends Y_5 and the router computes: s(Y_5) = F(5, 5)
6. The router has now authenticated the client through authenticating Y_5

Note that using this method, only $log_2 n$ transmissions are required to authenticate. However, only half of the transmissions are actually required because the router is generating half of the values itself.

To recap, the client transmits to the mesh router the secret token Y_i and the path to the root. The root is public so there is no need to transmit that. The client is authenticated by the fact that the mesh router is able to regenerate the value of the root based on the hash function *s()* and the path provided by the client (Merkle, 1979).

Secure Hash Functions

Public key algorithms use expensive modular arithmetic, exponential operations and are therefore not good fits for mesh clients (Santhanam et al., 2008). An alternative to the use of resource-hungry, quantum computer-vulnerable public key authentication is a system based on Merkle trees. It is well known that hash based algorithms like MD5 and SHA-2 are computationally less expensive than symmetric key algorithms, which in turn are computationally less expensive that public key algorithms.

Popular cryptographic hash functions like SHA-1 or MD5 work much like block ciphers. That is they take plain text and split them into fixed sized blocks then iterated by way of a function for some number of rounds (Stamp, 2011). They are considered secure if no collisions have been found; SHA-1 was broken in 2005 (https://www.schneier.com/blog/archives/2005/02/sha1_broken.html). Hash functions must be fast and have the effect that small changes to the input result in large changes in the output. This is known as the *avalanche effect* (Stamp, 2011).

A cryptographic hash function must provide:

1. **Compression:** The input file can be of any size, but the output must always be the same size.
2. **Efficiency:** It must be relatively easy for the computer to compute the output.
3. **One-Way:** Given only y of $y = s(x)$, it must be computationally infeasible to compute x.
4. **Weak Collision Resistance:** It is not feasible to modify a message without changing its hash value. That is, given *x* and *s(x)* to find any *y*, with $y \neq x$ and $s(x) = s(y)$ is infeasible.
5. **Strong Collision Resistance:** We cannot find any two inputs that produce the same hash output. That is, it is infeasible to find any *x* and *y*, such that $y \neq x$ and $s(x) = s(y)$.

The last item here refers to how resistant the hash function is to the *birthday attack*.

The Birthday Attack

The birthday paradox is a classic topic in probability, the result being that with only 23 people in a room you have a 50% chance of having two people with the same birthday. The paradoxical part of this problem is that at first glance it would appear 23 is too small a number.

The number of comparisons required with n people in a room is:

$$\frac{n(n-1)}{2} \approx n^2$$

There are 365 days in a non-leap year and we get the following:

$$n^2 = 365$$
$$n = \sqrt{365} \approx 19$$

Appling this to hash functions, if we have $s(x)$ that has an output with n bits, then there are 2^n different possible hash values—all values being equally likely. Since

$$\sqrt{2^n} = 2^{n/2}$$

Then by the birthday problem we can expect to have a collision after $2^{n/2}$ different inputs. As a consequence to prevent this sort of attack, n must be substantially so large that a brute force attack is not reasonable (Stamp, 2011).

The goal of the birthday attack on a hash function is not to find a message x such that $s(x) = s(y)$, rather it is to find two random messages x and y such that $s(x) = s(y)$ (Schneier, 1996). "The strength of a hash function against brute-force attack depends solely on the length of the hash code produced by the algorithm" (Stalling, 1999). This is a key point; to defend against a quantum attack the hash code only needs to be increased in length.

ANALYSIS AND PERFORMANCE EVALUATION

This section first presents the complexity analysis, which includes the analyses of time, memory, and message complexities of Merkel trees and RSA. It then describes the experiment setup, including WMN representing a smart grid network, the Merkle tree for authentication nodes, and the RSA implementation. Finally it illustrates the experimental results consisting of build time and authentication time.

Complexity Analysis of Merkle Trees

Complexities of Build-Time and Authentication-Time

Since a Merkle tree is a complete binary tree the number of nodes at height h is 2^h. The height of the tree with n leaves is $log_2 n$. The number of internal nodes in such a tree of height h is:

$$1 + 2 + 2^2 + \ldots + 2^{h-1} = \sum_{i=0}^{h-1} 2^i = \frac{2^h - 1}{2 - 1}$$

Therefore, there are $(2^h - 1)$ internal nodes (Cormen et al., 2009). To build a Merkle tree in each node we have an asymptotic upper bound of $O(2^h)$ with additional cost for the hash function.

For our experiment the *hash()* function available with the *tr1/functional* library of *C++* was used. *C++* uses *MurmurHashNeutral2* as its hash function, which uses a "Merkle-Damgard-esque" construction for its hash (https://sites.google.com/site/murmurhash/). This has a padding scheme on the front end to make sure all input into the compression function is of the same length. The input is broken into blocks that are then compressed. The compression involves taking the result so far and combining it with the next block. Many cryptographic hash functions work this way (http://en.wikipedia.org/wiki/Merkle-Damgard_construction). We can say that asymptotically the time complexity of the hash function is $O(\beta)$, where β is the key size.

The total build time is therefore $O(2^h) + O(\beta)$. The time to authenticate is bounded by the height of the tree, as illustrated in the previous section and Figure 1, and the hash function, i.e., $O(\beta h)$.

Memory Complexity

The amount of memory a Merkle tree requires is proportional to the size of the tree and the key size. Its memory complexity is therefore:

$$\beta * (2^h + 1) = O(\beta \, 2^h).$$

Message Complexity

As shown in previous sections, the Merkle tree sends an authenticating path back to the request. Each entry is $O(\beta)$ and there are h entries in this path, so we have $O(\beta h)$ message complexity.

Complexity Analysis of RSA

Computational Time Complexity

Public-private key generation relies on modular exponentiation. This is when an operation is raising one number to a power modulo another number. This is resource heavy, i.e., time, power and processor resources. Assume the *public key: (N, e)* and *private key: d*, satisfy:

$$\lg e = O(1), \lg d \leq \beta \text{ and } \lg N \leq \beta$$

Applying a public key requires $O(1)$ modular multiplications and uses $O(\beta^2)$ bit operations. Therefore the build time complexity is $O(1) + O(\beta^2) = O(\beta^2)$.

For authentication time, to apply a secret key requires $O(\beta)$ modular multiplications, for a total of $O(\beta^3)$ bit operations (Cormen et al., 2009).

Memory Complexity

In terms of memory consumption RSA does hold an advantage since it does not require a tree, and with one set of keys it can authenticate with an unlimited number of devices. Each node only needs to hold their own private key. Since public keys are public, the nodes do not need to retain that information. Therefore the amount of memory used is $O(\beta)$.

Message Complexity

RSA works in three exchanges. The message complexity is therefore also $O(\beta)$.

Comparison of Complexities

Table 1 summarizes the time, memory and message complexities of Merkle tree and of RSA.

Performance Experimental Setup

The experiments were set up using ns-3, a discrete event network simulator widely used in industry and academia for the purposes of testing and evaluating networks. Both Merkle tree and RSA authentication schemes were added into ns-3. This experiment was run on a MacBook Air running OS X 10.8.5, with a 1.8 GHz Intel Core i5 and 4 GB 1600MHz DDR3 of memory.

Wireless Mesh Network

In industry today we are starting to see utilization of WMN particularly in wireless lighting control systems. Currently these networks are limited to discrete sections of buildings, not entire buildings, and are often limited in size. For this reason we defined this experiment to have a network of 64 nodes.

Merkle Trees

The Merkle tree algorithm was coded as described in the previous sections. The Merkle trees were added into the existing ns-3 node structure, which represent devices in the WMN; this would be the build time. Later when the nodes are being linked into a network, we add a functionality of authentication of nodes; this would be the authentication time.

Table 1. Complexity analysis

		MERKLE TREE	RSA
COMPLEXITIES	BUILD TIME	$O(2^h) + O(\beta)$	$O(\beta^2)$
	AUTH TIME	$O(\beta\,h)$	$O(\beta^3)$
	MEMORY	$O(\beta\,2^h)$	$O(\beta)$
	MESSAGE	$O(\beta\,h)$	$O(\beta)$

The initial assumption was that a Merkle tree with 16 leaves (depth of 4) would be sufficient. Assuming a network of 64 devices, and if every node can authenticate with 16 other nodes around it, that should be sufficient to create a robust system. Deep trees are no more secure than shallow ones.

RSA

The RSA software used was obtained from *rsa Project* (https://code.google.com/p/rsa/). In the RSA scheme a private key is stored at the node. The public key is made public so there is no need for it to be stored in the node. This functionality was added in the same locations as the Merkle tree in ns-3.

RSA is able to use a public-private key pair to authenticate itself with any number of other nodes; this is an advantage over Merkle trees. That is, the Merkle tree scheme needs to know ahead of time how many nodes (devices) it will need to be able to authenticate with.

RSA key generation calculations depend on the length of the keys. For the sake of this test we choose 32 bits. We also have the length of our Merkle root at 32 bits. Albeit this would not be secure in a real system, it gives us good modeling data in a reasonable amount of time. We do test larger keys to see what impact the length has on calculation times.

Performance Results

The authors wanted to evaluate how the size of a Merkle tree effected build and authentication times. A large Merkle tree offers more authentication tokens, but takes longer to build and traverse. RSA on the other hand can authenticate with an unlimited number of devices, yet it requires intensive calculations to generate and use. To evaluate the Merkle tree time measurements were taken during the construction of the node, that is, when the Merkle tree is also built. Then when the node is linked into the network, this is the authentication time.

Build Time

Figure 2 shows that RSA is very slow to build compared to Merkle, taking on the order of 350,000 milliseconds to build. When compared to a Merkle tree of shallow depth, we see the Merkle scheme has a clear advantage. The Merkle scheme does slow down as the tree grows larger. Around a depth of 16 we start to see noticeable slowing in the Merkle scheme. At a depth of 16 each node has 65,536 leaves to authenticate with.

It was not possible to see at what depth the Merkle tree equaled RSA's time because at depth 25, the computer that was running the tests started to report memory problems, then seized up. At that depth we were building a Merkle tree with 33,554,432 leaves.

Authentication Time

For the Merkle trees we can see from Figure 2 that the larger the tree the more traversing of the tree we need to do to provide our authentication path. Still Merkle continues to do better than RSA for authentication. In these plots RSA is using a 32-bit key. With the 256-bit key, RSA did much worse than the Merkle tree taking about 3 minutes to authenticate one single node. This number would then be proportional to the size of the network and number of links. What we can see from all of this is that Merkle trees are a viable alternative to the use of public key for authentication.

Figure 2. Build time comparison

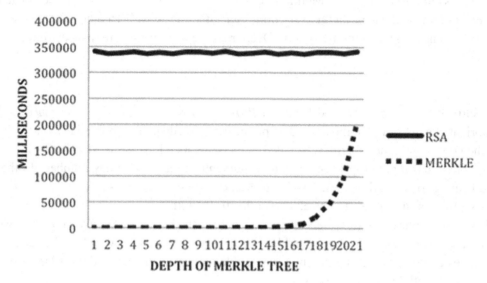

Figure 3. Authentication time comparison

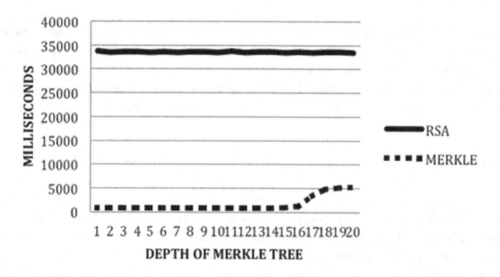

FUTURE RESEARCH DIRECTIONS

For this chapter the authors proposed and evaluated Merkel tree-based authentication, to offer an alternative where public-key encryption would be vulnerable to quantum attack (Kaku, 2008). The immediate next step would be to build a network with an RSA key of up to 2048 bits, which today is considered a secure length, and compare with Merkel tree approach.

A study on public key encryption systems that are not vulnerable to a quantum computer attack, such as the NTRU Cryptosystem (http://tbuktu.github.io/ntru/), would also be useful. Yet, it seems reasonable that both RSA and NTRU-based systems would be slower than a Merkle tree scheme.

Another future direction would be to look at the alternatives that improve over the use of Diffie-Hellman key exchange. Diffie-Hellman is based on the discrete log problem and allows users to establish a shared symmetric key (Stamp, 2011). It is part of the NIST-approved cryptographic techniques, known as NSA Suite B, and is approved for use on the smart grid (NIST, 2014). Finding the pros and cons of Diffie-Hellman and providing superior alternatives would be valuable for future realization of secure smart grid systems.

CONCLUSION

"Cybersecurity is one of the key technical areas where the state of the art falls short of meeting the envisioned functional, reliability, and scalability requirements of the smart grid" (NIST, 2014). It is understood that public key encryption may not be desirable for use in the smart grid. Issues related to key servers and certificate authorities are high on the concerns.

Although people see the threat of a quantum computing attack to be low, it is understood to be a long-term possibility (NIST, 2014). An evident is the recent launch of quantum satellite by China, which has shown that the era of quantum computing (and therefore its enabling of cybersecurity attacks) is no longer in a far-distant future (Wall Street Journal, August 2016).

The main objective of this chapter is to discourage the use of discrete log and factorization-based public key encryption that is vulnerable to quantum-computing attacks in smart grid communication domains. The build-time and authentication-time complexities, memory and message complexities of RSA, a public key authentication method, and our proposed Merkel-tree-based authentication methods are analyzed and compared based on build and authentication times. The proposed Merkel tree-based method took less time to build and to authenticate than RSA. These studies show that Merkle tree-based authentication is lightweight, secure, resistant to quantum computer attacks and should be considered for use in smart grid applications.

An important factor in the quality of our lives in the future will depend on energy; how we get it, how we use it, how we distribute it. Smart grid is an important step toward a future with a quality of life better than the one we have today. Smart grid will take a generation to complete yet everything that is to come must be built on a solid foundation of information security.

REFERENCES

Berger, L. T., & Iniewski, K. (Eds.). (April 2012). *Smart Grid - Applications, Communications and Security*. John Wiley and Sons.

Cormen, T., Leiserson, C., Rivest, R., & Stein, C. (2009). *Introduction to Algorithms* (3rd ed.). Cambridge, MA: The MIT Press.

Fernandes, E., Jung, J., & Prakash, A. (2016). *Security Analysis of Emerging Smart Home Applications*. Retrieved from https://cdn2.vox-cdn.com/uploads/chorus_asset/file/6410049/Paper27_SP16_Camera-Ready_SmartThings_Revised_1_.0.pdf

Gaur, S., Moh, M., & Balakrishnan, M. (December 2013). Hiding behind the Clouds: Efficient, Privacy-Preserving Queries via Cloud Proxies. In *Proc. of International Workshop on Cloud Computing Systems, Networks, and Applications.* 10.1109/GLOCOMW.2013.6825035

Hellemans. (2016). Europe Bets €1 Billion on Quantum Tech. *IEEE Spectrum.*

Hu & Gharavi. (2014). Smart Grid Mesh Network Security Using Dynamic Key Distribution With Merkle Tree 4-Way Handshaking. *IEEE Transactions on Smart Grid, 5.* doi:10.1109/TSG.2013.2277963

IEEE 802.11s. (2011). *Part11: Wireless LAN medium access control (MAC) (PHY) specifications amendment 10: Mesh networking.* IEEE Press.

IEEE-USA Board of Directors. (2010). *Building a Stronger and Smarter Electrical Energy Infrastructure.* Author.

Kaku, M. (2008). *Physics of the Impossible.* New York: Anchor Books.

Kapoor, A., & Moh, M. (2015). Implementation and evaluation of the DFF protocol for Advanced Metering Infrastructure (AMI) networks. *Proceedings of 11th IEEE International Conference on Design of Reliable Communication Networks.*

Khaund, K. (2015). *Cybersecurity in Smart Buildings.* Frost & Sullivan Collaborative Industry Perspective. Retrieved from http://23873b0b5ea986687186-fddd749ce937721293aa13aa786d4227.r31.cf1.rackcdn.com/Documentation/Cybersecurity%20in%20Smart%20Buildings_White%20Paper.pdf

Kim, Kim, Lim, Ko, & Lee. (2012). Improving the Reliability of IEEE 802.11s Based Wireless Mesh Networks for Smart Grid Systems. *Journal of Communications and Networks, 14*(6).

Kowalenko (2010). The Smart Grid: A Primer. *The Institute, IEEE.*

Kozen, D. (1997). *Automata and Computability.* Ithaca, NY: Springer. doi:10.1007/978-1-4612-1844-9

Li, H., Lu, R., Zhou, L., Yang, B., & Shen, X. (2013). An Efficient Merkle-Tree-Based Authentication Scheme for Smart Grid. *IEEE Systems Journal, 8*(2), 655–663. doi:10.1109/JSYST.2013.2271537

Merkle, R. (1979). *Secrecy Authentication and Public Key Systems.* Information Systems Laboratory, Stanford Electronics Laboratories. Retrieved from http://www.merkle.com/papers/Thesis1979.pdf

Monroe, C., & Kim, J. (2013, March). Scaling the Ion Trap Quantum Processor. *Science, 339*(6124), 1164–1169. doi:10.1126cience.1231298 PMID:23471398

Muñoz, M., Moh, M., & Moh, T.-S. (2014). Improving Smart Grid Security using Merkle Trees. *IEEE Conference on Communications and Network Security* (CNS). 10.1109/CNS.2014.6997535

Muñoz, M., Moh, M., & Moh, T.-S. (2014). Improving Smart Grid Authentication using Merkle Trees. *Proc. IEEE International Conference on Parallel and Distributed Systems.* 10.1109/PADSW.2014.7097884

NIST 7628. (2010). *Guidelines for Smart Grid Cyber Security.* Retrieved from http://www.nist.gov/smartgrid/upload/nistir-7628_total.pdf

NIST 7628 Revision 1. (2014). *Guidelines for Smart Grid Cyber Security.* Retrieved from http://nvlpubs.nist.gov/nistpubs/ir/2014/NIST.IR.7628r1.pdf

Rieffel, E., & Polak, W. (2011). *Quantum Computing, A Gentle Introduction*. Cambridge, MA: The MIT Press.

Rosen, K. (1995). *Discrete Mathematics And Its Applications* (3rd ed.). New York: McGraw-Hill, Inc.

Santhanam, L., Xie, B., & Agrawal, D. (2008). Secure and Efficient Authentication in Wireless Mesh Networks using Merkle Trees. *33rd IEEE Conference on Local Computer Networks*. 10.1109/LCN.2008.4664310

Schneier, B. (1996). *Applied Cryptography* (2nd ed.). New York: Wiley & Sons Inc.

Sectoral e-Business Watch. (2009). *Case study: Smart grid journey at Austin Energy, Texas, USA*. Author.

Shor, P. (1997, October). Polynomial-Time Algorithms for Prime Factorization and Discrete Logarithms on a Quantum Computer. *SIAM Journal on Computing, 26*(5), 1484–1509. doi:10.1137/S0097539795293172

Siddiqui, M. S., & Huong, C. S. (2007). Security Issues in Wireless Mesh Networks. *International Conference on Multimedia and Ubiquitous Engineering (MUE)*.

Stajic, J. (2013, March). The Future of Quantum Information Processing. *Science, 339*(6124), 1163. doi:10.1126cience.339.6124.1163 PMID:23471397

Stallings, W. (1999). *Cryptography and Network Security* (2nd ed.). Upper Saddle River, NJ: Prentice Hall.

Stamp, M. (2011). *Information Security Principles and Practices* (2nd ed.). Hoboken, NJ: Wiley & Sons Inc. doi:10.1002/9781118027974

Tanenbaum, A. (1990). *Structured Computer Organization* (3rd ed.). Englewood Cliffs, NJ: Prentice Hall.

The Wall Street Journal. (2016). *China's Latest Leap Forward Isn't Just Great—It's Quantum. Beijing launches the world's first quantum-communications satellite into orbit*. Retrieved 8/17/2016 from: http://www.wsj.com/articles/chinas-latest-leap-forward-isnt-just-greatits-quantum-1471269555

U.S.-Canada Power System Outage Task Force. (2004). *Final Report on the August 14, 2003 Blackout in the United States and Canada: Causes and Recommendations*. Retrieved from: http://energy.gov/sites/prod/files/oeprod/DocumentsandMedia/BlackoutFinal-Web.pdf

Wang, X., & Yi, P. (2011, December). Security Framework for Wireless Communications in Smart Distribution Grid. *IEEE Transactions on Smart Grid, 2*(4), 809–818. doi:10.1109/TSG.2011.2167354

Wong, R., Moh, T.-S., & Moh, M. (2012). Efficient Semi-Supervised Learning BitTorrent Traffic Detection: An Extended Summary. In *Proc. of 13th Int. Conf on Distributed Computing and Networking – ICDCN 2012 (LNCS)*, (vol. 7129). Springer. 10.1007/978-3-642-25959-3_40

Xu & Wang. (2013). Wireless Mesh Network in Smart Grid: Modeling and Analysis for Time Critical Communications. *IEEE Transactions on Wireless Communications, 12*(7), 3360 – 3371.

Yan, Y., Qian, Y., Sharif, H., & Tipper, D. (2012, January). A Survey on Cyber Security for Smart Grid Communications. *Communication Surveys and Tutorials, IEEE, 14*(4), 998–1010. doi:10.1109/SURV.2012.010912.00035

Yang, L., & Moh, M. (2011). Dual Trust Secure Protocol for Cluster-Based Wireless Sensor Networks. In *Proc. IEEE 45th Asilomar Conference on Signals, Systems and Computers*. 10.1109/ACSSC.2011.6190298

Zhang, Y., Sun, W., Wang, L., Wang, H., Green, R. II, & Alam, M. (2011). A multi-level communication architecture of smart grid based on congestion aware wireless mesh network. *43rd North American Power Symposium (NAPS)*.

ZigBee Alliance. (2008). *ZigBee Specifications 053474r17*. Retrieved from http://www.zigbee.org/

KEY TERMS AND DEFINITIONS

Factor: To decompose an integer into a product of primes.

National Institute of Standards and Technology (NIST): A measurement standards laboratory and part of the U.S. Department of Commerce.

One-Way Hash Function: A function that takes a variable length input and converts it to a fixed length output.

Public Key Encryption: Type of encryption where encrypting and decrypting are done with different keys.

Quantum Computing: Theoretical computing system that makes use of quantum mechanics to perform operations.

Ralph Merkle: Computer scientist and pioneer in the field of cryptography.

Tree: A connected acyclic graph.

Wireless Mesh Network (WMN): A wireless network topology where all nodes are peers that relay data for the network.

This research was previously published in Security Solutions and Applied Cryptography in Smart Grid Communications edited by Mohamed Amine Ferrag and Ahmed Ahmim; pages 117-136, copyright year 2017 by Information Science Reference (an imprint of IGI Global).

Chapter 16
Secure Speaker Recognition using BGN Cryptosystem with Prime Order Bilinear Group

S. Selva Nidhyananthan

Mepco Schlenk Engineering College, India

M. Prasad

Mepco Schlenk Engineering College, India

R. Shantha Selva Kumari

Mepco Schlenk Engineering College, India

ABSTRACT

Speech being a unique characteristic of an individual is widely used in speaker verification and speaker identification tasks in applications such as authentication and surveillance respectively. In this paper, framework for secure speaker recognition system using BGN Cryptosystem, where the system is able to perform the necessary operations without being able to observe the speech input provided by the user during speaker recognition process. Secure speaker recognition makes use of Secure Multiparty Computation (SMC) based on the homomorphic properties of cryptosystem. Among the cryptosytem with homomorphic properties BGN is preferable, because it is partially doubly homomorphic, which can perform arbitrary number of addition and only one multiplication. But the main disadvantage of using BGN cryptosystem is its execution time. In proposed system, the execution time is reduced by a factor of 12 by replacing conventional composite order group by prime order group. This leads to an efficient secure speaker recognition.

DOI: 10.4018/978-1-7998-1763-5.ch016

INTRODUCTION

Speech is one of the most private forms of personal communication. A sample of a person's speech contains information about the gender, accent, ethnicity, and the emotional state of the speaker apart from the message content. Speech processing technology is widely used in biometric authentication in the form of speaker verification. In a conventional speaker verification system, the speaker patterns are stored without any obfuscation and the system matches the speech input obtained during authentication with these patterns. If the speaker verification system is compromised, an adversary can use these patterns to later impersonate the user. Similarly, speaker identification is also used in surveillance applications. Most individuals would consider unauthorized recording of their speech, through eavesdropping or wiretaps as a major privacy violation. Yet, current speaker verification and speaker identification algorithms are not designed to preserve speaker privacy and require complete access to the speech data.

In many situations, speech processing applications such as speech recognition are deployed in a client-server model, where the client has the speech input and a server has the speech models. Due to the concerns for privacy and confidentiality of their speech data, many users are unwilling to use such external services. Even though the service provider has a privacy policy, the client speech data is usually stored in an external repository that may be susceptible to being compromised. The external service provider is also liable to disclose the data in case of a subpoena. It is, therefore, very useful to have secure speech processing algorithms that can be used without violating these constraints.

The objective of this paper is to develop a design for secure speaker recognition based on the homomorphic properties of BGN cryptosystem with low execution time. Usually, the main constraint in secure speaker recognition is the execution time which is dependent on the encryption of the speaker models. In existing work (Manas, 2013), they have used BGN cryptosystem and implemented it using composite order groups of larger size, which take large time to execute. In the proposed system, composite order group is replaced with prime order group of small size which gives the same security as composite order group implementation and reduces the execution time by a factor of 12. So we can obtain efficient secure speaker recognition using the proposed system.

LITERATURE SURVEY

Mel Frequency Cepstral Coefficient (MFCC) works better in noisy environment than that of Linear LPC as per Reynolds (1995). HMM needs higher computation than GMM but while considering the performance results they both are almost same. The ML parameter estimation using Expectation Maximization (EM) algorithm is used iteratively to estimate GMM parameters. It is also noted that the initial parameter for GMM is not making much difference to the final results. The speech feature vectors are separated into segments for performance evaluation. The performance of different models is compared with GMM.

BGN cryptosystem is a somewhat fully homomorphic cryptosystem which can perform arbitrary number of addition and only one multiplication (Boneh, Goh & Nissim, 2006). It is based on both Paillier and Okamoto Uchiyama encryption schemes. The cryptosystem depends on Subgroup decision problem of Composite order bilinear groups. The BGN cryptosystem is applied for calculation of 2-DNF formula, Private information retrieval, efficient election protocol without random oracles and universally verifiable computation.

Secure Multiparty Computation (SMC) can be used to compute secure speech recognition (Smaragdis & Shashanka, 2007). Using primitives for computing scalar products and maxima, secure protocols for classification using Gaussian mixture models was proposed. Secure protocols for the forward-backward algorithm, the viterbi algorithm and HMM training was proposed. The protocols are defined modularly in terms of primitives so that future advances in cryptography, which will hopefully provide more robust and efficient protocols, can be readily employed by straightforward replacement. The approach have taken also illustrates the process required to transform a signal processing algorithm to its privacy preserving version. Other data processing and classification algorithms can also be described in terms of secure primitives and easily reformulated for secure multiparty computations.

The protocols that enable both practical privacy preserving inference and classification with HMMs are described by Pathak, Rane, Sun & Raj (2011). A natural progression is to extend the protocols to more complete inference, including decoding from large HMMs with privacy preservation. Other extensions include privacy preserving inference from generalizations of HMMs such as dynamic Bayes networks. Applications for such technologies are myriad. One area where HMM technology is the basis for most applications, is the processing of voice, which is arguably the most personal and private medium of communication. Yet, most current voice processing systems require full, unobscured access to the voice of the user.

The privacy-preserving protocol for GMM-based algorithm for speaker verification using homomorphic cryptosystems such as BGN and Paillier encryption was developed by Pathak & Raj (2013) .The system observes only encrypted speech data, and hence, cannot obtain information about the user's speech. Both interactive and non-interactive variants of the protocol are constructed. The interactive variant is relevant in the case of semi-honest adversary and the non-interactive variant is necessary in the case of malicious adversary. During the exchanges required by the protocols, the user only observes additively or multiplicatively masked data, and does not gain any information about the user's speech from it. The protocols are also found to give results which are same up to a high degree of precision compared to a non-private GMM adaptation based scheme. The interactive protocol is more efficient than the non-interactive protocol as the latter requires homomorphic multiplication using BGN cryptosystem.

An abstract framework that encompasses the key properties of bilinear groups of composite order that are required to construct secure pairing-based cryptosystems, and use prime-order elliptic curve groups to construct bilinear groups with the same properties was shown by Freemann. In particular, a generalized version of the subgroup decision problem and give explicit constructions of bilinear groups in which the generalized subgroup decision assumption follows from the decision Diffie- Hellman assumption, the decision linear assumption, and/or related assumptions in prime-order groups. We apply our framework and our prime-order group constructions to create more efficient versions of cryptosystems that originally required composite-order groups. Specifically, the Boneh-Goh- Nissim encryption scheme, the Boneh-Sahai-Waters traitor tracing system, and the Katz-Sahai-Waters attribute-based encryption scheme.

GAUSSIAN MIXTURE MODEL

A Gaussian Mixture Model (GMM) is a parametric probability density function represented as a weighted sum of Gaussian component densities. A Gaussian mixture density is weighted sum of M component densities, given by the equation,

$$P(x \mid \lambda) = \sum_{i=1}^{M} p_i b_i(x)$$

where x is D-dimensional random vector, $b_i(x)$ $i=0,1,...,M$ are component densities and p_i are the mixture weights.

$$b_i(x) = \frac{1}{(2\Pi)^{D/2} \mid \Sigma_i \mid^{1/2}} \exp\{\frac{-1}{2}(x-\mu_i)'\sum_i^{-1} x - \mu_i\}$$

The Gaussian Mixture Model is given by,

$$\lambda = \{p_i, \mu_i, \Sigma_i\}$$

There are several variants on the GMM shown in Equation (3). The covariance matrices, Σ_i, can be full rank or constrained to be diagonal. Additionally, parameters can be shared, or tied, among the Gaussian components, such as having a common covariance matrix for all components, The choice of model configuration is often determined by the amount of data available for estimating the GMM parameters and how the GMM is used in a particular biometric application.

Maximum *A* Posteriori Parameter Estimation

In addition to estimating GMM parameters via the EM algorithm, the parameters may also be estimated using Maximum *A* Posteriori (MAP) estimation. MAP estimation is used, for example, in speaker recognition applications to derive speaker model by adapting from a Universal Background Model (UBM). It is also used in other pattern recognition tasks where limited labeled training data is used to adapt a prior, general model.

Like the EM algorithm, the MAP estimation is a two-step estimation process. The first step is identical to the "Expectation" step of the EM algorithm, where estimates of the sufficient statistics of the training data are computed for each mixture in the prior model. Unlike the second step of the EM algorithm, for adaptation these "new" sufficient statistic estimates are then combined with the "old" sufficient statistics from the prior mixture parameters using a data-dependent mixing coefficient. The data-dependent mixing coefficient is designed so that mixtures with high counts of new data rely more on the new sufficient statistics for final parameter estimation and mixtures with low counts of new data rely more on the old sufficient statistics for final parameter estimation.

The specifics of the adaptation are as follows. Given a prior model and training vectors from the desired class, $X=\{x1,...,xT\}$, we first determine the probabilistic alignment of the training vectors into the prior mixture components. That is, for mixture i in the prior model, we compute $\Pr(i|X_l, \lambda=prior)$.

We then compute the sufficient statistics for the weight, mean and variance parameters:

Weight, $n_i = \sum_{t=1}^{T} \Pr(i \mid x_t \mid, \lambda_{prior})$

$$\text{Mean, } E_i(x) = \frac{1}{n_i} \sum_{t=1}^{T} \Pr(i \mid x_t \mid, \lambda_{prior}) x_t$$

$$\text{Variance, } E_i(x^2) = \frac{1}{n_i} \sum_{t=1}^{T} \Pr(i \mid x_t \mid, \lambda_{prior}) x_t^2$$

This is the same as the "Expectation" step in the EM algorithm.

Lastly, these new sufficient statistics from the training data are used to update the prior sufficient statistics for mixture i to create the adapted parameters for mixture i with the equations:

$$\text{Adapted mixture weight, } \hat{w}_i = [\alpha_i^w n_i / T + (1 - \alpha_i^w) w_i] \gamma$$

$$\text{Adapted mixture mean, } \hat{\mu}_i = \alpha_i^m E_i(x) + (1 - \alpha_i^m) \mu_i$$

$$\text{Adapted mixture variance, } \hat{\sigma}_i^2 = \alpha_i^v E_i(x^2) + (1 - \alpha_i^v)(\sigma_i^2 + \hat{\mu}_i^2) - \hat{\mu}_i^2$$

The adaptation coefficients controlling the balance between old and new estimates are $\{\alpha_i^w, \alpha_i^m, \alpha_i^v\}$ for the weights, means and variances, respectively. The scale factor, γ, is computed over all adapted mixture weights to ensure they sum to unity. Note that the sufficient statistics, not the derived parameters, such as the variance, are being adapted.

BGN CRYPTOSYSTEM

Boneh, Goh, and Nissim described a cryptosystem that permitted arbitrary number of additions and one multiplication, without growing the ciphertext size [2]. Below we refer to this scheme as the BGN cryptosystem. Security of the BGN cryptosystem is based on the subgroup-membership problem in composite-order groups that admit bilinear maps. This cryptosystem immediately implies an efficient protocol for evaluating 2DNF formula (or more generally bilinear forms). Boneh et al. also described applications of the BGN cryptosystem to improving the efficiency of Private Information Retrieval schemes (PIR) and for a voting protocol.

Asymmetric ciphers, or public-key cryptosystems, are perhaps the most celebrated contribution of modern cryptography. They certainly have had the most impact. It is hard to imagine what the world would be like without their revolutionary approach to key distribution. All public-key cryptosystems in wide use today can trace their roots to the Diffie- Hellman key exchange protocol or the RSA cryptosystem. The former depends on cyclic groups with particular properties. The latter, though using similar arithmetic operations, relies on different principles. For example, RSA uses groups that are not cyclic and requires that the order of the group to be unknown to the attacker.

Roughly speaking, bilinear maps, or pairings, give cyclic groups additional properties. Initially, in the 1990s, these additional properties were seen as detrimental as they could be exploited to break cryptosystems, but it was later discovered that they could also be exploited to build cryptosystems. Rather than avoiding pairings, one can seek them out to construct new schemes. Boneh and Franklin's identity-based encryption scheme is perhaps the most famous early example of what could be achieved using bilinear maps, though not the first. Shamir first discussed identity-based encryption in 1984, but researchers were unable to build a practical scheme by conventional means for approximately twenty years.

Boneh and Franklin found an elegant solution using bilinear maps. Extending the basic idea leads to identity-based schemes with additional useful properties such as authenticated or hierarchical identity-based encryption. More generally, so many cryptographic applications of the pairing have been identified that this area of research is sometimes considered its own field called pairing-based cryptography. We note that an identity-based scheme based on quadratic residues and not bilinear maps has since been proposed, albeit one that is significantly less practical. However, this is the exception rather than the rule. In general it is not known how to find conventional equivalents of a given pairing-based cryptosystem.

One of the key ideas in the BGN system is to use elliptic curve groups whose order is a composite number n that is hard to factor. (In all previous systems we required the group order to be prime. We can generate such a curve as follows: pick two secret primes q and r, and publish $n=qr$. Then find a small integer l such that $4ln - 1$ is a prime p, and let E be the elliptic curve $y^2=x^3+x$ over F_p. Since $p \equiv 3 \pmod 4$ the curve E is supersingular with $\#E(F_p)=p+1=4ln$, and thus there is a point $P \in E(F_p)$ of order n. (We can compute such a point by choosing a random $P' \in E(F_p)$ and setting $P = [4l]P'$.

We now describe the system:

Gen (): Choose large primes q,r and set $n=qr$. Find a supersingular elliptic curve E/F_p with a point P of order n as described above, and let $G = \langle P \rangle$. Choose $Q' \xleftarrow{R} G \setminus \{\infty\}$ and set $Q = [r]Q'$; then Q has order q. Let $\hat{e} : G \times G \to \mu_n \subset F_{p^2}$ be the modified Weil pairing (constructed from the Weil pairing using a distortion map). Output the public key pk $= (E, \hat{e}, n, P, Q)$ and the secret key $sk = q$.

Enc(*pk,m*): Choose $t \xleftarrow{R} [1,n]$ and output C=[m]P+[t]Q.

Dec(*sk,C*): Compute $\tilde{P} = [q]P$ and $\tilde{C} = [q]C$, and output $m' = \log_{\tilde{P}} \tilde{C}$.

Decryption is correct since if C=[m]P+[t]Q, then $\tilde{C} = [mq]P + [qt]Q = [mq]P = [m]\tilde{P}$. Note that for efficient decryption we require the message space to be small as in the ElGamal variant.

Add(*pk,C_1,C_2*): Choose $t' \xleftarrow{R} [1,n]$ and output $C' = C_1 + C_2 + [t']Q \in G$.

Mult(*pk,C_1,C_2*): Choose $u \xleftarrow{R} [1,n]$ and output $D = \hat{e}(C_1, C_2).e(Q,Q)^u \in \mu_n$.

It is easy to see that if C1=[m1]P+[t1]Q is an encryption of m_1 and C2=[m2]P+[t2]Q is an encryption of m2, then Add(*pk*,C_1,C_2) is a (rerandomized) encryption of m_1+m_2. With the same setup, we have,

$$\begin{aligned}
\text{Mult(pk;C1;C2)} &= \hat{e}([m1]P + [t1]Q,[m2]P + [t2]Q) .\hat{e}(Q;Q)^u \\
&= \hat{e}(P; P)^{m_1 m_2} \hat{e}(P,Q)^{m_1 t_2 + t_1 m_2} \hat{e}(Q,Q)^{t_1 t_{2+u}}
\end{aligned}$$

METHODOLOGY

The whole system as shown in Figure 1 for secure speaker recognition can be implemented using C libraries. The input for the system is speech signal and the output of the system is the probability scores. Spro Library is used for feature extraction. ALIZE Library is used for speaker recognition. PBC Library is used to implement BGN cryptosystem. The possible way of implementing BGN Cryptosystem is by using PBC Library. The C libraries are more flexible. The curves used in BGN Cryptosystem are optimized to less time during pairing.

SPro is a speech signal processing toolkit which provides runtime commands implementing standard feature extraction algorithms for speech and speaker recognition applications and a C library to implement new algorithms and to use SPro files within your own programs. The library does not provide for high-level feature extraction functions which directly convert a waveform into features, mainly because such functions would require a tremendous number of arguments in order to be versatile. However, it is rather trivial to write such a function for your particular needs using the SPro library.

ALIZE is an open-source platform for speaker recognition. The ALIZE library implements a low-level statistical engine based on the well-known Gaussian mixture modeling. The toolkit includes a set of high level tools dedicated to speaker recognition based on the latest developments in speaker recognition such as Joint Factor Analysis, Support Vector Machine, i-vector modeling and Probabilistic Linear Discriminant Analysis.

The PBC library is designed to be the backbone of implementations of pairing-based cryptosystems, thus speed and portability are important goals. It provides routines such as elliptic curve generation, elliptic curve arithmetic and pairing computation. Thanks to the GMP library, despite being written in C, pairings times are reasonable. On a 1GHz Pentium III, the fastest pairing time is 11ms and slowest pairing time is 30ms.

The features from the input speech signal are extracted using Spro Library. The extracted features are processed using ALIZE library to find the GMM model. The GMM model is encrypted during enrollment phase and features are encrypted during verification phase with BGN cryptosystem using PBC library. Finally, scores are calculated using the homomorphic properties of BGN cryptosystem.

SECURE SPEAKER RECOGNITION

In the proposed system as shown in Figure 2, the train features are GMM modeled and encrypted using BGN cryptosystem with prime order group. During verification test features are encrypted and used to calculate scores homomorphically with encrypted GMM.

Speaker verification proceeds in two separate phases: enrollment and verification. In the enrollment phase, each user submits enrollment samples to the system, and in the verification phase, a user submits a claimed identity along with a test sample which the system compares to the enrollment samples for the claimed user to arrive at the decision to accept/reject the user. The system uses the UBM and adapted model framework to represent the speaker model.

The design of the privacy preserving speaker verification system with a motivation to satisfy the privacy constraints discussed. In the enrollment phase, the user and the system are assumed to be semi-honest. To start with, user generates a public/private key pair and sends the public key to the system. Assume that the system trains a UBM λ_U on publicly available data and stores it with itself as plaintext.

Figure 1. Flow chart for secure speaker recognition

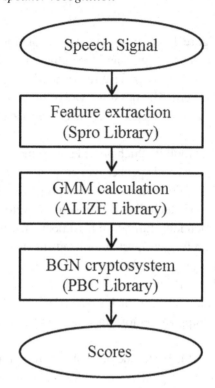

In the enrollment protocol, the system sends the UBM to the user in plaintext and the user performs the adaptation. The user then encrypts the adapted model with its key and sends it to the system. After executing the enrollment protocol with all users, the system has encrypted models for all users along with the UBM. At the end of the protocol, require the user to delete the enrollment data from its computation device in order to protect it from an adversary who might gain unauthorized access to it.

The user device only has the encryption and decryption keys. Similarly, as the server stores only the encrypted speaker models, it is also protected against an adversary who might compromise the system to gain the speaker models, in order to impersonate the user later. If an adversary compromises the user device as well as the system, consider the system to be completely compromised as the adversary can use the decryption key to obtain the speaker model in plaintext.

In the verification protocol, the user produces a test speech sample x and encrypts it using its key and sends it to the system along with the claimed identity. The system evaluates the encrypted test sample with the UBM and the encrypted model for the claimed speaker it had obtained in the enrollment protocol using the homomorphic operations and obtains two encrypted scores. The system makes its decision by comparing the difference between the two encrypted scores with a threshold using the compare protocol. This arrangement is sufficient for a semi-honest user, who provides the correct speech input while evaluating both the UBM and the speaker model.

In the verification phase, the user could also be malicious in the case it is represented by an imposter. A malicious user can gain an advantage in authenticating himself/herself by submitting different inputs during the evaluation of the UBM and the speaker models. Therefore, need a protocol where the user

Figure 2. Block diagram of Secure Speaker Recognition

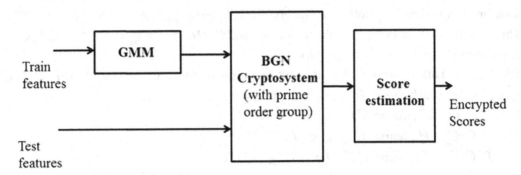

gets to submit only one speech sample as input and the system can evaluate it on both the models without requiring any further participation from the user. The non-interactive private verification protocol was created to address malicious users.

BGN Cryptosystem Using Prime Order Groups

Bilinear groups of composite order are a tool that has been used in the last few years to solve many problems in cryptography. The concept was introduced by Boneh, Goh, and Nissim, who applied the technique to the problems of private information retrieval, online voting, and universally variable computation. Subsequent authors have built on their work to create protocols such as non-interactive zero-knowledge proofs, ring and group signatures, attribute-based encryption, traitor tracing schemes, and hierarchical identity-based encryption. At a security level equivalent to 80-bit AES, ciphertexts in the Boneh-Goh-Nissim system can be up to three times smaller when instantiated using our prime-order construction than in the original composite-order system. At the 256-bit security level the improvement can be as large as a factor of 12.

BGN cryptosystem is based on subgroup decision problem. To create BGN cryptosystem with prime order we can use Decision Diffie-Hellman(DDH) or decision linear assumption.

BGN cryptosystem has the feature that given two ciphertexts, one can create a new ciphertext that encrypts either the sum or the product of the corresponding plaintexts. The product operation can only be carried out once; the system is thus partially doubly homomorphic.

Step 1 of the conversion process is to write the scheme in the abstract framework and transfer it to asymmetric groups. In the original BGN protocol any ciphertext may be paired with any other ciphertext, so in the asymmetric setting each computation in G must be duplicated in H. We must use a projecting pairing, as the decryption algorithm requires projection away from a certain subgroup. (Indeed, we defined the projecting property by using the BGN scheme as our model.)

KeyGen(λ): Let G be a projecting bilinear group generator. Compute
$(G, G_1, H, H_1, G_t, G_t', e, \pi_1, \pi_2, \pi_t) \leftarrow G(\lambda)$. Choose $g \xleftarrow{R} G$, $h \xleftarrow{R} H$ and output the public key $PK=(G, G_1, H, H_1, G_t, e, g, h)$ and the secret key $SK=(\pi_1, \pi_2, \pi_t)$.

Encrypt(PK,m): Choose $g_1 \xleftarrow{R} G_1$ and $h_1 \xleftarrow{R} H_1$. (Recall that the output of G allows random sampling from G_1 and H_1.) Output the ciphertext $(C_A, C_B) = (g^m, g_1, h^m, h_1) \in G \times H$. *Multiply(PK, C_A, C_B):* This algorithm takes as input two ciphertexts $C_A \in G$ and $C_B \in H$. Choose $g_1 \xleftarrow{R} G_1$ and $h_1 \xleftarrow{R} H_1$, and output $C = e(C_A, C_B).e(g, h_1).e(g_1, h) \in G_t$.

Add(PK, C, C'): This algorithm takes as input two ciphertexts C, C' in one of G, H or G_t. Choose $g_1 \xleftarrow{R} G_1$ and $h_1 \xleftarrow{R} H_1$, and do the following:

1. If $C, C' \in G$, output $C.C'.g_1 \in G$.
2. If $C, C' \in H$, output $C.C'.g_1 \in H$.
3. If $C, C' \in G_t$, output $C.C'.e(g, h_1).e(g_1, h) \in G_t$

Decrypt(SK;C): The input ciphertext C can be an element of G, H, or G_t.

1. If $C \in G$, output $m \leftarrow \log_{\pi_1(g)}(\pi_1(C))$.
2. If $C \in H$, output $m \leftarrow \log_{\pi_2(g)}(\pi_2(C))$.
3. If $C \in G_t$, output $m \leftarrow \log_{\pi_t(e(g,h))}(\pi_t(C))$.

It is clear that if C, C' are encryptions of m, m' respectively, then the Add algorithm gives a correctly distributed encryption of $m + m'$. Furthermore, it follows from the bilinear property of the pairing that if $C_A \in G$, $C_B \in H$ are the left and right halves of encryptions of m, m' respectively, then the multiply algorithm gives a correctly distributed encryption of $m.m'$. Since there is no pairing on G_t we can only perform the multiplication once.

Correctness of decryption of ciphertexts in G and H follows from the fact that G_1, H_1 are in the kernels of π_1, π_2, respectively. Correctness of decryption of ciphertexts in G_t follows from both projecting properties of G; for example, we have

$$\pi_t(e(g, h_1)) = e(\pi_1(g), \pi_2(h_1)) = e(\pi_1(g), 1) = 1.$$

Step 2 of the conversion process is to translate the security assumptions to asymmetric bilinear groups. In this case, semantic security of ciphertexts in G follows from the subgroup decision assumption on the left for G. Intuitively, if G satisfies the subgroup decision assumption on the left, then an adversary cannot distinguish the real system from a fake system in which $g \in G_1$. Semantic security then follows from the fact that in the fake system the ciphertext element C_A will be a uniformly random element of G_1 and thus will contain no information about the message m. The same argument holds for ciphertexts in H, and semantic security of ciphertexts in G_t follows from semantic security in G and H.

Step 3 is to translate the assumption to prime-order groups.

Let P be a prime-order bilinear group generator, and let G_p be the projecting bilinear group generator constructed from P. If P satisfies the DDH assumption in G_1 and G_2, then the BGN cryptosystem instantiated with $G = GP$ is semantically secure.

When instantiated with either G_{BGN} or G_P, decryption in the BGN system requires taking discrete logarithms in a group of large prime order. Thus to achieve efficient decryption the message space must be small (i.e., logarithmic in the group size). It is an open problem to find a bilinear group generator .. for which the subgroup decision assumption holds and for which discrete logarithms can be computed in a subset of $\pi_1(G)$ whose size is a constant fraction of the full group order. If we carry out the tensor product construction for any k and $n \geq k+1$, we obtain an instantiation of the BGN cryptosystem whose security depends on the k- Linear assumption. Since ciphertexts will consist of n elements of G_1 or G_2 or n^2 elements of G_t, these systems will in general be less efficient than the system constructed using G_p, which has $(n,k) = (2,1)$. We do note, however, that if $k \geq 2$ we can use a group with a symmetric pairing, in which case the Encrypt algorithm needs only to output the ciphertext C_A.

Matrix Representation of Multivariate Gaussian

The following construction from the multivariate Gaussian $N(x;u,\Sigma)$ computed on any d-dimensional vector x can be represented in terms of a *(d + 1) x (d + 1)* matrix W.

$$\tilde{W} = \begin{bmatrix} -\frac{1}{2}\Sigma^{-1} & \Sigma^{-1}\mu \\ 0 & w^* \end{bmatrix}$$

$$where \quad w^* = -\frac{1}{2}\mu^T\Sigma^{-1}\mu - \frac{1}{2}\log|\Sigma|.$$

This implies $\log N(x;u,\Sigma) = x\tilde{W}x^T$, where x is an extended vector obtained by concatenating 1 to x. The computation reduced to a single inner product $x^T W$, where the extended feature vector x consists of all pairwise product terms $x_i, x_j \in x$ and W is obtained by unrolling $\tilde{W}$ into a vector. In this representation

$$\log p(x|i) = \log N(x;u,\Sigma) = x^T W$$

Assume that the user computes MFCC features from the speech samples. In the following discussion, the MFCC features are referred as the speech sample itself.

Secure Enrollment Protocol

Assume that the system already has access to the UBM, λ_U trained on a collection of publicly available speech data. The speaker verification algorithm requires a speaker model obtained from adapting the UBM to the enrollment data provided by the speaker. The speaker model is kept with the system only after it is encrypted by the user's key. The enrollment protocol is outlined below.

Inputs:
1. User has the enrollment samples $x_1, ..., x_n$ and both encryption key $E[.]$ and decryption key $E^{-1}[.]$.
2. System has the UBM $\lambda_U = W_i^U$ i for i = 1,..., N, mixing weight α, and the encryption key $E[.]$.

Output:
System has the encrypted user model $E[\lambda_S] = E[W_i^S]$, for $i = 1,..., N$.

1.   The system sends the UBM λ_U to the user.
2.   User performs the model adaptation of λ_U with the enrollment samples $x_1, ..., x_n$ to obtain the adapted model λ_S.
3.   The user represents the mixture components of the adapted model using the $\hat{W}_i$ matrix representation described above.
4.   The user encrypts $\hat{W}_i$ using its encryption key and sends it to the system.

Secure Verification Protocol

In the verification protocol, the system needs to evaluate the probabilistic score of the given test sample using the UBM λ_U and the adapted model λ_S. This score is evaluated for all frames of the test sample; for a test sample $x = \{x_1 \ldots x_T\}$ and the model λ, this score is given by

$$P(x\,|\,\lambda) = \prod_t \sum_j w_j N(x_t; \mu, \Sigma)$$

The score uses log domain to prevent numerical underflow,

$$\log P(x\,|\,\lambda) = \sum_t \log \sum_j P(x_t\,|\,j) = \sum_t \log \sum_j e^{x_t^T w_j}$$

using the W matrix representation from Equation 12. In our privacy model, assume that the user has the speech sample x and the system has the encrypted matrices W_j. The verification protocol proceeds as follows: the user sends the encrypted frame vectors $E[x_t]$ to the system which the server uses to homomorphically compute the inner products $E[x_t^T W_j]$. In order to use the inner products to compute the log scores, need to perform an exponentiation operation on ciphertext. As our cryptosystem only supports homomorphic additions and a single multiplication, it is not possible to do this directly, and therefore use the logsum protocol which requires user participation in the intermediate steps.

RESULTS AND DISCUSSION

Implementation of Speaker recognition

The block diagram for the implementation of speaker recognition is shown in Figure 3. The feature extraction from speech signal was implemented using Spro library and the rest of GMM-UBM was implemented using ALIZE library.

The speaker recognition experiment is done using TIMIT corpus database. The Universal Background Model is calculated using 100 speakers and 30 speakers other than the speakers used for UBM is used for training. For testing the speech signal of the same 30 speakers is used again and tested against all trained models. The experiment is carried out with different number of mixture components. According to results, 16 number of mixture components are performing better as per Table 1.

Figure 3. Block diagaram of Speaker recognition implementation

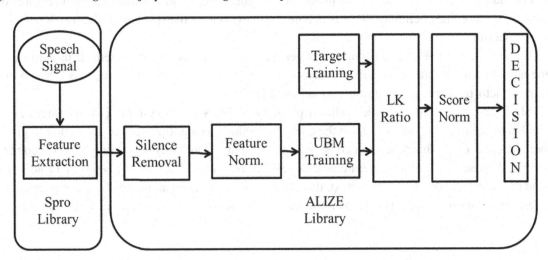

Table 1. Speaker Recognition results

No. of Mixture Components	% of Correct Identification
16	91
32	90
64	90
Average	90.33

The percentage of correct identification is calculated with the formula given by,

$$\% \text{ of correct identification} = \frac{\text{number of correct identification trail}}{\text{total number of trails}} \times 100$$

Implementation of BGN Cryptosystem

The results of experiments with the privacy preserving speaker verification protocols described above. The prototype implementations of the non-interactive verification protocols in C++ using the pairing-based cryptography (PBC) library to implement the BGN cryptosystem was created. The experiments on a 2.4 GHz Intel Core i5 Duo machine with 3 GB RAM running 64-bit Ubuntu was performed.

The measured the execution times for the verification protocols using BGN encryption keys of sizes 256 and 512-bits were measured. The BGN cryptosystem for the non-interactive protocol, as the private inner product is needed. The interactive protocol is faster than the non-interactive protocol. This is due to the execution of the private inner product for each frame vector needed for the non-interactive protocol. The system requires to perform multiplicative homomorphic operations to obtain the inner product. These operations in turn require the computation of a bilinear pairing which is much slower than homomorphically multiplying plaintexts with ciphertexts as do in the interactive protocol. In both protocols, observe that the UBM evaluation is significantly faster than the speaker model evaluation:

this is because the UBM is available in plaintext with the system and the inner product requires only additive homomorphic operations. This is in contrast to evaluating the speaker model that is only available in ciphertext.

Table 2 gives the public and private keys generated using BGN Cryptosystem. It uses to random prime numbers of 512 bits to produce a order of size 1024 bits. The size of the order is large so that it cannot be factorized. The prime number q1 act as the private key.

Table 3 gives the homomorphic addition property of BGN cryptosystem. Two messages are encrypted in to ciphertext C_A and C_B. Then the encrypted values are multiplied with each other to give the ciphertext value C_{A+B}. This property can be used to calculate probability scores in speaker recognition process. Likewise, BGN cryptosytem can also perform one multiplication as shown in Table 4. Here instead of multiplication of two ciphertext, the two ciphertext are bilinear mapped to get ciphertext $C_{A.B}$. The restriction in this process is that the message must be within the message space $1 \leq M \leq n - 1$.

Table 2. Public and private keys of BGN cryptosystem

PARAMETER	VALUE
Large prime q1	2306786701449964571703086538614026535569676498604371566813192732438330563180854244288360 6640957557579903805466875085381236084677308561540535357371410928 09
Large prime q2	2470337419191252904288837604837624124951366189913296090148934392879387441503219081306951 3824764714234559594196739777489227171006266725461041629002807583295815034073955109368161 7190017502272487962394478114945938143595569442948462784499731264262781992346058307565435 9218884758115899012366112250127634454 9671401
n=q1.q2	2470337419191252904288837604837624124951366189913296090148934392879387441503219081306951 3824764714234559594196739777489227171006266725461041629002807583295815034073955109368161 7190017502272487962394478114945938143595569442948462784499731264262781992346058307565435 9218884758115899012366112250127634454 9671401
Public Key (n,G,G1,e,g,h)	2470337419191252904288837604837624124951366189913296090148934392879387441503219081306951 3824764714234559594196739777489227171006266725461041629002807583295815034073955109368161 7190017502272487962394478114945938143595569442948462784499731264262781992346058307565435 9218884758115899012366112250127634454 9671401[2095926756619299857996098115011647894544261 3410546405521178442139835095041877377308248371352266089506439008437264286959792144397368 8251608153094971140582007758088815291246540775213003974250233756275752408600836279135555 4664617790384858022354583558300342394782461625982720253669079247562185172002799169224837 588,37215608595958589150723260564614538835573182900789346661338341421635445422143 2052981 4730148618854760899921845122720176798526328829024057227661623743192050076544387029926152 8777479694672101233447560728801129312995549488462626962714069020199982009230546230250247 9942854742619258247356559669204773595995474948449 2][1360092471046952921172502479628675 57 7222180353572499683845680087612908955015594082095309314136322550431676022386333003256615 2477724904157400618665256990333339512761891822038171046446170042811653734692555482614124 2801335990025689341552385613254563446450327039461528638320712908368011154904388104641381 98577338505,8924931979230694530441461239286388 09544028509231962683245976294481407389593 3 6783954245706169368372418531042884693287513552037556780704614219650358058514220573573026 10496420944292700188742991322478411240919611028262623231078194994210635427945398587138038 6908857345999313230143592596166525574094818162104 01858099]
Private Key q1	2306786701449964571703086538614026535569676498604371566813192732438330563180854244288360 6640957557579903805466875085381236084677308561540535357371410928 09

Table 3. Homomorphic Addition

PARAMETER	VALUE
A	100
B	50
Ciphertext *Ca*	9587593007706728368619473355072743938286950125729340053982280691925829458124006434634752499138595198556157916764204575793233800045320348958456865142846607628794309594430868846538908291890817403379687489977543396299653780030985727066080752469644578976320225017051494287569291231109967533657124587689029818755508,255781919832565313248950797922192027674464364749135512934858166958780861259312069710525622571698208666882875392864568971343812827213201693391288221340120363079955069178274626481271004248872865090963011844212063255148483369692978236572949714893884283565428322532912562413832064663385272475959796468929513741794 2]
Ciphertext *Cb*	8852127261784534914462022043759922164751821627187227316829298496942571532649433096515869752572199817597988918198010543502849665290001468598098686597042399265784577885850407262323017615831807451488609446137301845308898429488986146004503832615381785942185445034921444742313311522800530174770589212137633759555196,1017849114925782682687987278849342066664316785190261938692934072341875008275242326927739974147086781278889606968052022171040919702263496137681745284278152543792787841387526919116669663515176513468649088357016126063617460747251744641140818956353154412086164428314450387204119072427142193780882579673580557217143]
Ciphertext *C=Ca.Cb*	5189206234144165029976718349774642821851805921816084829202009955883814242553993816336738417881228660736977107686609549147620253684995133913183199701700036499327337592559152294216238420325598320955935226584894531826315453722690529133176243813418945366371078906449531091040590380305351683343738131623862713383150 5,1242393607075562547526542112095733542400914336744174588125405431375479962837811017668200342151037706663242429616025924451785085054016659430834310116831059271514601982314058606757197550534254705421971798619672517051553620882491791734392394671432819949223469590914755465802727864099879533035182407077 804696199793 3]
Plaintext *x=logC^q1=A+B*	150

Table 4. Homomorphic Multiplication

PARAMETER	VALUE
A	100
B	50
Ciphertext *Ca*	[3458557122760721508028418995742805223938721657930684084390603406165928864898837805138244213845870550491274494557998924860756714780302971949044910522209280773734389466070523736184802621490094503328796103680351828896732647303601770793603674100874543562541170746932711999404633909793777601542479683491675591569696 1,57487258717433037405771587785155091489095670665868537023810312299625549181459308043758626508954761159336133028333644672642032037985458429388570892603954388158254514976410427246492828581359023591632892669017492098216638166481578791091730740284814114937267295103051991893174553420360557130573176073333554720002 369]
Ciphertext *Cb*	[7322913430605976825556347679941730417702108071715018116608917556821459226891585429675783031337270554468968164403180258373647620713493090377148155728103339666551052639193067132680968281651531907594599888461579832634234474981429745938172134039623598360606262251492684658822703486402262108036094039482535218922306 9,4971853226877375960796908547893814981160818082429751623357422649048763057684624042344606308550556040301419822997667678449662937933147026835372165852651190732609914705624674826098675631345349851409289145367037974879406022068030688389341420183341922025790734034019639928313282537681671620535371319671977784364840 866]
Ciphertext *C*	[6105377167792565317894820825334865979282778521104813990973017927580771089171420716124432971287081967377304084165532069859607030779939092611464113211394161751809074214213716200478900599915947371209438059665796527775060530738457303686178392222213486621955512626444700413187053504749255500993302390430508283548055 8,18940542280720594098306386311830535220573392895249582865082809816879946277616578754316544381532774657205760051237009568768170444990034870247709952560343024142558983251708221804614277944686643554377661564428917232403836544236435395303581844490578719553693929568572201695782586637348707336128531815997372727058 993]
Plaintext *x=logC^q1=A.B*	5000

CONCLUSION AND FUTURE WORK

The GMM-UBM based speaker recognition was implemented using C libraries Spro and ALIZE and its performance was measure using different number of Gaussian mixture components. sing 16 mixture components gives better results than the other. The BGN Cryptosystem was implemented using PBC library, a C library for Pairing based cryptosystem. The additive and multiplicative homomorphic properties of BGN Cryptosystem were analyzed. The result shows secure speaker recognition can be implemented using BGN cryptosystem.

In the timing experiments for both speaker verification and speaker identification, observation shows that the parties spend a large amount of time performing encryption operations. This could be substantially reduced by using prime order bilinear groups to implement BGN cryptosystem and using a parallel computation framework such as graphics processing units. The tools and techniques used in this work can be used create secure protocols for other speaker recognition algorithms, e.g., super vectors with NAP and GMM-UBM with JFA. By using these algorithms the EER can be reduced and make the system more efficient.

REFERENCES

Aggarwal, C. C., & Yu, P. S. (Eds.). (2008). *Privacy Preserving Data Mining: Models and Algorithms, ser. Advances in Database Systems* (Vol. 34). New York: Springer. doi:10.1007/978-0-387-70992-5

Atallah, M. J., Kerschbaum, F., & Du, W. (2003). *Secure and private sequence comparisons* (pp. 39–44). Workshop Privacy Electron. Soc.

Bimbot, F., Bonastre, J. F., Fredouille, C., Gravier, G., Magrin-Chagnolleau, I., Meignier, S., ... Reynolds, D. A. (2004). A tutorial on text-independent speaker verification. *EURASIP Journal on Applied Signal Processing*, *4*(4), 430–451. doi:10.1155/S1110865704310024

Boneh, D., Goh, E.-J., & Nissim, K. (2006). Evaluating 2-DNF formulas on cipertext. *Proceedings of the Theory of Cryptography Conference* (pp. 325-341).

Campbell, W. M., Sturim, D. E., Reynolds, D. A., & Solomonoff, A. (2006). SVM based speaker verification using a GMM supervector kernel and NAP variability compensation. *Proc. ICASSP* (pp. 97–100). 10.1109/ICASSP.2006.1659966

Douglas, A. R., & Richard, C. R. (1995). Robust text-independent speaker identification using Gaussian mixture speaker models. *IEEE Transactions on Speech and Audio Processing*, *3*(1), 72–83. doi:10.1109/89.365379

El-Gamal, T. (1985). A public-key cryptosystem and a signature scheme based on discrete logarithms. *IEEE Transactions on Information Theory*, *IT-31*(4), 469–472. doi:10.1109/TIT.1985.1057074

Erkin, Z., Franz, M., Guajardo, J., Katzenbeisser, S., Lagendijk, I., & Toft, T. (2009). *Privacy-preserving face recognition* (pp. 235–253). Privacy Enhanc. Technol.

Freeman, D.M. (n. d.). Converting Pairing-Based Cryptosystems from Composite-Order Groups to Prime-Order Groups. *Research conducted at CWI and Universiteit Leiden, Netherlands, and supported by a National Science Foundation International Research Fellowship.*

Gentry, C. (2009). Fully homomorphic encryption using ideal lattices. *Proceedings of the ACM Symp. Theory of Comput.* (pp. 169–178).

Gentry, C. (2010). Computing arbitrary functions of encrypted data. *Communications of the ACM, 53*(3), 97–105. doi:10.1145/1666420.1666444

Gentry, C. (2010). Toward basing fully homomorphic encryption on worst case hardness. *Proc. of CRYPTO* (pp. 116–137). 10.1007/978-3-642-14623-7_7

Kenny, P., Ouellet, P., Dehak, N., Gupta, V., & Dumouchel, P. (2008). A study of inter-speaker variability in speaker verification. *IEEE Trans. Audio, Speech, Lang. Process., 16*(5), 980–988.

Lauter, M., Naehrig, Y., & Vaikuntanathan, V. (2011). Can homomorphic encryption be practical? *Proc. ACM Cloud Comput. Security Workshop.*

Manas A. Pathak & Bhiksha Raj. (2013). Privacy preserving Speaker verification and identification using Gaussian Mixture Models. *IEEE Transactions on Audio, Speech and Language processing, 21*(2), 397-406.

Nagar, A., Rane, S., & Vetro, A. (2010). *Alignment and bit extraction for secure fingerprint biometrics. SPIE Electron. Imaging, Media Forensics.* Security.

Paillier, P. (1999). Public-key cryptosystems based on composite degree residuosity classes. *Proc. of EUROCRYPT.* 10.1007/3-540-48910-X_16

Pathak, M., & Raj, B. (2011). *Privacy preserving speaker verification using adapted GMMs.* Proc. Interspeech.

Pathak, M., Rane, S., Sun, W., & Raj, B. (2011). Privacy preserving probabilistic inference with hidden Markov models. *Proc. of ICASSP* (pp. 5868–5871). 10.1109/ICASSP.2011.5947696

PBC Library. (n. d.). Retrieved from http://crypto.stanford.edu/pbc/

Pellom, B., & Hansen, J. (1999). An experimental study of speaker verification sensitivity to computer voice-altered imposters. *Proc. of ICASSP* (pp. 837–840). 10.1109/ICASSP.1999.759801

Reynolds, D. A. (1995). Speaker identification and verification using Gaussian mixture speaker models. *Speech Communication, 17*(1–2), 91–108. doi:10.1016/0167-6393(95)00009-D

Reynolds, D. A. (1997). Comparison of background normalization methods for text-independent speaker verification. *Proc. of Eurospeech* (Vol. 2, pp. 963–966).

Sang, Y. & Shen, H. (2009). Efficient and secure protocols for privacy-preserving set operations. *ACM Trans. Inf. Syst. Security*, 13(1), 9:1–9:35.

Smaragdis, P., & Shashanka, M. (2007). A framework for secure speech recognition. *IEEE Trans. Audio, Speech. Lang. Process., 15*(4), 1404–1413. doi:10.1109/TASL.2007.894526

Sundermann, D., Hoge, H., Bonafonte, A., Ney, H., Black, A., & Narayanan, S. (2006). Text-independent voice conversion based on unit selection. *Proc. of ICASSP* (pp. 81–84). 10.1109/ICASSP.2006.1659962

Vaidya, J., Clifton, C. W., & Zhu, Y. M. (2006). *Privacy Preserving Data Mining, ser. Advances in Information Security* (Vol. 19). New York: Springer.

Yao, A. (1982). Protocols for secure computations. *Proc. of FOCS*.

This research was previously published in the International Journal of Information Security and Privacy (IJISP), 9(4); edited by Michele Tomaiuolo and Monica Mordonini; pages 1-19, copyright year 2015 by IGI Publishing (an imprint of IGI Global).

Chapter 17
A Pairing–based Homomorphic Encryption Scheme for Multi–User Settings

Zhang Wei

Engineering University of Chinese Armed Police Force, China

ABSTRACT

A new method is presented to privately outsource computation of different users. As a significant cryptographic primitive in cloud computing, homomorphic encryption (HE) can evaluate on ciphertext directly without decryption, thus avoid information leakage. However, most of the available HE schemes are single-user, which means that they could only evaluate on ciphertexts encrypted by the same public key. Adopting the idea of proxy re-encryption, and focusing on the compatibility of computation, the authors provide a pairing-based multi-user homomorphic encryption scheme. The scheme is a somewhat homomorphic one, which can do infinite additions and one multiplication operation. Security of the scheme is based on subgroup decision problem. The authors give a concrete security model and detailed security analysis.

1. INTRODUCTION

Aiming on storage and computation outsourcing, cloud computing is revolutionizing the entire field of information technology. Clients outsource their data to the cloud to take advantage of the unlimited virtualized storage space and the low management cost. And the mighty computation ability can greatly alleviate the user's load. But the cloud is also posing new security and privacy challenges. Users want to gain reliability and availability for the remotely stored data, thus gives system designer a new challenge to provide security and credit, without service quality slacking.

During the past several years, since the first fully homomorphic encryption (FHE) scheme presented by Gentry (Gentry, 2009), homomorphic encryption has been a vibrant domain in cryptography. As a useful cryptographic primitive, homomorphic encryption can allow specific types of computations to be carried

DOI: 10.4018/978-1-7998-1763-5.ch017

out on ciphertexts and obtain an encrypted result which matches the result of operations performed on the plaintext after decryption. The idea of HE first presented by Rivest, Adleman and Dertouzos (Rivest, Adleman & Dertouzos, 1978), they found that some of the classical public key cryptosystem, such as RSA and ElGamal, are multiplication homomorphic, which means we can multiply two ciphertexts, and get the ciphertext of two plaintexts' multiplication.While RSA cannot permit addition on ciphertexts. This property is called semi-homomorphic, means only permit one operation (addition or multiplication).

BGN scheme was brought forward by Boneh, Goh and Nissim (Boneh, Goh & Nissim, 2005), it was the first semantic secure somewhat homomorphic encryption scheme that allows both addition and multiplication. This type is called *somewhat homomorphic*, because the time of multiplications is strictly limited, often once.If an encryption system permits unlimited additions and multiplications, then it is called *fully homomorphic*. During the past 30 years, the problem of constructing fully homomorphic encryption (FHE) schemes remains open. After the breakthrough work of Gentry in 2009, there has been numerous works on FHE. Some candidate schemes (Gentry, 2013, Yagisawa, 2015, Brakerski 2011) have been constructed, with security and efficiency been carefully analyzed.

However, most of the available HE or FHE schemes could only operate on ciphertexts of the same user. But in the practical world, it is often needed to operate on ciphertexts that was encrypted by different keys. In other word, we are facing such a scenario:

Suppose there are *n* clients that store their data in clouds. They wish to use these data as input to compute a function, with no personal information revealed. This is called *secure multiparty cloud computation* (SMCC), which is different from secure multiparty computation and server-aided multiparty computation in that it emphasizes that the server could not decrypt, yet the bulk computation should carry on the server.

SMCC is formulated as the following (Zheng & Zhang, 2012).

Secure Multiparty Cloud Computation (SMCC) Consider that k clients $p_1,...,p_k$, store their data $x_1,...,x_k$ in clouds in an encrypted form, they wish to cooperate together in order to efficiently and securely compute the function $f(x_1,...,x_k)$ by utilizing the computation capability of clouds.

This process is described in Figure 1.

Homomorphic encryption can be used to solve the problem of SMCC, however, the solution involves homomorphic evaluation on ciphertexts encrypted by different encryption keys, namely multi-key homomorphic encryption. The idea of multi-key homomorphic encryption is first presented by López-Alt, Tromer and Vaikuntanathan (López-Alt, Tromer & Vaikuntanathan, 2012). They constructed a multi-key fully homomorphic encryption (FHE) scheme from NTRU, and indicated that in theory, most of the existing FHE schemes can be changed into multi-key schemes, but in the resulting scheme, the size of ciphertext grows exponentially, thus cannot use in practice anyway. In 2014, Clear and McGoldrick (Clear & McGoldrick, 2014) put forward a multi-key leveled FHE basing on LWE assumption. They also point out that the ciphertext sizes of the multi-key FHE schemes are too long to be use in practice.

In addition to the above work, there's another way to obtain multi-key homomorphic encryption. That is, using the idea of proxy re-encryption to build an encryption scheme that can evaluate on two or more user's ciphertexts. The concept of proxy re-encryption, with a goal of securely enabling the re-encryption of ciphertexts from one key to another, first comes from the work of Blaze, Bleumer and Strauss (Blaze, Bleumer & Strauss, 1998).In 2005, Ateniese et.al. proposed a few new re-encryption schemes and discussed its several potential applications. Since then, many excellent schemes have been proposed, including re-encryption schemes in certificate based setting, in identity based setting and in hybrid setting (Wang et al, 2012, Matsuo,2007, Chandran,2015, Srinivasan & Rangan, 2014) .In 2012,

Figure 1. Secure multiparty cloud computation

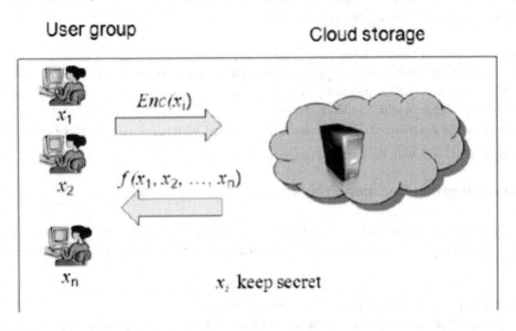

Zheng and Zhang(Zheng & Zhang, 2012) introduced homomorphic threshold proxy re-encryption into multiparty cloud computation. They constructed an efficient somewhat homomorphic encryption scheme, which can be used in multiparty cloud computation combing with proxy re-encryption and threshold decryption. .

To address the problem of secure multiparty cloud computing, we construct a multiuser homomorphic encryption scheme from BGN. Specifically, we construct an efficient multi-key somewhat homomorphic encryption scheme basing on BGN, and following the idea of proxy re-encryption to realize homomorphic operation between ciphertexts that was encrypted under different keys.

2. PRELIMINARIES

2.1. Bilinear Group and Bilinear Mapping

As a useful tool, bilinear mapping is applied in many cryptographic primitives.

Definition 1 (Bilinear Map) A map $e: G \times G \rightarrow G_1$ is a bilinear map if:

1. G, G_1 are groups of the same prime order q;
2. For all $a, b \in Z_q^*$, $g \in G$, $e(g^a, g^b) = e(g, g)^{ab}$;
3. The map is no-degenerate, i.e., if $G = \langle g \rangle$, then $G_1 = \langle e(g, g) \rangle$;
4. e is efficiently computable.

BGN scheme use finite groups of composite order that support a bilinear map.

Given an integer n, n is not a square of any integer, and is not divisible by 3, then a bilinear group and bilinear mapping is constructed as follows:

1. Find the smallest positive integer $l \in \mathbb{Z}$ such that $p=ln-1$ is prime and $p=2 \bmod 3$.
2. Consider the group of points on the (super-singular) elliptic curve $y^2=x^3+1$ defined over F_p. While $p=2\bmod 3$, the curve has $p+1=ln$ points in F_p. Therefore the group of points on the curve has a subgroup of order n which is denoted by G.
3. Let G_1 be the subgroup of $F_{p^2}^*$ of order n, the modified Weil pairing on the curve gives a bilinear map $e: G \times G \rightarrow G_1$ with the required properties.

2.2. The Subgroup Decision Problem

Given a security parameter $\tau \in \mathbb{Z}^+$, the following algorithm g can output a tuple (q_1,q_2,G,G_1,e) where G, G_1 are groups of order $n=q_1q_2$ and $e: G \times G \rightarrow G_1$ is a bilinear map. On input τ, algorithm g works as follows:

1. Generate two random τ-bit primes q_1,q_2 and set $n=q_1q_2 \in \mathbb{Z}$.
2. Generate a bilinear group G of order n as described at 2.1. Let g be a generator of G and $e: G \times G \rightarrow G_1$ be the bilinear map.
3. Output (q_1,q_2,G,G_1,e).

Let $\tau \in \mathbb{Z}^+$, and let (q_1,q_2,G,G_1,e) be a tuple produced by g (τ). The following problem is called *subgroup decision problem*: given (n,G,G_1,e) and an element $x \in G$, output '1' if the order of x is q_1, and output '0' otherwise. Namely, decide if an element x is in a subgroup of G without knowing the factorization of the group order n. The subgroup decision problem is considered hard, and the security of BGN scheme and our scheme relies on this assumption.

2.3. Revisit the Original BGN Scheme

BGN scheme is described as the following (Boneh et al, 2005):

KeyGen(τ): Given a security parameter $\tau \in \mathbb{Z}^+$, run g (τ) to obtain a tuple (q_1,q_2,G,G_1,e). Let $n=q_1q_2$. Pick two random generators $g,u \xleftarrow{R} G$ and set $h = u^{q_2}$. Then h is a random generator of the subgroup of G of order q_1. The public key is $pk=..$, and private key is $sk =q_1$.

Encrypt(pk, m): The message space of BGN is an integer set $\{0, 1, ..., T\}$ with $T<q_2$. To encrypt a message m using public key pk, pick a random $r \xleftarrow{R} \{0,1,\cdots,n-1\}$ and compute ciphertext c as $c=g^m h^r \in G$.

Decrypt(sk, c): To decrypt a ciphertext c using private key $sk =q_1$, observing that

$$c^{q_1} = \left(g^m h^r\right)^{q_1} = \left(g^{q_1}\right)^m$$

To recover m, it suffices to compute the descrete log of c^{q_1} base g^{q_1}. Using Pollard's lambda method (Boneh et al, 2005), this takes expected time $\tilde{O}\left(\sqrt{T}\right)$.

2.4. Proxy Re-Encryption and Hybrid Re-Encryption

Proxy re-encryption schemes are generally implemented in a very specific mathematical setting and find practical applications in secure e-mail forwarding or distributed storage systems.

In a proxy re-encryption scheme, a semi-trusted proxy converts a ciphertext for Alice into a ciphertext for Bob without seeing the underlying plaintext. The fundamental property of proxy re-encryption schemes is that the proxy is not fully trusted, i.e., it does not know the secret key of Alice or Bob and does not learn the plaintext during conversion. In such a scheme, Alice is called adelegator and Bob adelegatee.

In order to obtain the above goal, Alice or a trusted third party generates a re-encryption key and use it to transform Alice's ciphertext into a form that can be decrypted by Bob. Thus the key point of scheme constructing is how to generate the re-encryption key and how to use it.

A proxy re-encryption scheme consists 5 algorithms, KeyGen, ReKeyGen, Encryption, Reencryption, Decryption. They are defined as:

KeyGen: Given a security parameter τ, this algorithm generate the public key and private key of users.
ReKeyGen: Generate a re-encryption key to be used in re-encryption.
Enc: Given a plaintext, use Alice's public key to encrypt it.
ReEnc: Re-encrypt the ciphertext by the re-encryption key.
Dec: use Bob's private key to decrypt the above ciphertext.

In our scheme, the main point is to add and multiply the ciphertext of two users. We borrow the idea of proxy re-encryption and define a model of hybrid re-encryption.This model is similar to the above one, but differs in the re-encryption phase. .

Specifically, the re-encryption is re-defined as:

ReEnc: On input a message *m*, using the re-encryption key to generate a new ciphertext of Alice.

3. A BGN-TYPE MULTI-USER HOMOMORPHIC ENCRYPTION SCHEME

The aim of our scheme is to permit homomorphic operations between ciphertexts that was encrypted under different keys. In the original BGN scheme, different users may have different bilinear groups, and thus different ciphertext spaces. To operate on two user's ciphertext, we must solve the compatibility of multiplication. This involves modifying the parameters, constructing new bilinear groups and new encryption schemes.

We first show how to operate on two user's ciphertexts, then extend this method to the context of three or more users. Specifically, noted that the bilinear groups used in BGN must has an *n*-order subgroup, to achieve compatibility, we can make the bilinear group has a subgroup of order $n_1 n_2$ in the setup phase, and then constrains the ciphertext spaces of two users be two subrings of a same ring. Thus can add and multiply two ciphertexts encrypted under different keys. Details following.

3.1. Scheme Construction

Suppose there are two users Alice and Bob, the global parameter of the scheme is an integer n satisfies $n=n_1n_2$, where $n_1=q_{1A}q_{2A}$, $n_2=q_{1B}q_{2B}$, and $q_{1A},q_{2A},q_{1B},q_{2B}$ are secure primes. Find the least integer $l \in \mathbb{Z}$ such that $p=ln_1n_2+1$ is a prime, and $p=2\bmod3$. Then the super-singular elliptic curve $y^2=x^3+1$ has ln_1n_2 points in field F_p, and these points constitute a ln_1n_2-order group G. Moreover, G has subgroups G_A, G_B with order n_1,n_2 respectively. Here we also impose that $G_A \cap G_B \neq \Phi$. Let $G_A{}'$ be an n_1-order subgroup of $F_{p^2}^*$, and $G_B{}'$ be an n_2-order subgroup of $F_{p^2}^*$. Let $e_1 : G_A \times G_A \to G_A{}'$, $e_2 : G_B \times G_B \to G_B{}'$ be the modified Weil pairing on the elliptic curve.

Basing on the above parameters, we present a BGN-type two-user homomorphic encryption scheme which is compromised of 5 algorithms.

KeyGen(τ): Choose two generators $gA \ uA \in GA$, let $h_A = u_A{}^{\alpha \cdot q_{2A}}$, then h_A is a generator of the q_{1A}-order subgroup of G_A, here α is not specified. The public key of Alice is $pk_A = \left(n_1, G_A, G_A{}', e_1, q_A, h_A\right)$, and private key is $sk_A=q_{1A}$. Bob's public key pk_B and private key sk_B is generated similarly. But there's one more constraint that the generator g_B belongs to G_A, namely $g_B \in G_A \cap G_B$. And because G_A, G_B are two subgroup of a same group G, this happens with high probability.

ReKeyGen(u_A,q_{2B}): This algorithm generate a re-encryption key $rk_{A \to B} = h_A{}'$, which is used to re-encrypt a message and generate Alice's second level ciphertext.

Alice's ciphertext, so that it can be decrypted by Bob. Let g be a generator of G, then there exist a, $b \in \mathbb{Z}$ such that $u_A=g^a \in G$ and $u_B=g^b \in G$. Compute $h_A = u_A{}^{\alpha \cdot q_{2A}} = g^{a \cdot \alpha \cdot q_{2A}}$ and the re-encryption key is defined as

$$rk_{A \to B} = h_A{}' = h_A{}^{bq_{2B}} = u_A{}^{\alpha \cdot q_{2A} \cdot b \cdot q_{2B}} = \left(g^b\right)^{a \cdot \alpha \cdot q_{2A} \cdot q_{2B}} \in G_B$$

Enc(m): Suppose the plaintext space is $\{0,1,\ldots,T\}$, with $T<\min\{q_{2A},a_{2B}\}$. Given a message m, the encryption process is the same with the original BGN scheme, that is, randomly choose $r \xleftarrow{R} \{0,1,\cdots,n-1\}$ and compute ciphertext as

$$c_A = g_A{}^m h_A{}^r \in G_A$$

or

$$c_B = g_B{}^m h_B{}^r \in G_B$$

In order to operate on Alice and Bob's ciphertext, we need to re-encrypt a message so that the resulting ciphertext can be added and multiplied. The re-encryption is specified as the following.

Hybrid ReEnc(*m*): Given a message *m*, encrypt it using h_A' and g_B, and the ciphertext is computed as

$$c = g_B^m \left(h_A'\right)^{r_1}.$$

This process borrows the idea of proxy re-encryption, but has some differences. The key point is not transforming Alice's ciphertext, but encrypting a message under a new key $rk_{A \to B}$. The result can be decrypted by Bob's private key q_{1B}, and because $g_B \in G_A \cap G_B$, it could also be decrypted by Alice's private key q_{1A}. So this is not a generic proxy re-encryption process, and we call it a *hybrid re-encryption*.

Dec(*c*): To decrypt a ciphertext that has the above form using Bob's private key $q_{1,B}$, it only needs to compute

$$\left(c\right)^{q_{1B}} = \left(g_B^m \cdot g^{b \cdot a \cdot \alpha \cdot q_{1A} q_{2B}}\right)^{q_{1B}} = \left(g_B^{q_{1B}}\right)^m$$

To recover *m*, it suffices to compute the discrete log of $\left(c\right)^{q_{1B}}$ base $g_B^{q_{1B}}$. According to Pollard's Lambda method, the time complexity of decryption is $\widetilde{O}\left(\sqrt{T}\right)$ with $0 \le m \le T$. Moreover, this ciphertext could also be decrypted by Alice's secret key with the same method.

3.2. Homomorphic Properties of the Scheme

Suppose that the ciphertext of plaintext m_1 under the above re-enc key is denoted by c_1, and that of plaintext m_2 under Bob's encryption key is denoted by c_2, then $c_1 = g_B^{m_1}\left(h_A'\right)^{r_1}, c_2 = g_B^{m_2}\left(h_B\right)^{r_2}$, we will do homomorphic operations on these two ciphertexts.

- Homomorphic addition

The arithmetic product of c_1 and c_2 is

$$c_1 \cdot c_2 = g_B^{m_1+m_2}\left(h_A'\right)^{r_1} h_B^{r_2} = g_B^{m_1+m_2} \cdot u_B^{a \cdot \alpha \cdot q_{2A} \cdot q_{2B} \cdot r_1} u_B^{\beta \cdot q_{2B} \cdot r_2}$$

Considering that u_B is a generator of group G_B, and its order in G_B is $q_{1,B}q_{2,B}$, so the above $c_1 \bullet c_2$ is a natural ciphertext of m_1+m_2, and can be decrypted by Bob's private key q_{1B}.

- Homomorphic multiplication

The ciphertext space of the scheme is a multiplication group, and addition of ciphertexts is a natural one. To implement multiplication, we will make use of the bilinear mapping defined in section 2.1.

The multiplication is grounded on the fact that G_A and G_B are two subgroups of a same group, and the operations in these two subgroups are identical. To multiply two ciphertexts c_1 and c_2, we need to compute the bilinear mapping e_2 on $c_1 \cdot c_2$, namely, its suffices to compute

$$
\begin{aligned}
e_2\left(c_1, c_2\right) &= e_2\left(g_B^{m_1}\left(h_A'\right)^{r_1}, q_B^{m_2} h_B^{r_2}\right) \\
&= e_2\left(g_B^{m_1} u_B^{a \cdot \alpha q_{2A} q_{2B} r_1}, g_B^{m_2} u_B^{\beta q_{2B} r_2}\right) \\
&= g_B^{m_1 m_2} u_B^{\hat{r}} \in G_B'
\end{aligned}
$$

Decrypting the result by Bob's private key q_{1B}, and we can obtain a plaintext of $m_1 m_2$.

Through the above discussion, we can see that the ciphertexts of Alice and Bob can be added and multiplied, thus implement a two-user homomorphic encryption scheme. If we modify the parameters and let n has more divisors, then can obtain a scheme that can operate on ciphertexts of more users.

3.3. Security Analysis

The security of BGN lies on the subgroup decision problem: let G be a group with order n, $n = q_1 q_2$, and q_1 and q_2 are secure primes. Given $x \in G$, deciding if x belongs to some q_1-order subgroup is computationally infeasible.

Similar to BGN, security of our scheme also relies on the subgroup decision assumption, but has some difference. However, the main difference lies on that in our scheme, the modulus n has two factors n_1 and n_2, thus the security also relies on integer factoring assumption. And the latter is a well-studied problem, and is deemed as hard.

We now turn to proving semantic security of the system under the subgroup decision assumption.

Theorem 1: The multi-user homomorphic encryption scheme in Section3 is semantically secure assuming the algorithm g in section 2.2 satisfies the subgroup decision assumption.

Proof: Suppose a polynomial time algorithm B breaks the semantic security of the system with advantage ϵ. We construct an algorithm A that breaks the subgroup decision assumption with the same advantage. Given (q_1, q_2, G, G_1, e) as input, algorithm A works as the following:

1. A picks a random generator $g \in G$ and gives algorithm B the public key

$$
pk_A = \left(n_1, G_A, G_A', e_1, q_A, h_A\right).
$$

2. B outputs two messages $m_0 m_1 \in \{0, 1, \ldots, T\}$ to which A responds with the ciphertext $c = g^{m_b} h_A^{r} \in G$ for a random b and random $r \xleftarrow{R} \{0, 1, \cdots, n-1\}$.

3. Algorithm B outputs its guess $b' \in \{0, 1\}$ for b. If $b' = b$, then A outputs 1 (this means x is uniform in a subgroup of G); otherwise A outputs 0 (meaning x is uniform in G).

When x is uniformly distributed in G, the challenge ciphertext C is uniformly distributed in G and is independent of the bit b. Hence, in this case $\Pr[b' = b] = 1/2$.

On the other hand, when x is uniform in a subgroup of G, then the public key and challenge C given to B are as in a real semantic security game. In this case, by the definition of B, it holds that $\Pr[b' = b] > 1 / 2 + \epsilon$. It follows that A breaks the subgroup decision assumption with advantage ϵ.

4. CONCLUSION

In this article, we present a multi-user homomorphic encryption scheme that can operate on ciphertexts from different users. This scheme is a somewhat homomorphic one, however, comparing to the available NTRU-based multi-key FHE, the ciphertext length in our scheme grows linearly, and in applications such as multi-party cloud computation, our scheme is more practical.

5. FUTURE RESEARCH DIRECTIONS

Homomorphic encryption is a new research area, which has a variety of problems unresolved. For example, how to improve the efficiency so as to make the schemes practical, how to combine the application with special encryption schemes, and how to build fully homomorphic IBE and ABE schemes, etc. These problems are all promising and interesting, and our future research will focus on building fully homomorphic IBE and ABE schemes.

ACKNOWLEDGMENT

This research was financially supported by the National Science Foundation of China (Grant No. 61272492).

REFERENCES

Applebaum, B., Cash, D., Peikert, C., & Sahai, A. (2009). Fast cryptographic primitives and circular secure encryption based on hard learning problems. Proceedings of CRYPTO (pp. 595–618). doi:10.1007/978-3-642-03356-8_35

Blaze, M., Bleumer, G., & Strauss, M. (1998). Divertible Protocols and Atomic Proxy Cryptography. Proceedings of Advances in Cryptology- Eurocrypt '98, LNCS (Vol. 1403, pp. 127–144). Springer–Verlag. doi:10.1007/BFb0054122

Boneh, D., & Franklin, M. (2003). Identity based encryption from the Weil pairing. *SIAM Journal on Computing*, *32*(3), 586–615. doi:10.1137/S0097539701398521

Boneh, D., Goh, E. J., & Nissim, K. (2005). Evaluating 2-DNF Formulas on Ciphertexts. *Proceedings of TCC 2005, LNCS* (Vol. *3378*, pp. 325–341).

Brakerski, Z. (2013). When homomorphism becomes a liability. In *Theory of Cryptography* (pp. 143–161). Springer. doi:10.1007/978-3-642-36594-2_9

Brakerski, Z. and Vaikuntanathan, V. (2011). Fully homomorphic encryption from ring-LWE and security for key dependent messages. Proceedings of Advances in Cryptology CRYPTO2011 (pp. 505-524).

Canetti, R., & Hohenberger, S. (2007). Chosen-Ciphertext Secure Proxy Re-Encryption., *Proceedings of the 2007ACM Conference on Computer and Communications Security CCS '07* (pp. 185-194).

Chandran, N., Chase, M., & Liu, F. H. (2015). *Re-encryption, functional re-encryption, and multi-hop re-encryption: A framework for achieving obfuscation-based security and instantiations from lattices.* Cryptology ePrint Archive: http://eprint.iacr.org/2015/491.pdf

Chatterjee, A., Kaushal, A., & Sengupta, I. (2013, December 7-10). Accelerating sorting of fully homomorphic encrypted data. *Proceedings of Progress in Cryptology -INDOCRYPT 2013 - 14th International Conference on Cryptology in India*, Mumbai, India (pp. 262–273). 10.1007/978-3-319-03515-4_17

Cheon, J. H., & Kim, M. (2014). Search-and-compute on encrypted data. Cryptology ePrint Archive Report2014/812 (2014). Retrieved from http://eprint.iacr.org/2014/812

Clear, M. and McGoldrick, C. (2013). Multi-Identity and Multi-Key Leveled FHE from Learning with Errors. Cryptology ePrint Archive, 2013.

Ducas, L. and Micciancio, D. (2015). FHEW: Bootstrapping Homomorphic Encryption in less than a second. *Proceedings of Advances in Cryptology-EUROCRYPT '15*. Springer.

Gentry, C. (2009). Fully homomorphic encryption using ideal lattices. Proceedings of STOC '09 (pp. 169–178). doi:10.1145/1536414.1536440

Gentry, C., Sahai, A., & Waters, B. (2013). Homomorphic encryption from learning with errors: Conceptually-simpler, asymptotically-faster, attribute-based. In R. Canetti & J.A. Garay (Eds.), Proceedings of CRYPTO 2013, LNCS (Vol. 8042, pp. 75-92). Springer.

López, A., Tromer, E., & Vaikuntanathan, V. (2012). On-the-fly multiparty computation on the cloud via multikey fully homomorphic encryption. *Proceedings of the 44th symposium on Theory of Computing. STOC '12*, New York, NY, USA (pp. 1219-1234). ACM. 10.1145/2213977.2214086

Lyubashevky, V. Peikert, C. Regev, O. (2013). A Toolkit for Ring-LWE Cryptography. *Proceedings of Advances in Cryptology-EUROCRYPT '13*. Springer.

Matsuo, T. (2007). Proxy Re-encryption Systems for Identity-based Encryption. Proceedings of Pairing-Based Cryptography-Pairing'07, LNCS (Vol. 4575, pp. 247-267). Springer-Verlag. doi:10.1007/978-3-540-73489-5_13

Nuida, K. (2015). *A Simple Framework for Noiseless Fully Homomorphic Encryption on Special Classes of Non-Commutative Groups. Proceedings of Advances in Cryptology- Asiacrypt '15*. Springer.

Rivest, R. L., Adleman, L., & Dertouzos, M. L. (1978). On Data Banks and Privacy Homomorphisms. In Foundations of Secure Computation (pp. 169-177).

Srinivasan, A., & Rangan, C. P. (2014). Certificateless Proxy Re-Encryption Without Pairing: Revisited. Cryptology ePrint Archive http://eprint.iacr.org/2014/933.pdf

Wang, X. A., Huang, X., Yang, X., Liu, L., & Wu, X. (2012). Further observation on proxy re-encryption with keyword search. *Journal of Systems and Software*, *85*(3), 643–654. doi:10.1016/j.jss.2011.09.035

Yagisawa, M. (2015). Fully Homomorphic Encryption on Octonion Ring. Retrieved from http://eprint.iacr.org/2015/733.pdf

Yagisawa, M. (2015). Fully homomorphic encryption without bootstrapping [Technical report]. Cryptology ePrint Archive, Report 2015/474. Retrieved from http://eprint.iacr.org/2015/474

Zheng, Q., & Zhang, X. (2012). *Multiparty Cloud Computation*. Cryptology ePrint Archive, arXiv: 1206, 3717.

This research was previously published in the International Journal of Technology and Human Interaction (IJTHI), 12(2); edited by Anabela Mesquita and Chia-Wen Tsai; pages 72-82, copyright year 2016 by IGI Publishing (an imprint of IGI Global).

Chapter 18
A Secure Cloud Storage using ECC–Based Homomorphic Encryption

Daya Sagar Gupta

Indian Institute of Technology (ISM) Dhanbad, India

G. P. Biswas

Indian Institute of Technology (ISM) Dhanbad, India

ABSTRACT

This paper presents a new homomorphic public-key encryption scheme based on the elliptic curve cryptography (HPKE-ECC). This HPKE-ECC scheme allows public computation on encrypted data stored on a cloud in such a manner that the output of this computation gives a valid encryption of some operations (addition/multiplication) on original data. The cloud system (server) has only access to the encrypted files of an authenticated end-user stored in it and can only do computation on these stored files according to the request of an end-user (client). The implementation of proposed HPKE-ECC protocol uses the properties of elliptic curve operations as well as bilinear pairing property on groups and the implementation is done by Weil and Tate pairing. The security of proposed encryption technique depends on the hardness of ECDLP and BDHP.

1. INTRODUCTION

Public-key encryption (PKE) came into existence in the year 1976. Firstly, Diffie & Hellman (1976) asked whether it is possible to have two different keys; one for encryption (a public key *PK*) and another for decryption (a secret key *SK*) in their seminal paper entitled "New Directions in Cryptography". This paper includes the concepts of PKE to design a new homomorphic encryption technique mainly for cloud security. By homomorphic property, we mean that $E(m_1 \, o_m \, m_2) = E(m_1) \, o_c \, E(m_2)$ where E denotes the encryption and $o_c \, / \, o_m$ denote the binary operations.

DOI: 10.4018/978-1-7998-1763-5.ch018

In this paper, the authors use the properties of the elliptic curves and bilinear map to secure the network communication. The security of ECC algorithms is independently given by Kapoor, Abraham & Singh (2008). The authors of this paper propose a new cryptographic encryption/decryption technique with homomorphic property based on the hardness assumptions Elliptic Curve Diffie-Hellman Problem (ECDHP) and Bilinear Diffie-Hellman Problem (BDHP). The cloud security is the main objective of this proposed paper. Thus, for security issues on the clouds, the authors of this paper include the homomorphic encryption technique. They have presented four algorithms: *key generation, encryption, decryption, and evaluation* to implement this proposed work. In the *key generation*, the key pair (public and private key) for their proposed scheme is generated. *Encryption* algorithm of this scheme simply encrypts the message using the public key of the receiver and the encrypted message is stored on the cloud storage. Since the stored messages are encrypted, a cloud server is not able to understand these messages, *i.e.* security to the stored messages is provided so that the cloud system could not see the original message. *Decryption* algorithm takes the encrypted message as input and uses receiver's private key to decrypt the encrypted message to get the authentic message. At last, the *evaluation* algorithm is mainly used to design the homomorphic property for the proposed protocol. For the evaluating process of the proposed work, an authentic user requests the cloud for encrypted data which includes the addition or multiplication of original authentic messages stored on cloud storage. The cloud system, in return, performs some computation on the files stored in it and responds with computed files. The authentic user, in turns, performs the decryption algorithm to generate the addition or multiplication of original files.

1.1. Literature Review

Gentry (2009) proposed a fully homomorphic encryption. He shows that his scheme computes a function on encrypted data and also homomorphism is preserved. He uses the hard lattices to design his protocol. He firstly designed a somewhat homomorphic "boostrappable" encryption scheme and later showed the how boostrappable encryption is converted into a fully homomorphic encryption. Van Dijk, Gentry, Halevi & Vaikuntanathan (2010) proposed a modular arithmetic based fully homomorphic encryption scheme. They use Gentry (2009)'s technique to include "boostrappable" somewhat encryption. Their scheme is based on the addition and multiplication on integers. Brakerski & Vaikuntanathan (2014) an LWE based fully homomorphic encryption scheme. Smart & Vercauteren (2010) presents a fully homomorphic encryption scheme in which the size of key and cipher text is smaller. Their scheme uses Gentry (2009) technique to design a somewhat encryption to a fully homomorphic encryption scheme. Gentry, Sahai & Waters (2013) proposed a new technique which is used to design a fully homomorphic encryption scheme. They called this new technique as approximate eigenvector method. Ducas & Micciancio (2015) proposed a fully homomorphic encryption which works on bit operations and continuously refresh it. Bendlin, Damgard, Orlandi & Zakarias (2011) proposed a semi-homomorphic encryption scheme. Bos, Lauter, Loftus & Naehrig (2013) designed a new fully homomorphic scheme which removes this non-standard assumption and based on lattice and circular security problems.

Coron, Lepoint & Tibouchi (2014) proposed a scheme which presented a key policy attribute-based encryption (ABE) using a fully homomorphic encryption scheme and security of their scheme is given by LWE problem. Wei (2016) provided the security to the cloud system using a pairing-based homomorphic encryption scheme. A faster fully homomorphic encryption is proposed by Stehlé & Steinfeld (2010). Their scheme described the improvement in Gentry's homomorphic encryption. They provide a complex analysis of the hardness problem and proposed probabilistic decryption algorithm. Tebaa & Hajji (2014) proposed a homomorphic scheme which provides the protection of privacy on the data stored on a cloud. Their protocol insures a secure cloud computation using the homomorphic encryption.

1.2. Organization of the Paper

The paper is organized in the following manner. We defined some related definitions like elliptic curve cryptography, bilinear maps, HE and some related hard computational problems in Sect. 2. Section 3 describes the proposed HPKE-ECC schemes with its correctness in detail. The security analysis is done in Sect. 4. Finally, in Sect. 5, the paper is concluded.

2. BACKGROUNDS

This section gives a brief idea about the properties and definitions that have been used in the proposed HPKE-ECC.

2.1. Elliptic Curve

The elliptic curve, related to mathematics, has some interesting properties that are used in the field of cryptography. The points of these curve show an abelian group property with addition operation. A standard "elliptic curve" used in the cryptography is well-defined by the following equation:

$$y^2 = x^3 + ax + b; \quad 4a^3 + 27b^2 \neq 0$$

where *x, y, a* and *b* are some real numbers. The elliptic curves have two operations: an addition and a scalar multiplication on their points. The formulation of these operations is described here.

Let two points P and Q are on an elliptic curve. The addition of these two points *i.e. (P+Q)* is calculated as the following steps:

A. Let $P=(x_1,y_1)$ and $Q=(x_2,y_2)$ *i.e.* P and Q has the different abscissa and ordinate. The addition of these two points *(P+Q)* is another point R on the elliptic curve. To find R, join P and Q as a straight line which intercepts corresponding elliptic curve on a point $-R$. The mirror image of this point $-R$ about x-axis is the point R *i.e.* $R=P+Q$.

B. Let $P=(x_1,y_1)$ and $Q=(x_1,y_1)$ *i.e.* P and Q be the same points on the elliptic curve *(P = Q)*. The addition of these two points *(P+Q)* is another point R on the elliptic curve. To find R, a tangent is drawn to the point P or Q which intercepts corresponding elliptic curve on a point $-R$. The mirror image of this point $-R$ about x-axis is the point R *i.e.* $R=P+Q$.

C. Let $P=(x_1,y_1)$ and $Q=(x_1,-y_1)$ *i.e.* P and Q are the inverse of each other *(P = −Q)*. The addition of these two points *(P+Q)* is another point O on the elliptic curve. To find O, join P and Q as a straight line which doesn't intercepts corresponding elliptic curve but suppose to intercept at a point of infinity O. This point is called additive identity of elliptic curve group, i.e. $P + (-P) = O$.

To find the scalar multiplication with a point P of an elliptic curve, *i.e.* rP; $r \in Z$, simply add the given point P, r times using above described steps to get rP.

2.2. Bilinear Pairing

The bilinear pairing maps two elements of a group to an element of a different group. Let two groups G, G_1 and G_2 are three groups of same order n where G is an additive elliptic curve group, G_1 and G_2 are two multiplicative groups.

1. A bilinear map $\hat{e}_1$: $G \times G \to G_1$ is defined by following three properties:
   - **Bilinear Property:** $\hat{e}_1 (aP, bQ) = \hat{e} (P, Q)^{ab}$ for all $P, Q \in G$, and all $a, b \in Z_n$
   - **Non-degeneration Property:** There exists a P in G such that $\hat{e}_1 (P, P) \neq 1$.
   - **Computable Property:** There must be an efficient algorithm to compute $\hat{e}_1 (X, Y)$ for any $X, Y \in G$.
2. A bilinear map $\hat{e}_2$: $G_1 \times G_1 \to G_2$ is defined by following three properties:
   - **Bilinear Property:** $\hat{e}_2 (u^a, v^b) = \hat{e} (u, v)^{ab}$ for all $u, v \in G_1$ and all $a, b \in Z_n$
   - **Non-degeneration Property:** There exists a g in G_1 such that $\hat{e}_2 (g, g) \neq 1$.
   - **Computable Property:** There must be an efficient algorithm to compute $\hat{e}_2 (u, v)$ for any u, $v \in G_1$.

A bilinear mapping which satisfies these three properties is known to be an admissible bilinear map.

2.3. Homomorphic encryption

The public key encryption (PKE) with a special property of homomorphism is known to "homomorphic encryption". A PKE is defined by three algorithms namely; key generation, encryption, and decryption. In homomorphic encryption, evaluation algorithm is included with these three algorithms. Homomorphic encryption is defined by following four algorithms:

- **Key generation (t):** This algorithm is used to generate the keys. After taking a security parameter t, it outputs key pair for encryption/decryption as the public key (*PK*) and private key (*PR*).
- **Encryption (PK, m):** The encryption algorithm encrypts the given message m with the public key of receiver *PK* and outputs an encrypted message c.
- **Decryption (PR, c):** The decryption algorithm is used to decrypt the incoming cipher text c with the receiver's private key *PR* to get the message m.
- **Evaluation (PK, c_i, f):** This algorithm is used to show the homomorphic property. It performs some computation on a set of cipher texts c_i using the public key *PK*. The result of the computation gives the encryption of a function f on the original messages.

2.4. Hard Assumptions

This sub-section defines some hard assumptions which are incorporated with the proposed work. These assumptions are hard to solve.

- Discrete *logarithm problem (DLP):* For any given u, $v \in G_1$ and $v = u^r$; $r \in Z_q^*$, finding the value of r is hard.
- *Elliptic curve* discrete *logarithm problem (ECDLP):* For any given P, $Q \in G$ and $Q = rP$; $r \in Z_q^*$, finding the value of r is hard.
- *Bilinear Diffie-Hellman problem (BDHP):* For any given $(P, rP, sP, tP) \in G$; $r, s, t \in Z_q^*$, finding $\hat{e}(P, P)^{rst}$ is hard to compute.
- *Computational Diffie-Hellman problem (CDHP):* For any given $(P, rP, sP) \in G$; $r, s \in Z_q^*$, finding rsP is hard.

3. PROPOSED HPKE-ECC

This section presents the proposed homomorphic public-key encryption scheme based on the elliptic curve cryptography (HPKE-ECC). The main motive of this proposed scheme is cloud security. The proposed protocol, used in cloud computing, evaluates (add/multiply) on cipher texts without any decryption and thus no information is leaked about the original file. The steps of the proposed protocol is described by the following four algorithms:

3.1. Key Generation

This algorithm generates the public/private key pair in the following manner:

1. This random algorithm takes a security parameter $t \in Z^+$ and obtains a tuple $< q_1, q_2, G, G_1, G_2, \hat{e}_1, \hat{e}_2 >$ as system parameters where q_1 and q_2 are two t-bit random primes and let $n = q_1 q_2$.
2. Let P be a base point in group G and g and g_1 are primitive roots of G_1 and G_2 respectively. Calculate $Q = q_2 P$.
3. The key pair generated is: the public key $PK = (n, G, G_1, G_2, \hat{e}_1, \hat{e}_2, P, Q)$ and the private key $PR = q_1$.

3.2. Encryption

The message space $M = \{0, 1, 2, 3 \ldots I\}$ where $I < q_2$. To encrypt a message $m \in M$, a sender (Alice) selects a random $r < n$ and calculates $E = (mP + rQ) \in G$ and $E_1 = \hat{e}_1(E, P) \in G_1$. He then, sends E_1 to a receiver (Bob) and stores $<E, E_1>$ on the cloud storage.

3.3. Decryption

After receiving the encrypted message E_1, Bob uses her private key $PR = q_1$ and decrypt the message in the following manner: She computes $E_1^{q_1}$ and gets $(g^{q_1})^m$. Since m is small, she recovers the message m by computing the discrete logarithm of $E_1^{q_1}$ base g^{q_1}. This computation takes $O\sqrt{I}$ time using Pollard's lambda method.

Verification of the decryption process is done by the following manner:

$$E_1^{q_1} = \hat{e}_1 \left(E, P \right)^{q_1}$$
$$= \hat{e}_1 \left(\left(mP + rQ \right), P \right)^{q_1}$$
$$= \hat{e}_1 \left(\left(mP + rq_2 P \right), P \right)^{q_1}$$
$$= \hat{e}_1 \left(P, P \right)^{(m + rq_2)q_1}$$
$$= g^{(m + rq_2)q_1}$$

(Since $\hat{e}_1 \left(P, P \right) = g$)

$$= g^{mq_1} g^{rq_1 q_2}$$
$$= g^{mq_1}$$

(Since $q_1 q_2 = n$ and $g^n = 1$)

3.4. Evaluation

This algorithm shows the homomorphic property of the presented scheme. In this proposed work, the authors of this paper on the two properties (addition and multiplication) of homomorphism which are described below in detail.

3.4.1. Homomorphism

This sub-section provides the homomorphic properties of the proposed HPKE-ECC protocol. Let us consider, Alice, the sender store a number of cipher text pairs (*<E_a, E_{1a}>, <E_b, E_{1b}>, <E_c, E_{1c}>, ...*) on the cloud.

1. Let Bob, the receiver requests to the remote cloud for an encrypted file of the addition of two original messages. The cloud system simply computes the addition $A = E_a + E_b$ where $E_a = m_a P + r_a Q$ and $E_b = m_b P + r_b Q$ and calculates the encrypted file $A_1 = \hat{e}_1 \left(A, P \right)$. It, then responds with returning A_1 to the Bob. Bob, on the other hand, decrypts A_1 using decryption algorithm to get ($m_a + m_b$) mod *n*.
2. The request for an encrypted file of multiplication of two original messages is made by the Bob to the remote server (cloud). The remote server, in response to the request, calculates

$$B = \hat{e}_2 \left(E_{1a}, E_{1b} \right)$$
$$= \hat{e}_2 \left(g^{(m_a + r_a q_2)}, g^{(m_b + r_b q_2)} \right)$$
$$= \hat{e}_2 \left(g, g \right)^{m_a m_b + q_2 (r_a m_b + r_b m_a + r_a r_b q_2)}$$
$$= \hat{e}_2 \left(g, g \right)^{m_a m_b + q_2 \beta}$$

where

$$\beta = r_a m_b + r_b m_a + r_a r_b q_2$$
$$= g_1^{\,m_a m_b + q_2 \beta}$$

Then, it responds with returning B to the Bob. Bob, on the other hand, decrypts B using decryption algorithm and gets $m_a m_b \bmod n$.

4. IMPLEMENTATION OF PROPOSED HPKE-ECC

The implementation of the proposed scheme is based on the elliptic curve operations and bilinear mapping. The proposed protocol uses the operations on points of a standard elliptic curve described in the section 2.1. These operations can be easily computed using Kapoor, Abraham & Singh (2008). Now, in our scheme, decryption algorithm is based on the bilinear map discussed in section 2.2. This map is firstly introduced by Boneh & Franklin (2001). The computation of bilinear map is done using Weil and Tate pairing. Thus, the proposed HE protocol is easily implemented by using the addition operation on points of a elliptic curve and pairing methods.

5. SECURITY ANALYSES

In this section, the authors of this paper present the security proofs of the proposed HPKE-ECC schemes discussed in section 3. An HPKE-ECC scheme ε is known to be secure against an eavesdropper if no polynomial-time randomizes eavesdropper $\hat{A}$ has the success probability of following attacks greater than negligible:

1. Attack on Bob's secret key
2. Attack on Alice's random (session key)

The following theorem shows that our presented HPKE-ECC is secure against $\hat{A}$ under ECDLP and BDHP assumptions.

Theorem 1: The proposed ECC based homomorphic public-key encryption (HPKE-ECC) scheme ε is said to be probably secure against an eavesdropper attack if every polynomial-time randomizes eavesdropper $\hat{A}$ has a negligible probability of attacking the secrets.

Proof: Let the presented HPKE-ECC scheme may be written as:

$$\langle Alice\ (r),\ Bob\ (q_1) \rangle\ (n,\ G,\ G_1,\ G_2,\ \hat{e}_1,\ \hat{e}_2,\ P,\ Q) = \langle E,\ E_1 \rangle$$

Where the above expression denotes the communication system between Alice and Bob. Alice, the sender, takes r as input and Bob, the receiver, takes q_1 as input. $\langle E, E_1 \rangle$ are the outputs of the encryption process and $(n,\ G,\ G_1,\ G_2,\ \hat{e}_1,\ \hat{e}_2,\ P,\ Q)$ are the public parameters.

Let the *view* of the eavesdropper $\hat{A}$ be (i, j) which is the information exchanged between Alice and Bob on an insecure medium. Thus, *view* (<*Alice* (*r*), *Bob* (q_1)> (*n, G, G$_1$, G$_2$, ê$_1$, ê$_2$, P, Q*)) = (*i, j*)

1. Let adversary $\hat{A}$ attacks on the private key of Bob. The success probability of this attack is computed as:

Pr [$\hat{A}$ (*n, G, G$_1$, G$_2$, ê$_1$, ê$_2$, P, Q, view* (<*Alice* (*r*), *Bob* (q_1)> (*n, G, G$_1$, G$_2$, ê$_1$, ê$_2$, P, Q*))) = q_1]

= Pr [$\hat{A}$ (*n, G, G$_1$, G$_2$, ê$_1$, ê$_2$, P, Q*, (*i, j*)) = q_1]

= Pr [$\hat{A}$ (*n, G, G$_1$, G$_2$, ê$_1$, ê$_2$, P, Q*, <*E, E$_1$*>) = q_1]

= Pr [$\hat{A}$ (*n, G, G$_1$, G$_2$, ê$_1$, ê$_2$, P, Q*, <(*mP+rQ*), $\hat{e}_1\left(E,P\right)$>) = q_1] < *negl*

where, *negl* is a negligible function and the above inequality hold under hardness of ECDLP and BDHP assumption.

2. Let adversary $\hat{A}$ is willing to attack the Alice's session key. The success probability of this attack is calculated as:

Pr [$\hat{A}$ (*n, G, G$_1$, G$_2$, ê$_1$, ê$_2$, P, Q, view* (<*Alice* (*r*), *Bob* (q_1)> (*n, G, G$_1$, G$_2$, ê$_1$, ê$_2$, P, Q*))) = *r*]

= Pr [$\hat{A}$ (*n, G, G$_1$, G$_2$, ê$_1$, ê$_2$, P, Q*, (*i, j*)) = *r*]

= Pr [$\hat{A}$ (*n, G, G$_1$, G$_2$, ê$_1$, ê$_2$, P, Q*, <*E, E$_1$*>) = *r*] < *negl*

where, *negl* is a negligible function and the above inequality hold due to the hardness of ECDLP and BDHP assumption.

6. CONCLUSION

In this paper, the authors proposed an HPKE-ECC scheme to secure the cloud database. This proposed method performs a computation on the encrypted file stored in the cloud which, in turns, returns the encryption of addition or multiplication of original files. The scheme presented is simple and secure because the ECC is used to implement the proposed protocol. The scheme stores the encrypted files on a remote cloud system but the cloud system can't see the original message. The cloud server does some computation on stored files and returns the computed files to the authentic user. The authors also made a security analysis and showed the security of proposed protocol under various attacks. The security of this proposed scheme depends on the hard assumptions of ECC.

REFERENCES

Bendlin, R., Damgard, I., Orlandi, C., & Zakarias, S. (2011, May). Semi-homomorphic encryption and multiparty computation. *Proceedings of the Annual International Conference on the Theory and Applications of Cryptographic Techniques* (pp. 169-188). Springer.

Boneh, D., & Franklin, M. (2001, August). Identity-based encryption from the Weil pairing. *Proceedings of the Annual International Cryptology Conference* (pp. 213-229). Springer.

Boneh, D., Goh, E. J., & Nissim, K. (2005). Evaluating 2-DNF formulas on ciphertexts. In Theory of cryptography (pp. 325-341). Springer.

Bos, J. W., Lauter, K., Loftus, J., & Naehrig, M. (2013, December). Improved security for a ring-based fully homomorphic encryption scheme. *Proceedings of the IMA International Conference on Cryptography and Coding* (pp. 45-64). Springer. 10.1007/978-3-642-45239-0_4

Brakerski, Z., & Vaikuntanathan, V. (2014). Efficient fully homomorphic encryption from (standard) LWE. *SIAM Journal on Computing, 43*(2), 831–871. doi:10.1137/120868669

Coron, J. S., Lepoint, T., & Tibouchi, M. (2014, March). Scale-invariant fully homomorphic encryption over the integers. *Proceedings of the International Workshop on Public Key Cryptography* (pp. 311-328). Springer. 10.1007/978-3-642-54631-0_18

Diffie, W., & Hellman, M. (1976). New directions in cryptography. *IEEE Transactions on Information Theory, 22*(6), 644–654. doi:10.1109/TIT.1976.1055638

Ducas, L., & Micciancio, D. (2015, April). FHEW: bootstrapping homomorphic encryption in less than a second. *Proceedings of the Annual International Conference on the Theory and Applications of Cryptographic Techniques* (pp. 617-640). Springer. 10.1007/978-3-662-46800-5_24

Gentry, C. (2009). A fully homomorphic encryption scheme [Doctoral dissertation]. Stanford University.

Gentry, C., Sahai, A., & Waters, B. (2013). Homomorphic encryption from learning with errors: Conceptually-simpler, asymptotically-faster, attribute-based. In *Advances in Cryptology–CRYPTO 2013* (pp. 75–92). Springer. doi:10.1007/978-3-642-40041-4_5

Gupta, D. S., & Biswas, G. P. (2015). Secure Computation on Cloud Storage: A Homomorphic Approach. [JCIT]. *Journal of Cases on Information Technology, 17*(3), 22–29. doi:10.4018/JCIT.2015070103

Gupta, D. S., & Biswas, G. P. (2016). Cryptanalysis of Wang et al.'s lattice-based key exchange protocol. *Perspectives on Science, 8*, 228–230. doi:10.1016/j.pisc.2016.04.034

Kapoor, V., Abraham, V. S., & Singh, R. (2008). Elliptic curve cryptography. *Ubiquity, 2008*(May), 7. doi:10.1145/1386853.1378356

Smart, N. P., & Vercauteren, F. (2010, May). Fully homomorphic encryption with relatively small key and ciphertext sizes. *Proceedings of the International Workshop on Public Key Cryptography* (pp. 420-443). Springer. 10.1007/978-3-642-13013-7_25

Stehlé, D., & Steinfeld, R. (2010, December). Faster fully homomorphic encryption. *Proceedings of the International Conference on the Theory and Application of Cryptology and Information Security* (pp. 377-394). Springer.

Tebaa, M., & Hajji, S.E. (2014). Secure cloud computing through homomorphic encryption. arXiv preprint arXiv:1409.0829

Van Dijk, M., Gentry, C., Halevi, S., & Vaikuntanathan, V. (2010, May). Fully homomorphic encryption over the integers. *Proceedings of the Annual International Conference on the Theory and Applications of Cryptographic Techniques* (pp. 24-43). Springer.

Wei, Z. (2016). A Pairing-based Homomorphic Encryption Scheme for Multi-User Settings. *International Journal of Technology and Human Interaction*, *12*(2), 72–82. doi:10.4018/IJTHI.2016040106

This research was previously published in the International Journal of Information Security and Privacy (IJISP), 11(3); edited by Michele Tomaiuolo and Monica Mordonini; pages 54-62, copyright year 2017 by IGI Publishing (an imprint of IGI Global).

Chapter 19
Homomorphic Encryption as a Service for Outsourced Images in Mobile Cloud Computing Environment

Mouhib Ibtihal
MoulaySmail University, Morocco

El Ouadghiri Driss
MoulaySmail University, Morocco

Naanani Hassan
Ben'msik University, Morocco

ABSTRACT

The integration of cloud computing with mobile computing and internet has given birth to mobile cloud computing. This technology offers many advantages to users, like Storage capacity, Reliability, Scalability and Real time data availability. Therefore, it is s increasing fast and it is inevitably integrated into everyday life. In MCC, data processing and data storage can be migrated into the cloud servers. However, the confidentiality of images and data is most important in today's environment. In this paper, we mainly focus on secure outsourcing of images. For this purpose, we propose a secure architecture composed by two clouds a private cloud dedicated for encryption/decryption and a second public cloud dedicated for storage. We have implemented the first cloud using openstack while respecting the encryption as a service concept. As an encryption scheme, we have used paillier's homomorphic cryptosystem designed specifically for images. The test of the homomorphic property is done by applying the Watermarking algorithm DWT.

DOI: 10.4018/978-1-7998-1763-5.ch019

INTRODUCTION

Mobile cloud computing has emerged as new technology to empower the mobile computing functionality. As a combination of mobile computing and cloud computing (Buyya, Yeo, Venugopal et al., 2009; Aljawarneh, 2011). The MCC allows to mobile users an empowered the storage capacity, the reliability, scalability and real time data availability. Due to the limited storage and processing capabilities of mobile devices, many user start to save their data as videos, photos and music on clouds. The stored data in public cloud can be accessible by anyone without efficient protection mechanism. Consequently, serious question of security and trust issues has to be addressed. Even if encryption is used to protect sensitive data requires complex process to perform processing on encrypted data. Besides we cannot deny another drawback of hiding the important relationship between documents during the encryption process. In this paper, we are more interested in privacy issue of outsourced images because many images may include private information (Wang, Zhang, Ren & Roveda, 2013; Aljawarneh at el, 2015). Most of encrypted image schemes use the traditional cryptographic which does not provide secure solution to solve the images privacy problem. In this context, we propose as solution a secure architecture based on the encryption as a service concept and the homomorphic encryption. The main advantage in using homomorphic encryption is its computational ability that allows doing an arbitrary number of additions and multiplications on encrypted information without knowing decryption system where the secret key belongs only to the client. the first fully homomorphic encryption scheme was proposed in (Gentry, 2009), Others researchers proposed the variants of Gentry's model with some improvement (Smart, & Vercauteren, 2010) (Van Dijk, Gentry, Halevi, & Vaikuntanathan, 2010) (Stehlé, & Steinfeld, 2010) .There are several partially homomorphic crypto-systems like Goldwasser and Micali (Goldwasser, & Micali, 1984), ElGamal (ElGamal, 1984) and Paillier (Paillier, 1999) on the one hand Partial homomorphic encryption scheme perform one type of operation(addition or multiplication), on the other hand fully homomorphic encryption scheme use both operations. However, despite the good performance of fully homomorphic encryption, it requires a huge generated key using huge calculation number that consequently affect the calculation speed which exceeds 1000 times slower than the non-homomorphic operations. Several researches were constructed in order to improve the effectiveness of the cryptosystem in term of the consumed calculation time and the size of the keys (Naehrig, Lauter, & Vaikuntanathan, 2011). In this study, we are interested particularly by using Paillier cryptosystem because this scheme and its variants are famous for their efficiency" (Fontaine & Galand, 2007; Aljawarneh at el, 2016).

In our paper, we propose a secure architecture to resolve privacy issue for images stored in mobile cloud servers. For this we follow next steps:

1. Implementation of a private cloud using OpenStack (openstack.org) dedicated to encryption services and verified the Encryption as a service concept (Mouhib, ElOuadghiri, & ZineDine, 2016).
2. Development and implementation of a specific program on C language to encrypt/decrypt images by Paillier cryptosystem and implementation on nova hypervisor.
3. Development and implementation of a second program, also on C based on implemented discrete wavelet transform (DWT) on the encrypted domain, this program aim to test homomorphic property of our scheme.

This paper is organized as follows. Section 2 gives a literature overview about different concept used in our architecture and encryption techniques. Section 3 describe the proposed architecture. In section 4, we will present simulations results. Finally, the conclusion and future work are in section 5.

LITERATURE REVIEW

Openstack for Building a Private Cloud

OpenStack (openstack.org) is an open source project used to build a private/public cloud infrastructure. It supports all major virtualization platforms, including Xen, Kernel-based Virtual Machine (KVM), VMware, Hyper-V and container virtualization. This platform has six necessary core components (Lian, Zhang, Zhang, & Zhang,2015), there are computing components (Nova), ghost storage components (Glance), block storage components (Cinder), network service components (Neutron), dashboard components (Horizon) and identification components (Keystone). Openstack can be deployed in three different modes (Ristov, Gusev, & Donevski, 2013):

- **Single Node**: All nova-services are deployed on only one physical server which hosts also all the virtual machine instances.
- **Dual Node**: It consists of two physical servers the Cloud Controller Node which runs all the nova-services except for nova compute and the Compute Node which is deployed with nova-compute to instantiate virtual machine instances.
- **Multiple Node**: Particular number of CNs can be installed resulting in a multiple node installation.

For having an efficient private cloud, we have deployed OpenStack in the three nodes, compute, network and controller node as shown in Figure 4.

Paillier Cryptosystem: Basic Scheme and its Variants

Paillier cryptosystem (Paillier,1999) which is an additive homomorphic cryptosystem. It is a semantically secure cryptosystem based on composite residuosity classes, whose computation is believed to be computationally difficult. In its most basic form, Paillier scheme is described in Table 1.

Fast Decryption Paillier (Catalano,Gennaro, Howgrave-Graham, & Nguyen, 2001) has the advantage to Encrypt and decrypt faster, a single modular exponentiation for encryption against two in the original system, Table 2 describe it scheme.

PROPOSED ARCHITECTURE AND SIMULATIONS RESULT

We propose a hybrid architecture constructed by two clouds: First one is used as private cloud dedicated for the encryption/ decryption process, and the second one is a public cloud used to store encrypted image. To ensure the security of image outsourcing through this architecture, we propose the following

Table 1. Basic Paillier scheme

	Basic Paillier
Key generation	Alice generates two large prime numbers p and q and computes N = pq and $\lambda=\lambda(N)= lcm(p-1, q-1)$. She chooses randomly g: $pgcd\left(\dfrac{\left(g^{\lambda}modN^2\right)-1}{N},N\right)=1$
Public key	(g, N)
Private Key	(p, q)
Encryption	To encrypt a message $m\in\mathbb{Z}_N$ Bob uniformly randomly chosen $r\in\mathbb{Z}_N^*$, calculates and sends $c=g^m r^N modN^2$ to Alice.
Decryption	Alice decrypts the message received by calculating $m=\dfrac{c^{\lambda}modN^2}{g^{\lambda}modN^2}modN$

Table 2. Fast Decryption Paillier scheme

	Fast Decryption Paillier
Key Generation	$N=pq$ and $=\lambda(N)= lcm(p-1, q-1)$. Either $g\in\mathbb{Z}_{N^2}$ random order $\alpha\in\{1,...,\lambda\}$.
public key	(g, N)
private key	(p, q, α)
Encryption	To encrypt a message $m\in\mathbb{Z}_N$ Bob uniformly randomly chosen $r\in\mathbb{Z}_N^*$,, calculates and sends $c=g^{m+Nr}modN^2$ to Alice.
Decryption	Alice decrypts the message received by calculating $m=\dfrac{c^{\lambda}modN^2}{g^{\lambda}modN^2}modN$,

three steps: First we implement the private cloud, then we provide into this cloud the encryption cryptosystem, and finally we store it in the public cloud. In order to testify the homomorphic characteristic, we use a watermarking method as an extra step.

Small Exponent Paillier: Similarly to RSA, Catalano, Gennaro, Howgrave Graham, and Nguyen (2011) suggested using a public exponent, with a small weight, to accelerate the encryption process. On the other hand, the latter can be further optimized by choosing $g=N+1$ d so that $g^m=(1+mN)modN$. The decryption becomes $=g^m y^e=y^e(1+mN)modN^2$, with a low exponentiation and a modular multiplication.

The Discrete Wavelet Transform (DWT)

The discrete wavelet transform (DWT) is a mathematical tool frequently used in signal processing. The DWT can be used as interesting tool to extract various kinds of information from digital media in the encrypted domain. In our case, we are interested to apply it for secure image watermarking. DWT can be expressed recursively using Mallat's algorithm (Mallat,1989) as follows:

$$a_j\left(k\right) = \frac{1}{\sqrt{2}}\sum_{l \in \mathbb{Z}} h_d\left(2k - l\right)a_{j-1}\left(l\right)$$

$$d_j\left(k\right) = \frac{1}{\sqrt{2}}\sum_{l \in \mathbb{Z}} g_d\left(2k - l\right)a_{j-1}\left(l\right)$$

where *hd (k)* and *gd(k)* are the low-pass and high-pass decomposition filter coefficients, respectively, *j* is the decomposition level of the transformation, $j = 1, 2, 3, \ldots$, *a j (k)* and *d j (k)* are the approximation coefficients and detail coefficients, respectively. *a0(l)* is defined as the input signal *x(l)*. For convenience, we use *X j (k)* to represent both *a j (k)* and *d j (k)*.

We have implemented A watermarking scheme based on the 2D discrete Haar wavelet transform on encrypted domain.

Step 1: Implementing the Private Cloud

The private cloud is implemented using openstack. This type of cloud imposes restrictions on the network and user access which allows to the users more control over the infrastructure in secure manner. Besides, the processed data within such architecture aren't affected by the network bandwidth's limitations while the processing procedure, and also protected against legal issues. In addition, the private cloud is often designed to guarantee the availability of the services for specific purpose according to the firm objectives. There are many frameworks which are used according to the user and application requirements. In this work, we utilize OpenStack framework to design and implement the infrastructure as a service.

In our architecture, we have deployed the encryption server on OpenStack Version. The test bed consists of a controller node (as can be seen in Figure 1), a network node (as depicted in Figure 2) and finally Figure 3 shows the compute nodes.

After lunching the three nodes, we accede to our cloud via the authentication interface by entering a login and password (as shown in Figure 5) and then accede to the interface of administrator. (See Figure 6).

Step 2: Implementing of Paillier Cryptosystem in an Encryption as a Service Architecture See Figure 7.

As mentioned before, the data security and privacy issues are addressed using an encryption system. Consequently, our encryption system as a service should ensure the security of offload image against external/ internal attacks. For this we intend to encapsulate Paillier cryptosystem into Nova Hypervisor.

Step 3: Storing the Encrypted Images on the Public Cloud

See Figure 8.

Once the images are encrypted, there are stored on an external local server that represents the public cloud. In this work, paillier cryptosystem is implemented on Node Controller (see Figure 8), especially on Nova Hypervisor.

Figure 1. Controller node of openstack

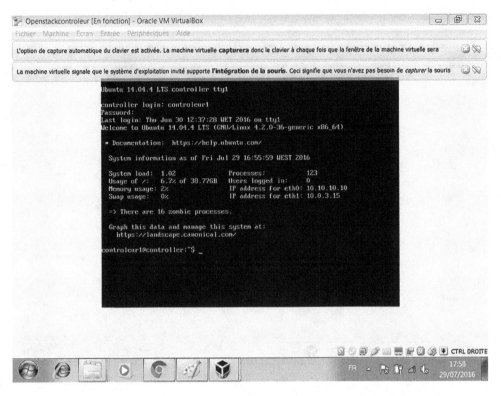

Figure 2. Network node of openstack

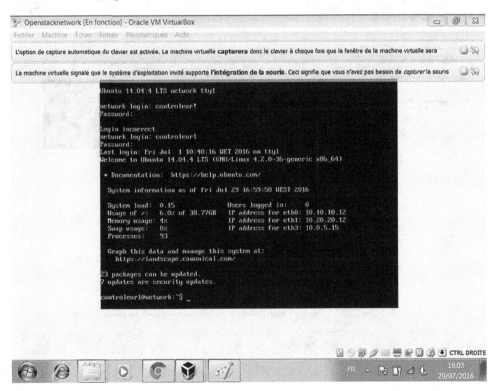

Figure 3. Compute node of openstack

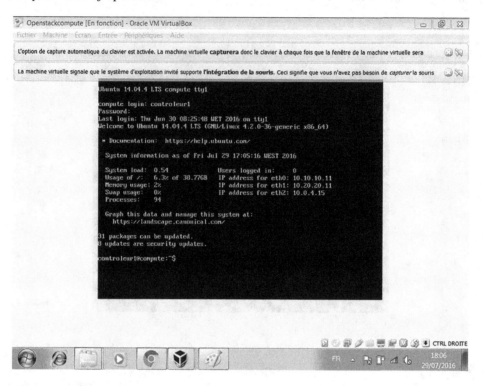

Figure 4. Our private cloud openstack with three nodes

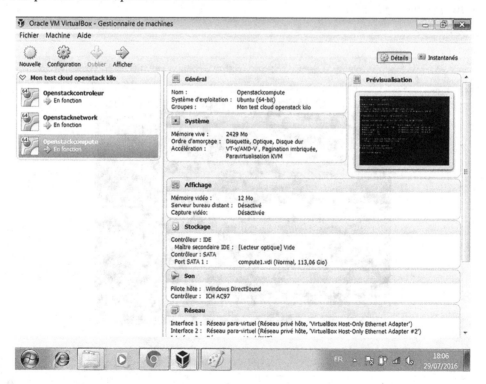

Figure 5. Authentication's interface

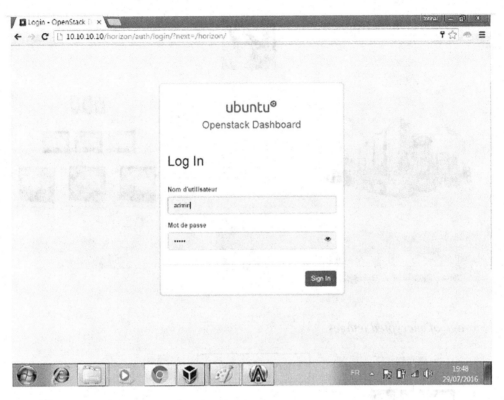

Figure 6. Administrator's interface

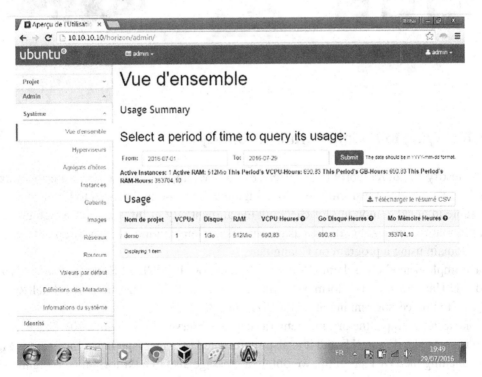

Figure 7. Encryption as a service architecture (Mouhib, ElOuadghiri, & ZineDine, 2016)

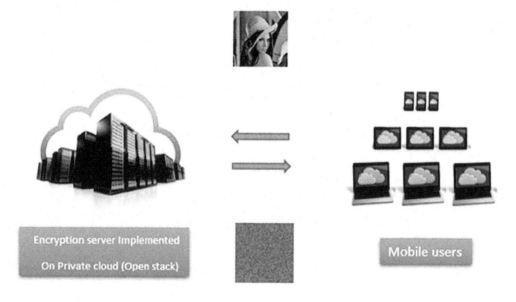

Figure 8. Storage of encrypted images

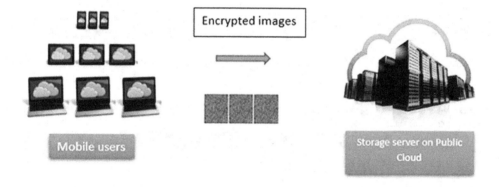

Step 4: Testifying the Homomorphic Property

In order to testify the homomorphic propriety of our system, we choose the watermarking method based on discrete wavelet transform DWT. See Figure 9. This method proves to be most effective and implementable in cloud computing for checking the authenticity of information, which guarantees the integrity, originality, and legality of data usage. In our implementation, we have implemented DWT on Encrypted domain using a program on C language.

We have implemented our scheme using C language on the ECLIPSE 4.2.2. The encrypted algorithm and 2-D Haar wavelet transform algorithm is conducted on a computer with Intel(R) Core(TM) i7-3720QM CPU processor running at 2.60 GHz, 8 G RAM.

If we take as an example the original lena (as can be observed from Figure 10). The cryptogram of this image is showed in Figure 11, and it is also represented by a message in txt format (see Figure 12).

After launching the DWT program, we obtain a message also in a txt format (see Figure 13).

Figure 9. Watermarking on Encrypted Images

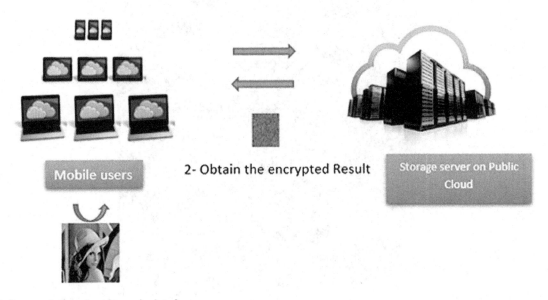

1-Execute program of DWT on encrypted images

2- Obtain the encrypted Result

Mobile users

Storage server on Public Cloud

3-Decrypt the result and obtain

the original Image

Figure 10. Original Lena

Figure 11. Encrypted Lena

Figure 12. Encrypted_Lena.txt

The experimental results have proven that time process for encrypted images is boosting with the expansion of images size and their features (as can be seen in Figure 14 and Figure 15), which means that encryption takes time when it comes to complex images.

CONCLUSION

In this present paper, we propose an architecture to secure outsourced images in mobile cloud computing environment. This architecture is based on encryption as a service concept in which a private cloud is dedicated to encryption and decryption. We implemented an additive homomorphic encryption scheme (paillier crysptosystem) and then we tested the functionality of our scheme by implementing a water-marking method (DWT) on a local server. The results show that the method doesn't take a long time in encryption and decryption processing, so it can be used as a solution of data security/privacy in such environment.

Figure 13. DWT on Encrypted_Lena.txt

Figure 14. Encryption processing

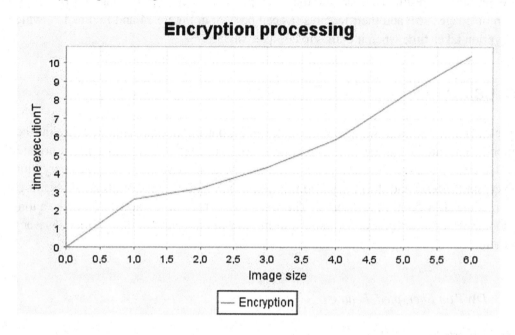

Figure 15. Decryption processing

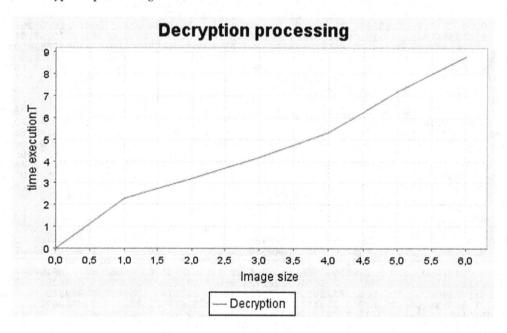

REFERENCES

Aljawarneh, S. (2011). Cloud Security Engineering: Avoiding Security Threats the Right Way. *International Journal of Cloud Applications and Computing, 1*(2), 64–70. doi:10.4018/ijcac.2011040105

Aljawarneh, S., Alshargabi, B., Hayajneh, M. A., & Imam, A. (2015). Integration of E-learning and Cloud Computing Platform Through Software Engineering. *Recent Patents on Computer Science, 8*(2), 100–105. doi:10.2174/2213275908666150706174305

Aljawarneh, S. A., Moftah, R. A., & Maatuk, A. M. (2016). Investigations of automatic methods for detecting the polymorphic worms signatures. *Future Generation Computer Systems, 60,* 67–77. doi:10.1016/j.future.2016.01.020

Buyya, R., Yeo, C. S., Venugopal, S., Broberg, J., & Brandic, I. (2009). Cloud computing and emerging IT platforms: Vision, hype, and reality for delivering computing as the 5th utility. *Future Generation Computer Systems, 25*(6), 599–616. doi:10.1016/j.future.2008.12.001

Catalano, D., Gennaro, R., Howgrave-Graham, N., & Nguyen, P. Q. (2001, November). Paillier's cryptosystem revisited. *Proceedings of the 8th ACM conference on Computer and Communications Security* (pp. 206-214). ACM.

ElGamal, T. (1984, August). A public key cryptosystem and a signature scheme based on discrete logarithms. *Proceedings of the Workshop on the Theory and Application of Cryptographic Techniques* (pp. 10-18). Springer.

Fontaine, C., & Galand, F. (2007). A survey of homomorphic encryption for nonspecialists. *EURASIP Journal on Information Security, 2007*(1), 1-10.

Gentry, C. (2009). *A fully homomorphic encryption scheme, PhD thesis.* Stanford University.

Goldwasser, S., & Micali, S. (1984). Probabilistic encryption. *Journal of Computer and System Sciences, 28*(2), 270–299. doi:10.1016/0022-0000(84)90070-9

Lian, L., Zhang, Y., Zhang, H., & Zhang, S. (2015). Constructing virtual network attack and defense platform based on openstack. *Proceedings of the 2015 International Conference on Automation, Mechanical Control and Computational Engineering.* 10.2991/amcce-15.2015.21

Mallat, S. G. (1989). A theory for multiresolution signal decomposition: The wavelet representation. *IEEE Transactions on Pattern Analysis and Machine Intelligence, 11*(7), 674–693. doi:10.1109/34.192463

Mouhib, I, & ElOuadghiri, D, & ZineDine, K. (2016). Data Encryption as a Service in Mobile Cloud Computing. *Journal of Information Assurance & Security, 11*(3).

Naehrig, M., Lauter, K., & Vaikuntanathan, V. (2011, October). Can homomorphic encryption be practical? *Proceedings of the 3rd ACM workshop on Cloud computing security workshop* (pp. 113-124). ACM. 10.1145/2046660.2046682

Paillier, P. (1999, May). Public-key cryptosystems based on composite degree residuosity classes. *Proceedings of the International Conference on the Theory and Applications of Cryptographic Techniques* (pp. 223-238). Springer. 10.1007/3-540-48910-X_16

Ristov, S., Gusev, M., & Donevski, A. (2013). Openstack cloud security vulnerabilities from inside and outside. In *Cloud Computing* (pp. 101-107).

Smart, N. P., & Vercauteren, F. (2010, May). Fully homomorphic encryption with relatively small key and ciphertext sizes. *Proceedings of the International Workshop on Public Key Cryptography* (pp. 420-443). Springer. 10.1007/978-3-642-13013-7_25

Stehlé, D., & Steinfeld, R. (2010, December). Faster fully homomorphic encryption. *Proceedings of the International Conference on the Theory and Application of Cryptology and Information Security* (pp. 377-394). Springer.

Van Dijk, M., Gentry, C., Halevi, S., & Vaikuntanathan, V. (2010, May). Fully homomorphic encryption over the integers. *Proceedings of the Annual International Conference on the Theory and Applications of Cryptographic Techniques* (pp. 24-43). Springer.

Wang, C., Zhang, B., Ren, K., & Roveda, J. M. (2013). Privacy-assured outsourcing of image reconstruction service in cloud. *IEEE Transactions on Emerging Topics in Computing*, *1*(1), 166–177. doi:10.1109/TETC.2013.2273797

This research was previously published in the International Journal of Cloud Applications and Computing (IJCAC), 7(2); edited by B. B. Gupta and Dharma P. Agrawal; pages 27-40, copyright year 2017 by IGI Publishing (an imprint of IGI Global).

Section 4
Steganography

Chapter 20
Digital Image Steganography:
Survey, Analysis, and Application

Chitra A. Dhawale

P. R. Pote College of Engineering and Management, India

Naveen D. Jambhekar

S. S. S. K. R. Innani Mahavidyalaya, India

ABSTRACT

Digital data transmitted over the insecure communication can be prone to attacks. Intruders try various attacks to unauthorized access of the confidential information. The Steganography is such as security system that provide the protection to the images, text and other type of data digitally transferred through the data communication network. This chapter elaborates the basics of Digital Image Steganographic techniques from ancient era to digital edge, types of images used for the steganography, payload used for the steganography, various attacks and different algorithms that can provide the information security. The performance analysis of the various Digital Image Steganographic algorithms are discussed. The current applications and their necessities are discussed in this chapter.

INTRODUCTION

Digital data in the form of text, images, audio and video are transmitted over the internet by means of communication links. The confidentiality of secret data should be preserved from intruders. Steganography contains a group of methods with which different algorithms are available to embed the secret data under the cover medium such as image, without any detectable indications on the cover image. Many algorithms are designed to provide the security for the communication of data over the Internet. The good steganographic algorithm is identified by the performance of the algorithm measured with the help of the parameters such as PSNR, MSE, robustness and capacity to hide the information in the cover image. This chapter explores the steganographic methods used from many years, the methods used currently and the capabilities of steganography in future. The crucial part of the steganographic algorithms are the carrier and its payload. There are various types of carriers available for the steganographic applications.

DOI: 10.4018/978-1-7998-1763-5.ch020

Steganography is the technique that covers the confidential data under the cover medium such as image, without reflecting any clue on the cover image (Chan & Cheng, 2004). Secrete Message transmission is possible by the technique steganography with the help of entities such as a secret message, message carrier and the embedding algorithm who embed the secret message in the cover message i.e. image. The Message is the secret data which is being hidden and carrier is the entity that covers the secret message (Valandar, Ayubi & Barani, 2015). Using the image steganographic method, the secret message is covered by an image in such way that the secret message can be easily extracted as well as the cover image does not lose its visibility (Bender, Morimoto & Lu, 2010). The variations are done slightly, that do not reflect the visual changes in the image.

The mathematical techniques, available in the cryptography have some limitations and can prone to crack mathematically. The image steganography is more secure, but the processing and extraction of the secret message from the cover image need some more processing time. The good steganographic algorithms are able to hide the sensitive data under the cover medium such as image, without remaining any noticeable clue to the intruders (Sun & Liu, 2010). The strength of the steganographic algorithms is to keep the confidential information under an image such a way that, no any steganalysis method, or tool extracts the original message from the cover image without the proper stego key (Mishra, Tiwari & Yadav, 2014).

In the spatial domain, the spatial based methods carried out by the image pixel base using the techniques such as Least Significant Bit (LSB) insertion, SVD and spread spectrum methods. In the frequency based methods, the Discrete Cosine Transformation (DCT), Discrete Wavelet Transformation (DWT), Discrete Fourier Transformation (DFT) and Integer Wavelet Transformation (IWT) steganographic transformation based methods hide secret image i.e. the payload to another cover image (Verma, 2011).

The efficiency of the above steganographic algorithms can be analyzed by comparing the cover image with the stego image. This comparison is carried out by calculating the parameters viz. Peak Signal to Noise Ratio (PSNR), Mean Squared Error (MSE) with the help of programming the code in MATLAB (Gonzalez, Woods & Eddins, 2010). Figure 1 shows the digital image steganographic algorithms.

The steganographic algorithms are classified using text, digital image, audio, video, internet protocols and 3d domain as shown in the Figure 1. This chapter explores the Digital Image Steganographic Algorithms by evaluating using image (spatial) domain and transform (frequency) domain. The spatial or image domain consists of the LSB insertion, PVD and spread spectrum methods while the transform or frequency domain consists of DWT, DCT, DFT and IWT methods which are discussed below (Barni, 2001).

Effective and efficient steganographic algorithms are those who hide the sensitive data under the cover medium such as image, without leaving any detectable clue to the intruders. The strength of the steganographic algorithms is to keep the confidential information under an image such a way that, no any steganalysis method, or tool extracts the original secret message from the cover image without finding right stegokey (Denemark, Boroumand, &Fridrich, 2016). Stegokey is used to merge the secret data under the cover image. The stegokey is unique and used for encryption and same for decryption. This stegokey must be preserved by both sender and receiver (Khan et al., 2014). Recently, many researchers have worked on steganography and written the benefits of the different steganographic algorithms.

Steganography is a group of methods used for securing the secret information under the cover medium such as an image using some translation rules. Here the translation rules merge the selected text into the image, that makes the simple text secure and no one can easily plunder the secret information.

Figure 1. Digital image steganographic algorithms

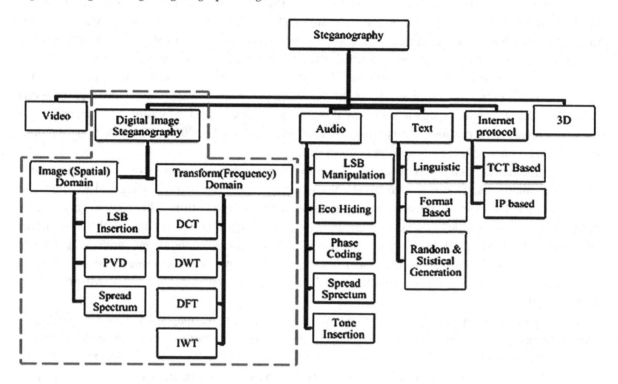

Because of steganography, two communication sides transfer the confidential data secretly where attacker unknown the secret message covered in other medium such as cover images. Steganography is the technique in which the original message which is being transmitted over the unsecured communication channel will be masked into the cover medium such as image, audio or video such that any human being, the device or the specialized software cannot predict the original hidden data. In steganography, the secret message transmission is possible using two entities such as the original message to be transmitted and the message carrier used to cover the transmitting message (Chakrabarti & Samanta, 2015).

Using the digital image steganographic method, the secret message is covered by an image in such way that the original message cannot predict by the intruders. The variations are done slightly that do not reflect the visual changes on the cover image.

STEGANOGRAPHY ON THE EARLY AGE

The Steganography suggest itself as a Greek word made from steganos - covered or secret and graphy - writing or drawing. The first steganographic technique was coming in the history of ancient Greece around 440 B.C. The Greek swayer Histaeus use the steganography in a new way to hide secret messages by shaving messenger's head, waiting to grow hair again, then again shaving the head and waiting to grow hair, so that the it will hide the secret message under long hair. On the other side, recipient finding the secret message by trimming hairs of messenger. The recipient was also using the same method to reply.

During 480 B.C. the next steganographic technique was evolved. Demerstus use the technique of writing the secret message to the Spartans that warns high intrusions by Xerxes. The secret message was put on the surface of wooden wax tablet and again covered with fresh wax. This tablet was delivered to the destination place with its hidden secret message.

Johannes Trithemius (1 February 1462 – 13 December 1516) is a first person who was the German Renaissance humanist, advisor to Emperors in Germany, the founder of scientific bibliography and one of the founders of modern cryptography also wrote the "Steganographia". He is a first author of the first printed work on cryptography, the Polygraphia.

With the publication of Auguste Kerchoffs', cryptography militaire, although this work was mostly about cryptography, but describes the principal that was helpful in designing the new steganographic system, known as Kerchoff's principal regarding the steganography. During both world wars, steganography helped to hide the confidential message using invisible ink which would gleam by keeping on the flame.

DIGITAL STEGANOGRAPHY TODAY

Thereafter the ancient steganographic techniques, many researchers discovered the steganographic algorithms that provide the high security features to secure the digital document. Intruders also develop methods that evacuate the safe message known as the steganalysis. Moreover, the ultimate use of the internet for the communication of the digital document was coming into existence in the recent days. Due to intensive use of internet- an unsecured communication channel, the sensitive data is not safe today.

The mathematical techniques that available in the cryptography, have some limitations and can prone to crack mathematically by anyone with little efforts. The digital image steganography is more secure, but the processing and extraction of the secret message from the cover image required some processing time. However, in the present digital era, by using the advanced computer systems with massive processing speed, this task is under control. Today the secret sharing over the internet is possible by applying the steganography, by carrying the following process effectively.

- Confidential data to be transmitted firmly.
- Cover image selection to hold secret message.
- Selection and implementation of the method that merge the secret message in the cover medium.
- The key that is used for the conversion method and also to uncover the secret message.

To secure the text using the steganographic techniques, the original text message is scrambled, shuffled or mixed with other text data with the help of mathematical function. Only the legal receiver can reverse this process to extract the message. The digital image steganographic technique hides the secret information under the cover image. In audio steganography, the multimedia such as text, image or sound can be put in the other cover audio signals that do not give the impression of this mixing (Tayel, Gamal & Shawky, 2016). This is similar for the video steganography, where two videos intermix with each other, or any carrier date like text, image or audio signals are merged with the covert video.

The algorithms used today to secure the digital document, commonly follows the steganographic rules as the one shown in the following figures.

Figure 2 and Figure 3 show the steganographic system.

Figure 2. Sender side steganographic system

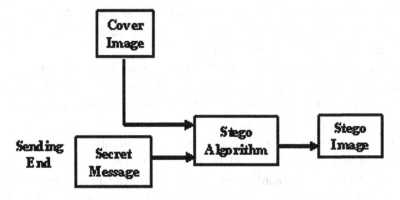

Figure 3. Receiving side steganographic system

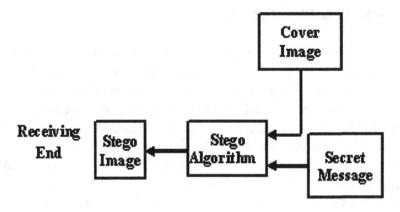

BASICS OF STEGANOGRAPHY

Terminology

1. **Digital Image:** A digital image is a series of pixels having different intensity can be represented by the hexadecimal value for every pixel. The image can be monochrome or colour image. The image can be 8, 16 or 32 bit image and can be represented by the pixel's intensity at different position where the image I is a represented by the function $I(x, y)$ where x and y are the address of pixel.

2. **Cover Image:** It is a carrier image which keep the secret image or message during transmission. The cover image can be large enough to keep the secret message or image.

3. **Secret Key:** The secret key can be optional. The work of secret key is to provide a special function even if the use of the specific steganographic algorithm.

4. **Payload:** The secret message or image to be hidden into the cover image.

5. **Stego Image:** The image that keep the secret image or message and used for the the actual transmission. The receiver end extract the confidential data from this stego image.

6. **Steganographic Algorithm:** The selected method that hide the payload in the cover image.

Steganographic Performance Evaluation Criterions

The use of steganographic functions for the secure data transmission depends on some criterions that define the efficiency of specific algorithm. These criterions are payload capacity, security, robustness, time complexity, consistency and efficiency (Cheddad, Condell, Curran & McKevitt, 2010). Figure 4 depicts the evaluation criterions.

Payload Capacity

The number of bits to be hidden inside the cover image. The capacity of payload i.e. the secret message or image is smaller than the cover image. Therefore, it can be easily hidden inside the cover image without disturbing the visual quality of the cover image.

Security

The secret image or message should not revealed in the cover image and preserve the security. Any digital image steganographic algorithm must accurate in its security assistance, otherwise it helps to the intruders to break the confidentiality. The security of the algorithms is measured through the algorithmic complexity.

Robustness

The secret message or image remain original and extracted accurately even if the stego image goes through worst transmission conditions, cropping, compression, rotation and filtering. The robustness of the steganographic algorithm must maintain even if the use of different size of payload with different types of cover images.

Figure 4. Steganographic Performance Evaluation Criterions

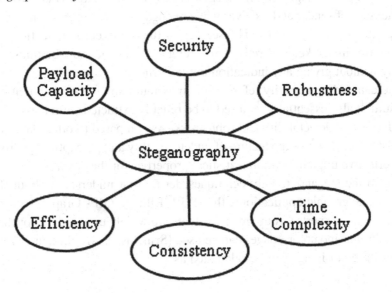

Time Complexity

The time complexity plays a crucial role during the stego message transmission. Large time complexity can generates the bigger message. The transmission can be affected by the bandwidth of the network. However, the large time required to embed the secret data inside the cover image can be due to the big size of the payload and the high security of the steganographic algorithm.

Consistency

The steganographic algorithm used at both the ends of the transmission must be consistent in it working. The data embedded at one end must be extracted accurately that proves the consistency of the steganographic algorithm.

Efficiency

How much size of payload embedded in the cover object is the efficiency of the steganographic algorithm. Also, the quality of cover image that keep the secret message or image is the efficiency of the steganographic algorithm.

Steganographic Data Hiding Capacity and Cover Selection

The primary goal of image steganography is to embed the secret image in another image known as a cover image. The selection of the cover is completely dependent on the size of the secret image. The cover image is large enough to hold the secret image (Fang, Liu, Gu & Tang, 2011). To select the cover image, the distortion measure along with a threshold value has been analyzed. Before embedding an image, the quality of the cover image is tested against the measures such as MSE, PSNR results into the efficient distortion less embedding which tends to the stego image undetectable by any steganalyzer. The steganalyzer verify the stego image for the micro changes and distortion in the image to guess and extract the secret message or image from the stego image (Provos & Honeyman, 2003). The cover image selection is the issue of sender and receiver who are engaged in the secret communication using the digital image steganographic algorithms. The secrecy of the secret communication is depends on the key image i.e. the cover image keep secretly. This secret cover image must be transferred from sender to receiver secretly without giving any indication to the intruders.

Steganographic data hiding capacity refers to the maximum amount of data that can be embedded into a cover-medium. It also essentially required to be reliably extracted from the stego-object in terms of perceptual perfection, undetectability and robustness. As compared to other data hiding system, the steganographic system must posses the feature of undetectability and perceptual quality that can be possible through the effective implementation statistical properties for the cover medium.

Before moving to the steganographic techniques, let us first understand about the digital image formats. For the steganographic applications, the BMP- Bitmap, GIF- Graphics Interchange Format, JPEG- Joint Photographic Experts Group image formats are widely used today. For the steganographic applications monochrome and color images can be used (Srinivasan, Arunkumar & Rajesh, 2015). The time complexity of the color image can be calculated as

$$C = (C_r + C_g + C_b) / 3 \tag{1}$$

where C is the complexity and r, g & b are the intensity of the pixels available for complexity analysis.

- **BMP: Bitmap** - Most operating systems support bitmap images with 1, 4, 8, 16, 24 and 32 bits per pixel. Here, the concentration is largely on the monochrome i.e. grayscale images and 24 bit color images because of the requirement of processing power, storage and transmission capacity of the network.
- **GIF: Graphics Interchange Format** - GIF is CompuServe's standard that defines the generalized color raster images. This Graphics Interchange Format permits high-quality, high-resolution graphics compatible for a variety of graphics hardware and is proposed as an exchange and display mechanism. It uses up to 256 colors from the 24-bit RGB color space, and stores both the palette and the pixel matrix.
- **JPEG: Joint Photographic Experts Group** - It is the most commonly used standard for lossy and lossless compression till today. It is very efficient photographic image technique and can make an excellent quality image even if it is a lossy compression technique. Because of the lossy compressed nature, some visual quality is lost in the compression process. With the lossless compression, the quality is great. The images used for the steganography are the 8-bit grayscale images as well as color images.

The steganographic methods used today are categories into image domain, transform domain, spread spectrum domain and statistical technique.

DIGITAL IMAGE STEGANOGRAPHIC ALGORITHMS

Secret data hiding through the digital image steganographic techniques can be preformed through the spatial and frequency domain as depicted using figure 3.

A steganographic security system can be represented as

$$Y = f(C, M, K) \tag{2}$$

where

Y is the stego object,
C is the cover medium,
M is the message embedded in the C,
K is the security key, and
f is the steganographic function.

Here, the security key K is optional and not required during some of the steganographic algorithms. The digital image steganographic algorithms are discussed below.

Image or Spatial Domain

The image or spatial domain is the field through which the embedding of secret message can be performed by using working with the pixel of the image, by embedding the secret image in the pixels intensity. The techniques covered under the spatial domain are

Least Significant Bit Insertion (LSB)

The LSB insertion technique implants secret information in a cover image by changing the intensity of Least Significant Bits (Ker, 2005). Image's every Least Significant Bits are somewhat randomly noisy and when replaced or modified, do not affect the visual quality of the image. The pixel value of the digital image can be represented as

$$P_i = \sum_{n=0}^{7} b_n X 2^n \tag{3}$$

where P represents the pixels at a specific position and b_n represents the number of bits in each pixels. The above equation represents the pixels value using 8-bits of binary data.

Using the LSB substitution technique, the secret message in binary format is first permuted and then substituted in the image in place of every bytes least significant bit place, bit by bit fashion (Chan & Cheng, 2004). The bit insertion depends on the bits available in the secret message. If the message is bigger, then the cover image should be enough bigger to hide it (Kong, 2009). The LSB substitution is suitable for BMP images where they are lossless. Digital images are commonly available in 8 bits, 16 bits and 24 bits. The embedding can be possible for one, two and three bits for each image pixel for the 8 bits, 16 bits and 24 bits images respectively. The embedding positions are the LSB for each byte. Some or every byte of cover image can hide one bit of secret image information (Singh & Singh 2015).

The following is the procedure to embed a secret message under a digital image.

LSB Substitution Algorithm

Step 1: Scan the secret message (text or image) along with the cover image.
Step 2: Convert secret message to binary data.
Step 3: Permute the binary bits of secret message
Step 4: Calculate LSB position of every byte of the cover image.
Step 5: Substitute every bit of cover image to the LSB of the cover image bit by bit.
Step 6: Save the image after LSB substitution and is the Stego image.

The following procedure is used to extract the secret message hidden under the digital image

LSB Algorithm to Read the Secret Message from Stego Image

Step 1: Scan the Stego image.
Step 2: Estimate LSB position of each byte of Stego image.
Step 3: Extract each LSB bit and convert each 8 bits into a character.

The hiding and extracting of the secret data in the least significant bit position of the cover image is carried out by converting the secret data to pixels data. The hiding and unhiding principal is depicted below.

The secret message embedding is carried with the help of following procedure.

The secret and cover image bit position is calculated by Secret(i,j) and Cover(i,j).

Three possibilities are calculated as

if LSB(Cover(i,j)) = MSB(Secret(i,j)) then no change and continue to next position

if LSB(Cover(i,j)) >MSB(Secret(i,j)) then LSB(Stego(i,j)) = LSB(Cover(i,j)) - 1

if LSB(Cover(i,j)) <MSB(Secret(i,j)) then LSB(Stego(i,j)) = LSB(Cover(i,j)) + 1

Here the new image after embedding is the stego image similar with the cover image. The similarity is because of the change in the LSB of the cover image, which cannot affect the visual perception of the cover image. Here Stego(i,j) is the stego image.

The process of extracting secret image bits from stegoimage is straightforward.

if LSB(Stego(i,j)) = 0 then MSB(Secret(i,j)) = 0

if LSB(C(i,j)) = 1 then MSB(S(i,j)) = 1

For this embedding process, the cover image large enough to hold the secret image's all bits.

Pixel-Value Differencing (PVD)

Secret data hiding in digital images with the help of the pixel-value differencing (PVD) method gives higher embedding capacity without reflecting any clue on the cover image. The pixel-value differencing (PVD) method was originally developed for hiding the secret messages into 8 bits grayscale images (Wu & Tsai, 2003). Even though the large amount of secret information is embedded, the PVD produces high definition stego image. PVD partitions the cover image into non overlapping blocks with two consecutive non overlapping pixels. The embedding of secret message get started using PVD with upper left corner of the cover image that reads the cover image in a zigzag fashion as shown in Figure 5. Each two-pixel blocks are used to maintain the smoothness properties of the cover image. There is a difference in the edge and the block pixels. If the difference is larger, more bits can be embedded in the cover image pixels pair. From each block the difference value d_i is calculated by subtracting P_i from P_i+1. The difference values are in between -255 to 255.

Following algorithm describes the PVD embedding process.

PVD Algorithm

Step 1: Difference between two consecutive pixels p_i and p_{i+1} is calculated as $di = |p_i - p_{i+1}|$
Step 2: Determine the number of bits to be embedded d_i in the quantization range table.
Step 3: Read secret bits s_i from secret stream and convert into decimal value b

Figure 5. Blocks of images with zigzag scan

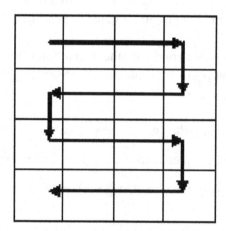

Step 4: Calculate the new difference $s_i = l_i + b$ where l_i is the lower bound of the range table and d_i and s_i must be in the range

Step 5: The new pixel value can be determined as

$$\left(s_i, s_{i+1}\right) = \left(p_i + \left\lceil \frac{\left|s_i - d_i\right|}{2} \right\rceil, p_{i+1} + \left\lfloor \frac{\left|s_i - d_i\right|}{2} \right\rfloor \right), \quad \text{if} \quad p_i \geq p_{i+1}, s_i \succ d_i \left(s_i, s_{i+1}\right)$$

$$\left(s_i, s_{i+1}\right) = \left(p_i + \left\lfloor \frac{\left|s_i - d_i\right|}{2} \right\rfloor, p_{i+1} + \left\lceil \frac{\left|s_i - d_i\right|}{2} \right\rceil \right), \quad \text{if} \quad p_i \prec p_{i+1}, s_i \succ d_i$$

$$\left(s_i, s_{i+1}\right) = \left(p_i + \left\lceil \frac{\left|s_i - d_i\right|}{2} \right\rceil, p_{i+1} + \left\lfloor \frac{\left|s_i - d_i\right|}{2} \right\rfloor \right), \quad \text{if} \quad p_i \geq p_{i+1}, s_i \leq d_i$$

$$\left(s_i, s_{i+1}\right) = \left(p_i + \left\lfloor \frac{\left|s_i - d_i\right|}{2} \right\rfloor, p_{i+1} + \left\lceil \frac{\left|s_i - d_i\right|}{2} \right\rceil \right), \quad \text{if} \quad p_i \prec p_{i+1}, s_i \leq d_i$$

Step 6: Repeating steps 1 to 5 for complete embedding of secret bits.

Spread Spectrum

In spread spectrum techniques, data hidden inside the cover image is spread completely making undetectable. Using this technique, the message is planted in noise and then mixed with the cover image producing the stego image. The cover image has powerful signals than the embedded signals. Therefore, it is difficult to notice by the human eye or even by the computer system (Marvel, Boncelet Jr. & Retter, 1999).

Here the secret data are dispersed throughout the cover image, without modifying the statistical parameters of the cover image. Most steganographic applications now use the spread spectrum techniques because of its extreme mathematical and complex approach.

Using spread spectrum method, secret information is distributed around the cover image therefore it is difficult to locate the secrets. Using spread spectrum method, the data from secret image is planted in noise and then mixed with the cover image to generate the stego image. Here the secret image data are embedded having lower signal than the cover image, the secret image is not noticeable by human as well as steganalyzer. The Spread spectrum technique is statistically strong and proves the robustness practically, even if the secret data is scattered all over the cover image, without modifying the statistical properties.

Transform Domain Techniques

Transform domain provides the robust watermarking feature because of its data embedding technique and greater capacity. Transforms domain techniques include the discrete cosine transform (DCT), discrete Fourier transform (DFT) and discrete wavelet transform (DWT). When data inserted or embed using the transform techniques, the secret data can stay in the robust zones, scattered across the cover image and provides safety against any signal processing attack.

The transform or frequency domain methods hide a secret message in the significant parts of the cover image which makes the stego image more robust. In this, the image is transformed from pixel domain to frequency domain. The following methods are the frequency domain techniques used in the digital image steganography.

Discrete Cosine Transformation

Digital steganography for images can be done with the help of two techniques- spatial domain and transform domain. The DCT is an orthogonal transformation for the digital and signal processing (Hashad, Madani & Wahdan, 2005). During 2-dimensional DCT, the image is divided into 8 x 8 blocks and then each block is transformed to the DCT domain. The different equal size band of the image is selected such as low, middle and high frequency bands (Figure 6).

DCT coefficients are organized frequency wise by zigzag fashion so that the frequency positions 0 to 63 can be acquired.

Figure 6. Bands of an image

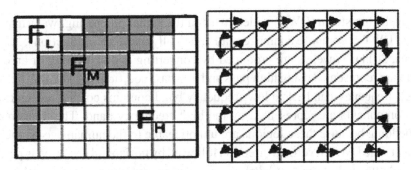

Thereafter, it is easier to embed secret image to the selected frequency band(s). The visual part is kept under the low frequency. The low and high frequency bands are targeted for the compression and noise removal (Sakr, Ibrahem, Abdullkader & Amin, 2012). Therefore, the middle frequency bands are more suitable for embedding because the secret image resides in without any loss and it cannot affect the visibility of the image. JPEG compression is accomplished with the help of DCT coefficients. It divide the cover image into portions. It translates cover image from the image domain to the frequency domain.

The following equation shows the 2-dimensional DCT

$$F\left(u, v\right) = \frac{c(u)c(v)}{4} \sum_{i=0}^{7} \sum_{i=0}^{7} \cos\left(\frac{\left(2i+1\right)\mu\pi}{16}\right) \cos\left(\frac{\left(2j+1\right)\mu\pi}{16}\right) f\left(i, j\right) \tag{4}$$

$$c\left(e\right) = \begin{cases} \dfrac{1}{\sqrt{2}} & \text{if } \begin{matrix} e = 0 \\ e \neq 0 \end{matrix} \\ 1 \end{cases} \tag{5}$$

Here, f(u,v) and f(i,j) present a DCT coefficient at the (u,v) coordinate and a pixel value at the (i,j) coordinate, respectively. f(0,0) is the DC component, which corresponds to an average intensity value of each block in the spatial domain. f(u,v) is the AC component, in which u $\neq$0 and v $\neq$0.

Input: Cover and secret image
Output: Stego image embedded with secret image

```
while end of secret image file do
        read adjacent f(i,j) of cover image
        if f(i,j) = 0 and f(i,j)= 1 then
            get adjacent LSB of secret image
            replace DCT LSB with secret image bit
        end if
        insert f(i,j)  into stego image
end while
```

Discrete Wavelet Transformation

The Discrete Wavelet transform (DWT) widely used in the signal processing, watermarking and image compression. The DWT decompose an image mathematically into a set of functions, known as wavelets (Demirel & Jafari, 2011). Wavelets are produced by converting and expanding of an existing original wavelet. The data are represented using high pass and low pass coefficients. The DWT divides the signal into low and high frequency bands. The low frequency band contains coarse information of the signal while the edge components are represented by the high frequency band. The high frequency band is suitable for embedding because these regions are unnoticeable to the human eye on their edges. In two dimensional object, The DWT in vertical direction followed by horizontal direction is performed (Kumar & Kumar, 2010). At the end of the first level decomposition, the four sub-bands: LL1, LH1, HL1, and

HH1 are generated. The previous level decomposed LL band is used as input for the next successive decomposition (Shejul & Kulkarni, 2010). To carry DWT for second level, The DWT on LL1 & for third Level decomposition is performed and the DWT on LL2 is applied & finally 4 sub band of third level that are LL3, LH3, HH3, HL3 is collected.

Discrete Fourier Transformation

The embedding of a secret message into cover image is done by converting the cover image from the spatial domain to frequency domain. Then divide the image into equal blocks 2x2 pixels. Then the secrete message data get hidden in the LSB part of the real image using the DFT method. Thereafter the conversion is done from frequency domain to spatial domain to generate the stego image. The frequency domain works in the analog nature of the image. The image is the collection of pixels, while the DFT converts image into the analog signals.

Integer Wavelet Transformation

Integer Wavelet Transformation (see Figure 7) is a frequency domain method efficiently produces the lossless compression. It represents the image coefficient into an integer number. The IWT uses a complete technique of DWT but maps integers to integers in the output (Ghasemi, Shanbehzadeh & ZahirAzami, 2011). In discrete wavelet transform, the wavelet filter has the floating point coefficients. When the secret information is stored, then data loss occurs because of the truncation of integer value due to floating point coefficient (Hemalatha, Acharya, Renuka & Kamath, 2012). This loss cannot persist in the Integer Wavelet Transformation, because it maps integer to integer in the output.

Figure 7. Three level discrete wavelet decomposition

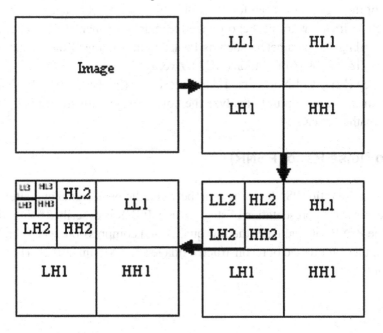

Statistical Method

Encrypt valuable information by applying specific statistical functions on a cover image and performing the variable possible test to extract the hidden information.

Patchwork

This uses statistical method to create a redundant pattern of secret data scattered over the cover image. In this, two different sections of cover image selected, where the secret message will completed embedded on two different patches. The implementation is redundant because, if any patch get destroyed, then the secret message can be easily available from other patch. But if the message is bigger, then only the single patch is possible depending on the size of the cover image. All this procedure is done on the grayscale image, because of the time, speed and space complexity of the algorithms and processors. This patch work is done by increasing the pixel intensity of one patch and decreasing the pixel intensity of another patch, also known as masking approach. Here the change is not noticeable and do not affect the quality of the cover image.

Because of its robustness, it is advantageous over the malicious manipulation of images. Because of the secret data distributed over various parts of the cover image and if the data is lost due to cropping of modification in the image, then it can be accessed through other part because of the multiple copies embedded as patches. Patchwork is beneficial to transfer highly sensitive small amount data.

The steganographic system is efficient enough to secure the hidden messages, but many researchers are working on the Steganalysis that accept the challenge to break the security to extract the secrets.

PERFORMANCE PARAMETERS

The performance of the algorithms used for the embedding of secret image on the cover, is measured by analyzing the cover image with the stego image (Kumar & Kumar, 2010). The analysis can be effictively done by finding the parameters such as Peak Signal to Noise Ratio (PSNR), Mean Squared Error (MSE), Normalized Cross-Correlation (NCC), Average Difference (AD), Structural Content (SC), Maximum Difference (MD) and Normalized Absolute Error (NAE) (Joseph & Vishnukumar, 2015). The following parameters are helpful to analyze the cover image with stego image and the difference will be calculated mathematically.

Peak Signal to Noise Ratio (PSNR)

The Peak Signal-to-noise ratio (PSNR) is the ratio between the peak signal and alteration noise signals that affects the accuracy of its presentation of stego image. PSNR is described using logarithmic decibel scale. The lower the PSNR rate indicates the low quality and compression, where higher the PSNR, the better the quality of the compressed or reconstructed image (Yoo & Ahn, 2012). The PSNR is calculated by following formula

$$PSNR = \log_{10}\left(\frac{MAX_i^2}{MSE}\right) \tag{6}$$

The PSNR is calculated via Mean Squared Error (MSE). Here, MAX_1 is the highest existing pixel value. If pixels are defined by a 8 bit value, then it becomes 255.

Mean Squared Ratio (MSE)

The MSE is the successively incremented squared error between the stego and the cover image. The Mean Squared Error (MSE) is used to quantify the difference between values implied by an estimator and the true values of the quantity being estimated. It is calculated by following formula

$$MSE = \frac{1}{mn}\sum_{i=0}^{m-1}\sum_{j=0}^{n-1}\left[l(i,j) - k(i,j)\right]^2 \tag{7}$$

where $I(i,j)$ am the original image and $K(i,j)$ is the stego image. The m & n are the dimensions of the images. If MSE is low, then errors are less having high quality.

Normalized Cross-Correlation (NCC)

Normalized cross correlation is used to match template, i.e. it is a process used to find the relevancy of the structure or object in an image. Correlation is widely used as an effective similarity measure in matching tasks. This function returns the normalized cross correlation between the calling data series and the argument, the input data series. It is calculated by following formula:

$$NCC = \frac{\sum_{j=1}^{m}\sum_{k=1}^{n}\left(l(x,y) - l'(x,y)\right)^2}{\sum_{j=1}^{m}\sum_{k=1}^{n}\left(l(x,y)\right)^2} \tag{8}$$

Average Difference (AD)

It is an average difference between the two selected pixel values of cover and stego image. If it is lower, both images match the correctness and without noise. It is calculated by following formula

$$AD = \frac{1}{M*N}\sum_{i=1}^{m}\sum_{j=1}^{n}\left(S(i,j) - C(i,j)\right) \tag{9}$$

Structural Content (SC)

The structural correlation or Content measures the similarity between the cover and stego image by analyzing the small areas having nearest low level structural information. The similarity is measured by counting the number of similar regions. If similar regions are large, then both images are more similar. The large value indicates the low quality and small value indicates the high quality. It is calculated by following formula:

$$SC = \frac{\sum_{j=1}^{M} X_i \sum_{k=1}^{N} l\left(x,y\right)^2}{\sum_{j=1}^{M} X_i \sum_{k=1}^{N} l'\left(x,y\right)^2} \tag{10}$$

Maximum Difference (MD)

It is used to measure the cover and stego images and the compressed quality of stego image. Large value indicates poor quality. It is calculated by following formula

$$MD = \max(|x_j, k - x_j, k|) \tag{11}$$

Normalized Absolute Error (NAE)

It is the statistical difference between the cover and stego image. The large value indicates the low quality and small value indicates the high quality. It is calculated by following formula

$$NAE = \frac{\sum_{j=1}^{M} \sum_{k=1}^{N} \left|X_j, k - X_j, k\right|}{\sum_{j=1}^{M} \sum_{k=1}^{N} \left|X_j, k\right|} \tag{12}$$

ATTACKS ON STEGANOGRAPHY: A STEGANALYSIS

Steganalysis is the technique with which, anyone can extract the secret message from the cover image. But the requirement is only the right algorithms or method to unhide the information from the cover image. Many researchers work on the steganalysis to break the hidden system of steganography and extract the secret message (Wang & Wang, 2004). The attacks on the steganography in the form of steganalysis are discussed below.

- **Stego-Only Attack:** Only the Stego image is analyzed and feasible methods are applied to discover the secret signals.

- **Known Cover Attack:** Both cover and stego object is compared and pattern differences are detected suck as the secret image and the image with the hidden information are selected for comparison.
- **Known Message Attack:** The sample stego image with known secret hidden message is analyzed. The similar technique will be applied to extract the hidden message from other stego images.
- **Chosen Stego Attack:** The hidden information is known with respect to the stego object and the steganographic method (tools) to extract it.
- **Chosen Message Attack:** The stego object is generated from the chosen message using the steganographic tools. This type of attack checks the matching patterns of the newly generated stego object and can determine the particular steganographic algorithm or tools used.
- **Known Stego Attack:** The verification of actual and stego object is done using known stegonography algorithms or tool.

APPLICATIONS OF STEGANOGRAPHY

Security plays a vital role for every individual who resides and communicate digitally over the insecure communication channels. Steganography plays a crucial role in securing the confidential information. Some of the applications needs high security while some needs moderate. Depending on the security need, capacity and type of data to be hidden, the type of steganographic algorithms are available. Some of the applications that require steganographic security are

- **Military:** Early years in the military data security suffers from the confidential data transmission. The transmission was possible through the paper courier medium. With the advanced technology, the transmission is done through the electronic medium. The hacking of confidential messages by the intruders are done frequently. The steganography gives the assurance to transmit images, text, audio and video security by keeping them in the competent cover medium without reflecting any clue to intruder. Military data can be hidden into the cover medium before transmission to the destination.
- **Business:** Business data such as online money transaction between authorized parties, stock market data and personnel information can be protected by the steganographic means. This is a secure medium where the legal party get the data without revealing to the intruder.
- **Government:** Government confidential information such as departmental files, pan cards, government resolutions and orders can be protected by the steganography.
- **Medical:** The medical records such as DNA reports, patients pathological reports can be protected by the steganography therefore intruder cannot tamper it.
- **Academic and Research:** Most of the research and valuable academic record are completely online can be prone to attack. The steganography protect the confidential research and their design interested to intruder.
- **Intellectual Property:** The patents, logos, copyrights and other intellectual properties valuable for any nation can be efficiently protected by various steganographic algorithms such as digital watermarking.

CONCLUSION

The steganography itself is a secret for many hundred years. The appearance and use it in secret writing or hiding is different. The secrets are something that baffles understanding and cannot be explained is in existence because of the steganography. In the current era, efficient algorithms are designed that helps to keep the intruders away from the secret information hidden in the cover image. Many steganalysis methods are developed to extract the hidden information. The effectiveness of the steganographic algorithms will be increased by Security Enhancement discuss in this paper such as efficient embedding, reducing distortion, suitable cover selection. Therefore, no any type of steganographic attack breaks the security mechanism implemented by the advanced steganographic algorithm.

This chapter elaborates different digital image steganographic technique along with the type of images required. The payload capacity and the cover image richness have been discussed. The performance parameters used for the analysis of images before and after the steganographic activity have been discussed. Various digital image steganographic applications have been discussed in terms of the security and confidentiality.

REFERENCES

Chan, C.-K., & Cheng, L. M. (2004). Hiding data in images by simple LSB substitution. *Pattern Recognition Society, 37*(3), 469–474. doi:10.1016/j.patcog.2003.08.007

Barni, M. (2001). Improved Wavelet-Based Watermarking Through Pixel-Wise Masking. *IEEE Transactions on Image Processing, 10*(5), 783-791.

Kong, F.-H. (2009). Image Retrieval using both Color and Texture Features. *Proceedings of the Eighth International Conference on Machine Learning and Cybernetics*, 4, 12-15. 10.1109/ICMLC.2009.5212186

Demirel, H., & Jafari, G. A. (2011). Image Resolution Enhancement by Using Discrete and Stationary Wavelet Decomposition. *IEEE Transactions on Image Processing, 20*(5), 1458–1460. doi:10.1109/TIP.2010.2087767 PMID:20959267

Fang, J., Liu, Gu, W., & Tang, Y. (2011). A method to improve the image enhancement result based on image fusion. *International Conference on Multimedia Technology (ICMT)*, 55-58.

Provos, N., & Honeyman, P. (2003). Hide and seek: An introduction to steganography. *Security & Privacy. IEEE Journals & Magazines, 1*(3), 32–44.

Bender, D. G., Morimoto, N., & Lu, A. (2010). Techniques for data hiding. *IBM Systems Journal, 35*(3 & 4), 313–336.

Ker, A. D. (2005). Steganalysis of LSB matching in grayscale images. *Signal Processing Letters, IEEE, 12*(6), 441–444. doi:10.1109/LSP.2005.847889

Cheddad, A., Condell, J., Curran, K., & McKevitt, P. (2010). Digital image steganography: Survey and analysis of current methods. *Signal Processing, 90*(3), 727–752. doi:10.1016/j.sigpro.2009.08.010

Yoo, J.-C., & Ahn, C. W. (2012). Image matching using peak signal-to-noise ratio-based occlusion detection. *IEEE. Image Processing, IET, 6*(5), 483–495. doi:10.1049/iet-ipr.2011.0025

Gonzalez, R. C., Woods, R. E., & Eddins, S. L. (2010). *Digital Image Processing Using Matlab* (2nd ed.). New Delhi: Tata McGraw Hill Education Private Limited.

Wu, D.-C., & Tsai, W.-H. (2003). *A steganographic method for images by pixel-value differencing. In Pattern Recognition Letters 24* (pp. 1613–1626). Elsevier.

Wang, H., & Wang, S. (2004). Cyber warfare: Steganography vs. Steganalysis. *Communications of the ACM, 47*(10).

Marvel, L. M., Boncelet, C. G. Jr, & Retter, C. (1999). Spread Spectrum Steganography. *IEEE Transactions on Image Processing, 8*(8).

Chan, C. K., & Cheng, L. (2004). Hiding data in images by simple LSB substitution. *Pattern Recognition Society, 37*(3), 469–474.

Hashad, A. I., Madani, A. S., & Wahdan, A. E. M. A. (2005). A robust steganography technique using discrete cosine transform insertion. *Enabling Technologies for the New Knowledge Society: ITI 3rd International Conference on Information and Communications Technology,* 255-264.

Sakr, A. S., Ibrahem, H. M., Abdullkader, H. M., & Amin, M. (2012). A steganographic method based on DCT and new quantization technique. *22nd International Conference on Computer Theory and Applications (ICCTA),* 187-191. 10.1109/ICCTA.2012.6523567

Kumar, V., & Kumar, D. (2010). Performance evaluation of DWT based image steganography. *IEEE 2nd International Advance Computing Conference (IACC),* 223-228.

Shejul, A. A., & Kulkarni, U. L. (2010). A DWT Based Approach for Steganography using Biometrics. *International Conference on Data Storage and Data Engineering (DSDE),* 39-43. 10.1109/DSDE.2010.10

Ghasemi, E., Shanbehzadeh, J., & ZahirAzami, B. (2011). A steganographic method based on Integer Wavelet Transform and Genetic Algorithm. *International Conference on Communications and Signal Processing (ICCSP),* 42-45. 10.1109/ICCSP.2011.5739395

Hemalatha, S., Acharya, U. D., Renuka, A., & Kamath, P. R. (2012). A secure image steganography technique using Integer Wavelet Transform. *World Congress on Information and Communication Technologies (WICT),* 755-758. 10.1109/WICT.2012.6409175

Sun, F., & Liu (2010). Selecting Cover for Image Steganography by Correlation Coefficient. *Second International Workshop on Education Technology and Computer Science (ETCS),* 2, 159-162. 10.1109/ETCS.2010.33

Mishra, M., Tiwari, G., & Yadav, A. K. (2014). Secret Communication using public key steganography. *IEEE International Conference on Recent Advances and Innovations in Engineering (ICRAIE-2014),* 1-5.

Verma, N. (2011). Review of Steganographic Techniques. *International Conference and Workshop on Emerging Trends in Technology (ICWET–TCET),* 990-993. 10.1145/1980022.1980237

Srinivasan, B., Arunkumar, S., & Rajesh, K. (2015). A Novel Approach for Color Image Steganography Using NUBASI and Randomized. *Secret Sharing Algorithm. Indian Journal of Science and Technology, 8*(S7), 228–235. doi:10.17485/ijst/2015/v8iS7/64275

Khan, A. S., Fisal, N., Bakar, Z. A., Salawu, N., Maqbool, W., Ullah, R., & Safdar, H. (2014). Secure Authentication and Key Management Protocols for Mobile Multihop WiMAX Networks. *Indian Journal of Science and Technology, 7*(3), 282–295.

Chakrabarti, S., & Samanta, D. (2015). A novel approach to Digital Image Steganography of key-based encrypted text. *IEEE International Conference on Electrical, Electronics, Signals, Communication and Optimization (EESCO)*, 1-6. 10.1109/EESCO.2015.7254009

Singh, A., & Singh, H. (2015). An improved LSB based image steganography technique for RGB images. *IEEE International Conference on Electrical, Computer and Communication Technologies (ICECCT)*, 1-4. 10.1109/ICECCT.2015.7226122

Valandar, M. Y., Ayubi, P., & Barani, M. J. (2015). High secure digital image steganography based on 3D chaotic map. *7th Conference on Information and Knowledge Technology (IKT)*, 1-6. 10.1109/IKT.2015.7288810

Denemark, T. D., Boroumand, M., & Fridrich, J. (2016). Steganalysis Features for Content-Adaptive JPEG Steganography. IEEE Transactions on Information Forensics and Security, 11(8), 1736-1746.

Tayel, M., Gamal, A., & Shawky, H. (2016). A proposed implementation method of an audio steganography technique. *18th International Conference on Advanced Communication Technology (ICACT)*.

Joseph, P., & Vishnukumar, S. (2015). A study on steganographic techniques. *Global Conference on Communication Technologies (GCCT), 206-210.* 10.1109/GCCT.2015.7342653

This research was previously published in Advanced Image Processing Techniques and Applications edited by M. Arun, S. Anand, N. Suresh Kumar, and Arun Kumar Sangaiah; pages 324-346, copyright year 2017 by Information Science Reference (an imprint of IGI Global).

APPENDIX: QUESTIONS AND ANSWERS

Q1: What is Steganography?

Ans. Steganographic system contains a group of methods with which different algorithms are available to embed the secret data under the cover medium such as image, without any detectable indications on the cover image. The steganography is a way to hide any type of digital object such as image, audio, video, text to the digital cover object.

Q2: What is digital image steganography?

Ans. Digital image Steganography is the technique that covers the confidential data under the cover medium such as digital image, without reflecting any clue on the cover image. Secret data hiding through the digital image steganographic techniques can be preformed through the spatial and frequency domain techniques.

Q3: Does Steganography advantageous over Cryptography?

Ans. The mathematical techniques available in the cryptography have some limitations and can prone to crack mathematically. These cryptographic techniques are not suitable for the digital data such as images, audio and videos.

The steganographic techniques are basically meant for the digital data such as images, audio and video, where the methods are work on the spatial and frequency domains. The concept of security in steganography is possible by hiding the digital secret material under the other digital cover object, without reflecting any perception to the intruders.

Q4: What are the types of Steganographic methods?

Ans. Steganography is a group of methods used for securing the secret information under the cover medium such as an image using some translation rules. Secret data hiding through the digital image steganographic techniques can be preformed through the spatial and frequency domain techniques. The spatial domain techniques deal with the digital images. These techniques are Least Significant Bit insertion (LSB), Pixel Value Differencing (PVD), Spread Sprectrum (SS). Where, the transform or frequency domain techniques include the discrete cosine transform (DCT), discrete Fourier transform (DFT) and discrete wavelet transform (DWT).

Q5: What is Payload?

Ans. The payload is the number of bits to be hidden inside the cover image. The capacity of payload i.e. the secret message or image must smaller than the cover image. Therefore, it can be easily hidden inside the cover image without disturbing the visual quality of the cover image.

Q6: What are the criterion for evaluation of Steganographic system Performance?

Ans. The use of steganographic functions for the secure data transmission depends on some criterions that define the efficiency of specific algorithm. These criterions are payload capacity, security, robustness, time complexity, consistency and efficiency.

Q7: Which digital image steganographic algorithm is superior?

Ans. The Average Difference i.e. noise is higher in using spatial domain methods as compared to the frequency domain methods such as medium in DCT and lower in the DWT. The DWT has lower difference and ideal for steganography. The lower invisibility of the secret image is occured using the DWT method. DWT is robust due to the lower noise impression on the stego image. DWT method is distortion less with less noise and greater image quality because of the Average Difference and Structural Content.

Though the spatial methods are simple and more suitable but the transform domain method such as DWT is more attractive as compared to all the steganographic methods.

Q8: Which digital image steganographic algorithm is suitable for data hiding in terms of low overhead processing?

Ans. The spatial algorithm such as LSB insertion is more suitable because of its simplicity and suitability. The extra overhead processing to compute the cover object structure and embedding process is less using the LSB insertion.

Q9: Which parameters are effective in comparing the performance of the digital image before and after steganographic operation?

Ans. The performance of the algorithms used for the embedding of secret image on the cover, is measured by analyzing the cover image with the stego image. The analysis can done by finding the parameters such as Peak Signal to Noise Ratio (PSNR), Mean Squared Error (MSE), Normalized Cross-Correlation (NCC), Average Difference (AD), Structural Content (SC), Maximum Difference (MD) and Normalized Absolute Error (NAE).

Q10: What is steganalysis?

Ans. Steganalysis is the technique with which, anyone can extract the secret message from the cover image. But the requirement is only the right algorithms or method to unhide the information from the cover image.

Chapter 21
Improved Secure Data Transfer Using Video Steganographic Technique

V. Lokeswara Reddy

K.S.R.M College of Engineering, India

ABSTRACT

Information security using data hiding in video provides high embedding capacity and security. Steganography is one of the oldest data protecting methodologies deals with the embedding of data. Video Steganography hides secret information file within a video. Present day communications are treated to be "un-trusted" in terms of security, i.e. they are relatively easy to be hacked. The proposed technique is invented to hide secret information into a video file keeping two considerations in mind which are size and security of the cover video file. At the sender side, the secret information which is to be hidden is encoded into cover video file. Double layered security for the secret data can be achieved by encrypting confidential information and by embedding confidential information into cover video file frames using encrypted embedding technique.

1. INTRODUCTION

1.1. Overview of Steganography

The aim of digital Steganography is to modify a digital medium (cover) to encode and conceal a sequence of bits (Secret data) to facilitate covert communication. In the traditional architecture there existed only the client and the server. In most cases the server was only a data base server that can only offer data. Therefore, majority of the business logic, i.e., validations, etc., had to be placed on the clients' system. This makes maintenance expensive. Such clients are called as 'fat clients'. This also means that every client has to be trained as to how to use the application and even the security in the communication is also the factor to be considered. Since the actual processing of the information takes place on the remote client the information has to be carried over the network, which requires a secured format of

DOI: 10.4018/978-1-7998-1763-5.ch021

the transfer method. A Steganography system, in general, is expected to meet three key requirements, namely, imperceptibility of hiding data, accurate recovery of hidden secret data, and huge payload. In a pure Steganography framework, the technique of encoding confidential data should be unidentified to anyone other than the receiver and the sender. An effective Steganography should possess the following characteristics (Suneetha, Hima Bindu, Sarath Chandra, 2013): Secrecy: Extraction of embedded secret data from the host medium should not be possible without the knowledge of the proper secret key used at the extracting. Imperceptibility: After hiding the confidential data in the cover file, it should be imperceptible from the original file. High capacity: The maximum size of the embedded secret information that can be hidden can be as long as possible. Resistance: The embedded secret information should be able to survive when the host medium has been manipulated. Accurate extraction: The extraction of the embedded secret data from the medium should be reliable and accurate. This paper explains a way in which so that a video file is used as a host medium to embed secret information without changing the file structure and content of the video file. Because degradation in the quality of the cover medium leads to noticeable change in the cover medium which may leads to the failure of objective of Steganography. The contents are processed during video embedding and de-embedding. This makes less vulnerable to video steg analysis methods. A single bit is embedded in the least significant bit of each motion vector.

In this digital world the information security and secret data communication is changing and advancing day by day. Broad band internet connections almost an errorless data transmission, which helps people to distribute large multimedia files and makes identical data copies of them. Sending secret information and secret files over the internet are carried in an unsecured form but everyone has got something to keep in secret. The aim of Steganography is to embed the secret information inside the cover file without changing the overall quality of cover file. In Steganography actual confidential data is not maintained in its original format but it is transformed in such a way that it can be embedded inside multimedia cover file e.g. image, video, audio. The current industries mainly demand for finger printing and digital watermarking of image, audio and video Steganography. The music and movie industries are continually searching for new methods for Steganography. In "broadcast monitoring" broadcast detectors are used to retrieve the watermark of a given file and report to the broadcasting events to notify the owner or distributor of broadcast status (medium played, time and date). Since internet is now the major medium for the communication and data transfer purpose it become necessary for each nation to make some counter measures to prevent the foul use of internet (Sunil Moon, Rajesree Raut, 2014). The cybercrimes are also informing immediately nowadays hence the steganographic methods should be that much effective and secure so that crimes can be minimized for that cryptography should be mixed with Steganography for the confidentiality of the secret data. Information Hiding is the process of embedding secret information into a host medium. In general, visual media is preferred due to their wide presence and the tolerance of human perceptual systems involved. For instance, audio/video data embedding share many common points; however, video data hiding demands more complex designs as a result of the additional temporal dimension. Therefore, video secret information embedding continues to constitute an active research area. LSB audio Steganography with location identification and it provides good audio quality and robustness (Pathak, Nag, 2014). Steganography helps not only to keep others from understanding that the secret data exists but also to bypass drawing suspicion to hide the information (Johnson, and Jajodia, Sushil, 1998 & Provos. and Honeyman, 2001). The rest of the paper is organized as follows: in Section 1 we overview the literature survey of Steganography and its methods. The proposed method and algorithm is given in Section 2 followed by the experimental results and analysis in Sections 3 and 4. Finally, the paper is concluded in Section 5.

1.2. Cryptography vs. Steganography

Security has different aspects, such as confidentiality, integrity and availability. For instance, one can use either cryptography or Steganography to address confidentiality requirements. Basically, the purpose of cryptography and Steganography is to provide secret communication. To make a steganographic communication even more secure the message can be encrypted before being hidden in the carrier. However, Steganography is not the same as cryptography. The comparison between "Steganography" and "Cryptography" by considering various parameters is shown in Table 1. In Steganography, the interest is in concealing the existence of a message from a third party, while in cryptography the purpose is to make a message unreadable by a third party. Cryptography means that original data is replaced with some other data using a key which can be recovered only with that key. Applications of cryptography can be ATM cards, computer password, electronic commerce. The use of Cryptography and Steganography is to enable secure communication. The term Cryptography means "secret writing" whereas Steganography means "cover writing". Steganography conceal the existence of the message whereas Cryptography embeds the secret information even from a malicious people. Cryptography secret message can be read when attacker breaks the system. Steganography is used for security communication. Once it is detected that there is any data hidden, complete file can be destroyed so that the data cannot be delivered to the receiver. To break a Steganography, the system requires the intruder to identify the Steganography which is used and is capable to scan the embedded information. Breaking a steganographic system needs the attacker to detect that Steganography has been used and is able to read the embedded message. The cryptography protects the contents of a message whereas Steganography protect both messages and communicating parties. Steganogrpahy can also enhance individual privacy. It is effective only if the hidden communication is not detected.

Table 1. Comparison of steganography and cryptography

Criterion/Method	Steganography	Cryptography
Carrier	Any digital media	Usually text based, with some extensions to image files
Objective	Secret communication	Data protection
Key	Optional	Necessary
Input Files	At least two unless in self embedding.	One
Result	Stego file	Cipher text
Type of attack	Steganalysis	Cryptanalysis
Authentication	Full retrieval of data	Full retrieval of data
Visibility	Never	Always
History	Very ancient except its digital version	Modern era
Message passing	Unknown	Known
Technology	Little known	Common

1.3. Literature Survey

Secret information can be embedded inside a video file using many suitable methods. The cover medium is video file. Video file is generally a collection of images and sounds, so most of the presented methods on image and audio can be applied to video files too. The combined evaluations i.e., the evaluations for image and audio Steganography can be taken together for the evaluation of video Steganography (Bandyopadhyay, Bhattacharyya, Ganguly et al., 2009). The great advantages of video are the large amount of data that can be hidden inside and the fact that it is a moving stream of images and sounds. A video stream consists of collection of frames and the confidential data is hidden in these frames as payload (Mandal & Dutta, 2012).

Mamta Juneja and Parvinder Singh Sandhu (2009) have given a robust Steganography method based on LSB substitution and Rivest, Shamir and Adleman (RSA) encryption techniques. For user's library based on their suitability as cover objects for some data, this paper ranks images in user's library. After matching this data to an image, there is a rare chance for an attacker to get back the data. This application first encrypts it before hiding the data.

A new polynomial-based image sharing method with two achievements was proposed by Z. Eslami and J. Zarepour Ahmadabadi (2011). The block size is dynamically determined depending on the size of embedded secret information and the size of the cover images is used for information embedding. A novel chaining type which achieves 15/16 as its alter detection ability with the usage of two authentication bits is proposed. This chaining as a feedback mechanism allows altering in one block affecting the secret information of the next block also.

A new steganographic technique is proposed by Huan Xu et al (2010) in which a resistant programming approach was employed to find an optimum solution for the pair-wise LSB matching method. By implementing this proposed method, the distortion of the stego image gets reduced and the visual quality gets improved and decreases the probability of detection. The new LSB matching method increases the PSNR value of the stego images and enhances the quality and decreases the probability of detection.

A new system for the combination of Steganography with watermarking was proposed by Shivani Kosla and Paramjeet Kaur (2014). The proposed High secured system using Steganography and watermarking is tested by taking message and hiding them in images/frames of input video. The authors recorded the results that are obtained from the experiments. In this paper authors take two videos as input and can embed secret message in both.

Andrew D. Ker (2007) proposed steganalysis methods of LSB insertion to both of the two minimum bit planes in images. The author showed how standard LSB replacement can be adapted to such embedding, and how the methods of structural steganalysis, giving the most sensitive detectors for standard LSB replacement are applied to make more purpose-built detectors for two bit plane Steganography. The author compares the detection of standard LSB embedding with the two methods of embedding in the lower two bit planes with new detectors of high accuracy resulting in the two lowest bit planes embedding into one.

Nilanjan Dey et al (2016) presented a comprehensive study for the behavior of some well-established watermarking algorithms in frequency domain for the preservation of stroke-based diagnostic parameters. Two different sets of watermarking algorithms namely: two correlation-based (binary logo hiding) and two singular value decomposition (SVD)-based (gray logo hiding) watermarking algorithms are used for embedding ownership logo. The diagnostic parameters in atherosclerotic plaque ultrasound video are namely: (a) bulb identification and recognition which consists of identifying the bulb edge points in far and near carotid walls; (b) carotid bulb diameter; and (c) carotid lumen thickness all along the carotid artery. The tested data set consists of carotid atherosclerotic movies taken under IRB protocol from University of Indiana Hospital, USA-AtheroPoint™ (Roseville, CA, USA) joint pilot study. ROC (receiver operating characteristic) analysis was performed on the bulb detection process that showed an accuracy and sensitivity of 100% each, respectively. The diagnostic preservation (DP$_{system}$) for SVD-based approach was above 99% with PSNR (Peak signal-to-noise ratio) above 41, ensuring the retention of diagnostic parameter devalorization as an effect of watermarking. Finally, the authors said that the fully automated proposed system proved to be an efficient method for watermarking the atherosclerotic ultrasound video for stroke application.

A new steganographic scheme based on the old and top numerical model was proposed by S. Geetha et al (2011). In this scheme, the embedded data is divided into numerals, each having variable information-carrying capacity. The proposed method provides a clear visual quality apart from high payload capacity. The generated stego medium get least perceptual distortion apart from high payload capacity.

Two novel secret information hidden algorithms based on using some histogram properties of raw digital video streams was proposed by Ozdemir Cetin et al (2009). Several different formats like '.xls', '.mp3', '.html', '.pdf', '.doc' and '.rar' can be taken by using secret information files in the hiding procedure. The '.rar' files provide a roboust compression type supporting strong encryption methods to some range. Comparitively the proposed algorithms result in an enhanced spatial and temporal perception levels in resulting the stego-video offering huge secret information hiding capacity.

A Hash-LSB steganographic method for embedding the secret message into cover video without producing any changes of quality of video was proposed by Manpreet Kaur and Amandeep Kaur (2014). In this work, secret information was embedded in a video file with more security. In the proposed technique the author applied a cryptographic method i.e. RSA algorithm to secure a secret message which is not easy to break.

Secret data embedding and de-embedding process for AVI videos was proposed by Arup Kumar Bhaumik et al (2009). This provided right security to information during broadcasting. In this, at sender side and at receiver side two different methods are used for hiding and retrieving. These procedures use the key for information hiding and unhiding. It is highly configurable, resulting in high data capacities.

The use of data embedding techniques in digital videos was described by Mohammed Elsadig Eltahir et al (2009). The authors described how to use LSB insertion method in video images and frames are added to the naked eye system to enhance the size of the information hidden in video file.

1.4. Steganography Techniques

Over the past few years, numerous Steganography techniques that embed hidden messages in multimedia objects have been proposed (Johnson, & Jajodia, 1998). There have been many techniques for hiding information or messages in multimedia object using many suitable techniques. As a cover object, image, audio or video file is selected. Depending on the type of the cover object, definite and appropriate techniques are followed in order to obtain security. In this section, different techniques or methods which are often used in image, audio and video Steganography are discussed.

1.4.1. Image Steganography

The image file is the most widely used cover object in Steganography. To a computer an image file is simply a file that shows different colors and intensities of light on different areas of an image. The images are divided into three types: Binary (Black & White), Grayscale and RGB (Red-Green-Blue). The binary image has only one bit value per pixel, '0' represents black and '1' represents white. While the grayscale image has 8 bits per pixel, 00000000 represents black pixel and 11111111 represents white pixel. The RGB image has 24 bits per pixel, 00000000 (R), 00000000 (G) and 00000000 (B) represents black pixel and 11111111 (R), 11111111 (G), 11111111 (B) represents white pixel. The RGB image is the most suitable image file format for Steganography, because it contains a lot of redundant information that helps in hiding secret information with a bit change in the image resolution which does not affect the image quality. Image domain techniques can be divided into two groups (Silman, 2001):

1.   Spatial domain
2.   Transform domain

Spatial domain technique embeds messages in the intensity of the pixels directly, while Transform domain also known as Frequency domain embeds information in transform coefficients of the cover images. Classification of image Steganography is shown in Figure 1

To hide information, straight message insertion may encode every bit of information in the image. The message may also be scattered randomly throughout the image. A number of ways exist to hide information in an image. Common approaches include:

- **Least significant bit insertion:** Least significant bit (LSB) insertion is a common and simple approach to embed information in an image file. In this method the LSB of a byte is replaced with a message bit. This technique works good for image, audio and video Steganography. To a human eye, the resulting stego image will look identical to the cover image (Johnson, Jajodia, 1998; Bandyopadhyay et al, 2008).

Figure 1. Categories of image steganography (Morkel, Eloff, Olivie)

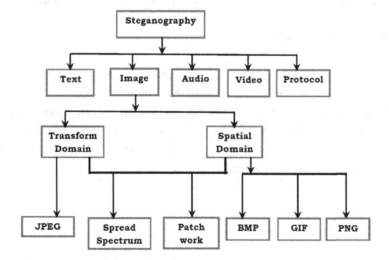

- **Masking and filtering:** Masking and filtering techniques are mostly used on RGB and grey scale images. They hide information in a way similar to watermarks on actual paper and are sometimes used as digital watermarks. Masking images entails changing the luminance of the masked area. The smaller the luminance change, the less of a chance that it can be detected. Masking techniques embed information in significant areas so that the hidden message is more integral to the cover image than just hiding it in the "noise" level. This makes it more suitable for instance, lossy JPEG images.

- **Redundant Pattern Encoding**: Patchwork and other similar tools do redundant pattern encoding, which is a sort of spread spectrum technique. It works by scattering the message throughout the picture. This makes the image more resistant to cropping and rotation. Smaller secret images work better to increase the redundancy embedded in the cover image, and thus make it easier to recover if the stego-image is manipulated.

- **Encrypt and Scatter:** The Encrypt and Scatter technique tries to emulate white noise. It is mostly used in image Steganography. White Noise Storm is one such program that employs spread spectrum and frequency hopping. It does this by scattering the message throughout an image on eight channels within a random number that is generated by the previous window size and data channel. The channels then swap rotate, and interlace amongst each other. Each channel represents one bit and as a result there are many unaffected bits in each channel. In this technique it is harder to extract a message out than an LSB scheme, because to decode, presence of hidden image is to be detected and then the bit pattern has to be extracted from a file. While that is true for any stego-image we need the algorithm and stego key to decode the bit pattern, both of which are not required to recover a message from LSB. Even though White Noise Storm provides extra security against message extraction it is just as susceptible as straight LSB to image degradation due to image processing (Johnson, & Jajodia, 1998; Bandyopadhyay et al, 2008).

- **Algorithms and transformations:** LSB modification technique for images does hold good if any kind of compression is done on the resultant stego-image. JPEG images use the discrete cosine transform to achieve compression. DCT is a lossy compression transform because the cosine values cannot be calculated exactly, and repeated calculations using limited precision numbers introduce rounding errors into the final result. Variances between original data values and restored data values depend on the method used to calculate DCT (Westfeld, 2001).

1.4.2. Audio Steganography

Audio Steganography is a technique that ensures confidential information broadcasting between parties normally in Internet community. In an audio Steganography system, confidential data is embedded in digital sound. The secret message is embedded by slightly altering the binary sequence of a sound file. Embedding secret messages in digital sound is usually a more difficult process than embedding messages in other media, such as digital images. In order to conceal secret messages successfully, a variety of methods for embedding information in digital audio have been introduced. These methods range from rather simple algorithms that insert information in the form of signal noise to more powerful methods that exploit sophisticated signal processing techniques to hide information. The list of methods that are commonly used for audio Steganography are listed and discussed below:

1. **Low-bit coding:** Low bit coding is also called as LSB coding. LSB coding is the simplest way to embed information in a digital audio file. In this technique LSB of binary sequence of each sample of digitized audio file is replaced with binary equivalent of secret message. By substituting the least significant bit of each sampling point with a binary message, LSB coding allows for a large amount of data to be encoded. In LSB coding, the ideal data transmission rate is 1Kbps per 1KHz. In some implementations of LSB coding, however, the two least significant bits of a sample are replaced with two message bits. This increases the amount of data that can be encoded but also increases the amount of resulting noise in the audio file as well. Using the least-significant bit is possible, as modifications will usually not create audible changes to the sounds. Another method involves taking advantage of human limitations. It is possible to encode messages using frequencies that are inaudible to the human ear. Using any frequencies above 20,000 Hz, messages can be hidden inside sound files and will not be detected by human checks (David Kahn, 1996).

2. **Parity coding:** Instead of breaking a signal down into individual samples, the parity coding method breaks a signal down into separate regions of samples and encodes each bit from the secret message in a sample region's parity bit. If the parity bit of a selected region does not match the secret bit to be encoded, the process flips the LSB of one of the samples in the region. Thus, the sender has more of a choice in encoding the secret bit, and the signal can be changed in a more unobtrusive fashion.

3. **Phase coding:** Human Auditory System (HAS) cannot recognize the phase change in audio signal as easy it can recognize noise in the signal. The phase coding method exploits this fact. Phase coding addresses the disadvantages of the noise inducing methods of audio Steganography. Phase coding relies on the fact that the phase components of sound are not as perceptible to the human ear as noise is. This technique encodes the secret message bits as phase shifts in the phase spectrum of a digital signal, achieving an inaudible encoding in terms of signal-to-noise ratio. Phase coding is explained in the following procedure (Poulami Dutta, Debnath Bhattacharyya, and Tai-Hoon Kim, 2009):

   ○ The original sound signal is broken up into smaller segments whose lengths equal the size of the message to be encoded.

   ○ A Discrete Fourier Transform (DFT) is applied to each segment to create a matrix of the phases and Fourier transform magnitudes.

   ○ Phase differences between adjacent segments are calculated.

   ○ Phase shifts between consecutive segments are easily detected. In other words, the absolute phases of the segments can be changed but the relative phase differences between adjacent segments must be preserved. Therefore the secret message is only inserted in the phase vector of the first signal segment as follows:

$$phase\_new = \begin{cases} \pi/2 & if \quad message \quad bit = 0 \\ -\pi/2 & if \quad message \quad bit = 1 \end{cases}$$

   ○ A new phase matrix is created using the new phase of the first segment and the original phase differences.

   ○ Using the new phase matrix and original magnitude matrix, the sound signal is reconstructed by applying the inverse DFT and then concatenating the sound segments back together.

○   To extract the secret message from the sound file, the receiver must know the segment length. The receiver can then use the DFT to get the phases and extract the information. One disadvantage associated with phase coding is a low data transmission rate due to the fact that the secret message is encoded in the first signal segment only. This might be addressed by increasing the length of the signal segment. However, this would change phase relations between each frequency component of the segment more drastically, making the encoding easier to detect. A characteristic feature of phase coding is the low data transmission rate owing to the fact that the secret message is encoded only in the first segment of the audio signal. Hence, the phase coding method is normally used only for a small amount of data hiding.

4. **Spread spectrum:** Spread Spectrum is another method used to conceal information inside of an audio file. This method works by adding random noises to the signal. The information is concealed inside a carrier and spread across the frequency spectrum. In the context of audio Steganography, the basic spread spectrum method attempts to spread secret information across the audio signal's frequency spectrum as much as possible. This is analogous to a system using an implementation of the LSB coding that randomly spreads the message bits over the entire sound file. However, unlike LSB coding, the Spread spectrum method spreads the secret message over the sound file's frequency spectrum, using a code that is independent of the actual signal. As a result, the final signal occupies a bandwidth in excess of what is actually required for transmission J. Bogdan Falkowski.

5. **Echo Hiding:** Echo Hiding is yet another method of hiding information inside an audio file. In echo hiding, information is embedded in a sound file by introducing an echo into the discrete signal. This method uses the echoes in sound files in order to try and hide information. By simply adding extra sound to an echo inside an audio file, information can be concealed. Like Spread Spectrum coding, echo hiding allows for a higher data transmission rate and provides superior robustness when compared to the noise-inducing methods. To successfully hide the data, three parameters of the echo need to be altered: amplitude, decay rate and offset (delay time) from the original signal. The echo is not easily resolved as all the three parameters are set below the human audible threshold limit. Also, the offset is altered to represent the binary message to be hidden. The first offset value represents a one (binary), and the second offset value represents a zero (binary) (Natarajan Meghanathan and Lopamudra Nayak, 2010). If only one echo was produced from the original signal, only one bit of information could be encoded. Therefore, the original signal is broken down into blocks before the encoding process begins. Once the encoding process is completed, the blocks are concatenated back together to create the final signal. Also, a message can be encoded using musical tones with a substitution scheme. A normal musical piece can now be composed around the secret message or an existing piece can be selected together with an encoding scheme that will represent a message.

1.4.3. Video Steganography

Video files are generally a collection of images and sounds, so most of the presented techniques on images and audio can be applied to video files too. So, video Steganography is nothing but a combination of image and audio Steganography. The combined evaluations i.e., the evaluations for image and audio Steganography can be taken together for the evaluation of video Steganography. Important benefit of video Steganography is the large amount of data that can be hidden inside and the fact that it is a moving stream of images and sounds. Therefore, any small but otherwise noticeable distortions might go by unobserved by humans because of the continuous flow of information (David Kahn, 1996). A video stream consists of collection of frames and the secret data is embedded in these frames as payload (J.K. Kousik Dasgupta Mandal and Paramartha Dutta, 2012).

1.5. Characterizing Secret Data Hiding Methods

Steganography is a kind of technique which can embed a message inside a cover object. There are a number of features that characterizes the merits and demerits of the embedding techniques. The way they are applied decides the importance of each and every feature. Set of criteria's are proposed to define the invisibility of an algorithm. The criteria's are as follows:

- **Invisibility:** The imperceptibility of a steganographic algorithm is the first and foremost necessity, since the quality of Steganography lies in its capacity to be unnoticed by the human eyes.
- **Payload Capacity:** Steganography techniques used aim at hiding the embedded secret data and also maximize the amount of confidential information embedded. The amount of confidential information that is hidden is called payload capacity.
- **Hiding Capacity:** Concealing capacity is the size of data that could be concealed with respect to the size of the cover object. A vast concealing capacity permits the use of smaller cover images and thus decreases the data transmission needed to transmit the stego image.
- **Perceptual Transparency:** The inability of an eavesdropper to detect hidden data is referred by Perceptual transparency.

1.6. Steganography Applications

Steganography is very useful in the area of information technology because it is used for the purpose of network security. It keeps data integrity which means that there will be no modification in the content of information during communication. It is also used for message authentication that means message is coming from a authorized person and will be transmitted to an intended receiver. Apart from that, it keeps secrecy and privacy as well. Steganography techniques can be used for the purpose of watermarking. There are several applications for Steganography including secret communication, copyright protection and feature tagging. Watermark or copyright notice could be inserted inside a multimedia file to recognize it as protected property. If somebody attempts to utilize this multimedia file without authorization, we can recognize by retrieving the watermark. Other applications of Steganography include multimedia watermarking, secure military communications and fingerprinting applications for authentication purposes to curb the problem of video-audio synchronization, digital piracy and TV broadcasting. Steganography on a large scale used by terrorists, who embed their secret information in innocent, cover sources like image, audio and video to spread terrorism across the country. It come in concern that terrorists using Steganography when the two articles titled "Terrorist instructions hidden online" and "Terror groups hide behind Web encryption" were published in newspaper.

This proposed system is to provide a good, efficient method for embedding the secret data and sent data to the destination in secure manner. The proposed method is very useful technique for secure communication over the Internet. In the process of Steganography, the message which is hidden is invisible. The sender and receiver only know how to hide and unhide the data into the carrier files. No other intermediate person will even know that there is a second message inside the carrier file. The sender and receiver only know the commands to hide and unhide. Steganography can be used for hidden communication. The "Video Steganography" is an application developed to embed text file in video file. It is concerned with hiding confidential data in an innocuous cover and in a secure robust manner. This system makes the secret files more secure by using the concepts of Steganography and cryptography. The proposed technique will not change the size of the cover video file even after encoding and also suitable for any type of video file format. Encryption and Decryption methods have been used to make the security system more robust. In this proposed technique secret information file is first encrypted and then embedded in to cover video file with the help of steganographic system.

2. PROPOSED SYSTEM

Among different data hiding methods proposed to embed secret data within video file, LSB coding technique is the simplest way to embed secret data in a video file by replacing the LSB of multimedia file frames with a binary message. Hence LSB method allows huge amount of secret information to be encoded in a video file. The proposed method provides a basic view of multimedia steganographic process at receiver and sender side. At the sender side the secret text message is encrypted by using Data Encryption Standard (DES) algorithm using a key shared by both sender and receiver. Symmetric encryption is an efficient process for providing security to the secret message. The encrypted message is passed to embedding phase. In the proposed technique the cover video file is broken down in to multiple frames. In embedding phase the encrypted message will embedded into the frames of cover video file. The embedded stego video file contains the encrypted text message which is extracted at the receiver side. At the receiver side stego video file is passed to de embedding phase. In extraction process encrypted text will be extracted from embedded video file and encrypted text is decrypted using decryption.

2.1. Embedding and Extracting

First, a video file is selected and loaded into the steganographic system. The cover video file is then broken down into frames. Now the LSB technique is applied to conceal the data in the carrier frames. The proposed technique takes bits of secret data and conceals them in LSB of RGB pixel value of the carrier frames. The process will run until the entire text message is inserted into multimedia file.

Algorithm for Embedding confidential data in Video file:
Step-1: Input cover video file, secret message.
Step-2: Break the video file into frames.
Step-3: Convert the secret message into cipher text by using DES algorithm.
Step-4: Find LSBs of each RGB pixels of the cover frame.
Step-5: Convert the encrypted text message into bits.
Step-6: Embed the bits of the secret message into bits of LSB of RGB pixels of the cover frame.
Step-7: Continue the process until the message is fully embedded into video file.
Step-8: Regenerate video file frames.

Algorithm for Extracting Secret message from Video file:
Step-1: Input stego video file.

Step-2: Break the stego video file into frames.

Step-3: Find and retrieve the LSBs of each RGB pixels of the stego frame.

Step-4: Continue the process until the message is fully extracted from video file.

Step-5: Decrypt the message to get original secret message.

Step-6: Reconstruct the secret information.

Step-7: Regenerate video file frame.

3. EXPERIMENTAL WORK AND RESULTS

In this section, we are going to implement Steganography technique on the following images and video files. The images and video files tested in the present experiment are displayed. When the system is executed Graphical User Interface (GUI) is displayed. The hiding process at sender side is shown in Figure 2 and 3. The hiding window provides a provision for selecting secret message file and cover medium file. The secret information file contains text. The un-hiding process at receiver side is shown in Figure 4 and 5. To get the original secret information click on un-hiding button. Comparing stego video with cover video requires a measure of video quality. Commonly used measure is Histogram. Figure 6 and 7 are the histograms of cover video file and stego video file. A text field with browse button to browse the secret information file. Second text field with browse button is used to browse video file as cover. This will open file chooser to select a video file. Third textbox is for choosing the destination path of the output video file which contains the secret message. Hiding button is used to hide confidential data in to cover video file and un-hiding button is used to retrieve secret information from stego video file. After successful encoding the dialog box in Figure 3 shows name of the output video file. The textbox with a browse button in Figure 5 is used to browse the stego video file containing the secret information.

Figure 2. Data hiding process at sender side

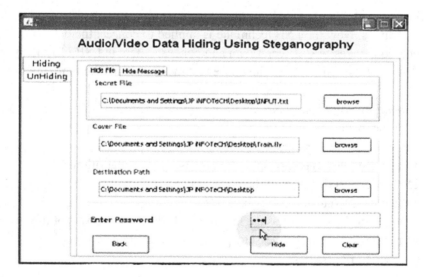

Figure 3. Data hidden successfully

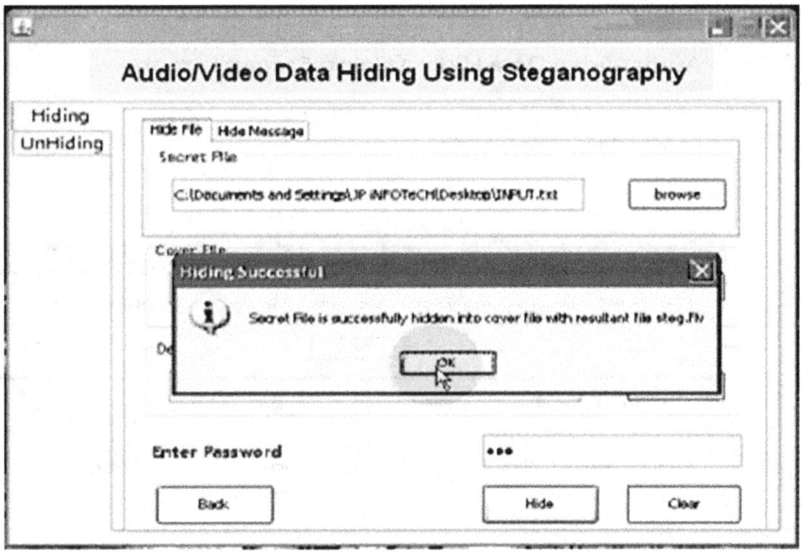

Figure 4. Un-hiding process at receiver side

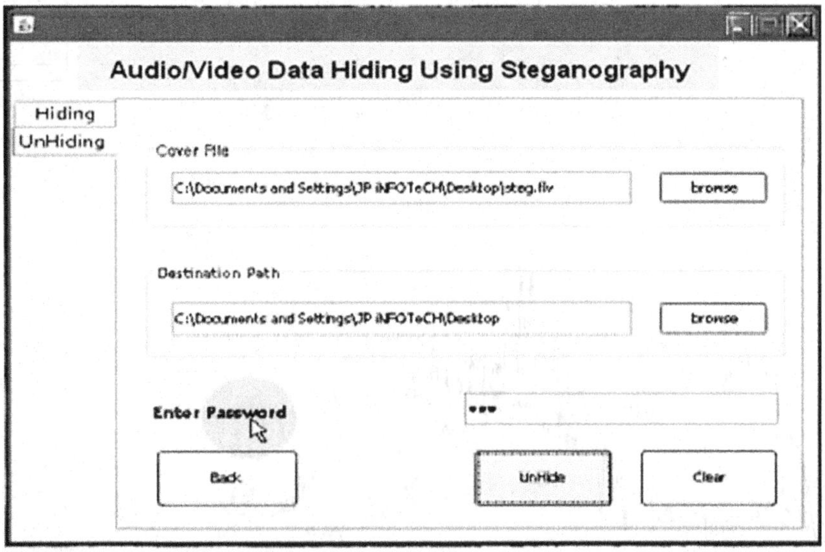

Figure 5. Retrieved the secret file

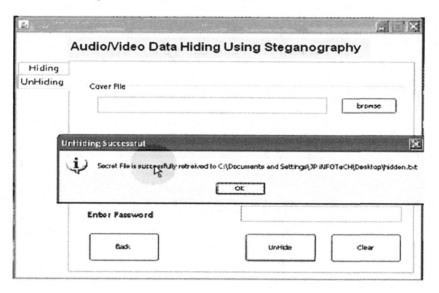

Figure 6. Histogram of cover video file

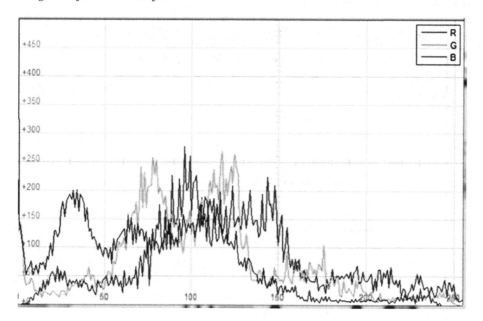

Figure 7. Histogram of Stego video file

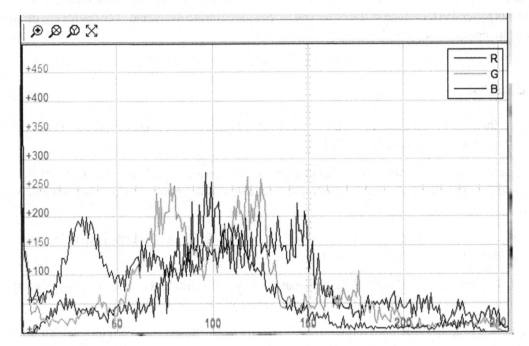

4. ADVANTAGES

The proposed technique combines the power of Cryptography and Steganography. Since the data are encrypted before being hidden into the cover video file, the steganalysis becomes very difficult. It uses a cryptographic algorithm DES (Symmetric encryption) using a key shared by both sender and receiver. This proposed technique also takes care to see that the quality and size of the output video stego file is almost similar to that of the original video file. Since the data to be hidden could be anything. However, with Steganography the user can send the stego video file to multiple recipients without them even realising that the video file contains hidden data, and only the intended recipient can be made aware of this contents and the means of how to retrieve the data.

5. CONCLUSION

In the era of fast information interchange using internet and World Wide Web (WWW), video Steganography has become essential tool for information security. In this study, we have clarified the knowledge of data hidden field. Furthermore, we have presented the history of the Steganography since ancient times until the present day. In this paper we have presented a new system for the combination of Steganography with Cryptography which could be proven as a highly secured technique for secure data transfer in near future. The proposed high secured system using Steganography and Cryptography is tested by taking secret message and hiding them in frames of input video file. The results that are obtained from these experiments are recorded. The Proposed algorithm provides more security in comparison to previous algorithms. Future Work may be further enhancement of results by applying some other algorithm than used in this paper. Performance of the cover and stego video file are evaluated. The results are in expected line and are comparable with the already existing results.

REFERENCES

Bandyopadhyay, S. K., Bhattacharyya, D., Ganguly, D., Mukherjee, S., & Das, P. (2008). Tutorial Review on Steganography. *Proceedings of, IC3*, 105–113.

Bandyopadhyay, S. K., Bhattacharyya, D., Ganguly, D., Mukherjee, S., & Das, P. (2009, June). A Tutorial Review on Steganography. *Proceedings of the International Conference on Comtemporary Computing* (IC3'09) (pp. 105-114).

Bhaumik, A. K., Choi, M., Robles, R. J., & O'Balitanas, M. (2009, June). Data Hiding in Video. *International Journal of Database Theory and Application*, 2(2), 9–16.

Cetin, O., & Ozcerit, A. T. (2009). A new Steganography algorithm based on color histograms for data embedding into raw video streams. *Computers & Security*, 28(7), 670–682.

Dasgupta, K., Mandal, J. K., & Dutta, P. (2012, April). Hash Based Least Significant Bit Technique for Video Steganography (HSLB). *International Journal of Security. Privacy and Trust Management*, 1(2), 1–11.

Dey, N., Bose, S., Das, A., Chaudhuri, S. S., Saba, L., Shafique, S., . . . Suri, J. S. (2016, April). Effect of Watermarking on Diagnostic Preservation of Atherosclerotic Ultrasound Video in Stroke Telemedicine. *Journal of Medical Systems*. PubMed

Dutta, P., Bhattacharyya, D., & Tai-hoon, K. (2009, June). Data Hiding in Audio Signal: A Review. *International Journal of Database Theory and Application*, 2(2).

Eltahir, M. E., Miss, L. M. K., Zaidian, B. B., & Zadian, A. A. (2009, April). High Rate Video Streaming Steganography. *Proceedings of the IEEE International Conference on Information Management and Engineering* (pp. 3550-3553).

Eslami, Z., & Ahmadabadi, J. Z. (2011). Secret image sharing with authentication-chaining and dynamic embedding. *Journal of Systems and Software*, 84(5), 803–809. doi:10.1016/j.jss.2011.01.002

Falkowski, J.B. (2002, July). Lossless binary image compression using logic functions and spectra. *Computers and Electrical Engineering*, 30(2004), 17-43.

Geetha, S., Kabilan, V., Chockalingam, S. P., & Kamaraj, N. (2011). Varying radix numeral system based adaptive image Steganography. *Information Processing Letters*, 111(16), 792–797. doi:10.1016/j.ipl.2011.05.013

Johnson, N. F., & Jajodia, S. (1998, February). Exploring steganography: Seeing the unseen. *The Computer Journal*, 31(2), 26–34. doi:10.1109/MC.1998.4655281

Johnson, N. F., & Jajodia, S. (1998, April). Steganalysis of Images Created Using Current Steganography Software. *Proceeding for the Second Information Hiding Workshop* (pp. 273-289). doi:10.1007/3-540-49380-8_19

Johnson, N. F., & Jajodia, S. (1998). Exploring Steganography: Seeing the unseen. *Computer*, *31*(2), 26–34. doi:10.1109/MC.1998.4655281

Juneja, M., & Sandhu, P. S. (2009, October). Designing of Robust Image Steganography Technique Based on LSB Insertion and Encryption. *Proceedings of the IEEE International Conference on Advances in Recent Technologies in Communication and Computing* (pp. 302-305). doi:10.1109/ARTCom.2009.228

Kahn, D. (1996, June). The History of Steganography. *Proc. of First Int. Workshop on Information Hiding*, Cambridge, UK, LNCS (Vol. 1174). doi:10.1007/3-540-61996-8_27

Kahn, D. (1996, June). The History of Steganography. *Proc. of First Int. Workshop on Information Hiding*, Cambridge, UK, LNCS (pp. 1174). doi:10.1007/3-540-61996-8_27

Ker, A. D. (2007, March). Steganalysis of Embedding in Two Least-Significant Bits. *IEEE Transactions on Information Forensics and Security*, *2*(1), 46–54. doi:10.1109/TIFS.2006.890519

Kosla, S., & Kaur, P. (2014, June). Secure Data Hiding Technique Using Video Steganography and Watermarking. *International Journal of Computers and Applications*, *95*(20), 7–12. doi:10.5120/16708-6861

Kosla, S., & Kaur, P. (2014, June). Secure Data Hiding Technique Using Video Steganography and Watermarking. *International Journal of Computers and Applications*, *95*(20), 7–12. doi:10.5120/16708-6861

Lee, Y. K., & Chen, L. H. (2000, June). High capacity image steganographic model. *Proceedings of the IEEE Vision, Image and Signal Processing*, *147*(3), 288–294. doi:10.1049/ip-vis:20000341

Meghanathan, N., & Nayak, L. (2010, January). Steganalysis Algorithms for Detecting the Hidden Information in Image, Audio and Video Cover Media. *International Journal of Network Security & Its Application*, *2*(1), 43–55.

Moon, S. K., & Raut, R. D. (2014). Application of data hiding in Audio-Video using anti forensics techniques for authentication and data security. *Proceedings of the IEEE International Advanced Computing Conference (IACC)*.

Morkel, T., Eloff, J. H. P., & Olivie, M. S. (2005). *An Overview of Image Steganography. Information and Computer Security Architecture (ICSA) Research Group*. Pretoria, South Africa: Department of Computer Science, University of Pretoria.

Pathak, P. A. K., & Nag, A. (2014). A New Audio Steganography Scheme based on Location Selection with Enhanced Security. *Proceedings of the ACES First International Conference*. doi:10.1109/ACES.2014.6807979

Provos, N., & Honeyman, P. (2001, August). CITI Technical Report.

Silman, J. (2001). *Steganography and Steganalysis: An Overview*. SANS Institute.

Suneetha, B., Hima Bindu, C. H., & Sarath Chandra, S. (2013). Secured Data Transmission Based Video Steganography. *International Journal of Mechanical and Production Engineering*, 2(1), 78–81.

Westfeld, A. (2001). F5-a steganographic algorithm: High capacity despite better steganalysis. *Proc. 4th International Workshop Information Hiding* (pp. 289–302). doi:10.1007/3-540-45496-9_21

Xu, H., Wang, J., & Kim, H. J. (2010). Near-optimal solution to pair-wise LSB matching via an immune programming strategy. *Information Sciences*, 180(8), 1201–1217. doi:10.1016/j.ins.2009.12.027

This research was previously published in the International Journal of Rough Sets and Data Analysis (IJRSDA), 4(3); edited by Nilanjan Dey; pages 55-70, copyright year 2017 by IGI Publishing (an imprint of IGI Global).

Chapter 22
Secure Group Message Transfer Stegosystem

Mahinder Pal Singh Bhatia
Netaji Subhas Institute of Technology, India

Manjot Kaur Bhatia
University of Delhi, India

Sunil Kumar Muttoo
University of Delhi, India

ABSTRACT

Grid environment is a virtual organization with varied resources from different administrative domains; it raises the requirement of a secure and reliable protocol for secure communication among various users and servers. The protocol should guarantee that an attacker or an unidentified resource will not breach or forward the information. For secure communication among members of a grid group, an authenticated message transferring system should be implemented. The key objective of this system is to provide a secure transferring path between a sender and its authenticated group members. In recent times, many researchers have proposed various steganographic techniques for secure message communications. This paper proposes a new secure message broadcasting system to hide the messages in such a way that an attacker cannot sense the existence of messages. In the proposed system, the authors use steganography and image encryption to hide group keys and secret messages using group keys in images for secure message broadcasting. The proposed system can withstand against conspiracy attack, message modification attack and various other security attacks. Thus, the proposed system is secure and reliable for message broadcasting.

DOI: 10.4018/978-1-7998-1763-5.ch022

1. INTRODUCTION

Security is one of an important issue and essential requirement in grid environment. Grid allows users from multiple domains to work in groups by sharing information with each other. Secure group communication is applicable in various applications such as interactive simulations, multiparty military actions, government discussions on critical issues and real time information services. To secure communication among members of a group working on collaborative tasks, grid environment requires implementation of additional security mechanisms. Secure group communication in grid needs to guarantee confidentiality and validity of the message to confirm the receiver that message is forwarded by the authorized user.

The main objective of secure group message transferring system is to create a secure environment between the sender and the authorized receivers for sharing some information in a secure way. In the secure group message transferring protocol, the message communication among the sender and the receivers forming the group must be confidential. Thus, only the authorized group members can extract the message, and the unauthorized members cannot access any important information. This brings the need of secure communication protocol responsible for generating secure group key and providing authenticated secure message transferring between group members. To provide these security functions, secure communication protocol needs to generate a group key/session key for the group members based on their secret information.

Our Secure group message transferring stegosystem (SGMS) protocol is based on steganography and image encryption technique to mask secure messages in such a way that an attacker could not know that any message is being communicated in the group. This paper extends our previous work (Bhatia et al., 2013) and proposes a new secure group message transferring stegosystem that can guard the group communication in grid environment against various security attacks, such as conspiracy attack, message modification attack. As a result, the proposed stegosystem not only has advantages of the secret message transferring system, but also is more protected and realistic in comparison to already proposed message transferring system. The remainder of this paper is organized as follows: Section 2 discusses group communication protocols already proposed by various researchers. Section 3 presents brief outline of our already proposed secure group communication protocol. The newly proposed stegosystem is presented in Section 4, while Sections 5 discusses its security features. Section 6 presents the simulation and experimental results and performance, respectively. Finally, Section 7 concludes the paper.

2. RELATED WORK

Researchers have proposed different protocols for secure group communication between grid entities. Researchers used either centralized or distributed group key management protocols for secure group communication. Most of the researchers have used encryption schemes/algorithms to provide secure group communication among various group members. Dual Level Key Management protocol (DLKM) that uses access Control Polynomial (ACP) and one-way functions to provide flexibility, security and hierarchical access control was proposed by Zoua (Zoua et al., 2007). Researchers used encryptions to update the group key for forward and backward secrecy. Li (Li et al., 2007) proposed a scalable service scheme using digital signatures and used Huffman binary tree to provide security and integrity. In this approach, Huffman binary tree is used to distribute and manage keys in VO and complete binary tree is used to manage keys in administrative domain. Park, (Park et al., 2010) have proposed an ID-based key distribution scheme that uses cryptographic algorithms to offer security and offer scalability. Li (Li et al., 2008) have proposed an authenticated encryption mechanism for group communication with basic characteristics of group communication in grid in terms of the basic theory of threshold signature. Several researchers have proposed various systems (Liao, 2007; Huang, 2010; Liaw, 1999) based upon different cryptographic techniques. Most of these systems encrypt the messages and send it to the members of its group. Liaw (Liaw, 1999) proposed a secure broadcasting cryptosystem based on the RSA and symmetric encryption algorithms, which allows addition of new users into the active groups. Tseng and Jan (Tseng and Jan, 2001) pointed out that Liaw's broadcasting system is not secure against conspiracy attack; an intruder can break its security and can obtain the master secret key. To overcome this problem, Tseng and Jan proposed a modified broadcasting cryptosystem. Masque and Peinado (Masque and Peinado, 2006) pointed out some problems of incorrect arithmetic in Tseng and Jan's broadcasting cryptosystem and presented a redefined Liaw's broadcasting cryptosystem. Zhu and Wu (Zhu and Wu, 2008) showed that Masque and Peinado broadcasting cryptosystem is still insecure, in that system an unauthorized user can obtain the secret session key of other group but did not provide any solution to that redefined Liaw's broadcasting cryptosystem.

2.1. Globus Toolkit: A Computational Grid Environment

Globus Toolkit is open source tool provided by the US R& D project Globus, it facilitates the construction of computational grids and grid based applications. The Globus ToolKit is used by many Grid Communities as a technology base (Foster and Kesselman, 1998). It allows sharing of resources, user authentication and communication. It includes components and protocols to provide basic set of services needed by Grid applications- resource management, information services, data management, and security. Grid Security Infrastructure (GSI), a part of open grid services architecture (OGSA) provides confidentiality and security based on public key encryption, X.509 certificates and the secure socket layer(OpenSSL) for authentication and secure communication over the Internet(Foster et al., 1998). The component GSI (Grid Security Layer) in Globus Toolkit is used to resolve various security issues. The GSI layer provides methods for authenticating grid users and resources, single sign on, data encryption, secure communication between grid users and delegation of authorities among others.

GSI uses public key cryptography scheme as the basis for executing above mentioned functionalities. Public key cryptography works on two keys in a way that one key is used to encrypt a message, the other key must be used to decrypt the message. The GSI assumes the user's private key to be stored in a file in the local computer's storage. To protect the private key from other users, the file containing the key is encrypted via a password. The other users need to know the password to decrypt the file.

GSI by default does not set up confidential communication between users. For secure communication GSI trust on mutual authentication process. When parties that need to communicate have certificates and both parties trust the signing authority, the two parties then can authenticate their identities to each other. This is known as mutual authentication. Once mutual authentication is over, users can communicate directly without the overhead of regular encryption and decryption. GSI can be used to set up a shared key for encryption when confidential communication is required.

3. BACKGROUND: PROPOSED PROTOCOL FOR SECURE GROUP COMMUNICATION

This section briefly describes the already proposed secure group communication protocol (SGCP) (Bhatia et al., 2013a). In SGC protocol, we considered a centralized key management center (KMC). Each user needs to submit an image IM to the KMC for registration in a grid group. KMC generates unique IDs and computes unique passwords for the users using the images submitted by the users. Each user's password is embedded in user's image and stego image (embedded password) is transferred to user. User uses this login information for authentication. After the completion of authentication process, KMC computes the group key and send it every member of the group for secure communication.

The computation of group key involves summation of soft dipole representation value S_I of every image IM. Soft dipole representation of an image IM is a function that uniquely represents that image[Chubb C. et al., 2002]. A soft dipole representation of an input image IM is a triple SI(d, α, β), where d is an integer-valued displacement and α and β are pixel intensities [Bhatia et al., 2013b]. The soft dipole representation of any one-dimensional image IM with N pixels can be calculated using equation (1), the displacement d ranges from 0 to N-1(N: total no. of pixels), so any value of the d can be chosen[Bhatia et al., 2013b].

N-1 N-1-d

$$S_I = \sum \left(\sum \left(I[r] \right) \left(I[r+d] \right) \right) \tag{1}$$

d=0 r=0

the displacement d ranges from 0 to N-1(N: total no. of pixels), so any value of the d can be chosen.

4. PROPOSED SECURE GROUP MESSAGE TRANSFERRING STEGOSYSTEM (SGMS)

This section proposes a new secure group message transferring stegosystem(SGMS) which is an extension of our previously proposed secure group communication protocol(SGCP) explained in Section 3. The main purpose of a message transferring system is to provide a secure communication channel to a sender for transferring messages to its intended receivers. In the group message transferring system, sender can share secret information with its group members by hiding it from other group members. Then, only group members of the sender's group can sense the presence of the message and can extract the message. The other grid users cannot acquire any important information from the forward message. Figure 1 shows the proposed secure group message transferring stegosystem.

Figure 1. SGMS architecture: Architecture of secure group message transferring stegosystem

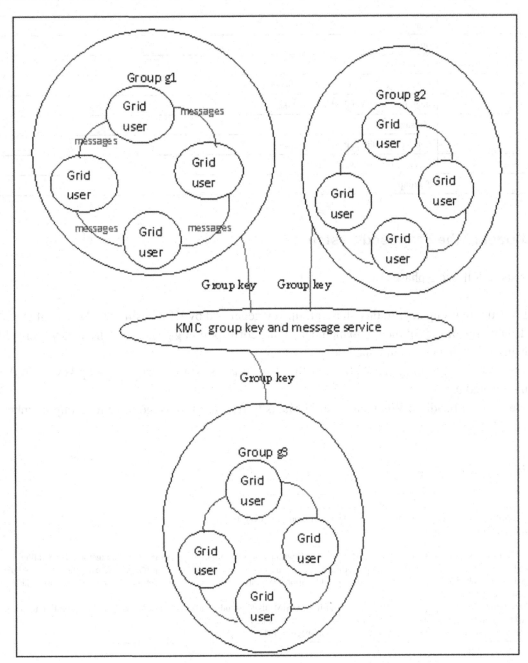

Table 1. Notations used

U_i	i^{th} user
IM	Image
GK	group key
GK_new	Updated group key on member join/leave
Stmg	stego image with embedded group key
M	Message
SIM	stego image with embedded message
ESIM	encrypted stego image SIM
g_i	i^{th} group

4.1. Model of the Proposed System

It consists of following phases

I. Embedding group key: In this phase group key generated by KMC using SGC protocol is embedded into the images of the group members of the corresponding group. The group key is embedded using DCT steganographic method.

II. Transferring group key: KMC transfer the stego-images (stmg) carrying group key to all the authenticated users.

III. Message embedding: When any user U_i wants to transfer a message M to its group members g_k: {U1, U2, ..,Um}:

Algorithm 1. Embedding

Input: cover image, stego key(i.e. group key), Message, iterations(for encryption)
Output: Encrypted-stego image

Step1. Ui embeds its message M into an image IMi using LSB with pseudorandom locations steganographic method. Embedding message bits in to the continuous pixel locations of the cover image can lead to serious security problems. To overcome this problem, message bits are embedded into the unique random pixel locations generated by the 'Random locations generator algorithm' (Table 2) using group key as stego key.
Step2. After embedding message, Ui encrypts the stego-image (SIM) using standard map and logistic map image encryption technique.
Step3. Ui transfer encrypted-stego image ESIM to its group members {U1, U2, ..,Um}.
(iv) Message extraction: To access the message hidden in image ESIM, users {U1, U2, ..,Um}

Algorithm 2. Extraction

Input: Encrypted-stego image, stego key, iterations (for encryption)
Output: original message

Step1. decrypts the image ESIM using image decryption method, resulting in stego-image SIM.
Step2. generate random locations using stego-key.
Step3. extract message from SIM using already shared extraction method.

Table 2. Pseudorandom locations generator algorithm [Johnson, 2000]

| Random locations generator: random[GK,IM]
{
j[1]=10
    For i=1 to m
    {
    a=j[i] div u
    b=j[i] mod u
    a=(a+h$_{k1}$(b)) mod v
    b=(b+h$_{k2}$(a)) mod u
    a=(a+h$_{k3}$(b)) mod v
    loc[i]=au+b
    j[i+1]=j[i]+5
    Print loc[i]
    }
} | Notations used in algorithm:
length(IM): total no of pixels in an image IM
j: j is any value between 1…. Length(IM)
u,v: length(IM) can be represented as length(IM)= u*v
m: total no of message bits
Gk: group key
GK is divided into three keys k1, k2, k3
h$_{k1}$(x): hash function value of x using key k1
h$_{k1}$(x)=x%k1 |

Figure 2. SGMS communication model1: shows the communication steps between the sender and the receivers

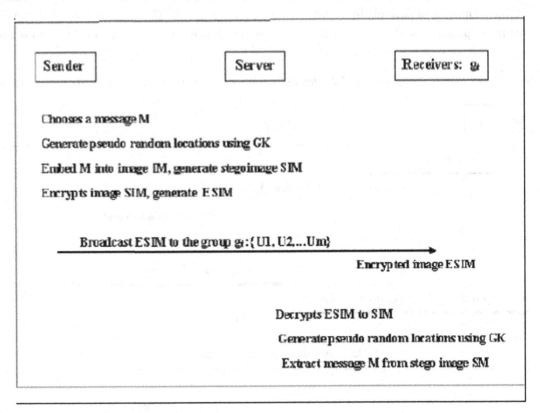

4.2. Secure Message Communication Between Grid Domains

In above proposed protocol groups are formed based on the users working on the same application. Grid environment allows users to change its group and join/leave any group. In our protocol, KMC is responsible for regenerating new group key when a new member joins or an old member leaves the group.

Our proposed protocol supports dynamic join/leave of the group members. To enables dynamism in the groups it provides facility of updating of group keys on change in the number of group members.

5. ANALYSIS OF PROPOSED ALGORITHMS

Analysis of algorithm indicates predicting the resource requirement of the algorithm. There are various resources associated with the execution of an algorithm such as memory, communication bandwidth and the most important computational time that we would like to measure. In computer science, the time complexity of an algorithm quantifies the amount of time taken by an algorithm to run as a function of the length of the string representing the input (Michael, 2006). In general, time complexity is used to compare the efficiency of several algorithms proposed for a problem. The time complexity of an algorithm mainly depends upon its input size and the input size depends on the problem. The running time

Figure 3. SGMS communication model 2: steps of communication when a user joins/leaves a group

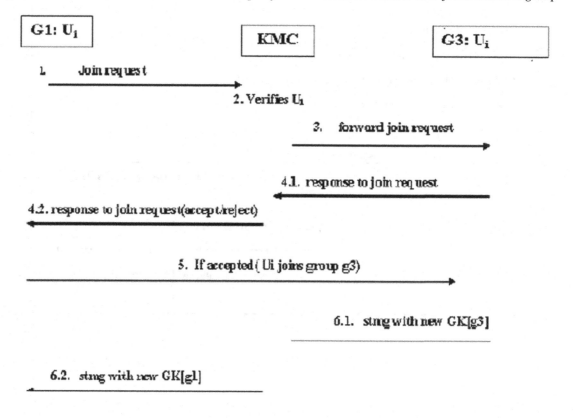

Algorithm 3. Group Key updation: User U_i of group g_j wants to join the group g_k

---

Input: User ID of U_i, g_j, g_k
Output: updated group keys of g_j and g_k i.e. GK_new$_j$, GK_new$_k$

Step1. U_i sends its request to KMC to leave group **g_j** and join group **g_k** with its user ID.
Step2. KMC verifies the identity of the user U_i.
Step3. After verification, KMC forwards its join request to members of group **g_k**.
Step4. KMC intimates U_i on acceptance of join request from members of group g_k, U_i then leaves group g_j and joins group g_k.
Step5. When a new member joins or an old member leaves the group, KMC regenerates the group key.
Step5.1. Updated group keys for gj and gk are:
The regeneration of group key of any group **g_i** involves re-computation of soft dipole representation value S_I again for every user's image IM_i of that group by changing the displacement factor d. Here, we changed the value of d randomly for every image using random sequence generator function. This gives unique value of **S_I** for same image also. For computation of new group key GK_new, summation is carried out on new S_I values of images of all the group members using equation no. 3.1 or 3.2 generating GK_updated .
If U_i left the group **g_j** and joined group **g_k**. KMC regenerates the group keys for groups **g_j** and group **g_k** as:
Step5.2. GK_updated[gj]= $\sum(S_{I(i)})$ where m=(1,2,...t$_j$)–U_i (group members for the
iem Jth group leaving U_i (2.1)
➢ *GK_new$_j$=XNOR(GK_updated[gj],Loc[i](**random[rand,IM$_j$]**)) (2.2)*
Step5.3. GK_updated[gk]= $\sum(S_{I(i)})$ where n=(1,2,...t$_j$)+U_i group members for
ien the Kth group including U_i (3.1)
➢ *GK_new$_k$=XOR(GK_updated[gk],(Loc[i](**random[rand,IM]**)) (3.2)*
Where i=1 …. Length(IM)
Step6. KMC embeds the **GK_new$_i$** into images of group members of ith group and **GK_new$_j$** into images of group members of jth group.
Step7. Transfer stego-images **stmg** hiding new group key to the members of the ith and jth groups.

Algorithm 4. GK_updated (Bhatia et. al., 2013b)

Input: No. of group members K, Images IM_1, IM_2, …. IM_K
Output: GK_updated

For i=1 to K
{
Generate random no. r(i) where r(i)= 1… N
For d=0 to r(i)
{
For j=0 to N 1 d
{
operations on pixels of IM_i
}
}
Compute $S_{I(i)}$
Gk_updated= $\sum(S_{I(i)})$
}

---

of an algorithm on a particular input is the number of steps executed and the steps in an algorithm are machine independent (cormen et. al., 2009). We generally focus on computing the worst case running time. Worst case time is the maximum running time for input size n and it assures that the algorithm can never take more time than the worst case time for any input. Big O notation is used to represent worst case time complexity of an algorithm (cormen et. al., 2012). Based on this notion, we computed the worst case time complexity for our proposed algorithms:

5.1. Complexity Analysis for Message Embedding Algorithm i.e. algo 4.1

Step 1: Generate m pseudo random locations for hiding m message bits.
   i.e. (m)
Step 2: Message is embedded into cover image using LSB steganography method. To embed message bits m in the cover image, m bits of the pixels at random locations in the cover image are replaced by the message bits.
   i.e. O(m)
Step 3: Image encryption of image obtained from step 2. The image encryption algorithm involves two steps.
   (i)   The no. of iterations t i.e. no. of times encryption function to be repeated on the image.
   (ii) The encryption function is applied on all the image pixels N.
       i.e. O(t*N)

Total time complexity of message embedding algorithm:
   Time complexity of the algorithm is sum of time complexities of all the above steps:

i.e. O(m+m+t*N) = O(2m+t*N)
   no. of message bits m and no. of iterations t, can be ignored as it is asymptotically very less than the no. of pixels in an image.
i.e. m <<N and t<<N
   so, ignoring m and t, worst case time complexity of the algorithm is: O(N)

5.2. Complexity Analysis for Message Extraction Algorithm i.e. algo 4.2

Message extraction algorithm includes all the steps of message embedding algorithm in reverse order. The worst case time complexity of message extraction algorithm is O(N).

5.3. Complexity Analysis for Group Key Updating Algorithm i.e. algo 4.3

Group Key updating algorithm generates new group key in case any user leaves a group or joins any new group. The group key updating includes algorithm 4.4: GK_updated.
   Complexity analysis for GK_updated i.e. algo 4.4
   Total time complexity:

$$O\left(\sum_{i=1}^{K} \left(r(i)(N - r(i)) \right) \right) \tag{4.1}$$

where r(i) denotes random number

$$= O\left(\sum_{i=1}^{K} (Nr(i) - r(i)^2 \right) = O\left(\sum_{i=1}^{K} (N\,E[r(i)] - E[r(i)]^2 \right) \tag{4.2}$$

where E[r(i)] denotes expected value of random number
Expected value of r(i) is the mean value of it's uniform distribution

Therefore $E\left[r\left(i\right)\right] = \sum_{j=1}^{N}\left(x_j p_j\right)$ (4.3)

where $x_j \in \{ x_1, x_2, x_3, \ldots\ldots x_N \}$ are the possible values of r(i)

$p_j \in \{ p_1, p_2, p_3, \ldots\ldots p_N \}$ are the probabilities of the value of x_j

because the probability of occurrence of each number is same=1/N

therefore $E\left[r\left(i\right)\right] = \sum_{j=1}^{N}\left(x_j \frac{1}{N}\right)$ (4.4)

$= \frac{1}{N}\sum_{j=1}^{N}x_j = \frac{1}{N}\left(1+2+3+\ldots\ldots+N\right)$ (4.5)

$= \frac{1}{N}\left[\frac{N\left(N+1\right)}{2}\right]$, because $\sum_{l=1}^{N}i = \left(\frac{N\left(N+1\right)}{2}\right)$ (4.6)

Substituting the value of $E\left[r\left(i\right)\right]$ in equation 4.2

$= O\left(\sum_{i=1}^{K}\left(\left(\frac{N\left(N+1\right)}{2}\right)-\left(\frac{N+1}{2}\right)^{2}\right)\right)$ (4.7)

$= O\left(\frac{1}{2}\sum_{i=1}^{K}\left(N^{2}+N-\frac{N^{2}}{2}-\frac{1}{2}+N\right)\right)$ (4.8)

$= O\left(\frac{1}{2}\sum_{i=1}^{K}\left(\frac{N^{2}}{2}+2N-\frac{1}{2}\right)\right)$ (4.9)

$= O\left(\frac{1}{4}\sum_{i=1}^{K}N^{2}+\sum_{i=1}^{K}N-\frac{1}{4}\sum_{i=1}^{K}1\right)$ (4.10)

$$= O\left(\frac{KN^2}{4} + KN - \frac{K}{4}\right) \tag{4.11}$$

Ignoring lower degree terms of N in equation 4.11

$$= O\ (KN^2) \tag{4.12}$$

Because number of users i.e. K are asymptotically very less than the number of pixels N in an image. i.e. K << N, ignoring K in equation 4.12

Worst case time complexity of Group Key updating algorithm is $O(N^2)$.

6. SECURITY OF THE PROPOSED PROTOCOL (SGMS)

6.1. Security Features

A new generated group key should be known only to the present group members. The proposed method of new group key generation fulfills the important security requirements of group key:

1. **Group Key Secrecy:** Even if the group key is changed *q* number of times, such as GK= {GK_1, GK_2, ..., GK_q}, it is computationally infeasible for unauthorized group member to compute any group key GK_i because computation of group key involves secret passwords of all the group members. The secret password of individual user is known to that user only. The group key computed using proposed protocol is secure against brute force attack. The brute force attack on the group key is handled by increasing the keysize of the group key. The keysize of the group key depends upon the keysize of the users' secret passwords that further depends upon the value of the displacement factor d ranges from 0 to N-1, as shown in equation 1. Here, in our proposed protocol we are choosing the unique value of d generated through random sequence generator, every time when we are updating the group key.

2. **Forward Secrecy:** means that new members will not be able to compute the already used old group keys. Our protocol ensures that it is computationally infeasible for any new group member to compute any old group key from the set of *q* old group keys such as GK={GK_1, GK_2, ..., GK_q }.When a new member joins/leaves a group, group key is updated for that group. Computation of new group involves generating new S_I value for the images of all the group members of that group. Calculations of S_I values of users' images depend upon the unique value of displacement factor d, generated by KMC using random sequence generator. This value is *XORED* with unique pixel location computed from the image of user U_i using algorithm 1 to generate new group key. So it is mathematically impracticable for any group member to compute new group key.

3. **Backward Secrecy:** Protocol ensures that any former group member should not be able to compute new group key for group with new set of group members. It is computationally infeasible for any user to know values of displacement factor d and compute the S_I values for all the present members of the group to compute GK_updated. The GK_updated is further *XNORED* with unique pixel location computed from the image of user U_i using algorithm 1 to generate new group key.

The attacker could not derive the group key because it is two-level secured

I.   It is computationally infeasible to generate group key as it is based on the passwords of group members and it is computed by trusted KMC.

II. The group key transferred to the group members is hidden into the images in such a way that attacker could not suspects the existence of it.

6.2. Security Analysis

1. Our protocol can handle group key modification attack. Since group key broadcasted to the group members is embedded into an image through steganography and it is infeasible for a human eye to detect the presence of information hidden in an image.

2. The proposed protocol is also secure from message modification attack with the use of two level security systems for hiding messages. First, the message is embedded into image using secure steganography technique and the embedding locations of the message bits depend upon the group key. Second, the stego image created after embedding message is encrypted using standard map and logistic map image encryption method.

3. The proposed protocol is secured from active attackers. An active attacker not able to extract the secret information can try to destroy it by applying image processing techniques. This can be avoided by using robust steganography technique. Here, we used robust steganographic system and stored group key in the discrete cosine transform coefficients of an image.

4. To protect the information from malicious attackers, the embedding method needs to be dependent on some secret key shared by sender and receiver. In our proposed protocol message bits are embedded into the image at pixel positions generated by the algorithm 1. This algorithm uses group key as secret key to generate the message embedding positions and only the group members can access the group key and message. So, proposed protocol is secured from malicious attackers.

7. SIMULATION RESULTS

For simulating the above proposed protocol, it is divided into following phases: (i) embedding group keys in users images (ii) broadcasting stego-images(stmg) with group keys (iii) extraction of group keys from stego-images by group users (iv) embedding message in image using group keys (v) encrypting stego-image(SIM) with message (vi) broadcasting encrypted image(ESIM) to group users.

7.1. Simulation of Proposed Protocol SGMS

The experiments are done considering five groups in grid environment with different number of users in each group. The simulation is done using java programming and Matlab. We used java programs for computing group keys with different no. of users. Matlab is used for embedding group keys, messages in the users' images and extracting group keys, messages from stego images (stmg, SIM). Matlab is also used for encryption of stego images SIM and decryption of encrypted images ESIM. It is assumed that the method used for decryption of encrypted image ESIM and extraction of information from the stego image(stmg) is already shared with the group members physically. The algorithm is tested on number of images of different images formats such as .jpg, .tif, .jpg and .png. The metric PSNR is used to measure the quality of the stego-image. The Peak-Signal-to-Noise Ratio (PSNR) is used to evaluate the visual quality of stego- images generated with the simulated method. PSNR is defined as follows:

$$PSNR = 10 \times \log 10 \frac{255^2}{MSE} \ dB \tag{5}$$

$$MSE = \frac{MSE_R + MSE_G + MSE_B}{3} \tag{6}$$

$$MSE_R = \sum_{i=0}^{M-1}\sum_{j=0}^{N-1} 1\left(X_r(i,j) - I'_r(i,j)^2\right) \tag{7}$$

where $X_r(i, j)$ represent the pixel values on the original image and $I'_r(i, j)$ signify the pixel values of the stego image located at (i, j) respectively. M and N represent height and width of the images. PSNR value is calculated to measure the similarity between cover and stego images, images with PSNR value greater than 30 dB is considered to be similar. In this case, it is hard to distinguish stego image from its corresponding cover image through human eyes. 7.2. Experimental ResultsTable 3 shows the group keys of five groups with different no. of group members. Table 4 shows the experimental results for the first three phases of the proposed protocol. Table 5 gives the experimental results for the next three phases of the proposed protocol. The PSNR of cover and stego image with embedded group key are shown in the Table 6. Table 7 gives the PSNR of cover and stego image with embedded message for proposed algorithm.

8. CONCLUSION

This paper proposes a protocol for secure message transferring in a group between the sender and the members of its group. Most of the researchers have used cryptography to provide secure group communication in grid environment. To overcome the weakness of cryptography that encrypted messages no

Table 3. Group keys of groups with different no. of users

Group ID	No. of users	Group key
g1	20	984969
g2	50	405487
g3	40	275923
g4	100	271098
g5	200	342226

Table 4. A user Ui left group g3 and moves to group g5

Group ID	No. of users	Group key	updated group key
g1	20	984969	
g2	50	405487	
g3	39	275923	427689
g4	100	271098	
g5	201	342226	267109

Table 5. A user Ui left group g4 and moves to group g2

Group ID	No. of users	Group key	updated group key
g1	20	984969	
g2	**51**	**405487**	**437665**
g3	39	275923	427689
g4	99	271098	166207
g5	**201**	**342226**	**267109**

Table 6. Group IDs, Cover image (IM), Group Key to be embedded, Stego image (SIM), PSNR of IM and SIM

Group ID	Image(IM)	Group Key	Stego-image(SIM)	PSNR
g1		984969		57
g2		405487		35
g3		275923		55
g4		271098		30
g5		342226		46

Table 7. Group IDs, Cover image (IM), message to be embedded, Stego image (SIM), PSNR of IM and SIM, Encrypted image (ESIM)

Group ID	Image(IM)	Message(M)	Stego-image(SIM)	PSNR	Encrypted Image (ESIM)
G1		After verification, KMC		45	
G1		KMC verifies the identity of the user U_i		35	
G2		The experiments are done		43	
G2		the file is embedded		48	
G3		Grid environment allows users can change its group		37	
G3		Our proposed protocol supports dynamic join/leave		41	
G4		Join these two files		38	
G4		Enter the data in these two files		44	
G5		Group key is updated		35	

matter how strong are arouse the suspicion, here, we used image steganography for hiding the group key and messages and transferring it securely to the group members. The protocol is secure against session key modification attack and message modification attack; message broadcasted to the group members is dual secured. To enhance the security of the communicated message, protocol embeds the message into image and further encrypts the stego-image. Receivers on the other end receive the encrypted image. The proposed protocol is suitable for secure message communication in grid environment. The protocol is simulated using Java programming language and Matlab.

REFERENCES

Bhatia, M., Muttoo, S. K., & Bhatia, M. P. S. (2011). Secure group communication protocol. *International Journal of Advanced Engineering Sciences and Technologies, 11*(1), 221–225.

Bhatia, M., Muttoo, S. K., & Bhatia, M. P. S. (2012). Steganography based secure communication. *Proceedings of the Second International Springer Conference on Soft Computing for Problem Solving (SocProS 2012)*, India.

Bhatia, M., Muttoo, S. K. and Bhatia, M.P.S. (2013a, May). Secure Group Communication with Hidden Group Key. *Information Security Journal: A Global Perspective, 22*(1), 21-34.

Bhatia, M., Muttoo, S. K., & Bhatia, M. P. S. (2013b). Secure Requirement Prioritized Grid Scheduling Model. *International Journal of Network Security, 15*(6), 478–483.

Burmester, M., & Desmedt, Y. G. (1994). A Secure and Efficient Conference Key Distribution System. Proceedings of Eurocrypt '94 Workshop Advances in Cryptology (pp. 275-286).

Chubb, C., & Yellott, J. I. (2002). Dipole statistics of discrete finite images: Two visually motivated representation theorems. *Journal of the Optical Society of America. A, Optics, Image Science, and Vision*, (May): 2002. PMID:11999958

Cody, E., Sharman, R., Rao, R. H., & Upadhyaya, S. (2008). Security in grid computing: A review and synthesis. *Decision Support Systems, 44*(4), 749–764. doi:10.1016/j.dss.2007.09.007

Cormen, T. H., Leiserson, C. E., Rivest, R. L., & Stein, C. (2009). *Introduction to Algorithms* (3rd ed.). MIT Press and McGraw-Hill.

Foster, I., Kesselman, C., Tsudik, G., & Tuecke, S. (1998). A security architecture for computational grids. *Proceedings of fifth ACM Conference on Computers and Security* (pp. 83-91). 10.1145/288090.288111

Huang, K., & Zhang, D. (2010). DHT-based lightweight broadcast algorithms in large scale computing infrastructures. *Future Generation Computer Systems, 26*(3), 291–303. doi:10.1016/j.future.2009.08.013

Johnson, N. F., & Katzenbeisser Stefan, C. (2000). *A survey of steganographic techniques*. Artech House Books.

Li, Y., Jin, H., Zou, D., Chen, J., & Han, Z. (2007). A scalable service scheme for secure group communication in grid. *Proceedings of 31st Annual International Computer Software and Applications Conference (COMPSAC 2007)* (pp. 31 – 38). 10.1109/COMPSAC.2007.38

Li, Y., Jin, H., Zou, D., Liu, S., & Han, Z. (2008). An authenticated encryption mechanism for secure group communication in grid. *Proceedings of the International Conference on Internet Computing in Science and Engineering*, USA (pp. 298-305). 10.1109/ICICSE.2008.80

Liao, L., & Manulis, M. (2007). Tree-based group key agreement framework for mobile adhoc networks. *Future Generation Computer Systems*, *23*(6), 787–803. doi:10.1016/j.future.2007.01.001

Liaw, H. (1999). Broadcasting cryptosystem in computer networks. *Computers & Mathematics with Applications (Oxford, England)*, *37*(6), 85–87. doi:10.1016/S0898-1221(99)00078-4

Martinelli, F., & Mori, P. (2010). On usage control for GRID systems. *Future Generation Computer Systems*, *26*(7), 1032–1042. doi:10.1016/j.future.2009.12.005

Masque, J., & Peinado, A. (2006). 'Cryptanalysis of improved Liaw's broadcasting cryptosystem'. *Journal of Information Science and Engineering*, *22*, 391–399.

Park, H., Yi, W. S., & Lee, G. (2010). Simple ID-based key distribution scheme. *Proceedings of Fifth International Conference on Internet and Web Applications and Services* (pp. 369–373). 10.1109/ICIW.2010.61

Perez, J., Bernabe, J., Calero, J., Clemente, F., Perez, G., & Skarmeta, A. (2011). Semantic-based authorization architecture for Grid. *Future Generation Computer Systems*, *27*(1), 40–55. doi:10.1016/j.future.2010.07.008

Sipher, M. (2006). *Introduction to the Theory of Computation*. Course Technology Inc.

Smith, M., Schmidt, M., Fallenbeck, N., Dornemann, T., Schridde, C., & Freisleben, B. (2009). Secure on-demand grid computing. *Future Generation Computer Systems*, *25*(3), 315–325. doi:10.1016/j.future.2008.03.002

Tseng, Y., & Jan, J. (2001). Cryptanalysis of Liaw's broadcasting cryptosystem. *Computers & Mathematics with Applications (Oxford, England)*, *41*(12), 1575–1578. doi:10.1016/S0898-1221(01)00122-5

Zhu, W., & Wu, C. (2008). Security of the redefined Liaw's broadcasting cryptosystem. *Computers & Mathematics with Applications (Oxford, England)*, *56*(7), 1665–1667. doi:10.1016/j.camwa.2008.03.025

Zou, D., Zheng, W., Long, J., Jin, H., & Chen, V. (2010). Constructing trusted virtual execution environment in P2P grids. *Future Generation Computer Systems*, *26*(5), 769–775. doi:10.1016/j.future.2009.05.020

Zoua, X., Dai, Y. S., & Rana, X. (2007, July). Dual-Level Key Management for secure grid Communication in dynamic and hierarchical groups. Future Generation Computer Systems. *Science Direct*, *23*(6), 776–786.

This research was previously published in the International Journal of Information Security and Privacy (IJISP), 9(4); edited by Michele Tomaiuolo and Monica Mordonini; pages 59-76, copyright year 2015 by IGI Publishing (an imprint of IGI Global).

Chapter 23
Implementation and Evaluation of Steganography Based Online Voting System

Lauretha Rura
Swinburne University of Technology, Malaysia

Biju Issac
Teesside University, UK

Manas Kumar Haldar
Swinburne University of Technology, Malaysia

ABSTRACT

Though there are online voting systems available, the authors propose a new and secure steganography based E2E (end-to-end) verifiable online voting system, to tackle the problems in voting process. This research implements a novel approach to online voting by combining visual cryptography with image steganography to enhance system security without degrading system usability and performance. The voting system will also include password hashed-based scheme and threshold decryption scheme. The software is developed on web-based Java EE with the integration of MySQL database server and Glassfish as its application server. The authors assume that the election server used and the election authorities are trustworthy. A questionnaire survey of 30 representative participants was done to collect data to measure the user acceptance of the software developed through usability testing and user acceptance testing.

1. INTRODUCTION

One of the most important concerns in elections is to have an efficient and secure voting procedure. Even though it could be achieved by implementing an e-voting system, its ability to complete voting process faster than the paper ballot procedure alone does not guarantee its security. E-voting systems must be able to earn user's trust and confidence by providing enhanced security features without affecting us-

DOI: 10.4018/978-1-7998-1763-5.ch023

ability, efficiency and reliability. The system should offer some level of transparency to the user without allowing any breach of trust and privacy. To fulfil this condition, e-voting systems must provide both individual and universal verifiability. Individual verifiability is the ability of an e-voting system to offer vote verifiability to the voter through the implementation of vote receipt, whereas universal verifiability is the ability to offer election transparency to its users. Such systems are categorised under End-to-End (E2E) verifiable voting system (Adida, 2008). End-to-end verifiability represents a change in electronic voting, allowing a way to verify the integrity of the election by permitting the voters to use the system generated information, rather than trusting that the system has behaved correctly (Ryan, Schneider & Teague, 2015). In this paper, we propose an improved E2E verifiable voting system called as eVote software. This voting software could deliver a secure, reliable, convenient, and efficient voting system. As a research objective, we want to improve the quality of election procedure in an electronic voting system that relates to security and usability aspects, by using visual cryptography and image steganography in the system architecture. We also want to evaluate the developed online system through usability testing.

The outcome of evaluating an Internet voting system in the Canton of Zurich shows the need to rely on more advanced technology and centralised infrastructure (Beroggi, 2014). In the work (Azougaghe, Hedabou & Belkasmi, 2015) an electronic voting system based on homomorphic encryption to ensure privacy and confidentiality are proposed. The eVote software differs from previous online voting systems with the usage of cryptography and steganography to secure the data transmission during the election. The difference between cryptography and steganography lies in the way data is processed. Cryptography generates a ciphertext, while steganography produces a stego-object which is not perceptible by Human Visual System (HVS). In electronic voting, cryptography is a commonly used technique as it is a good defence against threats. In this paper, the authors introduce a novel approach to enhance E2E Voting System's security by combining visual cryptography with image steganography. Image steganography is chosen due to its capability to use data transmitted over the network. During the election voting process, the image steganography protects the existence of the message as a secret (Wang and Wang, 2004), offering a good solution for threats and risks that might occur. The combination of these two schemes is expected to produce an improved and secure approach (Morkel et al., 2005). Petcu & Stoichescu (2015) proposed a mobile biometric-based design that uses techniques such as Secure Sockets Layer encryption, certificate keys and security tokens. This paper is organised as follows. Section 2 discusses the E2E verifiable voting system and related works, section 3 is the proposed eVoting system, section 4 is the software testing and the usability analysis done, and section 5 is the conclusion and limitations.

2. E2E VERIFIABLE VOTING SYSTEM

Various E2E systems have been proposed and are widely used these days (Ryan et al., 2009; Chaum, 2004; Adida, 2008; Chaum et al., 2008; Hubbers, Jacobs, & Pieters, 2005). A verifiable voting system allows blind voters and voters in remote locations to cast fully secret ballots in a verifiable way (Burton, Culnane & Schneider, 2016). In principle, E2E voting system offers assurance to the voters over their cast vote. This is done by distributing vote receipt of encoded cast vote to each of the voters for verification purpose. To support this verification process, E2E systems implemented bulletin board which is a secure append-only broadcast media where each of the encoded votes would be posted once the voters completed the voting process. To verify their cast votes, they need to match the encoded value on their receipt against the values shown on the bulletin board. However, the vote receipt cannot be used as a

Figure 1. Basic E2E voting system's mechanism

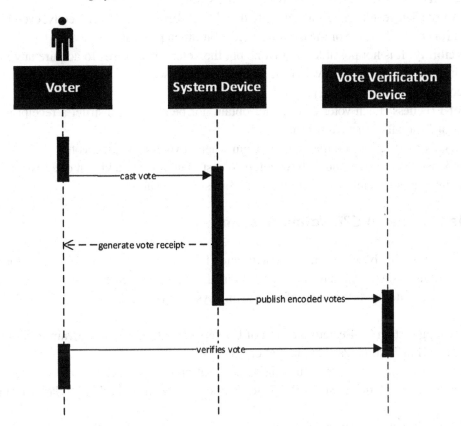

proof of vote buying or vote coercion because it is encoded. As a result, the E2E voting system would protect the voter's privacy and supports incoercibility that preserves the integrity and impartiality of the election result. This mechanism is illustrated in Figure 1.

2.1. E2E Voting Systems Requirements

Every e-voting system has numerous requirements to be fulfilled to ensure its primary characteristics – individual and universal verifiability is intact. These requirements are mostly categorized as non-functional requirements. Listed as follows are the non-functional requirements of E2E verifiable voting system in general (Fujioka et al., 1992; Benaloh, 2006; Gritzalis, 2002; Cetinkaya, 2008; Kofler et al., 2003; Aditya, 2005):

- **Completeness:** All valid votes are counted correctly.
- **Soundness:** A dishonest voter cannot disrupt the voting.
- **Privacy:** All votes must be secret.
- **Un-Reusability:** No voter can vote twice.
- **Eligibility:** Only authorised voters are allowed to vote.
- **Fairness:** Nothing must affect the voting. (i.e. no one can indicate the tally before the votes are counted)

- **Verifiability:** No one can falsify the result of the voting.
- **Robustness:** The result reflects all submitted and well-formed ballots correctly, even if some voters and (or) possibly some of the dishonest election officials cheat.
- **Incoercibility:** It is not possible for anyone but the voters themselves to acquire any information regarding their secret ballots; even if the voters are untrustworthy (the election process is assumed to be conducted by the voter in private).
- **Receipt-Freeness:** Each voter can neither obtain nor be able to construct a receipt to prove the content of their ballot to anyone else.
- **Mobility:** No restrictions on the location from where a voter can cast a vote.
- **Convenience:** The system must allow voters to cast their votes quickly, in one session with minimal equipment or special skills without compromising its usability.

2.2. Related Works on E2E Voting Systems

E2E voting systems vary based on their security and flexibility levels. In this section, four different types of E2E voting systems that have been used in medium to large-scale real-world elections will be discussed to give a better understanding of E2E voting system. They are:

1. Helios voting system for Recteur election of Université Catholique de Louvain in Belgium,
2. Scantegrity II in Takoma Park municipal election,
3. Student Council election at Princeton University that makes use of Prêt à Voter system, and
4. Rijnland Internet Election System (RIES) for public election in Netherlands (Carback et al., 2010).

Helios Voting System is an open-source web-based voting system that offers verifiable online elections (Adida, 2008). It was designed to ensure a clean election setting through the open-audit election, unlike a typical traditional election where only the election officials are entitled to do the observation throughout the election process. Its latest version offers a better approach to protecting system's privacy by appointing multiple trustees, given the main assumption that the trustees will remain truthful. This enhancement was inspired by the simple, verifiable voting protocol proposed by Benaloh, in which they implemented Sako-Killian mix-net scheme and threshold decryption cryptosystem. Each trustee has to decrypt the final tally of the election by using advanced cryptographic techniques. This open-audit election also ensures universal verifiability. Individual verifiability is done through the implementation of vote (receipt) verification feature called ballot tracking centre where users can verify whether their votes have been received and tallied correctly. This vote receipt is shown to the users in ciphertext format.

Unlike Helios, Scantegrity II increases election integrity through a novel use of confirmation codes printed on ballots in invisible inks (Chaum et al., 2008). It is a practical enhancement for the initial optical scan voting systems – Punchscan and Scantegrity. The physical ballot of Scantegrity II consists of a voting portion and a receipt portion. Just as the traditional paper ballot voting procedure, the voters are given conventional paper ballot where they need to mark their chosen candidate with a special pen that uses invisible ink. This technology allows the voters to retain their receipts in a secure and secret manner with the help of unique confirmation codes on each ballot that no attackers would be able to coerce. The confirmation codes on voter's ballot are kept secret and will only be visible to the voters when they cast their votes. No information regarding the confirmation codes would be accessible to anyone before the votes are cast. Due to this feature, Scantegrity II can earn more trust and confidence of the voters which results in individual verifiability by the voters themselves. Besides that, the system also provides universal verifiability for everyone to reconfirm the computation of the tally and ensures that votes are not altered or deleted for manipulating the final tally of a particular election. Through the implementation of invisible ink in its vote verification feature, Scantegrity II could prevent some of the issues raised by the Punchscan and Scantegrity, like phantom votes and randomization attack.

Besides introducing Scantegrity II and its predecessors, Chaum also published a paper on Secret-Ballot Receipt Election (2004) which inspired Peter Ryan and his fellow researchers to develop Prêt a Voter System (2009). It implemented the same concept as Chaum's secret-ballot receipt scheme with visual cryptography approach proposed by Naor and Shamir (1994) in a simpler way. Prêt a Voter System was introduced to provide more accurate and faster tallying process to cut unnecessary election cost and to increase voter participation. The election auditability feature allows any of the system's users including the audit teams to evaluate its integrity by checking distinct stages of voter authentication, ballot preparation and vote processing. This system supports both universal and individual verifiability. Similar to other E2E voting systems, Prêt à Voter assure the voters that their votes have not been altered. Votes were collected and counted correctly in the tally by giving each of the voters a unique encrypted receipt. This receipt will not leak out the ballot; it can only be used to check the vote status against the read-only bulletin board. With the support of some security components, vote verifiability could be ensured. These security techniques give a better security where internal sources of threats could be anticipated and handled properly. The security components include encryption schemes such as RSA, ElGamal and Paillier and few other cryptographic methods like threshold decryption cryptosystem, zero-knowledge proofs, homomorphic encryption, etc. Thus, the vote would remain secret, and the possibilities of election fraud could be averted.

The last E2E voting system that we want to discuss is RIES (Rijnland Internet Election System). Similar to other E2E voting systems, the RIES was developed to increase the actual number of voters participating and to decrease the unnecessary cost of the conventional election via mail (Hubbers, Jacobs & Pieters 2005). The system was initially designed by Herman Robers for the completion of his master's thesis (Robers 1998). It was then implemented at a local election in the Delft University of Technology. Soon after Hoogheemraadschap van Rijnland, a local water management authority in Netherlands continued its development. RIES allows eligible voters to cast their votes in two distinct techniques - either by mail or electronically. Based on this key feature RIES allows its users to independently verify the election's result. RIES voting system which was implemented in water boards election differs from the initial system by Robers because of the implementation of some features to ensure that it provides internet voting in a simple, straightforward and transparent way without sacrificing the system's reliability, performance and maintenance cost. Those changes are the elimination of multifunction smartcard to authenticate the voters, which was substituted by digitalized secret key and the supplementary feature of vote by regular mail integration and additional user's type in the system. The use of RIES is abolished as security problems were found in the implementation.

As discussed, all E2E voting systems were designed to fulfil two main objectives, to provide individual-verifiability (also known as voter-verifiability) and universal-verifiability. The four voting systems reviewed are equipped with both features. However, the authors are proposing a novel E2E voting system that is capable of fulfilling all the requirements of the E2E voting system without compromising its integrity, security and usability.

3. THE PROPOSED SYSTEM

The eVote software is an improved version of the existing end to end verifiable voting system. While the existing E2E voting systems cater to different scales of the election, eVote is intended to assist the voting process in small to medium scale election. It not only offers secure and reliable voting system, but it also provides a flexible platform for the election officials to set up and maintain it based on their needs. System users are divided into three distinct types (levels) – voters, polling officers and system administrators. Its technology and system stages are described below.

3.1. System Technology

The eVote voting system is built as a web application that can be accessed through a computer or a tablet. Due to its low platform dependency as well as other characteristics such as security, robustness and scalability, Java EE 6 has been chosen for the eVote's system architecture. Security is very important in the development of an E2E Verifiable Voting System. Voting procedures in an online election rely on various information security building blocks that have to do with cryptography. Cryptography is used due to its general defence against electoral frauds like ballot box tampering and other attacks. We also introduce steganography to complement the cryptography schemes. Steganography offers better protection against threats and attacks similar to vote tampering by maintaining secret communication between two parties (client-side and server-side). It is used to protect the data transmitted between the voter and the server to ensure that it would not be accessible to anyone but the voters. Image steganography is used in our proposed system. The various implemented technologies are discussed as follows.

3.2. Password Hashed-Based Scheme

Password hashed-based scheme is applied to secure user's password in registration and authentication stage. It does not require extensive computation, yet it is proven to be cryptographically secure (Wagner & Goldberg, 2000). Hashed-based algorithms are one-way functions, and the ciphertext form of hashed value is not reversible into the original plaintext. The server is only required to compare the hashed value calculated from user input with the hashed value stored in the database for user authentication. To enhance this protocol and make it even more difficult to be compromised by known attacks (like dictionary and brute force attack on stored pre-computed passwords), salt value and key stretching are implemented alongside its algorithms. To generate a completely secure salt value, reliable Pseudo-Random Number Generator (PRNG) is used. In eVote's development, Java EE SecureRandom Class was used with 24 bytes of salt value. However, even with the enhancement of salt value, the intruder still can steal the user's password by running dictionary or brute-force attacks on each password hashed. Therefore, PBKDF2 key stretching technique is introduced to strengthen the password. In Java EE, SecretKeyFactory Class supports this technique. This class constructs secret keys by using PBKDF2 function found in RSA Laboratories' Public-Key Cryptography Standard (PKCS) #5 v2.0. The standard name for this secret-key algorithm in Java documentation is PBKDF2WithHmacSHA1.

3.3. Visual Cryptography

Visual cryptography (Naor & Shamir, 1994) was implemented to prevent vote buying or selling, as well as vote coercion by providing direct assurance to each of the voters through digital vote receipt. The plaintext (in this case the ballot), will be encrypted to two shares of ciphertext. The ciphertext has two separated layers of pixel symbols. For an additional layer of security of the ciphertext shares, Java EE SecureRandom Class was applied in secret message distribution over the shares. This class produces cryptographically strong random numbers by implementing its Pseudo-Random Number Generator (PRNG) algorithm - SHA1PRNG. It uses the SHA-1 hash function as the foundation of the PRNG. One share will be given to the voter as their vote receipt, and the other share is to be stored in the database. To decrypt these shares, visual cryptography decryption algorithm is to be executed. This mechanism was adopted from Chaum's secret-ballot receipt (Chaum, 2004). A simple amendment is made to the applied mix-net scheme used by Chaum (2004) due to its extensive process.

3.4. Threshold Decryption Cryptosystem

Even with the implementation of cryptography based security, attacks and threats still cannot be averted. There are enormous numbers of possible attacks in a remote e-voting system. Besides using visual cryptography and password hashed-based scheme, the eVote software also implemented threshold decryption cryptosystem as an additional layer of security. Shamir developed threshold decryption cryptosystem in 1979. A (k, n) threshold scheme secures and provides reliable key management for a cryptographic system. By having robust security and protection over the key management itself, the security of a cryptographic system itself could be ensured. Threshold scheme would be implemented in the ballot decryption process of the tallying stage to ensure that only authorised personnel can have access to the vote tallying process. To perform this decryption process, the private key, which has been divided and distributed to a few appointed personnel, must be merged before each of the election officials as well as the election administrator can gain access to the summary ballot list which is also known as the 'ballot box'.

3.5. Image Steganography

Steganography is the science of hiding information when two parties communicate, where others in between would be unaware of the hidden information. Image steganography provides an enhanced security technique of data encoding with the digital image file as the cover file. Based on our previous work (2011), F5 image steganography algorithm (Westfeld, 2001) as in Figure 2, is considered to be more efficient for secure data transmission compared to the other image steganography schemes.

F5 Steganography technique has better characteristics compared to the other image steganography algorithms namely - LSB, Palette-based and Spread Spectrum. One of the evaluations conducted was the comparison of initial and stego-image sizes for different image steganography techniques as shown in Figure 3 and F5 looks better overall. The F5 stego-image size is small and hence can transmit the embedded stego-image to the election server faster (Rura, Issac & Haldar, 2011). The other comparison is carried out to examine the robustness of each image steganography techniques against visual attack and statistical attacks namely - Regular Singular (RS) analysis and Binary Similarity Measures (BSM) test respectively.

Figure 2. Message encoding process of F5 steganography algorithm
Westfeld, 2001.

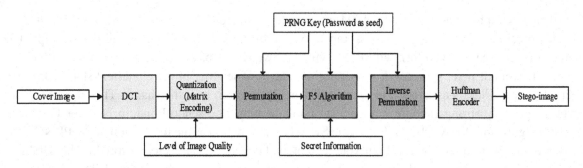

Figure 3. Comparison of initial and stego-image size on different implementation of image steganography techniques

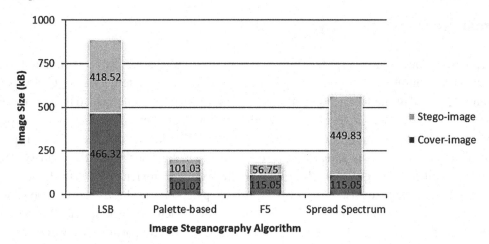

Based on the results displayed in Table 1, where robustness of each image steganography methods is ranked from low to high, it can be seen that F5 is not highly subject to visual attack. F5 also eliminates the possibility of Chi-square (χ^2) attack (Bateman, 2008). Considering Figure 3 and Table 1, F5 image steganography algorithm was chosen in our system. Fridrich, Goljan & Hogea (2002) explained breaking the F5 algorithm in their paper, but the authors Fard, Akbarzadeh-T & Varasteh-A (2006) discusses a new genetic algorithm (GA) approach for secure steganography.

3.6. The System Stages

The electoral process in the eVote software consisted of five stages – registration, authentication, voting, tallying and vote verification. The process flow diagram of the software is shown in Figure 4. Further explanation of each stage of the software is as follows.

Table 1. Robustness of different image steganography methods to visual and statistical attacks

Image Steganography Methods	Steganalysis Method Used	Visual Attack	Statistical Attack
LSB	RS Analysis	Low	High
Palette-based	BSM Test	Low	High
F5	BSM Test	Medium	High
Spread Spectrum	BSM Test	High	High

Figure 4. Process flow diagram of the eVote software system

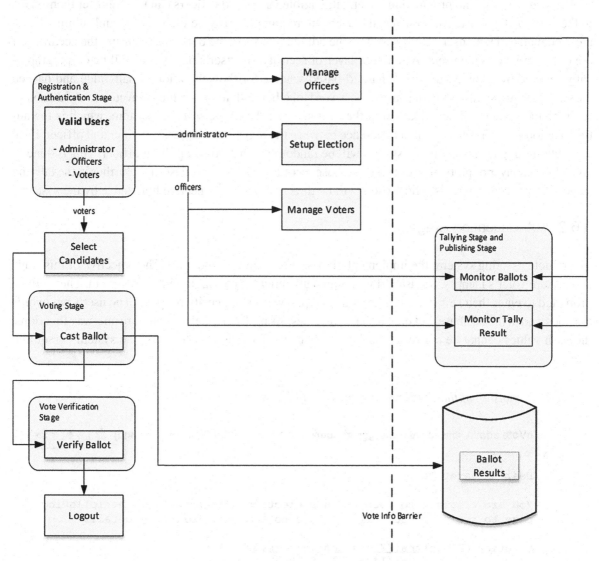

3.6.1. Registration Stage

In this stage, all constraints for the election are prepared by the voters and polling officers. Before this stage, system administrators must prepare the election setup by adding the details of the election and the candidates for each election category. Besides that, the system administrators also need to add the records of eligible voters and polling officers in the database. This record includes their username, Identification Card (IC) number and valid email address. Upon successful attempts, eligible users will receive emails from system administrator notifying their eligibility to register into the eVote system as shown in Figure 5.

By accessing the link provided in the email, eligible voters and officers can now register themselves in the system. To register themselves, the users are required to provide their details and submit. These are then matched with user details saved by the administrators in the database to ensure the accuracy of the details given by the users. As another layer of security, the user's passwords will be cryptographically secured by applying password hashed-based scheme for the generation of salt value and hashed password. By using this, only the hashed password together with its salt value is saved into the database. Its implementation will be explained in the next stage of the eVote software system, which is the authentication stage. There is a slight difference between the registration process of voter and officer. Each voter attempting to register in the system will be randomly assigned to a polling officer. This is done as an additional layer of protection over the database records which will be described further in the tallying stage. After successful registration, users will be directed to their respective homepage by the system.

3.6.2. Authentication Stage

In a remote e-voting system, the implementation of this stage is mandatory. The objective of this stage is to ensure voter's identity. Registered voters are authenticated by logging into the system. They will be prompted to enter their self-defined username and password for security purpose. The user's passwords are not saved in the database, but only its hashed values. As hash-based algorithms are one-way functions, the hash values cannot be converted back to a plaintext. To authenticate users, the system is required

Figure 5. Screenshot of the email received by an eligible voter

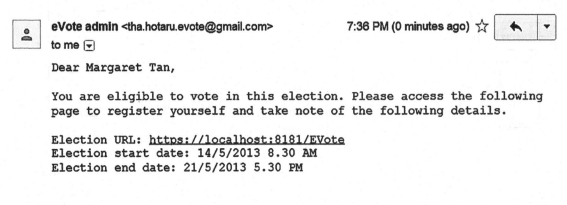

Figure 6. Screenshot of voter homepage upon successful registration

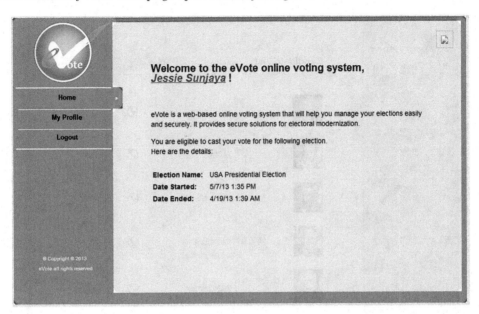

to compare the hashed value calculated from user input with the hashed value stored in the database. Once a user has been identified as a registered voter and has successfully logged into the system, he will see a welcome screen which shows the user account status and a menu panel where a user can navigate through features offered depending on the user level. Figure 6 shows the homepage screenshot for a voter.

3.6.3. Voting Stage

This stage is carried out by forming a secured ballot electronically and sending it to the election server where all the ballots would be collected and stored. After completing the two stages mentioned above, voters can then log on to the system and access the voting page. They can cast their vote by selecting their desired candidates for each category listed on that page. The voter's ballot is generated every time the chosen candidates are reviewed or updated. Figure 7 shows the voting page, where the voter can choose one candidate.

During the ballot generation, F5 image steganography algorithm would be applied as shown in Figure 8. The voter's chosen candidates would be encrypted in a stego-image format for their ballot. This ballot will, later on, be sent over to the tally server.

Once received by the server, the ballot would be decrypted to reveal the candidate names before they are encrypted again with visual cryptography as an additional security level to earn voter's direct trust by providing the vote receipt. The decrypted stego-image (ballot) would be encrypted with visual cryptography technique by splitting the vote into two shares. The stand-alone share would not reveal any information to anyone, but once the shares are overlaid or combined using a visual cryptography decryption algorithm, the voter's casted vote would be revealed. Basically each voter would be given one layer or share of the image as their receipt which will be sent to their respective email account as displayed in Figure 9, while the other separated layer of the vote would be kept by the administrator for ballot counting purpose and to disconnect the relation of each voter with their own ballot.

Figure 7. Screenshot of voting page accessible only for the voters

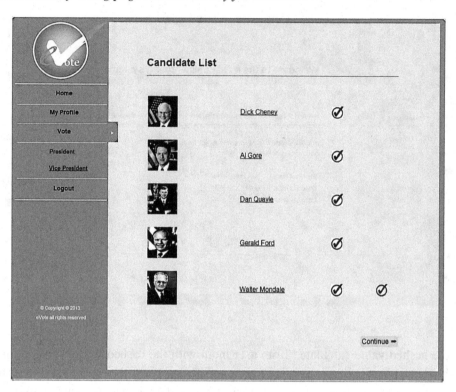

Figure 8. Pseudo-code of F5 Image steganography algorithm applied in the voting stage
Provos & Honeyman, 2003.

Input: message, shared secret, cover image
Output: stego-image
initialize PRNG with shared secret
permutate DCT coefficients with PRNG
determine k from image capacity
calculate code word length $n \leftarrow 2k - 1$
while data left to embed **do**
get next k-bit message block
   repeat
   $G \leftarrow \{n$ non-zero AC coefficients$\}$
   $s \leftarrow k$-bit hash f of LSB in G
   $s \leftarrow s \oplus k$-bit message block
     if $s \neq 0$ **then**
       decrement absolute value of DCT coefficient Gs
       insert Gs into stego image
     end if
   until $s = 0$ or $Gs \neq 0$
insert DCT coefficients from G into stego image
end while

Figure 9. Screenshot of the voter's vote receipt received by the voter

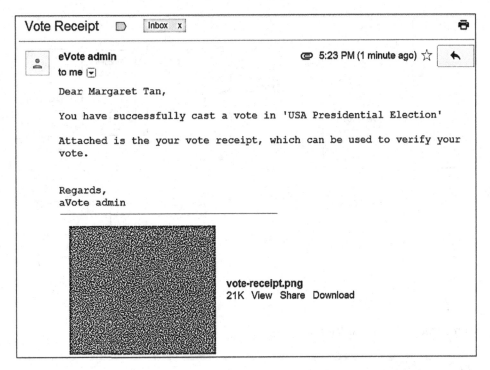

In the eVote software, the voting stage process is finished when the voting summary page is shown. The overall process flow of the eVote's voting stage is shown in Figure 10.

3.6.4. Tallying Stage

Tallying stage follows the voting stage. After the votes are cast, ballots are securely stored in the database. Users cannot access the ballots before the completion of the tallying stage. The tally determined at this stage is obtained by polling officers with help from system administrators. Each polling officers holds a unique secret key to retrieve ballot records from the database. These keys are pre-distributed by the system administrators during the election setup. System administrators generate these keys by utilising UUID utility.

To access the tally list, polling officers must perform 'decryption' process by merging their secret keys. This method is called the threshold decryption cryptosystem (Shamir, 1979). Only after each of the polling officers has submitted their secret keys, the result tally list (bulletin board) is accessible to the system administrators and the polling officers for monitoring. This tally list is only readable and does not show any relation between the ballot and its voter. Threshold scheme is implemented in the ballots decryption process to ensure that only the authorised personnel can count the vote. The tally is shown in Figure 11.

Figure 10. Process flow diagram of voting stage

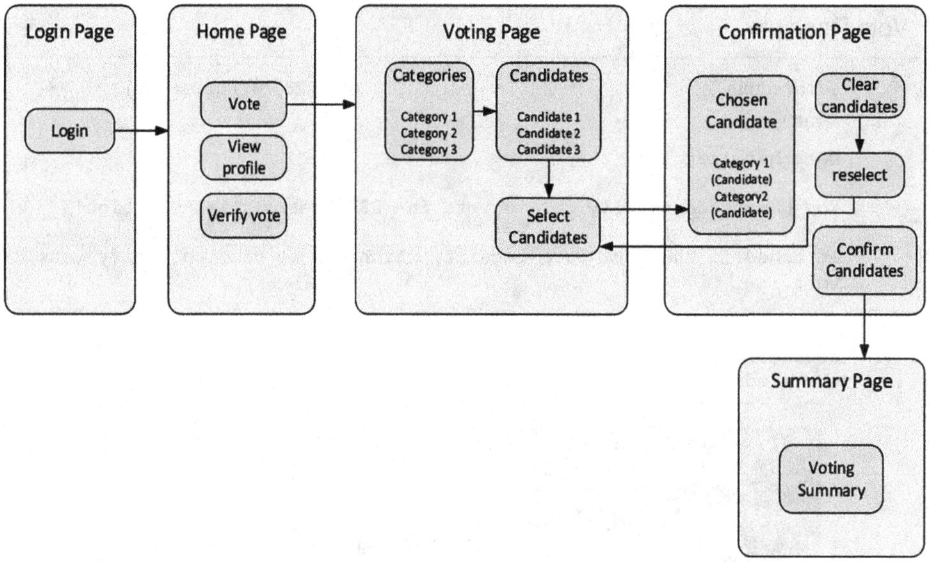

Figure 11. Screenshot of tally results page

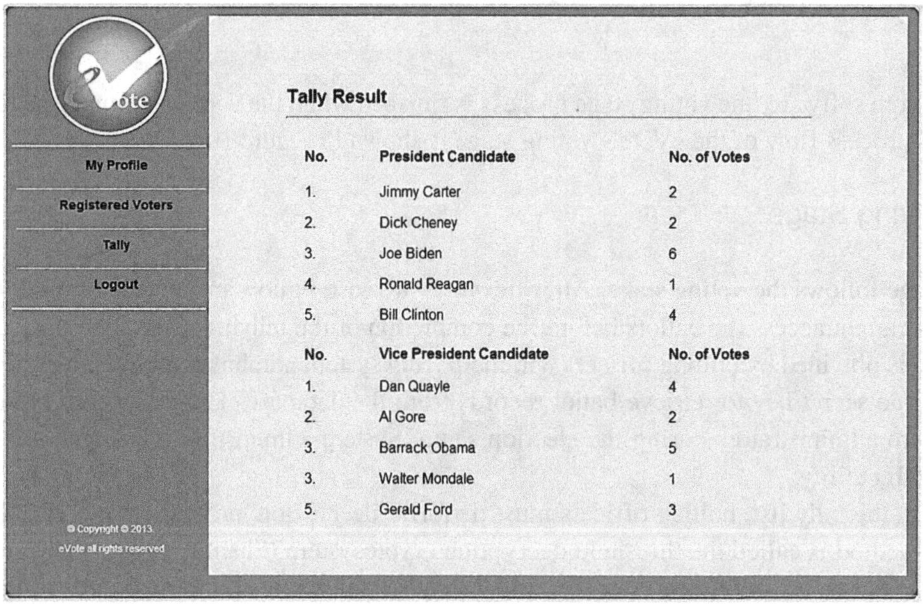

3.6.5. Vote Verification

In a traditional paper-based voting, once the tally process is done, authorised personnel will announce the result of the election. However, voters will not be able to verify their votes. As a result, voters cannot be assured that their submitted ballot is counted as cast. This may affect the turnout in subsequent elections. To solve this problem, voter receipt is implemented in the system development of the E2E voting system. This receipt is not revealed in their ballots. It can be used by each voter to ensure that the ballot cast is properly used by the system. Each user can only obtain one share of the visual cryptography encrypted image. The other half of the shares is automatically saved in the database. The combined shares would be used to retrieve and verify the voter's ballot. Voters of such a system can verify their votes by submitting the vote receipt into the system. The verification feature is supported by visual cryptography scheme. The vote receipt submitted by the voters will be matched (decrypted) against the other half of the encryption share saved in the database during the voting stage to verify an individual's vote. The server storing the share is assumed to be secure. The vote verification is shown in Figures 12 and 13 (Rura, Issac & Haldar, 2011).

4. SOFTWARE TESTING AND ANALYSIS

This section evaluates the three main properties that need to be ensured by the eVote software besides security namely effectiveness, efficiency and usability. It is done with two distinct types of software testing namely, usability testing and user acceptance testing. Testing the usability of a Moodle-based learning platform is discussed in the paper (Ternauciuc & Vasiu, 2015). In usability testing, the user's experience was examined by assessing Nielsen's five quality components of usability (Nielsen, 2012). On the other hand, user's acceptance was measured by using Davis' Technology Acceptance Model (TAM). Both have been commonly used as a standard for many empirical studies on user experience and acceptance. Here the data is collected through questionnaire before applying Cronbach's alpha test to measure its reliability scale (Cronbach, 1951). For the questionnaire survey, 30 representative individuals from different demographic groups participated. They were recruited based on the consideration of few significant aspects such as gender, the level of education and basic knowledge of information security and usability. The users are also chosen based on the minimum voting age requirement by the

Figure 12. Screenshot of vote verification page for the voters

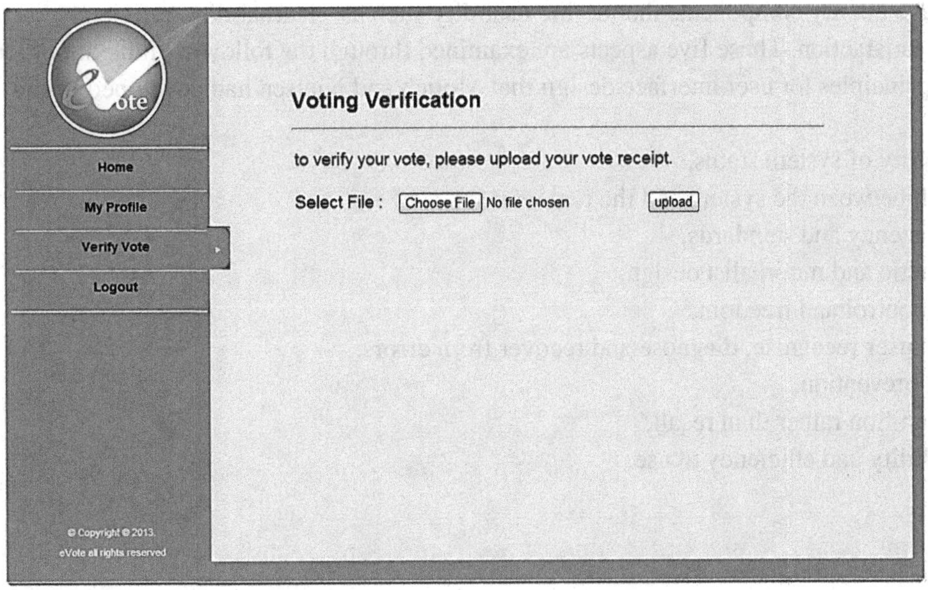

Figure 13. Screenshot of vote verification page upon successful verification

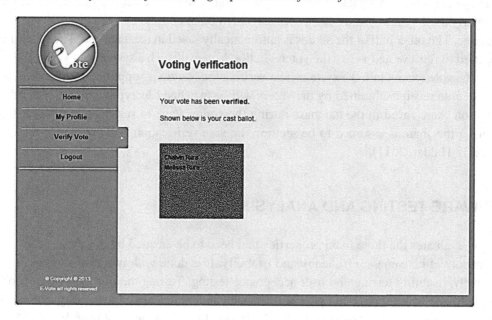

Malaysian law. The summary of participant's demographic information is shown in Figures 14 and 15. Each of the participants is required to complete a set of voter's tasks assigned to them and also to fill in a questionnaire in not more than thirty minutes. This questionnaire was constructed for the intended users to evaluate the eVote voting software's effectiveness, efficiency and reliability. The test results are discussed in detail in the following sections.

4.1. Usability Testing

Usability testing measures the concerns of the user about the system. According to Nielsen (2012), there are five quality components that define usability such as - learnability, efficiency, memorability, errors and satisfaction. These five aspects are examined through the following nine out of ten usability heuristics principles for user interface design that Molich and Nielsen had developed (1990).

- Visibility of system status,
- Match between the system and the real world,
- Consistency and standards,
- Aesthetic and minimalist design,
- User control and freedom,
- Helps user recognise, diagnose and recover from errors,
- Error prevention,
- Recognition rather than recall,
- Flexibility and efficiency to use.

Figure 14. Summary of participants based on their age

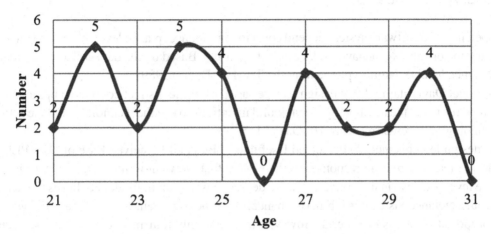

Figure 15. Summary of participants based on their gender and highest level of education

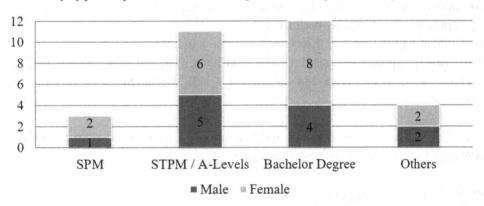

From the observation of usability testing carried out by 30 participants with good computer literacy, data collection is done. Illustrated in Table 2 are its derived results. The information presented in Table 2 illustrate user's perspective regarding the learnability, efficiency and satisfaction of the system interface. Based on the three sets of the task given to them, they evaluate the navigation process of the eVote software. Users give a positive feedback for their first experience to use the eVote. They can understand the system and navigate through different processes in the three distinct user levels easily. The neat layout with simple, consistent and understandable menu arrangement is one of the factors that supported this.

The other factor that needs be ensured by a system to support user's accessibility is proper error handling. It must be done properly to meet the user requirements. The eVote software provides a number of error-handling mechanisms. JavaScript handles some of them on the client-side, while the others are supported on the server-side. The 30 participants have a satisfactory experience with its error-handling mechanism, and there is room for improvement based on the survey. The last factor that the users evaluated is their effectiveness in using the eVote software for the second time or also referred to as memorability. This is the main reason why they are asked to complete three different set of tasks from each user level of the software. Due to its similar layout design and the straightforward functionalities, it offered, users agree that the software is able to provide efficient election procedures.

4.1.1. User Acceptance Testing

The competency of a software system depends on a lot on user acceptance level. User acceptance testing is conducted to consider the behavioural factors of the users. Based on the data collected we identify the user acceptance level through implementing the TAM by Davis (1989).

In his model Davis claimed that design features are part of the distinct cognitive appraisals of user's attitudes towards using the technology, behavioural intentions to use the technology and the actual usage of the technology as shown in Figure 16 (Davis, 1989).

Those design features include Perceived Usefulness (PU) and Perceived Ease of Use (PEU). These are the design features and the responses to the system that we want to measure to determine the user acceptance level. PU (extrinsic motivator) is the degree to which an individual believes that a particular system would enhance his or her job performance. As a measurement tool to obtain PU value, Davis initially proposed six items or criteria. However, there are only four most commonly used criteria, as follows:

1. Using application increases my productivity,
2. Using application increases my performance,
3. Using application enhances my effectiveness on the job, and
4. Overall I find the application useful. On the other hand, PEU (intrinsic motivator) is the degree to which a user believes that the use of a particular system would require less effort compared with other systems.

Similar to the PU, there are four out of six most commonly used items or criteria that Davis proposed as a measurement tool. The PEU criteria are as follows:

1. Learning to operate the application is easy for me,
2. I find it easy to get the application to do what I want to do,
3. The application is rigid and inflexible to interact with, and
4. Overall I find the application easy to use.

Figure 16. TAM model (Davis, 1989)

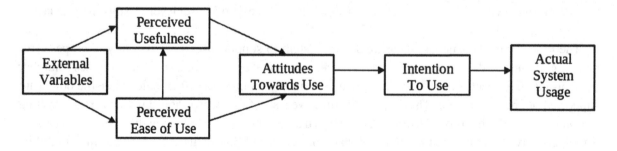

Table 2. Results of the usability testing conducted based on Molich and Nielsen's usability heuristics for user interface design

Heuristic Principles	Sub-Principles	Strongly Agree	Agree	Neutral	Disagree	Strongly Disagree
Visibility of System Status	Ability to understand the interface easily	21	9	0	0	0
	Ability to use the system easily	17	10	3	0	0
Match between the System and the Real World	The function of each icon/ button is understandable	8	16	6	0	0
	Ability to follow the order of the system	25	5	0	0	0
Consistency and Standards	Interface layout is arranged in a logical order	22	8	0	0	0
	Poor arrangement of icons/ buttons in the interface	0	0	1	6	23
Aesthetic and Minimalist Design	Existence of irrelevant information in the system	0	0	0	10	20
	Experience of user-friendliness from the system design	7	18	2	0	3
User Control and Freedom	Ability to navigate to another page once error is made	8	15	2	5	0
Help User Recognize, Diagnose and Recover from Errors	Ability to handle errors once occurred	0	16	11	3	0
Error Prevention	Errors are occasionally made	0	0	0	19	11
	Ability to handle error once occurred	0	14	12	4	0
Recognition Rather than Recall	Expected functions are available	23	7	0	0	0
	Ability to recognize the function rather than recall	17	13	0	0	0
Flexibility and Efficiency to Use	Capability of inexperienced user to use the system	6	14	10	0	0
	Ability to operate more effectively at the second time	25	5	0	0	0

Molich & Nielsen, 1990.

In this research, the two main aspects of TAM were evaluated based on these eight criteria. The collected data were analysed as follows.

The Cronbach's alpha test was used to determine the internal reliability of PU and PEU of the survey questionnaire. Its results are derived from the equation shown in Equation 1, where n is the number of items, V_i is the variance of item scores, and V_t is the variance of test scores (Cronbach, 1951).

$$\alpha = \frac{n}{n-1}\left(1 - \frac{\Sigma VI}{Vt}\right)$$

(1)

These results subsequently determine the reliability of user's acceptance level. Nunnally (1978) and Hair et al. (1998) recommends the value of 0.60 to 0.70 and above as the standard reliability coefficient. However, with the number of items or criteria applied, the coefficient value should be increased accordingly. It should then be calculated with the formula shown in Equation 2, where r_d is the desired reliability, r_e is the reliability of the existing instrument, and k is the number of times the test would have to be lengthened to obtain the desired reliability (Nunnally, 1978).

$$k = \frac{r_d\left(1 - r_e\right)}{r_e\left(1 - r_d\right)} \tag{2}$$

Based on the evaluation conducted, the results of Cronbach's alpha test for eVote on PU and PEU are shown respectively in Table 3 and 4. Both portrays good results of 0.89 for PU's measurement and 0.88 for PEU's measurement. These values are higher than the benchmark values of 0.6 to 0.7 that is set as standard, which means the results of the questionnaire conducted is reliable. Specifically, the user's acceptance of the system can be concluded as very good. From the comments gathered during the survey, most of the participants prefer to use the remote E2E voting system, compared to the polling booth provided in a traditional voting system to cast their votes. This is mostly due to the convenience and practicality it offered. According to them, the implementation of vote receipt is more reliable and offers more assurance to them, compared to the implementation of indelible ink commonly used in the traditional voting system. There are many ways counterfeit votes can be cast using indelible ink.

On the other hand, the implementation of vote receipt only requires the involvement of system administrators and polling officers who are assumed to be trustworthy. Besides that, most of the participants are also assured that their votes have been counted as cast and are kept securely by the eVote voting system. From the survey conducted, we also concluded that vote receipt in visual cryptography image format is more preferable compared to ciphertext format. It is more practical and convenient to be used by the voters.

Table 3. Results of the user acceptance test (PU's measurement) conducted based on Davis TAM

PU Items	Strongly Agree	Agree	Neutral	Disagree	Strongly Disagree	Rate Variance
Using application increases my productivity	5	9	10	4	2	11.5
Using application increases my performance	7	11	8	3	1	16
Using application enhances my effectiveness on the job	9	17	2	2	0	49.5
Overall I find the application useful	10	12	3	3	2	21.5
Total	31	49	23	12	5	98.5
Mean	24					
SD	17.18					
SD of TAM Items	295					
Cronbach's Alpha Value	0.89					

Davis, 1989.

5. CONCLUSION AND LIMITATIONS

The development of the eVote system addresses the common problems that arose in the traditional voting procedure. The main contribution of this work lies in the simplicity and user-friendliness the eVote software offers without compromising system security, efficiency and performance. The usability and user acceptance testing done has shown that the developed system is favoured by the users. The technology behind the voting system is as follows. Password hashed-based scheme was applied to secure user's password in registration and authentication stage. The plaintext of the ballot was encrypted using visual cryptography to two shares of ciphertext. One share was given to the voter as their vote receipt, and the other share was stored in the database. Visual cryptography decryption algorithm was executed to decrypt these shares. It also provides improved vote receipt mechanism. The vote receipt in our system is shown as visual cryptography image format. The voter's receipt is segmented into two parts. The voters only possess a part of that receipt, and the other part is kept secure in the database. The only individual who has access to their votes is the voters themselves, and it can only be done through the vote verification feature. Threshold decryption scheme was implemented in the ballot decryption process of the tallying stage to ensure that only authorised personnel can have access to the vote tallying process. F5 image steganography provided an enhanced security technique of data encoding with the digital image file as the cover file. Image steganography is used to ensure voters' receipts are only accessible to the voter themselves. The system works well assuming that the server used to store the information and the authorities involved are trustworthy.

On the limitation side, there are security attacks possible on the online voting system. If a group of polling officers work in unethical ways, the system can be compromised. But one polling officer alone cannot compromise the system because to access the voting tally list, the polling officers must perform 'decryption' process by merging their unique secret keys. Only after each of the polling officers has submitted their unique secret keys, the result tally list is accessible to the system administrators and the polling officers for monitoring. The distributed denial of service (DDoS) attacks could overload the servers on the election day, the hackers could eavesdrop the network traffic and could potentially imper-

Table 4. Results of the user acceptance test (PEU's measurement) conducted based on Davis TAM

PEU Items	Strongly Agree	Agree	Neutral	Disagree	Strongly Disagree	Rate Variance
Learning to operate the application is easy for me	9	16	3	1	1	42
I find it easy to get the application to do what I want to do	6	18	3	2	1	48.5
The application is flexible to interact with	6	7	14	3	0	27.5
Overall I find the application easy to use	8	17	3	1	1	46
Total	29	58	23	7	3	164
Mean	24					
SD	21.86					
SD of TAM Items	478					
Cronbach's Alpha Value	0.88					

Davis, 1989.

sonate normal users through spoofing attacks to cast false votes. The web application could be attacked through shell-injection vulnerability or other web technology flaws. The attackers could get through by attacking the payloads and through attacking the network infrastructure. There are other attacks possible on specific technologies used like F5 image steganography and visual cryptography that we have not discussed. But there are various countermeasures that can be implemented to secure the network and network resources (Haynes, 2014), including an additional layer of biometric authentication. These discussions can be long and are beyond the scope of this paper.

REFERENCES

Adida, B. (2008). Helios: Web-based Open-Audit Voting. *Proceedings of the 17th Conference on Security Symposium*, Berkeley, USA (pp. 335-348).

Aditya, R. (2005). Secure Electronic Voting with Flexible Ballot Structure [PhD Thesis]. Queensland University of Technology, Australia.

Ambler, S.W., & Sadalage, P.J. (2006). *Refactoring Databases: Evolutionary Database Design*. Addison-Wesley Professional.

Azougaghe, A., Hedabou, M., & Belkasmi, M. (2015). An electronic voting system based on homomorphic encryption and prime numbers. *Proceedings of the 11th International Conference on Information Assurance and Security (IAS)*, Marrakech, Morocco (pp. 140-145). 10.1109/ISIAS.2015.7492759

Bateman, P. (2008). Image Steganography and Steganalysis [Master's Thesis]. University of Surrey, UK.

Benaloh, J. (2006). Simple Verifiable Elections. *Proceedings of the USENIX/Accurate Electronic voting Technology Workshop 2006 on Electronic Voting Technology Workshop*, Berkeley, USA (pp. 5-5).

Beroggi, G. E. G. (2014). Internet Voting: An Empirical Evaluation. *Computer, 47*(4), 44–50. doi:10.1109/MC.2013.224

Burton, C., Culnane, C., & Schneider, S. (2016). vVote: Verifiable Electronic Voting in Practice. *IEEE Security and Privacy, 14*(4), 64–73. doi:10.1109/MSP.2016.69

Carback, R., Chaum, D., Clark, J., Conway, J., Essex, A., Herrnson, P. S., ... Vora, P. L. (2010). Scantegrity II Municipal Election at Takoma Park: The First E2E Binding Governmental Election with Ballot Privacy. *Proceedings of the 19th USENIX Conference on Security*, Berkeley, USA (p. 19).

Cetinkaya, O. (2008). Analysis of Security Requirements for Cryptographic Voting Protocols. *Proceedings of Third International Conference on Availability, Reliability and Security 2008*, Piscataway, USA (pp. 1451-1456). 10.1109/ARES.2008.167

Chaum, D. (2004). Secret-Ballot Receipts: True Voter-Verifiable Elections. *IEEE Security and Privacy, 2*(1), 38–47. doi:10.1109/MSECP.2004.1264852

Chaum, D., Carback, R., Clark, J., Essex, A., Popoveniuc, S., Rivest, R. L., ... Sherman, A. T. (2008). Scantegrity II: End-To-End Verifiability for Optical Scan Election Systems Using Invisible Ink Confirmation Codes. *Proceedings of the Conference on Electronic Voting Technology*, Berkeley, USA.

Cronbach, L. J. (1951). Coefficient Alpha and the Internal Structure of Tests. *Psychometrika*, *16*(3), 297–334. doi:10.1007/BF02310555

Davis, F. D. (1989). Perceived Usefulness, Perceived Ease of Use, and User Acceptance of Information Technology. *Management Information Systems Quarterly*, *13*(3), 319–340. doi:10.2307/249008

Fard, A. M., Akbarzadeh-T, M. R., & Varasteh-A, F. (2006). A New Genetic Algorithm Approach for Secure JPEG Steganography. *Proceedings of IEEE International Conference on Engineering of Intelligent Systems*, Islamabad (pp. 1-6). 10.1109/ICEIS.2006.1703168

Fridrich, J., Goljan, M., & Hogea, D. (2002). Steganalysis of JPEG Images: Breaking the F5 Algorithm. *Proceedings of the 5th International Workshop, IH 2002 Noordwijkerhout*, The Netherlands, (pp. 310-323).

Fujioka, A., Okamoto, T., & Ohta, K. (1992). A Practical Secret Voting Scheme for Large Scale Elections. *Proceedings of the Workshop on the Theory and Application of Cryptographic Techniques: Advances in Cryptology* (pp. 244-251). Springer-Verlag.

Gritzalis, D. A. (2002). Principles and Requirements for a Secure E-Voting System. *Computers & Security*, *21*(6), 539–556. doi:10.1016/S0167-4048(02)01014-3

Hair, J. F., Anderson, R. E., Tatham, R. L., & Black, W. C. (1998). *Multivariate analysis*. Englewood: Prentice Hall International.

Haynes, P. (2014). Online Voting: Rewards and Risks. Atlantic Council, Intel Security, Washington DC. Retrieved from http://www.mcafee.com/us/resources/reports/rp-online-voting-rewards-risks.pdf

Hubbers, E., Jacobs, B., & Pieters, W. (2005). RIES — Internet Voting in Action. *Proceedings of the 29th Annual International Computer Software and Applications Conference* (pp. 417-424). IEEE Computer Society, Washington DC., USA.

Kofler, R., Krimmer, R., & Prosser, A. (2003). Electronic Voting: Algorithmic and Implementation Issues. *Proceedings of the 36th Annual Hawaii International Conference on System Sciences*. IEEE Computer Society, Washington DC., USA.

Morkel, T., Eloff, J. H., & Olivier, M. S. (2005). An overview of image steganography. *Proceedings of the Fifth Annual Information Security South Africa Conference*, Sandton, South Africa.

Naor, M., & Shamir, A. (1994). Visual Cryptography. *Proceedings of Workshop on the Theory and Application of Cryptographic Techniques*, *LNCS* (p. 112). Springer-Verlag.

Nielsen, J. (2012). Usability 101: Introduction to Usability. Retrieved from http://www.nngroup.com/articles/usability-101-introduction-to-usability/

Nielsen, J., & Molich, R. (1990). Heuristic evaluation of user interfaces. *Proceedings of the SIGCHI Conference on Human Factors in Computing Systems* (pp. 249-256).

Nunnally, J. (1978). *Psychometric methods*. New York, NY: McGraw-Hill.

Petcu, D., & Stoichescu, D. A. (2015). A hybrid mobile biometric-based e-voting system. *Proceedings of 9th International Symposium on Advanced Topics in Electrical Engineering (ATEE)*, Bucharest (pp. 37-42). 10.1109/ATEE.2015.7133676

Provos, N., & Honeyman, P. (2003). Hide and seek: An Introduction to Steganography. *IEEE Security and Privacy, 1*(3), 32–44. doi:10.1109/MSECP.2003.1203220

Rura, L., Issac, B., & Haldar, M. K. (2011). Online Voting Verification with Cryptography and Steganography Approaches. *Proceedings of IEEE International Conference on Computer Science and Network Technology 2011 (ICCSNT '11)* (pp. 125-129). 10.1109/ICCSNT.2011.6181923

Rura, L., Issac, B., & Haldar, M. K. (2011). Analysis of Image Steganography Techniques in Secure Online Voting. *Proceedings of IEEE International Conference on Computer Science and Network Technology 2011 (ICCSNT '11)* (pp. 120-124). 10.1109/ICCSNT.2011.6181922

Ryan, P.Y.A., Bismark, D., Heater, J., Schneider, S. & Zhe Xia (2009). Prêt à Voter: a Voter-Verifiable Voting System. *IEEE Transactions on Information Forensic and Security, 4*(4), 662-673.

Ryan, P. Y. A., Schneider, S., & Teague, V. (2015). End-to-End Verifiability in Voting Systems, from Theory to Practice. *IEEE Security and Privacy, 13*(3), 59–62. doi:10.1109/MSP.2015.54

Shamir, A. (1979). How to Share a Secret. *Communications of the ACM, 22*(11), 612–613. doi:10.1145/359168.359176

Ternauciuc, A., & Vasiu, R. (2015). Testing usability in Moodle: When and How to do it. *Proceedings of the IEEE 13th International Symposium on Intelligent Systems and Informatics (SISY)*, Subotica (pp. 263-268). 10.1109/SISY.2015.7325391

Wagner, D., & Goldberg, I. (2000). Proofs of Security for the Unix Password Hashing Algorithm. *Proceedings of Lecture Notes in Computer Science* (pp. 560–572). London, UK: Springer-Verlag. doi:10.1007/3-540-44448-3_43

Wang, H., & Wang, S. (2004). Cyber Warfare: Steganography vs. Steganalysis. *Communications of the ACM, 47*(10), 76–82. doi:10.1145/1022594.1022597

Westfeld, A. (2001). F5- A Steganographic Algorithm. *Proceedings of the 4th International Workshop on Information Hiding (IHW '01)* (pp. 289-302). Springer-Verlag. 10.1007/3-540-45496-9_21

This research was previously published in the International Journal of Electronic Government Research (IJEGR), 12(3); edited by Nripendra P. Rana; pages 71-93, copyright year 2016 by IGI Publishing (an imprint of IGI Global).

Section 5
Visual Cryptography

Chapter 24
Exploiting the Homomorphic Property of Visual Cryptography

Xuehu Yan
Hefei Electronic Engineering Institute, China

Song Wan
Hefei Electronic Engineering Institute, China

Yuliang Lu
Hefei Electronic Engineering Institute, China

Wanmeng Ding
Hefei Electronic Engineering Institute, China

Lintao Liu
Hefei Electronic Engineering Institute, China

Hanlin Liu
Hefei Electronic Engineering Institute, China

ABSTRACT

In this paper, homomorphic visual cryptographic scheme (HVCS) is proposed. The proposed HVCS inherits the good features of traditional VCS, such as, loss-tolerant (e.g., (k, n) threshold) and simply reconstructed method, where simply reconstructed method means that the decryption of the secret image is based on human visual system (HVS) without any cryptographic computation. In addition, the proposed HVCS can support signal processing in the encrypted domain (SPED), e.g., homomorphic operations and authentication, which can protect the user's privacy as well as improve the security in some applications, such as, cloud computing and so on. Both the theoretical analysis and simulation results demonstrate the effectiveness and security of the proposed HVCS.

INTRODUCTION

Secret sharing encrypts the user data into different secret shadows (also called shares or shadow images) and distributes them to multiple participants, which has attracted more attention of scientist and engineers. Shamir's polynomial-based scheme (Li, Ma, Su & Yang, 2012; Li, Yang, Wu, Kong & Ma, 2013; Lin et al., 2007; Shamir, 1979; Thien & Lin, 2002; Yang & Ciou, 2010) and visual cryptographic scheme (VCS) (Naor et al., 1994; Tuyls et al., 2005; Wang et al., 2007, Wang, Arce, & Di, 2009, Weir & Yan, 2010; Yan et al., 2014), are the primary branches in secret sharing. A (k,n) threshold secret sharing scheme was first proposed by Shamir (1979) through encrypting the secret into the constant coefficient

DOI: 10.4018/978-1-7998-1763-5.ch024

of a random (k -1)-degree polynomial. The secret image can be perfectly reconstructed using Lagrange's interpolation. Inspired by Shamir's scheme, Thien and Lin (2002) reduced share size 1/k times to the secret image utilizing all coefficients of the polynomial for embedding secret. The advantage of Shamir's polynomial-based schemes (Li, Ma, Su & Yang, 2012; Li, Yang, Wu, Kong & Ma, 2013; Lin et al., 2007; Shamir, 1979; Thien & Lin, 2002; Yang & Ciou, 2010) is that, the secret image can be recovered losslessly. Although Shamir's polynomial-based schemes only need k shares for reconstructing the distortion-less secret image, it requires more complicated computations, i.e., Lagrange interpolations, for decoding. The limitation makes it useless without computational device and unsuitable for light-weight devices, such as, mobile phone, smart device and so on.

Naor and Shamir [14] first proposed the threshold-based VCS. In their scheme, a secret image is generated into n random shares which separately reveals nothing about the secret other than the secret size. The n shares are then printed onto transparencies and distributed to n associated participants. The secret image can be visually revealed based on human visual system (HVS) and probability by stacking any k or more shares, while less than k shares give no clue about the secret, even if infinite computational power is available.

Unfortunately, traditional VCS has the limitation of the pixel expansion 错误!未找到引用源. The pixel expansion will increase storage and transmission bandwidth. In order to remove the pixel expansion, probabilistic VCSs (Cimato, 2006; Ryo et al., 1999; Yang, 2004) and random grids (RG)-based VCSs (Chen & Tsao, 2013; Guo et al., 2013; Kafri & Keren, 1987; Shyu, 2007; Weir & Yan, 2010; Wu & Sun, 2013) were proposed. Main properties of VCS are simple recovery method and the alternative order of the shadow images. Simply reconstructed method means that the decryption of secret image is light-weighted or completely based on HVS without any cryptographic computation.

On the other hand, recently, rapid technological developments in areas such as cloud computing, online applications, social networking, and distributed processing have raised important concerns about the security (privacy) of user-related content (Lagendijk et al., 2013).

Traditional cryptographic technologies aim to protect data, but fail if the processor itself is untrusted (Lagendijk et al., 2013). In providing a service that needs personal information, the service provider may gain a lot about a user's past behavior, preferences, and biometrics. On the one hand, in order to use the service, the user must trust the service provider requiring his personal data. On the other hand, the service provider may be untrusted. Thus, the use of personal information becomes more varied with more flexibility in presentation and processing.

In particular, biometric techniques (Rao et al., 2008; Revenkar et al., 2010; Ross & Othman, 2011) such as, face recognition/authentication, are increasingly employed to verify the identity of a person with digital photos. Aiming to automatically match the faces of people shown on surveillance images against a database of known suspects, surveillance cameras in public areas led to the high interest in face recognition technologies (Lagendijk et al., 2013). The widespread use of biometrics raises privacy risks if the face recognition process is performed or stored at untrusted or only a central server. The faces might be used in criminal behavior.

To address this issue, signal processing in the encrypted domain (SPED) technologies (Barni, 2012) such as, homomorphic encryption (Bao & Zhou, 2015; Erkin et al., 2007; Li et al., 2012; Naehrig et al., 2011; Smart & Vercauteren, 2014) and authentication, are proposed, whose main motivator is to process the sensitive signals at potentially untrusted sites, minimally or without leaking information.

However, similarly as traditional cryptography, homomorphic encryption and authentication are not loss-tolerant and require more complicated computations for decryption. Homomorphic VCS (HVCS) may be an alternative way to solve the problem, which will be introduced in this paper. In addition, in HVCS, secret images are processed through the shares, i.e., in the encrypted domain, which shows the security of the proposed HVCS compared with traditional VCS.

The main motivation of this paper is to introduce HVCS which exploits the homomorphic property of traditional VC, thus the proposed HVCS achieves the features of both homomorphic encryption and visual secret sharing. The contribution of this paper lies in: 1) HVCS is first introduced; 2) the homomorphic property of traditional VC is exploited; 3) some operations of traditional VCS are proved or validated to support HVC operations. As an example, the proposed schemes exploit traditional RG-based VCS to support HVC operations. The proposed schemes have homomorphic property where the result of a specific signal processing operation performed on the secret image is equivalent to that of the decryption of the same (probably different) signal processing operation performed on the shares. In addition, they allow the authentication to be carried out by utilizing the shares instead of the original secret image. Simulations results and analysis are given to show the advantages and effectiveness of our methods.

The rest of the paper is organized as follows. Section II introduces the preliminary techniques as the basis for our method. In Section III, the proposed schemes are presented in detail. Section IV is devoted to experimental results. Finally, Section V concludes this paper.

PRELIMINARIES

In this section, we give some definitions and review RG-based VCS (Kafri & Keren, 1987; Wu & Sun, 2013) which are the basis for our method. In what follows, symbols $\oplus$ and $\otimes$ denote the Boolean XOR and OR operations, respectively. $\bar{b}$ is a bit-wise complementary operation of a bit b. The binary secret image denoted as S with pixel value $S(i,j)$, $1 \leq i \leq M$, $1 \leq j \leq N$, is shared among n (n ≥ 2, n$\in$Z$^+$) shares $SC_1, SC_2, \ldots, SC_n$, and the reconstructed secret image S' is reconstructed from t ($2 \leq t \leq n$, t$\in$Z$^+$) shares. Here '0' denotes white pixel and '1' denotes black pixel.

For a certain pixel x in a binary image X with size of M×N, i.e., x = X (i, j), the pixel color is transparent or white (0), say (x = 0), and the same for that pixel color is opaque or black (1). Besides,

$$\left(X=0\right)=1-\frac{1}{MN}\sum_{i=1}^{M}\sum_{j=1}^{N}X\left(i,j\right), 1 \leq i \leq M, 1 \leq j \leq N .$$

The generation and recovery phases of one original (2, 2) RG-based VCS (Kafri & Keren, 1987) are described below.

- Generation:
  - **Step 1:** Randomly generate 1 RG SC_1.
  - **Step 2:** Compute SC_2 using Equation 1.
- Recovery:

$S' = SC_1 \otimes SC_2$ using Equation 2. If a certain secret pixel of S (i, j), simply denoted as s, is 1, the recovery result $SC_1 \otimes SC_2 = 1$ is always black. If s is 0, the recovery result $SC_1 \otimes SC_2 = SC_1$ (i, j) $\otimes SC_1$ (i, j) has half chance to be black or white since SC_1 are generated randomly.

$$SC_2(i,j) = \left\{ \begin{array}{ll} SC_1(i,j) & \text{if } S(i,j) = 0 \\ \overline{SC_1(i,j)} & \text{if } S(i,j) = 1 \end{array} \right. \tag{1}$$

$$S'(i,j) = SC_1(i,j) \otimes SC_2(i,j) = \left\{ \begin{array}{ll} SC_1(i,j) \otimes SC_1(i,j) & \text{if } S(i,j) = 0 \\ SC_1(i,j) \otimes \overline{SC_1(i,j)} = 1 & \text{if } S(i,j) = 1 \end{array} \right. \tag{2}$$

HOMOMORPHIC VISUAL CRYPTOGRAPHY

In this section, we first introduce the motivation and definition of the proposed HVCS, then some HVC operations and their analyses are given in detail.

Motivation

There are various applications in which HVCS is useful. Below we describe two application scenarios that can use HVCS.

1. A lady had breast disease. Due to personal privacy and treatment needs, breast medical diagnosis image can be viewed with the agreement of both her and her personal physician. Later, according to the disease development needs, multiple experts' consultation needs to see the affected area of the image by a projector in order to optimize the treatment. Meanwhile the lady does not want the remaining part of the private area of the image to be publicly viewed. Therefore, this scenario has the similar property like a (2, 2)-HVCS for one secret image with cutting operation. The image is encrypted into two secret shares distributed to the lady and her personal physician. The lady and her personal physician then store the two shares in two different service providers (e.g., cloud computing parties). Each service provider cannot obtain any formation of the image since each share separately gives no clue about the secret image. Prior to show the image to multiple experts' consultation, the lady and her personal physician can ask service providers to cut the remaining part of the private area from the shares. The result of a cutting operation performed on the shares is equivalent to that of the same cutting operation on the secret image. Then the image can be visually revealed by projector based on HVS without cryptographic knowledge and computational devices through superimposing the two shares. Thus, we achieve privacy protection.
2. In biometrics applications, in order to protect the privacy of the individual organism, template is generally stored instead of the original secret image. Template protection is also important as the template disclosure may be used by others to achieve authentication, while if the template is stored in only one or untrusted database which can expressly or directly use the template to verify, thus there are significant security risks. Our method can be used to solve this problem. In general, the authentication can be performed based on Boolean XOR operation. The template is encrypted into two secret shares stored in two databases, respectively. Each service provider cannot obtain any formation of the template. Similarly, the verified template can be processed. The proposed HVCS for two secret images allows storing ciphertext and the authentication to be carried out by utilizing the shares instead of the original template. As a result, the security will be improved.

There are more examples that can apply HVCS, when some operations need to be performed on the shares instead of the original secret image for privacy protection. Therefore, HVCS has potential applications and deserves studying.

Definition of HVCS

We denote all the participants as P={1,2,...,n}. The original binary secret image S is shared among n (n ≥2, n∈Z+) shadow images $SC_1, SC_2, ..., SC_n$, by generation function E, that is $(SC_1, SC_2, ..., SC_n)$ = E (S); while the recovered secret image is recovered from t (1≤t≤n, t∈Z+) shadow images by recovery function D, that is S' =D($SC_{i_1}, SC_{i_2}, ..., SC_{i_t}$), where ($i_1, i_2, ..., i_t$) is the subsequence of (1, 2,... n) and t = 1 means SC_i=S or S' = S.

The definition of HVCS is introduced as follows.

Definition 1 (HVCS)

A VCS is a HVCS if there exist $f_1()$ and $f_2()$ satisfying one of the following two conditions:

1. For one secret image. $f_1(S') = D\left(f_2(SC_{i_1}, SC_{i_2}, \cdots SC_{i_t})\right)$.
2. For two secret images. $f_1(S_1', S_2') = D\left(f_2(S_1C_{i_1}, S_1C_{i_2}, \cdots S_1C_{i_t}, S_2C_{i_1}, S_2C_{i_2}, \cdots S_2C_{i_t})\right)$.

where, $f_1()$ and $f_2()$ denote two operations which are also called HVC operations in VCS. S1' and S2' indicate two original recovered secret image without operations corresponding to the original two secret image S1 and S2, respectively.

The above two conditions imply:

1. The result of the operation $f_1()$ on the original revealed secret image S' is the same as that of the decryption of the operation $f_2()$ on the corresponding random shares.
2. The result of the operation $f_1()$ on the two original revealed secret images S1' and S2' is the same as that of the decryption of the operation $f_2()$ on the corresponding random shares.

Based on definition 1, a HVCS is a VCS with HVC operation. The above definition can be extended to share more than two secret images based on repeatedly applying definition 1.

Remark: in our HVCS, we can only perform one operation on encrypted data (shares), thus our HVCS belongs to partial homomorphic encryption (Ogburn et al., 2013) from the non-strict sense.

HVC Operations for One Secret Image

The secret image is encrypted pixel by pixel in traditional VCS, thus pixel-based operations will belong to HVC operations. Some HVC operations for one secret image are stated as follows.

1. Cutting operation: the act of removing part of S' or shares.
2. Darkening operation: making S' or shares become darker.
3. Brightening operation: the act of making S' or shares lighter or brighter.

a. Based on the result of darkening or brightening operation, we can approximate the result of noise operation.
4. Rotation operation: a transformation in which the coordinate axes are rotated by a fixed angle about the origin.
5. Scaling operation: enlarging the size of S′ or shares.
6. Permutation operation: the act of changing the arrangement of pixels in S′ or shares. Based on the HVC permutation operation, the permutation encryption of the original secret image can be performed on the ciphertext shares instead of the plaintext secret image. In addition, after the secret image is encrypted by the HVC permutation operation, the contrast also can be computed in the encrypted domain rather than the plaintext domain.

The above HVC operations are also suitable for (k, n) threshold or general access structure. For case (k, n), the secret recovery of our method is based on stacking $(\otimes)$ or HVS when directly stacking k or more shares. Besides, if less than k shares are stacked, the original secret image will not be revealed.

HVC Operation for Two Secret Images

Herein, first we will prove that XOR operation is a HVC operation when both two secret images need protection, where both $f_1()$ and $f_2()$ denote the XOR operation. Then some other HVC operations for two secret images are proved when only one secret image S1 needs protection.

In fact, Equation 1 is equal to

$$sc_2 = sc_1 \oplus s \text{ or } s = sc_1 \oplus sc_2 \qquad (3)$$

since if s = 0, we have

$$sc_2 = sc_1 \oplus 0 \Rightarrow sc_2 = sc_1 \qquad (4)$$

else s = 1,

$$sc_2 = sc_1 \oplus 1 \Rightarrow sc_2 = \overline{sc_1} \qquad (5)$$

Thus, better image quality or perfectly reconstructed secret can be obtained by applying the XOR-based VCS (XOR recovery) (Wang et al., 2007; Yang, 2004; Yang & Wang, 2014).

The same equation can be extended to $s = sc_1 \oplus sc_2 \oplus \cdots \oplus sc_k$ and the same approach can be extended to (k, k) RG-based VCS by applying the above process repeatedly for the first k bits (Chen & Tsao, 2011).

Based on the above discussions, when XOR operation is applied for two secret images S_1 and S_2, we have:

$$S_1 = S_1C_1 \oplus S_1C_2$$
$$S_2 = S_2C_1 \oplus S_2C_2$$

(6)

Thus,

$$S_1 \oplus S_2 = \left(S_1C_1 \oplus S_2C_1\right) \oplus (S_1C_2 \oplus S_2C_2)$$

(7)

As a result, based on definition 1 XOR operation is a HVC operation for two secret images S_1 and S_2, where both $f_1()$ and $f_2()$ denote the XOR operation and the recovery function D () indicates XOR operation. The feature can be applied for authentication in encrypted domain, which can improve the security. An application diagram is illustrated in Figure 1. In the enrollment step, the template is generated into two random shares, which are stored in two different databases respectively.

Figure 1. An application diagram of the proposed HVC operation for two secret images

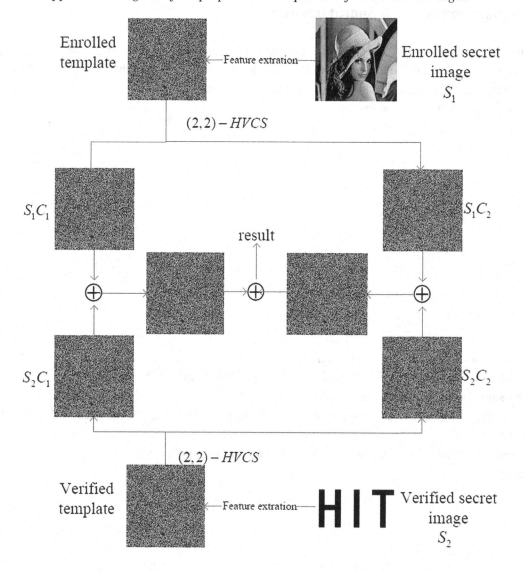

For authentication, the input template is also generated into two shares by the same procedure as (2, 2) RG-based VCS. Then, based on the proposed HVC operation, the authentication can be achieved by the shares instead of the original secret image. Thus, the original secret image and the template are protected in a degree.

The above HVC operation can protect both enrolled secret image and the verified secret image, if only the enrolled secret image needs protection, i.e., the verified secret image might be plaintext. We can handle this situation by two cases. Case 1: based on XOR operation; Case 2 based on AND (&) operation.

Case 1: based on XOR operation.

$$S_1 \oplus S_2 = S_2 \oplus \left(S_1 C_1 \oplus S_1 C_2\right) = \left(S_2 \oplus S_1 C_1\right) \oplus S_1 C_2 \tag{8}$$

Thus, XOR operation is a HVC operation when only one secret image needs protection, where both $f_1()$ and $f_2()$ denote the XOR operation and the recovery function D () indicates XOR operation.

Case 2: based on & operation.

$$S_2 \& S_1 = S_2 \& \left(S_1 C_1 \oplus S_1 C_2\right) = \left(S_2 \& S_1 C_1\right) \oplus \left(S_2 \& S_1 C_2\right) \tag{9}$$

Hence, & operation achieves HVC operation when only one secret image needs protection, where both $f_1()$ and $f_2()$ denote the & operation and the recovery function D() indicates XOR operation.

In addition, both $f_1()$ and $f_2()$ denote the & operation and the recovery function D() indicates operation, which will be proved to be a HVC operation by the following equation:

$$S_2 \& \left(S_1 C_1 \otimes S_1 C_2\right) = \left(S_2 \& S_1 C_1\right) \otimes \left(S_2 \& S_1 C_2\right) \tag{10}$$

Here we noted that, in the above applications, we should exclude the cheaters for security.

In summary, the features of the proposed HVCSs for biometrics privacy protection lie in:

1. The template is generated into two shares and the two shares are stored in two different databases respectively that separately reveals nothing about the template, which outperforms that they are stored in only one central database. In addition, our approach can be extended to generate k shares.
2. We don't make any pixel expansion in the proposed HVCSs, which could reduce the storage and transmission bandwidth. In addition, the VCS with meaningful shares (Yang & Yang, 2014) can be applied in the proposed scheme, because it can increase the efficiency of management and decrease the suspicion of secret image encryptions.
3. We achieve the authentication by the shares without reconstructing the original secret template, which can decrease the risk of template leakage.
4. Compared with traditional recognition technologies, one advantage of biometrics is to realize the recognition or authentication without preserving and showing an ID card. Different shares can be generated by the same user for each validation.
5. No encryption key is used in the proposed HVCSs.

EXPERIMENTAL RESULTS

In this section, based on traditional RG-based (2, 2) VCS (Kafri & Keren, 1987), experiments and analysis are conducted to evaluate the effectiveness of our method. Since sharing a binary secret image is the basic issue in VCS, in the experiment we only focus on binary secret images.

Simulation result by traditional RG-based (2, 2) VCS (Kafri & Keren, 1987) is presented in Figure 2. The secret image S is illustrated in Figure 2(a). Two generated shares SC1 and SC2 which are noiselike are demonstrated in Figure 2(b) to Figure 2(c). The stacking result denoted as S′ by the two shares is shown in Figure 2(d), which reveals the secret. S′, SC_1 and SC_2 will be utilized to show the effectiveness of the proposed HVC operations for one secret image.

Simulation result of HVC cutting operation for one secret image is shown in Figure 3. Figure 3(a) shows the original recovered secret image S′ performed the HVC operation. The shares performed the HVC operation are demonstrated in Figure 3(b) to Figure 3(c). The stacking result by the two shares is illustrated in Figure 3 (d), which reconstructs the secret performed the HVC operation. Thus, cutting operation is a HVC operation for one secret image.

Figure 2. Simulation result of traditional RG-based (2, 2) VCS (Kafri & Keren, 1987). (a) The secret image S; (b)--(c) two random shares SC_1 and SC_2; (d) stacking result S′ by two shares (SC_1 and SC_2)

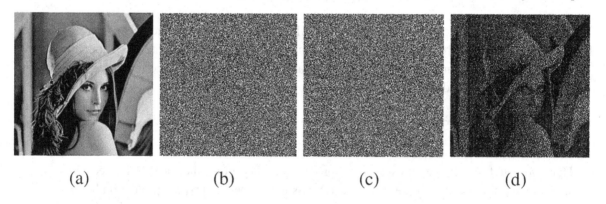

(a)   (b)   (c)   (d)

Figure 3. Simulation result of HVC cutting operation for one secret image. (a) The original recovered secret image S′ performed the HVC operation; (b)--(c) two shares SC_1 and SC_2 performed the HVC operation; (d) stacking result by (b) and (c)

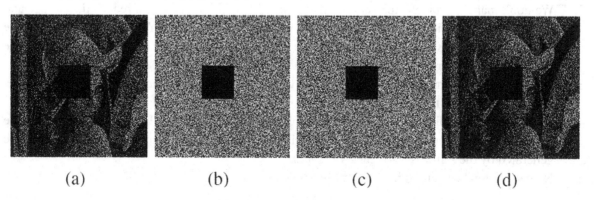

(a)   (b)   (c)   (d)

CONCLUSION

This paper proposed homomorphic visual cryptographic scheme (HVCS) with loss-tolerant, simply reconstructed method and homomorphic feature, where the result of a HVC operation performed on the secret image is equivalent to that of the decryption of the same HVC operation performed on the shares. Simulations results show that the proposed HVCS allows signal processing in the encrypted domain (SPED), e.g., homomorphic operations and authentication, which can protect the privacy in cloud computing and so on. Exploiting more useful HVC operations and HVCS will be the future work.

ACKNOWLEDGMENT

The authors would like to thank the anonymous reviewers for their valuable discussions and comments. This work is supported by the National Natural Science Foundation of China (Grant Number: 61602491).

REFERENCES

Bao, L., & Zhou, Y. (2015). Image encryption: Generating visually meaningful encrypted images. *Information Sciences*, *324*, 197–207. doi:10.1016/j.ins.2015.06.049

Barni, M., Kalker, T., & Katzenbeisser, S. (2013). Inspiring New Research in the Field of Signal Processing in the Encrypted Domain [From the Guest Editors]. *IEEE Signal Processing Magazine*, *30*(2), 16–16. doi:10.1109/MSP.2012.2229069

Chen, T. H., & Tsao, K. H. (2011). Threshold visual secret sharing by random grids. *Journal of Systems and Software*, *84*(7), 1197–1208. doi:10.1016/j.jss.2011.02.023

Cimato, S., De Prisco, R., & De Santis, A. (2006). Probabilistic visual cryptography schemes. *The Computer Journal*, *49*(1), 97–107. doi:10.1093/comjnl/bxh152

Erkin, Z., Piva, A., Katzenbeisser, S., Lagendijk, R. L., Shokrollahi, J., Neven, G., & Barni, M. (2007). Protection and retrieval of encrypted multimedia content: When cryptography meets signal processing. *EURASIP Journal on Information Security*, *2007*(1), 17. doi:10.1186/1687-417X-2007-078943

Guo, T., Liu, F., & Wu, C. (2013). Threshold visual secret sharing by random grids with improved contrast. *Journal of Systems and Software*, *86*(8), 2094–2109. doi:10.1016/j.jss.2013.03.062

Kafri, O., & Keren, E. (1987). Encryption of pictures and shapes by random grids. *Optics Letters*, *12*(6), 377–379. doi:10.1364/OL.12.000377 PMID:19741737

Lagendijk, R. L., Erkin, Z., & Barni, M. (2013). Encrypted signal processing for privacy protection: Conveying the utility of homomorphic encryption and multiparty computation. *IEEE Signal Processing Magazine*, *30*(1), 82–105. doi:10.1109/MSP.2012.2219653

Li, L., El-Latif, A. A. A., & Niu, X. (2012). Elliptic curve ElGamal based homomorphic image encryption scheme for sharing secret images. *Signal Processing*, *92*(4), 1069–1078. doi:10.1016/j.sigpro.2011.10.020

Li, P., Ma, P. J., Su, X. H., & Yang, C. N. (2012). Improvements of a two-in-one image secret sharing scheme based on gray mixing model. *Journal of Visual Communication and Image Representation*, *23*(3), 441–453. doi:10.1016/j.jvcir.2012.01.003

Li, P., Yang, C. N., Wu, C. C., Kong, Q., & Ma, Y. (2013). Essential secret image sharing scheme with different importance of shadows. *Journal of Visual Communication and Image Representation*, *24*(7), 1106–1114. doi:10.1016/j.jvcir.2013.07.005

Lin, S. J., & Lin, J. C. (2007). VCPSS: A two-in-one two-decoding-options image sharing method combining visual cryptography (VC) and polynomial-style sharing (PSS) approaches. *Pattern Recognition*, *40*(12), 3652–3666. doi:10.1016/j.patcog.2007.04.001

Naehrig, M., Lauter, K., & Vaikuntanathan, V. (2011, October). Can homomorphic encryption be practical? *Proceedings of the 3rd ACM workshop on Cloud computing security workshop* (pp. 113-124). ACM. 10.1145/2046660.2046682

Naor, M., & Shamir, A. (1994, May). Visual cryptography. *Proceedings of the Workshop on the Theory and Application of of Cryptographic Techniques* (pp. 1-12). Springer.

Ogburn, M., Turner, C., & Dahal, P. (2013). Homomorphic encryption. *Procedia Computer Science*, *20*, 502–509. doi:10.1016/j.procs.2013.09.310

Rao, Y. S., Sukonkina, Y., Bhagwati, C., & Singh, U. K. (2008, November). Fingerprint based authentication application using visual cryptography methods (improved id card). Proceedings of the 2008 IEEE Region 10 Conference TENCON '08-(pp. 1-5). IEEE.

Revenkar, P. S., Anjum, A., & Gandhare, W. Z. (2010). Secure iris authentication using visual cryptography. arXiv:1004.1748

Ross, A., & Othman, A. (2011). Visual cryptography for biometric privacy. *IEEE transactions on information forensics and security, 6*(1), 70-81.

Ryo, I. T. O., Kuwakado, H., & Tanaka, H. (1999). Image size invariant visual cryptography. *IEICE Transactions on Fundamentals of Electronics, Communications and Computer Science, 82*(10), 2172–2177.

Shamir, A. (1979). How to share a secret. *Communications of the ACM, 22*(11), 612–613. doi:10.1145/359168.359176

Shyu, S. J. (2007). Image encryption by random grids. *Pattern Recognition, 40*(3), 1014–1031. doi:10.1016/j.patcog.2006.02.025

Smart, N. P., & Vercauteren, F. (2014). Fully homomorphic SIMD operations. *Designs, Codes and Cryptography, 71*(1), 57–81. doi:10.100710623-012-9720-4

Thien, C. C., & Lin, J. C. (2002). Secret image sharing. *Computers & Graphics, 26*(5), 765–770. doi:10.1016/S0097-8493(02)00131-0

Tuyls, P., Hollmann, H. D., Lint, J. V., & Tolhuizen, L. M. G. M. (2005). XOR-based visual cryptography schemes. *Designs, Codes and Cryptography, 37*(1), 169–186. doi:10.100710623-004-3816-4

Wang, D., Zhang, L., Ma, N., & Li, X. (2007). Two secret sharing schemes based on Boolean operations. *Pattern Recognition*, *40*(10), 2776–2785. doi:10.1016/j.patcog.2006.11.018

Wang, Z., Arce, G. R., & Di Crescenzo, G. (2009). Halftone visual cryptography via error diffusion. *IEEE transactions on information forensics and security*, *4*(3), 383-396.

Weir, J., & Yan, W. (2010). A comprehensive study of visual cryptography. In *Transactions on data hiding and multimedia security V* (pp. 70–105). Springer. doi:10.1007/978-3-642-14298-7_5

Wu, X., & Sun, W. (2013). Improving the visual quality of random grid-based visual secret sharing. *Signal Processing*, *93*(5), 977–995. doi:10.1016/j.sigpro.2012.11.014

Yan, X., Wang, S., & Niu, X. (2014). Threshold construction from specific cases in visual cryptography without the pixel expansion. *Signal Processing*, *105*, 389–398. doi:10.1016/j.sigpro.2014.06.011

Yang, C. N. (2004). New visual secret sharing schemes using probabilistic method. *Pattern Recognition Letters*, *25*(4), 481–494. doi:10.1016/j.patrec.2003.12.011

Yang, C. N., & Ciou, C. B. (2010). Image secret sharing method with two-decoding-options: Lossless recovery and previewing capability. *Image and Vision Computing*, *28*(12), 1600–1610. doi:10.1016/j.imavis.2010.04.003

Yang, C. N., & Wang, D. S. (2014). Property analysis of XOR-based visual cryptography. *IEEE Transactions on Circuits and Systems for Video Technology*, *24*(2), 189–197. doi:10.1109/TCSVT.2013.2276708

Yang, C. N., & Yang, Y. Y. (2014). New extended visual cryptography schemes with clearer shadow images. *information. The Sciences*, *271*, 246–263.

This research was previously published in the International Journal of Digital Crime and Forensics (IJDCF), 9(2); edited by Feng Liu; pages 45-56, copyright year 2017 by IGI Publishing (an imprint of IGI Global).

Chapter 25
Basic Visual Cryptography Using Braille

Guangyu Wang

Chinese Academy of Sciences, China & Auckland University of Technology, New Zealand

Feng Liu

Chinese Academy of Sciences, China

Wei Qi Yan

Chinese Academy of Sciences, China & Auckland University of Technology, New Zealand

ABSTRACT

As a significant part of information security, Visual Cryptography (VC) is a secret sharing approach which has the advantage of effectively obscuring hints of original secret. In VC, a secret image is separated into partitions which are also known as VC shares. The secret is only able to be revealed by superimposing certain shares. Since Basic VC is in a structure which is similar to that of Braille where white and black dots are arranged in certain orders, it is feasible to utilize the feature of Braille for the authentication of VC. In this paper, the authors will conduct an experiment embedding Braille into grayscale and halftone images as well as VC shares. The result indicates that the embedding of Braille has little impact on VC secret revealing and enhances the security of VC shares.

1. INTRODUCTION

Visual Cryptography (VC) was firstly invented and researched by Naor and Shamir in 1994 to deal with the problem of secret sharing (Wei & Yan, 2012; Shamir, 1979; Yang & Laih, 1999). As equipped with the ability to divide secret image into several images which show no hint of the secret, VC is now playing an important role in information security. The aim of VC is to provide efficient approaches for image secret sharing (Naor & Pinkas, 1997). In VC, encryption and decryption are the two significant processes.

DOI: 10.4018/978-1-7998-1763-5.ch025

The decryption problem in VC is defined as a secret sharing problem. By stacking certain number of the shares together, secret image is revealed visually. VCS result is perceived by Human Visual System (HVS) (Naor & Shamir, 1995; Tuyls, Hollmann, Van Lint & Tolhuizen, 2005; Memon & Wong, 1998). On the contrary, secret remains undiscovered if the amount of given shares is fewer than the required number. Different from original secret image in which the secret can be easily identified, the stacked secret is perceived by using the contrast between the secret and its background.

There are three main types of VC: traditional VC, grayscale and color VC, multi-secret VC. Traditional VC aims at analyzing one secret image which has only black and white color. As two important expansions, while grayscale VC is studied to resolve the images consisting of multiple colors or intensity (Wei & Yan, 2010), multi-secret VC attempts to reveal more than one secret (Wei & Yan, 2010; Shyu et al, 2007).

Despite VC significantly assists secret protection, it appears to be difficult for participants to validate all shares and the secret, thereby given cheaters the opportunity to create unauthorized share. The role of cheater in VC as well as the authentication and successful cheat in VC are defined by Horng, Chen and Tsai (2006). According to their definition, a cheater is someone who releases a fake share that is different from the one (s)he received from the dealer during the process of secret reconstruction. Thus cheating prevention approaches are necessary in association with VC to prevent those cheating practices. There are two authentication methods available for checking shares and secret (Wei & Yan, 2012). The first type is to use an additional share to check the authentication of the revealed secret. This authentication method enables verification of the shares before the process of secret restoration. The other available authentication method is to use a blind authentication technique which aims at preventing the prediction of genuine shares' structure. As the inconvenience of producing and carrying additional shares, the first type of authentication is hard to be implemented. By contrast, using blind authentication methods such as cipher text is widely accepted in researches and applications.

In this paper, we will introduce Braille encoding and explain how it is applied to handle the authentication problem in VC. Our contribution is to use Braille for VC. To the best of our knowledge, this is the first time Braille has been applied to the area of VC. The remaining sections will be: Section 2 will introduce our related work, Section 3 will depict the contributions, our results will be provided in Section 4, discussions and conclusion will be presented in Section 5.

2. RELATED WORK

Even though the security nature of VC, attack approaches have been investigated and proved to be effective. Hu and Tzeng (Hahn & Jung, 2006) explained numerous cheating methods and each of the methods is capable of cheating VC schemes. A vast number of other researchers have also attempted to develop practical applications including one involving biometrics (Hegde et al, 2008; Hu & Tzeng, 2007; Jin, Yan & Kankanhalli, 2004; Lee & Chen, 2012; Tuyls et al, 2005; Weir 7 Yan, 2009; Liu, Wu & Lin, 2008; Horng et al, 2006).

In this paper, we focus on developing a new scheme of VC authentication method by using Braille as the cheating prevention tool. In 1824, a French visually impaired person Louis Blair invented Braille which is designed specifically for the visually impaired person to read by tactile perception (Yin, Wang & Li, 2010). In Braille, the alphabet is written in the form of blocks of the six dots which are also called Braille cells (Goldberg & Swan, 2011). Braille cells are small, flat, rectangular objects of a standard size.

The surface of each point can either be flat or salient. Each letter of the alphabet is uniquely represented in Braille cells by a pattern of six black dots (Goldberg & Swan, 2011; Sterr et al, 1998; Sadato et al, 1996; Charoenchaimonkon, Paul & Vatcharin, 2009; Van et al, 2000; Nolan & Kederis, 1969; Sadato et al, 1998; Hermelin & O'connor, 1971).

While open circles indicate the flat positions in each cell, filled circles indicate salient dots in the cell. The American Library of Congress has published explicit unified standard for Braille print (Goldberg & Swan, 2011).

Visually impaired people read Braille articles by using their fingers padding over Braille cells and perceiving the characters by the dots arrangement in Braille cells. While Braille is very useful for visually impaired people, individuals can hardly understand the content on Braille passages if they have no experience in reading Braille (Goldberg & Swan, 2011). Subsequently Braille appears to be only unrecognizable signs for people who lack the knowledge of Braille. Therefore, Braille can be treated as a cipher text for normal people.

Our contribution in this paper is to propose a scheme dealing with the issue of VC authentication by seeking the assistance from Braille. By analyzing the similarities between Braille and VC shares, we found an ideal method for replacing the pixels on VC shares by using Braille. At the same time of offering a method of VC authentication, embedding Braille into VC shares also provides an approach of recognizing VC shares and authentication information in a dark environment with dim light.

3. OUR CONTRIBUTIONS

As for the embedding process, we firstly define how salient points on Braille are related to the pixels on VC shares. In order to facilitate the identification of Braille on images, each block of six pixels on VC shares represents a Braille cell and salient points are only embedded into black pixels. Figure 1 shows examples of the correspondence between Braille cells and blocks of six pixels on VC shares:

The Braille also support for grayscale VC. Character 'a' is able to represent the pixel with grayscale value of 1 and character 'b' or 'c' tends to be used for expressing pixels whose grayscale value is 2. In a similar way, Braille of other alphabetic characters is utilized to represent pixels with certain grayscale values based on the number of their black dots. Furthermore, color images are separated into R, G, B chancels and each of the RGB channels is able to be represented by Braille on the basis of depth of red, green and blue in the picture.

As Braille cell has three rows, there is also a problem that the height of share may not be multiple of three. Two possible ways are presented. The first is to expand the resolution of VC shares to its triple size. The benefit of this operation is that the Braille can be used to occupy the whole space of VC shares.

Figure 1. Samples of Braille

However, it would spend much time on recreating another share. Another way is to change the last one or two rows to be all white. This solution is more preferable than the former choice. The first reason is that a character of space is comprised by two columns of three dots therefore visually impaired people can easily differentiate this extra line from a character of space. Further, this method would not increase the size of VC shares, thereby keeping the consistency with the original shares and secret, it also saves time than that of the first method. The flowchart of embedding Braille into a share is shown in Figure 2.

The process of embedding Braille into VC is divided into two main sub-processes. First, using basic VC scheme separates the secret into two shares and one of the shares is replaced by Braille input. The second sub-process is to use the replaced share (New Share2) so as to determine the appearance of the other share. The whole process of embedding Braille focuses on input meaningful Braille information and the secret recovery result.

Since VC secret is obtained by superimposing its shares together, it is possible to get one of the shares by reversing the operation on the other VC share and the original secret image.

Figure 2. Flowchart of embedding Braille into VC shares

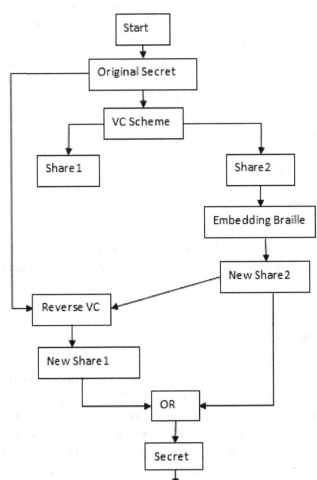

Figure 3. Regions of VC share are replaced by Braille: "AUT is", the red rectangles are used to indicate Braille cells

Figure 3a

Figure 3b

```
Algorithm 1. Embedding Braille into a VC share
Input:    Braille string A, VC share Img
Output:   A VC share embedded with Braille Img'
Procedure:
i=0;
While (i < Length of A)
{
    Judge and find whether A[i] is a capital letter or a number
    If A[i] is capital then A[i] add one Braille cell in Img according to
Braille rules of capital letter;
    If A[i] is number then A[i] add one Braille cell in Img according to
Braille of number;
        Map A[i] to Baille characters;
    If the lower case of A[i] is from 'a' to 'z' then change the pixel order
in every Braille cell-shaped region in Img complying to Braille coding rules.
    If A[i] is from '0' to '9' then change the pixels in Img according to the
order of characters from 'a' to 'j';
    i++;
}
```

Algorithm 1 illustrates how Braille cells are embedded into VC shares. According to Braille rules, capital characters and numbers hold two Braille cells. Besides, every alphabetic character appears to have its own arrangement in the cell.

4. RESULTS AND ANALYSIS

In this paper, we use Matlab as our programming platform to conduct this experiment. The dataset of original secret image contains six images as our test bed. These images are transferred into binary images for further analyzing. Figure 4 shows the images (gray and color) which are presented by Braille. The tested images and their restored images as VC secrets using Braille are shown in Fig 5.

In the process of embedding Braille, it is important to count the number of the Braille cells to be implanted in VC share since the scale of VC share is in a limited size. Current study of VC shows that it lacks of the strength of authentication process. Major benefits of embedding Braille into VC shares include helping visually impaired people understand the content on VC shares, enhancing decryption

Figure 4. Braille for VC

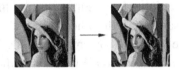

Figure 4a

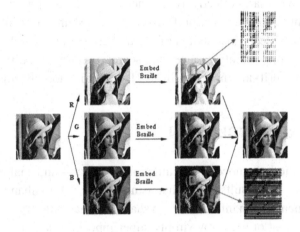

Figure 4b

Figure 5. Test set of embedding Braille into VC shares

Figure 5a

Figure 5b

Figure 5c

Figure 5d

Figure 5e

Figure 5f

ability in dark environment and authentication information being coded as Braille and embedded into VC shares. And also, Braille can be regarded as a cipher text. Authentication information can be coded as Braille and embedded into a VC share. At the same time, the other share also tends to have authentication.

Table I shows the degree how secret image is affected by embedding the Braille. This table indicates the similarity between the original secret and the recovered VC secret in the test bed. From the results in Table 1, it is obvious that secret revealing has only been affected slightly after embedding Braille into one of the VC shares.

Embedding Braille in VC shares effectively enhances the VC authentication process. While dealer is able to extract the authentication information from embedded shares, it is difficult for cheaters to realize how the shares are encrypted. This method of VC authentication by embedding Braille solely gives authorized participants the opportunity of accessing secret revealing. Modified and fake shares are able to be easily recognized by verifying the correctness of authentication information.

5. DISCUSSIONS AND CONCLUSION

This paper provides a method of embedding Braille into VC shares and analyses the effect of Braille on VC shares by experiments. The results reveal that using Braille helps enhancing authentication process of VC by embedding authentication information on shares and has little effect on the shares. Participants are also able to get every dot of secret by simply superimposing the correspondence pixel values on each of the shares.

Current study of VC shows that it lacks of the strength of authentication process. Major benefits of embedding Braille into VC shares include helping visually impaired people understand the content on VC shares, enhancing decryption ability in dark environment and authentication information being coded as Braille and embedded into VC shares. And also, Braille can be regarded as a cipher text. Authentication information can be coded as Braille and embedded into a VC share. At the same time, the other share also tends to have authentication.

Even though the advantages of Braille in VC, there are drawbacks of Braille in VC needed to be paid attention to. As meaningful authentication information is embedded into one of the VC shares, the Braille on the other share is possibly meaningless and hard to be verified. Moreover, this paper mainly contributed to the (2, 2)–VCS, further related researches are expected to have more investigation on other types of VC.

Table 1. The accuracy of recovered secret image

Samples	Sample Size	Accuracy (%)
1	231×219	94%
2	480×360	93%
3	294×282	96%
4	1024×946	96%
5	1154×906	95%
6	396×522	94%

REFERENCES

Charoenchaimonkon, E., Janecek, P., & Hamratanaphon, V. (2009, April). Using advanced encryption standard to secure the content dissemination of electronic Braille books. *Proceedings of the 3rd International Convention on Rehabilitation Engineering & Assistive Technology* (p. 32). ACM. 10.1145/1592700.1592737

Chen, Y.-C., Tsai, D.-S., & Horng, G. (2012). A new authentication based cheating prevention scheme in Naor–Shamir's visual cryptography. *Journal of Visual Communication and Image Representation*, *23*(8), 1225–1233. doi:10.1016/j.jvcir.2012.08.006

Goldberg, L., & Swan, L. (2011). A biosemiotic analysis of Braille. *Biosemiotics*, *4*(1), 25–38. doi:10.100712304-010-9092-y

Hahn, H., & Jung, J. (2006) Improving performance of the decoder for two-dimensional barcode symbology PDF417. In J. Braz, H. ArauJo, A. Vieira, A., & B. Encarnaçao (Eds.), Informatics in control, automation and robotics I (pp. 233-237). Springer Netherlands. doi:10.1007/1-4020-4543-3_28

Hegde, C., Manu, S., Shenoy, P., Venugopal, K., & Patnaik, L. (2008) Secure authentication using image processing and visual cryptography for banking applications. *Proceedings of the 16th International Conference on Advanced Computing and Communications* (pp. 65–72). 10.1109/ADCOM.2008.4760429

Hermelin, B., & O'connor, N. (1971). Functional asymmetry in the reading of Braille. *Neuropsychologia*, *9*(4), 431–435. doi:10.1016/0028-3932(71)90007-8

Horng, G., Chen, T., & Tsai, D.-. (2006). Cheating in Visual Cryptography. *Designs, Codes and Cryptography*, *38*(2), 219–236. doi:10.100710623-005-6342-0

Hu, C. M., & Tzeng, W. G. (2007). Cheating prevention in visual cryptography. *IEEE Transactions on Image Processing*, *16*(1), 36–45. doi:10.1109/TIP.2006.884916

Jin D., Yan W., & Kankanhalli M. (2004). Visual cryptography for print and scan applications. *Proceedings of IEEE ISCAS '04*.

Lee, Y.-S., & Chen, T.-H. (2012). Insight into collusion attacks in random-grid-based visual secret sharing. *Signal Processing*, *92*(3), 727–736. doi:10.1016/j.sigpro.2011.09.015

Liu, F., Wu, C., & Lin, X. (2011). Cheating immune visual cryptography scheme. *IET Information Security*, *5*(1), 51–59. doi:10.1049/iet-ifs.2008.0064

Memon, N., & Wong, P. W. (1998). Protecting digital media content. *Communications of the ACM*, *41*(7), 35–43. doi:10.1145/278476.278485

Naor, M., & Pinkas, B. (1997). Visual Authentication and Identification. In B. S. Kaliski Jr., (Ed.), *CRYPTO 1997. LNCS* (Vol. 1294, pp. 322–336). Heidelberg: Springer.

Naor, M., & Shamir, A. (1995) Visual cryptography. In Advances in Cryptology—EUROCRYPT'94 (pp. 1-12). Springer Berlin Heidelberg. doi:10.1007/BFb0053419

Nolan, C. Y., & Kederis, C. J. (1969). Perceptual Factors in Braille Word Recognition. (American Foundation for the Blind. Research Series No. 20).

Sadato, N., Pascual-Leone, A., Grafman, J., Deiber, M. P., Ibanez, V., & Hallett, M. (1998). Neural networks for Braille reading by the blind. *Brain, 121*(7), 1213–1229. doi:10.1093/brain/121.7.1213

Sadato, N., Pascual-Leone, A., Grafmani, J., Ibañez, V., Deiber, M. P., Dold, G., & Hallett, M. (1996). Activation of the primary visual cortex by Braille reading in blind subjects. *Nature, 380*(6574), 526–528. doi:10.1038/380526a0

Shamir, A. (1979). How to share a secret. *Communications of the ACM, 22*(11), 612–613. doi:10.1145/359168.359176

Shyu, S. J., Huang, S.-Y., Lee, Y.-K., Wang, R.-Z., & Chen, K. (2007). Sharing multiple secrets in visual cryptography. *Pattern Recognition, 40*(12), 3633–3651. doi:10.1016/j.patcog.2007.03.012

Sterr, A., Müller, M. M., Elbert, T., Rockstroh, B., Pantev, C., & Taub, E. (1998). Changed perceptions in Braille readers. *Nature, 391*(6663), 134–135. doi:10.1038/34322

Tuyls, P., Hollmann, H. D., Van Lint, J. H., & Tolhuizen, L. M. G. M. (2005). XOR-based visual cryptography schemes. *Designs, Codes and Cryptography, 37*(1), 169–186. doi:10.100710623-004-3816-4

Van Boven, R. W., Hamilton, R. H., Kauffman, T., Keenan, J. P., & Pascual–Leone, A. (2000). Tactile spatial resolution in blind Braille readers. *Neurology, 54*(12), 2230–2236. doi:10.1212/WNL.54.12.2230

Wang, G. (2014) Content based Visual Cryptography [Unpublished Master Thesis]. Auckland University of Technology, Auckland.

Wang, G., Liu, F., & Yan, W. (2014) Braille for Visual Cryptography. Proceedings of IEEE ISM '14, Taiwan.

Wei, J., & Yan, W. (2010). *A comprehensive study of visual cryptography* (pp. 70–105). Springer Transactions on Data Hiding and Multimedia Security.

Weir, J., & Yan, W. (2009) Sharing multiple secrets using visual cryptography. *Proceedings of the IEEE International Symposium on Circuits and Systems ISCAS '09* (pp. 509-512). 10.1109/ISCAS.2009.5117797

Weir, J., & Yan, W. (2012). Authenticating visual cryptography shares using 2D barcodes. In Y. Shi, H.-J. Kim, & F. Perez-Gonzalez (Eds.), *Digital Forensics and Watermarking* (Vol. 7128, pp. 196–210). Springer Berlin Heidelberg. doi:10.1007/978-3-642-32205-1_17

Weir, J., & Yan, W.-Q. (2009). Dot-Size Variant VC. In A. T. S. Ho, Y. Q. Shi, H. J. Kim, & M. Barni (Eds.), *IWDW 2009, LNCS* (Vol. 5703, pp. 136–148). Heidelberg: Springer.

Yang, C., & Laih, C. (1999) Some new types of visual secret sharing schemes. Proceedings of the *National Computer Symposium (NCS 1999)* (Vol. 3, pp. 260–268

Yin, J., Wang, L., & Li, J. (2010) The research on paper-mediated Braille automatic recognition method. *Proceedings of the Fifth International Conference on Frontier of Computer Science and Technology (FCST)* (pp. 619-624).

Chapter 26
Threshold Secret Sharing Scheme for Compartmented Access Structures

P. Mohamed Fathimal
Manonmaniam Sundaranar University, India

P. Arockia Jansi Rani
Manonmaniam Sundaranar University, India

ABSTRACT

In the realm of visual cryptography, secret sharing is the predominant method of transmission and reception of secure data. Most of the (n, n) secret sharing schemes suffer from one common flaw — locking of information when the all- n number of receivers are not available for some reason. This paper proposes a new method of compartmented secret sharing scheme where some threshold number of equally privileged from each compartment can retrieve data. This scheme rules out regeneration of secret image at the single compartment thereby eliminating the danger of misusing secret image. The key features of this scheme are: better visual quality of the recovered image with no pixel expansion; non-requirement of half toning of color images; less computational complexity by reconstructing secret through XORing and simple addition of all share images. This scheme is highly beneficial in applications where data has to be stored securely in a database and in cloud computing to synchronize information passed to different groups or clusters from a single host.

INTRODUCTION

In today's information and networking era, secret sharing is a fundamental issue in network security. Many applications such as distributed file storage, key management and multi-party secure computation use secret sharing scheme to share a secret among a set of participants. Shamir (1979) and Blakley (1979) introduced this secret sharing scheme in 1979. In this threshold (t, n) secret sharing scheme, secret

DOI: 10.4018/978-1-7998-1763-5.ch026

shares are distributed to n participants and the secret image is reconstructed by combining more than t of them. In this scheme, all participants have equal privileges and cannot be distinguished according to trust or authority and only the number of the participants involved is important for recovering the secret.

Multi-level secret sharing scheme is a scheme in which each participant is assigned a level — a positive integer — and at least r participants of each level are required to access the secret. There are two categories of multi-level access structure. The first category is the hierarchical structure in which the participants differ in their authority or level of confidence and the presence of higher-level participants are authoritative to allow the recovery of the secret. The electronic fund transfer in a bank may require the signature of two vice-presidents or three senior tellers for authentication. If there are only two senior tellers available, then the third senior teller role can be played by a vice-president.

The second category of multi-level secret sharing scheme is multipartite or compartmented secret sharing scheme in which every compartment or part has some number of equally privileged participants. The reconstruction of the secret requires a specified level of concurrence by participants in all the compartments. When two companies agree to sign the secret document through a secret sharing scheme, regeneration of the secret document is possible only when at least threshold number of the participants from both companies pool their shares together.

This paper proposes an ideal compartmented secret sharing scheme using magic square for situations requiring the agreement of several parties to recover the color secret image.

RELATED LITERATURE REVIEW

Many researchers introduced new secret sharing scheme based either on Shamir's scheme (1979) or with new concepts. Shamir introduced multipartite access structures in his seminal work for weighted threshold access structures. Blakely (1979) introduced geometric threshold secret sharing scheme. Mignotte (1983) and Asmuth-Bloom (1983) developed threshold secret sharing scheme based on the Chinese remainder theorem.

Mignotte's threshold secret sharing scheme (1983) uses special sequences of integers, referred to as Mignotte sequences. A (k, n)-Mignotte sequence is a sequence of positive integers $m_1 < \cdots < m_n$ such that $(m_i, m_j) = 1$, for all $1 \leq i < j \leq n$, and $m_n - k + 2 \cdots m_n < m_1 \cdots m_k$. The scheme proposed by Asmuth and Bloom (1983) also used special sequences of integers. More exactly, a sequence of pairwise coprime positive integers $r, m_1 < \cdots < m_n$ is chosen such that $r \cdot m_n - k + 2 \cdots m_n < m_1 \cdots m_k$. This scheme was generalized for allowing modules that are not necessarily pairwise coprime in an obvious manner.

Brickell (1990) proposed an elegant solution by choosing the secret S as a combination of m compartment secrets and using a threshold secret sharing scheme for each compartment. In the reconstruction phase, if the number of participants from the jth compartment is greater than or equal to the k_j, for all $1 \leq j \leq m$, then all compartment secrets can be recovered and thus the secret S can be obtained. Brickell proved that all multilevel and compartmented access structures are ideal. He proved that every structure in one of those families admits a vector space secret sharing scheme over every large enough field. Even though the proof is constructive, this scheme did not explain how to construct efficiently.

Simmons (1990) introduced two families of multipartite access structures, the so-called multilevel and compartmented access structures by generalizing the geometrical threshold scheme by Blakely (1979) and he speculated that this was possible for all of them. He has presented the example of an official action that requires at least two Americans and at least two Russians for its initiation.

Kaya (2007) introduced functional Secret sharing scheme to share the RSA signature and the ElGamal and Paillier decryption functions using the Asmuth–Bloom (1983) Secret sharing scheme. Ching-Fang Hsu et al. (2014) extended both Asmuth–Bloom and Kaya schemes to bipartite access structures and investigated the design of CRT-based secret sharing schemes realizing multipartite access structures.

Graham Enos and Yuliang Zheng (2012) introduced an id based Signcryption Scheme with Compartmented Secret Sharing for Unsigncryption. If an organization have different compartments, this scheme allows any member of a specific compartment to participate in the unsigncryption. Moreover, each member of a compartment has information unique to that individual. Thus, this scheme uses identity-based encryption, extends it into a compartmented scheme, allowing a sender to address a message to an organization O and requires different compartments to cooperate for the message's recovery.

Oriol Farr`as et al. (2012) proposed a scheme to optimize the ratio between the maximum length of the shares and the length of the secret value in secret sharing schemes for general access structures. This method uses linear programming to compute lower bound for every given bipartite access structure and obtains the best lower bound using combinatorial method. In addition, this scheme presented new general lower bounds on the optimal complexity of bipartite access structures to construct optimal secret sharing schemes for a family of bipartite access structures. Cheng Guo (2012) suggested a hierarchical threshold secret sharing scheme based on Birkhoff Interpolation. This scheme generates meaningful share images. The drawback of this scheme is high computational complexity for the regeneration process.

The proposed compartmented secret sharing scheme addresses the problems in the existing schemes with low computational complexity, accuracy in the reconstructed image, security and no pixel expansion. The organization of this paper is as follows. Section III explains discussion of the proposed scheme. Section IV discusses Experimental Results. Finally, section V concludes the paper.

PROPOSED WORK

This section describes the proposed multipartite or compartmented secret sharing scheme in detail. The scheme consists of two processes -Sharing and Recovery. Sharing Process involves weight Initialization for each compartment, Key Generation and Distribution of shares in each compartment. The Recovery Process involves verification and Regeneration.

Sharing Process

Algorithm 1 explains the sharing process to generate unequal weighted shares for each compartment and equally weighted share for all participants in each compartment. This scheme uses (n, n) secret sharing scheme for sharing secret image among a set of compartments and (t, n) secret sharing scheme for further sharing among the participants in each compartment.

Using Lagrange interpolation polynomial, the dealer generates unique key$(x, f(x))$ for each participant to ensure authentication for each participant and to validate his or her shares during regeneration. This avoids fabrication of shares from hackers, as it requires the correct unique key value $(x, f(x))$.

Every participant unique value is generated using $f(x) = (a_0 + a_1 x + a_2 x^2 \ldots + a_{k-1} x^{k-2}) \bmod 255$ where the coefficients $a_0\, a_{1\ldots}\, a_{k-1}$ are random numbers in the range of [1,255]. The dealer then computes $y(x) = (x, f(x))$.i.e. $y(1)=(1,f(1)), y2=(2,f(2))\ldots y(n)=(1,f(n))$.

This authentication unique id is a pair of two integers with the condition that $x \neq 0$. If any k of n participants gathers, they can reconstruct the coefficients.

Let *n* be the number of compartments, the dealer divides each pixel of the secret image into n unique values by performing arithmetic modulo operations on the values in a row or column of a $n*n$ magic square. As the row or column is selected based on the user's choice and the modulus key value is with the dealer, the hackers or dishonest compartment participants cannot guess the ratio using which the other compartment's values are divided and the other compartment values cannot be regenerated without the dealer's knowledge.

Similarly, the compartment key and the shares in each compartment are permuted using the coefficients of the polynomial. Therefore, the compartment shares can be retrieved only when threshold number of participants in each compartment are involved in regeneration. Different polynomials are used in each compartment and thus ensures one compartment's participant cannot play the role of other compartment's participant.

Algorithm 1

Input:

  a. Number of Compartments/parts N
  b. Number of participants N_c in each compartment $c,(c=1..N)$
  c. No. of shares required to recover the shares t_c in each compartment c
  d. Secret Image S of size $m_1*m_2*d,$
  e. set of N_c unique ids $y(1),....y(N_c)$ and coefficients $a_0, a_1... a_{tc-1}$ of polynomial $f(x)$ for each participant in each compartment c

Output: *N_c shares of size m_1*m_2*d for each compartment c*
  Step 1: Initialization of Main Key

Initialize the random generated main key K_m and a zero matrix S' of size m_1*m_2*d, copy all pixel values in S to S'. Select all pixels in the secret image S_{ij} which have the intensity less than $(N^3 +N)/2$, add the value $(N^3+N)/2$ with that pixel value. XOR the value with the original value and store it in the corresponding cell position in K_m.

$$S'_{ij} = \left(S_{ij} \oplus K_{mij} \right) + \left(N^3 + N \right)/2$$

$$K_{mij} = K_{mij} \oplus S_{ij} \oplus S'_{ij}$$

  Step 2: Generation of Compartment weights Generate a magic square of size N. Choose any row or column randomly. Assign each cell of a selected row or column in the magic square as weights of each compartment or parts (W_c).
  Step 3: Each cell value in S' is added with W_c and $(N^2+1)/2$ to generate each compartment's secret share S'_c.

$$S'_c = S' + W_c + (N^2+1)/2$$

Step 4: Share Distribution in each compartment c. Subtract each cell value S'_c from it modulus t_c -1(threshold number of shares in each compartment). XOR the output generated with compartment shares. Each compartment's key share K_c is generated by XOR ing S'_c with R_c obtained in step 5. R_c is divided by t_c -1 to obtain Z_c.

$$R_c = S'_c - \left(S'_c \bmod \left(t_c - 1 \right) \right)$$

$$K_c = S'_c \oplus R_c$$

$$Z_c = R_c / (t_c - 1)$$

Step 5: In order to aid authentication and to avoid fabrication of shares, this resultant value Z_c is then right shifted by the unique key ($f(x) * a_{x \bmod 255}$) mod 255 and distributed to each participant x.

$$y_x = \left(a_{x \bmod (tc-1)} * f(x) \right) \bmod 255$$

$$Sh_{c,x} = rightcircularshift(Z_c, y_x) \text{ where } 2 \leq x \leq N_c$$

Step 6: Similarly, each compartment key is right shifted by the constant term of the polynomial of degree t_c -2.

$$y_0 = (a_0) \bmod 255$$

$$Sh_{c,1} = rightcircularshift(K_c, y_0)$$

Step 7: In the dealer side, the main keys K_m and compartment keys $Sh_{1,1} \ldots SH_{N,1}$ of size $m_1 * m_2 * d$ are stored in the database as key share for regenerating the secret image.

Recovery Process

The Recovery Process involves computation of each compartment shares after authenticating each participant's shares. This authentication process solves the polynomial of degree $(t_c - 2)$ using the $(t_c - 1)$ unique key $(x, f(x))$. It then performs reverse permutation - left circular shift of each share by $\left(a_{x \bmod tc-1} * f(x) \right) \bmod 255$ and checks whether all threshold shares are equal. If the threshold shares are equal, the dealer shall add all threshold minus 1 number of participants and XORed with the compartment's key share. Similarly all compartments shares are generated and XORed with the main key leading to the recovery of secret image without any loss.

Algorithm 2

Input:

1. t_c -1 number of participant share images $S_{c,x}$ in each compartment c of size $m_1 * m_2 * d$
2. Mainkey and each compartment's key share from the dealer's database K_m and $Sh_{1,1} ... Sh_{N,1}$ of size $m_1 * m_2 * d$
3. set of N_c unique ids $y(1), ... y(N_c)$ (for each participant)

Output: *Secret Image S_{rec} of size $m_1 * m_2 * d$*

Step 1: with the knowledge of t_c-1 pairs of $(x, f(x))$, determine the (t_c-2) degree polynomial $f(x)$ and the coefficients are calculated using the following equation.

$$s = f(0) = \prod_{j=1 j!=i}^{k} \frac{(-xi)}{xi - xj} \mod p$$

Step 2: Authenticate shares and check the integrity of the share image by calculating

$$y_x = \left(a_{x \mod tc-1} * f(x) \right) \mod 255$$

$$S_{rec_{c,x}} = leftcircularshift \left(S_{c,x}, y_x \right) \text{ where } 2 \leq x \leq k.$$

Step 3: if all t_c-1 shares $S_{rec_{c,x}}$ in each compartment are same, the shares are not modified and share from the database can be accessed.

$$y_1 = (a_0) \mod 255$$

$$S_{rec_{c,1}} = leftcircularshift \left((Sh_{c,1}), y_1 \right)$$

Step 4: Calculate compartment shares by adding all participants' shares and XOR with key share.

$$S_{rec_c} = S_{rec_{c,1}} \oplus S_{rec_{c,2}} + S_{rec_{c,3}} + ... S_{rec_{c,tc}}$$

Step5: Similarly, all compartment shares are calculated and added. The resultant value is then XORed with the main key K_m.

$$S_{rec} = K_m \oplus \left(S_{rec_1} + S_{rec_1} + ... S_{rec_N} \right)$$

Meaningful Share Images

This proposed scheme can generate the meaningless shares for each participant with the size of shares same as the secret image size. To make the shares meaningful, XOR each bits of the secret image and reduce it into single bit can preprocess the secret image and the XORed values are stored as main key. For Preprocessing, the 4 Least Significant Bits(LSB) are XORed with 4 MSB bits of each pixel and the value is stored as 4 bits MSB in the main key. Similarly, first two LSB bits are XORed with the next two LSB bits of every pixel and stored in 4th and 3rd bit of main key, 2nd bit is XORed with 1st bit and stored as second bit in the main key. The First LSB bit in each pixel of the main key is always set as zero. The LSB of the secret image are considered and the successive eight pixel's LSB are combined to form a pixel of the reduced secret image. This reduces the size of the secret image 8 times. The share distribution algorithm produces shares for this reduced image. Each random shares bit replaces LSB of the cover image to make meaningful share images.

Experimental Results and Analysis

This section explains the results of the tests to determine the feasibility of the proposed scheme. The algorithm described in this paper is implemented in *Matlab 10.0* running on *Windows 8, i5 Processor* with *4 GB* of memory. The criteria for the visual quality of the image is the Peak Signal to Noise Ratio (PSNR) which is defined as

$$\text{Mean Square Error } MSE = \frac{1}{mn}\sum_{1}^{m}\sum_{1}^{n}\left[I_{ij} - I'_{ij}\right]^2$$

$$PSNR = 20 * \log_{10}(\max_f / sqrt(MSE))$$

Legend:
  I-original image of size $m \times n$
  I'-recovered image of size $m \times n$
  $\max_f$- maximum intensity value that exists in the original image (255).

The higher the PSNR value, better the quality of the reconstructed image. This scheme satisfies the criteria such as correctness, security, less recovery time with no Pixel Expansion.

Correctness

As the secret image is divided by tc -1 value in each compartments and the remainder is XORed with the compartment key, secret image can be regenerated without any loss. The correctness of the algorithm for regeneration of the secret image is measured by PSNR and MSE value. This algorithm regenerates the original image with PSNR of infinity.

Security

As each participant's share are encrypted using the coefficients and the f(x), only the participants can involve in regeneration and the hackers cannot fabricate the shares as it is required to provide the private key f(x) of the participants which can be generated only when all the coefficients of the LaGrange polynomial are known.

When a dishonest compartment tries to generate the remaining compartment's shares to recover the secret image, the dishonest compartment has to find the dealer's main key (K_m) and the weights (W_c) of other compartments which is calculated based on the magic square and the main key. Therefore, without the knowledge of the other compartments and the dealer, it is impossible to recover the secret image.

Complexity

The regeneration algorithms require n operations for simple addition of threshold number of shares and XORed with compartment key in each compartment and all compartment values are then added and XOR ed with main key. Authentication of each participant involves solving polynomial leading to n^2 operations for onetime. Thus, the complexity of the algorithm is O (n) when compared to existing scheme, which requires O (n^2) operations.

Pixel Expansion

The size of the share images are the same size as the secret image when it does not involve preprocessing. For generating meaningful share images, the secret image is preprocessed and reduced by 8 times and the cover images size is also same as the secret image. Thus there is no pixel Expansion and the cover image is less distorted with PSNR of 50.8 dB. The recovered secret image has better visual quality with no loss and infinite PSNR value.

Figure 1 shows the experimental results of the proposed compartmented scheme. Lena test image is the input image. Shares for three compartments and the main key generated is shown in Figure 1. (b-e), Figure 1. (f – h) shows the shares given to each participant in compartment 1. Figure 1. (i-k) and Figure 1. (l-m) shows the shares for participants in compartment 2 and compartment 3 respectively. Figure 1. (n-p) shows the recovered Image after combining threshold shares from each compartment. In this test (t, n) value is (2, 3) for compartment 1 and 2 and (1, 2) for compartment 3. So this proposed algorithm does not reveal the secret image after combining less than k shares. Thus, it ensures confidentiality. Only when the right key from the dealer is XOR-ed with the combined 3-compartmented shares, the secret image can be recovered and the recovered image is shown in Figure 1 shows the recovered image after combining all compartments shares with the wrong main key.

The above results prove that this scheme regenerates secret image without any loss and no pixel expansion.

Table 1 shows the comparison of the proposed Scheme with the existing Cheng Guo's hierarchical Threshold Secret Sharing Scheme (Guo, Chang & Qin, 2012).

25 color test images with various file formats are used and the PSNR of the some stego images for t_c =2and N_c =3 in a compartment c(c=1) are obtained in Table 2. From the table, it is observed that average PSNR is 51dB for cover images with no pixel expansion.

Figure 1. Input Secret Image, Main key, Shares of the 3 compartments and recovered image

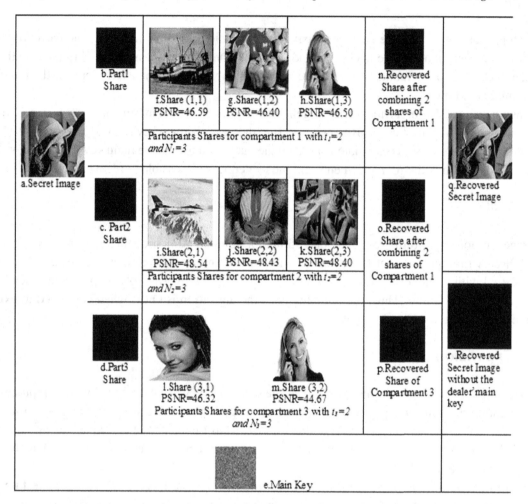

Table 1. Comparison of the proposed scheme with the existing scheme

	Cheng Guo'Scheme	Proposed Scheme
Functionality	Hierarchical	Compartmented
Average PSNR of Cover Images	38dB	50.8dB
Meaningful shadow Images	Yes	Yes
Embedding Capacity	[M*n/max{ri}]*tm	M*N/8
Complexity	$O(n\log^2 n)$	$O(n)$
Pixel Expansion	4	1

Table 2. PSNR of cover images for different test images in the proposed scheme

Secret Image 256*256	Boat.bmp 256*256	Baboon.bmp 256*256	Barbara.bmp 256*256
Im1.bmp	52.46	52.39	52.37
Im2.tiff	51.28	51.13	51.15
Im3.png	52.66	52.55	52.56
Im4.bmp	51.28	51.13	51.15
Im5.bmp	52.51	52.49	52.37

CONCLUSION

The new compartmented secret sharing scheme proposed in this paper emphasizes five capabilities: Confidentiality, authentication, availability and correctness, Integrity and no pixel expansion. The computational complexity of the Shamir secret sharing scheme is $O(k \log^2 k)$ times ARITHMETHIC $(GF(q))$ for recovery whereas this scheme has very less computational complexity of $O(k)$ as it includes simple addition and XOR operation. The experimental result shows that recovered image has superior quality compared to the existing algorithms. This research can be extended for making hierarchical secret sharing scheme. This scheme can be applied in a situation where the shared secret could be an expected return message to acknowledge receipt of important information.

REFERENCES

Asmuth, C. A., & Bloom, J. (1983). A modular approach to key safeguarding. *IEEE Transactions on Information Theory*, *29*(2), 208–210. doi:10.1109/TIT.1983.1056651

Blakley, G. R. (1979). Safeguarding cryptographic keys. *Proceedings of the American Federation of Information Processing Societies National Computer Conference* (Vol. 48, pp. 313–317).

Brickell, E. F. Some ideal secret sharing schemes. In J.-J. Quisquater & J. Vandewalle (Eds.), *Advances in Cryptology, LNCS* (Vol. 434, pp. 468–475). Springer-Verlag; doi:10.1007/3-540-46885-4_45.

Hsu, C.-F., & Harn, L. (2014). Multipartite Secret Sharing Based on CRT. *Wireless Personal Communications*, *78*, 271–282.

Enos, G., & Zheng, Y. (2012). An id based Signcryption Scheme with Compartmented Secret Sharing for Unsigncryption. Retrieved from https://eprint.iacr.org

Farras, O., & Ruth, J. Metcalf-Burton, Padr'o, C., & V'azq, L. (n. d.). On the Optimization of Bipartite Secret Sharing Schemes. Retrieved from www.ma4.upc.edu

Fathimal, P.M., & Arockia Jansi Rani, P. (2015, May). Design of Block based Visual Secret sharing scheme for color Images. International Journal of Applied Engineering Research.

Fathimal. P.M., & Arockia Jansi Rani, P. (2014). Bidirectional Serpentine Scan Based Error Diffusion Technique for Color Image Visual Cryptography. *International Journal of Science, Engineering and Technology Research.*

Fathimal, P. M., & Arockia Jansi Rani, P. (2015, March). K out of N Secret Sharing Scheme for Gray and Color Images. *Proceedings of the IEEE International Conference on Electrical, Computer and Communication Technologies.* doi:10.1109/ICECCT.2015.7226019

Fathimal, P.M., & Arockia Jansi Rani, P. (2015, June). (N, N) Secret Color Image Sharing Scheme with Dynamic Group. *International Journal of Computer Network and Information Security.*

Fathimal, P.M., & Arockia Jansi Rani, P. (2015, December). K out of N Secret Sharing Scheme with Steganography and Authentication. *Advances in Intelligence Systems and Computing, Springer.*

Fathimal, P.M., & Arockia Jansi Rani. P(2016,April)K out of N Secret Sharing Scheme for Multiple Images with Steganography and Authentication. *International Journal of Imaging and Graphics, World Scientific.*

Guo, C., Chang, C. C., & Qin, C. (2012). A Hierarchical Threshold secret image sharing. *Pattern Recognition Letters, 33*(1), 83–91. doi:10.1016/j.patrec.2011.09.030

Kaya, K., & Selçuk, A. A. (2007). Threshold cryptography based on Asmuth–Bloom secret sharing. *Information Sciences, 177*(19), 4148–4160. doi:10.1016/j.ins.2007.04.008

Mignotte, M. (1983). How to share a secret. In T. Beth (Ed.), *Cryptography-Proceedings of the Workshop on Cryptography, LNCS* (Vol. 149, pp. 371–375). Springer-Verlag; doi:10.1007/3-540-39466-4_27.

Shamir, A. (1979, November). How to Share a Secret. *Communications of the ACM, 22*(11), 612–613. doi:10.1145/359168.359176

Simmons. (1990). How to (Really) Share a Secret. In S. Goldwasser (Ed.), Advances in Cryptology, LNCS (Vol. 403, pp. 390–448). Springer-Verlag.

This research was previously published in the International Journal of Information Security and Privacy (IJISP), 10(3); edited by Michele Tomaiuolo and Monica Mordonini; pages 1-9, copyright year 2016 by IGI Publishing (an imprint of IGI Global).

Chapter 27
An Improved Size Invariant (n, n) Extended Visual Cryptography Scheme

Rahul Sharma
Indian School of Mines, India

Ayush Khare
Indian School of Mines, India

Nitesh Kumar Agrawal
Indian School of Mines, India

Arup Kumar Pal
Indian School of Mines, India

ABSTRACT

In this paper, the authors have presented a (n, n) extended visual cryptography scheme where n numbers of meaningful shares furnish a visually secret message. Initially they have converted a grayscale image into binary image using dithering method. Afterwards, they have incorporated pixel's eight neighboring connectivity property of secret image during formation of meaningful shares. The scheme is able to generate the shares without extending its size. This approach has enhanced the visual quality of the recovered secret image from n numbers of shares. The scheme has been tested with some images and satisfactory results are achieved. The scheme has improved the contrast of the recovered secret image than a related (n, n) extended visual cryptography scheme.

1. INTRODUCTION

A *n* out of *n* visual cryptography scheme *((n,n)*-VCS), defined by Naor and Shamir (1994) in which the image is first encrypted into n shares and someone with all *n* shares can only decrypt the secret image, while stacking less than *n* number of shares will not reveal any information about the secret image. In a *(2, 2) Visual Cryptography* experiment defined by Naor and Shamir (1994), a codebook comprising of all code words of size *(2, 2)* sub-pixels is taken. The secret image is then encrypted into two shares where the size of each share is four times the size of the original secret mage. An example illustrating

DOI: 10.4018/978-1-7998-1763-5.ch027

the *(2,2)* Visual Cryptography codebook is shown in Figure 1 where the secret image is shown in Figure 1(a) and the two shares are shown in Figure 1(b) and Figure 1(c). The final stacked result of the two generated shares is shown in Figure 1(d).

The overlapping of encrypted shares can be of two types; namely *Stack based* and *XOR-based* In *Stack based visual cryptography scheme*, the logical OR of the generated shares has been chosen whereas in *XOR-based visual cryptography scheme*, the XOR operation on the generated shares are performed to reveal the secret image (Ou et al., 2015). According to the research, many unresolved issues on OR-based visual cryptography scheme have been extensively studied, such as meaningless share, poor contrast quality of revealed secret image, perfect reconstruction of the black pixels and the cheating prevention issue (Chen and Tsao, 2009). To overcome the above mentioned problems, a random grid-based size-invariant visual cryptography scheme (RGVCS) was introduced by Kafri and Keren (1987) in which a secret image is encoded into two random-liked shares. The size of each share is same as that of the original secret image for solving the problem of pixel expansion. Furthermore, areas of research include improving the visual quality of RGVCS and constructing RGVCS with the abilities of OR and XOR decryption. Contrast is one of the main factor in evaluating the visual quality of the revealed secret image. In OR-based visual cryptography scheme, the contrast achieved is at most 50% of the secret image. In order to achieve better visual quality of the revealed secret image, XOR-based visual cryptography scheme was introduced (Ou et al., 2015). In XOR-based visual cryptography scheme, only small, cheap and lightweight computational devices are needed. Decryption of secret image using XOR-based operation improves the visual quality of the revealed secret image and solves the alignment problem, some drawbacks like meaningless shares still exist in this scheme. We can generate the meaningful shares with the help of multiple cover images. To generate meaningful shares, the light transmission of a share is adjusted according to an independent cover image. Moreover, the visual quality of both the shares and the revealed secret image is still poor.

To overcome the aforementioned problem, in this paper, a size invariant XOR-based visual cryptography scheme has been proposed with a notion of improved visual quality of the meaningful shares as well as the revealed secret image. Firstly, a basic algorithm for (n, n) XOR-based visual cryptography scheme has been presented. Teng Guo et. al. (2014) have suggested a (n,n) random grid based extended visual cryptography scheme. Introduction of randomness in share generation process of random-grid based visual cryptography scheme (RGVCS) have degraded the visual quality of the generated meaningful shares and the revealed secret image. To overcome the peculiarities associated with above problem, we have introduced a new method in which we have considered the probability of the neighboring pixel of cover image to determine whether a pixel should be black or white. The proposed method improves the visual quality of the generated shares and the revealed secret image considerably. In this paper, we have improved the to the algorithm proposed in Teng Guo et al. (2014) in terms of improvement of visual quality of the generated meaningful shares as well the revealed secret image by introducing some improvement in the above (n, n) *XOR-based Visual Cryptography* algorithm and secondly perfect regeneration of the black pixels associated with the black pixel in the revealed secret image.

This paper is organized as follows. In section 2, we provide the detailed method of RG-based VCS and RG-based EVCS. In section 3, we provide a proposed method of RG-based EVCS is given. In section 4, a performance analysis of the algorithm provided in section 3 is done. Section 4 provides the experimental results of algorithm proposed in section 3. The conclusion of the paper is given in section 5.

Figure 1. An example of VC scheme proposed by Naor and Shamir (1994). (a) Secret Image, (b, c) Encoded shares, (d) Reconstructed Image

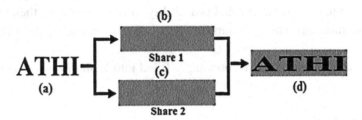

2. RELATED WORK

2.1. (2, 2) Random Grid-based VCS

In $(2, 2)$ random grid visual cryptography scheme, a binary secret image S can produce two random grids RG_1 and RG_2 in such a way that pixel in them is either black or white with equal probability. Generally, any of the individual share provide no information of S individually, but they reveal S when stacked properly.

Algorithm 1
Input: A secret binary image S.
Output: Two random grids R_1 and R_2.
Step1: Generate a random grid R_1 where R_1 (i, j) $\in_r$ (0,1).
Step2: For each pixel $S(i, j)$, compute $R_2 = R1(\text{i, j})$ if $S(\text{i, j})=0$ else $\sim R1(\text{i, j})$.
Step 3: Output $(R1, R2)$.

2.2. (K, K) Random Grid-based Extended VCS (T. Guo et al (2014))

This algorithm takes one secret image S and K cover images as input and generate K meaningful shares corresponding to the K cover images. Share image (S_i) shows the content of the cover image (C_i) or $1 \leq i \leq K$ with reduced visual quality, while stacking of shares $S_1, S_2, ..., S_K$ reveals the content of the secret image (S) whose visual quality is also reduced. In this algorithm, the parameter β is used to set a tradeoff between share images and revealed secret image, on one hand, the larger β value implies that the cover images are be *more* visual in shares and reduced the visual quality of revealed secret image, on the other hand, smaller β value implies that cover images are *less* visual in shares and improved visual quality of revealed secret image.

Algorithm 2
Input: A secret binary image S and K cover images C_j $(1 \leq j \leq K)$.
Output: K random grid shares.
Step 1: For each pixel $S(i, j)$ of secret image do:
Step 2: Generate a bit x which is 0 with probability β and 1 with probability $1-\beta$.
Step 3: If x is equal to 1
Step 4: Call *Algorithm 1* to encode pixel $S(i, j)$ so that two pixel q_1 and q_2' are produced. Encrypt $q2$' similarly to produce q_2 and q_3'. Repeat until all K shares are generated where q_k is the bit q_k'.

Step 5: Else if x is equal to 0

Step 6: Generate K pixels $b_1, b_2, ..., b_K$ such that, if $C_f (1 \leq f \leq K)$ is white, then we generate a pixel for $S_f (I, j)$ that is either white or black with equal probability, else if C_f is black, then we generate K pixels are all white, we randomly choose a number $(1,2,....,K)$, say r, and set the r-th pixel to black.

Step 7: End if.

Step 8: All the generated pixels are correspondingly filled into K shares where r-th pixel is filled into $S_r(i, j)$.

Step 9: End for

Step 10: Output all the K shares.

3. PROPOSED XOR-BASED EXTENDED VCS SCHEME

In *Algorithm 2*, the visual quality of the revealed secret image as well as the generated meaningful shares is deteriorated. To overcome this problem, we propose a scheme to improve the visual quality of both by considering the probability of neighboring pixels. We have considered that if all the neighboring pixels of the cover image corresponding to the pixel to be processed is black, then the probability of that pixel to be black in share image is more. This method improves the visual quality of the meaningful shares. The above fact is verified using different experimental results of contrast and average light transmission ratio in section 4. We have uses the near-neighbor connectivity of a pixel, which is 8 for inner pixels and 6 for the boundary pixels. The schematic diagram of the proposed scheme is shown in Figure 2. The algorithmic steps of the proposed VCS are summarized below:

Algorithm 3

Input: A secret binary image S and K cover images C_i where $(1 \leq i \leq K)$.

Output: K meaningful shares $S_1, S_2, ... S_K$.

Neighbor function *(Image1,i,j)*: Return number of pixels that are white in the neighboring connectivity of pixel (i,j) of image1.

Step 1: For each pixel $S(i, j)$ of secret image do:

Step 2: Generate a bit x which is 0 with probability β and 1 with probability $1-\beta$.

Step 3: If x is equal to 1

Step 4: Call *Algorithm 1* to encode pixel $S(i, j)$ so that two pixel q_1 and q_2' are produced. Encrypt q2' similarly to produce q_2 and q_3'. Repeat until all K shares are generated where q_k is the bit q_k'.

Step 5: Else if x is equal to 0

Step 6: Generate K pixels $b_1, b_2, ..., b_K$ such that, if $C_f (1 \leq f \leq K)$ is white, then we generate a pixel for $S_f(i,j)$ that is either white or black with probability Neighbor_fucntion(C_{fl}, i,j)) /pixel_Connectivity, else if C_f is black, then we generate K pixels are all white, we randomly choose a number $(1,2,....,K)$, say r, and set the r-th pixel to black.

Step 7: End if.

Step 8: All the generated pixels are correspondingly filled into K shares where r-th pixel is filled into $S_r(i,j)$.

Step 9: End for

Step 10: Output all the K shares.

Figure 2. The proposed VCS scheme

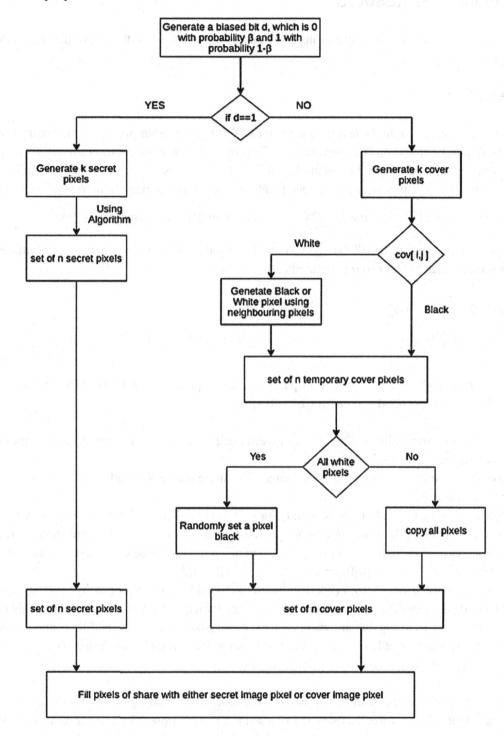

4. EXPERIMENTAL RESULTS

In this section, we present some definitions and tools using which we will analyze the results derived from *Algorithm 3*.

4.1. Definitions

Definition 1: (Average Light Transmission, Shyu (2007)) For a certain pixel p in the binary image S, the probability of pixel p is transparent, say Prob (p=0), represents the light transmission of pixel p, which is denoted as l[p]. For example, the light transmission of a transparent pixel p is l[p]=1, while the light transmission of an opaque pixel x is l[p]=0. The average light transmission of image S is defined as $L[S] = (1/[h*w])* \sum_{i=1}^{h}\sum_{j=1}^{w} l(i,j)$, in which the size of image S is h*w.

Definition 2: (Contrast, Shyu (2007)) To evaluate the visual quality of the revealed secret image R for the secret image S, contrast α is defined as

$$\alpha = \frac{L\left[R\left[S(0)\right]\right] - L\left[R\left[S(1)\right]\right]}{1 + L\left[R\left[S(1)\right]\right]}$$

where R(0) (resp. R(1) denotes all the transparent(resp. opaque)pixels in R and S[A(0)(resp. opaque) denotes all the pixels encoded from R(0) (resp. R(1)).

Definition 3: (Contrast condition, Chen and Tsao (2011)): The reconstructed image S reveals the content of the original secret image R if $\alpha > 0$.

Definition 4: (Contrast Condition for share image) The share image S reveals the content of the cover image R if $\alpha > 0$.

Definition 5: (Security Condition, Chen and Tsao (2011)) A (K,n) RG-based Visual Cryptography Scheme is secure if the stacking of any r (r<K) share pixels $x_{i1}, x_{i2}, ..., x_{ir}$ that are encoded from the same secret pixel, which is either $\alpha(0)$ (transparent) or $\alpha(1)$ (opaque), will result in the same light transmission $l(x_{i1}, x_{i2}, ..., x_{ir}[\alpha[0]] = l(x_{i1}, x_{i2}, ..., x_{ir}[\alpha[1]] = 1/2^{r}$.

Definition 6: (Security Condition) A (k,k) RG-based Extended Visual Cryptography Scheme is secure if given a fixed combination of cover pixels $c_1, c_2, ..., c_K$ (where $c_i \in (0,1)$), the stacking of any r (r<K) share pixels $x_{i1}, x_{i2}, ... x_{ir}$ that are encoded from cover pixels $c_1, c_2, ..., c_K$ and the same secret pixel $\alpha(0)$ (transparent) or $\alpha(1)$ (opaque), will result in the same light transmission $l(x_{i1}, x_{i2}, ..., x_{ir}[\alpha[0], c_1, c_2, ..., c_K]] = l(x_{i1}, x_{i2}, ..., x_{ir}[\alpha[1], c_1, c_2, ..., c_K]]$.

Figure 3 shows the outcome of the proposed VCS scheme. We have generated 5 shares and subsequently the secret image is revealed using the five shares. The contrast values of revealed secret images with respect to different values are presented in Table 1. The proposed scheme achieved better results compared to other schemes. In addition, the visual effect is depicted Figure 4 and in our experiment we have achieved better results.

Figure 3. Encoding of secret image using Improved (n, n) Algorithm

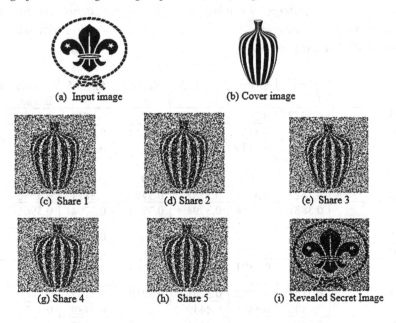

Figure 4. (a) Reconstructed Image using T. Guo et al (2014), (b) Reconstructed image using proposed OR based Scheme, (c) Reconstructed image using proposed XOR based VC scheme

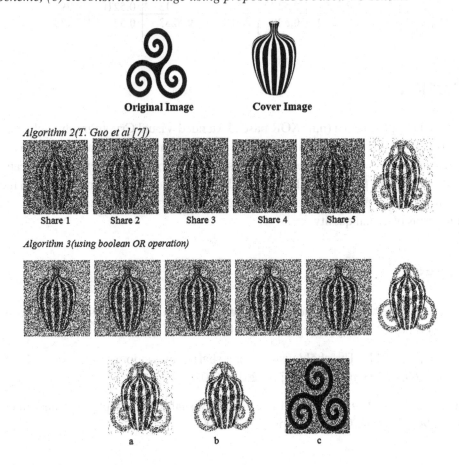

Table 1. The contrast Result of the share images and the decoded image that are generated by Algorithm 3 of (K,K) access structure with different β's, where S_1, S_2,S_3,S_4 and S_5 denote the five share images and $S_1+S_{2+}S_3+S_4+S_5$ denotes the decoded image. (a) T. Guo et al VC scheme, (b) Proposed Boolean OR based scheme, (c) Proposed XOR based scheme.

□		Share 1	Share 2	Share 3	Share 4	Share 5	Reconstructed image
0.2	A	0.2657	0.2681	0.2698	0.2716	0.2700	0.3968
	B	0.3135	0.3136	0.3118	0.3114	0.3123	0.3992
	C	0.3111	0.3119	0.3104	0.3136	0.3144	0.5347
0.4	A	0.2967	0.2960	0.2942	0.2972	0.2945	0.3584
	B	0.3822	0.3802	0.3787	0.3799	0.3821	0.3646
	C	0.3881	0.3814	0.3794	0.3783	0.3794	0.3961
0.5	A	0.3062	0.3067	0.3072	0.3074	0.3063	0.3402
	B	0.4148	0.4131	0.4160	0.4147	0.4159	0.3453
	C	0.4154	0.4171	0.4155	0.4167	0.4166	0.3326
0.6	A	0.3185	0.3202	0.3201	0.3210	0.3192	0.3260
	B	0.4486	0.4466	0.4449	0.4468	0.4489	0.3453
	C	0.4454	0.4465	0.4471	0.4477	0.4459	0.2712
0.8	A	0.3455	0.3435	0.3476	0.3451	0.3484	0.2874
	B	0.5217	0.5229	0.5215	0.5213	0.5210	0.2933
	C	0.5210	0.5205	0.5228	0.5233	0.5235	0.1368

5. CONCLUSION

In this paper, we have proposed a (n,n) XOR based Extended Visual Cryptography Scheme with meaningful shares by considering the neighboring pixel probability in the cover images. The visual quality of the generated shares have been improved and the visual quality of reconstructed images can be adjusted by setting suitable value of β. The visual quality of the reconstructed image increases as β increases. We can set a specific value of parameter β as per the required application. The schemes have improved the exiting one in terms of visual quality.

REFERENCES

Chen, T., & Tsao, K. (2009). visual secret sharing by random Grids Revisited. *Pattern Recognition, 42*(9), 2203–2217. doi:10.1016/j.patcog.2008.11.015

Chen, T., & Tsao, K. (2011). Threshold visual secret sharing by random Grids. *Journal of Systems and Software, 84*(7), 1693–1703. doi:10.1016/j.jss.2011.02.023

Guo, T., Liu, F., & Wu, C. (2014). K out of K extended Visual Cryptography by Random Grids. *Signal Processing, 94*, 90–101. doi:10.1016/j.sigpro.2013.06.003

Kafri, O., & Keren, E. (1987). Encryption of pictures and shapes by Random Grids Optics. *Letters*, 12(6), 377-379.

Naor, M., & Shamir, A. (1994). Visual Cryptography. In *EUROCRYPT'94, LNCS* (Vol. 950). Berlin: Springer-Verlag.

Ou, D., Sun, W., & Wu, X. (2015). Non-expansible XOR based Visual Cryptography Scheme with meaningful shares. *Signal Processing*, *108*, 604–621. doi:10.1016/j.sigpro.2014.10.011

Shyu, S. (2007). Image encryption by Random grids. *Pattern Recognition*, *40*(3), 1014–1031. doi:10.1016/j.patcog.2006.02.025

Zohu, Z., Arce, G., & Crescenzo, G. D. (2006). Halftone Visual Cryptography. *IEEE Transactions on Image Processing*, *15*(8), 2441–2453. doi:10.1109/TIP.2006.875249 PMID:16900697

This research was previously published in the International Journal of Business Data Communications and Networking (IJBDCN), 12(2); edited by Zoubir Mammeri; pages 80-88, copyright year 2016 by IGI Publishing (an imprint of IGI Global).

Chapter 28
A Methodological Evaluation of Crypto–Watermarking System for Medical Images

Anna Babu
M. G. University, India

Sonal Ayyappan
SCMS School of Engineering and Technology, India

ABSTRACT

Health care institution demands exchange of medical images of number of patients to sought opinions from different experts. In order to reduce storage and for secure transmission of the medical images, Crypto-Watermarking techniques are adopted. The system is considered to be combinations of encryption technique with watermarking or steganography means adopted for safe transfer of medical images along with embedding of optional medical information. The Digital Watermarking is the process of embedding data to multimedia content. This can be done in spatial as well as frequency domain of the cover image to be transmitted. The robustness against attacks is ensured while embedding the encrypted data into transform domain, the encrypted data can be any secret key for the content recovery or patient record or the image itself. This chapter presents basic aspects of crypto-watermarking technique, as an application. It gives a detailed assessment on different approaches of crypto-watermarking for secure transmission of medical images and elaborates a case study on it.

INTRODUCTION

Crypto-Watermarking is an evident area of research especially with the advent of medical related technologies. Health care institution demands exchange of medical images of number of patients to sought opinions from different experts. In order to facilitate storage and secure transmission of the medical images the applications related to telemedicine, transfer medical images by the aid of efficient crypto-watermarking system (Acharya, R., Bhat, P. S., Kumar, S., & Min, L. C, 2003). Since the transfer of

DOI: 10.4018/978-1-7998-1763-5.ch028

medical imageries between hospitals and additionally among totally different consultants is common occurrence, the security and confidentiality of medical images is demanded. Crypto-watermarking helps in providing the appropriate information embedded in the medical images without creating an opportunity to defame an institution by rightful delivery of medical images to intended owner. The images can be protected while transmitting through channel when encryption is done. After the images get decrypted at the recipient side, it's prone to security breaches which can be protected by the use of watermarking. Thus crypto-watermarking is technique in which cryptography is combined with watermarking. In recent time, Crypto-watermarking techniques are gaining popularity as its finding importance in certain sensitive areas like healthcare, military communication and law-enforcement (Khan, A., Siddiqa, A., Munib, S., & Malik, S. A., 2014).

The utilization of internet for information spreads has created the vital call for security. Numerous robust encryption techniques for plain messages have been industrialized to fund this request. Privacy protection could be ensured with encryption and embedding the symmetric key in the encrypted domain. Encryption is the key for confidentiality and authentication of medical images transmitted. Encryption converts a data into unintelligible form. When an image with some secrecy need to be transmitted is encrypted, the provider unknown of the secret data tries to compress the encrypted image.

BACKGROUND

The Need for Crypto-Watermarking

The need for crypto-watermarking system is to give testimony concerning the security and confidentiality of images especially in sensitive areas like medical and military. In medical field the use of crypto-watermarking comes to play when the security of electronic patient records needs to be guaranteed along with privacy, authenticity and security of respective medical image. The regulations used for checking the protection of these data are the *Health Insurance Portability and Accountability Act (HIPAA)* of US government and the European Data Protection Directive 95/46/EC (Fernández-Alemán, J. L., Señor, I. C., Lozoya, P. Á. O., & Toval, A., 2013).

Crypto-Watermarking system has many applications which include the transfer of images whose security and confidentiality need to be verified also transfer of medical data for patients to undergo proper service regarding the health issues from various specialists. The use of crypto-watermarking in both areas is studied simultaneously in this chapter i.e. secure image transfer having details to preserve and secure electronic patient record transfer along with image. The medical data is protected by the aid of encryption and data hiding algorithms.

Medical field requires the transfer of medical data among practitioners for integrated checkups for patients around the globe. To aid these system EPR facilities for the hospital helps a lot for centralized access of patient records. EPRs give the opening for patients to take improved synchronized care from health providers and admission to their health material becomes easier. Electronic Patient Record (EPR) is a way to make things easier for all and to be better-quality informed and more involved in the patient's general health care. Providing EPRs among the different opinion collectors becomes critical with questions and apprehensions around the confidentiality and security of patient's condition information as well as hospitals fame.

Specific to protecting the information stored in EPRs, the HIPAA Security Rule of US government requires the health care providers to take up physical, administrative, and technical safeguards to protect a subject's electronic health information. Some safety measures that may be built in to EPR systems include:

In order to protect the data hold on in EPRs, the HIPAA Rule concerning security of US government needs the health care suppliers to take up physical, admin body, and technical safeguards to guard a subject's electronic health data. Some safety measures which will be in-built to EPR systems follow the mechanisms given below:

1. "Admittance controls mechanisms" like password keys and access PIN numbers, acts as a protective layer to limit access to one's confidential information's or limiting unauthorized access;
2. "Encryption" of information includes many patients health data cannot be easily interpreted or read except by authorized who can ``decrypt" it, using a secret ``key" or any special type of key using symmetric or asymmetric methods;
3. "Review trail" which makes a note of who retrieved the info, what variations were completed and when.

The proposed method is motivated by the following observations: Next generation medical care technologies implies the need for security, confidentiality and privacy that will provide many benefits for health care delivery, but with advent of medical industry and its standards there are number of hindrances to privacy and security provisions that must be safeguarded in order to maintain basic virtuous principles in medical industry and its social existence (Zhang, X., 2011). Intention taken is to develop a technique that pools encryption of image and information (relevant data) hiding algorithm for benign transmission (Jaeger et al., 2014). Convenience of stream cipher motivates to use symmetric RC4 algorithm for EPR data encryption. The quick analysis and extraction of medical images and the relevant data also requires confidentiality to be preserved.

The chapter includes the transfer of image and EPR securely by the means of crypto –watermarking technique. Image is transferred securely after encryption by RC4. The secret key used for encryption by RC4 is in turn encrypted using a different technique - ElGamal crypto – system. Efficiency of this crypto -system is the major research paradigm in many works. The key encrypted by ElGamal is then entrenched in the image by the robust frequency DCT based – Spread spectrum watermarking approach. When EPR data needs to be embedded in the image it follows a different approach. The EPR security is other case study requirement for which different watermarking methodology is adopted based on size of data handled. When EPR is needed to be transmitted, the embedding algorithm can be differed as data varies considerably. Spatial pixel manipulations with research in area of Prediction – Error Domain is done for watermarking the EPR to images.

Thus case study in this chapter includes image encryption with secret key embedding with DCT based approach also EPR data embedding can be done in spatial prediction error domain using Rhombus prediction scheme as future scope. Analysis of results is done with quality metrics used as Peak Signal to Noise Ratio (PSNR) and Mean Square Error (MSE) values.

Image Encryption Techniques

Encryption is process of converting the message into a form that is illegible for any unauthorized personnel unless the key to decode the message is obtained which is only present with the authorized user. So it confirms the properties of authentication, integrity and confidentiality. Encryption can be based on *symmetric key encryption* and *public key encryption* scheme that can be applied to streams or blocks. Stream cipher is faster compared to block cipher methods. The keys used for encryption can be secret key, public-private key and shared key. RC4 is an example of stream cipher algorithm based on a symmetric secret key, RSA is an example of public-private key scheme, and Diffie Hellman key algorithm is worked upon shared secret key.

The encryption practice can be asymmetric, symmetric or hybrid. It can be functional to *blocks* or *streams*. The block encryption scheme applied to images, can meet with basically three inconveniences. The first and foremost one is when there is encryption of identical zones, they are found to be similar. The problem that is found next is that block encryption schemes are not vigorous to noise. The data integrity preservation is the third problem (Puech, Chaumont, & Strauss, 2008). The combination of encryption and watermarking can solve these types of problems.

Use of cryptography in images will make pixel intensity information to be transmitted in a form different from the original details so that only authorized personnel can view the image by using proper key and validate the image data. Thus image data included in as pixel information to be transmitted into an illegible form by different image encryption techniques as discussed above. Apart from these there are many more types of algorithms used for incorporating the image encryption. Different techniques of image encryption are incorporated that preserves the security of images. Algorithms based on both chaos and non-chaos image encryption schemes have been proposed. Of the both chaos based and non-chaos based, chaos is considered to be efficient and promising. The image encryption based on chaotic algorithm uses properties of dynamics that is deterministic and behavior that is not predictable. Encryption techniques are namely of three types permutation, reversal or replacement and techniques that include both substitution and transposition. There is change in the pixel values in substitution or replacement schemes while shuffling of pixel intensities is done in permutation. Improved security is uaranteed by combining both techniques. An image encryption scheme is proposed in (Guan, Huang, & Guan, 2005) which use Arnold cat map and Chen's chaotic system. Combinations of three permutation schemes is discussed, which can be in levels of bits, in levels of pixel and in block level permutations are introduced in any order (Mitra, Rao, & Prasanna, 2006). Key stream generator is added for enhancement in AES algorithm used in image encryption in (Zeghid et al., 2007). The scheme used in (Zhu, Z. L., Zhang, W., Wong, K. W., & Yu, H., 2011) does shuffling of bits which is chaos based. Shuffling of bits not only changes the position of bits of pixel intensities but also changes its pixel value. Total permutation is done in (Zhang, G., & Liu, Q., 2011) used for a novel encryption scheme for images. Security of encryption in images is improved by the combination of 2 logistic maps in (Ismail, Amin, & Diab, 2010). Multiple chaotic encryption systems are used in (Alsafasfeh & Arfoa, 2011). The custom image encryption schemes can be taken into account such as based on Rubik's cube and many more.

Digital Watermarking Approach

Watermarking is the process of embedding a signal into a multimedia content of text, image, audio or video types; and signal used as watermark can be of any format- text, image or audio signal. It can be viewed as a data hiding technique. The data hiding can be done in two domains - *spatial* and *frequency* domain. It can be basically reversible and irreversible. The properties to be satisfied by watermarking include robustness, capacity and imperceptibility. The robustness against attack is possible when the embedding is done in frequency domain and if capacity is of major concern spatial domain can be of great help. The message is imperceptibly embedded using watermarking and without any change in image size or format (Pal, Ghosh & Bhattacharya, 2013). In case of digital images, the information embedded can be either *invisible* or *visible* from the user perspective. As the security and confidentiality is primary concern, concentration is on imperceptible watermarks. Digital Watermarking technology is fit for being used as a form of copyright protection and a preventing those who have illegal in order intention to get a hold of confidential multimedia data including images disproportionately. The watermarking is based on spatial and frequency domain. *Reversible data hiding* focuses on data embedding and extraction (Zhang, X., 2011). There are number of schemes in spatial domain where additional data including images, notations are added within the encrypted image. In these schemes it's hopeful that original content is recovered without any change. In a scheme, watermarking is opted to share data (Coatrieux, G et al., 2000). When watermarking is applied to images, it allows the insertion of a message by modifying the pixel gray-scale values of the image in an imperceptible manner. Data-hiding is done in both steganography and watermarking with only a narrow line of difference in which watermarking safeguards the elimination of secret information in the cover medium whereas latter requires the existence of secret information to be unknown (Khan, A., Siddiqa, A., Munib, S., & Malik, S. A., 2014).

In the writing, a significant couple of calculations are anticipated to fulfill the property of change-ableness. The ordinary techniques square measure upheld modulo 256 option used in (Puech, Chaumont & Strauss, 2008), lossless multi-determination revamp (Coatrieux, G., Le Guillou, C., Cauvin, J. M., & Roux, C., 2009), lossless pressure (Puech & Rodrigues, 2004), (Stinson, 2005), invertible commotion including (Schneier, 2007), qualification development (Cox et al., 1997), (William & Stallings, 2006),whole number undulating revamp (Coatrieux et al., 2000), alteration of histogram (Jaeger et al., 2014), then forward. All in all, these calculations target advanced pictures that square measure keeps as whole numbers from zero to 255. The best approach to reversibly floating so as to bring information into the items diagrammatically or settled point numbers, similar to the 3D models comprising of directions (e.g., (Zhang, X., 2011).) furthermore the high-dynamic-range pictures as indicated by (Acharya, R., Bhat, P. S., Kumar, S., & Min, L. C, 2003), has once in a while been explored. Be that as it may, reversible hiding in any style of learning is interesting to maintain a strategic distance from information misfortune. Since the vast majority of the overarching procedures trade out of the attributes of advanced pictures, straightforwardly floating so as to apply them to the articles diagrammatical or settled point numbers may experience troubles or cause an outsized contortion. In the preparatory work (Khan, A., Siddiqa, A., Munib, S., & Malik, S. A., 2014), the idea of keeping the balance information inside of the watermarked article is embraced in quantization-based inserting. Moreover, we tend to execute it on 3D network models so the main lattice model will pretty much be recouped. The condition for the exact recuperation is given in (Zhang, W., Ma, K., & Yu, N., 2014), furthermore the recuperation strategy might be performed with no particular information of the primary article. Indeed, even along these lines, it's capability to gauge the quantizer used inside of the regulation by the connected arithmetic investigation of the watermarked object, as appeared inside of the accompanying segment. Hence, the insurance of the algorithmic project must be expanded to thwart the potential data escape from the watermarked object.

Crypto-Watermarking Approaches

The method recognized in (Qian & Zhang, 2014) is one of the scheme of crypto-watermarking in which data hiding is done in encrypted images. The stream cipher technique for encryption followed by data hiding in which chosen bits are taken from the encoded picture to implant the mystery information.

Zhang, W., Ma, K., and Yu, N. (2014) had advised a scheme in which certain pixels are selected for estimating the errors and data hiding is done into these estimated errors. Standard stream cipher algorithm AES is used to encrypt the pixels of the image and special scheme is used to encrypt the estimation errors. The efficiency and feasibility of the scheme is computed by PSNR and embedding rate.

Pal, K., Ghosh, G., and Bhattacharya, M. (2013) had embedded the patient record including patient's name, diagnostic and region of interest into the cover image by the use of discrete cosine transform in frequency domain and RSA public-private key algorithm The infected region to be the ROI is detected through an amalgamation of contour detection algorithm and region growing. The embedded information is found to be obtained with exact similarity even from several attacked image.

The scheme described in Lakrissi, Y., Erritali, M., and Fakir, M. (2013) is based on the arrangement of encryption algorithms using secret keys and public-private keys including watermarking. The algorithm for image encryption is done using stream cipher technique with secret key encrypted with an asymmetric cipher technique. The watermarking algorithm is used to insert this encrypted secret key into the encrypted image.

The system explained by Bouslimi et al. (2012) moves towards a watermarking algorithm which is substitutive, the quantization index modulation (QIM) and an encryption algorithm which is stream or block cipher technique. In Joint Watermarking/Encryption scheme watermark is embedded during the encryption process. It allows verifying the image reliability in both encrypted and spatial domains. Here encryption and data embedding is conducted together at the stage for protection, decryption and data extraction can be applied in parallel.

The Medical image watermarking preserves image quality that is mandatory for medical diagnosis and treatment in Rao and Kumari (2011) highlights needs that are essential for medical image watermarking with a go over of developments since 2000 and simulated experiments to exhibit the significance of watermarking in management of medical information.

Puech, Chaumont, and Strauss (2008) portrayed the framework with encryption or information concealing calculations, the assurance of media information. The transmission time can be decreased by the utilization of the information pressure. This work, give answers for consolidate picture encryption and pressure. Utilization of reversible information concealing calculations on encoded pictures wish to evacuate the implanted data before the decoding of picture. The utilization of bit substitution-information concealing strategy helps for this reason. Keeping in mind the end goal to evacuate the watermarked information amid the unscrambling step, nearby standard deviation examination of the watermarked scrambled pictures is finished. Sharing of therapeutic picture in applications, for example, remote analysis help or e-learning, Coatrieux, g., Le Guillou, C., Cauvin, J. M., and Roux, C. (2009) proposes to make the picture more usable while watermarking it with related information digest. Watermarking is utilized to push in the Knowledge Digest (KD) into the dim scale pixel estimations of the related pictures. When it is shared through web, watermarking transmits dependability verifications of a picture and it's KD.

CRYPTO-WATERMARKING

Technologies are evolving for providing security to multimedia applications especially medical data or images that needs proper confidentiality, integrity and authenticity to be ensured. The popular among these technologies include combinations of cryptography and digital watermarking. Cryptographic methods and primitives allow access that is conditional for the protection of multimedia applications and data. The robustness of digital watermarking enables the data that is confidential cannot be removed or destroyed.

Challenges

Cryptography and watermarking are married in the system for crypto-watermarking (Sadeghi, 2008). To deal with various security issues in multimedia applications Crypto-Watermarking is one of the measures that involves great deal of study. The application which is in concern with current chapter work is health care imagery means. The major challenge posed by the system involves secure hiding of confidential information and proper extraction of the data in untrusted environment. The ownership proofs are also on the issues that must be dealt with these systems. The use of encryption and decryption using stream or block ciphers help in protection of data or images corresponding to the medical imagery. The chapter focuses on the works with combination of cryptographic and data hiding schemes so that it enables not to reveal sensitive data other than for those authorized to do so.

In application scenarios the watermark embedding phase requires the watermark extraction phase to know the key or the watermark itself for extraction of the information. This includes the dispute for ownership which can be relatively resolved by the use of public private crypto-system for encryption of secret key or watermark. Limitation in robustness of watermarking undermines the security.

Another challenge in this system is that the encryption and watermarking mechanisms should with stand compression. Because of this, medical mages cannot be communicated when this kind of risk persists. The solution to this kind of problem is encryption (Puech, 2008). Many techniques for encryption of images and data exist. In this chapter the need of the cryptographic and watermarking principles essential to confirm the security of medical imageries and statistics is discussed.

Applications

The application that makes use of Crypto-Watermarking System includes defense, health care institutions for medical imagery. The promise to the protection of medical images during transfer and during the archiving is the main objective. Watermarking accompanied by cryptography in medical imagery helps in increasing the security and provide authentication. Applications can vary from biomedicine, radiology, teradialogy in medicine and plenty more. Health data management can be done properly through multiple watermarking and secret key encryptions.

Case Study

The case study for this method systematically does the encryption and watermarking of medical images efficiently with confidentiality assured. A scheme for reversible crypto-watermarking for safe transfer of images include the biomedical image to be encrypted and the key used for encryption is subsequently ELGamal encrypted for confidentiality and security policy implication preservation. A medical image is selected for transmission in scenario of practioner and medical specialist. Before transmission following steps are done systematically. This constitutes encryption of image based on secret key using stream cipher method RC4. Then the encrypted image is watermarked using spread spectrum coding in DCT after the key itself being encrypted using public-private crypto-system. The encrypted and watermarked image is finally transmitted. The proposed methodology is depicted using a detailed diagram (*Figure 1*). Encrypting images using asymmetric methods are not suitable because they are computationally complex. So a conventional symmetric key encryption, with channel to transfer the key is used (Lakrissi, Y., Erritali, M., & Fakir, M., 2013). The projected method combines algorithm for symmetric image

Figure 1. Proposed methodology

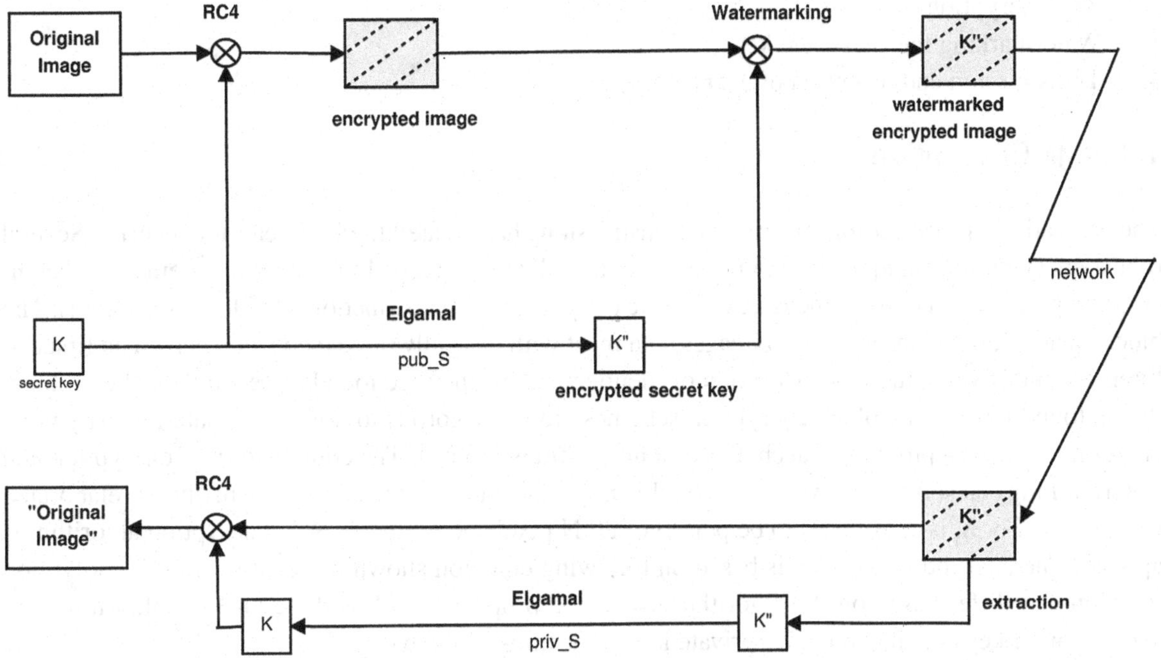

encryption, secret key encryption using asymmetric public-private scheme and spread spectrum coding algorithm in discrete cosine transform for watermarking. RSA being the traditional asymmetric method based on public-private keys and being probe to several security issues, the secret key is encrypted using ELGamal public-private cryptosystem.

Combining image or data encryption with watermarking technique for reliable transmission of medical images including scan and other medical informations and ensuring confidentiality and authenticity is the major intention to address.

- Encryption and Watermarking is the most combined techniques for safe transmission of images (Qian, Z., & Zhang, X., 2014).
- Efficient crypto-system is most essential for secure transmission.
- Stream cipher – symmetric key cipher is used due to it benefits for image encryption.
- ElGamal being stronger crypto-system due to randomization employed is more resistant to attacks and could be replaced for traditional RSA cryptosystem used (Stinson, D. R., 2005).
- The quick analysis and extraction of medical images also requires confidentiality to be preserved.
- Because of the addition of noise by the any watermarking methodology, Robust Spread spectrum approach which reduces the noise input to images need to be employed

Basically, four steps are basically involved in the case study conducted for studying the crypto-watermarking technique. This is general methodology which could be revisited in various orders a further extension to this method is incorporated through the encryption of electronic patient record (EPR) into encrypted or non-encrypted images which can be done as part of future extension, a certain portion of this is carried out here. So general methodology is as follows:

1. Image encryption
2. Key encryption
3. Watermarking the encrypted key.
4. Transmission and reception of encrypted image.

1. Image Encryption

The utilization of internet for information transmissions has created the basic call for security. Several robust encryption techniques for plain messages have been developed to supply this demand. The encryption practice can be asymmetric, symmetric or hybrid. It can be functional to blocks or streams. The block encryption scheme applied to images, can meet with basically three inconveniences. The first and foremost one is when there is encryption of identical zones, they are found to be similar. The problem that is found next is that block encryption schemes are not vigorous to noise. The data integrity preservation is the third problem (Puech, Chaumont, & Strauss, 2008). The combination of encryption and watermarking can solve these types of difficulties. The brief idea of the encrypting method is elaborated in *Figure 2*. For X_i is considered to be poised of all N pixels of an image, RC4 encryption algorithm is applied. The encryption function is based on following equation shown in Equation 1. The encryption function can differ based on the algorithm used. The proposed work is done on RC4 algorithm and encryption of key is done on public-private key algorithm- ELGamal

$$Y = E_k(X)$$

where $E_k()$ is the purpose for encryption with k as the secret key and Y is the equivalent cipher-text. The RC4 stream cipher method used is explained in following section especially the key generation and XOR operation.

a. Stream Cipher - RC4

RC4 could be a radial cipher designed for RSA Security in 1987 by West Chadic Rivest. It's a stream cipher algorithmic rule with variable key size, simple and very quick. Usually Stream cipher algorithms are accustomed to assemble the bits of plain text with a secret key stream of bits issued from a Pseudo Random Number Generator (PRNG), with typical use of XOR operation. The generation of key depends on one key which remains a secret, creating stream cipher algorithms as a part of varied techniques for

Figure 2. Encryption and Watermarking

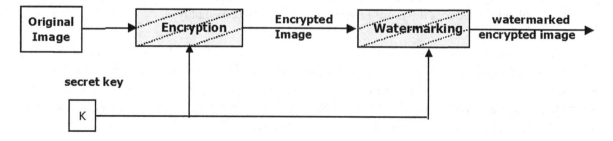

radial coding. The specificity of such stream cipher algorithmic rule strictly depends on, however the bit key stream is created by the PRNG. The RC4 PRNG encompasses 2 steps:

1. Initialization
2. Byte key stream generation.

Key Scheduling Algorithm

To begin, the entries of S are set adequate to the values from zero through 255 in ascending order; that is; S[0] contains zero, S[1] contains 1 and so on. A variable T, which is a vector, is booted up. Now taking a key of length to be 256 bytes, which is transferred to variable T. Else if the length is different one, the first subsequent length of key is changed to components of T and then K is perennial as again and again so as to fill the vector T. These preliminary operations are briefed as in *Table 1*.

After which a gentle swapping is done to get permuted result.

Byte Stream Generation

The input key is not used once Sb is given a initial permuted value. The generation of stream includes starting with Sb[0] and going up to to Sb[255], and, replacing Sb[i] with alternative byte takes place for all S[i] per a theme as configured of S. This process repeats as method continues.

This process generates a sequence of pseudo-random values. Then the input stream is XORed with the pseudo-random values produced by the algorithm. The encryption and decryption process is the same as the process of XORing data stream with the generated key sequence. If it is fed in an encrypted message, i decrypted message will be generated as output, and if it is fed in plain text message, it will produce the encrypted version (William & Stallings, 2006).

In RC4 module each value of k is generated based on RC4 key stream generation algorithm and the entries in S box are once again permuted. Encryption is done by XORing the key value k with the bytes of plain text image pixels. Decryption is done again by XORing the key value k cipher text rounding based on bytes.

2. Key Encryption

The secret key taken based on PRNG is the key to decrypt the medical image sent to the specialist so that he can view the image for diagnosis or further processing, so there is a great need to secure this key at the same time the key needs to be obtained by the specialist fast. The security is guaranteed through public-private key algorithm. In order to increase the security the proposed method use a strong algorithm known as ELGamal which increases the randomization involved in the cipher text also it is difficult against cryptanalysis. The practioner M takes the public key of Specialist S and encrypts the secret key and embeds the encrypted secret key in image using either watermarking or steganography principles. The basics of ELGamal crypto-system is explained in detail in following subsection.

Table 1. Key scheduling step

for j = 0 to 255 do Sb[j] = j; Tb[j] = Key[j mod len];

a. ELGamal Cryptosystem

An ELGamal crypto-system functions in a very finite cyclic cluster group (Schneier, 1996) (Diffie & Hellman, 1976). An ELGamal cryptosystem are often represented by a 4-tuple (p, g, x, y), wherever p may be a massive prime and describes that group or cluster Z_p is employed, g is a part of order n in Z_p, x may be a random integer with $1 <= x <= n-1$, and $y = g^x$. The steps within the ELGamal crypto-system area unit as follows:

1. Key generation: Pick a massive prime p, generator g of Z_p, private key is a random x such that $1 <= x <= p-2$ and public key is 4 tuple (p, g, $y = g^x \bmod p$).
2. Encryption: Pick random k such that, $1 <= k <= n-1$ and encryption function is defined as

$$E(m) = (g^k \bmod p,\ m y^k \bmod p) = (\gamma, \delta)$$

3. Decryption: Given cipher text (γ, δ), compute $\delta \gamma^{-x} \bmod p$ and recover m such that:

$$m = \delta \gamma^{-x} \bmod p$$

3. Watermarking the Encrypted Key

Digital Watermarking technology is fit for being used as a form of copyright protection and a preventing those who have illegal in order intention to get a hold of confidential multimedia data including images disproportionately. The watermarking is based on spatial and frequency domain (Cox, Miller, Bloom, & Honsinger, 2002). The frequency domain being more robust to attacks, the work is done on Discrete Cosine Transform. The encrypted secret key is embedded in DCT domain using spread spectrum approach a traditional method discussed by (Cox, Kilian, Leighton & Shamoon, 1997) as the basic watermarking principle. For an input image, the DCT frequency components are computed using the Equation. 4 shown below:

$$y(u,v) = \sqrt{\frac{2}{M}} \sqrt{\frac{2}{N}} C_u C_v \sum\nolimits_{u=0}^{M-1} \sum\nolimits_{v=0}^{N-1} x(m,n) \cos \frac{(2m+1)u\pi}{2M} \cos \frac{(2n+1)u\pi}{2N}$$

In the equation, with size of N x M pixels, $x(m,n)$ is the spatial intensity at corresponding position of the image, and is the DCT frequency coefficient at corresponding point of the DCT matrix.

The inverse DCT operation is done for watermarked image to restore the image to cover image extracting the watermark information applying the Equation 5 shown below:

$$x(m,n) = \sqrt{\frac{2}{M}} \sqrt{\frac{2}{N}} C_u C_v \sum\nolimits_{u=0}^{M-1} \sum\nolimits_{v=0}^{N-1} y(u,v) \cos \frac{(2m+1)u\pi}{2M} \cos \frac{(2n+1)u\pi}{2N}$$

Vital visual details are included in low frequency bands of the image and geometrical modifications could eliminate high frequency coefficients of the image – basically compression. The watermark is embedded by changing the frequency elements of the mid –band frequencies so that the visual excellence of the image will not be distorted and the watermark cannot be removed by geometrical changes.

a. Spread Spectrum Watermarking

The proposed watermarking calculation in the change area i.e. DCT space is spread range system. In the first place, the best place for supplement the watermark bits is found by file sorting for getting the primary n high recurrence coefficients. The watermark is spread over to numerous containers gathering recurrence so that the vitality in any canister is insignificant and can't be recognized. The watermark ought not be set in locales of inconsequentiality. Watermark is known as a sign transmitted through the recurrence space of the picture. The vigor and security of watermark is guaranteed by, setting the watermark expressly in the most noteworthy coefficients of the picture perceptually. Keeping in mind the end goal to place watermark of length n into a NxN picture, coefficients are registered for the NxN picture utilizing DCT and setting the watermark into extent coefficients with high values. Make a watermark where every worth xi is picked freely as per N (0, 1). The extricated from host advanced picture, an arrangement of qualities Vi, into which a watermark xi is embedded to acquire a balanced grouping of qualities Wi. Watermark insertion results in watermarked image W, with a scaling parameter α used to specify, the extent to which watermark alters the cover image. Formula for computing watermarked signal is shown in Equation 6. A large value of α will cause perceptual degradation in the watermarked image.

$$W_i = V_i = \alpha x_i$$

where V_i is DCT coefficient value of the image and α is scaling factor denotes the imperceptibility degree. The extraction is reverse of the process of insertion including deviation analysis. For each watermarked cipher text Y_i, applying the decoding function for two possible values (0 or 1) while analyzing the local standard deviation. The bit value is selected where local standard deviation is least.

4. Transmission and Reception of Encrypted Image

Transmission and reception includes the last phase of the Crypto-Watermarking system when the sender transmits the medical image with secret data watermarked which can be secret key or any other patient record whose confidentiality and integrity needs to be assured. The intended recipient actually extracts the watermark which includes the confidential data as well as the key to decrypt it. After which he or she could view the imagery.

SOLUTIONS AND RECOMMENDATIONS

The reversible crypto-watermarking system has been implemented using python - OpenCV library running on an Ubuntu 14.04 platform with the support of Intel core 3 and 4GB RAM. The performance of each step in combined crypto-watermarking techniques is evaluated using the dataset described in next section.

1. Dataset

The reversible crypto-watermarking approach is applied on more than 200 gray level images that are obtained from one (Candemir et al., 2014) (Jaeger et al., 2014) and other sources. The proposed method is applied on a chest image (396 x 400 pixels) and the medical image (512 x 512 pixels) which is shown in Figure 3 and in Figure 4 respectively. The watermark data is encrypted key data which is variable length ranging up to 126bits. The results are evaluated using mean-square-error (MSE), peak-signal-to noise- ratio (PSNR) and entropy for evaluating encryption efficiency.

2. Comparison and Evaluation

Stream cipher method is applied to encrypt the input image. The encryption of the original image Figure 3 is done by using the RC4 algorithm to get the encrypted image illustrated in *Figure 5*. Using stream cipher method shows just few seconds as time for encryption. In this encrypted image, bits of encrypted key are embedded to get the watermarked encrypted image illustrated in *Figure 6*. On reception of image by the specialist the watermark is extracted from the image which is embedded secret key k' and this secret key is used to decrypt the image to view the initial image. The watermark extracted image and corresponding decrypted image is shown in *Figure 7* and *Figure 8* respectively.

The *Table 2* shows the execution time for each step done on input images *Figure 3* and *Figure 4*.

Table 2. Execution time for rc4

RC4 – Image Encrytion	First Image	Second Image
Time	3 msec	2.3msec

Figure 3. First input   *Figure 4. Second input*

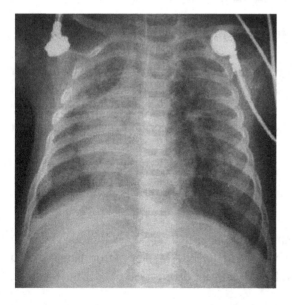
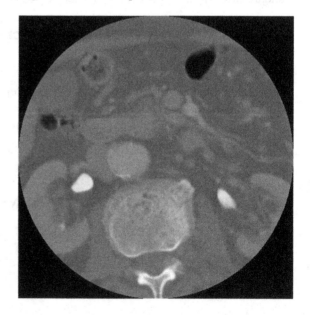

Figure 5. Encrypted image

Figure 6. Watermarked image

Figure 7. Key Extracted image

Figure 8. Decrypted image

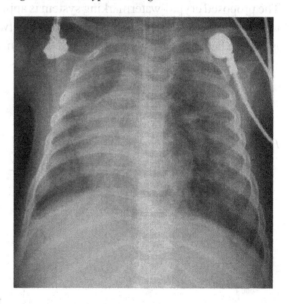

3. Results

In order to interpret the results obtained, it is necessary to develop tools to measure the error between embedded and original image. Among these strategies histogram analysis, entropy analysis and PSNR ratios respectively are used. Gray image is having 256 gray scale levels and the theoretical value of entropy is 8bits. Entropy is issue to know the security and strength concerned within the cryptography method for images. Entropy for encrypted image is near 7.9bits/pixel. *Table 3* shows the entropy of input image and encrypted image respectively.

Table 3. Entropy for medical image and its encrypted image

Image	Entropy(bits/pixel)
Chest image	7.21
Encrypted image	7.99

A histogram is a graphical representation of a continuous variable distribution. So the difference can be noted clearly from the histogram of original images and encrypted image shown in *Figure 9* and *Figure 10* respectively. Uniform distribution of pixels are done, which can resist attacks. So, efficiency of algorithm is ensured due to the security it guarantees with secure transmission of confidential information.

By the comparison of both histograms that of the initial image, Figure 9 and that of the image encrypted, Figure 10, with remark that the probabilities of occurrence of gray levels in the image are equally distributed also shown respectively.

4. Quality Analysis

The proposed crypto-watermarking system is applied to chest image. Quality Metrics used is Peak Signal to Noise Ratio and to evaluate the similarity between the Decrypted image and original image. Bigger is PSNR, better is quality of image. PSNR for image with size M x N is given by Equation 7:

Figure 9. Histogram(chest)

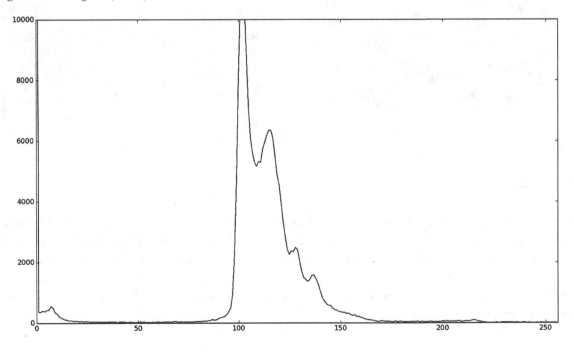

Figure 10. Histogram(Encrypted)

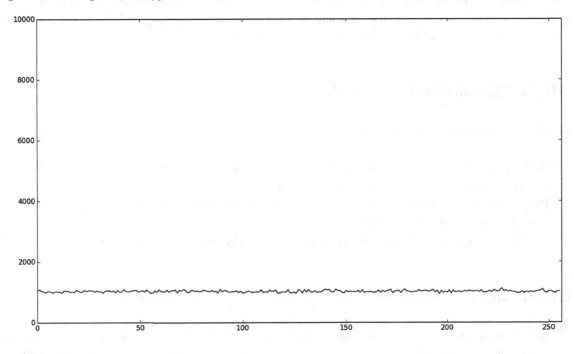

$$PSNR = 10\log_{10}\left(\frac{\displaystyle\sum_{x=1}^{M}\sum_{y=1}^{N}E^2_{\max}}{\displaystyle\sum_{x=1}^{M}\sum_{y=1}^{N}(f(x,y)-f'(x,y))^2}\right)$$

where, $f(x,y)$ are pixel gray values of original image. $f'(x,y)$ is pixel gray values of watermarked image. M and N are image pixel dimensions. PSNR value obtained for the decrypted image is high.

The value for α is taken to be 0.5 in the whole experiment. For different values, the result is not accurate. The watermarked chest image shown in the *Figure: 6* shows a PSNR value of 70.18dB which is high compared to other approaches discussed in literature. If the amount of data embedded is increased to 15242 bits the same image shows a PSNR value of 61.08dB which is good value with less distortion in image quality. Decryption of key involves the authentication through the ELGamal crypto-system thereby safeguarding the confidentiality in its reality.

INFERENCE

The combination of cryptography, information-hiding and integrity verification is projected and evaluated for safe transmission of medical data with the individual image. The stream cipher technique is strong to moderate noise with top quality issue. Within the field of cryptography and image watermarking, crypto-watermarking is a vital space of analysis in medical mental imagery that helps in protecting confidentiality, genuineness and integrity of medical information. DCT domain is employed to embed the key attributable to its physical property and hardiness to geometric distortions. The management of magnitude relation between the capacity and distortion got to be addressed more that is initiated with our future analysis direction. The management of ratio between the capacity and distortion need to be addressed further which is initiated with our future research direction.

FUTURE RESEARCH DIRECTIONS

The following are some suggestions for future study.

- A comparative study between all the different Crypto-Watermarking schemes based on different encryption and data hiding schemes can be done.
- Proposed system can also be applied to other domains other than discrete cosine transform i.e. in prediction error domain of spatial system.
- Variety of techniques can be applied to eliminate the addition of unnecessary noise.

FUTURE CASE STUDY: EPR EMBEDDING IN SPATIAL DOMAIN

In EPR embedding, the EPR encrypted data is embedded into the cover image based on prediction errors exploiting the sorting according to the local variances μ. The local variance $\mu_{i,j}$ has several features like this value remain unchanged after data hiding also this value is proportional to the magnitude of prediction error of the cell under consideration. Cell is unit of pixels in which data should be embedded. Using the prediction scheme allows efficient embedding of data with low distortion. Each pixel of the cover image can be used for data hiding, so capacity can be increased considerably. Low prediction error values are ideal for data hiding.

The security priorities have increased with increased use of computer networks and wireless technologies. EPR data include various patient information that is relevant for the medical treatment, through its communication can be used for proper diagnostics by opinion gathering. Data include notes from physicians, scan reports - MRIs, CT scan, and clinical observation results. The patient's data can be accessed by medical specialist, by the patient at home, and other medical practitioners. This can help improve overall quality of health care delivery; the welfares of this technology must be well-adjusted with the privacy and security implications. Thus encryption, access control mechanisms are used to safeguard the EPR data for facilitating. Techniques of message encryption have been developed to meet this demand. The original image is embedded with EPR data encrypted using a secret key. This encrypted data is embedded with cover image and transferred to the network. The transferred image is received and the encrypted data is extracted reversibly before which the hash is calculated and compared with the extracted hash value. The integrity check is done here. Also the algorithm must be lossless scheme for extracting the encrypted data properly. With the secret key decryption of EPR data is done.

CONCLUSION

In the field of cryptography and image watermarking, crypto-watermarking is an important area of research in medical imagery which helps in preserving security, confidentiality, authenticity and integrity of medical data. It's a process of enabling data hiding by the aid of encryption. Encryption is done using various methods which can be block cipher or stream cipher. Watermarking of the encrypted data or image can be done in various domains taking into account various features of respective domain and it depends on the applications that perform.

The proposed Crypto-Watermarking System processed the medical images for its safe transfer. Encryption of image using standard stream cipher algorithm is done which is very fast and reliable. Being robust to moderate noise stream cipher algorithm is efficient with high quality factor. The secret key used for encryption is then watermarked in DCT domain by the use of spread spectrum coding algorithm due to its imperceptibility and robustness to geometric distortions. The additional security is guaranteed by the use of ELGamal public-private key crypto-system for secret key encryption which is stronger than traditional RSA system. The system is verified using 250 input images and result is presented and high PSNR value obtained concludes the method to be efficient. Future work is to try the same on various other transform domains and by increasing the embedding rate.

REFERENCES

Acharya, R., Bhat, P. S., Kumar, S., & Min, L. C. (2003). Transmission and storage of medical images with patient information. *Computers in Biology and Medicine*, *33*(4), 303–310. doi:10.1016/S0010-4825(02)00083-5 PMID:12791403

Alsafasfeh, Q. H., & Arfoa, A. A. (2011). Image encryption based on the general approach for multiple chaotic systems. *Journal of Signal and Information Processing*, *2*(03), 238–244. doi:10.4236/jsip.2011.23033

Bouslimi, D., Coatrieux, G., Cozic, M., & Roux, C. (2012). A joint encryption/watermarking system for verifying the reliability of medical images. *Information Technology in Biomedicine. IEEE Transactions on*, *16*(5), 891–899.

Candemir, S., Jaeger, S., Palaniappan, K., Musco, J. P., Singh, R. K., Xue, Z., ... McDonald, C. J. (2014). Lung segmentation in chest radiographs using anatomical atlases with nonrigid registration. *IEEE Transactions on Medical Imaging*, *33*(2), 577–590. doi:10.1109/TMI.2013.2290491 PMID:24239990

Celik, M. U., Sharma, G., & Saber, E. (2002). Reversible data hiding. In *Image Processing. 2002. Proceedings. 2002 International Conference on* (Vol. 2, pp. II-157). IEEE. 10.1109/ICIP.2002.1039911

Cheung, Y. M., & Wu, H. T. (2007). A sequential quantization strategy for data embedding and integrity verification. *Circuits and Systems for Video Technology. IEEE Transactions on*, *17*(8), 1007–1016.

Coatrieux, G., Le Guillou, C., Cauvin, J. M., & Roux, C. (2009). Reversible watermarking for knowledge digest embedding and reliability control in medical images. *Information Technology in Biomedicine. IEEE Transactions on*, *13*(2), 158–165.

Coatrieux, G., Maitre, H., Sankur, B., Rolland, Y., & Collorec, R. (2000). Relevance of watermarking in medical imaging. In *Information Technology Applications in Biomedicine, 2000. Proceedings. 2000 IEEE EMBS International Conference on* (pp. 250-255). IEEE. 10.1109/ITAB.2000.892396

Cox, I., Miller, M., Bloom, J., Fridrich, J., & Kalker, T. (2007). *Digital watermarking and steganography*. Morgan Kaufmann.

Cox, I. J., Kilian, J., Leighton, F. T., & Shamoon, T. (1997). Secure spread spectrum watermarking for multimedia. *Image Processing. IEEE Transactions on, 6*(12), 1673–1687.

Cox, I. J., Miller, M. L., Bloom, J. A., & Honsinger, C. (2002). *Digital watermarking* (Vol. 53). San Francisco: Morgan Kaufmann.

De Vleeschouwer, C., & Macq, B. (2003). Circular interpretation of bijective transformations in lossless watermarking for media asset management. *Multimedia. IEEE Transactions on, 5*(1), 97–105.

Diffie, W., & Hellman, M. E. (1976). New directions in cryptography. *Information Theory. IEEE Transactions on, 22*(6), 644–654.

Fernández-Alemán, J. L., Señor, I. C., Lozoya, P. Á. O., & Toval, A. (2013). Security and privacy in electronic health records: A systematic literature review. *Journal of Biomedical Informatics, 46*(3), 541–562. doi:10.1016/j.jbi.2012.12.003 PMID:23305810

Fridrich, J., Goljan, M., & Du, R. (2001, August). Invertible authentication. In Photonics West 2001-Electronic Imaging (pp. 197-208). International Society for Optics and Photonics.

Goljan, M., Fridrich, J. J., & Du, R. (2001, January). Distortion-free data embedding for images. In *Information Hiding* (pp. 27–41). Springer Berlin Heidelberg. doi:10.1007/3-540-45496-9_3

Guan, Z. H., Huang, F., & Guan, W. (2005). Chaos-based image encryption algorithm. *Physics Letters. [Part A], 346*(1), 153–157. doi:10.1016/j.physleta.2005.08.006

Honsinger, C. W., Jones, P. W., Rabbani, M., & Stoffel, J. C. (2001). *U.S. Patent No. 6,278,791*. Washington, DC: U.S. Patent and Trademark Office.

Ismail, I. A., Amin, M., & Diab, H. (2010). A digital image encryption algorithm based a composition of two chaotic logistic maps. *International Journal of Network Security, 11*(1), 1–10.

Jaeger, S., Karargyris, A., Candemir, S., Folio, L., Siegelman, J., Callaghan, F., ... Thoma, G. (2014). Automatic tuberculosis screening using chest radiographs. *IEEE Transactions on Medical Imaging, 33*(2), 233–245. doi:10.1109/TMI.2013.2284099 PMID:24108713

Khan, A., Siddiqa, A., Munib, S., & Malik, S. A. (2014). A recent survey of reversible watermarking techniques. *Information Sciences, 279*, 251–272. doi:10.1016/j.ins.2014.03.118

Lakrissi, Y., Erritali, M., & Fakir, M. (2013). A Joint Encryption/Watermarking Algorithm for Secure Image Transfer. *International Journal of Computer Networking and Communication, 1*(1). doi:10.1109/TCSVT.2015.2418611

Levoy, M., Pulli, K., Curless, B., Rusinkiewicz, S., Koller, D., Pereira, L., ... Fulk, D. (2000, July). The digital Michelangelo project: 3D scanning of large statues. In *Proceedings of the 27th annual conference on Computer graphics and interactive techniques* (pp. 131-144). ACM Press/Addison-Wesley Publishing Co. 10.1145/344779.344849

Macq, B., & Dewey, F. (1999, October). Trusted headers for medical images. In DFG VIII-D II Watermarking Workshop (Vol. 10). Erlangen.

Menezes, A. J., Van Oorschot, P. C., & Vanstone, S. A. (1996). *Handbook of applied cryptography*. CRC Press. doi:10.1201/9781439821916

Mitra, A., Rao, Y. S., & Prasanna, S. R. M. (2006). A new image encryption approach using combinational permutation techniques. *International Journal of Computer Science, 1*(2), 127–131.

Ni, Z., Shi, Y. Q., Ansari, N., & Su, W. (2006). Reversible data hiding. *Circuits and Systems for Video Technology. IEEE Transactions on, 16*(3), 354–362.

Pal, K., Ghosh, G., & Bhattacharya, M. (2013, December). A new combined crypto-watermarking technique using RSA algorithm and discrete cosine transform to retrieve embedded EPR from noisy bio-medical images. In *Condition Assessment Techniques in Electrical Systems (CATCON), 2013 IEEE 1st International Conference on* (pp. 368-373). IEEE.

Pérez-Freire, L., Comesana, P., & Pérez-González, F. (2005, January). Information-theoretic analysis of security in side-informed data hiding. In *Information Hiding* (pp. 131–145). Springer Berlin Heidelberg. doi:10.1007/11558859_11

Pérez-Freire, L., & Pérez-González, F. (2009). Spread-spectrum watermarking security. *Information Forensics and Security. IEEE Transactions on, 4*(1), 2–24.

Puech, W. (2008, October). An Efficient Hybrid Method for Safe Transfer of Medical Images. In E-MEDISYS'08: E-Medical Systems.

Puech, W., Chaumont, M., & Strauss, O. (2008, February). A reversible data hiding method for encrypted images. In *Electronic Imaging 2008* (pp. 68191E–68191E). International Society for Optics and Photonics.

Puech, W., & Rodrigues, J. M. (2004, September). A new crypto-watermarking method for medical images safe transfer. In *Signal Processing Conference, 2004 12th European* (pp. 1481-1484). IEEE.

Qian, Z., & Zhang, X. (2014). *Reversible Data Hiding in Encrypted Image with Distributed Source Encoding*. Academic Press.

Rao, N. V., & Kumari, V. M. (2011). Watermarking in medical imaging for security and authentication. *Information Security Journal: A Global Perspective, 20*(3), 148-155.

Sadeghi, A. R. (2008). The marriage of cryptography and watermarking—beneficial and challenging for secure watermarking and detection. In *Digital Watermarking* (pp. 2–18). Springer Berlin Heidelberg. doi:10.1007/978-3-540-92238-4_2

Schneier, B. (1996). *Applied cryptography*. New York: Wiley.

Schneier, B. (2007). *Applied cryptography: protocols, algorithms, and source code in C*. John Wiley & Sons.

Shahid, Z., Chaumont, M., & Puech, W. (2011). Fast protection of H. 264/AVC by selective encryption of CAVLC and CABAC for I and P frames. *Circuits and Systems for Video Technology. IEEE Transactions on, 21*(5), 565–576.

Stinson, D. R. (2005). *Cryptography: theory and practice*. CRC Press.

Thodi, D. M., & Rodriguez, J. J. (2004, October). Prediction-error based reversible watermarking. In *Image Processing, 2004. ICIP'04. 2004 International Conference on* (Vol. 3, pp. 1549-1552). IEEE. 10.1109/ICIP.2004.1421361

Tian, J. (2003). Reversible data embedding using a difference expansion. *IEEE Transactions on Circuits and Systems for Video Technology*, *13*(8), 890–896. doi:10.1109/TCSVT.2003.815962

William, S., & Stallings, W. (2006). *Cryptography and Network Security, 4/E*. Pearson Education India.

Wu, H. T., & Cheung, Y. M. (2005, September). A reversible data hiding approach to mesh authentication. In *Web Intelligence, 2005. Proceedings. The 2005 IEEE/WIC/ACM International Conference on* (pp. 774-777). IEEE.

Wu, H. T., & Cheung, Y. M. (2010). Reversible watermarking by modulation and security enhancement. *Instrumentation and Measurement. IEEE Transactions on*, *59*(1), 221–228.

Xuan, G., Zhu, J., Chen, J., Shi, Y. Q., Ni, Z., & Su, W. (2002). Distortionless data hiding based on integer wavelet transform. *Electronics Letters*, *38*(25), 1646–1648. doi:10.1049/el:20021131

Zeghid, M., Machhout, M., Khriji, L., Baganne, A., & Tourki, R. (2007). A modified AES based algorithm for image encryption. *International Journal on Computer Science and Engineering*, *1*(1), 70–75.

Zhang, G., & Liu, Q. (2011). A novel image encryption method based on total shuffling scheme. *Optics Communications*, *284*(12), 2775–2780. doi:10.1016/j.optcom.2011.02.039

Zhang, W., Ma, K., & Yu, N. (2014). Reversibility improved data hiding in encrypted images. *Signal Processing*, *94*, 118–127. doi:10.1016/j.sigpro.2013.06.023

Zhang, X. (2011). Reversible data hiding in encrypted image. *Signal Processing Letters, IEEE*, *18*(4), 255–258. doi:10.1109/LSP.2011.2114651

Zhu, Z. L., Zhang, W., Wong, K. W., & Yu, H. (2011). A chaos-based symmetric image encryption scheme using a bit-level permutation. *Information Sciences*, *181*(6), 1171–1186. doi:10.1016/j.ins.2010.11.009

KEY TERMS AND DEFINITIONS

Computer Vision: It is an area that contains procedures for obtaining, handling, examining, and understanding images and, high dimensional facts from the real world in order to produce mathematical or representational data.

Crypto-Watermarking: Crypto-Watermarking is the synonym used for techniques which binds watermarking with cryptographic features.

Digital Watermarking: Digital watermarking is a convenient way of embedding covertly noises into multimedia signals such as an audio, video or image data. It is typically used to identify ownership of the copyright of such signal.

Discrete Cosine Transform: The discrete cosine transform (DCT) is a technique for converting a signal into elementary frequency components. It is widely used in image compression. Here we develop some simple functions to compute the DCT and to compress images.

Encryption: It is an effective method for data security in which one converts the data into a form that is not easily understood called the cipher text. Data encrypted can be accessed by secret key or passwords that allows subsequent decryption of encrypted file. File that is not encrypted is called plain text.

Health Insurance Portability and Accountability Act (HIPAA): Efficiency and effectiveness of health care system was ensured by the act enacted by United States Congress on August 21 1996.

Peak-Signal-to-Noise-Ratio(PSNR): The term peak signal-to-noise ratio (PSNR) is an expression for the ratio between the maximum possible value (power) of a signal and the power of distorting noise that affects the quality of its representation.

Pseudo Random Number Generator (PRNG): Pseudo Random Number Generator is a random generator used to generate bits randomly that have properties similar to random numbers.

Steganography: Steganography is concerned with hiding secret data into the media.

Stream Cipher: A stream cipher is a symmetric key cipher where plaintext digits are combined with a pseudorandom cipher digit stream (key stream). In a stream cipher each plaintext digit is encrypted one at a time with the corresponding digit of the key stream, to give a digit of the cipher text stream.

This research was previously published in Cloud Computing Systems and Applications in Healthcare edited by Chintan M. Bhatt and S. K. Peddoju; pages 189-217, copyright year 2017 by Medical Information Science Reference (an imprint of IGI Global).

Chapter 29
Reversible Watermarking in Medical Image Using RDWT and Sub–Sample

Lin Gao
Tianjin Chengjian University, China

Tiegang Gao
Nankai University, China

Jie Zhao
Tianjin Chengjian University, China

ABSTRACT

This paper proposed a reversible medical image watermarking scheme using Redundant Discrete Wavelet Transform (RDWT) and sub-sample. To meet the highly demand of the perceptional quality, the proposed scheme embedding the watermark by modifying the RDWT coefficients. The sub-sample scheme is introduced to the proposed scheme for the enhancement of the embedding capacity. Moreover, to meet the need of security, a PWLCM based image encryption algorithm is introduced for encrypting the image after the watermark embedding. The experimental results suggests that the proposed scheme not only meet the highly demand of the perceptional quality, but also have better embedding capacity than former DWT based scheme. Also the encryption scheme could protect the image contents efficiently.

INTRODUCTION

Digital watermark has been widely used in the copyright protection of digital image. In medical area, reversible watermarking scheme is more preferred than irreversible scheme because of the highly demand on the perceptional quality of the image. Based on the algorithm used to achieve reversible embedding, the reversible watermarking scheme could be categorized into three types: lossless compression based schemes, difference expansion (DE) based schemes and histogram shifting / histogram modifying (HS/ HM) based schemes.

DOI: 10.4018/978-1-7998-1763-5.ch029

The lossless compression based schemes first compressed the cover image using lossless compressing scheme(Kountchev, Todorov, Kountcheva, & Milanova, 2006; Maxwell, Handel, & Bradley, 1998; Shih & Wu, 2005). After the compression the size of the cover image has been reduced, the watermark could be embedded into the image by exploit the space generated by the compression. During the extraction process, the watermark was extract from the image, then the compressed image was decompressed using the lossless compression algorithm.

Lossless compression based schemes are easily to achieve. The performance of these schemes is highly depends on the performance of the lossless compression algorithm. The draw back of lossless compression based scheme are robustness and perceptional quality. Because the compressed cover image is vulnerable to the tamper of the stego-image, this kind of scheme usually is not robust against tampering attack. Moreover, since the cover image had been compressed, the visual quality of the stego-image is significantly deduced, which made lossless compression based schemes not suitable for used in medical image watermarking.

Difference expansion based scheme was first proposed by Tian(Tian, 2003) .The main idea of Tian's scheme is as follows: For an 8-bit grayscale image, a pixel pair (x, y) is used to embed a secret bit S, $S \in \{0,1\}$. In the embedding phase, the difference value h and the integer average value l are defined as:

$$h = x - y, l = \left\lfloor \frac{x+y}{2} \right\rfloor \tag{1}$$

The inverse transform is

$$x = l + \left\lfloor \frac{h+1}{2} \right\rfloor, y = l - \left\lfloor \frac{h}{2} \right\rfloor \tag{2}$$

Next, the new difference h' is obtained as follows:

$$h' = 2 \times h + S \tag{3}$$

Finally, the stego-pixel pair (x', y') is obtained by the following transform:

$$x' = l + \left\lfloor \frac{h'+1}{2} \right\rfloor, y' = l - \left\lfloor \frac{h'}{2} \right\rfloor \tag{4}$$

In order to prevent underflow and overflow, the absolute of new difference $|h'|$ after a secret bit S has been embedded must satisfy the following condition:

$$|h'| \leq \min\left(2 \times (255 - l), 2 \times l + 1\right) \tag{5}$$

DE based scheme was initially proposed and used in spatial domain embedding. Since it is easy to achieve, lots of researches had been done and several improvements have been made based on Tian's scheme. For example, Alattar et al. introduced DE scheme into quad of pixels(Alattar, 2004). By expanding pairs to quads, Alattar's scheme improved the embedding capacity from 0.5 bpp to 0.75 bpp at best case. Other researches using the same method including Lee's(Lee, Wu, Tsai, & Chu, 2008) and Chang's (Chang & Lu, 2006) scheme. These schemes tried to expand pairs of pixels to quads or even more pixels. These improved schemes could generate more differences than original DE scheme, which means higher embedding capacity.

DE based scheme's draw back including relatively lower embedding capacity and undetermined size of the location map(LM). Because DE using the differences between the pair or quad of pixels/coefficients, the embedding capacity is lower than other schemes such like HS/HM based schemes. Also, since the amount of the overflow/underflow pairs is depend on the distribution of the pixel/coefficients values, the size of the LM are vary by the cover images. One of our previous work tried to apply DE in the DCT coefficients, the results also proved the DE has the disadvantages above(Lin, Tiegang, Guorui, Yanjun, & Li, 2012).

The HS/HM based scheme was first proposed by Ni(Ni, Shi, Ansari, & Su, 2006).The core idea of HS/HM based scheme is find the peak and gap in the histogram of the pixel/coefficient values, then shift or modify the peak and gap values to embed the watermark. The original scheme used the pixel values for embedding. By locate and shift the peak and gap values of the pixels, the original scheme achieved relatively higher embedding capacity and better visual quality than former schemes. An other advantage of applying HS/HM in spatial domain is the PSNR of stego-image has a estimated lower bondage, which means that the worst case of the visual quality could be estimated before the embedding(Ni et al., 2006).

The embedding capacity of the HS/HM based scheme is decided by the distribution of the corresponding pixel/coefficient values. Several methods are proposed to make the distribution of the corresponding values more concentrate, including prediction-error expansion(PEE)(X. Chen, Sun, Sun, Zhou, & Zhang, 2013) and sub-sample(Kim, Lee, Lee, & Lee, 2009). PEE is an improvement of DE technique (Tian, 2003). It is first proposed by Thodi and Rodriguez(Thodi & Rodríguez, 2007), who utilized prediction-error instead of difference value for expansion embedding. Unlike in DE where only the correlation of two adjacent pixels is considered, the local correlation of larger neighborhood is exploited in PEE. Moreover, Thodi and Rodriguez suggest incorporating expansion embedding with histogram shifting to ensure the reversibility. In this way, compared with Tian's approach, the location map used for blind extraction is remarkably compressed. Afterwards, Thodi and Rodriguez's method is developed by Hu et al. (Hu, Lee, & Li, 2009) by constructing a payload dependent location map, where the compressibility of location map is further improved. Besides these works, several PEE-based methods are also proposed recently(M. Chen, Chen, Zeng, & Xiong, 2009; Fallahpour, 2008; Luo, Chen, Chen, Zeng, & Xiong, 2010; Tai, Yeh, & Chang, 2009; Tsai, Hu, & Yeh, 2009), and in principle, they differ in the employed prediction algorithm. The mechanism of PEE-based embedding can be described as follows. First, image pixels are predicted to get the prediction-error histogram which is a Laplacian-like distribution centered at 0. Then, a capacity-parameter is determined according to the capacity, and one gets the so-called inner region and outer region. Finally, each pixel of inner region is expanded to carry 1 bit, and pixels of outer region are shifted to eliminate ambiguity. Here, expanding or shifting a pixel means to expand or shift its prediction-error in the prediction-error histogram. In summary, PEE can embed a large payload by exploiting the prediction-error histogram, and control the distortion by utilizing expansion embedding and/or histogram shifting. By using a proper predictor, the embedding capacity would meet the need of high capacity embedding. Another way to get a concentrated distributed coefficients is using sub-sample method. Sub-sample method exploited the fact that adjacent pixels/coefficients usually have same value. The differences between the pixel of same location in different sub-images usually has a more concentrated distribution than in the corresponding original image, which is ideal for HS/HM embedding.

This paper proposed a reversible watermarking scheme using HS/HM based method in RDWT domain. Applying HS/HM in frequency domain would achieve better perceptual quality than in spatial domain. However, since modify the coefficients would resulted changes to several correlated pixels, the prevention of overflow or underflow should be take more consideration. The proposed scheme using pre-process to avoid over/underflow of pixel values. For a better performance of embedding capacity, sub-sampling method is also introduced into the proposed scheme. As mentioned before, sub-sampled images could generated more concentrated distribution of coefficients. This property means higher embedding capacity in HS/HM based scheme. To enhance the security of the proposed scheme, a PWLCM (Piecewise Linear Chaotic Map)based image encryption method is introduced to the proposed scheme to meet the need of security. The image could be encrypted after the embedding of watermark, enhanced the security of the image content, which related to the patient's privacy.

RELATED WORKS

Redundant Discrete Wavelet Transform (RDWT)

Discrete Wavelet Transform is commonly used transform in watermarking. Because of the excellent spatial-frequency localization properties the DWT has, it is very useful to locate the areas in the original image where the watermark can be imperceptibly inserted. However, one major disadvantage of the DWT is shift variant. The down sampling process after each level of filtering caused a significant change in the wavelet coefficients of the image even for minor shift in it. This disadvantage made the DWT-based watermark scheme fragile against geometrical attacks.

To deal with the disadvantage of the DWT, Redundant Discrete Wavelet Transform (RDWT) is proposed and introduced into robust watermarking schemes. RDWT is also named as the over complete DWT (ODWT), the undecimated DWT(UDWT), the discrete wavelet frames (DWF) and the shift-invariant DWT (SIDWT) .RDWT can be implemented in many methods, the core idea of it is avoid the down sampling process of DWT while keeping other advantages of it. The size of the each sub-band of the RDWT coefficients maintains the same size as the original image. This made the capture of the local texture of the RDWT domain can be done more precisely than in DWT domain. And more important, this feature made RDWT shift-invariant.

General 1-D DWT is shown in Figure 1. The low pass and high pass analysis filters are h[-k] and g[-k] and the corresponding low pass and high pass synthesis filters are h[k] and g[k].The cj and dj are the low-band and high-band output coefficients at the level j.

DWT analysis:

$$c_j[k] = \left(c_{j+1}[k] * h[-k] \right) \downarrow 2 \tag{6}$$

And

$$d_j[k] = \left(c_{j+1}[k] * g[-k]\right) \downarrow 2 \tag{7}$$

where * indicates convolution, and ↓2 indicates down sampling. That is, if $y[n]=x[n]\downarrow2$, then

$$y[n] = x[2n] \tag{8}$$

DWT synthesis

$$c_{j+1}[k] = \left(\left(c_j[k] \uparrow 2\right) * h[k] + \left(d_j[k] \uparrow 2\right) * g[k]\right) \tag{9}$$

↑2 here denote to the up sampling process. That is, if $y[n]=x[n]\uparrow2$, then

$$y[n] = \begin{cases} x\left[\dfrac{n}{2}\right], & n \text{ even} \\ 0, & n \text{ odd} \end{cases} \tag{10}$$

Figure 2 shows the 1-D RDWT and its inverse transform. One significant difference between DWT and RDWT is RDWT removes down sampling and up sampling of coefficients. At each level, the number of the output coefficients doubles the numbers of the input. Therefore, the filters for scale j are:

$$h_j[k] = h_{j+1}[k] \uparrow 2 \tag{11}$$

And

$$g_j[k] = g_{j+1}[k] \uparrow 2 \tag{12}$$

Figure 1. Two level 1-D DWT analysis and synthesis filter banks

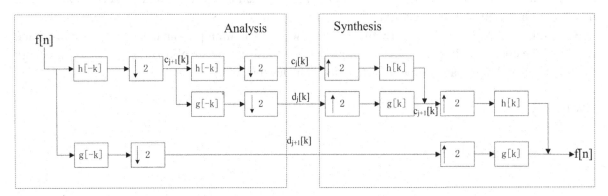

RDWT analysis

$$c_j[k] = \left(c_{j+1}[k] * h_j[-k]\right) \tag{13}$$

And

$$d_j[k] = \left(c_{j+1}[k] * g_j[-k]\right) \tag{14}$$

RDWT synthesis

$$c_{j+1}[k] = \frac{1}{2}\left(c_j[k] * h_j[k] + d_j[k] * g_j[k]\right) \tag{15}$$

PWLCM (Piecewise Linear Chaotic Map)

PWLCM has been widely used in the image encryption, generation of image hashing and many other applications for its high efficiency and security. The PWLCM proposed and analyzed by Xiao et al. is defined as:

$$X_{t+1} = F_p\left(X_t\right) = \begin{cases} X_t/p, & 0 \le X_t < p \\ \left(X_t - p\right)/\left(0.5 - p\right), & p \le X_t < 0.5 \\ \left(1 - X_t - p\right)/\left(0.5 - p\right), & 0.5 \le X_t < 1 - p \\ \left(1 - X_t\right)/p, & 1 - p \le X_t \le 1 \end{cases} \tag{16}$$

where $X_t \in [0,1]$ and $p \in (0,0.5)$ denote the iteration trajectory value and the current iteration parameter, respectively. This PWLCM has been proved to be a suitable sequence generator for security of watermark.

Figure 2. Two level 1-D RDWT analysis and synthesis filter banks

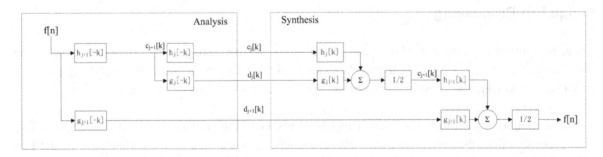

Another PWLCM analyzed by Li et al. is defined as

$$F(X_t, p) = \begin{cases} X_t / p, & X_t \in [0, p) \\ (X_t - p)/(1/2 - p), & X_t \in [p, 1/2) \\ F(1 - X_t, p), & X_t \in [1/2, 1] \end{cases}$$
(17)

It also has been shown that it has the same properties as the PWLCM proposed by Xiao et al. These two PWLCM definitions are imported in the proposed scheme, and they are both evaluated by the experimental results for comparison.

Sub-Sampling Scheme

Sampling is the process of selecting units (e.g., pixels, coefficients) from an image. Suppose that an image of size N×M pixels is denoted by I(x, y), where x = 0, ..., M − 1 and y = 0, ..., N − 1. Two sampling factors, u and v set the desired sub-sampling intervals in a row and column direction, respectively. The 2-D image could be sampled at uniform intervals. This process is called as sub-sampling and each sub-sampled image S_k of size N/u × M/v is obtained as follow:

$$S_k(i, j) = I\left(i \bullet \Delta v + floor\left(\frac{k-1}{\Delta u} \right), j \bullet \Delta u + ((k-1) \bmod \Delta u) \right)$$
(18)

If N/u or M/v is not an integer value, we slightly modify the size of all sub-sampled images by flooring. For example, when M = N = 512 and u = v = 3, the size of the sub-sampled image is set at the nearest integer less than or equal to the number: [512/3]=170 in both width and height. The residue of pixels is neither included in any sub-sampled images nor targeted embeddable components An example of sub-sample is given in Figure 3.

PROPOSED SCHEME

Image Pre-Processing

Image pre-processing algorithm should be performed on the cover image before the embedding of the watermark. The pre-processing algorithm check every pixel of the cover image, then mapping the pixel may underflow/overflow to avoid the under/over flow. The detailed algorithm is given below:

1. Location map generation. Location map(LM) is used to record the location of mapped pixels. The proposed algorithm using a zero-matrix which has the same size of the cover image as the LM initially.
2. Select the mapping threshold T. Then check every pixel of the cover image and adjust the pixel value p as following:

Figure 3. An example of sub-sampling scheme

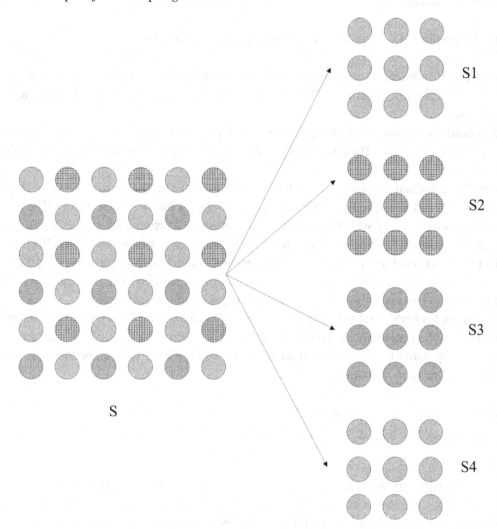

$$p' = \begin{cases} p + T, & p \in [0, T] \\ p, & p \in (T, L - T) \\ p - T, & p \in [L - T, L] \end{cases} \tag{19}$$

where p is the original pixel value, p' is the adjusted value. T is the mapping threshold, L is the scale of the image pixel value. For each adjusted pixel, the corresponding location in the LM was changed from 0 to 1.

3. Compression of the LM. When the whole image was scanned and adjusted, the LM was compressed and coded for the embedding.

Watermark Embedding

The detailed algorithm of watermark embedding is given as following:

1. **Image Pre-Processing:** Adjusting the pixels may underflow/overflow according to the threshold value T. The LM was generated at the same time. Encoding the LM then calculate the length of coded LM.
2. **Watermark Generation:** Encoding the watermark provided by the user, then calculate the length of the coded watermark. The total length of the coded LM and watermark is used as the length of the watermark.
3. **Image Transformation:** Perform the RDWT on the adjusted image, the coefficients generated is LL,LH,HL and HH. The LL sub-band was remain intact for the visual quality. The other three sub-bands are processed with 4-sub-sample, the sub-sample scheme divide the original sub-band coefficient matrixes to 4 sub-matrixes, which is $S1_i, S2_i, S3_i, S4_i$, where $i \in \{LH, HL, HH\}$.
4. **Differences Generation:** For each sub-band, generated the differences matrixes $diff1_i, diff2_i, diff3_i$ by calculate the differences between the S1 and other sub-matrixes. The total amount of the zeros in the diff matrixes is the maximum embedding capacity of the cover image.
5. **Watermark Embedding:** First compare the maximum embedding capacity of the cover image and the length of the watermark. If the total length of the watermark exceeded the maximum embedding capacity, notify the user then terminate the whole algorithm, else, embedding the watermark to the cover image as following:

$$diff = \begin{cases} diff - 1, & diff < 0 \ or \ diff = 0 \text{ and } w = 0 \\ diff + 1, & diff > 0 \text{ or } diff = 0 \text{ and } w = 1 \end{cases} \tag{20}$$

where diff is the corresponding value in the difference matrixes, w is the corresponding value in the coded watermark sequence. For each sub-band, the proposed algorithm check every value in the three differences matrixes. Each difference not equal to zero was shifted by one far from the zero point. The differences equal to zero are used for watermark embedding. These differences are either plus one or minus one according to the watermark bit embedded.

After embedded the watermark sequence to the cover image, the order of the sub-sample and the length of the watermark are recorded with the threshold T as the key corresponding to the image.

6. **Stego-Image Generation:** Perform the inverse-RDWT using the original LL and modified LH,HL and HH sub-bands, generated the stego-image.

Watermark Extracting

The detailed algorithm of watermark extraction is given as following:

1. **Parameter Extraction:** Extract the order of sub-sample, length of the watermark sequence and threshold T from the key corresponding to the stego-image.

2. **Watermark Extraction:** Perform 1-level RDWT on the stego-image, then using the same method as the embedding procedure to generate the differences matrixes. Extract the watermark sequence by detect the 1 and -1 in the differences matrixes. While extracting the watermark sequence, the coefficients of differences matrixes were reverse shifted to restore the original value.
3. **Watermark Decoding:** Divide the watermark sequence into watermark and LM according to the length recorded in the key. Then decoding the watermark and LM separately.
4. Image restoration. Perform 1-level inverse-RDWT using the restored coefficients generated in step 2. Then reverse adjusting the boundary pixels according to the LM and threshold T.

The watermark extraction algorithm extract the watermark from the stego-image while restore the image to the original state. From the above it is obviously that the proposed scheme only rely on the parameter stored in the key, so this scheme is a blind watermark scheme.

Image Encryption

To enhance the security of the proposed scheme, a PWLCM based image encryption algorithm is introduced to the proposed scheme. The image first scrambled using the PWLCM sequence, then each of the image's pixel value was encrypted by the PWLCM based algorithm. The detail of the encryption algorithm is given as following:

1. **Sequence Generation:** Generate the PWLCM sequence using PWLCM. The proposed algorithm used the PWLCM function proposed by Xiao et al., which given as following:

$$X_{t+1} = F_p(X_t) = \begin{cases} X_t/p, & 0 \leq X_t < p \\ (X_t - p)/(0.5 - p), & p \leq X_t < 0.5 \\ (1 - X_t - p)/(0.5 - p), & 0.5 \leq X_t < 1 - p \\ (1 - X_t)/p, & 1 - p \leq X_t \leq 1 \end{cases} \tag{21}$$

where $X_t \in [0,1]$, $p \in (0,0.5)$ is the initial value for iteration. Suppose the image has the dimension of M by N pixels, then the total number T the image has is $M \times N$. Number each pixel of the image by a integer X as indexing number from top to bottom and left to right, $X \in \{0,1,2,...,T\}$. Then calculate the iterating number n using the scale of the pixel value L and T by $n = L \times T$. Generate the sequence $S = \{X_1, X_2, ..., X_n\}$ by iterate the PWLCM n times.

2. **Index Generation:** Generate the scrambling index using sequence S. Sort S in ascending order to get a new sequence $\{\widehat{X}_1, \widehat{X}_2, ..., \widehat{X}_T\}$. By picking up each address number of Xi from the the new sequence, a sequence $I = \{t_1, t_2, ..., t_n\}$ was generated for scramble.
3. **Image Scramble:** Scrambling the image P using index I. Suppose the indexing number of current pixel is i, then the corresponding indexing number in the scrambled image Ps is I(i). The scrambling process changed the spatial correlation of the pixels. The pixel values are remain intact.
4. **Pixel Value Encryption:** Generate the encrypting sequence $E = \{XX_1, XX_2, ..., XX_n\}$ using sequence S and the following threshold function:

$$XX_i = \begin{cases} 0, S_i > 0.5 \\ 1, S_i \leq 0.5 \end{cases} \tag{22}$$

where $i \in \{1,2,\ldots,n\}$, XXi is the ith element of E. Each element of sequence E has the value 0 or 1.

The scrambled image Ps then encrypted using E. Each pixel value of Ps was first convert to binary form then perform bit-wise XOR with corresponding element in sequence E. Then convert the results to decimal form to get the encrypted image Pe.

The image encryption algorithm not only remove the spatial correlation of the pixels, but also encrypted the pixel value. This guaranteed the security of the image content and the watermark embedded in it.

EXPERIMENTAL RESULTS AND ANALYSIS

The proposed scheme has been tested with MATLAB 2013a platform on i5-2500 processor with 16GB RAM. Six 512 by 512 pixels 8-bit gray scale medical images are used as cover image (Figure 4). For comparison, a Integer DWT based scheme proposed by Xuan et al.(Xuan et al., 2006) using histogram shifting was also tested for comparison.

Figure 4. Images used in the test

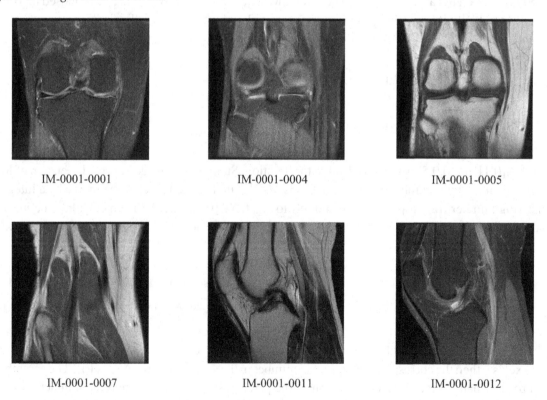

IM-0001-0001   IM-0001-0004   IM-0001-0005

IM-0001-0007   IM-0001-0011   IM-0001-0012

Embedding Capacity

The embedding capacity of Xuan et al.'s scheme and the proposed scheme are given in Table 1 and Table 2.

Table 1 shows the statistics of embedding capacity of Xuan et al's scheme. T is the threshold value used for the embedding control. With the increment of T, the embedding capacity increased.

Table 2 shows the embedding capacity of the proposed scheme. To show the differences between the DWT and RDWT, the same algorithm was tested both using DWT and RDWT. It is obvious that the RDWT supported larger embedding capacity.

From Table 1 and Table 2 it could be concluded that the proposed scheme has the largest embedding capacity than DWT based and Xuan et al's scheme.

Visual Quality

The visual quality of the stego image is critical for the evaluation of the medical image watermarking scheme. To evaluate the visual quality of the proposed scheme and Xuan et al.'s scheme. The PSNR(Peak Signal Noise Ratio) and SSIM(Structural Similarity) index are introduced.

Table 1. Embedding capacity of Xuan et al.'s scheme

Image Number	T					
	0	1	2	3	4	5
IM-0001-0001	10083	21798	31238	38441	40920	43398
IM-0001-0004	8214	16781	24483	31318	37121	41851
IM-0001-0005	8340	17033	24760	31407	36889	41494
IM-0001-0007	8672	18073	26575	33717	39736	43666
IM-0001-0011	10143	23881	25890	27328	28883	31028
IM-0001-0012	11053	16232	27511	26677	29746	30655

Table 2. Embedding capacity of the proposed scheme

Image Number	DWT				RDWT			
	Capacity	Size of LM	Size of Coded LM	Net Capacity	Capacity	Size of LM	Size of coded LM	Net Capacity
IM-0001-0001	20481	1761	10040	10441	47859	1761	10040	37819
IM-0001-0004	16897	962	5657	11240	41915	962	5657	36258
IM-0001-0005	17202	1000	5956	11246	42260	1000	5956	36304
IM-0001-0007	18013	1024	6073	11940	44034	1024	6073	37961
IM-0001-0011	15263	1512	8324	6939	31448	1512	8324	23124
IM-0001-0012	16302	1216	6353	9949	32604	1216	6353	26251

PSNR was initially proposed for the measurement of noise in the channel of communication. Using PSNR in the evaluation of the image quality could reflect the distortion caused by the embedding of the watermark.

The PSNR is computed as following:

$$PSNR = 10 \log_{10} \left(\frac{MAX^2}{MSE} \right)$$

(23)

$$MSE = \frac{1}{M \times N} \sum_{x=1}^{M} \sum_{y=1}^{N} \left(I(x,y) - I'(x,y) \right)^2$$

(24)

where, MAX denotes the max pixel value of the image, M and N denotes the width and height of the image, $I(x,y)$ and $I'(x,y)$ denotes the pixel value of the position (x,y) in the Cover-image and Stego-image, respectively.

The SSIM is developed based on the HVS (Human Visual System). This made SSIM a suitable measurement of the perceptional quality.

The SSIM index of two images x and y is defined as:

$$SSIM(x,y) = \frac{\left(2\mu_x \mu_y + C_1 \right)\left(2\sigma_{xy} + C_2 \right)}{\left(\mu_x^2 + \mu_y^2 + C_1 \right)\left(\sigma_x^2 + \sigma_y^2 + C_2 \right)}$$

(25)

where x and y is two non-negative image signals, μ_x and μ_y are mean value of the pixel values of image x and y, σ_x and σ_y are standard deviation of the image's pixel value, respectively. The σ_{xy}, C_1 and C_2 is calculated as follow:

$$\sigma_{xy} = \frac{1}{N-1} \sum_{i=1}^{n} \left(x_i - \mu_x \right)\left(y_i - \mu_y \right)$$

(26)

$$C_1 = (K_1 L)^2$$

(27)

$$C_2 = (K_2 L)^2$$

(28)

where K_1 and K_2 are two small constants satisfy $K_1, K_2 \ll 1$ and L is the scale of the image pixel value. The SSIM has the value between 0 and 1. Zero means the two images are not visually connected and 1 means the two images are visually same.

Table 3 and Table 4 shows the statistics of PSNR and SSIM corresponding to Xuan et al's and the proposed scheme. To evaluate the perceptional quality of the corresponding scheme, a PWLCM based pseudo-random sequence was generated and used as the watermark. The length of the sequence was decided by the capacity calculated in Table 1 and Table 2. To generate the PWLCM based 0-1 sequence, first a combo of initial value was selected, then a PWLCM sequence S is calculated according to the initial value. Finally the 0-1 sequence S' was generated as following:

$$S'_i = \begin{cases} 0, S_i > 0.5 \\ 1, S_i \leq 0.5 \end{cases} \tag{29}$$

where S_i and S'_i is the element of the corresponding sequece.

Table 3 and Table 4 suggested that the proposed scheme has the best visual quality comparing to DWT based and Xuan et al's scheme. It should be noted that the proposed scheme also has the largest embedding capacity according to Table 1 and Table 2.

Security

The PWLCM-based image encryption algorithm was introduced into the proposed scheme. To test the algorithm, the test images are encrypted using the algorithm, than the NC and SSIM between the original and processed image are calculated. The NC between image A and B can be defined as:

Table 3. PSNR and SSIM of Xuan et al.'s scheme

Visual Quality				
Image number	PSNR	SSIM	T	S
IM-0001-0001	44.7381	0.9691	5	-5
IM-0001-0004	42.5887	0.9668	5	-5
IM-0001-0005	45.5195	0.9798	5	-5
IM-0001-0007	46.0221	0.9697	5	-5
IM-0001-0011	48.6928	0.9795	5	-5
IM-0001-0012	47.2906	0.9965	5	-5

Table 4. PSNR and SSIM of the proposed scheme

Image Number	DWT		RDWT	
	SSIM	PSNR	SSIM	PSNR
IM-0001-0001	0.9860	46.3620	0.9877	48.9631
IM-0001-0004	0.9869	46.3680	0.9886	49.1924
IM-0001-0005	0.9865	46.3467	0.9879	49.1279
IM-0001-0007	0.9854	46.3380	0.9878	49.1161
IM-0001-0011	0.9948	49.9656	0.9965	50.2915
IM-0001-0012	0.9947	47.0940	0.9967	50.1944

$$NC(A,B) = \frac{\sum_m \sum_n \left(A_{mn} - \overline{A}\right)\left(B_{mn} - \overline{B}\right)}{\sqrt{\left(\sum_m \sum_n \left(A_{mn} - \overline{A}\right)^2\right)\left(\sum_m \sum_n \left(B_{mn} - \overline{B}\right)^2\right)}} \tag{30}$$

where m and n are pixel coordinates of image A and B, $\overline{A}$ and $\overline{B}$ are the mean value of image A and B, respectively.

The correlation coefficient between A and B can have the value between -1 and 1. If the value is near 1, A and B are strongly correlated. If it is near -1, A and B are also strongly correlated but it looks similar to negative film. If it is near 0, A is totally uncorrelated with B. The results of NC and SSIM are given in Table 5.

Table 5 suggests that the proposed scheme could encrypting the image efficiently. The NC and SSIM indexes of the encrypted and original image are close to zero, which means there's no visual or statistical connection between the original and encrypted image.

However, the security of the proposed scheme is not only depends on the relationship between the original and encrypted image, but also depends on the scale of the encrypting scheme's key space. Since the encrypting sequence used in the proposed scheme are all generated by the PWLCM, the key space could be estimated by analyzing the PWLCM.

Figure 5 to Figure 8 shows the absolute difference of the PWLCM sequence based index with minimum modification on the initial values. The initial value X_t and p are changed with 10^{-16}, then a index sequence is generated using the method proposed in index generation. The absolute value of the differences between each item of the index are calculated. The result suggests that when the difference between the initial values is 10^{-16}, the corresponding sequences show significant differences. When the variance between the initial values is 10^{-17} there are no difference between the corresponding sequences any more.

The results also show that different PWLCM function has the same chaos property in the generation of the indexes. This permits the user change the PWLCM function without affecting the security of it.

The scale of the proposed scheme's key space can be estimated as follows. Since the initial values are acted as the key of the scheme, the space of the initial value can be used to represent the proposed scheme's key space. From the above, it could be concluded that the minimum variance of the initial value with the chaos property is 10^{-16}, which is approximately 2^{-50}. This means that for each initial value there are 2^{50} possibilities, because every key is a combination of 2 initial values Xt and p, the scale of the key space could be approximately 2^{100}. This key space is huge enough to resist the exhaustive searching attack.

Table 5. The NC and SSIM between the original and processed images

Image Number	Scrambled		Encrypted	
	NC	SSIM	NC	SSIM
IM-0001-0001	-0.00087023	0.0379	-0.00082014	0.0268
IM-0001-0004	0.0029	0.0973	0.00062118	0.0331
IM-0001-0005	-0.0011	0.03	-0.0028	0.0317
IM-0001-0007	0.0035	0.1691	-0.00053077	0.0308
IM-0001-0011	-0.00028359	0.0556	-0.0014	0.0273
IM-0001-0012	-0.0018	0.124	-0.0004666	0.0269

Figure 5. Absolute differences of the PWLCM generated index with Xiao's PWLCM (Xt changed from 0.323232 to 0.3232320000000001)

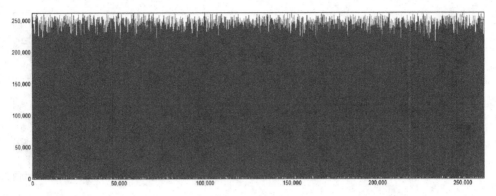

Figure 6. Absolute differences of the PWLCM generated index with Xiao's PWLCM (p changed from 0.252525 to 0.2525250000000001)

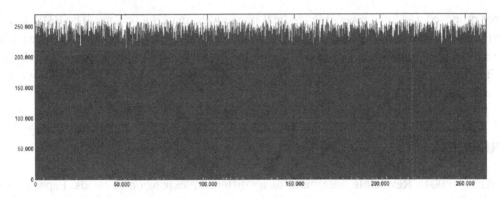

Figure 7. Absolute differences of the PWLCM generated index with Li's PWLCM (Xt changed from 0.323232 to 0.3232320000000001)

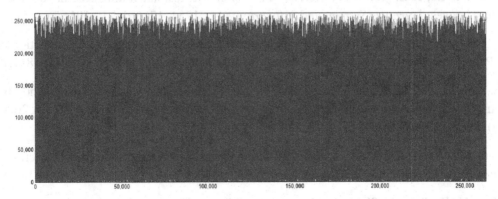

Figure 8. Absolute differences of the PWLCM generated index with Li's PWLCM (p changed from 0.252525 to 0.2525250000000001)

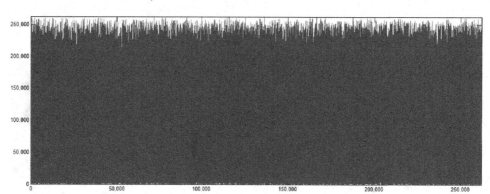

CONCLUSION

This paper proposed a secured reversible medical image watermarking scheme. The RDWT was introduced to the proposed scheme to meet the highly demand of the visual quality. To guarantee the security of the image and the watermark, a PWLCM based image encryption algorithm was introduced to the scheme. The experimental results shows that the proposed scheme has better visual quality, embedding capacity and security than former scheme.

REFERENCES

Alattar, A. M. (2004). Reversible watermark using difference expansion of quads. Paper presented at the IEEE International Conference on Acoustics, Speech, and Signal Processing (ICASSP'04). 10.1109/ICASSP.2004.1326560

Chang, C.-C., & Lu, T.-C. (2006). A difference expansion oriented data hiding scheme for restoring the original host images. *Journal of Systems and Software*, 79(12), 1754–1766. doi:10.1016/j.jss.2006.03.035

Chen, M., Chen, Z., Zeng, X., & Xiong, Z. (2009). Reversible data hiding using additive prediction-error expansion. Paper presented at the 11th ACM workshop on Multimedia and security. 10.1145/1597817.1597822

Chen, X., Sun, X., Sun, H., Zhou, Z., & Zhang, J. (2013). Reversible watermarking method based on asymmetric-histogram shifting of prediction errors. *Journal of Systems and Software*, 86(10), 2620–2626. doi:10.1016/j.jss.2013.04.086

Fallahpour, M. (2008). Reversible image data hiding based on gradient adjusted prediction. *IEICE Electronics Express*, 5(20), 870–876. doi:10.1587/elex.5.870

Hu, Y., Lee, H.-K., & Li, J. (2009). DE-based reversible data hiding with improved overflow location map. Circuits and Systems for Video Technology. *IEEE Transactions on*, 19(2), 250–260.

Kim, K.-S., Lee, M.-J., Lee, H.-Y., & Lee, H.-K. (2009). Reversible data hiding exploiting spatial correlation between sub-sampled images. *Pattern Recognition*, 42(11), 3083–3096. doi:10.1016/j.patcog.2009.04.004

Kountchev, R., Todorov, V., Kountcheva, R., & Milanova, M. (2006). Lossless compression of biometric image data. Paper presented at the 5th WSEAS international conference on Signal processing.

Lee, C.-C., Wu, H.-C., Tsai, C.-S., & Chu, Y.-P. (2008). Adaptive lossless steganographic scheme with centralized difference expansion. *Pattern Recognition*, *41*(6), 2097–2106. doi:10.1016/j.patcog.2007.11.018

Lin, G., Tiegang, G., Guorui, S., Yanjun, C., & Li, F. (2012, July 15-17). A new reversible watermarking scheme based on Integer DCT for medical images. Paper presented at the International Conference on Wavelet Analysis and Pattern Recognition (ICWAPR).

Luo, L., Chen, Z., Chen, M., Zeng, X., & Xiong, Z. (2010). Reversible image watermarking using interpolation technique. Information Forensics and Security. *IEEE Transactions on*, *5*(1), 187–193.

Maxwell, T. S. I., Handel, T. G., & Bradley, J. N. (1998). Compression embedding: Google Patents.

Ni, Z., Shi, Y.-Q., Ansari, N., & Su, W. (2006). Reversible data hiding. Circuits and Systems for Video Technology. *IEEE Transactions*, *16*(3), 354–362.

Shih, F. Y., & Wu, Y.-T. (2005). Robust watermarking and compression for medical images based on genetic algorithms. *Information Sciences*, *175*(3), 200–216. doi:10.1016/j.ins.2005.01.013

Tai, W.-L., Yeh, C.-M., & Chang, C.-C. (2009). Reversible data hiding based on histogram modification of pixel differences. Circuits and Systems for Video Technology. *IEEE Transactions*, *19*(6), 906–910.

Thodi, D. M., & Rodríguez, J. J. (2007). Expansion embedding techniques for reversible watermarking. Image Processing. *IEEE Transactions*, *16*(3), 721–730.

Tian, J. (2003). Reversible data embedding using a difference expansion. *IEEE Transactions on Circuits and Systems for Video Technology*, *13*(8), 890–896. doi:10.1109/TCSVT.2003.815962

Tsai, P., Hu, Y.-C., & Yeh, H.-L. (2009). Reversible image hiding scheme using predictive coding and histogram shifting. *Signal Processing*, *89*(6), 1129–1143. doi:10.1016/j.sigpro.2008.12.017

Xuan, G., Yao, Q., Yang, C., Gao, J., Chai, P., Shi, Y. Q., & Ni, Z. (2006). *Lossless data hiding using histogram shifting method based on integer wavelets Digital Watermarking* (pp. 323–332). Springer.

This research was previously published in the International Journal of Digital Crime and Forensics (IJDCF), 7(4); edited by Feng Liu; pages 1-18, copyright year 2015 by IGI Publishing (an imprint of IGI Global).

Chapter 30
Video Saliency Detection for Visual Cryptography–Based Watermarking

Adrita Barari
Defence Institute of Advanced Technology, India

Sunita V. Dhavale
Defence Institute of Advanced Technology, India

ABSTRACT

The aim of this chapter is to review the application of the technique of Visual cryptography in non-intrusive video watermarking. The power of saliency feature extraction is also highlighted in the context of Visual Cryptography based watermarking systems for videos. All schemes in literature related to Visual cryptography based video watermarking, have been brought together with special attention on the role of saliency feature extraction in each of these schemes. Further a novel approach for VC based video watermarking using motion vectors (MVP Algorithm) as a salient feature is suggested. Experimental results show the robustness of proposed MVP Algorithm against various video processing attacks. Also, compression scale invariance is achieved.

1. INTRODUCTION

The rapid growth in digital video editing technologies has become a threat to the authenticity and integrity of video data. In case of wide range of applications, such as video surveillance, video broadcast, DVDs, video conferencing, and video-on-demand applications, protection of intellectual property rights of transmitted video data is vital. Digital watermarking technology has emerged in last decade as a well-known solution for video copyright protection (Hartung & Kutter, 1999). In digital watermarking technique (Hartung & Kutter, 1999; Petitcolas, F.A.P, 2000), a watermark representing the copyright information (w) is embedded into the cover video (x) to obtain new watermarked signal $\hat{x} = x + w$, practically indistinguishable from x, by people, in such a way that an eavesdropper cannot detect the presence of w in $\hat{x}$. At the

DOI: 10.4018/978-1-7998-1763-5.ch030

time of ownership dispute, the embedded watermark is extracted ($\hat{w}$) from the watermarked video ($\hat{x}$) and used for verification. Almost all digital video data today is distributed and stored in the compressed format. Hence, existing approaches in video watermarking can be categorized as uncompressed domain video watermarking (Sun & Liu, 2005; Chen & Leung, 2008; Blanchi & Piva, 2013) and compressed domain video watermarking (Ardizzone, E., La Cascia, M., Avanzato, A., & Bruna, A., 1999; Lin, Eskicioglu, Reginald, & Edward, 2005; Fang & Lin, 2006; Sejdic, Djurovic & Stankovic 2011; Aly, H., 2011).

A well-designed video watermarking system must offer both perceptual transparency and robustness (Petitcolas, F.A.P, 2000). Perceptual transparency means that the watermarked video should be perceptually equivalent to the original video. Robustness refers to a reliable extraction of the watermark even if the watermarked video is degraded during different intentional and non-intentional attacks. Assuring perceptual transparency is difficult in video compared to that with still images, due to the temporal dimension existing in video. Embedding different watermarks into video frames independently without taking the temporal dimension into account usually yields a flicker effect in video. This is due to the fact that the differences exist between the intensities of pixels at the same position in two successive video frames.

Of late, visual cryptography (VC) has come up as one of the novel solution for image and video watermarking which is capable of providing zero perceptual distortion along with good robustness towards attacks. VC is a cryptographic technique which allows visual information (for example images, text, etc.) to be split into n different shares with the help of simple mathematical techniques (Naor & Shamir, 1995). In case of watermarking, a secret watermark image w is split into master share M and ownership share O using VC technique. The master share M is generated based on the unique salient features of the host data h which needs to be watermarked. The ownership share O depends on both binary watermark secret w as well as master share M and is registered with certified authority CA. At the time of dispute over the rightful ownership of the attacked host data $\hat{h}$, ownership is identified by stacking the master share $\hat{M}$ (estimated based on $\hat{h}$) and ownership share O kept by the CA. Generation of master share M affects the robustness and security of VC based watermarking. As M is generated based on the unique salient features of the host data h, video saliency detection plays an important role in VC based watermarking.

This chapter provides a brief introduction to VC and application of VC in watermarking. The chapter also provides detail overview of existing VC based video watermarking techniques. In case of nonintrusive VC based video watermarking approaches, the importance of video saliency detection stage in generation of master share M is analyzed. Finally, a novel approach is suggested for VC based video watermarking techniques using motion vectors.

2. VISUAL CRYPTOGRAPHY IN WATERMARKING

In 1995, a novel visual secret sharing concept called Visual Cryptography (VC) was proposed by Moni Naor and Adi Shamir. VC is a technique which allows visual information (for example images, text, etc.) to be split into n different *shares* with the help of simple mathematical techniques. These shares are nothing but pseudo random noise-like structures which reveal no meaningful information if viewed in isolation as seen in Figure 1(a) and 1(b). However, when all the required shares are printed upon transparencies and overlaid one upon the other, they reveal the secret image as illustrated in Figure 1(c). The reconstruction of the secret visual information in this case can be done only with the help of the Human Visual System (HVS). This is the reason why the technique is called *visual* cryptography.

Figure 1a. Shares created by VC technique

Figure 1b. Shares created by VC technique

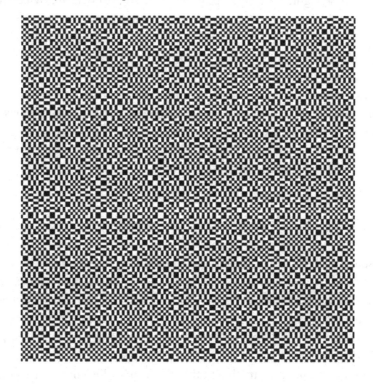

Figure 1c. Overlapping of shares to reveal watermark

The basic model of VC as suggested in (Naor & Shamir, 1995) is as follows. It consists of a printed page of *cipher text* (which can be sent by mail or faxed) and a printed transparency (which serves as a secret key). The original *clear text* is revealed by placing the transparency with the key over the printed page of the cipher text. Both the cipher text and the clear text are random noise-like structures. In a more general way, these pseudo random noise-like structures are called *shares*.

This model can be extended to the *k* out of *n* secret sharing problem. In this scheme, the secret image is split into *n* different shares. The secret information can be retrieved by overlaying $k(k \leq n)$ or more than *k* shares but any $(k - 1)$ shares give absolutely no information about the secret image.

The basic model can be considered to be a particular case of the (k,n) model described above. It can be considered to be a 2 out of 2 secret sharing scheme. The (2,2) VSS scheme can be explained as follows. A secret image with size $(M \times N)$ is divided into two shares with size $(2M \times 2N)$ where every pixel of the secret image is represented by a block of $(2 \times)$ pixels. In the encryption process, every secret pixel is turned into two blocks, and each block belongs to the corresponding share image. In the process, two share images are obtained. In the decryption process, two corresponding blocks of a pixel are simply stacked together to retrieve the secret pixel. Two share blocks of a white secret pixel are similar while share blocks of a black secret pixel are complementary. Figure 2 shows the concept of (2,2) VSS scheme.

This visual secret sharing scheme shares the secret into a predetermined number of shares so that the cooperation of the legitimate group of shareholders reveals the secret information. The retrieval of the secret information is impossible by an unauthorized group of shareholders.

The VC technique is gaining momentum and acceptance in the field of information hiding and security because of its benefits over normal cryptography and traditional watermarking techniques. The advantages of using visual cryptography in watermarking are as follows:

- VC based watermarking schemes are non-intrusive and do not alter the contents of the host image or video. Thus, VC does not deteriorate the quality of the host.
- VC based watermarking techniques can achieve large embedding capacity, that is, it can embed a large watermark (an image) into the cover images
- It can achieve high security.
- It has the ability to share a secret image between multiple users.

Figure 2. Concept of (2, 2) VSS scheme
(Rawat and Balasubramanian, 2012).

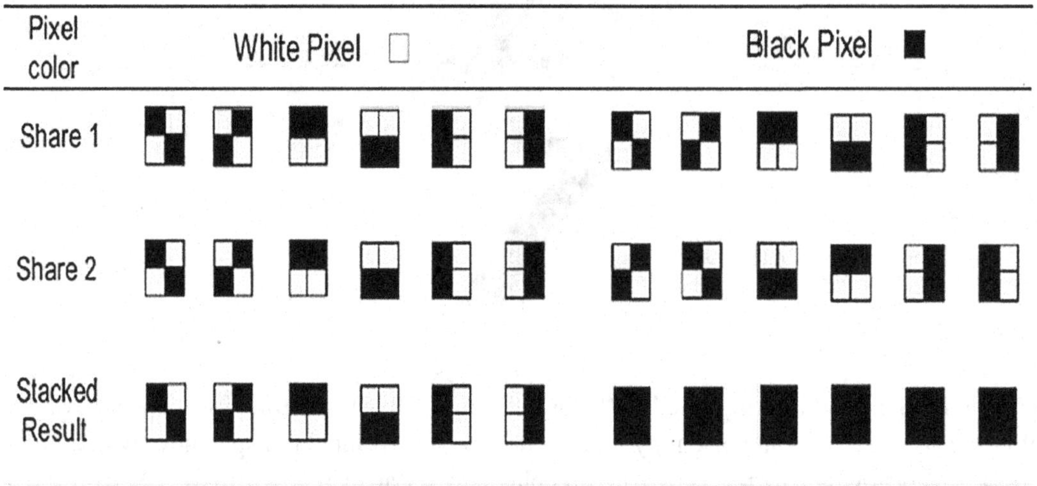

- The VC based scheme is easy to implement where preparation of shares does not require any complex cryptographic computations unlike normal cryptography where a lot of mathematical calculations need to be performed.
- VC requires no previous knowledge or experience of cryptography on the part of the person decoding the message since decoding can be done by the Human Visual System (HVS). By means of the shares, visual information is encrypted such that decryption becomes a mechanical operation.
- It is equally difficult for an unauthorized user to decode the message since secret message can be deciphered only if all shares are available to the attacker. The probability of this happening is very less since one of the shares has to be registered with a higher Certified Authority (CA).

As seen from above, one of the major advantages of the VC technique is that it does not modify the cover data at all. This property of VC makes VC based watermarking techniques an absolutely loss-less procedure. VC based watermarking may be used in applications where the cover image or video contains sensitive information whose integrity needs to be preserved. Though traditional watermarking techniques have been successful in proving the rightful ownership of a multimedia content, the process embedding of the watermark has been found to seriously degrade the quality of the host image or video. This is particularly undesirable in defence, military and medical sectors where classified information is conveyed through multimedia. For this reason, there was a need to develop a non-intrusive watermarking technique which would preserve the integrity of the host as well as successfully establish the owner-ship. This could be achieved with Visual Cryptography (VC) based watermarking techniques where a single image or text is split into Master share M and Ownership Share O. When M and O are overlaid one upon the other, the secret watermark information is revealed. VC based watermarking schemes have been developed by researchers worldwide for watermarking images and videos (Lou, Tso & Liu, 2007; Wang & Chen, 2009; Liu & Wu, 2011). Thus, VC finds some great applications in watermarking as will be discussed in the next section.

3. EXISTING VC BASED VIDEO WATERMARKING TECHNIQUES

Video watermarking schemes are used for various video applications such as copyright protection, copy control, fingerprinting, broadcast monitoring, video authentication, enhanced video coding etc. Here, a video is nothing but a sequence of images yet image watermarking techniques cannot be directly applied to videos owing to their three dimensional characteristics. In addition to their special preprocessing techniques, the temporal nature of videos has to be taken into account (Hartung & Kutter, 1999). Redundancy between frames and a large volume of data makes it all the more difficult to perform watermarking in videos. Further, real time implementations of video watermarking techniques are generally much more complex than that of image watermarking which becomes an important issue.

Some common forms of attack on videos are frame swapping, frame averaging, frame dropping, statistical analysis, interpolation etc. which are unknown to the domain of image watermarking. Inter-video collusion attacks and intra-video collusion attacks are also major issues in case of video fingerprinting applications. In collusion attacks, several compromised buyers can come together and use their authorized copies to generate a new copy. This process can remove the watermark from new copy thus making them evade punishment.

Almost all traditional video watermarking approaches modify the content of the host video which in turn affects the host video quality. Thus, instead of the traditional watermarking schemes, we can use VC based non-intrusive video watermarking approaches effectively for copyright protection. In this section, we present some of the existing VC based watermarking schemes for videos.

3.1 Work by Houmansadr and Ghaemmaghami, (2006)

One of the earliest VC based video watermarking approaches was proposed by Houmansadr and Ghaemmaghami, (2006). This approach was in the spatial domain and proved to be robust to collusion attacks and geometrical attacks. The proposed scheme is based on Naor and Shamir's (2,2) visual secret sharing scheme (Naor & Shamir, 1995) and can be broadly categorized into Embedding of Watermark and Detection of Watermark stages.

Within the embedding stage, the algorithm begins with the share creation phase wherein the binary watermark image is split into two noise-like pseudo random shares. The binary format (0,1) of the watermark information is converted to the (-1, +1) signed format which gives a pseudo-random watermark sequence which is approximately zero mean. In the following phase of the proposed algorithm, the frames of the video are temporally scrambled by the use of a Linear Feedback Shift Register (LFSR) as illustrated in Figure 3. Initial condition of the LFSR serves as the private key in the watermark detection stage.

A one to one mapping is maintained between the frames of the original video and the temporally scrambled video. The next phase which is the share insertion phase scales the shares by a parameter (α) that determines the strength of the watermark and combines them with the scrambled video frames. The final watermarked video sequence is produced by the inverse temporal scrambling process. The watermark detection stage, shown in Figure 4, begins with passing the watermarked video through a high pass filter (HPF) which preserves the high frequency components in the noise- like watermark sequence. Subsequently, the video is temporally scrambled once again such that the frames containing the shares now lie adjacent to each other. As a result $\frac{L}{2}$ stacked frames are obtained where a pixel by pixel com-

Figure 3. Embedding of watermark
(Houmansadr and Ghaemmaghami, 2006).

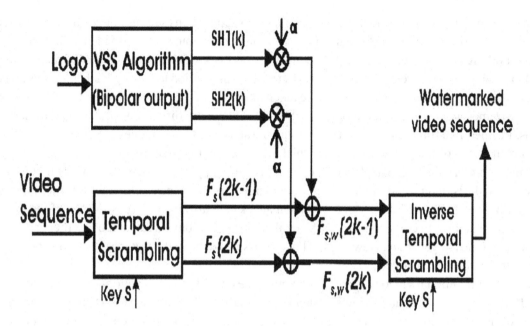

parison between the stacked frames are done, followed by a reduction of the stacked image from ($2M\times2N$) pixels to ($M\times N$) pixels. The detection algorithm uses the principle that stacking frames, containing corresponding shares of the logo, makes higher correlation with the logo, as compared to stacked frames containing non- relevant shares of the logo. The correlation between the $\frac{L}{2}$ stacked frames and the binary watermark is calculated to check the presence of the watermark.

In this simple and effective spatial domain method (Houmansadr and Ghaemmaghami, 2006), the inserted watermark shows high resilience against some attacks, such as geometrical distortions and collusion attacks. However, the scheme is in spatial domain which provides a lower robustness to steganalysis in comparison to VC based watermarking techniques of the transformed domain. Further, since the shares are embedded into the host video in the watermark embedding stage, the process alters the contents of the host and hence degrades it.

The strength of the algorithm is tested by performing several attacks. As mentioned above, the correlation between the $\frac{L}{2}$ stacked frames and the binary watermark is calculated to check the presence of the watermark. Tables 1-3 (Houmansadr and Ghaemmaghami, 2006) show a decrement in the correlation coefficient after performing attacks such as frame cropping, frame rotating and changing the aspect ratio of the watermarked video sequence . Also, the watermarked sequence is found to have good robustness against geometric distortions. Table 4 shows resistance of this scheme to frame scaling. Table 5 demonstrates the average true to false ratio detection ratio when the watermarked sequence is M-JPEG compressed with different quality factors.

Figure 4. Retrieval of watermark
(Houmansadr and Ghaemmaghami, 2006).

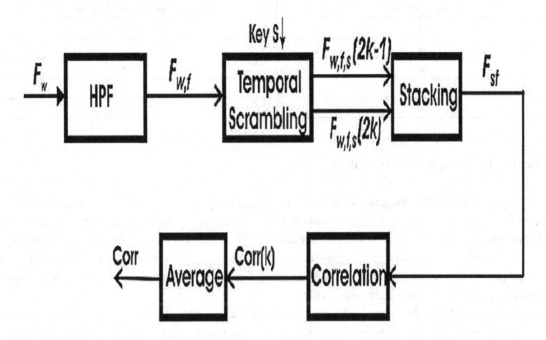

Table 1. Decrement of correlation coefficient after frame cropping (keeping middle of frames)

Cropping Percentage	Decrement of Correlation Coefficient(%)
10	8
20	10
30	6
40	11
50	16

Table 2. Decrement of correlation coefficient after frame rotation

Rotation Angle	Decrement of Correlation Coefficient(%)
10	8
20	10
30	6
40	11
50	16

Table 3. Decrement of correlation coefficient after changing the AR of 240 * 360 pixels watermarked frames

New Size Pixels	Decrement of Correlation Coefficient(%)
240 * 180	15
240 * 90	12
480 * 360	29

Table 4. Decrement of correlation coefficient after frame scaling

Scaling Ratio	Decrement of Correlation Coefficient(%)
2	29
4	31
8	39

Table 5. Average true to false detection ratio after M-JPEG compression for different quality factors

Quality Factor	Average True to False Detection Ratio
100	7.83
90	5.20
80	2.75
60	1.72
40	1.53

3.2 Work by Zeng and Pei, (2008)

Later, Zeng and Pei, (2008), suggested a novel video diagnosing method where the generation of crypto watermarks was carried out by using the concept of visual cryptography. Here, significant information in the form of crypto-watermarks is embedded into the video through a Dual Domain Quaternary Watermarking Algorithm which lends robustness to the scheme. The proposed method can identify the attack category (frame attack and temporal attack) and the video authentication type (whether video is a watermarked video or non-watermarked video).

The first stage of the algorithm is the generation of such crypto- watermarks while the next stage embeds the crypto-watermarks using the quaternary watermarking algorithm. The crypto-watermarks are generated through visual cryptography from binary images and have different resistances against different attacks. Four crypto-watermarks, namely first watermark (w_1), second watermark (w_2), intra-watermark (w_3) and inter-watermark (w_4) are generated as shown in Figure 5. Here, w_1 and w_2 form the quaternary watermark w_q. This quaternary watermark is added into the intra frame in the DCT domain in the embedding stage. During the watermark extraction stage at the receiver end, the data stream is divided into (8×8) non overlapping blocks and then w_q is extracted by calculating sample values in the DCT domain.

The bit-error-rate (BER) between the extracted watermarks of the suspected video and the original crypto watermarks is measured. Analysis of BER determines the nature of attack on the video. Based on a comparison of BER's between the first, second, intra and inter watermarks, status of frame attack is assigned. The status can be used to diagnose a video to be a non-watermarked video, authorized video, recompressed video and unauthorized frame inserted video.

Important applications of this methodology include dispute resolving, content identity verification and prevention of illegal video editing. However, the decryption process is not done by merely overlaying the shares. Since the watermark extraction process involves computations in the DCT domain followed by calculation of sample, it causes a computational overhead. Thus the inherent advantage of visual cryptography that is, extracting the secret information directly by the human visual system without the use of any complex computational process, is compromised. Also, similar to the method proposed by Houmansadr and Ghaemmaghami, (2006), this is an intrusive method and operates by directly embedding the watermark into the contents of the host.

Figure 5. Generation of crypto-watermarks
Zeng and Pei, (2008).

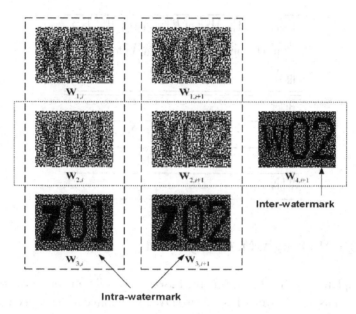

3.3 Work by Vashistha, Nallusamy, Das, & Paul (2010)

In both previous mentioned techniques, content of host audio is modified. Vashistha et.al (2010) proposed a method that employs (2,2) visual cryptography, scene change detection and extraction of features from scene to create *Verification Information (VI)*. The authors' have rightly coined the term *'non-intrusive watermarking'* for visual cryptographic schemes since the information of the watermark has been extracted by creation of shares applying the principles of visual cryptography rather than embedding watermark information directly into the cover content (host image or video). This is indeed a major advantage over the previously mentioned schemes of Houmansadr and Ghaemmaghami, (2006) and Zeng and Pei, (2008).

The process to generate *VI* for watermark pattern (*w*) of size (*h×l*) and an original 256 gray-leveled image (*I*) of size (*m×n*) with the help of a secret key (*S*) and by the rule shown in Figure 6. The *VI* is constructed by assembling all the (VI_1, VI_2) pairs. In the verification process, the authenticity of the image $(\hat{I})$ is assessed by using the inverse process. The above process is used in the context of videos by first performing scene change detection and then by forming a scene averaged image which is converted into grey scale for computing the *VI*. The number of scenes detected decides the number of *VI* vectors since these two values have to be necessarily equal. The *VI* vector is thus one of the shares generated from the watermark pattern and the secret image.

Since no data is embedded into the host video in this technique, the method is resilient to attacks aimed at distorting the data embedded into videos. The method is particularly effective against frame averaging, frame dropping, frame swapping and interpolation attacks. All watermarked scenes, and not just individual frames, need to be dropped for an effective attack. Dropping of scenes makes illegal copying and distribution pointless and thus automatically discourages malpractices. A major contribution of this scheme is that it can survive as much as a 50% frame drop attacks. However, the scheme is in the spatial domain which makes it less robust than its transform domain counterparts.

Figure 6. Rules for retrieval of watermark
Vashistha et.al (2010).

Color of ith pixel in W	The MSB of R_i^{th} pixel of image I	Assign (V_{i1}, V_{i2}) of VI to be
Black	1	(0,1)
Black	0	(1,0)
White	1	(1,0)
White	0	(0,1)

3.4 Work by Singh, R., Singh, M. & Roy (2011)

Singh et al. (2011) implemented VC based scheme based on DWT transform domain and scene change detection. Here, 1- level Discrete Wavelet Transform (DWT) is applied on averaged frame and features are extracted from LL sub band. The watermark is split into sub-watermarks, the number of sub-watermarks being equal to the number of detected scenes. Frame mean μ_k of all k frames in a scene and global mean (μ) of the frame mean in a scene are found by taking the average of all corresponding pixel values in all frames in the same scene and the average of all pixel values in the frame mean in the same scene respectively.

Next, the construction of owner's share is done by checking the pixel value of the binary watermark and comparing the pixel value of the frame mean of same scene of the video with the global mean. Since, different parts of a single watermark are used in different scenes while the same sub-watermark is used for the different frames of a same scene the algorithm becomes robust to frame attacks like frame averaging, frame dropping, frame swapping and interpolation attacks. The identification share is generated by comparing the frame mean $\hat{\mu}_k$ of the suspected video with the global mean μ of this frame mean. The stacking of both the shares reveals copyright information. An overview of this scheme is demonstrated in Figures 7(a) and 7(b). The robustness of DWT to noise attacks and the security and simplicity of VC makes this technique easy to implement.

Though all above mentioned VC based video watermarking schemes have tried to achieve high imperceptibility and robustness, they suffer from limitations imposed by VC technique itself. For any VC scheme, resolution of extracted secret watermark binary image is degraded due to pixel expansion (Naor & Shamir, 1995). Here, pixel expansion increases apparent randomness and security but often leads to a poorer quality of extracted watermark. Therefore, a compromise between security and resolution should be made for successful implementation of these VC based schemes. Also, certain VC schemes operate by dividing the host image or video into non-overlapping blocks and then by selecting only a few blocks on which the feature extraction techniques are applied (Singh et. al., 2011). When a smaller block size is chosen, the number of blocks obviously increases. Thus, there is more randomness in selecting the blocks which enhances the security of the scheme (Barari & Dhavale, 2013). On the other hand, a larger block size captures the features of the host more effectively as compared to a smaller block size. Therefore, a tradeoff needs to be achieved in between level of security and feature extraction accuracy too. A thorough performance comparison is given in Table 6.

Figure 7a. Overview of the watermarking process by Singh et.al (2011): generation of owner's share

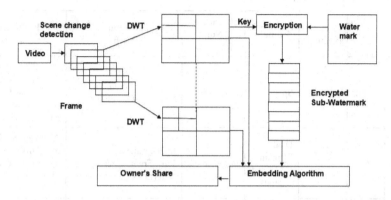

Figure 7b. Overview of the watermarking process by Singh et.al (2011): generation of identification share

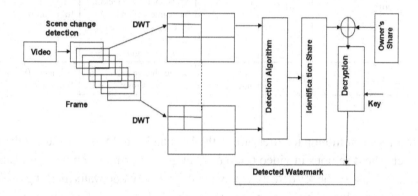

Visual Cryptography has proven to be a simple, robust and non-intrusive video watermarking technique. Utilizing the power of visual secret sharing methods for may offer a very attractive and robust solution for different sectors like defence or military video based communication services, music industries to establish their rightful copyright ownerships, digital video forensic applications etc.

In VC based techniques, identifying the salient features is a primary task, which helps in creation of the Master share M. Thus, saliency detection in videos in case of VC based video watermarking techniques is an important consideration. The following section explains the importance of video saliency detection in video watermarking schemes.

4. IMPORTANCE OF VIDEO SALIENCY DETECTION IN WATERMARKING

Saliency detection is widely used to extract regions of interest (ROIs) in images or in video frames for various image and video processing applications such as segmentation, classification, watermarking etc. The number of image saliency detection models proposed in literature is many during the last decade (Hou & Zhang., 2007; Guo & Zhang, 2010). Compared to image saliency detection, video saliency detection algorithms are much more computationally intensive since they have to account for motion in

Table 6. Performance comparison of various VC based watermarking schemes for videos

S. No.	Proposed Scheme	Year	No. of Shares	Domain	Intrusive /Non-Intrusive	Techniques Used	Performance Mentioned in Related Work
1	Houmansadr and Ghaemmag hami	2006	2	Spatial	intrusive	Temporal Scrambling, Stacking, Correlation	For 50% frame cropping decrement in correlation coefficient 16%; For 8 times frame scaling, decrement in correlation coefficient 39%;
2	Zeng and Pei	2008	4	Dual Domain (DCT and Spatial)	intrusive	Inter-Frame and Intra-Frame Crypto watermark generation	Average PSNR found to be 52.78 dB for original frames and 42.18 dB for watermark; capable of identifying different types of attacks.
3	Vashistha et al.	2010	2	Spatial	non-intrusive	Construction of Verification Information, Scene change detection by segmentation based on colour difference histogram, Scene averaging.	Survives as much as a 50% frame drop
4	Singh et al.	2013	2	DWT	non-intrusive	Scene change detection, scene averaging	NC above 0.95 for all kinds of frame attacks

between video frames since motion features attract the Human Visual System. Currently, several studies have tried to detect salient regions in video (Guo & Zhang, 2010; Shuai, Zhang, Liu, Liu, Feng, 2011).

As mentioned previously saliency detection plays a vital role in video watermarking. Video watermarking schemes use perceptually salient regions to embed the watermark information. According to some schemes suggested in literature (Fang, Lin,Chen, Tsai & Lin, 2013), a watermark must be placed in the perceptually significant components of the host signal for it to be robust to distortions and malicious attacks. Thus, the perceptually most significant components are the salient regions of the host signal and must be explicitly identified and extracted. In contrast to this view, a few other schemes claim that modification of perceptually significant components of the host signal may result in faster perceptual distortions. Thus, the watermark should be placed in the perceptually insignificant portions of the host image or video. Consequently, many watermarking schemes that focus on extracting the perceptually significant features were developed by researchers. Such techniques which aim at extracting regions of perceptual significance in images and videos are known as *Saliency Region Extraction* techniques (Fang et. al., 2013).

Previous schemes are based on uncompressed domain but most of the videos on the internet are available in compressed format. A few techniques have been developed in the recent years which perform video watermarking in the compressed domain. A scheme proposed in (Ding-Yu & Long-Wen, 2006) uses the phase angle of the motion vectors in the inter-frame as the salient features to embed data in a video. A different approach has been suggested in (Aly, 2011) to achieve a lesser distortion to prediction error and lower data size overhead in comparison to (Ding-Yu & Long-Wen, 2006). Here, motion vectors whose associated macroblocks prediction error is high are taken to be candidate motion vectors (CMV). The CMVs which become the salient features are then used to hide a bit of data in their horizontal and vertical components.

Shanableh (2012) later proposed two novel approaches to which gave a higher message extraction accuracy and payload. In the first approach message bits are concealed by modifying the quantization scale of the MPEG video. Feature extraction is performed by for individual macroblocks and a second order regression model is computed to predict the content of the hidden message. Though this procedure has a high level of prediction accuracy the payload is restricted to one bit per macroblock. The second approach proposed in (Shanableh, 2012) benefits from a high message payload with negligible drop in the PSNR levels. This solution uses Flexible Macroblock Ordering (FMO) to direct the encoder to create slice groups (independently coded and decoded units). This approach is compatible with H.264/AVC standards and is independent of the frame type being used (Intra frame Predicted frame or Bidirectional Frame), so it is advantageous from the point of view of implementation.

All of these schemes modify the content of the host video which in turn affects the host video quality. Instead of mentioned traditional watermarking schemes, we can use VC based techniques effectively for copyright protection. In VC based watermarking techniques, creating Master share M using the salient video features adds more robustness towards different kinds of video attacks. Thus, saliency detection in videos becomes an important consideration.

In the following section, we present a novel approach that uses motion vectors in the MPEG domain as salient features for generating master share for VC based video watermarking. Randomly selected motion vectors from the available motion vectors are used to create the Master Share M. M is further used to generate Ownership Share O.

5. PROPOSED VC BASED VIDEO WATERMARKING APPROACH USING MOTION VECTORS AS SALIENT FEATURES

All of the above VC based video watermarking techniques, depict watermarking of uncompressed videos wherein share creation is usually done by using pixel values of the individual frames or by applying some transform operations on the pixel values of frames. These techniques are good for the purpose of authentication, copyright protection or patenting a video. However, they fail to suggest a technique, where the required data can be hidden and retrieved by using the features of the video in compressed domain itself. Extraction of compressed domain features is expected increase the resilience towards compression attacks, thus making it compression invariant. Although the existing schemes show a good amount of robustness against most attacks, it is observed that their resilience against attacks involving the change of compression scale decreases rapidly with increase in the number of attacked frames of the video. To overcome this disadvantage of the above mentioned existing schemes, the salient features of the video in the compressed MPEG domain is targeted in the proposed work.

The novelty of the proposed scheme arises from the fact that it uses the salient MPEG domain motion features derived from the host video for the purpose of share creation. Here, the unique motion features that are extracted from the host video are the motion vectors. The reason for selecting motion vectors as unique features is that they are processed internally during the video encoding/decoding which makes it hard to be detected by image and video steganalysis methods. Also, motion vectors are loss less coded, thus they are not prone to quantization distortions (Shuai et. al. 2011). Hence, more robustness of the watermark against different malicious and non-malicious attacks, and more specifically against compression scale attacks, is ensured. Motion vectors are coded in the compressed stream and allow to reconstruct motion compensated macroblocks. Their extraction is very simple and fast and does not require a full decompression of the video stream which makes the algorithm computationally efficient (Shuai et. al. 2011). Further computational economy comes from having only one motion vector for each (16 x 16) macroblock.

In the following sections, the different modules of the proposed MVP Algorithm have been explained. The MPEG encoder flowchart is presented in the Figure 8. The MPEG encoder converts the video in raw Y4M/YUV format to compressed MPEG format.

5.1 Motion Feature Extraction

The proposed schemes use two distinct features of the motion vectors:

1. Length or magnitude, and
2. Phase of the motion vectors as its salient features.

The magnitude of a motion vector MV_i is computed as follows:

$$MV_i = \sqrt{MV_{iH}^2 + MV_{iV}^2} \tag{1}$$

where MV_{iH} is the horizontal component and MV_{iV} is the vertical component of the ith motion vector of a P frame. A large magnitude of a motion vectors indicates a fast moving object the modification of a motion vector with large magnitude is less perceivable than that of a smaller magnitude motion vector (Shuai et. al. 2011). The phase of a motion vector ϑ_i is computed as follows:

Figure 8. MPEG encoder

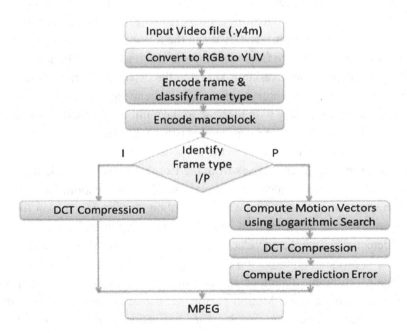

$$\theta_i = \arctan\left(\frac{MV_{iV}}{MV_{iH}}\right) \tag{2}$$

Figure 9 gives a diagrammatic representation of the phase of a motion vector MV_i.

Since phase angle of a motion vector gives us an impression of the change in the position of blocks from one frame to the next, a less phase angle changed motion vector indicates that the shapes of the objects in the next frame are same as the previous frame. The motion vectors are computed in the MPEG encoder during the motion estimation stage. They are retrieved through computer programming before the share creation phase. Following this, the magnitude and phase parameters of the selected motion vectors are computed for share creation.

5.2 Share Creation Module

As discussed in the previous section, motion vector information such as phase and magnitude is extracted from the MPEG encoded video. The phase or magnitude information of the randomly selected motion vectors is converted to a binary matrix B as per the rules which will be discussed in this section. The binary matrix B and the binary watermark image W are now compared on a pixel to pixel basis. B and W are the inputs to the Share Creation Module which creates the Master Share (M) according to the following rules:

If B_i is a white pixel, then $M_i = \begin{bmatrix} 1 & 0 \\ 0 & 1 \end{bmatrix}$

If B_i is a black pixel, then $M_i = \begin{bmatrix} 0 & 1 \\ 1 & 0 \end{bmatrix}$

Figure 9. Representation of phase of a motion vector

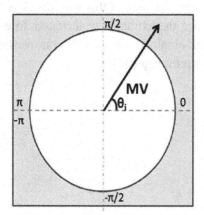

The M generated is of the size *(2m x 2n)* . After generating the M, we generate an Owner Share (O) by combining the M and the pixels of W. The construction of the O is as follows:

$$\text{If } W_i = 1 \text{ and } M_i = \begin{bmatrix} 1 & 0 \\ 0 & 1 \end{bmatrix} \text{then } O = \begin{bmatrix} 1 & 0 \\ 0 & 1 \end{bmatrix}$$

$$\text{If } W_i = 1 \text{ and } M_i = \begin{bmatrix} 0 & 1 \\ 1 & 0 \end{bmatrix} \text{then } O = \begin{bmatrix} 0 & 1 \\ 1 & 0 \end{bmatrix}$$

$$\text{If } W_i = 0 \text{ and } M_i = \begin{bmatrix} 1 & 0 \\ 0 & 1 \end{bmatrix} \text{then } O = \begin{bmatrix} 0 & 1 \\ 1 & 0 \end{bmatrix}$$

$$\text{If } W_i = 0 \text{ and } M_i = \begin{bmatrix} 0 & 1 \\ 1 & 0 \end{bmatrix} \text{then } O = \begin{bmatrix} 1 & 0 \\ 0 & 1 \end{bmatrix}$$

The O again is of the size *(2m x 2n)*. O should be registered with a higher authority for further authentication.

During creation of the share, the proposed scheme assumes that the binary watermark image W represents the ownership information like company logo image etc. In order to extend the usability of proposed algorithm for fingerprinting applications i.e. buyer specific watermarking, a secret unique key K_s can be maintained for recognizing each buyer. During share creation module, K_s will decide the selection of the motion vectors or/and will permute the binary watermark image W before creating share. In this case, the created Owner Share O can able to identify the compromised buyer among the set of legitimate buyers.

5.3 Watermark Extraction Module

At the receiving end, the watermark may be revealed by stacking M generated at the receiver end and the O retrieved from the *CA*. However, the size of this watermark is *(2m x 2n)* since both M and O are of this size. Thus, we need to reduce the extracted watermarks to get the original watermark. This is achieved by dividing the watermark obtained into *(2 x 2)* non-overlapping blocks. Let us denote these blocks by w'. Then, the reduced secret image W'' is

$$W''_{ij} = \left\{ 0 \, for \sum_i \sum_j w'_{i,j} < 2 \right\}$$

$$W''_{ij} = \left\{ 1 \, for \sum_i \sum_j w'_{i,j} \geq 2 \right\} \tag{3}$$

5.4 Proposed MVP Algorithm

In the proposed algorithm, initially Motion Vector Magnitude is used as the salient features of the MPEG domain. However, this algorithm was not able to sustain different types of attacks since a small variation in the magnitude of the selected motion vectors was enough to change the mean value of motion vectors. Consequently, there was a drop in the value of Normalized Correlation (*NC*). To overcome this drawback, Motion Vector Phase was used as a salient feature from the MPEG domain. Motion Vector Phase was able to overcome small perturbations in the value of motion features due to attacks. This made it much more robust to different kinds of attacks. However, on careful observation it was found that the outline of the watermark image was visible in the generated Owner Share. This was because while creating the shares, the phase values of motion vectors are used directly without any preprocessing and compared with the pixels of the watermark image on a one to one basis. This is dangerous in a situation where the malicious user has even the slightest hint or information about the watermark image. Thus, there was a need to devise an algorithm where the watermark information would be completely inconspicuous.

The proposed *MVP algorithm* stands for the Motion Vector Phase based VC video watermarking scheme. The salient features from the MPEG domain are motion vector phase features. MVP attempts to improve on the shortcomings of both the previous approaches by preprocessing the motion feature matrix instead of using the feature values directly. Here, the motion feature matrix is obtained by randomly selecting $(4 \times (m \times n))$ number of motion vectors. The motion feature matrix is then split into blocks of size (4×1) each. The blocks are transformed to the DFT domain. Following this, SVD is used on each of the blocks so that a single value is obtained for each of the four motion vector phase values in the motion feature matrix. This single value represents features of each of the 4 values of the block. While DFT prevents us from using the motion vector phase information directly, SVD gives us a single value for one to one comparison in the Share Creation Module. MVP has been explained in details in this section.

Preprocessing Stage:
1. The uncompressed video in YUV/Y4M video is converted to a compressed format as per MPEG coding standards.

Share creation stage:
1. Extract motion vectors from all P-Frames of the compressed host video h.
2. Select $(4 \times (m \times n))$ motion vectors, using a pseudo-random number generator. The randomly selected motion vector positions are now appended to form the secret key K, which has to be transmitted to the authenticated personnel at the receiver end, through a secured channel.
3. Enter the randomly selected motion vector phase values in a $(4 \times (m \times n))$ matrix called *MVP*hase.
4. Split *MVP*hase into blocks of (4×1) size. Perform DFT followed by SVD on each block. Store the first singular value obtained from each block in *SVD* First Valmatrix.
5. Calculate the binary matrix B from the matrix *SVD*FirstValmatrix as

$B_{ij} = 0$ if *SVD*FirstValmatrix< 180

$B_{ij} = 1$ otherwise

Here 180 is used to decide the pixel of B_{ij}, since on inspection it is found that the entire range of transformed values is between 0 and 360.

6.   Generate the *M* and the *O* according to the rules given in the Share Creation Module.
7.   The *O* is registered with a higher Certified Authority (*CA*) for retrieval in case of any dispute regarding the ownership.

The Share Creation Process of MVP has been shown in Figure 10.

Watermark Extraction Stage:

At the receivers end, *HV´* is the video received which may have been subjected to various malicious and non-malicious attacks. To establish rightful ownership, the watermark *W* needs to be extracted. The steps for watermark extraction are given as follows:

1.   Retrieve Key *K* from secure channel.
2.   Using *K*, identify the locations of the selected (4×(*m*×*n*)) number of motion vectors from *HV* and retrieve the magnitude of the corresponding locations from *HV´*.
3.   Store the selected motion vector phase values in an (4×(*m*×*n*)) matrix called *MV*AttPhase.
4.   Split *MV*AttPhase into blocks of (4 x 1) size. Perform DFT followed by SVD on each block. Store the first singular value obtained from each block in *SVD*FirstValAttMatrix.

Figure 10. Share creation process of the proposed approach

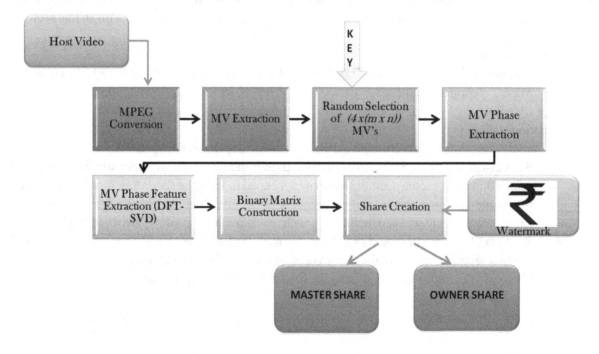

5. Calculate the binary matrix B from the matrix SVDFirstValAttMatrix as

$B_{ij} = 0$ if SVDFirstValAttMatrix < 180

$B_{ij} = 1$ otherwise

6. Again, the M' and the O' are created from B_{ij} and W_{ij} according to the rules explained in the Share Creation Module.
7. The O is retrieved from the CA and O and M' are stacked together to reveal the watermark W' by the process explained in Watermark Extraction Module. The size of W' is *(2m x 2n)*.
8. The secret image is reduced to *(m x n)* to get the retrieved watermark image.

The Watermark Extraction process in MVP has been shown in Figure 11.

The proposed MVP algorithm uses motion vector phase as its salient feature from the MPEG domain. MVP uses 4 times more the number of features from the host video. Following this, the use of DFT to convert each (4 x 1) block to the transform domain and the application of SVD to extract the robust feature from each block has ensured that imperceptibility of the watermark in the shares is preserved. Besides, the MVP algorithm also achieves a high value of NC for various kinds of attacks for the extracted watermark. The next chapter on experimental results and analysis validates all the proposed schemes against attacks.

This experiments carried by simulating the proposed algorithm in the MATLAB 2012 Platform. MPEG- 2 standards have been encoded and the code for MPEG-2 encoder (Steve Hoelzer) has been customized for implementing the VC based video watermarking schemes. Here, a source movie can be

Figure 11. Watermark extraction stage of the proposed approach

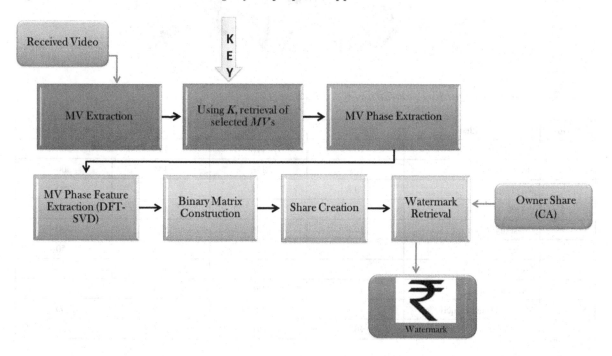

encoded into MPEG format and then can be decoded back into a MATLAB movie. A standard test video database consisting of movie sequences of the YUV and Y4M formats were selected for our analysis. The following video sequences which were used in the experiments as shown in Figure 12 are *Akiyo, Bowing, Carphone, Container, Coastguard, Flower, Foreman, Hall_Monitor, Mother_daughter* and *Silent*. The information regarding the format, height, width, size and number of frames has been tabulated in Table 7. Each of these videos is played at a frame rate of 30 frames per second (fps).

In our simulations, these raw uncompressed videos are encoded using a GOP of 10 frames length with a frame pattern of *"IPPPPPPPP"*. The scaling factor used in MPEG compression module is set to the fixed value of 31 and has been varied only while performing compression scaling attacks on the proposed schemes.

In these videos, the frame resolution is either (176 x 144) pixels or (352 x 288) pixels. Each frame is divided into macroblocks of the size (16 x16). The one to one correspondence in between the number of macroblocks and motion vectors has already been observed. Hence, the number of macroblocks and correspondingly the number of motion vectors is obtained by dividing the resolution with the macroblock size. For instance, in a video frame with frame resolution of (176 x 144), a set of 99 motion vectors per frame are extracted. The motion vectors which have been encoded from random frames of the test video sequence *carphone* have been plotted as shown in Figure 13.

Figure 12. Standard video database

Table 7. Information regarding standard video database

S. No.	Video	Size (MB)	Width	Height	No. of Frames
1	Akiyo_qcif	10.8	176	144	300
2	Bowing_qcif	10.8	176	144	300
3	Carphone	13.8	176	144	382
4	Container_qcif	10.8	176	144	300
5	Coastguard_qcif	10.8	176	144	300
6	Flower_cif	36.2	352	288	250
7	Foreman_qcif	7.25	176	144	300
8	Hall_monitor_qcif	10.8	176	144	300
9	Mother_Daughter_qcif	10.8	176	144	300
10	Silent_qcif	10.8	176	144	300

Figure 13a. Motion vectors from random frames of carphone: Frame 2

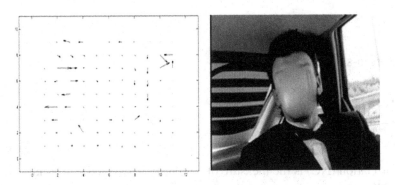

Figure 13b. Motion vectors from random frames of carphone: Frame 9

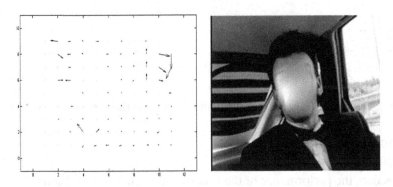

According to the proposed schemes, the salient features from the test video sequences are extracted, randomly selected, stored in a matrix and then compared on a pixel to pixel basis with the binary watermark image. This forms the basis for share creation. At the receiving end, M' and O are overlaid upon each other to reveal the watermark. The retrieved watermark is then evaluated on the basis of standard parameters which are discussed in the next subsection.

5.5 Watermark Evaluation Parameters

A watermarking scheme is evaluated on the basis of criteria like perceptibility, reliability, robustness, capacity, speed of implementation and statistical detectability. MSE (Mean Square Error), PSNR (Peak Signal to Noise Ratio) and NC (Normalized Correlation) are some of the popular metrics which are used for evaluating a watermark scheme (Petitcolas, F.A.P, 2000). While implementing the proposed algorithms, the algorithm was validated for robustness to various attacks based on these metrics.

Peak signal to noise ratio (PSNR) is used in this paper to analyze the visual quality of the extracted watermark W in comparison to the original watermark W. PSNR gives us a measure of the degree of distortion to the watermark and given as in Equation (4).

$$PSNR = 10 \log_{10} \left(\frac{255^2}{MSE} \right) db \tag{4}$$

where MSE is the mean-square error given as

$$MSE = \frac{1}{MN} \sum_{i=0}^{M-1} \sum_{j=0}^{N-1} \left[W_{i,j} - \hat{W}_{i,j} \right]^2 \tag{5}$$

Normalized Correlation (NC) is the measure of similarity between the original and extracted watermarks. The closer NC value is to 1, more is the similarity between W and W. The expression for NC is given in Equation (3).

$$NC = \frac{\sum_{i=0}^{m} \sum_{j=0}^{n} \overline{W_{i,j} \oplus \hat{W}_{i,j}}}{(m \times n)} \tag{6}$$

where denotes the exclusive-or (XOR) operation and *(m × n)* is the size of the watermark.

5.6 Performance against Attacks

In the following section, the performance of the watermark against various kinds of attacks is evaluated against these watermark evaluation parameters. MVP Algorithm is tested for robustness against various different types of attacks. NC, PSNR and MSE values are calculated to obtain a comprehensive quantitative analysis. The generated shares and retrieved watermarks for Frame drop attack and Gaussian noise attack have been shown.

5.6.1 Frame Drop Attack

An attacker can attempt to distort the video and yet conserve its visual quality by dropping a few frames. A large percentage of frame drops may create unnecessary suspicion for the attacker. Here in in Figure 14, the quality of the extracted watermark has been shown for a frame drop attack where 10 frames are dropped from a 300 frame video sequence. Figures 14 (a) and 14 (b), shows the generated Master shares and Owner shares while 14 (c) shows the extracted watermark retrieved by overlaying the two shares. The corresponding NC, MSE and PSNR values have also been shared.

5.6.2 Gaussian Noise Attack

To validate the proposed algorithms against Gaussian noise attack, frames of the video were subjected to Gaussian noise at zero mean and different local variances ranging from 0.01 to 0.1. The results for a Gaussian noise attack of 10 frames out of a 300 frame video being subjected to a Gaussian noise with a noise variance of 0.01, have been shown in Figure 15. Figures 15 (a) and 15 (b), shows the generated

Figure 14a. Master share
NC = 0.9404; MSE = 0.0596; PSNR = 54 db

Figure 14b. Owner share
NC = 0.9404; MSE = 0.0596; PSNR = 54 db

Figure 14c. Extracted watermark for frame drop attack for MVP
NC = 0.9404; MSE = 0.0596; PSNR = 54 db

Master shares and Owner shares while 15 (c) shows the extracted watermark obtained after overlaying the two shares. Also, the corresponding NC, MSE and PSNR values have also been shared.

A graphical representation of the performance MVP against 15 different types of attacks has been shown.

Here, the NC values for different attacks is plotted against the number of frames being subjected to that attack. It is observed that MVP sustains as much as 20% of frame attack without causing any severe distortion to the watermark. A high value of Normalized Correlation (NC) of the extracted watermark for attacks, particularly for frame drop, scaling, averaging and sharpening attacks, proves that MVP has a good amount of robustness against these attacks. See Figure 16 (a)-(p).

Figure 15a. Master share
NC = 0.9504; MSE = 0.0496; PSNR = 53 db

Figure 15b. Owner share
NC = 0.9504; MSE = 0.0496; PSNR = 53 db

Figure 15c. Extracted Watermark for Gaussian noise attack for MVP
NC = 0.9504; MSE = 0.0496; PSNR = 53 db

Table 8 tabulates the average values of NC and PSNR for all attacks when performed using the Standard Binary Test Image Database with images of size (64 x 64 size) shown in Figure 17. An important observation here is the MPEG Compression scale change attack which has been performed by varying the compression scale of the MPEG video from 1 to 112. It is observed that in spite of varying the compression through the entire range, there is no severe degradation in the quality of the extracted watermark. Thus, we may say that Compression Scale Invariance is achieved in the proposed algorithm.

Figure 16a.

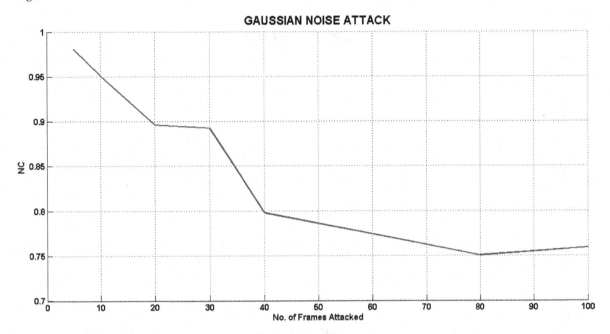

Figure 16b. Graphical analysis of performance of MVP algorithm against following attacks: frame drop

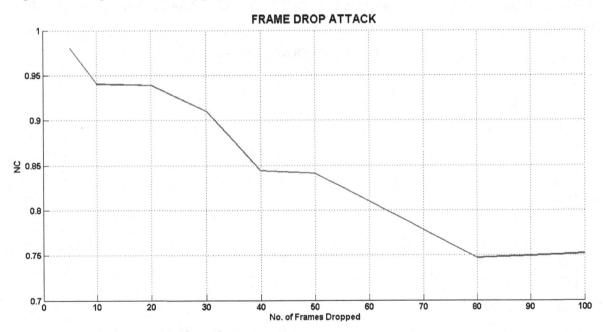

Figure 16c. Graphical analysis of performance of MVP algorithm against following attacks: averaging attack

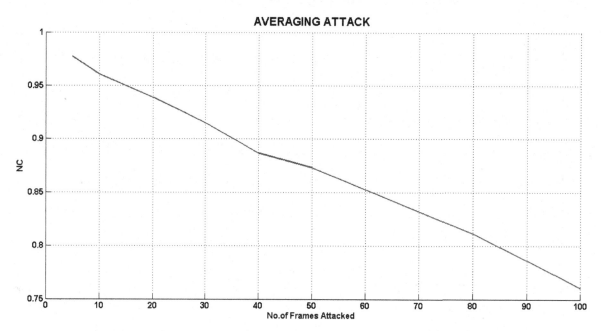

Figure 16d. Graphical analysis of performance of MVP algorithm against following attacks: salt & pepper noise

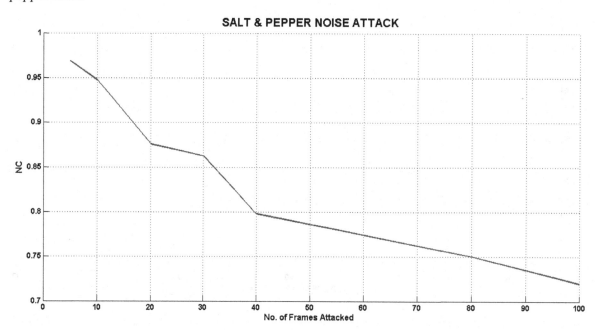

Figure 16e. Graphical analysis of performance of MVP algorithm against following attacks: Gaussian noise

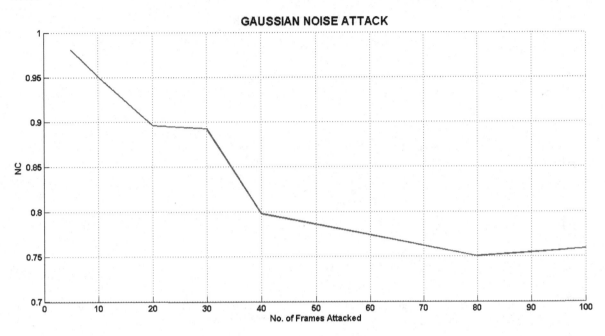

Figure 16f. Graphical analysis of performance of MVP algorithm against following attacks: motion blur

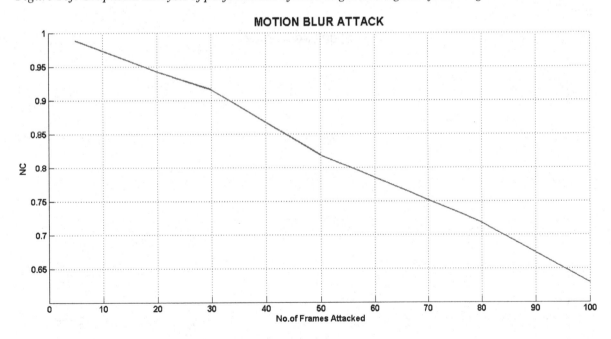

Figure 16g. Graphical analysis of performance of MVP algorithm against following attacks: sharpening attack

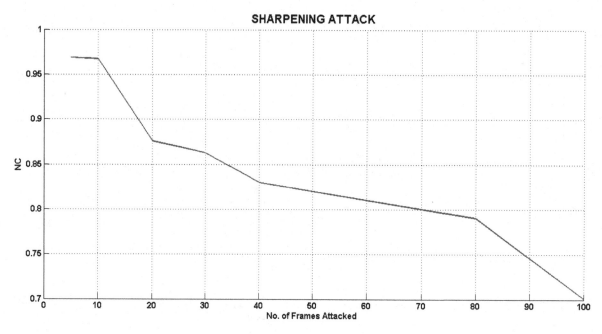

Figure 16h. Graphical analysis of performance of MVP algorithm against following attacks: blurring attack

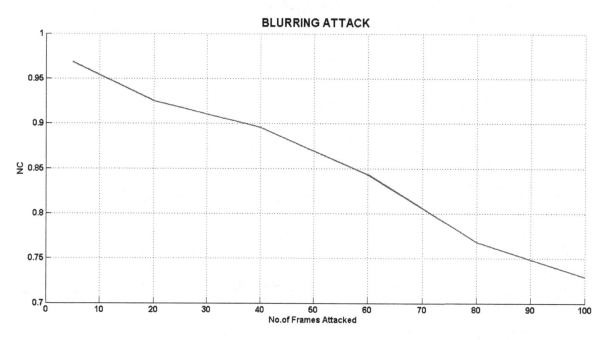

Figure 16i. Graphical analysis of performance of MVP algorithm against following attacks: histogram equalization

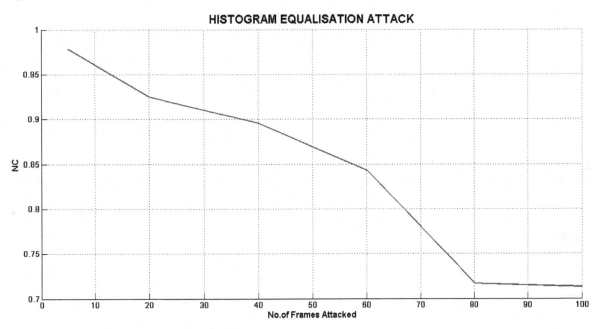

Figure 16j. Graphical analysis of performance of MVP algorithm against following attacks: cropping

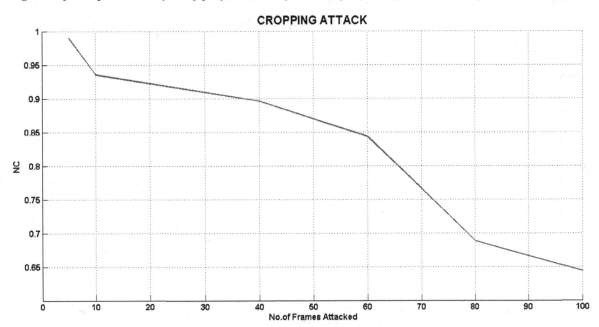

Figure 16k. Graphical analysis of performance of MVP algorithm against following attacks: image negative attack

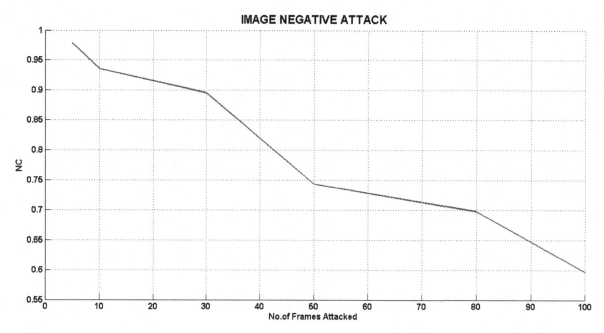

Figure 16l. Graphical analysis of performance of MVP algorithm against following attacks: rotation attack

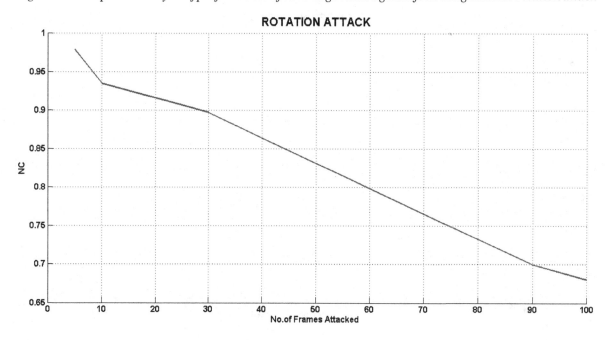

Figure 16m. Graphical analysis of performance of MVP algorithm against following attacks: scaling attack

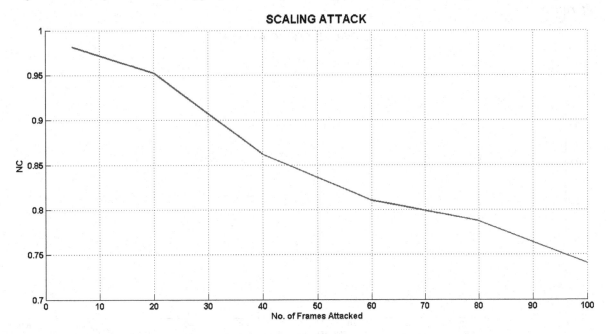

Figure 16n. Graphical analysis of performance of MVP algorithm against following attacks: gamma correction attack

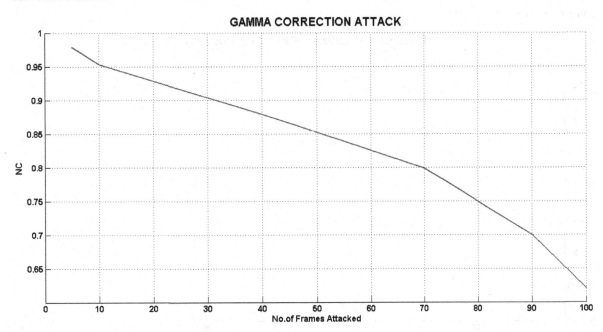

Figure 16o. Graphical analysis of performance of MVP algorithm against following attacks: median filtering attack

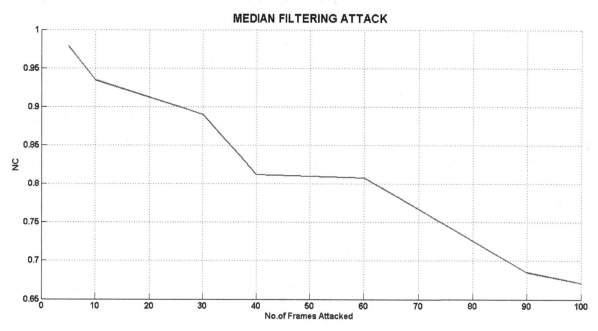

Figure 16p. Graphical analysis of performance of MVP algorithm against following attacks: MPEG compression scale change

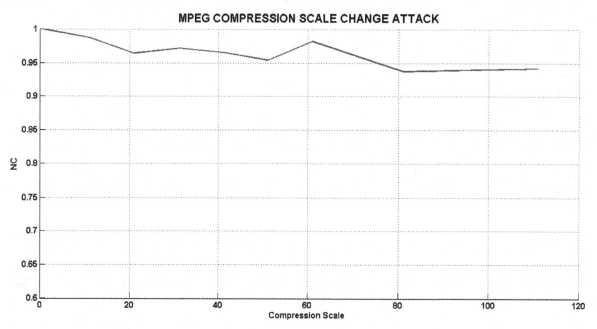

Table 8. Average NC and PSNR values for watermark retrieved using algorithm MVP

Attacks	MVP	
	NC	PSNR (dB)
Frame Drop	0.9379	54.17
Averaging Attack	0.9645	48.73
Salt & Pepper Noise	0.9457	53.78
Gaussian Noise	0.9553	53.05
Motion Blur	0.9420	54.87
Sharpening Attack	0.9645	49.73
Blurring	0.9278	57.63
Histogram Equalization	0.9271	57.78
Cropping	0.9369	56.01
Image Negative Attack	0.9271	56.08
Rotation Attack	0.9308	56.84
Scaling Attack	0.9817	43.08
Gamma Correction Attack	0.9364	55.67
Median Filtering Attack	0.9604	47.80
Compression Scale Change Attack	0.9845	41.73

Figure 17. Standard binary test image database (all of 64 x 64 size)

5.7 Performance Analysis

A payload of 1 bits per macro block is achieved in MVP Algorithm. The validation of the proposed scheme has been carried out by conducting 15 different types of attacks on the host video. It is found that the retrieved watermark is visually recognizable after all attacks which prove the robustness of the algorithm. Also, it is observed that change of quality scale of the MPEG from 1 to 112 by the attacker does not render the watermark unidentifiable as seen in Figure 16(p). Thus, compression scale invariance is also achieved. Since the feature extraction module is based on general MPEG coding, the proposed algorithms can be integrated in the MPEG Encoder for real time applications. Furthermore, the retrieval of the hidden data by an unauthorized person or malicious attacker is extremely difficult because the Ownership Share is registered with a CA. The proposed also method provides a good tradeoff between ease of implementation and security.

6. FUTURE RESEARCH DIRECTIONS

In all VC based video watermarking schemes, each host video corresponds to a secret image that is registered to a certified authority (CA). When the number of cover videos is large, it will be a heavy burden for the CA to store all the secret images. Hence in future a solution to this problem needs to be addressed.

Also a robust salient features need to be extracted from the video data in order to create the master share and hence to increase the robustness of the algorithm further. From simulation results of MVP Algorithm, it has been observed that as more number of salient features i.e. motion vectors are selected from the available motion vector set, there is a decrease in the robustness of the extracted watermark. This is because with increase in selected motion vectors, the randomness of watermark embedding decreases. Research may be carried out in future to increase the robustness of the proposed algorithms for a higher percentage of frame attacks.

7. CONCLUSION

In this chapter, importance of visual cryptography technique in non-intrusive video watermarking is evaluated. The chapter also states the pros and cons of the existing research works for non-intrusive video watermarking. Further the importance of saliency detection in general video watermarking and creation of master share in VC based watermarking has been discussed. Finally, a novel robust visual cryptography based video watermarking approach (MVP Algorithm) has been proposed which uses motion vector phase features of the video from the MPEG domain as salient features for creation of master share. Experimental results shows that the proposed MVP Algorithm provides a good trade off among different parameters like robustness, embedding payload capacity, ease of implementation and security.

REFERENCES

Aly, H. (2011). Data Hiding in Motion Vectors of Compressed Video Based on Their Associated Prediction Error. *IEEE Transactions on Information Forensics and Security*, 14-18.

Barari, A., & Dhavale, S. (2013). An Overview of Visual Cryptography based Video Watermarking Schemes: Techniques and Performance Comparison. In *Proceedings of International Conference on Advances in Computer Science, Association of Computer Electronics and Electrical Engineers*.

Bianchi, T., & Piva, A. (2013). Secure watermarking for multimedia content protection: A review of its benefits and open issues. *Signal Processing Magazine, IEEE, 30*(2), 87–96. doi:10.1109/MSP.2012.2228342

Chen, S., & Leung, H. (2008). Chaotic watermarking for video authentication in surveillance applications. *Circuits and Systems for Video Technology. IEEE Transactions on, 18*(5), 704–709.

Fang, D. Y., & Chang, L. W. (2006, May). Data hiding for digital video with phase of motion vector. In *Circuits and Systems, 2006. ISCAS 2006. Proceedings. 2006 IEEE International Symposium on*. IEEE.

Fang, Y., Lin, W., Chen, Z., Tsai, C. M., & Lin, C. W. (2014). A video saliency detection model in compressed domain. *Circuits and Systems for Video Technology. IEEE Transactions on, 24*(1), 27–38.

Guo, C., & Zhang, L. (2010). A novel multiresolution spatiotemporal saliency detection model and its applications in image and video compression. *Image Processing. IEEE Transactions on, 19*(1), 185–198.

Hartung, F., & Kutter, M. (1999). Multimedia watermarking techniques. *Proceedings of the IEEE, 87*(7), 1079–1107. doi:10.1109/5.771066

Hou, X., & Zhang, L. (2007, June). Saliency detection: A spectral residual approach. In *Computer Vision and Pattern Recognition, 2007. CVPR'07. IEEE Conference on* (pp. 1-8). IEEE. 10.1109/CVPR.2007.383267

Houmansadr, A., & Ghaemmaghami, S. (2006, April). A novel video watermarking method using visual cryptography. In *Engineering of Intelligent Systems, 2006 IEEE International Conference on* (pp. 1-5). IEEE. 10.1109/ICEIS.2006.1703171

Liu, F., & Wu, C. K. (2011). Robust visual cryptography-based watermarking scheme for multiple cover images and multiple owners. *IET Information Security, 5*(2), 121-128.

Lou, D. C., Tso, H. K., & Liu, J. L. (2007). A copyright protection scheme for digital images using visual cryptography technique. *Computer Standards & Interfaces, 29*(1), 125–131. doi:10.1016/j.csi.2006.02.003

Naor, M., & Shamir, A. (1995). Visual cryptography. In Advances in Cryptology—EUROCRYPT'94 (pp. 1-12). Springer Berlin/Heidelberg. doi:10.1007/BFb0053419

Petitcolas, F. A. (2000). Watermarking schemes evaluation. *Signal Processing Magazine, IEEE, 17*(5), 58–64. doi:10.1109/79.879339

Rawat, S., & Raman, B. (2012). A blind watermarking algorithm based on fractional Fourier transform and visual cryptography. *Signal Processing, 92*(6), 1480–1491. doi:10.1016/j.sigpro.2011.12.006

Shanableh, T. (2012). Data hiding in MPEG video files using multivariate regression and flexible macroblock ordering. *Information Forensics and Security. IEEE Transactions on, 7*(2), 455–464.

Shuai, B., Zhang, Q., Liu, J., Liu, X., & Feng, X. (2011, October). Saliency region extraction for MPEG video method based on visual selective attention. In *Image and Signal Processing (CISP), 2011 4th International Congress on* (Vol. 1, pp. 560-564). IEEE. 10.1109/CISP.2011.6099990

Singh, T. R., Singh, K. M., & Roy, S. (2013). Video watermarking scheme based on visual cryptography and scene change detection. *AEÜ. International Journal of Electronics and Communications, 67*(8), 645–651. doi:10.1016/j.aeue.2013.01.008

Sun, J., & Liu, J. (2005, September). A temporal desynchronization resilient video watermarking scheme based on independent component analysis. In *Image Processing, 2005. ICIP 2005. IEEE International Conference on* (Vol. 1, pp. I-265). IEEE.

University of Illinois at Chicago (UIC). (n.d.). Retrieved from http://www.cs.cf.ac.uk/Dave/Multimedia/Lecture_Examples/Compression/ mpegproj/

Vashistha, A., Nallusamy, R., Das, A., & Paul, S. (2010, July). Watermarking video content using visual cryptography and scene averaged image. In *Multimedia and Expo (ICME), 2010 IEEE International Conference on* (pp. 1641-1646). IEEE. 10.1109/ICME.2010.5583256

Wang, M. S., & Chen, W. C. (2009). A hybrid DWT-SVD copyright protection scheme based on k-means clustering and visual cryptography. *Computer Standards & Interfaces*, *31*(4), 757–762. doi:10.1016/j. csi.2008.09.003

Xu, C., Ping, X., & Zhang, T. (2006, August). Steganography in compressed video stream. In *Innovative Computing, Information and Control, 2006. ICICIC'06. First International Conference on* (Vol. 1, pp. 269-272). IEEE.

Zeng, Y. C., & Pei, S. C. (2008, May). Automatic video diagnosing method using embedded crypto-watermarks. In *Circuits and Systems, 2008. ISCAS 2008. IEEE International Symposium on* (pp. 3017-3020). IEEE.

ADDITIONAL READING

Al-Qaheri, H., Mustafi, A., & Banerjee, S. (2010). Digital Watermarking using Ant Colony Optimization in Fractional Fourier Domain. *Journal of Information Hiding and Multimedia Signal Processing*, *1*(3).

Ardizzone, E., La Cascia, M., Avanzato, A., & Bruna, A. (1999, July). Video Indexing Using MPEG Motion Compensation Vectors, *IEEE International Conference on Multimedia Computing and Systems*, 2,(725–729) 10.1109/MMCS.1999.778574

Ateniese, G., Blundo, C., De Santis, A., & Stinson, D. R. (1996). Visual cryptography for general access structures. *Information and Computation*, *129*(2), 86–106. doi:10.1006/inco.1996.0076

Bo, W., Ming, X., & Zhang, C.-C. (2011). Realization of Digital Image Watermarking Encryption Algorithm Using Fractional Fourier Transform, *The 6th International Forum on Strategic Technology*.

Chang, C. C., & Chuang, J. C. (2002). An image intellectual property protection scheme for gray-level images using visual secret sharing strategy. *Pattern Recognition Letters*, *23*(8), 931–941. doi:10.1016/S0167-8655(02)00023-5

Choudhary,S., Yadav, S., Sen,N., & Nasreen, G. (2012). A Study of Image Fingerprinting by Using Visual Cryptography, Computer Engineering and Intelligent Systems, 3(7).

Fang, W. P., & Lin, J. C. (2006). Progressive viewing and sharing of sensitive images. *Pattern Recognition and Image Analysis*, *16*(4), 638–642. doi:10.1134/S1054661806040080

Faragallah, O. S. (2013). Efficient video watermarking based on singular value decomposition in the discrete wavelet transform domain. *International Journal of Electronics.And Communication.*, *67*(3), 189–196. doi:10.1016/j.aeue.2012.07.010

Ghouti, L., Bouridane, A., Ibrahim, M. K., & Boussakta, S. (2006). Digital Image Watermarking Using Balanced Multiwavelets. *IEEE Transactions on Signal Processing*, *54*(4), 1519–1536. doi:10.1109/TSP.2006.870624

Gonzalez, R., & Woods, R. (2002). *Digital image processing* (2nd ed.). Upper Saddle River, N.J.: Prentice Hall.

Hadizadeh, H., & Baji'c, I. V. (2014, January). Saliency-Aware Video Compression. *IEEE Transactions on Image Processing, 23*(1), 19–33. doi:10.1109/TIP.2013.2282897 PMID:24107933

Hou, Y.-C., & Quan, Z.-Y. (2011, November). Progressive Visual Cryptography with Unexpanded Shares. *IEEE Transactions on Circuits and Systems for Video Technology, 21*(11), 1760–1764. doi:10.1109/TCSVT.2011.2106291

Hwang, R.-J. (2000). A Digital Image Copyright Protection Scheme Based on Visual Cryptography. *Tamkang Journal of Science and Engineering, 3*(2), 97–106.

Jianga, M., Maa, Z., Niua, X., & Yanga, Y. (2011). Video Watermarking Scheme Based on MPEG-2 for Copyright Protection, *3rd International Conference on Environmental Science and Information Application Technology (ESIAT 2011).* 10.1016/j.proenv.2011.09.136

Lee, K.-H. & Chiu,P.L.(2012). An Extended Visual Cryptography Algorithm for General Access Structures, *IEEE Transactions On Information Forensics And Security, 7*(1).

Lin, C.-C., & Tsai, W.-H. (2003). Visual cryptography for gray-level images by dithering techniques. *Pattern Recognition Letters, 24*(1-3), 349–358. doi:10.1016/S0167-8655(02)00259-3

Lin, E.-T., Eskicioglu, A. H., Reginald, L. L., & Edward, J. D. (2005, January). Advances in Digital Video Content Protection. *Proceedings of the IEEE, 93*(1), 171–183. doi:10.1109/JPROC.2004.839623

Lin, S.-F, & Chung,W.-H.(2012). A Probabilistic Model of *(t,n)* Visual Cryptography Scheme With Dynamic Group, *IEEE Transactions On Information Forensics And Security, 7*(1).

Ling, H., Wang, L., Zou, F., Lu, Z., & Li, P. (2011). Robust video watermarking based on affine invariant regions in the compressed domain. *Signal Processing, 91*(8), 1863–1875. doi:10.1016/j.sigpro.2011.02.009

Mehta, S., Vijayaraghavan, V., & Nallusamy, R. (2012). On-the-fly Watermarking of Videos for Real-time Applications, *IEEE International Conference on Multimedia and Expo Workshops.* 10.1109/ICMEW.2012.17

Oakes, M., & Abhayaratne, C. (2012, May). Visual saliency estimation for video. In Image Analysis for Multimedia Interactive Services (WIAMIS), 2012 13th International Workshop on (pp. 1-4). IEEE. 10.1109/WIAMIS.2012.6226751

Patel, S., & Yadav, A. R. (2011). Invisible Digital Video Watermarking Using 4-level DWT, *National Conference on Recent Trends in Engineering & Technology.*

Paul, R.T. (2011). Review of Robust Video Watermarking Techniques, *International Journal of Computer Applications Special Issue on "Computational Science - New Dimensions & Perspectives"..*

Sejdic, E., Djurovic, I., & Stankovic, L. (2011). Fractional Fourier transform as a signal processing tool:An overview of recent developments. *Signal Processing, 91*(6), 1351–1369. doi:10.1016/j.sigpro.2010.10.008

Shamir, A. (1979, November). How To Share A Secret. *Communications of the Association for Computer Machinery, 22*(11), 612–613. doi:10.1145/359168.359176

Wang, C.-C., & Lin, Y.-C. (2010). An automated system for monitoring the visual quality and authenticity of satellite video streams using a fragile watermarking approach. *Digital Signal Processing, 20*(3), 780–792. doi:10.1016/j.dsp.2009.10.005

Wang, L., Ling, H., Zou, F., & Lu, Z. (2012). Real-Time Compressed- Domain Video Watermarking Resistance to Geometric Distortions, *Multimedia in Forensics, Security, and Intelligence.* 70-79.

Yang, C.-N., Shih, H.-W., Wu, C.-C., & Harn, L. (2012). k Out of n Region Incrementing Scheme in Visual Cryptography. *IEEE Transactions on Circuits and Systems for Video Technology, 22*(5), 799–810. doi:10.1109/TCSVT.2011.2180952

Zheng, L., Shi, D., & Zhang, J. (2013). *CAF–FrFT: A center-affine-filter with fractional Fourier transform to reduce the cross-terms of Wigner distribution.* Signal Processing Elsevier Journals.

KEY TERMS AND DEFINITIONS

Compression Scale Change Invariance: The phenomenon where there is no degradation in the quality of the extracted watermark even after the MPEG Compression Scale is varied over the entire permissible range.

Digital Watermarking: The method of embedding data into digital multimedia content. This is used to verify the credibility of the content or to recognize the identity of the digital content's owner.

Motion Feature Extraction: The process of extraction of salient motion features from a video. These motion features may be motion vector magnitude features or motion vector phase features.

Normalized Correlation: The similarity between the extracted watermark and the original watermark.

Saliency Detection: The process of identifying visually or perceptually significant or salient regions in an image or video.

Visual Cryptography: A cryptographic technique which allows visual information (pictures, text, etc.) to be encrypted in such a way that decryption becomes a mechanical operation which does not require complex calculations. Decryption can be done visually.

This research was previously published in Innovative Research in Attention Modeling and Computer Vision Applications edited by Rajarshi Pal; pages 132-170, copyright year 2016 by Information Science Reference (an imprint of IGI Global).

Chapter 31
On the Pixel Expansion of Visual Cryptography Scheme

Teng Guo
University of International Relations, China

Jian Jiao
University of International Relations, China

Feng Liu
Chinese Academy of Sciences, China

Wen Wang
Chinese Academy of Sciences, China

ABSTRACT

In this paper, we first follow Ateniese et al.'s work that provides upper bounds of the pixel expansion of visual cryptography schemes(VCSs) for more kinds of graph access structures, in which we require that a subset of parties can determine the secret if they contain an edge of the graph G. The constructive upper bounds are derived by the graph decomposition technique. Then we generalize Ateniese et al.'s method of comparing the optimal pixel expansion of VCSs with two different access structures.

INTRODUCTION

Secret sharing schemes split a secret into several shares that are distributed to several parties (Blakley, 1979), so that certain qualified subsets of parties can determine the secret, while unqualified subsets of parties have no information about the secret (Shamir, 1979). Visual cryptography is a special type of secret sharing in which the secret can be decoded directly by the human visual system without needing any extra calculations (Naor & Shamir, 1995). The best way to understand visual cryptography scheme (VCS) is by an example. Basic VCSs have to deal with binary images that only contain white □ and black ■ pixels. In a (2, 2)-VCS, every □ is encoded into (□■, □■) or (■□, ■□) with equal prob-

DOI: 10.4018/978-1-7998-1763-5.ch031

ability, while every ■ is encoded into (□■, ■□) or (■□, □■) with equal probability. Observing a single share, we have ■□ and □■ with equal probability, no matter whether the secret pixel is □ or ■. This guarantees that we obtain no information about the secret from a single share. The underling pixel stacking rule is: □+□=□, □+■=■, ■+□=■, ■+■=■. Hence the decoded □ is □■ or ■□, while the decoded ■ is ■■. This guarantees that we can perceive the secret by properly aligning the two share images.

In general, a secret pixel has to be encoded into multiple pixels on each share to achieve the above goals. This number is called the pixel expansion and is usually denoted by m. In the above (2, 2)-VCS, the pixel expansion $m = 2$. Since the pixel expansion is directly related to the size of the shares, it is expected to be as small as possible and is extensively studied (Adhikari et al., 2004, Blundo et al., 2001, Blundo et al., 2006, Bose & Mukerjee, 2006, Bose & Mukerjee, 2010, Droste, 1996, Koga, 2002, Shyu & Chen, 2011, Verheul & Tilborg, 1997).

In a graph access structure, a subset of parties can determine the secret iff they contain an edge of the graph. In this paper, we first focus on the pixel expansion of graph access structure VCSs. Similar to the decomposition method in secret sharing, Ateniese et al. propose a method to build larger VCS from smaller schemes. Although the framework is easy to understand, but how to decompose (Blundo et al., 1995, Blundo et al., 1993, Stinson, 1994) and the properties of the decomposition are very tricky (Beimel et al., 2012). In addition to the star and bipartite graph access structures (Ateniese et al., 1996), VCSs based on trees, cycles and multi-partite graph access structures are studied. This paper is organized as follows. Some basic knowledge of VCS is given in Section II. The pixel expansion of some graph access structure VCSs is analyzed in Section III. The comparison of two access structures w.r.t. the optimal pixel expansion is discussed in Section IV. The paper is concluded in Section V.

PRELIMINARIES

This section contains two parts. The first part presents the basic concepts related to VCS. The second part reviews some previous results of graph access structure VCS.

Basic Definitions

We first give some knowledge of access structure. Denote all parties by $P = \{1, 2, \cdots, n\}$. $\Gamma = (Q, F)$ is called an access structure if $Q \subseteq 2^P$ and $F \subseteq 2^P$ and $Q \cap F = \emptyset$. The elements of Q are called qualified sets and the elements of F are called forbidden sets. If for any element of Q, all of its supersets are also in Q, then Q is said to be monotone increasing. If for any element of F, all of its subsets are also in F, then F is said to be monotone decreasing. $\Gamma = (Q, F)$ is said to be a strong access structure if Q is monotone increasing and F is monotone decreasing and $Q \cup F = 2^P$. $Q_0 = \{A \in Q: A' \notin Q$ for all $A' \subsetneq A\}$ represents the set of all minimal qualified sets. Q_0 is also called the basis. $FM = \{A \in F: A' \in Q$, for any $a \in P \setminus A$, $A' = A \cup \{a\}\}$ represents the set of all maximal forbidden sets.

Given a graph $G = (V(G), E(G))$, if each vertex is associated with a party in P, and the qualified sets on P are exactly the closure of the edge set of G, then we say G represents a graph access structure. A vertex cover of G is a subset of vertices $A \subseteq V(G)$ such that every edge has at least one endpoint in A. A graph $G' = (V(G'), E(G'))$ is called a subgraph of a given graph $G = (V(G), E(G))$ if $V(G') \subseteq V(G)$ and $E(G') \subseteq E(G)$. The complete graph K_n is a graph on n vertices such that any two vertices are joined by an edge. A clique of a graph G is any complete subgraph of G. The complete multipartite graph $K_{a_1, a_2, \ldots, a_n}$ is a graph on a set of $\sum_{i=1}^{n} a_i$ vertices, which is partitioned into n subsets of sizes a_i ($1 \leq i \leq n$) respectively, called partites, such that vertices w and v are joined by an edge iff they are from different partites. The complementary graph of a graph $G = (V(G), E(G))$ is denoted by G. A graph $G = (V(G), E(G))$ is called a complementary graph of a given graph $G = (V(G), E(G))$ iff $V(G) = V(G)$ and $wv \in E(G)$ iff $wv = \in E(G)$. The complementary graph of a complete multipartite graph is a vertex-disjoint union of cliques. The complete graph K_n can be seen as a complete multipartite graph with n partites of size 1. A path in a graph $G = (V(G), E(G))$ is a sequence of vertices $v_1, v_2, \ldots, v_k$ such that each consecutive pair v_i, v_{i+1} is joined by an edge in G, which is often denoted by P_k, where k is the length of the path. A path is called simple if all its vertices are distinct. Without a special statement, all pathes P_n are simple in this paper. A cycle in a graph $G = (V(G), E(G))$ is a simple path $v_1, v_2, \ldots, v_k$ with v_1 and v_k joined by an edge in G, which is often denoted by C_k. A graph G is connected if for any two vertices w, $v \in V(G)$, there exists a path from w to v.

In the following, we set up our notations. Let S be a $n \times m$ Boolean matrix and X be a subset of $P = \{1, 2, \cdots, n\}$ and Z be a subset of $M = \{1, 2, \cdots, m\}$ and $|X|$ be the cardinality of X. $S[X][Z]$ represents the $|X| \times |Z|$ matrix S constrained to rows in X and columns in Z. $S[X]$ represents the $|X| \times m$ matrix S constrained to rows in X. Let C be a collection of $n \times m$ Boolean matrices. $C[X]$ represents the collection of $|X| \times m$ matrices, which are matrices in C constrained to rows in X. The OR result of rows of $S[X]$ is denoted by S_X and its Hamming weight is denoted by $w(S_X)$.

If we denote a □ by 0 and denote a ■ by 1, then the share patterns for white and black pixels can be denoted by two collections of Boolean matrices. The stacking rule is simply the OR operation. The formal definition of general access structure VCS is given as follows:

Definition 1

Let $\Gamma = (Q, F)$ be an access structure on a set P of n parties. The two collections of $n \times m$ Boolean matrices (C_0, C_1) constitute a solution of (Γ, m)-VCS if they satisfy the following conditions:

1. **Contrast**: There exists a positive real number α and a set of thresholds $\{t_X \mid X \in Q\}$ such that for any party set $X \in Q$, we have $w(M_X^0) \leq t_X - \alpha m$ for each $M^0 \in C_0$ and $w(M_X^1) \geq t_X$ for each $M^1 \in C_1$.
2. **Security**: For any party set $Y \in F$, $C_0[Y]$ and $C_1[Y]$ contain the same matrices with the same frequencies.

Remark

The number α is called the *relative contrast* and m is called the *pixel expansion* and $r = \log(\max\{|C_0|, |C_1|\})$ is called the *randomness* of the scheme. In this paper, the base of logarithm is 2. r is roughly the number of independent bits necessary to share a pixel. If (C_0, C_1) can be obtained by permuting the columns of two $n \times m$ Boolean matrices (S_0, S_1) in all possible ways, then (S_0, S_1) are called *basis matrices* and $|C_0| = |C_1| = m!$ and $r = \log(m!)$. The minimum amount of randomness required by any Γ-VCS is denoted by $r^*(\Gamma)$. The minimum (optimal) pixel expansion required by any Γ-VCS is denoted by $m^*(\Gamma)$.

Previous Results

- **Theorem 1 (Ateniese et al., 1996)**

Given an access structure $\Gamma = (Q, F)$ on P, which can be decomposed into $\Gamma_1 = (Q_1, F_1)$, $\Gamma 2 = (Q_2, F_2)$, ..., $\Gamma_t = (Q_t, F_t)$, such that $Q_1 \cup Q_2 \cup ... \cup Q_t = Q$ and $F_1 \cap F_2 \cap ... \cap F_t = F$. Suppose the white and black basis matrices for a Γ_i-VCS ($1 \leq i \leq t$) are denoted by $\hat{S}_O^i$ and $\hat{S}_1^i$ respectively, then $S_0 = \hat{S}_0^1 \circ \hat{S}_0^2 \circ \cdots \circ \hat{S}_0^t$ and $S_1 = \hat{S}_1^1 \circ \hat{S}_1^2 \circ \cdots \circ \hat{S}_1^t$ are the white and black basis matrices for a Γ-VCS, where $\circ$ represents the concatenation operation.

Recall that a vertex cover of graph G is a subset of vertices $A \subseteq V(G)$ such that every edge has at least one endpoint in A. For a graph G, let $\beta(G)$ denote the minimum cardinality of a vertex cover of G, and let $m^*(G)$ denote the minimum pixel expansion required by any G-VCS.

- **Theorem 2 (Ateniese et al., 1996):** *For any graph* G, *we have that* $m^*(G) \leq 2\beta(G)$.
- **Corollary 1 (Ateniese et al., 1996):** Suppose G is a bipartite graph with bipartition (V_1, V_2). Then $m^*(G) \leq 2\min\{|V_1|, |V_2|\}$.

THE PIXEL EXPANSION OF SOME GRAPH ACCESS

Following the work of (Ateniese et al., 1996), we provide upper bounds on $m^*(G)$ for more kinds of graph access structures in this section.

- **Corollary 2**: For any tree G with vertex set V, we have that $\beta(G) \leq \left\lceil \left\| V_2 \right\| \right\rceil$.
  - **Proof:** From the breadth-first search (BFS) of G from the root, we know that every vertex is labeled with a level from 0 to some positive integer, say t. All odd level vertexes constitute a set V_{odd} and all even level vertexes constitute a set V_{even}. Since both V_{odd} and V_{even} constitute a bipartition of V, we have that either $|V_{odd}| \leq \left\lceil \left\| V_2 \right\| \right\rceil$ or $|V_{even}| \leq \left\lceil \left\| V_2 \right\| \right\rceil$ holds. Besides, both V_{odd} and V_{even} constitute a vertex cover of G, which leads to the conclusion.
- **Corollary 3**: For a circle C_n of length n, we have that $m^*(C_n) \leq 2\left\lceil n/2 \right\rceil$.
  - **Proof:** Suppose the sequence of vertices on the circle is denoted by $v_1, v_2, ..., v_n$ in clockwise order. The set V_{odd} of all vertices v_i with i being odd constitutes a vertex cover of C_n. Clearly, $|V_{odd}| \leq \left\lceil n/2 \right\rceil$. The conclusion follows immediately from Theorem 2.
- **Corollary 4**: Suppose G is a multipartite graph with t partition $(V_1, V_2, ..., V_t)$ of vertex set V. Then $m^*(G) \leq 2\min\{|V/V_1|, |V/V_2|, ..., |V/V_t|\}$.
  - **Proof:** Observe the fact that any of $V/V_1, V/V_2, ..., V/V_t$ constitutes a vertex cover of G. The conclusion follows immediately from Theorem 2.
- **Remark:** Corollary 1 in (Ateniese et al., 1996) is a special case of Corollary 4 with $t = 2$.

COMPARE THE OPTIMAL PIXEL EXPANSION OF VCS WITH TWO DIFFERENT ACCESS STRUCTURES

Suppose $\Gamma = (Q, F)$ is an access structure on P, its *induced* access structure Γ_A by $A \subseteq P$ is defined by $\Gamma_A = (Q_A, F_A)$, where $Q_A = \{X \in Q: X \subseteq A\}$ and $FA = \{X \in F: X \subseteq A\}$. The optimal pixel expansion of Γ_1-VCS is denoted as m_1, and the optimal pixel expansion of Γ_2-VCS is denoted as m_2.

- **Theorem 3 (Ateniese et al., 1996)**

  If Γ_1 is an *induced* access structure from Γ_2, then $m_1 \le m_2$.
  In this section, we generalized Theorem 3 in (Ateniese et al., 1996) by two kinds of minor operations.

Two Kinds of Minor Operations

We first introduce two kinds of minor operations to an access structure $\Gamma = (Q, F)$ on parties $P = \{1, 2 ,..., n\}$, and let $T \subseteq P$:

- $\Gamma\backslash T = (Q_T, F_T)$ on parties $P\backslash T$, where $Q_T = \{X: X\backslash T \in Q\}$ and $F_T = \{X: X\backslash T \in F\}$, which means a scenario that after the lost of shares hold by parties T, which subset of parties still can reconstruct the secret.
- $\Gamma/T = (Q_T, F_T)$ on parties $P\backslash T$, where $Q_T = \{X: X\cup T \in Q\}$ and $F_T = \{X: X\cup T \in F\}$, which means a scenario that after the exposure of shares hold by parties T, which subset of parties can reconstruct the secret now.
- **Remark:** The "*induce*" operation in (Ateniese et al., 1996) is the same as the \ operation. If Γ^- can be obtained by iteratively using a sequence of \ or / operations to Γ, then Γ^- is called a *minor* of Γ. Clearly, the *minor* operations are a strict generalization of the "*induce*" operation.
- **Theorem 4**: Let Γ be an access structure on $P = \{1, 2 ,..., n\}$, and Γ^- be a *minor* of Γ. If we have a Γ-VCS with pixel expansion m, then we have a Γ^--VCS with pixel expansion m.
  - **Proof:** Denote the white and black basis matrices of the given Γ-VCS by S_0 and S_1. Suppose Γ^- is obtained by sequentially use $f_1(T_1), f_2(T_2), ..., f_k(T_k)$ to Γ, where $f_1,...,f_k \in \{\backslash, /\}$ and $T_1,...,T_k$ are disjoint subsets of P. The following construction transforms a given Γ-VCS to a Γ^--VCS.
- **Construction 1**:
  Input: A Γ-VCS.
  Output: A Γ^--VCS.
  - **Step 1:** For $i = 1$ to $i = k$
  - **Step 2:** If $f_i == \backslash$
  - **Step 3:** For each of S_0 and S_1, throw its rows in T_i away.
  - **Step 4:** Else if $f_i == /$
  - **Step 5:** For each of S_0 and S_1, stack the rows in T_i to every still remaining row that is not in T_i, and then throw the rows in T_i away. Formally, for every $j \in P \backslash (T_1 \cup ... \cup T_i)$, $S_0[j] = (\bigoplus_{e \in Ti} S_0[e]) \oplus S_0[j]$ and $S_1[j] = (\bigoplus_{e \in Ti} S_1[e]) \oplus S_1[j]$.
  - **Step 6:** End if
  - **Step 7:** End for
  - **Step 8:** Output the modified S_0 and S_1, which are the white and black basis matrices of a Γ^--VCS.

- **Remark:** The minor operations $f_1(T_1), f_2(T_2), ..., f_k(T_k)$ satisfy the commutative law. All the \ operations can be merged into one.
  - The stacking of any qualified subset in $\Gamma^{\cdot}$ is equivalent to the stacking of some qualified subset in Γ, which ensures the satisfaction of the contrast condition. Besides, for any forbidden subset $Y^{\cdot}$ in $\Gamma^{\cdot}$, there is a forbidden subset Y in Γ such that each row in $Y^{\cdot}$ is the stacking result of some rows in Y. Hence the conclusion holds.
- **Theorem 5:** If Γ_1 is a *minor* of Γ_2, then $m_1 \leq m_2$.
  - **Proof:** From Theorem 4, we can build a Γ_1-VCS from a Γ_2-VCS with the same pixel expansion. Hence the conclusion holds.

    The following example gives an intuitive idea of the minor operations and Construction 1.
- **Example 1:** Let $\Gamma = (Q, F)$ be an access structure on $P = \{1, 2, 3, 4\}$, where $Q = \{\{1, 2, 4\}, \{1, 3, 4\}, \{2, 3\}\}$. The following two basis matrices S_0 and S_1 define a Γ-VCS.

$$S_0 = \begin{bmatrix} 0 & 1 & 1 & 0 & 0 \\ 1 & 0 & 1 & 0 & 0 \\ 1 & 0 & 1 & 0 & 0 \\ 1 & 1 & 0 & 0 & 0 \end{bmatrix} \text{ and } S_1 = \begin{bmatrix} 1 & 0 & 0 & 0 & 1 \\ 1 & 0 & 0 & 1 & 0 \\ 1 & 0 & 1 & 0 & 0 \\ 1 & 1 & 0 & 0 & 0 \end{bmatrix}$$

  - Let $\Gamma^2 = (Q^2, F^2)$ be an access structure on $P = \{1, 3, 4\}$, where $Q^2 = \{X: X \setminus \{2\} \in Q\} = \{\{1, 3, 4\}\}$. The following two basis matrices S_0^2 and S_1^2 define a Γ^2-VCS.

$$S_0^2 = \begin{bmatrix} 0 & 1 & 1 & 0 & 0 \\ 1 & 0 & 1 & 0 & 0 \\ 1 & 1 & 0 & 0 & 0 \end{bmatrix} \text{ and } S_1^2 = \begin{bmatrix} 1 & 0 & 0 & 0 & 1 \\ 1 & 0 & 1 & 0 & 0 \\ 1 & 1 & 0 & 0 & 0 \end{bmatrix}$$

  - Let $\Gamma^4 = (Q^4, F^4)$ be an access structure on $P = \{1, 2, 3\}$, where $Q^4 = \{X: X \cup \{4\} \in Q\} = \{\{1, 2\}, \{1, 3\}, \{2, 3\}\}$. The following two basis matrices S_0^4 and S_1^4 define a Γ^4-VCS.

$$S_0^4 = \begin{bmatrix} 1 & 1 & 1 & 0 & 0 \\ 1 & 1 & 1 & 0 & 0 \\ 1 & 1 & 1 & 0 & 0 \end{bmatrix} \text{ and } S_1^4 = \begin{bmatrix} 1 & 1 & 0 & 0 & 1 \\ 1 & 1 & 0 & 1 & 0 \\ 1 & 1 & 1 & 0 & 0 \end{bmatrix}$$

CONCLUSION

This paper advances the previous studies in the following ways:

1. We provide upper bounds on the optimal pixel expansion of more kinds of graph access structures, e.g. tree, circle, multipartite graph.
2. Two kinds of minor operations are introduced to compare the optimal pixel expansion of two different access structures, which strictly generalize the "induce" operation in (Ateniese et al., 1996).

ACKNOWLEDGMENT

This work was supported by the "Fundamental Research Funds for the Central Universities" grant No. 3262016T47 and the NSFC grant No. 61671448 and the key project of NFSC grant No. U1536207 and the "Strategic Priority Research Program" of the Chinese Academy of Sciences No. XDA06010701.

REFERENCES

Adhikari, A., Dutta, T. K., & Roy, B. (2004). A new black and white visual cryptographic scheme for general access structures. In A. Canteaut & K. Viswanathan (Eds.), *INDOCRYPT 2004, LNCS* (Vol. 3348, pp. 399–413). Springer. doi:10.1007/978-3-540-30556-9_31

Ateniese, G., Blundo, C., De Santis, A., & Stinson, D. R. (1996). Visual cryptography for general access structures. *Information and Computation*, *129*(2), 86–106. doi:10.1006/inco.1996.0076

Beimel, A., Farras, O., & Mintz, Y. (2012). Secret sharing schemes for very dense graphs. In R. S. Naini & R. Canetti (Eds.), *CRYPTO 2012, LNCS* (Vol. 7417, pp. 144–161). Springer. doi:10.1007/978-3-642-32009-5_10

Blakley, G. R. (1979). Safeguarding cryptographic keys. In R.E. Merwin (Ed.), *Proceedings of the National Computer Conference* (*Vol. 48*, pp. 313–317), American Federation of Information Processing Societies.

Blundo, C., Cimato, S., & De Santis, A. (2006). Visual cryptography schemes with optimal pixel expansion. *Theoretical Computer Science*, *369*(1-3), 169–182. doi:10.1016/j.tcs.2006.08.008

Blundo, C., De Bonis, A., & De Santis, A. (2001). Improved schemes for visual cryptography. *Designs, Codes and Cryptography*, *24*(3), 255–278. doi:10.1023/A:1011271120274

Blundo, C., De Santis, A., Stinson, D. R., & Vaccaro, U. (1993). Graph decomposition and secret sharing schemes. In R. A. Rueppel (Ed.), *EUROCRYPT 1992, LNCS* (Vol. 658, pp. 1–24). Springer.

Blundo, C., Gaggia, A. G., & Stinson, D. R. (1995). On the dealer's randomness required in secret sharing schemes. In A. D. Santis (Ed.), *EUROCRYPT 1994, LNCS* (Vol. 950, pp. 35–46). Springer. doi:10.1007/BFb0053422

Bose, M., & Mukerjee, R. (2006). Optimal (2, n) visual cryptographic schemes. *Designs, Codes and Cryptography*, *40*(3), 255–267. doi:10.100710623-006-0011-9

Bose, M., & Mukerjee, R. (2010). Optimal (k, n) visual cryptographic schemes for general k. *Designs, Codes and Cryptography*, *55*(1), 19–35. doi:10.100710623-009-9327-6

De Bonis, A., & De Santis, A. (2004). Randomness in secret sharing and visual cryptography schemes. *Theoretical Computer Science*, *314*(3), 351–374. doi:10.1016/j.tcs.2003.12.018

Droste, S. (1996). New results on visual cryptography. In N. Koblitz (Ed.), *CRYPTO 1996, LNCS* (Vol. 1109, pp. 401–415). Springer.

Koga, H. (2002). A general formula of the (t, n)-threshold visual secret sharing scheme. In Y. L. Zheng (Ed.), *ASIACRYPT 2002, LNCS* (Vol. 2501, pp. 328–345). Springer. doi:10.1007/3-540-36178-2_21

Naor, M., & Shamir, A. (1995). Visual cryptography. In A. D. Santis (Ed.), *EUROCRYPT 1994, LNCS* (Vol. 950, pp. 1–12). Springer.

Shamir, A. (1979). How to share a secret. *Communications of the ACM*, *22*(11), 612–613. doi:10.1145/359168.359176

Shyu, S. J., & Chen, M. C. (2011). Optimum pixel expansions for threshold visual secret sharing schemes. IEEE Transactions on Information Forensics and Security, 6(3), 960–969.

Stinson, D. R. (1994). Decomposition construction for secret sharing schemes. *IEEE Transactions on Information Theory*, *40*(1), 118–125. doi:10.1109/18.272461

Verheul, E., & Tilborg, H. V. (1997). Constructions and properties of k out of n visual secret sharing schemes. *Designs, Codes and Cryptography*, *11*(2), 179–196. doi:10.1023/A:1008280705142

This research was previously published in the International Journal of Digital Crime and Forensics (IJDCF), 9(2); edited by Wei Qi Yan; pages 38-44, copyright year 2017 by IGI Publishing (an imprint of IGI Global).

Chapter 32
A Novel Pixel Merging–Based Lossless Recovery Algorithm for Basic Matrix VSS

Xin Liu
Harbin Institute of Technology, China & Harbin University of Science and Technology, China

Shen Wang
Harbin Institute of Technology, China

Jianzhi Sang
Harbin Institute of Technology, China

Weizhe Zhang
Harbin Institute of Technology, China

ABSTRACT

Lossless recovery in visual secret share (VSS) is very meaningful. In this paper, a novel lossless recovery algorithm for the basic matrix VSS is proposed. The secret image is reconstructed losslessly by using simple exclusive XOR operation and merging pixel. The algorithm not only can apply to the VSS without pixel expansion but also can apply to VSS with pixel expansion. The condition of lossless recovery of a VSS is given by analyzing the XOR all columns of basic matrixes. Simulations are conducted to evaluate the efficiency of the proposed scheme.

INTRODUCTION

One of efficient secure methods for secret image protection is the visual secret sharing (VSS), also called visual cryptography scheme (VCS) (Wang, Zhang, Ma, & Li, 2007) (Naor, & Shamir, 1999). The original secret image is divided into different meaningless or meaningful shadows (shares) in VSS generating phase. The generated shares are distributed to a group of participants (Yang, 2004) (Cimato, Prisco & Santis, 2006) (Kafri, & Keren, 1987). If enough shadows collected, the secret image is performed by superposing all or some of shares. Based on human visual system (HVS) we can easily obtain the original secret image. However, less than th threshold coefficient[k] participants give nothing about the secret image.

DOI: 10.4018/978-1-7998-1763-5.ch032

Literature on VSS is quite rich (Liu, Guo, Wu, & Qian, 2012) (Shyu, 2009) (Li, El-Latif, & Niu, 2012) (Chen, & Tsao, 2011) (Yan, Jin, & Kankanhalli, 2004) (Li, Ma, Su, & Yang, 2012). The concept of the VSS is first introduced by Naor and Shamir (Naor, & Shamir, 1999), the shadow images are generated according to the basic matrixes and are expanded to the larger size than the secret image. Following Naor and Shamir's work, many research works focus on VSS own physical properties and problems of the VSS mechanism. The probabilistic VSS (ProbVSS) (Yang, 2004) and Random grid (RG)-based VSS (Kafri, & Keren, 1987) (Liu, Guo, Wu, & Qian, 2012) (Shyu, 2009) (Li, El-Latif, & Niu, 2012) (Chen, & Tsao, 2011) are proposed to solve the problem of the pixel expansion. The (Blundo, D'Arco, Santis, & Stinson, 2003) (Hou, & Quan, 2011) focus on the basic matrixes, (Yan, Jin, & Kankanhalli, 2004) (Li, Ma, Su, & Yang, 2012) (Yan, Liu, & Yang, 2015) and XOR-based VSS (XVSS) (Tuyls, Hollmann, & Lint, 2005) concentrate on improving the visual quality. The basic matrix-based VSS scheme is our research object.

It is worth noting that in a lot of situations the lossless recovery of secret image is necessary such as for transmission and storage of military secret images, private medical images, and so on. It is very meaningful to research the lossless recovery scheme which only uses simple computation in the phase of decrypting (recovering).

In the following, we discuss some related works and scope of the proposed work. Lossless recovery can reconstruct the secret losslessly if the light-weight computation device is available.

Chen et al. (Chen, Wang, Yan, & Li, 2014) proposed a progressive[(2, n)] VSS and the secret will be reconstructed losslessly by additive operation. Wu and Sun (Wu, & Sun, 2013) proposed a scheme having the abilities of OR and exclusive OR (XOR) decryptions and the secret could be recovered losslessly at the condition of collecting all n shares. Utilizing XOR operation, Yan et al. (Yan, Wang, El-Latif, & Niu, 2015) proposed a scheme which needs all n shares to reveal the distortion-less secret image. Nevertheless, none of these schemes (Chen, Wang, Yan, & Li, 2014) (Wu, & Sun, 2013) (Yan, Wang, El-Latif, & Niu, 2015) could recover the secret losslessly when the size of shadow images is expanded. The two-in-one VSS (TiOISS) (Lin, & Lin, 2007) only needs k shares to reconstruct the distortion-less secret image. However, it still requires knowing the order of shadow images and needing complicated computations, i.e., Lagrange interpolations, in the second decoding phase. In addition, in most literatures, the visual quality of the recovered image is always low and the secret image could not be losslessly recovery.

In this paper, a novel pixel merging-based lossless recovery algorithm for basic matrix-based VSS is proposed. The proposed algorithm just needs to use simple XOR operation and pixel merging in order to lossless recover the original secret image. In addition, the algorithm can be applied to the VSS with and without pixel expansion.

In our algorithm, firstly to analysis the ability of lossless recovery of a VSS by performing the simple XOR operation on all n columns of basic matrixes. According to the XOR theory, we can obtain the following conclusion. If all the XOR-ed result of the basic matrix M^0 is 0 and all the result of the basic matrix M^1 is 1, the secret image can be recovered losslessly for a VSS scheme. Otherwise, the secret image cannot be recovered losslessly for a VSS scheme. In the phase of recovery, the original secret image could be losslessly revealed by XOR-ing all the shadows. For the VSS scheme with pixel expansion, the recovery phase needs a pixel merging phase. The algorithm has lossless recovery feature at the same time maintains the merits of the original VSS scheme. Simulation results show the effectiveness of the proposed scheme. Comparisons with the previous approaches show the advantages of the proposed algorithm.

The rest of the paper is organized as follows. In Section 2, the proposed algorithm is presented in detail and gives the theory analyses of the algorithm. Section 3 is devoted to simulation results. Finally, Section 4 concludes this paper.

THE PROPOSED ALGORITHM AND ANALYSIS

In this section, we present the proposed lossless recovery algorithm based XOR operation and pixel merging. The generation phase and recovery phase of the proposed algorithm are depicted in details.

Firstly, we give Algorithm 1, which can be used to judge whether the basic matrixes VSS scheme can be losslessly recovered or not. The architecture of Algorithm 1 is illustrated in Figure 1 and detailed in Algorithm 1.

Algorithm 1. The proposed algorithm
Input: The basic matrixes $M^0(r{\times}c)$ and $M^1(r{\times}c)$, which are given in a VSS scheme
Output: The lossless recovery ability of a VSS
Step 1: First, we compute the XOR result of c columns of the matrix M^0. That is, we get:

$$XORM^0(1) = M^0(1,1) \oplus M^0(2,1) \oplus \cdots \oplus M^0(r,1)$$

$,\ldots,$

$$XORM^0(c) = M^0(1,c) \oplus M^0(2,c) \oplus \cdots \oplus M^0(r,c)$$

Figure 1. The architecture of Algorithm 1

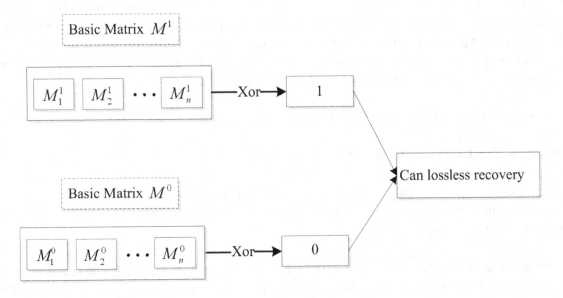

Step 2: For the basic matrix M^1, we execute the same operation:

$$XORM^1(1) = M^1(1,1) \oplus M^1(2,1) \oplus \cdots \oplus M^1(r,1)$$

$,\ldots,$

$$XORM^1(c) = M^1(1,c) \oplus M^1(2,c) \oplus \cdots \oplus M^1(r,c)$$

Step 3: If each result of $XORM^0(i)=0$ and $XORM^1(i)=1$ go to Step 4, else go to Step 5.
Step 4: Output the VSS can be reconstructed losslessly.
Step 5: Output the VSS cannot be reconstructed losslessly.

According to the basic matrix, we can directly estimate whether the VSS has the lossless recovery ability or not. In general, two matrixes denoted by M^0 and M^1 are designed, which represent the sharing basic matrix for white and black pixels of the secret image, respectively. The ability of lossless recovery of the VSS can be judged through XOR operation of all columns of the two basic matrixes (In most situation, the column of matrix represented a shadow image. However, if the row of matrix represented a shadow image in a VSS, then the ability of lossless recovery is judged by XOR of all n rows). If all the result from M^0 is 0 and M^0 is 1, then the VSS can recover the secret image losslessly. In the phase of recovery, the original secret image could be losslessly revealed based on the XOR operation and pixel merging.

The idea of Algorithm 1 can be described precisely as follows: In steps 1-2 of Algorithm 1, judging whether the VSS has ability of lossless recovery by executing XOR operation among n columns of matrixes. In step 3, according to the result of the XOR operation, we can determine whether the VSS scheme has lossless recovery ability. If each result of $XORM^0(i)$ is 0 and $XORM^1(i)$ is 1, the VSS has the lossless recovery ability. Otherwise, it has not. From the algorithm, the ability of lossless recovery are obtained. If the VSS scheme has pixel expansion, then the expansion coefficient will also be used in the recovery phase. In our paper, we focus on the basic matrix-based on VSS, which has pixel expansion. That means the expansion coefficient m also plays an important role in our recovery algorithm.

The proposed lossless recovery algorithmic steps are described in detailed as in Algorithm 2 and the corresponding architecture of the proposed scheme is illustrated in Figure 2.

Algorithm 2. The proposed recovery algorithm
Input: n shadow images $SC_1, SC_2, \ldots, SC_n$, m.
Output: A $M \times N$ binary secret image S'.
Step 1: XOR the n shadow images, $SCS_n = SC_1 \oplus SC_2 \oplus \cdots \oplus SC_n$.
Step 2: Executing pixel merging for '0' of SCS_n, the m '0' is merged into one '0'.
Step 3: Executing pixel merging for '1' of SCS_n, the m '1' is merged into one '1'.
Step 4: Output the binary image S'.

In the phase of recovery for the VSS with pixel expansion, if light-weight device is available and the number of shadows is equal to n, the secret could be reconstructed losslessly. In step 1, according to the XOR operation, we can recover a temp secret image which size is equal to the shadow image.

Figure 2. The architecture of lossless recovery algorithm for expansion VSS

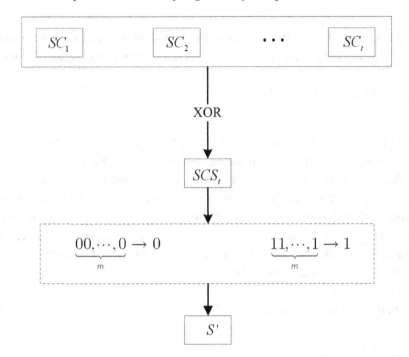

Obviously, the temp recovery image corresponding to the secret image has pixel expansion. So, pixel merging is executed in steps 2-3, the m '0' is merged into one '0' and the m '1' is merged into one '1'. In our algorithm, expansion coefficient m means one pixel of original secret image is translated into m pixels of shadow image. Step 4 outputs the secret binary lossless recovery image.

Remark

The proposed algorithm can also be applied to the VSS scheme without pixel expansion. Since we only need to consider this case as $m=1$. In the phase of recovery for the VSS without pixel expansion, if lightweight device is available and the number of shadows is equal to n, the secret could be reconstructed losslessly according to the above recovery algorithm.

THEORETICAL ANALYSES

Here, we give the theoretical analyses of the proposed algorithm:

Lemma 1: For the basic matrixes M^0 and M^1 given by a VSS scheme, two sets $XORM^0$ and $XORM^1$ are obtained from XOR all the columns of two matrixes M^0 and M^1, respectively. If $XORM^0$ only contains element 0 and $XORM^1$ only contains element 1, then the secret image S can be reconstructed losslessly.

Proof

Specifically, for this Lemma 1 to be proved, obviously, the shadow images are generated according to the basic matrix. Executing the simple XOR operation on n shadow images, we can get a new matrix:

$$XORSCS_n \left(XORSCS_n = SC_1 \oplus SC_2 \oplus \cdots \oplus SC_n \right)$$

Since the shadow images are generated from the basic matrix, each XOR results of shadow images are equal to the XOR results of the corresponding column of basic matrix. Again, in this Lemma 1, the condition $XORM^0$ only contains element 0 and $XORM^1$ only contains element 1 are established. For the two matrixes M^0 and M^1 represent the sharing basic matrix for white (0) and black pixels (1) of the secret image, respectively. Obviously, we can get the original secret image by XOR all the shadow images. We should note that since the basic matrix-based scheme has the pixel expansion, in the final step of recovering phase, there is the pixel merging procedure which ensures that the secret image can be recovered losslessly. In order to merge pixel, the coefficient m must be an integer. The m '0' is merged into one '0' and the m '1' is merged into one '1'.

For example, there is a basic matrix-based (2,2) VSS scheme, which the basic matrixes are:

$$M^0 = \begin{bmatrix} 0 & 1 \\ 0 & 1 \end{bmatrix}, M^1 = \begin{bmatrix} 0 & 1 \\ 0 & 1 \end{bmatrix} \tag{1}$$

Through the calculation, the XOR results of all columns of matrix M^0 are {0,0} and the XOR results of all columns of matrix $M1$ are {1,1}. Obviously, the secret image can be recovered losslessly.

SIMULATIONS AND ANALYSES

In this section, we perform the simulations to evaluate the effectiveness of the proposed scheme. The original binary secret images are shown in Figure 3 (a) (image1), Figure 4 (a) (image2) and in Figure 5 (a) (image3), with the size of 256×256, to test the efficiency of our scheme. In our experiments, the literature (Naor, & Shamir, 1999) (2,2) ($k=2$, $n=2$) threshold scheme with secret image1, (3,3) ($k=3$, $n=3$) threshold scheme with secret image2 and (Hou, & Quan, 2011) (2,4) ($k=2$, $n=4$) scheme with secret image3 are used to test the efficiency of proposed scheme. The basic matrix of (Naor, & Shamir, 1999) (2,2) threshold scheme is Equation 1 and (3,3) is Equation 2:

$$M^0 = \begin{bmatrix} 0 & 1 & 1 & 0 \\ 0 & 1 & 0 & 1 \\ 0 & 0 & 1 & 1 \end{bmatrix}, M^1 = \begin{bmatrix} 1 & 0 & 0 & 1 \\ 0 & 1 & 0 & 1 \\ 0 & 0 & 1 & 1 \end{bmatrix} \tag{2}$$

Figure 3. Experimental example of the (Naor, & Shamir, 1999) (2,2) scheme with our lossless recovery of the binary image1

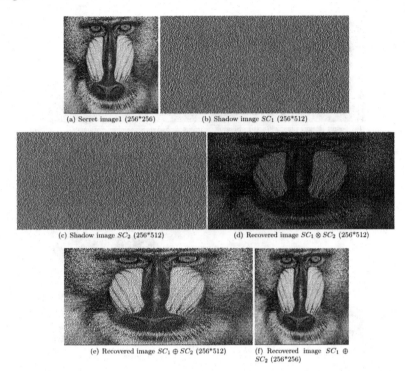

(a) Secret image1 (256*256) (b) Shadow image SC_1 (256*512)

(c) Shadow image SC_2 (256*512) (d) Recovered image $SC_1 \otimes SC_2$ (256*512)

(e) Recovered image $SC_1 \oplus SC_2$ (256*512) (f) Recovered image $SC_1 \oplus SC_2$ (256*256)

Figure 3 (b-c) show the 2 shadow images SC_1 and SC_2 are generated by the (Naor, & Shamir, 1999) (2,2) threshold scheme for binary secret image1. Figure 3 (d) show the revealed binary secret image with 2 shadow images with OR recovery. Figure 3 (e) shows the revealed temp recovery image with 2 shadow images by our scheme before processing of pixel merging. We can see all pixels of original secret image have been recovered, just one pixel is extended to two pixels. Figure 3 (f) shows the secret image revealed by all 2 shadow images is lossless.

Figure 4 (b-d) show the 3 shadow images SC_1, SC_2 and SC_3 are generated by the (Naor, & Shamir, 1999) (3,3) threshold scheme for binary secret image2. Figure 4 (e) show the revealed binary secret image with 3 shadow images with OR recovery. Figure 4 (f) shows the revealed temp recovery image with 3 shadow images by our scheme before processing of pixel merging. Similarly, all pixels of original secret image have been recovered, just an expanded lossless recovery image. Figure 4 (g) shows the secret image revealed by all 3 shadow images is lossless.

Figure 5 (b) show the shadow images are generated by (Hou, & Quan, 2011) scheme for binary secret image3. Figure 5 (c-e) show the revealed binary secret image with any 2 (taking 1 and 2 as an example), 3 (taking 1,2 and 3 as an example) or 4 shadow images with OR recovery. Figure 5 (i) shows the revealed secret image with 4 shadow images by our scheme, the secret image can be losslessly recovered.

The (2,2) VSS has been analyzed in the previous section. Now we give some discussion about (3,3) VSS and (Hou, & Quan, 2011) PVSS. According to the basic matrixes of the (3,3) VSS, we can easily obtain the XOR result for all columns of M^0 is $XORM^0=\{0,0,0,0\}$ and M^1 is $XORM^1=\{1,1,1,1\}$. Obviously, $XORM^0$ only contains one element 0 and $XORM^1$ only contains one element 1 and the secret image can be recovered losslessly.

Figure 4. Experimental example of the (Naor, & Shamir, 1999) (3,3) scheme with our lossless recovery of the binary image2

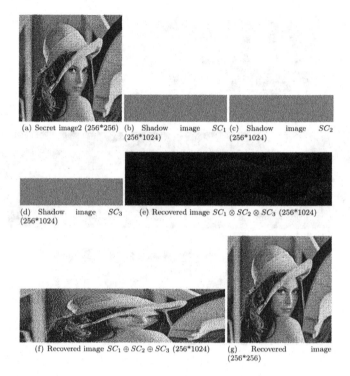

(a) Secret image2 (256*256)   (b) Shadow image SC_1 (256*1024)   (c) Shadow image SC_2 (256*1024)

(d) Shadow image SC_3 (256*1024)   (e) Recovered image $SC_1 \otimes SC_2 \otimes SC_3$ (256*1024)

(f) Recovered image $SC_1 \oplus SC_2 \oplus SC_3$ (256*1024)   (g) Recovered image (256*256)

Figure 5. Experimental example of the (Hou, & Quan, 2011) (2,4) scheme with our lossless recovery of the binary image3

(a) Secret image2 (256*256)   (b) Shadow image SC_1 (256*256)   (c) Recovered image $SC_1 \otimes SC_2$ (256*256)

(d) Recovered image $SC_1 \otimes SC_2 \otimes SC_3$ (256*256)   (e) Recovered image $SC_1 \otimes SC_2 \otimes SC_3 \otimes SC_4$ (256*256)   (f) Recovered image $SC_1 \oplus SC_2 \oplus SC_3 \oplus SC_4$ (256*256)

We note that the (Hou, & Quan, 2011) scheme is a (2,n) scheme and without pixel expansion. Since the rows of the matrix represented the shadow images, so the set is calculated by XOR of all n rows. From Table 1, the XOR result of the row of the M^1 is 1. However, for the M^0, if n is an even then the XOR result is 0 and if n is an odd then the XOR result is 1. So if n is an even, the (Hou, & Quan, 2011) scheme has ability of lossless recovery. As long as we can get all the n shadow images, according to proposed scheme, we can recover the secret image lossless. If n is an odd, it has not.

From the simulation results, we can see the secret image can be lossless recovered for the pixel expansion VSS, and the work of (Wu, & Sun, 2013) and (Yan, Wang, El-Latif, & Niu, 2015) cannot. In addition, all TiOISS schemes are based on polynomial evaluation and interpolation in decoding phase of lossless recovery, so their algorithmic complexity is $O(n\log^2 n)$. The generation phase of our scheme computes r columns of matrixes using XOR operation, its computation time is proportional to $r - 1$. The recovery phase of our scheme computes n shadow images also using addition operation, its computation time is proportional to n. In the process of pixel merging, the computation complexity is $O(m)$. The computation complexity is also proportional to the image size. Approximately, the computation complexity of our scheme is $O(n+m+r-1)$. Comparing with TiOISS schemes, our algorithm needs only simple calculation operation when recover the secret image. Table 2 summaries the above discussion. In summary, our scheme is feasible and fast and can be applied to real-time application.

Table 1. Two basic matrixes and the Hamming weight sets of (Hou, & Quan, 2011)

Secret Pixel	Basic Matrixes	XOR
0	$M^0 = \begin{bmatrix} 1 & 1 & \cdots & 1 \\ 0 & 0 & \cdots & 0 \\ \vdots & \vdots & \vdots & \vdots \\ 0 & 0 & \cdots & 0 \end{bmatrix}_{n \times n}$	$\begin{bmatrix} 1\ or\ 0 \\ 0 \\ 0 \\ 0 \end{bmatrix}$
1	$M^1 = \begin{bmatrix} 1 & 0 & \cdots & 0 \\ 0 & 1 & \cdots & 0 \\ \vdots & \vdots & \vdots & \vdots \\ 0 & 0 & \cdots & 1 \end{bmatrix}_{n \times n}$	$\begin{bmatrix} 1 \\ 1 \\ 1 \\ 1 \end{bmatrix}$

Table 2. Comparative results among TiOISS, (Wu, & Sun, 2013) and (Yan, Wang, El-Latif, & Niu, 2015), our algorithm

Scheme	Apply to Pixel Expansion VSS	Computation Complexity
TiOISS	No	$O(n\log^2 n)$
(Wu, & Sun, 2013) and (Yan, Wang, El-Latif, & Niu, 2015)	No	$O(n)$
Our algorithm	YES	$O(n+m+r-1)$

CONCLUSION

For the personal privacy images and military secrets, the lossless recovery is particularly important. There are some disadvantages such as complex computation, cannot apply to VSS with pixel expansion in the existing lossless recovery algorithms. To deal with those disadvantages, in this paper, a novel pixel merging-based lossless recovery scheme for basic matrix-based VSS is proposed. The algorithm can reconstruct the secret image losslessly according to the relationship of the matrixes M^0 and M^1. Simulations are conducted to show the efficiency of the proposed scheme. Designing the novel (2,4) lossless recovery scheme aiming at the VSS with pixel expansion is our future work.

ACKNOWLEDGMENT

The authors would like to thank the anonymous reviewers for their valuable discussions and comments. This work is supported by the National Natural Science Foundation of China (Grant Number: 61471141, 61361166006, 61301099, 61472108, 61672186, 61501148,), the National Key Research and Development Program of China (Grant Number: 2016YFB0800801), Key Technology Program of Shenzhen, China, (No. JSGG20160427185010977) and Basic Research Project of Shenzhen, China (Grant Number: JCYJ2015051351706561).

Shen Wang is a corresponding author on this article. He can be reached at the following email: shen.wang@hit.edu.cn.

REFERENCES

Blundo, C., DArco, P., Santis, A. D., & Stinson, D. R. (2003). Contrast optimal threshold visual cryptography schemes. *SIAM Journal on Discrete Mathematics*, *16*(2), 224–261. doi:10.1137/S0895480198336683

Chen, G., Wang, C., Yan, X., & Li, P. (2014). Progressive Visual Secret Sharing with Multiple Decryptions and Unexpanded Shares. In *Digital-Forensics and Watermarking* (pp. 376-386).

Chen, T. H., & Tsao, K. H. (2011). Threshold visual secret sharing by random grids. *Journal of Systems and Software*, *84*(7), 1197–1208. doi:10.1016/j.jss.2011.02.023

Cimato, S., Prisco, R. D., & Santis, A. D. (2006). Probabilistic visual cryptography schemes. *The Computer Journal*, *49*(1), 97–107. doi:10.1093/comjnl/bxh152

Hou, Y. C., & Quan, Z. Y. (2011). Progressive visual cryptography with unexpanded shares. *IEEE Transactions on Circuits and Systems for Video Technology*, *21*(11), 1760–1764. doi:10.1109/TCSVT.2011.2106291

Kafri, O., & Keren, E. (1987). Encryption of pictures and shapes by random grids. *Optics Letters*, *12*(6), 377–379. doi:10.1364/OL.12.000377 PMID:19741737

Li, L., El-Latif, A. A. A., & Niu, X. (2012). Elliptic curve ElGamal based homomorphic image encryption scheme for sharing secret images. *Signal Processing*, *92*(4), 1069–1078. doi:10.1016/j.sigpro.2011.10.020

Li, P., Ma, P. J., Su, X. H., & Yang, C. N. (2012). Improvements of a two-in-one image secret sharing scheme based on gray mixing model. *Journal of Visual Communication and Image Representation*, *23*(3), 441–453. doi:10.1016/j.jvcir.2012.01.003

Lin, S. J., & Lin, J. C. (2007). Vcpss: A two-in-one two-decoding-options image sharing method combining visual cryptography (vc) and polynomial-style sharing (pss) approaches. *Pattern Recognition*, *40*(12), 3652–3666. doi:10.1016/j.patcog.2007.04.001

Liu, F., Guo, T., Wu, C. K., & Qian, L. (2012). Improving the visual quality of size invariant visual cryptography scheme. *Journal of Visual Communication and Image Representation*, *23*(2), 331–342. doi:10.1016/j.jvcir.2011.11.003

Naor, M., & Shamir, A. (1999). Visual cryptography. In Advances in Cryptology, *LNCS* (Vol. *950*, pp. 1–12).

Shyu, S. J. (2009). Image encryption by multiple random grids. *Pattern Recognition*, *42*(7), 1582–1596. doi:10.1016/j.patcog.2008.08.023

Tuyls, P., Hollmann, H. D. L., Lint, J. H. V., & Tolhuizen, L. (2005). Xor-based visual cryptography schemes. *Designs, Codes and Cryptography*, *37*(1), 169–186. doi:10.100710623-004-3816-4

Wang, D., Zhang, L., Ma, N., & Li, X. (2007). Two secret sharing schemes based on Boolean operations. *Pattern Recognition*, *40*(10), 2776–2785. doi:10.1016/j.patcog.2006.11.018

Wu, X., & Sun, W. (2013). Random grid-based visual secret sharing with abilities of OR and XOR decryptions. *Journal of Visual Communication and Image Representation*, *24*(1), 48–62. doi:10.1016/j.jvcir.2012.11.001

Yan, W. Q., Jin, D., & Kankanhalli, M. S. (2004). Visual cryptography for print and scan applications. *Proceedings of the International Symposium on Circuits and Systems* (Vol. 5, pp. 572-575).

Yan, X., Liu, X., & Yang, C. N. (2015). An enhanced threshold visual secret sharing based on random grids. *Journal of Real-Time Image Processing*.

Yan, X., Wang, S., El-Latif, A. A., & Niu, X. (2015). Visual secret sharing based on random grids with abilities of and and xor lossless recovery. *Multimedia Tools and Applications*, *74*(9), 3231–3252. doi:10.100711042-013-1784-2

Yang, C. N. (2004). New visual secret sharing schemes using probabilistic method. *Pattern Recognition Letters*, *25*(4), 481–494. doi:10.1016/j.patrec.2003.12.011

This research was previously published in the International Journal of Digital Crime and Forensics (IJDCF), 9(3); edited by Wei Qi Yan; pages 1-10, copyright year 2017 by IGI Publishing (an imprint of IGI Global).

Chapter 33
A Contemplator on Topical Image Encryption Measures

Jayanta Mondal
KIIT University, India

Debabala Swain
KIIT University, India

ABSTRACT

Images unduly assist digital communication in this aeon of multimedia. During times a person transmits confidential images over a flabby communication network, sheer protection is an accost contention to preserve the privacy of images. Encryption is one of the practice to clutch the reticence of images. Image encryption contributes a preeminent bite to charter security for secure sight data communication over the internet. Our work illustrates a survey on image encryption in different domains providing concise exordium to cryptography, moreover, furnishing the review of sundry image encryption techniques.

INTRODUCTION

Information technology in the web is proliferating without warning, causing massive users communicating via interactive media, especially; image, audio, and video. Images immerse the ample snippet of digital communication and play a consequential role in communication, for instance; military, medical agencies and diplomatic concerns (Shannon, 1949). Images, carrying significant private information, needs absolute protection during transportation or storage. In short, an image entails protection from diverse security attacks. The major motive to safeguard images is to ensure confidentiality, integrity and authenticity. Various techniques are at disposal for keeping images secure and encryption is one of them. Encryption does transform images into a cipher images mostly by assistance of a key. Later, an authorized user can recover the original image by decryption, the reverse process of encryption. This process is a part of the study called cryptology. Cryptology is the addition of cryptography; science of making ciphers, and cryptanalysis; science of breaking ciphers.

DOI: 10.4018/978-1-7998-1763-5.ch033

The field of modern cryptography provides a theoretical upheld focused around which a person can comprehend what indubitably these concerns are, the finest approach to assess practices that fancy to light up them and the means to gather conventions in whose safety one can have conviction (Kumar, Aggarwal, & Garg, 2014). Modern automated progresses have made private information by and large available. Security concerns over internet data made cryptography the field of interest for the researchers. The traditional and basic issue of cryptography is to provide secure communication over an untrusted channel. A has to send a secret message to B over an unsecured media, which can be hacked. The late forge ahead in technology, exceptionally in automation and information industry, allowed huge business for electronic interactive multimedia data through the Internet. This advancement made the web highly accessible with its contents, which encouraged obvious security problems. Digital security is maintained by some methods used to protect the sight and sound substance (Shannon, 1948). This whole picture acutely centered on cryptography.

PRELIMINARIES

Cryptography is the art or science encompassing the principles and methods of transforming an intelligible message into one that is unintelligible, and then retransforming that message back to its original form.

- **Plaintext:** Plaintext is the original intelligible message.
- **Ciphertext:** Ciphertext is the transformed message.
- **Encryption:** Encryption is the process (algorithm) for transforming a plaintext into a ciphertext.
- **Decryption:** Decryption is the reverse process of encryption, i.e. transforming the ciphertext back to plaintext.
- **Key:** Key is the most important data used by encryption algorithms, known to the both authorized parties. Encryption mechanisms relies on the key. Encryption algorithms are available for all, so, attacker's objective is to achieve the key.

Basic cryptography process for a text message at its simplest form can be described as:

Plaintext $P=[P_1, P_2, ..., P_X]$ of length X, where X belongs to finite alphabet set. The key $K=[K_1, K_2, ..., K_Y]$ of length Y. Ciphertext $C=[C_1, C_2, ..., C_Z]$ of length Z. With message P and key K the encryption algorithm creates the ciphertext $C=EK(P)$. The plaintext can be achieved by $P=DK(C)$. D being the decryption algorithm.

A cryptosystem thus can be formulated mathematically as a five tuple *(P, C, K, E, D)* where the following should satisfy:

1. P is a finite set of possible plaintext.
2. C is a finite set of possible ciphertext.
3. K, the key space, is the finite set of possible keys.
4. E is encryption rule, and, D is decryption rule.
5. $\forall k \in K, \exists e_k \in E, \exists d_k \in D$

Each $e_k: P \rightarrow C$ and $d_k: C \rightarrow P$ are functions,
Such that $\forall x \in P, d_k(e_k(x))=x$

CRYPTOGRAPHIC GOALS

The primary goals of cryptography are confidentiality, i.e. hiding information from unauthorized access, Integrity, i.e. preventing information from unauthorized modification, and, availability, i.e. information should be available to authorized users. International Telecommunication Union-Telecommunication standardization sector (ITU-T) includes authentication, nonrepudiation, and access-control as important objectives of cryptography. ITU-T provides standardized some security mechanisms to achieve security services, namely, encryption, data-integrity, digital-signature, authentication, traffic-padding, routing-control, notarization, and, access-control.

TYPES OF ENCRYPTION

Encryption is by far the best mechanism to achieve most of the security goals. Encryption algorithms are primarily classified into two categories—Symmetric key and Asymmetric key encryption.

Symmetric Encryption

In symmetric cryptography same key is used in encryption is and in decryption. Hence the key has to be distributed before sending the encrypted message. The key has the most significant role to play in symmetric cryptography as security depends straight on the essence of the key. For existing examples there are a number of symmetric key algorithms such as AES, DES (Shannon, 1949), TRIPLE DES, RC4, RC6, BLOWFISH (Shannon, 1949) available and frequently used. Symmetric algorithms can be classified into two categories; Block ciphers and Stream ciphers (Menezes, van Oorschot, & Vanstone, 1996).

In block cipher the process maps n bit blocks of plaintext to n bit blocks of ciphertext. Here the block length is denoted by n. The process can be parameterized by k (a randomly chosen key of n bits), where $k \in K$ (the key space), will transform into Vk (k bit vector). To avoid data expansion equal sized blocks of plaintext and ciphertext are used.

In stream ciphers each and every of the plaintext get encrypted one by one. The encryption transformation process changes with time. Stream ciphers are less complicated and time efficient. It can be more appropriate at times as they hardly have any error propagation. When the probability of transmission errors is high stream ciphers are proved to be more advantageous (Menezes, van Oorschot, & Vanstone, 1996). Stream ciphers are generally of two types based on the key distribution process namely, synchronous stream ciphers or self-synchronizing stream ciphers.

Asymmetric Encryption

In Asymmetric or public-key encryption the sender and the receiver uses different keys. For encryption public key is used, which is available for all, and for decryption a private key is used, which is confidential and resides with the receiver only (Menezes, Oorschot, and Vanstone, 1997). Examples of well-established public key include: ElGamal, Diffie-Hellman, Cramer-Shoup, RSA etc.

Public Key algorithms are relied on mathematical problems that presently give no accurate solution. Asymmetric encryption undoubtedly more secure but are complex and time consuming.

Properties of a Good Cryptosystem

There are two properties that a good cryptosystem must follow: diffusion and confusion (Schneier, 1996). Diffusion is the measure of change reflected on the plaintext for a slight change in the ciphertext, or vice-versa. An encryption algorithm must have a high diffusion rate. If a character of the cipher text is changed, then a significant number of characters of the plain text should change. Confusion refers to the complexity of relation of the key with the ciphertext, i.e. the key should not relate in a simple way.to be more specific, each bit/letter of the ciphertext should rely on different parts of the key.

This paper is further organized as follows in section 2 we present general guide lines about image encryption. In section 3 we survey on some recently proposed research papers, finally we conclude in section 4.

IMAGE ENCRYPTION

Challenges in Image Encryption

In the web open wide, several security issues exists with the processing and transmission of sight and sound data. Hence it is highly essential to affirm the privacy and security of the digital image being in the internet. During recent past, many image encryption techniques have been put forward. Image encryption algorithms varies from data encryption algorithms (Kaur & Singh, 2013). All existing data encryption algorithms cannot be applied straight to the multimedia contents mainly because of their large size. Encryption of digital images are different and difficult due to some inherent features of the images. Images have bulk information capability, high correlation between pixels, and data redundancy that square measure typically tough to handle like a text message. Moreover, an important feature of digital image is their less sensitivity as matched to text data, i.e. a small alteration in a single pixel value does not bother the entire original image (Khan & Shah, 2014). Therefore, efficient techniques are necessary for ultimate security of images.

Approaches Towards Image Encryption

Image encryption techniques transform the original image to encrypted image that is difficult to understand. A number of approaches exists relying on diverse features towards image encryption, each of them having different techniques, such as pixel value modification (Öztürk and Soukpinar, n.d.), chaos theory, visual image encryption (Naor and Shamir, 1995), or key less approach (Srivastava, 2012). Belonging to the image splitting or pixel modification method the image encryption techniques are classified into three main types: transposition (position permutation), substitution (value transformation) and combination of transposition and substitution techniques. The transposition techniques randomly rearranges the pixel position within the original image and generally have less safety as histogram of the encrypted image does not alter. In the value transformation algorithms, the pixel values of the original image are altered, making it more secure and efficient. Lastly, the combination carries out both substitution and transposition, and achieve high measure of security.

The other approach for protecting digital images is centered chaotic functions. Recently, various image encryption algorithms have been suggested focused on chaotic maps to deal with image encryption problems. Theoretically in technical aspect, chaos is described as when the current decides the future, but the rough present does not approximately decide the future (Matthew, 1989). Chaos theory was introduced in cryptography for its ergodicity, sensitivity-dependency on starting condition, random behavior, complex structure and control parameters. Chaotic techniques give excellent mixture of high security, lesser time and computational overheads (Pareek, Patidar and Sud, 2006). For multimedia content encryption those ciphers are only granted efficient, which takes less time and provides absolute security. Chaos theory based modern algorithms are such ciphers.

Visual Cryptography is the approach where encryption of visual information like images, is done in such a way that decryption can be performed by human visual systems without high computational efficiency. Simple algorithms are performed without the necessity of complex computations. Concerning security problems it provides good amount of certainty against mediocre level of cryptanalytic attacks. Images are encrypted to split the original image into a fixed number of shares using a simple algorithm. At the time of decryption all the shares are required. Without a single share the whole image cannot be recovered. In some specific areas, a number of authorities follow this approach for image security; most importantly military and security services (Rakhunde & Nikose, 2014).

In mixed approach an image is first split into random shares with the help of using some kind of encryption key then pixel distribution happens. It includes some traditional encryption technique and visual cryptography together. Generally a keyless approach is applied for image share distribution. This approach involves low computation cost and keyless management offers a fresh approach (Malik, Sardana, & Jaya, 2012).

Spatial and Frequency Domain

In spatial domain method, the pixel comprising of image specifics are acknowledged and different methods are put in application straight on these pixels (Khan & Shah, 2014). The image processing procedure in the spatial domain can be formulated as

$$g(x,y) = T[f(x,y)],$$

where, the input image is represented as $f(x,y)$, $g(x,y)$ represents the processed output image, and, T is the operation on f performed on a neighborhood of (x,y).

The operation (T) also can be performed on multiple images at a time. In spatial domain, an alteration in position in the image does reflect a straight change in the scene-position. Distances between the pixels in the image correspond to actual distances in the scene. The frequency that changes image values is defined as the number of pixels periodically repeating a cycle.

In frequency domain every image value at a given position stands for the variation of distances over that position. Here, the change of position gives the rate of change in spatial frequency in the spatial domain image. High frequency components correspond to edges where as low frequency components correlates with the smooth regions in an image (Khan & Shah, 2014).

Spatial domain trades in with images as it is, where, the pixel-values changes against scenes. Whereas the frequency domain reflects the rate of pixel-value change spatial domain.

In some recent techniques hybrid domain (frequency and time domain) system is proposed to achieve better security.

Full Encryption and Partial Encryption

Information privacy is an important factor of image encryption. Privacy of the encrypted data correctly balanced in computational time and resource of the encryption technique will be the hard challenge worth achieving in image encryption. These issues have been differentiated in some works extending across the spatial domain (Nien et al., 2009; Rhouma, Arroyo, and Belghith, 2009; Ahmad & Alam, 2009; Wei, Fen-lin, Xinl, and Yebin, 2010; Kamali, Hossein, Shakerian, and Hedayati, 2010; Z, L, and Z, 2010; Rodriguez-Sahagun, Mercado-Sanchez, Lopez-Mancilla, Jaimes-Reategui, and Garcia-Lopez, 2010; Mastan, Sathishkumar, and Bagan, 2014; Pareek, Narendra and Patidar, 2011; Abugharsa & Almangush, 2011; Yadav, Beg, and Tripathi, 2013), frequency domain (Sinha and Singh, 2013; Zhou, Wang, Gong, Chen, and Yang, 2012; Aburturab, 2012; He, Cao, and Lu, 2013; Chen, Du, Liu, and Yang, 2013) and the hybrid domain (Yu, Zhe, Haibing, Wenjie, and Yunpeng, 2010; El-Latif, Niu, and Amin, 2012) techniques in full encryption schemes, where the full image is encrypted for privacy preservation (Jawad1 and Sulong, 2013).

Generally multimedia content security schemes are called fully layered, the entire content is encrypted. Selective encryption or partial encryption is a process which only encrypts a part of a sight and sound data. It includes encryption of a subset of the data. With the ability of partial encryption, various targets could be achieved. The selective encryption scheme unlike the full encryption scheme, encrypts solely significant parts of the image. The fundamental worth of the partial encryption technique will be that it can offer the exact security and computational needs without tradeoffs. Huge research (Jawad1 and Sulong, 2013) has been carried out centered around selective encryption. Some of the work on varied domain; spatial (Rao, Mitra, and Prasanna, 2006; Wong & Bishop, 2007; Oh, Yang, & KH, 2010; Steffi & Sharma, 2011; Parameshachari and Soyjaudah, 2012; Kumar, 2012; Rodrigues, Puech, and Bors, 2006; Ou, Sur, and Rhee, 2007), frequency (Yekkala, Udupa, Bussa, and Madhavan, 2007; Brahimi, Bessalah, Tarabet, and Kholladi, 2008; Krishnamoorthi and Malarchelvi, 2008; Kulkarni, Raman, and Gupta, 2008; Younis, Abdalla, and Abdalla, 2009; M. and Agaian, 2010; Sasidharan and Philip, 2011; Kuppusamy and Thamodaran, 2012; Munir, 2012; Taneja, Raman, and Gupta, 2011; Parameshachari, Soyjaudah, and Devi, 2013), and, hybrid (Kumar, Aggarwal, & Garg, 2014; Shannon, 1949), noted for reference.

Evaluation Parameters for Image Encryption Schemes

1. **Correlation Coefficient:** The correlation coefficient assesses the level of equivalence in two images. Correlation within one image is termed as self-correlation. The self-correlation of neighboring pixel for a relevant image is consistently lofty as the value of neighboring pixel is near to each other. The correlation analysis calculated on two diagonally adjoining, horizontally adjoining and vertically adjoining pixels of encrypted image as well as original image (Ruisong, 2011). Correlation coefficient is again used to measure the quality of cryptosystem. An acceptable encryption algorithm conceals all features of the actual image transforming the image to uncorrelated. When correlation coefficient is one, then the original image and cipher-image are totally identical. If it is zero or nearing zero then they are completely different.

2. **Entropy:** Entropy of an image gives details about the image itself. It points out the degree of uncertainty of a communication system. It is the randomness feature of the image (Shannon, 1949). Mathematically entropy can be formulated as –

$$E\left(s\right) = \sum_{i=0}^{2N-1} p\left(s_i\right) \log\left(\frac{1}{p\left(s_i\right)}\right)$$

whenever the value of the entropy in a method gets closer to 8(ideal value), the predictability becomes less and the security improves (Kaleem and Ahmed, 2007).

3. **Compression Friendliness:** Image compression plays an important part in image security. Image compression lessens the need of transmission bandwidth and repository space. Diverse compression approaches are used, focused on the entropy theory. When the encryption does not influence the compression effectiveness largely nor does it instigate extra data then it can be called compression friendly (Lian, 2008).

4. **Encryption Quality:** The quality of encryption is measured by calculating three factors Maximum Deviation (zaid and El-Fishawy, 2009), Irregular Deviation (Noaman & Alla, 2008), and, Deviation from the Uniform Histogram (Ahmed & Ahmed, 2012).

High maximum deviation is the better for the quality of encryption. A good encryption technique must randomize the input pixels in a same way. Irregular deviation is relied on how much deviation causes irregularity on encrypted image. It calculates the irregular deviation of pixels from the basic position. A good encryption algorithm has irregular deviation and nears to uniform distribution. If the histogram of the encrypted image after encryption is uniform then the algorithm is regarded as a good encryption technique.

5. **Diffusion Characteristic:** A little alteration in original image should change cipher-text image significantly. This characteristics is known as avalanche effect. Number of Pixel Change Rate (NPCR) (Ahmed & Ahmed, 2012) and Unified Average Change Intensity (UACI) (Mohamed & Kachouri, 2011) are the means to measure Diffusion Characteristic. Higher the value of NPCR and UACI, better is the algorithm. Mathematically they can be formulated as –

$$\text{NCPR} = \frac{\sum_{i,j} D\left(i,j\right)}{M \times N} \times 100\%$$

$$\text{UACI} = \frac{1}{M \times N}\left[\sum_{i,j} \frac{C_1\left(i,j\right) - C_2\left(i,j\right)}{255}\right] \times 100\%$$

where *M, N, $C_1(i,j)$* and *$C_2(i,j)$* respectively represents width of the plain-text image, height of the plain-text image, gray scale value of encrypted image C_1 and the gray scale value of encrypted image C_2.

6. **Key Space Analysis:** Key is the primary need for all kind of cryptology. The ultimate security of the system at the end depends on the key (Forouzan, 2011; Alvarez & Li, 2006). Therefore, larger the key space, better the security. The algorithm should be sensitive on its key. If a small change happens in the initial key, the encryption/decryption should result in drastic difference.

7. **Mean Square Error:** The mean square error measures the difference between the cipher image and the original image. The MSE value should be higher for better image security. MSE can be mathematically defined (Alvarez & Li, 2006) by –

$$\text{MSE} = \frac{1}{s \times s} \sum \sum (X_{ij} - Y_{ij})^2$$

S, X_{ij}, and Y_{ij} respectively represents size of the image and parameter values, original image, and cipher-image. The difference between two images will be evident when MSE>30dB.

LITERATURE REVIEW

A First Approach on an RGB Image Encryption

In Kumar, Mishra, and Sharma (2014), M Kumar, D.C. Mishra, and R.K. Sharma proposed a foremost step towards a new image encryption centered on RGB unscrambling using TSRMAC. For achieving high security during image transmission the random matrix affine cipher (RMAC) is being used in two steps combining with Discrete Wavelength Transformation (DWT). The new feature proposed is to introduce RMAC parameters in key distribution. This approach suits well foe large size images with a huge key space. Though affine cipher is highly regarded for text encryption but the proposed RMAC is specifically well suited for images in matrix format. The total number of choices for RMAC parameters get increased as it's done in two phases, makes the encryption stronger as well as decryption difficult for attackers. For decryption the correct number of RMAC parameters are essential with the right key. The proposed approach is highly sensitive on the key space. The security analysis proves this approach efficient with uniform histogram and low MSE value.

Multiple-Image Encryption Based on Optical Wavelet Transform and Multichannel Fractional Fourier Transform

In 2014, Kong et al, suggested a new image encryption strategy for multiple image encryption based on optical wavelet transform (OWT) and the multichannel fractional Fourier transform (Mfrft) is proposed in 2014. The technique enabled to fully utilize the multi-determination deterioration of wavelet transform (WT) and multichannel handling of Mfrft. The scheme makes use of the specified properties that can efficiently handle the encryption of multi-image and single image. Each and every image gets a unique autonomous key and their fractional request for transmission, after completion of the encryption process. Experimental testing of scrambled impacts has been found satisfactory. Furthermore, the exclusive effect of wavelet transformation and execution order of the multiple images are thoroughly examined with the application and examination of multichannel fractional Fourier transform proved to be proficient too.

Numerical reenactment substantiates the applicability of the theory and proves that the complication of insufficient limit is better fathomed. Therefore, the flexibility of techniques increases. In the proposed plan the authors used a straightforward opto-electronic mixed device for better understanding of the strategy. The proposed work achieves high security, increasing key sensitivity and efficiently overcomes the challenge of real-time image security, reducing the encryption time using multiple images at a time.

Interference-Based Multiple-Image Encryption by Phase-Only Mask Multiplexing with High Quality Retrieved Images

In 2014, Y Qin, H Jiang, and Q Gong in 2014, proposed a manageable advanced method fundamentally rooted on optical intrusion concept for multiple-image encryption. The particulars of miscellaneous images can be numerically encoded into two phase-only masks multiplexing (POMs) unaccompanied by some iterative process, and the secure keys, essential for decryption are achieved logically. The prosed work can be seen as the extension of (Qin & Gong, 2011), where similar technique is used for multiple image encryption, but the cross-talk noise has gravely demeaned the standard of the recovered images. Even though some digital techniques, like filtering, may be used to subdue the cross-talk noise, the standard is still unsatisfactory. Hence, its use is narrowed to binary image encryption. Therefore, it is wise developing new techniques that can utterly remove the cross-talk noise. In a current work (Wang, Guo, Lei, & Zhou, 2013), also primarily based on the interference-based encryption scheme has been proposed with a little advancement on multiple-image encryption, although the encrypted images are complex images, making decryption process much complex. Moreover, the degree of security achieved using POMs is also compromised. In this proposed work under the IBE scheme centered on phase only mask multiplexing is resistant to cross-talk noise and the secret keys which are also POMs increases the security level. Hence, for real time multiple grayscale image encryption this proposed approach is well suited, providing higher security through POMs, time saving without any iterative algorithm, no cross-talk noise and silhouette problem, and, with a fast decryption mechanism.

Novel Image Compression–Encryption Hybrid Algorithm Based on Key-Controlled Measurement Matrix in Compressive Sensing

In 2014, Nanrun Zhoua, Aidi Zhang, Fen Zheng, and, Lihua Gong, in the year 2014, proposed a new hybrid technique combining image compression and image encryption. The proposed algorithm is rooted on compressive sensing and random pixel exchanging. Compressive sensing (CS) is a brand-new sampling and then reconstruction process that finishes sampling and compressing side by side at the same time. Severel researchers have worked on CS and implemented their proposals in recent past. But all the CS-based encryption algorithms so far has followed the full measurement matrix as the key that makes the key colossal for distribution and memorization. Both the compression and encryption techniques in a few proposed methods are unable to execute at the same time. The authors proposed the concept of constructing a circulant matrix where the key will control the measurement matrix to prevail over these issues. The proposed algorithm divides the original image into four blocks for compression and encryption. Further, the changed blocks go through a scrambling process. The scrambling process is performed based on random pixel exchanging process, which is supervised by the random matrices.

The proposed algorithm is well-suited for square-sized images. The whole encryption-decryption process goes through five steps. Firstly, the image is divided into four blocks. Then two measurement matrices are constructed with keys for two pairs of non-neighboring blocks. Thereafter, the adjoining blocks are scrambled, guided by two random matrices to get the cipher image. For decryption the inverse scrambling is carried out in the reverse order prior to the utilization of SL0 algorithm for decryption and decompression.

The measurement matrices in CS in this proposed work are created by using the circulant matrices and availing logistic maps to supervise the primary row vectors of the circulant matrices. Simulation outcomes show the efficacy of the work. By introducing the random pixel exchanging and binding the random matrices with the measurement matrices higher security is achieved and throughput is increased by its compression friendliness.

Image Scrambling Using Non Sinusoidal Transform and Key Based Scrambling Technique

In 2014, Kekre et al, proposed a hybrid image encryption scheme in the year 2014, based on image scrambling which includes an amalgamation of spatial domain and frequency domain. The authors have focused on creating a robust and versatile technique for image encryption which leads them to combine spatial domain and frequency domain as the factors in transform domain provide much robustness compared to spatial domain.

The work goes through a survey of different hybrid methods then proposes a new image scrambling scheme in the transform domain. A detailed implementation has been made utilizing four different non sinusoidal transformation techniques. The used transformation techniques are Walsh (Kekre & Patil, 2008), Slant (Pratt, Chen, & Welch, 1974), Haar (Kekre, Thepade, & Maloo, 2010), and Kekre (Kekre et al., 2010) transforms. Different mode of transformations such as row transforms, column transforms, and full transforms are tried on each of the four transforms. A diverse sequence generation algorithm is used for the scramble-process based on plaintext image-size. All existing scrambling methods can be applied on the proposed scheme, which makes it a different, versatile and effective technique for image security. The experimental results for all four non sinusoidal transformation schemes show efficiency and almost similar energy distribution. Among the four applied transforms, Kekre transform is proved to be the best in terms of security, robustness, and energy distribution.

Threshold Visual Cryptographic Scheme with Meaningful Shares

In 2014, Shyong Jian Shyu in 2014 has proposed an effective and advanced method for gray-scale image encryption on Visual Cryptography (VC) domain. In VC (Naor & Shamir, 1995) a number of participants shares a confidential image where a threshold exists, out of the number of Visual Cryptographic Schemes (VCS) should be able to part the original image into same number of shares (diverse transparencies) that are accordingly allotted to each members in a way that a group containing minimum threshold number of members can recover the image by superimposing their shares, however, any lesser number of shares than the threshold achieves no meaningful data justifying the purpose of encryption. The decryption method is totally centered on human visual recognition of the superimposition of the required number of transparencies. Therefore, no complex calculation or digital computing is necessary, which makes VC dissimilar from other mainstream cryptographic schemes.

A viable VCS encrypts each and every pixels in the plaintext image into sub pixels, this process is termed as pixel expansion, in all shares based on a random column permutation. This permutation process is conducted based on basis matrices in such a way that the superimposition of threshold number of shares or more than that gives the original image but less number of shares do not reveal any clue about the confidential image. The challenges in making a practical VCS are to minimize pixel expansion and to design applicable basis matrices with lesser complexity.

This proposed work concentrates on defining and constructing a threshold VCS where the pixel expansion can be minimum and the superimposed image of threshold shares gives the original image information. In Shyu and Jiang (2013) a successful technique is implemented based on threshold access structure utilizing Integer Linear Programming (ILP). The author has made some advancements on that work. This proposed work provides a better implementation of the ILP that can efficiently constructs the basis matrices, besides giving the formal definition of Visual Cryptographic Schemes with Meaningful Shares (VCS-MS).

An Image Encryption Algorithm Utilizing Julia Sets and Hilbert Curves

In Sun et al., (2014), a novel image encryption algorithm combining Julia sets and Hilbert curves is proposed by Yuanyuan Sun, Lina Chen, Rudan Xu, and Ruiqing Kong in 2014. The approach uses Julia sets' parameters to originate a unusual order as the primary keys and acquires the resulting encryption keys by clambering the beginning keys by the Hilbert curve. The encrypted image is acquired by modulo arithmetic and diffuse operation. In the proposed algorithm, the Julia set is clambered in bit-level through the Hilbert curve to amplify the key sensitivity. The diffusion process is instrumented to counter cryptanalytic attacks.

Along a thorough survey of the tested outcomes, the following deductions are achieved:

1. Plentiful Julia-like images lessens the key storage, which are easily generated by a few parameters. Security of the encryption algorithm can be enhanced by a large extent by the chaotic behavior of the Julia images, giving the key absolute sensitivity. The experimental research shows the key sensitivity achieves 10215.
2. Security against attacks is extraordinarily increases with highly sensitive immense key space provided by the diffusion process.
3. The algorithm succeeds to achieve the ideal value as per cipher image entropy is concerned, resulting in good security, uniform distribution, and randomization of the cipher-image.

A Block-Based Image Encryption Algorithm in Frequency Domain Using Chaotic Permutation

In 2014, Rinaldi Munir in 2014 proposed a new algorithm for Images encryption in frequency domain based on chaotic permutation for achieving robustness against any image processing attacks. For this purpose the original image is first transformed and encrypted in 8×8 blocks. After encryption some image processing based modifications were made on the cipher image to check the robustness of the image. The author has suggested encryption in favor of frequency domain to resist general image processing functions. Therefore, when a modification is targeted on the encrypted image, only the low frequency pixels get affected a little. Discrete Cosine Transform (DCT) is used for the image transformation process. Each block is encrypted using chaos based permutation technique.

The algorithm proposed is a small modification of an existing simple image transformation algorithm. A JPEG grey scale image of $N \times N$ pixels is considered for encryption. The original image is split into blocks of size 8×8 pixels and a DCT is applied for each bock. Then, DCT coefficients of each block are scrambled, except the upper leftmost element, by iterating Arnold Cat Map m times. The upper leftmost element coefficient is not encrypted because it carries significant visual information. Finally, IDCT is applied on each block to get the ciphertext image. Experimental results shows the cipher image is still recognizable, therefore the author randomized the pixels of plain-image before encryption using Arnold Cat Map twice, the first for scrambling the pixels of plain-image in spatial domain, and the second for scrambling the DCT coefficients of each block 8×8, to overcome the weakness of the simple algorithm.

A Novel Image Encryption Scheme Based on Hyper Chaotic Systems and Fuzzy Cellular Automata

In Wei, Fen-lin, Xinl, and Yebin (2010), a new image encryption scheme based on hyper chaotic system and Fuzzy Cellular Automata is proposed by Samaneh Zamani et.al, in 2014. Chaos theory has an immense impact on recent image encryption scenario. Hyper chaotic system has been suggested in this paper, as it has more complex dynamical characteristics than chaos systems. Therefore, it suits safe sight data encryption schemes. In this technique the authors have made a worthy research to enhance the computational efficiency besides providing high security by using four hyper chaotic systems. The first level of security is provided by the transposition of pixels, bit prior to that, the original image is parted in four pieces, each having its own hyper chaotic system. Two neighbor parted-images are considered first for the pixel transposition centered on the sequence numbers generated by the different hyper chaotic systems. Fuzzy logic is used in the encryption process. The algorithm is based on right neighbor theory. For this process five numbers if one dimensional non-uniform Fuzzy Cellular Automata is used. For different cell types (odd/even), two different encryption methods are used. The implementation results, on a few USC-SIPI database images, shows that the proposed method achieves great security level providing confusion, diffusion, and key sensitivity.

Image Encryption Using Chaotic Maps in Hybrid Domain

In 2014, S. Ramahrishnan, B. Elakkiya, R. Geetha, P. Vasuki, S. Mahalingam in 2014 proposed a new chaos based encryption in hybrid domain seeking more security. Pseudo random images are obtained utilizing chaotic maps for secure encryption. In the proposed system two transformation process are used for two domains. Discrete Wavelength Transformation (DWT), for time and frequency domain, and, Discrete Fourier Transform (DFT), for frequency domain. To compute different parts of time domain signal varied in different frequencies DWT is used. In encryption process the plain image is decomposed using DWT, then, divided into seven sub-bands, each of which are applied to DFT. Thus, encryption is performed in two steps: Transformation by DFT, using tent map, and, Substitution by DWT which uses Bernoulli map. The system is analyzed through rigorous performance test. The tests on the encrypted image shows that the proposed method produce a uniform histogram, a correlation coefficient of 0.024, MSE value around 17952, NCPR value of 100, and UACI is 46.88. With all these result this proposed technique should be granted as a good Image Encryption method.

CONCLUSION

In this paper, we made a theoretical survey over image encryption. We reviewed from the beginning, starting from the basic idea, we have gone through the several approaches to diverse existing image encryption techniques in different domain, lastly we reviewed some of the most recently proposed work on total and selective image encryption approaches under spatial, frequency and hybrid domains. In the route of this survey, a few remarks were made, such as, full encryption schemes, chaos based algorithms ensures high level of security of encrypted data, though less time is spent in selective encryption process.

Conclusively, from the literature review, by a thorough theoretical analysis we can conclude all the recent proposed techniques are efficient on their own goals, some providing ultimate security and some are made for enhance robustness. Almost every current method relies on the chaotic nature and the hybrid schemes for maximum security, efficiency, and, robustness.

REFERENCES

Abd El-Latif, A., Niu, X., & Amin, M. (2012, October). A new image cipher in time and frequency domains. *Optics Communications*, *285*(21–22), 4241–4251. doi:10.1016/j.optcom.2012.06.041

Abugharsa, A. B., & Almangush, H. (2011). A New Image Encryption Approach using Block-Based on Shifted Algorithm. *International Journal of Computer Science and Network Security*, *11*(12), 123–130.

Abuturab, M. R. (2012, May). Securing color information using Arnold transform in gyrator transform domain. *Optics and Lasers in Engineering*, *50*(5), 772–779. doi:10.1016/j.optlaseng.2011.12.006

Ahmad, M., & Alam, M. (2009). A New Algorithm of Encryption and Decryption of Images Using Chaotic Mapping. *International Journal on Computer Science and Engineering*, *2*(1), 46–50.

Ahmed & Ahmed. (2012). Efficency Analysis and Security Evaluation Parameters of Image Encryption schemes. *International Journal of Video & Image Processing And Network Security, 12.*

Alvarez & Li. (2006). Some Basic Cryptographic requirement for Chaos-Based Cryptosystems. *International Journal of Bifurcation and Chaos, 16.*

Bd, P., Sunjiv Soyjaudah, K., & Devi, K. A, S. (2013). Secure Transmission of an Image using Partial Encryption based Algorithm. *International Journal of Computers and Applications*, *63*(16), 33–36. doi:10.5120/10553-5746

Brahimi, Bessalah, Tarabet, & Kholladi. (2008). A new selective encryption technique of JPEG2000 code stream for medical images transmission. *5th International Multi-Conference on Systems, Signals and Devices*, 1–4.

Chen, H., Du, X., Liu, Z., & Yang, C. (2013, June). Color image encryption based on the affine transform and gyrator transform. *Optics and Lasers in Engineering*, *51*(6), 768–775. doi:10.1016/j.optlaseng.2013.01.016

Flayh, Parveen, & Ahson. (2009). Wavelet based partial image encryption. *International Multimedia, Signal Processing and Communication Technologies (IMSPCT)*, 32–35.

Forouzan. (2011). *Cryptography and Network Security*. McGraw Hill Education Private Limited.

He, Cao, & Lu. (2012). Color image encryption based on orthogonal composite grating and double random phase encoding technique. *Optik - International Journal for Light and Electron Optics, 123*(17), 1592–1596.

Jawad, & Sulong. (2013). A Review of Color Image Encryption Techniques. *International Journal of Computer Science Issues, 10*(6).

JiangShyuand. (2013, May). General constructions for threshold multiple-secret visual cryptographic schemes. *IEEE Trans. Inf. Forensics Security, 8*(5), 733–743. doi:10.1109/TIFS.2013.2250432

Kaleem & Ahmed. (n.d.). Implementation of RC% block cipher algorithm for image cryptosystem. *International Journal of Information Technology, 3*.

Kamali, M. R. (2010). A New Modified Version of Advanced Encryption Standard Based Algorithm for Image Encryption. *International Conference on Electronics and Information Engineering (ICEIE), 1*, 141–145.

Kaur, R., & Singh, E. K. (2013). Image Encryption Techniques : A Selected Review. *Journal of Computer Engineering, 9*(6), 80–83.

Kekre, H. B. (2014). Image Scrambling Using Non Sinusoidal Transform And Key Based Scrambling Technique. *International Journal of Computers & Technology, 12*(8), 3809–3822.

Kekre, H. B., & Kavita, B. (2008). Walsh Transform over color distribution of Rows and Columns of Images for CBIR. *International Conference on Content Based Image Retrieval (ICCBIR)*. PES Institute of Technology.

Kekre, Thepade, & Maloo. (2010). Query by Image Content using Color-Texture Features Extracted from Haar Wavelet Pyramid. *IJCA*, 52-60.

Kekre, Thepade, Athawale, Shah, Verlekar, & Shirke. (2010). Energy Compaction and Image Splitting for Image Retrieval using Kekre Transform over Row and Column Feature Vectors. *International Journal of Computer Science and Network Security, 10*(1).

Khan, M., & Shah, T. (n.d.). *A Literature Review on Image Encryption Techniques*. Springer. DOI . doi:10.100713319-014-0029-0

Kong, D., & Shen, X. (2014). Multiple-image encryption based on optical wavelet transform and multichannel fractional Fourier transform. *Optics & Laser Technology, 57*, 343–349. doi:10.1016/j.optlastec.2013.08.013

Krishnamoorthi, R., & Malarchelvi, P. D. S. K. (2008). Selective Combinational Encryption of Gray Scale Images using Orthogonal Polynomials based Transformation. *International Journal of Computer Science and Network Security, 8*(5), 195–204.

Kulkarni, N. S., Raman, B., & Gupta, I. (2008). Selective encryption of multimedia images. *32th National Systems Conference*, 467–470.

Kumar, M., Aggarwal, A., & Garg, A. (2014). A Review on Various Digital Image Encryption Techniques and Security Criteria. *International Journal of Computer Applications, 96*(13).

Kumar, M., Mishra, D. C., & Sharma, R. K. (2014). A first approach on an RGB image encryption. *Optics and Lasers in Engineering, 52*, 27–34. doi:10.1016/j.optlaseng.2013.07.015

Kumar, P. (2012). RC4 Enrichment Algorithm Approach for Selective Image Encryption. *International Journal of Computer Science & Communication Networks, 2*(2), 181–189.

Kuppusamy, K., & Thamodaran, K. (2012). Optimized partial image encryption scheme using PSO. *International Conference on Pattern Recognition, Informatics and Medical Engineering*, 236–241. 10.1109/ICPRIME.2012.6208350

Lian, S. (2008). *Multimedia content encryption: techniques and applications*. CRC Press.

Mastan, J. M. K., Sathishkumar, G. A., & Bagan, K. B. (2011). A Color Image Encryption Technique Based on a Substitution Permutation Network. *Advances in Computing and Communications, 4*, 524–533. doi:10.1007/978-3-642-22726-4_54

Matthew, R. (1989). On the derivation of a chaotic encryption algorithm. *Cryptologia, 8*(1), 29–42. doi:10.1080/0161-118991863745

Menezes, A., van Oorschot, P., & Vanstone, S. (1996). *Applied cryptography*. Boca Raton, FL: CRC. doi:10.1201/9781439821916

Menezes, A. J., Oorschot, P. C. V., & Vanstone, S. A. (1997). *Handbook of applied cryptography*. Boca Raton, FL: CRC Press.

Mohamed, Zaibi, & Kachouri. (2011). Implementation of RC5 and RC6 block ciphers on digital images. *8th International Multi-Conference*. IEEE.

Munir. (2014). *A Block-based Image Encryption Algorithm in Frequency Domain using Chaotic Permutation*. IEEE.

Munir, R. (2012). Robustness Analysis of Selective Image Encryption Algorithm Based on Arnold Cat Map Permutation. *Proceedings of 3rd Makassar International Conference on Electrical Engineering and Informatics*, 1–5.

Naor, M., & Shamir, A. (1995). Visual cryptography. *Advances in Cryptography: Eurocrypt'94*.

Naor, M., & Shamir, A. (1995). Visual cryptography. *Proc. EUROCRYPT'94, 50*, 1–12.

Nien, H. H., Huang, W. T., Hung, C. M., Chen, S. C., Wu, S. Y., Huang, C. K., & Hsu, Y. H. (2009). Hybrid image encryption using multi-chaos-system. *7th International Conference on Information, Communications and Signal Processing (ICICS)*, 1–5.

Noaman & Alla. (2008). Encryption Quality Analysis of the RCBC Block Cipher Compared with RC6 and RC5 Algorithms. *International Journal of Imaging, 10*.

Oh, Yang, & Chon. (2010). A Selective Encryption Algorithm Based on AES for Medical Information. *Healthcare Informatics Research, 16*(1), 22–9.

Ou, Y., Sur, C., & Rhee, K. H. (2007). Region-Based Selective Encryption for Medical Imaging. *1st Annual International Workshop*, 4427(4613), 62–73.

Parameshachari, B. D., & Soyjaudah, K. M. S. (2012). Analysis and Comparison of Fully Layered Image Encryption Techniques and Partial Image Encryption Techniques. *Communications in Computer and Information Science*, 292, 599–604. doi:10.1007/978-3-642-31686-9_70

Pareek, Narendra, & Patidar. (2011). A Symmetric Encryption Scheme for Colour BMP Images. *International Journal of Computer Applications in Special Issue on Network Security and Cryptography*, 42–46.

Pareek, N. K., Patidar, V., & Sud, K. K. (2006). Image encryption using chaotic logistic map. *Image and Vision Computing*, 24(9), 926–934. doi:10.1016/j.imavis.2006.02.021

Pratt, Chen, & Welch. (1974). Slant Transform Image Coding. *IEEE Trans. Comm., 22*.

Qin, Y., & Gong, Q. (2013). Interference-based multiple-image encryption with silhouette removal by position multiplexing. *Applied Optics*, 52(17), 3987–3992. doi:10.1364/AO.52.003987 PMID:23759846

Qin, Y., Jiang, H., & Gong, Q. (2014). Interference-based multiple-image encryption by phase-only mask multiplexing with high quality retrieved images. *Optics and Lasers in Engineering*, 62, 95–102. doi:10.1016/j.optlaseng.2014.05.010

Rakhunde, S. M., & Nikose, A. A. (2014). New Approach for Reversible Data Hiding Using Visual Cryptography. *Sixth International Conference on Computational Intelligence and Communication Networks*. 10.1109/CICN.2014.180

Ramahrishnan, S., Elakkiya, B., Geetha, R., Vasuki, P., & Mahalingam, S. (2014). Image encryption using chaotic maps in hybrid domain. *International Journal of Communication and Computer Technologies*, 2(5), 44–48.

Rao, Y. V. S., Mitra, A., & Prasanna, S. R. M. (2006). A Partial Image Encryption Method with Pseudo Random Sequences. Lecture Notes in Computer Science: vol. 4332. International Commission on Intervention and State Sovereignty (ICISS), (pp. 315–325). Berlin: Springer.

Rhouma, Arroyo, & Belghith. (2009). A new color image cryptosystem based on a piecewise linear chaotic map. *6th International Multi-Conference on Systems, Signals and Devices*, 1–6.

Rodrigues, J. M., Puech, W., & Bors, A. G. (2006). A Selective Encryption for Heterogeneous Color JPEG Images Based on VLC and AES Stream Cipher. *3rd European Conference on Colour in Graphics, Imaging and Vision (CGIV'06)*, 1, 34–39.

Rodriguez-Sahagun, M. T., Mercado-Sanchez, J. B., Lopez-Mancilla, D., Jaimes-Reategui, R., & Garcia-Lopez, J. H. (2010). Image Encryption Based on Logistic Chaotic Map for Secure Communications. *IEEE Electronics, Robotics and Automotive Mechanics Conference*, 319–324. 10.1109/CERMA.2010.44

Ruisong, Ye. (2011). *An Image Encryption Scheme with Efficient Permutation and Diffusion Processes*. SpringerVerlag Berlin Heidelberg.

Sasidharan, S., & Philip, D. S. (2011). A Fast Partial Encryption Scheme with Wavelet Transform and RC4. *International Journal of Advances in Engineering & Technology*, 1(4), 322–331.

Schneier, B. (1996). *Applied cryptography: protocols algorithms and source code in C*. New York: Wiley.

Shannon, C. E. (1948). The mathematical theory of communication. *The Bell System Technical Journal*, *27*(3), 379–423. doi:10.1002/j.1538-7305.1948.tb01338.x

Shannon, C. E. (1949). Communication theory of secrecy systems. *The Bell System Technical Journal*, *28*(4), 656–715. doi:10.1002/j.1538-7305.1949.tb00928.x

Shyu, S. J. (2014, December). Threshold Visual Cryptographic Scheme with Meaningful Shares. *IEEE Signal Processing Letters*, *21*(12), 1521–1525. doi:10.1109/LSP.2014.2344093

Siddharth, Anjali, & Jaya. (2012). A Keyless Approach to Image Encryption. *International Conference on Communication Systems and Network Technologies*. IEEE.

Sinha, A., & Singh, K. (n.d.). *Image encryption using fractional Fourier transform and 3D Jigsaw transform*. Retrieved from http://pdfworld.net/pdf-2013/Image-encryption-using-fractionalFourier-transform-and-3D-Jigsaw-transform-pdf.pdf

Srivastava, A. (2012, June). A survey report on Different Techniques of Image Encryption. *International Journal of Emerging Technology and Advanced Engineering*, *2*(6), 163–167.

Steffi, M. A. A., & Sharma, D. (2011). Comparative Study of Partial Encryption of Images and Video. *International Journal of Modern Engineering Research*, *1*(1), 179–185.

Sun, Y., Chen, L., Xu, R., & Kong, R. (2014, January). Yuanyuan Sun1*, Lina Chen2, Rudan Xu1, Ruiqing Kong1, "An Image Encryption Algorithm Utilizing Julia Sets and Hilbert Curves. *PLoS ONE*, *9*(1), e84655. doi:10.1371/journal.pone.0084655 PMID:24404181

Taneja, N., Raman, B., & Gupta, I. (2011, March). Combinational domain encryption for still visual data. *Multimedia Tools and Applications*, *59*(3), 775–793. doi:10.100711042-011-0775-4

Wang, Q., Guo, Q., Lei, L., & Zhou, J. (2013). Multiple-image encryption based on interference principle and phase-only mask multiplexing in Fresnel transform domain. *Applied Optics*, *52*(28), 6849–6857. doi:10.1364/AO.52.006849 PMID:24085198

Wei, W., Fen-lin, L., Xinl, G., & Yebin, Y. (2010). Color image encryption algorithm based on hyper chaos. *2nd IEEE International Conference on Information Management and Engineering*, 271–274. 10.1109/ICIME.2010.5477430

Wong, A., & Bishop, W. (2007). Backwards Compatible, MultiLevel Region-of-Interest (ROI) Image Encryption Architecture with Biometric Authentication. *International Conference on Signal Processing and Multimedia Applications*, 324 – 329.

Yadav, R. S., Beg, M. H. D. R., & Tripathi, M. M. (2013). Image Encryption Techniques: A Critical Comparison. *International Journal of Computer Science Engineering and Information Technology Research*, *3*(1), 67–74.

Yekkala, A. K., Udupa, N., Bussa, N., & Madhavan, C. E. V. (2007). Lightweight Encryption for Images. *International Conference on Consumer Electronics*, 3, 1–2.

Younis, H. A., Abdalla, T. Y., & Abdalla, A. Y. (2009). Vector Quantization Techniques For Partial Encryption of Waveletbased Compressed Digital Images. *Iraqi Journal of Electrical and Electronic Engineering*, *5*(1), 74–89.

Yu, Z., Zhe, Z., Haibing, Y., Wenjie, P., & Yunpeng, Z. (2010). A chaos-based image encryption algorithm using wavelet transform. *2nd International Conference on Advanced Computer Control*, *2*(4), 217–222.

Zamani, Javanmard, Jafarzadeh, & Zamani. (2014). *A Novel Image Encryption Scheme Based on Hyper Chaotic Systems and Fuzzy Cellular Automata.* IEEE.

Zhou, N., Wang, Y., Gong, L., Chen, X., & Yang, Y. (2012, October). Novel color image encryption algorithm based on the reality preserving fractional Mellin transform. *Optics & Laser Technology*, *44*(7), 2270–2281. doi:10.1016/j.optlastec.2012.02.027

Zhou, N., Zhang, A., Zhen, F., & Gong, L. (2014). Novel image compression–encryption hybrid algorithm based on key-controlled measurement matrix in compressive sensing. *Optics & Laser Technology*, *62*, 152–160. doi:10.1016/j.optlastec.2014.02.015

This research was previously published in Security Breaches and Threat Prevention in the Internet of Things edited by N. Jeyanthi and R. Thandeeswaran; pages 189-212, copyright year 2017 by Information Science Reference (an imprint of IGI Global).

Index

A

Access control 143, 147-148, 158, 274, 374, 474

Adaptive Chosen-Ciphertext Attack (CCA2) 219, 237

Advanced Encryption Standard 70, 129-130, 132, 135, 139-141, 158, 435, 569

AES Modified Algorithm 133

anti-spyware software 143, 145, 158

Anti-virus 143, 145

AODV 72-76, 78, 82, 86-96

Asymmetric Cryptosystems 214

Authentication 19, 21-23, 36, 40, 46-47, 73-75, 77, 82, 84, 86, 99, 117, 123, 127, 139, 143, 145-147, 152-153, 157-158, 160, 163, 193-194, 257-258, 261, 263, 265-275, 277-278, 320, 323, 352, 358, 364, 371, 375-376, 395-396, 398, 400, 411-412, 416-419, 422-423, 425-426, 428-430, 432, 434-435, 439-442, 445, 447-448, 459, 461, 464, 473, 476-478, 503, 506, 511, 514, 532, 558, 572

Automatic Variable Key (AVK) 239, 249, 255

Availability 2, 78, 127, 142-145, 240, 250, 258, 295, 316-317, 320, 357, 412, 447, 558

B

Basic Matrix 545-546, 548, 550

BGN Cryptosystem 277-279, 281, 283, 285-286, 289-290, 292

Bilinear Mapping 297-298, 301-302, 309, 312

Bilinearity 231

Biometric 23, 39-42, 44, 46-47, 146, 278, 280, 412, 417, 426, 497, 572

Blackhole Attack 72, 84, 88, 93-94, 96

Braille 428-437

C

Cellular automata 99-101, 104-106, 117-119, 180-181, 183-187, 189-191, 567, 573

Chaos 7-8, 23-24, 37-39, 41, 46, 70, 99, 117-118, 256, 461, 494, 559-560, 566-568, 572

Chaos-Based Encryption 36, 40

Chaotic Encryption 1, 7-8, 17, 23, 190, 461, 570

Chosen Message Attack (CMA) 221, 237

Chosen-Ciphertext Attack (CCA1) 219, 237

Chosen-Plaintext Attack (CPA) 219, 237

Cloud Computing 37, 139, 255, 274, 295, 297, 310, 314, 316-317, 324, 327, 329-330, 416-417, 419, 425-426, 438, 479

Cloud Security 68, 258, 306-307, 310, 329-330

Compartmented Secret Sharing 438-440, 447

Complex systems 49, 99, 101

Compression Scale Change Invariance 536

compression scale invariance 498, 522, 531

Computer Vision 478, 533, 536

Confidentiality 22-23, 36, 73, 77, 80, 86, 99, 142-144, 148-149, 151, 157-158, 160, 193-194, 219, 258, 278, 316, 332, 337, 350, 356-357, 374-375, 392, 445, 447, 459-465, 469, 473-474, 556, 558

Content Protection 1, 532, 535

Cover Image 1-3, 6-7, 9-10, 17, 332-338, 340-348, 350, 353-354, 360-361, 382, 386-388, 444-445, 450-452, 454, 458, 463, 468-469, 474, 481, 486, 488, 490, 502

Cryptanalysis 63, 69, 106, 128, 143, 149-150, 157, 176-177, 180-181, 183, 185-190, 212, 236, 251, 314, 390, 467, 556

cryptic mining 255

Cryptographic Algorithms 67, 72, 104, 107, 117, 133, 142-144, 157, 159, 177, 201, 249, 262, 375

Cryptography 39-41, 46-47, 49-52, 67-70, 72-73, 76-80, 86-89, 93-96, 99-100, 103-106, 108, 114, 117-120, 122, 127-130, 142, 149, 151-153, 157-158, 160, 162-163, 167, 176-181, 189-190, 193-195, 212-215, 217, 236-237, 254-255, 257-258, 262, 275-276, 279, 281-282, 285, 289, 292, 295, 303-304, 306, 308, 310, 314, 330, 333, 335, 353, 355-357, 365, 369, 375, 386, 391-392, 395-397, 401, 405, 410-414, 416-417, 419, 425-428, 435-436, 438, 448-451, 454, 456-457, 459, 461, 463-464, 471, 473-474, 476-478, 498-499, 501-502, 506-507, 509, 532-537, 543-545, 554-558, 560, 565, 569-572

Cryptosystem 46, 50, 52, 60, 69, 71, 73, 77-79, 81, 87-88, 99, 106, 108-109, 112-114, 116-118, 120-121, 123, 127-128, 149, 189, 214-216, 218, 229, 235-241, 244-247, 249-250, 254-256, 272, 277-279, 281-283, 285-286, 288-290, 292, 296, 316-320, 329, 375, 390, 394-395, 397, 403, 465, 468, 557, 559, 561, 569, 571

CryptoWatermarking 458

Crypto-Watermarking 458-459, 462-465, 469-470, 472-475, 477-478

CUDA 193-194, 198-202, 204-205, 212-213

D

Data Security 22, 49, 99, 141-142, 160, 320, 327, 349, 371, 479

DCT 1-6, 17-18, 20, 23, 160, 163, 333, 343-344, 351, 353-354, 361, 378, 458, 460, 464, 468-469, 473, 475, 479, 482, 497, 506, 566-567

Decryption 10, 23, 28-29, 31, 35-36, 39, 42-43, 46, 49, 51-52, 59, 61, 63, 66-67, 79, 81, 100, 105-106, 109, 111, 113-114, 116-117, 121-122, 129-131, 135-136, 149, 151-152, 154, 156, 166-169, 194-195, 201-202, 204-205, 207-209, 211-212, 215, 217-222, 237, 244, 246-249, 254, 282, 284-287, 295-297, 299, 301, 306-312, 316-319, 327-328, 333, 365, 375, 385, 391, 394-395, 397, 401, 403, 411, 416-418, 420, 425, 428-429, 432, 434, 440, 450, 463-464, 467-468, 473-474, 479, 501-502, 506, 536, 556-558, 560, 563-565, 568

Digital Image Steganography 332, 335, 343, 350, 352-353

Digital Signature 93, 120, 122, 127, 152, 215, 217, 221, 236

Digital Watermarking 1-3, 18-19, 21, 349, 356, 458, 461-463, 468, 476-478, 497-498, 534, 536

Discrete Cosine Transform 1, 4, 159, 343, 351, 353, 361, 385, 463, 465, 468, 474, 477, 479, 566

Discrete Wavelet Transform 2, 19, 159, 317, 319, 324, 343-345, 353, 480, 483, 508, 534

DNA-based Cryptography 51, 67-68, 72-73, 93, 95

Dynamic Secret Sharing 438

E

ECC 160, 262, 306-307, 312-313

ECG 22-26, 28-32, 34-38

Electrocardiogram 19, 22-23, 37

Encrypted Image 43-44, 46, 53, 58, 61-66, 137, 316-318, 385, 388-389, 405, 459, 462-464, 466, 469-472, 477-478, 490, 494, 559, 561-562, 566-567

Encryption 1-3, 7-8, 17, 22-25, 27-32, 34-44, 46-53, 59-70, 73, 75, 77, 79, 88, 100, 102, 104-107, 109-110, 113-114, 116-118, 120-123, 127-132, 135-136, 138-141, 145, 151-156, 158-165, 167-169, 171, 176-178, 180, 186, 190, 194-195, 201-202, 204-207, 209, 211, 215, 217-225, 235-237, 244, 246-249, 254-258, 260-262, 272-273, 276, 278-279, 282, 284-289, 292-293, 295-297, 299-310, 312-320, 324, 327-330, 333, 358-359, 364-365, 369, 371, 373-375, 382, 385, 390, 392, 395, 405, 412, 416-418, 420-421, 423, 425-426, 428, 435, 440, 457-463, 465-468, 470, 474-480, 483, 485, 489-490, 493, 496, 501, 534, 545, 554-573

Exact Security 214, 216-217, 228-229, 237, 561

Exclusive 82, 545-546, 563

Execution Time 277-278, 470

Existential Forgery 221, 237

Extended Visual Cryptography Scheme 449-450, 454, 456

F

Factor 1, 6-7, 16-17, 49, 164, 244, 260, 273, 276-278, 281-283, 285, 355, 384, 407, 450, 469, 475, 518, 561

feature extraction 283, 288, 498, 508, 511-512, 531, 536

Fibonacci-Q matrix 239, 246

firewall 143, 145-146, 158, 264

FPGA 18, 99-100, 107-108, 112-113, 116, 129, 138-141, 163

G

Generic Group Model 214, 216-217, 231-232, 235, 237

GMM 277-280, 283, 292

GPGPU 193

Graph Access Structure 538

Grid Environment 373-375, 380, 385-386, 389

Group Key 373-374, 376, 378, 380-382, 384-387, 389-390

H

Health Insurance Portability and Accountability Act 459, 479
Health Insurance Portability and Accountability Act (HIPAA) 459, 479
Homomorphic Encryption 293, 295-297, 299-300, 302-309, 314-317, 327, 329-330, 392, 395, 412, 416-418, 420, 425-426
Homomorphic Visual Cryptography 416, 419
Homomorphy 277
Huffman 159-160, 162, 178, 375
Human Visual System 2, 392, 416-417, 428-429, 492, 499, 502, 506, 510, 537, 545

I

Image Encryption 23-24, 37-41, 46-47, 53, 64, 68, 70, 106, 373-374, 382, 385, 425-426, 457, 460-461, 463-466, 475-478, 480, 483, 485, 489-490, 493, 496, 545, 554-556, 559-561, 563-573
Image Scrambling 47, 565, 569
Image Security 39, 56, 560, 562-565
Image Steganography 332-333, 335, 338, 343, 350-353, 360-361, 370-371, 389, 391-392, 396-399, 401-402, 411-414
Indistinguishability or Semantic Security 237
Information Sharing 545
Integrity 22, 36, 73, 77, 79-80, 86-87, 99, 123, 127, 142-145, 148, 151-152, 160-161, 193-194, 217, 258, 324, 357, 364, 374, 392-395, 443, 447, 461, 463, 466, 469, 473-475, 498, 502, 556, 558

J

Java 159, 161, 167, 177, 385, 389, 391, 396-397
JPEG Compression 1, 3, 12, 16-17, 19, 344

K

key 7-8, 10, 31-32, 35-37, 39-44, 46-47, 49-53, 59, 61-63, 66-68, 71, 73, 77-82, 84, 86-88, 105-106, 118, 120-123, 125, 127-132, 139-140, 143-144, 146, 148-158, 160, 165-169, 177-178, 180-181, 184-185, 190, 193-196, 199, 204-205, 207, 209, 213-215, 217-219, 221-230, 235-245, 247-252, 254-262, 265-274, 276, 279, 281-285, 287-288, 290, 295-296, 298-304, 306-307, 309-310, 312-314, 317, 329-330, 332-333, 335-336, 338-339, 351-352, 356-357, 359, 361, 365, 369, 373-376, 378, 380-382, 384-387, 389-390, 395-397, 403, 423, 438, 440-447, 458-461, 463-471, 473-475, 478-479, 488-489, 494, 498, 501, 503, 507, 514-516, 536, 543, 554, 556-560, 563-567, 569
key length 7, 130, 155, 167-168, 237, 239-241, 243-244, 254
Key-Only Attack 221, 237
Known Signature Attack (KSA) 221, 237

L

Lossless Recovery 427, 545-549, 551-555

M

MANETs 72, 74-75, 77, 94-96
Matlab 11, 62, 161, 333, 351, 385, 389, 428, 432, 444, 490, 517-518
Meaningful Share 440, 444-445, 449
Meaningless Shares 438, 444, 450
Medical Image 20, 68, 459, 463-464, 467, 469-470, 472, 480-481, 491, 496
Mobile Cloud Computing 316-317, 327, 329
Modification 1-2, 5, 76, 120-122, 127-130, 132, 140, 144-145, 183, 217, 228, 265, 346, 361, 364, 373-374, 385, 389, 494, 497, 510, 512, 558-559, 566-567
Motion Feature Extraction 512, 536
motion features 498, 510-511, 515, 536

N

National Institute of Standards and Technology (NIST) 114, 257, 276
Negligible Function 237, 313
Neural Networks 180, 182, 185, 187-188, 436
non-intrusive watermarking 502, 507
Normalized Correlation 515, 519-521, 536

O

One-Way Hash Function 257, 266, 276
Online Voting System 391, 411
Openstack 316-318, 320-322, 329-330

P

Patterns 39-40, 51, 103, 112, 162, 180-181, 183-185, 188-190, 248, 251, 254, 278, 349, 539
Payload 332-333, 336-338, 350, 353, 356, 358-359, 364, 482, 511, 531-532
Peak-Signal-to-Noise-Ratio(PSNR) 479
Performance Analysis 89, 140, 158, 254, 332, 450, 531
Pixel Expansion 417, 423, 427, 438, 440, 444-445, 447, 450, 508, 537-543, 545-546, 548-550, 553-554, 566
Prime Order Bilinear Group 277
Privacy 22-23, 36-37, 40, 47, 97, 122, 144, 148, 158, 277-279, 283, 288-289, 292-295, 304, 308, 315, 317, 320, 327, 350, 357, 364, 370, 390, 392-394, 412, 414, 416-417, 419-420, 423, 425-426, 448, 459-460, 474, 476, 483, 554, 556, 559, 561
PRNG 99, 106, 109, 112-113, 396-397, 466-467, 479
Programmable cellular automata 99-100, 104, 117
Provable Security 214-215, 237
Proxy Re-encryption 295-297, 299, 301, 304-305
Pseudo Random Number Generator 466, 479
Pseudo Random Number Generator (PRNG) 466, 479
PSNR 10-11, 14, 41, 44, 46, 332-333, 338, 346-347, 354, 358-359, 386-388, 444-445, 447, 458, 460, 463, 470-473, 475, 479, 482, 491-493, 511, 519-522, 531
Public Key Cryptography 79, 151-152, 160, 178, 213-215, 217, 237, 255, 258, 314, 330, 375
Public Key Encryption 127, 160, 215, 217, 219, 221-223, 235, 237, 257-258, 260-262, 272-273, 276, 309, 375, 461
Public-Key Encryption (PKE) 306
PWLCM 480, 483, 485-486, 489, 492-496

Q

Quantum Computing 53, 258-259, 273, 275-276

R

Ralph Merkle 276
Random Oracle Model 214, 226-229, 235
Random-Oracle Model 216, 238
RDWT 480, 483-485, 488-489, 491, 496

Reconfigurable computing 117
Regression 180, 184-185, 187-189, 511, 533
Reversible Watermarking 475-476, 478, 480, 483, 496-497
Robustness 1, 3-4, 11-12, 15-17, 19-20, 34, 46, 130, 261, 332, 337-338, 343, 346, 353, 356, 363, 394, 396-399, 458, 461, 463-464, 475, 481, 498-499, 504, 506, 508, 511, 519-521, 531-532, 565-566, 568, 570
RSA 7, 40, 121-128, 146, 149, 160, 214, 217, 225-230, 255, 258, 262, 268-273, 281, 296, 319, 358-359, 375, 395-396, 440, 461, 463, 465-466, 475, 477, 558

S

Saliency Detection 498-499, 509-511, 532-533, 536
Secret Information 333, 335, 340-341, 343, 345, 350, 353, 355-360, 363-366, 374, 376, 385, 462, 501, 506
Secret Key 39, 42, 50, 53, 59, 77-80, 84, 105, 121-123, 151, 153-154, 168, 190, 217-218, 221-223, 225-226, 229, 238, 245, 265, 269, 282, 285, 299, 301, 306, 312, 317, 332, 336, 356, 375, 385, 395, 403, 458, 460-461, 463-470, 474-475, 479, 501, 507, 515
Secret Sharing 153, 335, 352, 416, 418, 425-429, 435, 437-440, 445, 447-449, 456, 499, 501, 503, 509, 534, 537-538, 543-545, 554-555
Secret Sharing Scheme 416, 426, 438-440, 445, 447-448, 501, 503, 544, 555
Secure Data Transfer 355, 369
Secure Group Communication 373-374, 376, 386, 389-390
Secure Inter Group Communication 373
Secure Message Broadcasting 373
Secure Multiparty Computation 277, 279, 296
Secure Socket Layer 122, 157, 375

Security 1-3, 7, 11, 16-18, 21-24, 29-30, 32-33, 35-37, 39-41, 46-50, 52-53, 56, 63-69, 71-75, 86-87, 92, 94-97, 99-100, 105, 107, 112, 116, 118, 120-123, 125, 127-130, 132, 138-149, 151-153, 157-161, 163, 167, 174, 176-181, 193-194, 202, 204, 207, 212-231, 235-240, 243, 245, 248-250, 254-255, 257-265, 273-276, 278, 281, 285, 287, 293-296, 298-299, 302-304, 306-310, 312-315, 317-318, 320, 327, 329-330, 332, 335, 337-339, 346, 349-350, 352-353, 355-357, 359, 361, 364-365, 369-371, 373-375, 384-385, 389-392, 394-397, 400-401, 405, 411-414, 416-419, 422-423, 425-429, 435-436, 438, 440, 444-445, 448, 454, 459-467, 469, 471-472, 474-480, 483, 485, 489-490, 493-494, 496-497, 499, 501, 508, 531-533, 535-536, 539, 544, 556-571, 573

Security Issues 49, 142, 144, 158, 275, 307, 375, 464-465, 559

Security Services 73, 86, 142, 144, 146, 157, 558, 560

Selective and Full Encryption 556

Selective Forgery 221, 238

share creation 498, 503, 511, 513-517, 519

Signal Processing in the Encrypted domain (SPED) 416-417, 425

Size Invariant Visual Cryptography 426, 449, 555

Soft Computing 100, 180-181, 189-190, 389

Sparse Matrix 239, 247-249

Spatial and Frequency Domain 339, 353, 461-462, 468, 556, 560

Speaker Recognition 277-278, 280, 283-285, 288-290, 292

Standard Model 167, 214, 235

Steganalysis 333, 335, 346, 348, 350-352, 354-355, 358, 369, 371-372, 412-414, 504, 511

Steganography 18, 21, 37, 52, 68-69, 332-336, 338-339, 343, 348-366, 369-374, 382, 385, 389, 391-392, 396-399, 401-402, 411-414, 448, 458, 462, 467, 476, 479, 534

Stego Image 333, 336-338, 340-349, 354, 358, 360, 364, 376, 385-388, 491

Stream Cipher 153-157, 167, 458, 460-467, 470, 473, 475, 479, 571

Subgroup Decision Problem 278-279, 285, 295, 298, 302

Sub-Sample 480, 482-483, 486, 488

SWMANETs 72-73

Symmetric key 52, 61, 81, 87, 118, 120, 129, 151, 155, 158, 193, 195, 239-240, 244-245, 247, 254-256, 267, 273, 459, 461, 464-465, 479, 558

Symmetric-RSA 120-121, 127

T

Tight Security 217, 228-229

Time variant key 239, 255

Total Break 221, 238

Tree 21, 74, 190, 258, 261, 265-266, 268-272, 274, 276, 374-375, 540, 542

U

Universal Forgery 221, 238

Usability Testing 391-392, 405-407, 409

V

Video Steganography 335, 355-356, 358-360, 363, 365, 369-372

video watermarking 18-19, 498-499, 503, 508-511, 515, 517, 532-536

Visual Cryptography 391-392, 395, 397, 401, 405, 410-413, 416, 419, 425-428, 435-436, 438, 448-451, 454, 456-457, 498-499, 501-502, 506-507, 509, 532-537, 543-545, 554-556, 560, 565, 570-571

Visual Secret Sharing 418, 425, 427, 435, 437, 447, 456, 499, 501, 503, 509, 534, 544-545, 554-555

W

Watermarking 1-4, 11-12, 16-21, 37, 163, 316, 319-320, 324-325, 327, 343-344, 349-350, 356, 358-359, 364, 370-371, 436, 458-469, 473-478, 480-481, 483, 491, 496-499, 501-504, 506-511, 514-515, 517, 519, 532-536, 554

Wireless mesh network 270, 275-276

Wireless Mesh Network (WMN) 276

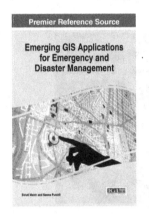